Karen —

As former CFO of two public companies, this book was helpful to me. Learning about and thinking about new things... you on it has been a pleasure... moving the US team for this upstairs.

I am sorry that you will know that you are always welcome as part of our business, and hopefully we can work together and continue to learn from one another.

I hope this book can give you some good thoughts and guidance in the years ahead, and maybe some day as the future CFO of Jafra Cosmetics! Happy 1998 Birthday!

Best wishes
Mike Ordonio
10-12-98

The CFO's Handbook

Editorial Advisory Board

The CFO's Handbook

Edited by

Richard F. Vancil
Assisted by **Marianne D'Amico**

and

Benjamin R. Makela

DOW JONES-IRWIN
Homewood, Illinois 60430

ISBN 0-87094-591-2
Library of Congress Catalog Card No. 85–71161

Printed in the United States of America

1 2 3 4 5 6 7 8 9 0 MP 3 2 1 0 9 8 7 6

To Betty, and to Gregg

Benjamin Makela

Consulting Editors

Buxbaum, William E., senior vice president—finance and CFO, E. I. du Pont de Nemours and Company

Calman, Robert F., vice chairman and CFO, IU International Corporation

Campbell, Robert E., executive committee member, Johnson & Johnson

Capone, A. William, senior vice president and CFO (retired), Koppers Company, Inc.

Dammeyer, Rod, senior vice president and CFO, Household International

de Palma, Robert A., senior vice president, CFO, and corporate director, Rockwell International Corporation

Dillon, Robert E., Jr., executive vice president—finance, Sony Corporation of America

Harrigan, Arthur W., executive vice president—finance (retired), International Paper Company

Hiser, Harold R., Jr., senior vice president—finance, Schering-Plough Corporation

Lee, Charles R., senior vice president—finance, GTE Corporation

McIntosh, Donald L., senior vice president—finance and administration (retired), NCR Corporation

Medhus, Sigurd D., executive vice president, First City Capital Corporation

Meehan, Joseph G., senior vice president and CFO, Rubbermaid Inc.

Meyer, Daniel J., vice president—finance and administration, Cincinnati Milacron Inc.

Murdy, James L., executive vice president, Gulf Oil Corporation

Nicholas, Nicholas J., Jr., executive vice president, Time, Inc.

Pettit, Raymond F., senior vice president and CFO, The Rockefeller Group

Robinson, Ryle G., senior vice president—finance and administration, William Natural Gas Company

Rogers, Marvin G., executive vice president and CFO, Control Data Corporation

Russler, D. W., senior vice president—finance and administration, NCR Corporation

vi

Shaffer, Fred W., vice president, CFO, and controller, Rohm and Haas Company

Skelly, Thomas F., senior vice president—finance, The Gillette Company

Spring, John B., executive vice president—finance and administration, National Car Rental System Inc.

Wirth, James W., senior vice president and CFO, Aluminum Company of America

Contributing Authors*

Alleman, Raymond H. (Chapter 10*)—*senior vice president and deputy comptroller, International Telephone and Telegraph Corporation*

Battaglia, Alfred J. (Chapter 3*)—*president, VACUTAINER Systems Division, Becton Dickinson and Company*

Beasman, Mark D. (Chapter 9*)—*director, operations planning and control, Marriott Corporation*

Beck, Douglas (Chapter 1*)—*vice president—political risk analysis, Data Resources, Inc.*

Bedford, Bruce Paul (Chapter 6)—*chairman, Flagship Funds Inc. (formerly vice president—financial affairs, The Mead Corporation)*

Bertocchi, Alfred M. (Chapter 7)—*vice president—finance and administration (retired), Digital Equipment Corporation*

Briggs, Roger T. (Chapter 5*)—*partner, Kelly Briggs and Associates (formerly vice chairman, Esmark, Inc.)*

Brinner, Roger (Chapter 1*)—*group vice president—U.S. Economic Services, Data Resources, Inc.*

Caine, Franklyn A. (Chapter 27*)—*staff vice president and assistant treasurer, RCA Corporation*

Canning, Robert J. (Chapter 24*)—*manager—corporate financial manpower operation (retired), General Electric Company*

Carl, John L. (Chapter 4*)—*vice president/controller, hospital sector, American Hospital Supply Corporation*

Cashel, William S., Jr. (Chapter 23*)—*chairman of the board, Campbell Soup Company (formerly vice chairman of the board AT&T)*

Chaikind, Leonard S. (Chapter 20*)—*assistant treasurer policy and administration, Shell Oil Company*

Chrenc, Robert J. (Chapter 22*)—*partner, Arthur Andersen*

Connor, Joseph E. (Chapter 19)—*chairman, Price Waterhouse*

Cornelius, James M. (Chapter 15*)—*vice president of finance and treasurer, Eli Lilly & Company*

Denny, James M. (Chapter 25)—*executive vice president and chief financial and planning officer, G. D. Searle & Co.*

---

*Denotes coauthor

Eckstein, Otto   (Chapter 1*)—*chairman of the board (deceased), Data Resources, Inc.*

Filippello, A. Nicholas   (Chapter 21*)—*director, financial relations and chief economist, Monsanto Company*

Fraser, Bruce D.   (Chapter 16*)—*formerly director, Lehman Brothers Kuhn Loeb International, Inc.*

Gelardin, Jacques P.   (Chapter 16*)—*managing director, Shearson Lehman Brothers International, Inc.*

Glucksman, Lewis L.   (Chapter 16*)—*formerly chairman, Lehman Brothers Kuhn Loeb Inc.*

Grobstein, Michael   (Chapter 15*)—*vice chairman accounting and auditing services, Ernst & Whinney*

Gross, Edward H.   (Chapter 29*)—*vice president—finance and CFO, Baker & Taylor Division, W. R. Grace & Co.*

Harlan, Neil E.   (Introduction)—*chairman and chief executive officer, McKesson Corporation*

Harrigan, Arthur W.   (Chapter 24*)—*executive vice president—finance (retired), International Paper Company*

Hickey, John T.   (Chapter 12*)—*executive vice president and CFO, Motorola Inc.*

Higgins, Jay F.   (Chapter 5*)—*managing director—mergers and acquisitions, Salomon Brothers, Inc.*

Hines, Paul   (Chapter 22*)—*executive vice president and director, E. F. Hutton & Company Inc.*

Howe, Thomas H.   (Chapter 23*)—*president, Management Analysis Center, Inc.*

Hunter-Henderson, Alastair I.   (Chapter 17)—*vice president, Morgan Guaranty Trust Company*

Kennedy, John H.   (Chapter 31*)—*senior vice president and CFO, Alco Standard Corporation*

Laughlin, William M.   (Chapter 31*)—*director of internal audit, Alco Standard Corporation*

Ledbetter, William J.   (Chapter 30)—*senior executive vice president—administration and planning, Textron Inc.*

Litle, Mary V.   (Chapter 29*)—*assistant treasurer, W. R. Grace & Co.*

Madero, Hernando   (Chapter 14*)—*vice president, Booz Allen & Hamilton International*

Marlantes, Lorian L.   (Chapter 27*)—*vice president—strategic planning and corporate development, The Rockefeller Group*

Miller, Richard W.   (Chapter 27*)—*executive vice president and CFO, RCA Corporation*

Milne, Garth L.   (Chapter 12*)—*vice president and director of treasury, Motorola Inc.*

---

*Denotes coauthor

Myers, Jerry K.   (Chapter 4*)—*executive vice president and chief administrative and financial officer, American Hospital Supply Corporation*

Povejsil, Donald J.   (Chapter 28*)—*vice president—corporate planning, Westinghouse Electric Corporation*

Reid, James A.   (Chapter 18*)—*vice president, AIRINC*

Roberts, Rennie   (Chapter 18*)—*senior vice president—corporate human resources, American Express Company*

Schmidt, Richard F.   (Chapter 2)—*executive vice president—finance and planning, The Dun & Bradstreet Corporation*

Schotanus, Gene L.   (Chapter 26*)—*senior vice president, financial services and CFO, Deere & Company*

Schwallie, Edward H.   (Chapter 14*)—*senior vice president and president of Booz Allen Acquisition Services, Booz Allen & Hamilton Inc.*

Semler, Bernard H.   (Chapter 8)—*chairman and president, Semler Associates, Inc. (formerly executive vice president—finance, Abbott Laboratories)*

Slacik, Karl F.   (Chapter 11)—*senior vice president and CFO, Levi Strauss & Co.*

Stroble, Francis A.   (Chapter 21*)—*senior vice president and CFO, Monsanto Company*

Thompson, Robert C.   (Chapter 20*)—*vice president—finance and CFO (retired), Shell Oil Company*

Umlauf, August   (Chapter 29*)—*president, Baker & Taylor Division, W. R. Grace & Co.*

Vos, Hubert D.   (Chapter 3*)—*president, Stonington Capital Corporation (formerly CFO, Becton Dickinson and Company)*

Wadsworth, John S., Jr.   (Chapter 13)—*managing director, investment banking division, Morgan Stanley & Co., Inc.*

Wilcox, Jarrod W.   (Chapter 26*)—*senior vice president, Batterymarch Financial Management*

Wilson, Gary L.   (Chapter 9*)—*executive vice president and CFO, Marriott Corporation*

Wurst, Charles M.   (Chapter 10*)—*director headquarters A&G and special projects, International Telephone and Telegraph Corporation*

Yochum, Leo W.   (Chapter 28*)—*senior executive vice president—finance, Westinghouse Electric Corporation*

---

*Denotes coauthor

Preface

This handbook has a tightly targeted mission: to serve the needs of a defined group of corporate executives, a group whose members increasingly carry the title of chief financial officer.

The CFO—in contrast to the dozens or hundreds of other financial managers in the organization—has a unique responsibility: the determination of financial policies and financial goals for the corporation. The perspective is corporate and strategic, rather than functional and technical. The twin tasks are to seek to ensure that (1) the corporate strategy is financially viable in a turbulent environment, and (2) the execution of that strategy is not constrained by lack of funds. Like other members of the corporate management team, the CFO is also responsible for maintaining a set of external relationships on behalf of the corporation, and for overseeing the day-to-day management of an important set of internal corporate resources. This handbook attempts to encompass all those duties by focusing on the policy and administration of corporate financial management.

To assist in fulfilling that objective, we have organized a group of contributors who are either current (or past) CFOs or senior advisers to such executives. Contributors in both categories are necessary, reflecting both the internal and external dimensions of the CFO's responsibilities. The fact that such a highly qualified set of individuals would volunteer to participate is testimony of their belief in the crucial importance of the CFO's function and of their desire to help improve the CFO's performance.

Most handbooks are designed as reference manuals, a source book to which the reader can turn to find a needed fact or a technical description of how to deal with a specific kind of problem. This handbook, because of its broad policy orientation, is more conceptual than technical. Our hope is that the

reader will turn to this book to stimulate thinking about an issue of current concern. The chapters are short and readable. Our
simple instruction to each author was, "assume that a CFO is
willing to invest 30 minutes reading your chapter before deciding (1) whether or not to launch a review of practices concerning your topic, or (2) how to design the main thrust of such a
review if he or she has already decided that some individual
initiative is necessary." This handbook is designed for the
proactive CFO, trying to help him or her decide whether or not
there is a problem and, if so, how to use the resources available
to deal with it.

One major focus of this handbook, which epitomizes our objective, deals with the emerging practical theory of corporate financial management. Fifteen years ago, academic inventions such
as the Capital Asset Pricing Model and the Sustainable Growth
Model were simply that: academic. Today, the power of those
models to help the CFO review and organize thinking about
corporate financial goals is an established reality. Chapters 3, 4,
9, and 28 are relevant to this point. If the reader is an expert on
this topic, he or she will be pleased to have the reaffirmation;
if not, he or she will learn even more. Sections I and III also
contain other chapters on specific topics related to the broad task
of establishing corporate financial goals.

This same policy-level focus is maintained in each of the other
sections of this handbook. Two sections focus on major substantive issues: setting financial policies (Section II) and international financing (Section IV). Two sections deal with the various aspects of the CFO's role, both externally (Section V) and
internally (Section VI). The final section is aimed specifically at
CFOs in diversified firms who must design a process for the financial management of the more-or-less autonomous divisions
and subsidiaries in their corporations.

In the introduction which follows, Neil E. Harlan has elo-
quently defined the role of the CFO. Our responsibility has been
to disassemble that awesome array of duties into accessible
pieces. We hope that the result will be eminently useful.

Personally, we would like to say that it has been an enormous pleasure to serve as the editors for this undertaking. Such
a project could only be attempted as a group activity; no one
individual—and certainly not an editor—has sufficient depth of
knowledge to write definitively on these 31 topics.

All of the participants are listed, of course, and the work of each contributing author is readily identifiable. The members of the editorial advisory board performed a special service. Without their willingness to begin, and their patience and counsel during the early months, the original idea would have died aborning. In addition, 24 CFOs played crucial roles as consulting editors. Their sharp criticism of the first drafts of each chapter served to stiffen our backbones in requesting revisions and improvements from busy authors. The result, we believe, is that this team has produced a handbook of unusually high quality; a book which we hope will be a real contribution to the profession of corporate financial management.

On behalf of all the participants, we would like to thank Marianne D'Amico for her cheerful and unflagging efforts in keeping this project on track. Located in Vancil's office in Boston, and also serving Makela in Florida and contributors throughout the country, she deserves great credit for the fact that we finally produced this result.

Richard F. Vancil
Benjamin R. Makela

Introduction

When I was approached about writing an introduction to *The CFO's Handbook*, I was asked to focus my attention on the *role* of the CFO. I agreed to that suggestion, as it seemed to me a sensible enough way to provide a brief background against which one might make use of the wealth of materials contained in the chapters that follow.

I am not sure that there is *a* role of the CFO, although I recognize that certain functional activities can clearly be identified as being among his or her responsibilities. I suspect that the role is, to a very important extent, determined by the individual filling it and, perhaps to a lesser extent, by the circumstances in which it is being filled. What I am much less uncertain about is that, if the role of the CFO continues to change as rapidly in the next few decades as it has in the last 10 to 20 years, this handbook will stand in need of frequent revision.

I will comment first on the rapid change in the nature of the CFO function in recent years and in the tools of his trade, and then go to what I believe to be the ultimate criterion for measuring the true effectiveness of the CFO—the role he or she plays in the top level of corporate decision making. I assume the functional responsibilities of the CFO, as indicated by the contents of this book, to include financing, accounting and reporting, the protection of the assets of the enterprise and the financial aspects of capital, and financial investment decisions.

It hasn't been many years—maybe 25 or 30—since the individual with the primary responsibility for financial matters was the treasurer—the person who looked after the treasury. He was more or less charged with somehow determining the amount of funds that would be needed to sustain the operations of the company (meaning any business enterprise); with raising those funds as efficiently as possible, that is, at the optimal combi-

nation of cost and risk; and with exercising without fail the cus-
todial care to ensure that the funds were put to their intended
use.

As late as the early 1950s finance courses in most business
school curricula also dealt almost entirely with projecting fund
requirements and providing those funds at the lowest cost consistent with the maintenance of a "sound" capital structure, that
is, one that would get the enterprise through the normal ups
and downs of its underlying business with an appropriate allowance for a not-so-normal blip or two along the way.

Lagging not far behind, the *practice* of corporate finance began to see the development of more sophisticated analytical tools
than had before been available or in general use. There were
certainly exceptions to this observation in such companies as
Standard Oil of New Jersey, General Electric Co., Du Pont,
General Motors Corp., and others where the concept, if not the
title, of the chief financial officer had begun to be developed years
earlier.

For an indication of the absence, before the 1950s, of the adap-
tion of any but the most basic mathematical or economic concepts to the analytical processes in corporate finance, one has
only to realize that even in the most advanced business schools
of the day the concept of the time value of money was just beginning to be applied to capital investment decisions. And, interestingly, the introduction of that concept at most of those institutions did not take place in traditional finance courses but
rather by faculty members, whatever their departmental affiliation, who had one foot at least partially planted in the field of
managerial economics.

Along with the notion of discounting future cash flows to their
present value came the need to decide on the discount rate to
be used, and thus the notion of the *cost of capital* for a given
business concern. Shortly thereafter, more theoretical notions
about the cash flow figures to be discounted led to the concept
of subjective *probability* assignments in dealing with the timing
and risks inherent in future cash flow estimates.

That is not to say, of course, that these analytical tools were
totally new and strange, although to many they indeed were.
Their influence had undoubtedly made partial inroads into some
corporate decision making through the intuitive judgments of
those making the decisions. In any event, I think few would

dispute the notion that this sophistication of the analysis of capital investment decisions in the corporate world developed very rapidly in the 1950s.

In the intervening years, we have seen a host of adaptations of mathematical and economic concepts in business decision making—the *sustainable growth model,* the *capital asset pricing model,* the *stock price formula,* and so on. Some of these have represented elaborations or refinements of earlier innovations, some the breaking of new ground.

This rapid rate of change has cut across the full breadth of the responsibilities of the CFO. For a number of years corporate finance had experimented with various forms of equity ownership—multiple classes of common stock and a variety of preferred, both straight and convertible. Until fairly recently, however, debt instruments had for the most part been straightforward. A business borrowed money for a specified period of time at a rate that reflected the financial condition of the business, the term of the debt being issued, and whether the debt was convertible into some form of equity.

In the 1970s, we began to hear of the "deep discount bond" and, later, the "zero coupon bond" (the ultimate in deep discounts!). Late in the 1970s, the "junk bond" made its way onto the scene. The term, *junk bond,* as originally used, had a pejorative connotation in that it tended to be applied to debt instruments whose terms needed to be scrutinized carefully because of the dubious quality of the instrument. While the junk bond has still not shed all of the suspicion with which it was originally regarded, it has come into extremely wide use, particularly in the financing of corporate takeover bids. With the growing array of bells and whistles being dreamed up for debt instruments, we may expect at any moment to see the emergence of the "punk bond."

And, we shouldn't forget the "blank check" preferred stock that now occupies a place among an expanding variety of "shark repellents" designed to divert, or at least deter, the corporate raider from his appointed rounds.

And finally, under the caption of exotic new tools, I cannot fail to mention the personal computer—the "PC". Its numbers in corporate offices across the country are growing at a phenomenal rate. The chief executive officer of a local company told me at a recent gathering that he believes that PCs reproduce at night when all the humans have left the office. They are awesome in the amount of work—good or bad—they enable their user to do, as well as in their ability to make the person who doesn't have one feel as inferior as the PC users around him assume him to be.

In the field of accounting, we have seen a reemergence of efforts to deal with the effects of inflation on reported earnings. It is hard to realize, with our more recent experience with inflation, that earlier interest in price level adjustment in accounting was spurred by the thought advanced in the mid 1950s by Professor Sumner Schlicter, among others, that it just might be possible that the United States would have to learn to live with a 2 *percent* inflation rate! With all the trial and effort that has gone into the question of price-level accounting, the only tangible progress has been in areas driven by tax considerations, LIFO inventory accounting being virtually the only example. Nevertheless, the accounting profession still struggles with the problem.

The amortization of goodwill was until fairly recently an accounting matter that received very little attention; there wasn't enough goodwill on anyone's books to make it worth worrying about. But now, the spate of acquisitions over the past couple of decades, combined more recently with high inflation rates, has left companies amortizing the cost of acquired goodwill at the same time those assets were gaining nominal value, sometimes at rapid rates. The result in many instances has been to penalize—at least in reported earnings—those who held shares while goodwill was being written off and to benefit those who held the stock when dispositions of the amortized assets were made at substantial gains!

The CFO of any corporate business enterprise, particularly one publicly held, should understand the growing list of new and sometimes complex concepts, or know someone who does—preferably a trusted adviser. The aspiring CFO should make them a part of his or her arsenal. To reject outright any of them as being too academic, too theoretical, or even too ludicrous to be of practical use is to assume, for any large and complex business concern, that the world is simpler than it in fact may be.

It is important, however to enter a word of caution. It is always possible for the imaginative and innovative analyst to fall prey to his own inventions, to become so mesmerized by the elegance of the models he brings to the decision process that he believes they will unerringly lead to good decisions. And this risk may be aggravated by the alluring—maybe even intimidating—computer printout that is often the culmination of the analytical process. The models can be indispensable in bringing rigor and consistency to decision making; but, like all models, they have nothing to say about the judgments that go into the selection of the data they process. Those judgments remain, in all respects, the prerogative and the responsibility of management.

It is the influence that the CFO brings to this critical juncture—between the functional areas of financial management and the decision making of general management—that establishes and measures his role in the important affairs of the business enterprise. I believe this to be true almost without regard to the specific nature of the decision to be made at the general management level. Most "operating" decisions of a corporate nature have financial content, and it is essential to the long run success of the enterprise that financial considerations not be overlooked. Conversely, most "financial" decisions also require inputs from operating people, and it is important that the CFO ensure that his organization understands and appreciates fully why those inputs must be made and how they can be made.

But it is in the strategic decisions of an enterprise—those that set the direction and determine the thrust of the enterprise—that the ultimate contribution of the CFO can be made.

It is, of course, absolutely essential that the CFO ensure that all of the functional activities of corporate finance be carried out with the highest level of professional competence. That they indeed are of that caliber can be a source of professional pride for the CFO. But to stop there is to provide a high quality *service* function. The enterprise will be supplied with the financing it needs and at an appropriate cost; its assets will be adequately protected; accounting reports will be reliable and timely; and the CFO can take pride in the way that part—the sine qua non—of his responsibility is being met.

But the CFO's job is not a service function. That it is treated so in some companies is ultimately a failure of the chief executive officer. My own observations tell me that it is first and fundamentally a failure of the CFO—a failure to demonstrate that his participation in major corporate decisions is indispensible—

that he can bring far more to the difficult strategic decisions of an enterprise than well processed information.

Having injected this note of caution—and perhaps leaned too hard on my own convictions—let me encourage you to explore, carefully and thoughtfully, the chapters of this handbook. For even the most seasoned chief financial officer, these materials can provide new perspectives and shed new light on familiar concepts. For those who are in the process of building toward a role as CFO, I recommend this volume as an addition to your list of essential reading. I know you will find the time you spend with it profitable.

Neil E. Harlan

Neil E. Harlan began his career as a professor at Harvard Business School and subsequently served as assistant secretary of the Air Force, financial vice president of Anderson, Clayton & Co., and a director of McKinsey & Co. He is currently chairman and chief executive officer of McKesson Corporation.

Contents

ings Retention (1–D). Leverage and Cost of Debt $(1 + R_1 + R_2) \times (1 - i/NIi)$. Integrated Financial Goals.

ties. Short-Term Debt. Accounts Payable. Other Current Liabilities. Macro Working Capital Management.

Integrating Debt Financing into Financial Goals and Capital
Structure. Considerations in Using Financial Service Insti-
tutions. New Financing Trends and Tools. Short-Term
Funding. Long-Term Funding.

Framework for Evaluation. Dividend Irrelevancy. Dividend
Increases Mean Increased Firm Value. Dividend Increases
Mean Decreased Firm Value. Dividend Irrelevancy Revis-
ited. Guidelines for the CFO. Equity Financing—Introduction. Methodology and Size. Choice of Type of Distribution. Common Stock Repurchase—Introduction. The Choice
of an Investment Bank.

Introduction. What Risk Means to a Company. Identifying
and Evaluating a Company's Risks. Management of Risk:
*Describe Industry Characteristics and Operating Strategies and
Forecast Future Government Goals. Match the Host Government's Goals and Policies against the Company's Desired Product
Characteristics to Identify Risks. Estimate the Economic Impacts
of Likely Political Risks on the Company. Assess the Political Risks
and Impacts on Competitors in Each Market Country. Estimate
the Overall Impact on Political Risks on the Company in Each
Market Country. Develop and Evaluate Alternative Operating
Strategies.* Implications for the Financial Executive.

Introduction. Environmental Risk Analysis: *Defining Risk
Factors. Effect of Size and Scope of Operations.* The Case for
Centralized Treasury Management: *Organizational Factors.
Ideas for Managing Exchange Risk.* The Focus of Controller-

ship: *Designing Financial Reporting Systems. Analyzing Operating Results.* Audit Role in International Control: *Cost/Benefit Considerations. Setting Audit Priorities.* Good Communications Are Critical. Summary.

The Effects of Inflation versus Changing Prices. Foreign Currency Translation. All-Inclusive Reporting of Obligations. International Accounting and Reporting Standards. Summary.

Background. Personal Views on Regulations and Regulators. Working with Regulatory Agencies: *From the Perspective of Business. From the Perspective of the Agency Itself.* Regulatory Agencies—Examples: *Securities and Exchange Commission (SEC). Federal Trade Commission (FTC). Department of Commerce (DOC). Department of Energy (DOE). Working Relationships—A Case Study. Financial Accounting Standards Board (FASB). New York Stock Exchange. State Agencies.* Working through Others. Regulatory Improvements. Sources and Materials. Conclusions. Bibliography.

What Information Must Be Communicated? *Product Portfolio and Markets Served. Current Business Conditions and Outlook. Corporate Strategy. Sources of Potential Surprise.* How to Carry Out Communications: *Written Communications to Shareholders. The Annual Meeting. Communications with Top Management. Financial Communications Abroad. The Financial Relations Staff.* Conclusion.

Introduction. When Outside Consultants Are Needed. The Professional Resource Network. Sources. Building Your Own Network. What to Look for in a Consultant: *Auditors. Investment Bankers.* When to Use Professional Resources. Managing Professional Relations. How to Be a Good Client. Engagement Letter. Summary and Conclusions.

List of Exhibits

Chapter 27

Chapter 28

Chapter 29

PART ONE

Corporate Strategy and
Financial Strategy

1

Environmental Analysis

*Otto Eckstein**

INTRODUCTION

The financial performance of a firm is affected both by the decisions made within the firm and by economic and political events outside the control of the company's management. While the chief financial officer (CFO) must concentrate on the decisions over which he/she has control, in today's environment those decisions cannot be made responsibly without anticipating developments in the economic and political arena. Fortunately, progress in information technology now makes it easier for the CFO to organize the data on the economic and political environment. The following sections of this chapter describe how to identify the impact of environmental parameters, how to as-

---

*Chapter 1 has been written according to the outline of the late Dr. Otto Eckstein by Mr. Donald McLaughlin, Dr. Douglas Beck, and Dr. Roger Brinner, all from Data Resources. Inc.

Otto Eckstein, Warburg Professor of Economics at Harvard University and a former member of President Johnson's Council of Economic Advisors, founded Data Resources, Inc. (DRI) in 1968. Donald McLagan joined DRI in 1969 and became executive vice president. Roger Brinner joined in 1975 and became group vice president—U.S. economic services. Douglas Beck joined DRI and became vice president—political risk analysis.

sess the elements of political risk, and how to harness information technology to make economic and political data relevant
to financial decisions. The data and the technology cannot eliminate risk, but they can help the CFO to anticipate the impact
of change and to plan for orderly growth.

ENVIRONMENTAL PARAMETERS

There are no businesses which are substantially isolated from
variations in the external environment. Therefore, the chief financial officer has a clear need to receive a continual flow of
information on this environment and to have a good model of
the linkage to the firm's cash flow and profits.

The environment, or the "macroeconomy" as economists describe external conditions, is likely to have at least as great an
impact on short-term profit performance as are the tactical decisions made by management. And for most firms, profitability
is the joint result of management decisions and the macroeconomy. It is hard to grow a firm's revenues faster than its market
growth for very long. It is not possible to isolate a firm's costs
from increasing national or regional norms; labor, energy, and
capital usage can be managed for efficiency, but the prices of
these services are closely tied to broader markets. Similarly, there
are limits on the extent to which diversification can average out
cyclical movements in specific markets and stabilize corporatewide performance. While there are tendencies for certain sectors to lag or to lead in a macroeconomic business cycle, these
lead-lag patterns are not uniform through time, and conventional recoveries and recessions are so broadly based that their
impacts cannot be avoided. Finally, an all-out effort to reduce
the cyclical correlation of a firm's businesses also logically implies a very low correlation of the fundamental activities across
business units and thus puts exceptional demands on the intelligence of any central management. If cyclicality cannot be diversified out or if individual shareholders can arguably better
perform such diversification for themselves, then dealing with
the effects of macroeconomic change is a fundamental fact of
life for CEOs.

Accepting the argument that the environment will strongly
influence the firm, the issue is then one of organizing the prompt

collection of macroeconomic data and then ensuring that this raw "data" is transformed into useful "information."

Creation and Distribution of Data

The federal government is the primary collector of macroeconomic data. Washington distributes its information directly through its own publications and computer tapes and indirectly through business information firms. The value-added of the private sector firms begins with their selection of the most useful data, their transformation of this data into more accessible print and computer formats, and their consulting support in setting up firm-specific monitoring reports and models. Often, the time lag in obtaining raw data and then transforming it into useful informtion can be shorter if the data is accessed through the private firms. This time element can be particularly important for the daily, weekly, or monthly data reports. However, even the quarterly and annual updates of important series often provoke financial market reactions when they contain important "news" on business conditions, and receiving that data quickly can be critical. Exhibit 1 summarizes the types of information which are available.

Data Organization and Interpretation

Work must be done to translate most, if not all, environmental information into the firm-specific numbers required by the chief financial officer. In some cases, this may be achieved by a simple, tabular display of a historical time series, such as the national rate on certificates of deposit. From this, the CFO can make his own judgments of whether the firm's banks are currently offering a competitive rate. In most cases, more elaborate displays and models will be required to identify historical patterns, to anticipate the range of future movements, and to infer the impacts on the firm's finances. For example, a prediction of where interest rates will be heading probably requires additional thoughts and modeling. The corporation's finance and planning departments can create models "from scratch," or they can collaborate with the consulting support teams from the business information firms.

Exhibit 1
Useful Databanks for Environmental Analysis

U.S. Economics
  National
    U.S. Central
    U.S. Cost Forecasting
    U.S. Flow of Funds
    U.S. Prices
    Conference Board
    Interindustry
  Regional
    U.S. Census 1980
    U.S. County
    U.S. County Business Patterns
    U.S. Regional
    California
    New York City

International Economics
  Economies
    Canada
    DRI–CEI
    Europe
    European Satellites
    IBRD World Tables
    International Cost Forecasting
    Japan
    Japan Prices
    LDC
    OECD Economic Outlook
    OECD Main Economic Indicators
    OECD National Income Accounts
  Trade and Finance
    Detailed Monthly Trade Monitor
    External Debt
    IMF Balance of Payments
    IMF Direction of Trade
    IMF International Financial
      Statistics
    IMF IFS Restated
    International Trade Information

Energy
  Domestic
    COALINK
    FPA Oil and Gas
    Gas
    Oil and Gas Drilling
    Oil Company
    U.S. Energy
  International
    Canadian Energy
    International Energy
    Japanese Energy
    Petroconsultants International
      Drilling
    Platt's

Financial
  Markets and Transactions
    Commodities
    DRI–FACS
    DRI–SEC
    DRI S&P 500 Forecasting Service
    IBES
    Merrill Lynch
    Robinson–Humphries
    Securities Industry
    Standard and Poor's Industrial
      Financial
    Toronto Stock Exchange
  Accounts and Firms
    DRI–BAS
    COMPUSTAT
    EXSTAT
    Financial Post
    Japan Financial
    SPI PIMS
    Value Line

Industrial/Sectoral
    Agriculture and Chemicals
    Computers and Communications
    F.W. Dodge Construction
    Defense
    Forestry and Wood Products
    Insurance and Health
    Metals
    Transportation

Good models are not black boxes: The best models are sets of clear-cut equations, with each equation a carefully constructed mathematical expression of business common sense tested against the reality of past experience. For example, a cash flow model might begin with an equation linking the firm's sales to a basket of categories of national expenditures (gross national product [GNP] components) as measured by the government. This sales equation would weight the GNP components to match the proportionate distribution of the firm's revenues across markets. Changes in the ratio of firm sales to the national basket value would indicate changes in market share. Statistical analysis can be used to measure trends in the market share and to quantify the linkages between changes in share and introductions of new products, advertising programs, and price changes. Companion equations can relate firm-specific labor, energy, and capital costs to relevant national measures and can introduce the influence of explicit corporate decisions on pay, hiring, equipment purchases, and construction activities. Other common modeling applications include acquisition and divestiture analyses, competitor monitoring, and predicting shareholder reactions to strategic decisions and financial results.

Types of Information

Demographics A good starting point for economic information is a compilation of the relevant information on labor force, employment, and household growth. Such data have one noteworthy advantage over other categories of information on the future, The prospective course of these numbers is fairly certain. With the exception of immigrants, everyone who will join the labor force between now and the end of this century has already been born. Likewise, all of the individuals who are likely to form households can be counted, and important age group cohorts can be enumerated year by year through any medium-term forecast horizon. The principal uncertainties surrounding population and labor force movements occur not at the national level but at the regional level. Understanding regional trends requires an appreciation of the economic forces encouraging movements from the stagnant areas to the prosperous areas in response to changing business opportunities, environmental at-

tractiveness, union strength, relative energy costs, and differential tax rates.

The CFO is most likely to encounter a need for demographic
information in conjunction with strategic rather than tactical
planning. Plant location, plant expansion, acquisitions, and divestitures may require an assessment of labor force and population outlooks. Business condition information of the type to
be discussed in subsequent sections is appropriate for both
strategic and tactical decision making.

Economic Fluctuations The U.S. economy has suffered seven
business recessions since 1950, with three occurring in the last
eleven years (Exhibit 2). Such turbulence is a persistent feature
of our economy, but the cycles do not arrive on an immutable
three- or four-year schedule. Moreover, when slumps do occur,
the depth and the duration are not homogeneous. The causes

Exhibit 2
Cycles in the U.S. Economy

Recessions	Length in Months	Percent Drop Industrial Output	Peak Jobless Rate
August 1929–March 1933	43	53.4	24.9
May 1937–June 1938	13	32.4	20.0
February 1945–October 1945	8	38.3	4.3
November 1948–October 1949	11	9.9	7.9
July 1953–May 1954	10	10.0	6.1
August 1957–April 1958	8	14.3	7.5
April 1960–February 1961	10	7.2	7.1
December 1969–November 1970	11	8.1	6.1
November 1973–March 1975	16	14.7	9.0
January 1980–July 1980	6	8.7	7.8
July 1981–November 1982	16	12.3	10.7

of business cycles are categorized by economists into five broad categories: (1) (fiscal) government tax and expenditure policy, (2) monetary policy, (3) natural resource availability and price, (4) foreign markets, and (5) random events, such as those relating to market psychology. If several business cycles coincide, the economy will fall well short of its potential performance. The character of each particular recession will reflect the relative importance of the five factors just noted. For example, the 1974–75 and 1981–82 recessions were brought on by the OPEC oil price shocks and thus were associated with unusually high inflation and relatively incomplete recoveries of employment. The 1957–58 and 1960–61 recessions resulted from fiscal and monetary policy errors and produced more traditional patterns of labor and product market price demand weakness followed by recovery.

Exhibit 3 displays the national economic patterns regularly reported by the government. The growth rates of final spending adjusted for inflation are reported sector by sector, as are several measures of the volatility of each sector and of the correlation of the sector with the national economy. Real growth and volatility measures do substantially differ across sectors and through time, suggesting the prospect of a significant payoff to firms capable of interpreting the repercussions of such environmental changes on their business operations.

The growth rates are reported on a peak-to-peak basis to avoid any distortions of the trend growth rates due to the business cycle. Inspection of the growth rates shows quite clearly the slower growth of the first half of the 1980s[1] due to both lower population growth and the incomplete economic recovery through 1984.

The columns labeled sector volatility reveal two aspects of the business cycle on a sector-by-sector basis. The column labeled standard deviation reports the standard deviation of the quarterly growth rates for each indicator. The proper interpretation is that approximately two thirds of the time, the sectoral growth rate should be within one standard deviation of its mean value. For example, the standard deviation of real GNP growth is 3.1 percent, indicating a very substantial range of fluctuations (approximately 0.3 percent to 6.5 percent encompasses the mean

---

[1] "1980s" refers to the growth from the last quarter of 1979 through the third quarter of 1984.

Exhibit 3
National Economic Patterns

	Average Growth Rate*					Sector Volatility	
	1950s	1960s	1970s	1980s	1950–84	Standard Deviation†	Correlation††
Real Gross National Product	3.6	3.8	3.4	2.2	3.4	3.1	1.0
Consumption	3.2	4.0	3.6	2.7	3.5	2.1	0.7
Durables	3.9	5.7	5.2	4.1	4.8	8.9	0.6
Motor Vehicles and Parts	5.8	5.1	4.5	5.1	5.1	15.0	0.5
Furniture and Appliances	2.1	5.8	6.0	3.8	4.4	6.7	0.6
Other Durables	3.8	7.0	5.4	2.4	4.9	5.8	0.6
Nondurables	2.6	3.1	2.6	2.0	2.7	1.9	0.6
Food	2.4	2.6	2.0	1.7	2.2	2.0	0.3
Clothing and Shoes	1.9	2.8	5.3	4.2	3.3	3.5	0.5
Gasoline and Oil	5.7	5.0	1.6	0.5	3.7	4.1	0.3
Services	3.7	4.5	4.0	2.7	3.9	1.2	0.6
Housing	5.6	4.7	4.7	2.8	4.7	1.2	0.5
Household Operation	4.4	4.4	3.9	1.4	3.9	2.5	0.4
Transportation	0.3	4.0	3.6	-1.4	2.0	3.4	0.5
Other Services	3.0	4.4	3.5	3.9	3.7	1.9	0.3

Investment	3.0	3.1	3.7	6.2	3.6	16.3	0.8
Fixed	2.8	3.8	4.2	3.5	3.5	8.5	0.8
Nonresidential	2.6	5.2	4.4	4.1	4.0	8.3	0.7
Equipment	1.7	6.1	5.8	4.8	4.4	10.0	0.8
Structures	3.9	3.9	1.7	2.3	3.1	7.5	0.5
Residential	3.2	0.8	3.7	1.6	2.4	17.6	0.5
Structures	3.2	0.6	3.6	1.6	2.3	18.0	0.5
Equipment	5.1	7.6	6.7	2.2	5.9	16.2	0.4
Exports	3.2	6.3	9.0	-0.8	5.0	10.0	0.3
Imports	6.0	7.4	5.9	9.5	6.8	9.0	0.7
Government	6.0	3.8	1.2	2.0	3.6	8.0	0.2
Federal	6.1	1.9	-0.5	4.5	2.9	15.9	0.2
Defense	9.2	1.2	-2.2	6.3	3.4	19.7	0.3
Nondefense	-2.0	5.4	3.9	0.6	2.0	19.8	-0.1
State and Local	5.8	5.6	2.5	0.4	4.1	3.2	0.0

*The intervals for the decades have been selected to run from one business cycle peak at the beginning of the decade to another peak near the end of the decade. The exact calendar quarters used are: 50s, 1948:3 to 1960:1; 60s, 1960:1 to 1970:3; 70s, 1970:3 to 1979:4; 80s, 1979:4 to 84:3 and 1950–84, 1948:3 to 1984:3.

†Standard deviation of the growth rates of real spending over all four-quarter intervals from 1948:3 to 1984:3.

††The simple correlation coefficient shows the sectoral growth rate correspondence to the aggregate GNP growth rate. A correlation of 1.0 suggests a perfect correspondence of sectoral ups and downs with GNP.

plus-or-minus one standard deviation). More stable components include the consumption of housing services and food—necessities whose purchase cannot vary substantially through a business cycle.

The investment categories are among the most volatile, particularly in the residential category. Home construction can be delayed much more easily in periods of tight money than can almost any other category of expenditure. Thus, the standard deviation of the growth rate is 18.0 percent, which is nearly six times the variation in total GNP growth.

Perhaps surprisingly, another sector with substantially greater than average variation is spending by the federal government. Two phenomena account for this. First, policy changes can be quite abrupt as administrations change; second, the government often tries to act in a countercyclical fashion to offset swings in the private sector.

Indeed, this countercyclical phenomena shows up clearly in the last column, which presents the correlation of growth in a given sector with overall GNP growth. Notice that nondefense purchases by the federal government are negatively related to growth in the overall economy. A correlation of −0.1. Defense spending has only weak positive correlation with the overall economy because multiyear defense programs have a different cycle of their own. The standard deviation is quite large because of the impact which policy shifts can have on the growth rate.

Exports and imports are also only weakly correlated with the growth in the rest of the economy. This flows from the impact of exchange rate changes on these categories and on differences in the global business cycle from U.S. performance. The exchange rate was largely fixed until the early 1970s; since then, major swings have occurred without any close correspondence to the general U.S. cycle. Export and import volumes have responded significantly to this variable as it has changed the relative price of U.S. and foreign goods. This factor is responsible for reducing the correlation of imports with GNP; the export correlation is even lower because Europe, Japan, OPEC, and the less developed countries have disparate cycles of their own.

The category most highly correlated with the fluctuations in macroeconomy is investment with a 0.8 correlation. The 0.8 correlation for business-fixed investment reflects the major influence of capital spending cycles on the economy and vice versa: Strength breeds strength and weakness multiplies through investment behavior. The lower correlation for the residential sector reflects the fact that housing typically leads the economy in to and out of recession by a margin of several quarters. Therefore, the contemporaneous correlation is low even though there is substantial variation around mean growth.

Financial Conditions External information regarding financial conditions should provide the chief financial officer with two types of intelligence. First, what cyclical changes are likely to occur in the near future based on past norms, and, second, what deviations from these norms are likely due to special factors of a particular cycle. As an example, the chief financial officer should recognize the tendency of short-term debt to decline as a share of total corporate debt during a business recovery. This suggests there will be a heavy schedule of corporate bond offerings during such periods, and, if the debt markets can be avoided by the corporation during the mature phase of recovery, the high interest rates of this phase can also be avoided.

However, there are occasions during which the federal government will produce anomalies in the financial markets; 1983 and 1984 are good cases in point. With the federal government trying to finance deficits on the order of $150 to $200 billion per year, there is fierce competition for funds. The nation's central bank, the Federal Reserve, refuses to accommodate this borrowing with massive purchases of Treasury debt because of its concern for adverse longerterm inflationary consequences of such action. Since 1979, Federal Reserve Chairman Paul Volcker has been unusually persistent in his anti-inflation zeal. Interest rates, as a result, are tending to be 5 percent to 8 percent above the rate of inflation for short-term borrowing compared to a normal range of 0 percent to 3 percent. This means that debt is very expensive relative to the firm's ability to raise prices to pay for it.

Equally important to the CFO are the unusual decisions by the U.S. Treasury on the maturity of their borrowing. From June 30, 1983, through June 30, 1984, for example, the Treasury increased the volume of publicly held Treasury securities with a maturity of one year or less by $2 billion while drawing $138 billion in longer maturities. This has so swamped the supply of funds at the long end of the market that long-term interest rates

Exhibit 4
National Inflation Rates

	Average Growth Rate*					Sector Volatility	
	1950s	1960s	1970s	1980s	1950–84	Standard Devia-tion†	Correla-tion††
GNP Deflator	2.1	2.8	6.8	6.3	4.1	2.8	1.0
Energy	0.3	1.2	17.7	6.7	5.6	13.0	0.7
Labor	5.0	5.1	8.1	7.1	6.1	2.2	0.9
Equipment	3.3	1.6	6.2	2.9	3.5	3.3	0.7
Structures	2.3	3.1	9.7	5.1	4.8	5.5	0.9
Agriculture	−1.9	1.4	9.0	0.6	2.1	10.2	0.4

*The intervals for the decades have been selected to run from one business cycle peak at the beginning of the decade to another peak near the end of the decade. The exact calendar quarters used are: 50s, 1948:3 to 1960:1; 60s, 1960:1 to 1970:3; 70s, 1970:3 to 1979:4; 80s, 1979:4 to 1984:3 and 1950–84, 1948:3 to 1984:3.

†Standard deviation of the inflation rates over all four-quarter intervals from 1948:3 to 1984:3.

††The simple correlation coefficient shows the sectoral inflation rate correspondence to the aggregate inflation rate given by the GNP deflator. A correlation of 1.0 suggests a perfect correspondence of sectoral ups and downs with PGNP.

have remained well above short-term interest rates—a striking difference from a traditional second year of economic recovery when the yield curve tends to flatten. CFO's response to this peculiar Treasury behavior has been to abort the transformation of balance sheets from short debt to long debt and to instead further increase the proportion of short-term corporate debt. Moreover, in mortgage markets his pressure has shown up as an inclination by the private sector to take out adjustable-rate mortgages rather than fixed-rate mortgages. Monitoring and understanding financial markets provide critical input to the cost of funds for a corporation and requirethe close and continuing attention of the CFO.

Costs and Prices It is not sufficient for the chief financial officer to have only a general knowledge of economywide changes in inflation. Cost inflation is not uniform across time intervals nor is there uniformity across the elements of cost. Exhibit 4 displays the inflation variation which has been observed over the past two decades and which is expected for the 1980s.

If competitors have different cost structures, the rates of cost inflation can shift competitive advantage. During the 1970s, companies which were energy intensive were at a disadvantage with respect to competitors who had more energy-efficient means of producing comparable goods or providing similar services. In the 1980s, with financing costs expected to run well ahead of the rate of inflation, companies with relatively capital-intensive production processes may find themselves at a substantial disadvantage to competitors who are more reliant on labor or energy. Detailed knowledge of specific inflation rates is therefore necessary to predict the evolution of costs within your own firm and in a competitor. Exhibit 5 shows how pieces of competitive information can be combined with the detailed analytical framework of a company's own cost to model future competitive cost and margin performance.

Exhibit 5a
Information on Competitor's Costs

Uses plastic instead of steel.	Has costs about the same as ours today.
Uses more equipment than we do.	
Uses fewer production people than we do.	Has about the same size and growth as we do.

Exhibit 5b
Can Be Compared with a Company's Own Income Statement

	1980 Our Company	1980 Competitor
Sales	$100	$100
Purchased materials	38	39
Value added	62	61
Direct labor costs	26	24
Overhead costs	7	6
Distribution expense	4	4
Selling expense	9	9
Depreciation	6	8
Net operating income	$ 10	$ 10
NOI margin	10%	10%

Exhibit 5c
And the Company's Detailed Schedule of Costs

Purchased Materials	Our Company Factor Weights	Competitor's Difference	Competitor's Factor Weights
Hot rolled carbon strip	.384	much less	.095
Fractional HP motors	.190	same	.190
Rubber and plastic	.095	much more	.384
Copper wire and cable	.083	same	.083
Natural gas and electricity	.079	more	.090
Ball and roller bearings	.054	same	.054
Malleable iron castings	.052	less	.041
Bolts, nuts, screws and rivets	.022	same	.022
Paint	.021	same	.021
Lumber and wood	.020	same	.020
Total	1.000		1.000

Government Tax and Expenditure Policies The final broad category of economic information with value to the CFO is that of fiscal policy. Changes in special incentives or general tax rates, increases in particular expenditure programs, and prospective federal deficits do have major impacts on industry performance.

Private vendors and the federal government continually release reports on prospective legislation. These can be valuably integrated into "scenario" analysis by the firm: for example, What

Exhibit 5d
To Simulate How Inflation May Shift Competitive Advantage: Our Company versus Competitor's Costs and Margins 1985

	1985 Our Company	1985 Competitor
Sales	$153.9	$153.9
Purchased materials	61.5	61.0
Value added	92.4	92.9
Direct labor costs	39.3	36.1
Overhead costs	11.2	9.5
Distribution expense	7.9	7.8
Selling expense	14.8	14.7
Depreciation	6.6	8.7
Net operating income	$ 12.6	$ 16.1
NOI margin	8.2%	10.5%

if energy taxes are increased? How will this affect the automotive industry by changing buyer preferences, reducing disposable income, changing inflation and interest rates?

With advance knowledge of policy initiatives under consideration, management can assess the impacts and may choose an activist position, including lobbying for favorable changes.

ASSESSING POLITICAL RISK

When considering the economic parameters discussed in the previous section, the CFO is concerned primarily with the influences of markets as they are affected by supply and demand. Political parameters, however, are quite different. A current understanding of how the political environment relates to a particular business requires a focus on the decisions within the political arena that affect policy change. Although it is often popular to focus upon the stability of governments when assessing the international political scene or upon the personalities of newly elected individuals at home, it is more important to assess how the political environment will change and how that change will affect the firm. A perfectly stable foreign government may in fact have even greater opportunity to impose policies unfavorable to a given business, while a tumultuous political environment may imply few changes in current policies.

Exhibit 6
Policy Effects on Corporate Income

Category	1985	Potential Policy Effects
Sales	$153.9	Policy on foreign competitors
Purchased materials	61.5	Foreign source import restraint
Direct labor costs	39.3	Wage policy, union policies
Overhead costs	11.2	Report requirements, health regulations
Distribution expense	7.9	Credit and interest rate policies
Selling expense	14.8	Transportation regulations
Depreciation	6.6	Tax policy
Operating income	$ 12.6	

Exhibit 6 shows how the political environment can affect a firm's income statement. Whether a firm is operating domestically or overseas, every line item of its balance sheet and income statement can be influenced dramatically by changes in domestic policy. In addition, a wide range of financial regulations can affect the capital position of the balance sheet and the financing options available to the treasurer, which are further confounded by exchange rate policies effects on cross-national accounting. Thus, correctly cataloging and anticipating the policy changes that can affect the firm is the key to assessing the effects of the political environment.

Merely keeping track of potential policy changes is not such a simple process, however. Too often, there is a tendency to focus on the pronouncements of the government in power or the most senior individuals in that government to predict policy movements. Yet the nature of politics is to produce decisions that are the result of competing pressures among many different groups, not just one or two players. Just as the president cannot guarantee that his preferred budget package will become law, neither would we naively assume that a foreign government's conditionality agreements with the IMF detailing agreed domestic economic policies will be followed to the letter despite domestic political pressure from groups opposed to the policies.

Consequently, keeping current on political parameters is a two-stage process. First is the identification of policies which may affect the outcome of operating and investment decisions. This is the organizational scheme around which any ongoing political analysis or evaluation should be directed. Second, given those policies, is the evaluation of how the players in the political arena might force changes in those policies, if at all. Finally, after these two stages, it is possible to consider the implications of these potential changes for the business.

What Are the Policies?

The starting point for keeping current on political parameters is to define the policy areas that affect your firm. This will serve to focus and organize any reading or analysis. The following are policies which affect the financial decisions of many companies. In general, we might suggest the following policy areas that may be applicable:

- Financial policy
    - Market institution regulation
    - Interest rate controls
    - Credit rationing
- Investment policy
    - Investment incentives
    - Local ownership levels
- Economic policy
    - Fiscal monetary trends
    - Foreign exchange controls
    - Changing tax policies
- Trade policy
    - Tariff/quota changes
    - Import licensing
    - Export assistance
- Operating policy
    - Domestic content requirements
    - Environmental regulations
- Labor policy
    - Wage policies
    - Unionization
    - Employment regulations

For each company, the list of relevant policies will vary. For example, the concern of an American high technology firm in Mexico may be wage policy decisions and local ownership requirements, while the same firm in Japan may be concerned with financial deregulation to aid in local financing, or the potential for import restrictions in the United States. While the broad, well-known political issues of how stable is the government or who will win the next election may provide important clues about the potential for policy change, it is the specific policy changes that take place within that environmental context that should bear the closest scrutiny. In 1984, some American firms, for example, continue to run profitable plants in El Salvador, certainly not because the overall political events are positive, but because the policies relevant to their particular plant operations continue to be favorable.

Four Elements to Monitor

In order to anticipate changes in the policies that significantly affect the firm, it is important to monitor four elements of the political environment—who the players are, what positions they are taking on each policy, what resources they have available to influence the policies, and how willing they are to expend those resources. Anticipating changes in these factors is the key to successful forecasting of policy movements that could affect your business environment in either a positive or negative manner.

Monitoring the players and their positions means more than keeping track of only the key players. On most policies, even key players must bend somewhat to the pressures brought to bear by other groups. Merely monitoring the policy pronouncements of the president or prime minister will often lead to a distorted picture of where the final policy outcome will move. In addition to key legislative or cabinet influences, policy change is often affected by industry or labor interest groups, as well as pressures from foreign sources. Even in governments dominated by strong leaders, it is highly unusual for policy outcomes to be affected by the pressures of less than a dozen players. Thus, for those policies that make a great difference to corporate operations, it is important to go beyond the typical newspaper coverage of the two or three best-known officials.

In addition to understanding the players and their positions on critical issues, assessing their relative degrees of political clout and their willingness to apply it provides an additional key to determining who most affects the policy outcome. Both of these elements are important because they determine the effective pressure that a group may apply toward a policy decision. Seemingly weak groups, such as narrow interest groups, can become extremely influential on particular decisions because they target all of their available resources toward a particular outcome.

In reality, policy decisions are formulated by balancing competing pressures which are a function of the player's issue positioning, resources, and willingness to apply those resources. A CFO who wishes to closely anticipate policy change or to select the best lobbying strategy on a particular issue must be aware of all of these elements of the policy process.

Keeping Current on Political Parameters

Keeping abreast of all of these parameters requires substantially more effort than is normally allotted for reading the daily newspaper. The successful anticipation of policy changes, however, can have dramatic effects on a firm's operations. Throughout the 1980s, we will be witnessing dramatic policy changes that will impact every business. Worldwide financial deregulation will continue to foster capital market expansion and new entries into the financial services industry. Protectionism is a constant threat to trade flows. As most nations seek to grapple with large public deficits, we will witness a host of new experiments in austerity and tax policies that affect both investment and operating decisions.

To keep track of U.S. policy developments, many large firms keep government relations offices in Washington to monitor critical issues in detail. Without such on-site information, however, it would be important to subscribe to policy-oriented journals that track issue developments in a detailed and consistent manner. This provides a significant information advantage over the more haphazard and "key player" reporting style of the news media.

Information on international political developments is now commonly provided by a number of services that have mushroomed since the fall of the Shah of Iran in 1979. Many of these so-called political risk services focus only on the broad political events. Other more comprehensive services go beyond the broad coverage to monitor all four political risk elements and to access their impact on a firm.

A more extensive description of this process is presented in Chapter 14, "Risk Assessment and Management."

HARNESSING INFORMATION TECHNOLOGY

Personal computing and on-line data bases have revolutionized the information resources available to the chief financial officer. The rapid spread of personal computers, the development of company information centers, and the availability of decision support software makes internal company information accessible for analysis by the CFO and his/her staff. The growth of on-line data bases brings external data on the economy, finance, markets, competitors, and costs into the company at electronic speeds. Harnessing this internal and external information technology can provide CFOs with early warning of change, with tighter financial control, and with the ability to plan for orderly growth.

Personal computers have become the symbol of the new availability of personal computing. These small, powerful, and flexible computers are commonplace in managers' offices, in their son's and daughter's classrooms, and even in television ads during the Super Bowl. Electronic spreadsheets have made computing literally visible as the effect of a cell change ripples across the rows and columns on the computer monitor. The accessibility of computing made possible by PCs has stimulated financial managers to test the application of these personal computing resources to their functions. Annual budgets, capital budgeting, and project analysis are typical uses of PCs in finance. While PCs cannot perform all the functions required by financial managers, they are becoming the workstation of choice. When PCs cannot perform the analyses, they are being used as terminals to the company's MIS mainframe and to external vendors' time-sharing and data banks. In this way, personal computers are the gateways to a much broader range of information resources for the finance department.

While PCs have garnered most of the publicity, other information technology changes have been taking place which extend the personal computing capabilities of financial managers.

Two of these capabilities are the availability of decision support system (DSS) software and the installation of internal company time-sharing computers. These two resources are often combined to support end user (personal) computing under the heading of an Information Center (IC). Decision support software provides a powerful array of mainframe capabilities operating through user-friendly commands and increasingly also through multiple choice menus to help new users get started. The DSS software typically includes report writing, graphics, financial modeling, statistics, and data management. Generally, this software is purchased by the MIS department and installed on a mainframe time-sharing computer dedicated to departments, such as finance, marketing, planning, and personnel.

The DSS and information center resources supplement PC capabilities. The information center can more easily make central data banks available to those with a legitimate need to access them than if these data were only available on PCs. Furthermore, the power of a mainframe computer beyond that of a PC is required for some large financial tasks, such as consolidating the budgets of all the business units or evaluating a large acquisition. By networking their PCs to the company information center, financial managers have access to the combined capabilities of the internal company data base, the power of a mainframe computer, and the flexibility and control of their own PC.

Another information technology to be harnessed is the power of the external data bases. On-line data bases from information vendors provide a wealth of economic, marketing, financial, competitor, and cost data. Together with internal mainframes and PCs and DSS software, these external data bases help financial managers develop economic assumptions for budget guidance, provide a market perspective on business unit growth plans, test vendor cost performance, monitor interest and exchange rates, compare financial performance against competitors, and evaluate company stock price changes. Most of the external information vendors provide the ability to download relevant data to PCs. Some of these vendors are helping information centers build and maintain comprehensive external databases on the information center time-sharing system so that the data are available for use by analysts throughout the company.

Combining PCs, DSS software on the company's information center, and external data provides comprehensive information technology support for financial managers. Economic change persists. Performance is not equal across business units. Vendors still look for opportunities to raise prices. Financial markets continue to move quickly. Competitors will always seek advantage, and stock price changes may portend important changes in investor attitudes towards the company. Harnessing the new information technology can give CFOs better understanding of their environment, improved control of their businesses, and the ability to plan for steady financial progress.

2

Industry and Competitive Analysis

Richard F. Schmidt

As a CFO, you are frequently called upon to recommend to your CEO requests for funding that will have a strong impact on your company's growth and profitability. These requests come to you in the form of budgets, strategic plans, capital appropriations, and acquisition proposals.

Often, you have to make your recommendations on the basis of inadequate information, as if doing a jigsaw puzzle with some of the pieces missing. Although you know a great deal about the intracompany forces that affect growth and profitability, you have little opportunity in the course of your daily work to learn about the external forces that can exert an even greater impact.

Environmental analysis, discussed in the preceding chapter,

Richard F. Schmidt is executive vice president—finance and planning of The Dun & Bradstreet Corporation, which he joined in 1969. In addition to a four-year assignment as a D&B division president, he has held both line and staff positions at other companies. He wishes to acknowledge the substantial contributions made to this chapter by Kenneth Marlin, David Morrison, and Elna Wallace.

can supply many of the missing pieces in the puzzle. Industry and competitive analysis can supply many more.

As a CFO, you are unlikely to perform industry and competitive analysis routinely yourself or even to oversee your staff's doing so. Such analysis requires specialized skills, plus a lot of legwork, which the typical financial department is not staffed to supply. But you will find it helpful to know how the analysis is done. That knowledge will sharpen your ability to identify the key factors that influence your company's success. This will come in handy as you review operating management's proposals, for it will lead you to ask the right questions.

A complete industry and competitive analysis answers three questions:

1. How much customer spending is potentially available to your product (or service)?
2. How can you convert the maximum amount of that potential spending into revenues for your product?
3. How can you minimize the cost of obtaining that revenue and thereby maximize your profitability?

An effective industry and competitive analysis is a blend of science and art. The science consists of knowing all the steps that must be taken to do a complete industry and competitive analysis for any product or service. The art consists of understanding which of these steps provides the greatest leverage—given the product being analyzed and its importance to your company and your resources—and thereby recognizing which steps can be slighted or omitted. This chapter will outline the science, while only someone thoroughly familiar with your product and your company can supply the art.

DETERMINING TOTAL CUSTOMER SPENDING

The first task of industry and competitive analysis is the measurement of total customer spending potentially available to your product. This measurement defines the marketplace and thus identifies the boundaries of success that your product may attain over time.

Distinguishing one marketplace from all others involves three steps:

1. Defining the product.
2. Identifying competitors.
3. Identifying customers.

Defining Your Product

For the purpose of industry and competitive analysis, a product is defined in terms of the customers' perception of the value it supplies to fill a specific need. You must know that value precisely in order to identify all other products providing similar value (competitors) and all individuals and organizations to whom that value is significant (customers).

The value of a product consists of the benefits it provides, offset by the price the customer has to pay.

Benefits There are many methods of defining the benefits provided by a product. One useful method is to begin by recognizing four generic benefits that every product provides to some degree: product performance, delivery, ancillary services, and exposure. Each of these benefits can then be examined by breaking it down into components.

Product Performance Product performance expresses how well the product fulfills its basic mission. In the case of automobiles, for example, the basic mission is transportation. (In the case of high-priced automobiles, an important secondary mission is status.)

For an automobile, the components of product performance are such qualities as reliability (freedom from breakdowns), appearance (sporty design), workmanship (doors that close the first time), durability (chrome that won't rust), power (speed and acceleration), and safety (protection from impact).

Product performance criteria are not limited to hard goods. Services must meet customer expectations for such characteristics as comprehensiveness, presentation, and reliability. In the credit information business, for example, customers demand information that is not only comprehensive but also accurate, reliable, timely, and presented in an easy-to-understand manner.

Delivery Whether the product is mousetraps, ice cream, or credit reports, customers require you to deliver your product speedily, reliably, and conveniently. How often will you buy the best ice cream in the world if you have to travel hours to get it? The trade-offs that customers are willing to make between product performance and accessibility can have a powerful impact on a firm's sales.

Ancillary Services Often, customers have needs that go beyond the receipt of the product. These needs include services after the purchase. Ancillary services include help with installation, advice on care, maintenance and usage of the product, and readily available repair facilities. In some industries (mainframe computers, for example), ancillary services may be the overriding factor in the decision to purchase.

Exposure Finally, customers need a benefit that we call exposure. This benefit consists of the efforts that sellers make to facilitate customers' access to the buying opportunity. Its components include information about the product provided to customers through salesmen; through displays in store windows, showrooms, catalogues, advertising, and the like; and through such aids as a free "800" telephone number for convenient order placement.

These four benefits—product performance, delivery, ancillary services, and exposure—are independent and must be considered separately if one is to analyze customers' value perceptions accurately.

Price The four product benefits offset a fifth aspect of value, price. Price consists of four elements: net payment to the seller (list price less discounts); any other costs of acquisition (transportation to the site, installation, etc.); the ongoing cost of owning the product (maintenance and repair); and the disposal costs.

You will have defined your product properly for purposes of an industry and competitive analysis once you have enumerated the components of each element of value in sufficient detail to be able to measure a customer's perception of your product's advantage or disadvantage compared with products offered by your competitors.

Identifying Competitors

Identifying your competitors is the second analysis required to define your product's opportunities, as well as the threats it must combat. This analysis requires two steps:

1. Identifying all products providing benefits similar to those provided by your product and assessing the degree of substitutability.
2. Measuring the size of competitors who supply each substitutable product.

Identifying Products That Provide Similar Benefits and Assessing Substitutability Taking the four benefits one at a time, ask yourself, "What other products offer this benefit in a similar enough form so that customers could substitute that product for ours or ours for it?"

As a simple example, if you are a manufacturer of baseboard radiators, the basic mission of your product is heating rooms. Other products that provide that benefit include upright radiators, electric heaters, and heat pumps.

To assess the degree of substitutability, compare the value of your product and others by considering both benefits and price.

Your success in the future will depend on whose product the difference in value favors and whether that difference gets larger or smaller. In the 1950s, the desktop calculator was an indirect competitor of the slide rule because it offered dissimilar benefits at a much higher price. Although the calculator provided greater computing power, it was not portable.

Over the next 20 years, however, changing technology reduced the calculator to pocket size. Thus, it offered the same portability as the slide rule, as well as superior computing power. As a result, the two products became more directly competitive. When, in addition, the calculator dropped in price, it substituted the slide rule out of business.

After you have completed your assessment of substitutability, you should have a list of products ranked by degree of substitutability—that is, divided into direct and indirect competitors. In addition, you might have a third category of "potential" competitors—products not yet on the market but soon to be made possible through advances in technology.

Measuring the Size of Competitors Your next step is to measure the size and, if possible, to forecast the growth rate of each competitor. This will define in the aggregate how large an opportunity you have over time for substituting your product for others, as well as how significant a threat you face from other products. Competitor size should be measured both in units and in dollars of revenue.

The sources of this information include: your sales force, competitors' annual reports, trade associations, government statistics, and independent research organizations that can interview both users and competitors. For a detailed discussion of techniques for analyzing customers and competitors, see Michael Porter, *Competitive Strategy* (New York: Free Press, 1980).

A convenient way of portraying the results of your analysis is shown in Exhibit 1. A complete analysis will depict the competitive situation not only as it is today but also as you expect it to exist some time in the future—that is, your projected market growth.

Exhibit 1
The Marketplace for Product "X"
$20 Billion

($ billion)

Percentage of revenue

100%	$3.2	$8.2	$5.0	$2.1	$1.5
80	All other competitors				
60					
	Third largest competitor				
40	Second largest competitor (your product)				
20					
	Largest direct competitor				
0					

Your industry	Industry A	B	C	D
Direct competitors				

Indirect competitors

High ◄— Degree of product substitutability (competitiveness) —► Low

Identifying Customers

Identifying customers—both current and potential—for all the products that compete with yours is the third analysis that defines the limits of your product's opportunities as well as its threats. This analysis requires finding out who the current customers are and why each one buys.

Who Are the Customers? Identifying your current and potential customers is key to developing a program to capture the largest possible portion of your industry's revenues for yourself.

Your research should result in a list of customers whose total spending equals the total revenue of your own product, plus that of all competitors. For this research, you can use much the same sources that you used earlier to measure your competitors' revenues.

In itself, this list will not be of significant usefulness to you. It is likely to include customers who buy from you or your competitors for very different reasons. For example, some customers will prize quality and care relatively little about price; others will be happy to do with less quality as long as the price is low. For that reason, the list by itself is going to give you few clues as to what you might do to improve customers' perception of the value of your product versus competing products. To uncover those clues, you must segment your customers by determining why each one buys the products he does.

Why Do They Buy? Customer segmentation requires measuring the relative importance customers attach to the elements of value in the product you and your competitors provide, and then grouping customers with similar profiles. When you know how each segment assesses value, you will know why customers in that segment may shift their purchases from other products to yours or vice versa.

Measuring the importance that customers attach to the elements of value requires two approaches: (1) asking customers how they rank the five elements of value, and (2) analyzing actual purchase patterns.

In many instances, you will have to divide each of the five elements of value into components—that is, characteristics specifically applicable to your product. For example, for a consumer hard good you will get meaningful results only if you ask customers how important reliability is to them or what level of workmanship or materials they expect.

Because customers often have difficulty articulating the relative importance of subtle or intangible product benefits, your questioning of customers will almost always have to be supplemented by an analysis of customers' actual purchases. This can be done using your own customer purchase records or collecting product purchase information during your interaction with the customer.

The result of your analysis will be a list of customers, segmented by their benefit priorities. Exhibit 2 shows one way of displaying the detailed preferences of one customer segment.

Exhibit 3 shows a simplified comparative analysis of two customer segments. These data might represent two of the segments in the overnight accommodations market. Segment I might be the middle-class family traveling on vacation. It is price sensitive and requires only basic levels of comfort, cleanliness, and safety. Segment II might be the business traveler who spends many nights on the road. This type of customer is relatively price insensitive but is fairly demanding in such areas as room amenities, expedited check-in and check-out services, ease of making reservations, and availability of room service.

The significance of these differences in perceptions of the elements of value is, of course, that customers will react differently to any change you or your competitors make in these elements. For example, if your price drops, the price-sensitive customers of your competitors may be persuaded to switch to your product. Quality-sensitive customers may not do so. The more aware you are of these differences in the customers' perception of value, the more likely you are to make correct competitive decisions.

This completes Part I of your industry and competitive analysis—that is, the determination of total customer spending on the benefits provided by your product and all of its competitors. You now know your market's size, growth, and potential, and your own market share. You also know enough about your competitors and your customers so that you can turn your attention to determining how you can attain the best combination of high revenue and low cost—that is, the revenue/cost position that will yield the highest sustainable profit for your product.

Exhibit 2
Relative Importance Attached to Selected Elements of Product Value—Customer Segment I

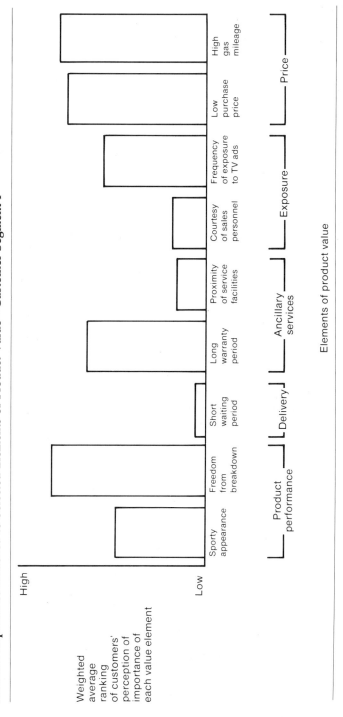

Elements of product value

Exhibit 3
Simplified Comparative Analysis of Two Customer Segments—Customer Segment I (Price-Oriented), Customer Segment II (Service-Oriented)

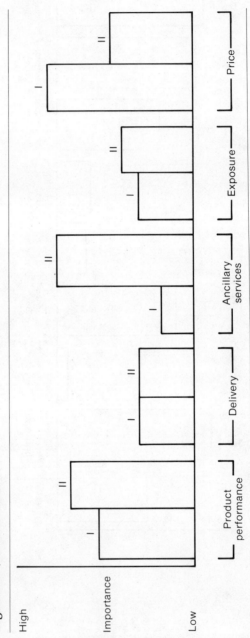

In the interest of clarity, the subjects of increasing revenue and attaining low costs relative to competition are treated separately in the following two sections of this chapter. In practice, of course, the analyses of these two topics are usually performed in tandem. A benefit-by-benefit analysis of revenue potential, together with the cost and time required to offer each benefit, will allow you to assess the profit contribution of each benefit and thereby maximize your overall, long-term, cash-generating capacity.

MAXIMIZING YOUR REVENUE

The second task in industry and competitive analysis is the definition of your product's revenue-growth potential. Defining that potential requires examining three options:

1. Gaining market share.
2. Expanding the market.
3. Tapping new sources of revenue.

Each of these steps is shown graphically in Exhibit 4 and described below.

Exhibit 4A
Options for Increasing Revenue: Gain Market Share

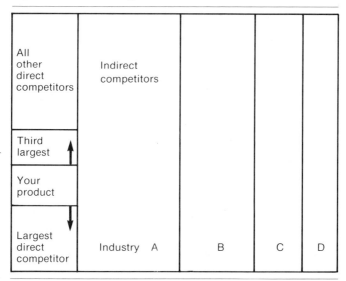

Exhibit 4B
Options for Increasing Revenue: Expand the Market

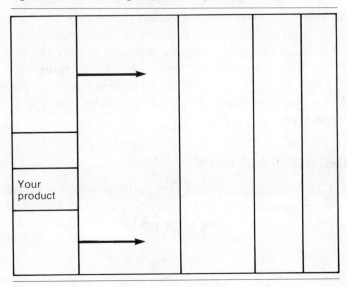

Exhibit 4C
Options for Increasing Revenue: Tap New Sources of Revenue

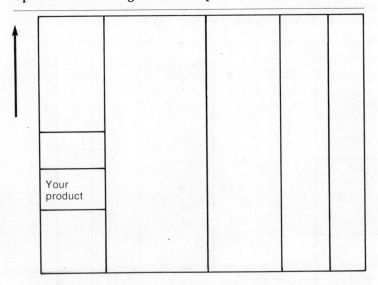

Gaining Market Share

Your first option for increasing your product's revenue-growth potential is to gain market share by drawing spending away from your direct competitors.

You can visualize this option as "expanding your product's rectangle" on the share/competition matrix as shown in Exhibit 4A.

Your success in gaining market share will depend on your ability to do a better job than your direct competitors in matching your product benefits and your price with your customers' desires. To identify opportunities for doing this, you will find it helpful to work with one customer segment at a time, with one competitor at a time, and with one element of value at a time in the following sequence of steps:

1. Measure the difference in customers' perception of the value of your competitor's product and your own.
2. Identify opportunities for better addressing customers' value priorities.
3. Estimate the additional revenue each opportunity is likely to generate for your product.

Obviously, you must also consider whether the additional revenue justifies the cost of implementing the opportunity. A later section of this chapter will deal with that question. Here, let us look at how one company went about taking the three steps listed above.

Operating in a rapidly growing region of the country, Beneco (a fictitious name for a real company) provided services to employee benefit departments of small companies. Although the CEO was convinced that his company was providing better services than its competitors, Beneco had stopped gaining market share when it reached a 15 percent share whereas its largest competitor had a 35 percent share.

To find a way of getting over this hurdle, the Beneco CEO performed an analysis in the following manner.

Measuring Customers' Perception of the Difference in Product Value Taking one customer segment and one component of value at a time, the CEO learned, first, that customers considered Beneco's prices competitive. They also considered Beneco's services at least as good as those of competitors on the counts of exposure, ancillary services, and delivery. Moreover, on most components of performance, Beneco's services were rated outstanding; for example, Beneco personnel processed paperwork more accurately than competitors, and they answered inquiries more quickly.

On one performance component, however, Beneco fell short of competitors and still shorter of what customers desired. That component was reliability or, to be specific, convincing evidence of staying power. Beneco was small, with annual volume of $6 million, and had been in business only a few years. How, customers asked, could they be confident that Beneco would stay the course? Would Beneco have the financial and managerial wherewithal to provide uninterrupted service over many years?

At this point, the CEO had a pretty good idea of where Beneco's product was strong and where it was weak in relation to both competitors' performance and customers' desires. The results of his analysis could be displayed as shown in Exhibit 5.

Now the CEO was ready to identify opportunities for changing customers' perceptions in Beneco's favor.

Identifying Opportunities for Addressing Customers' Value Priorities At first, the CEO considered improving the components on which Beneco was already strong—exposure, for ex-

Exhibit 5
What Beneco and Its Competitor Provide versus What Customers Desire

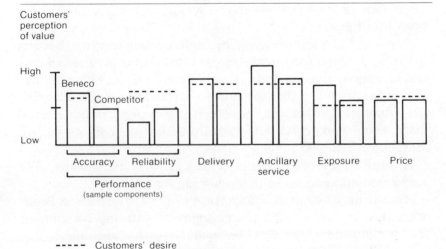

ample. He soon realized, however, that the key to improving customers' perception of a product's value is to concentrate on the element that customers consider either most important or least fulfilled. In Beneco's case, the greatest leverage would result from improving reliability. Since a reputation for reliability takes a long time to develop, Beneco decided to affiliate with a "ready-made" reputation. The CEO approached Megacorp, one of the oldest and best-established companies in the country, as a potential buyer.

Before consummating the purchase, Megacorp requested a projection of the additional sustainable revenue that its backing would enable Beneco to generate.

Estimating Additional Revenue Generation To estimate the additional sustainable revenue that the prestigious Megacorp name would attract, Beneco's CEO asked: How much, and for how long, will this improved product benefit increase the number of units that we can sell? Alternatively, he might have asked: How much, and for how long, will this improvement enable us to increase our price?

To find the answers, the CEO analyzed the likely reaction of both Beneco's customers and its competitors.

Reaction of Customers In assessing the likely reaction of customers, the CEO consulted his own sales force and a cross-segment sample of current and potential customers. The great majority of customers said they would consider Beneco's affiliation with Megacorp excellent evidence that Beneco would be in business for a long time. And many customers went so far as to say that the Megacorp name would carry more weight than the names of Beneco's competitors.

Reaction of Competitors In assessing the likely reaction of competitors, the CEO could not, of course, consult the competitors themselves. Therefore, he relied on his own informed judgment and that of his staff.

First, they asked themselves, "If we increase the perceived reliability of our service by affiliating with Megacorp, can our competitors follow suit?" Since the answer was "probably" (although attractive corporate suitors are just as hard to find as attractive corporate brides), they considered their competitors' likely intentions. "From what we know of our competitors' past behavior, are any of them likely to copy us and, if so, how soon?"

To this question, the answer was that the competitors, being larger and better established than Beneco, would probably see no need to form an affiliation in order to gain share.

The foregoing analysis gave Beneco solid evidence that correcting its one weakness, lack of convincing evidence of staying power, would tip the balance of customers' value perceptions in its favor. Further, Beneco had reason to believe that this advantage would be sustainable because its competitors would not act to nullify this effect.

Megacorp concluded, therefore, that Beneco (which was less than half as big as its largest competitor in 1978) could equal the largest competitor by 1982. As it turned out, this projection was conservative: By 1982, Beneco was twice as big as its largest competitor.

Expanding the Market

Your second option for increasing your product's revenue-growth potential is to expand your market—that is, to increase spending on your product and the products of your direct competitors at the expense of your indirect competitors.

This option can be visualized as "expanding your industry's rectangle" on the overall matrix as shown in Exhibit 4B. Success in exercising this option depends on convincing customers that your industry's products offer greater value than those of your indirect competitors.

Changing the perception of customers in this manner is usually the province of companies having very strong leadership positions in their industry. Nonetheless, it is useful for anyone doing an industry and competitive analysis to examine the list of his product's benefits for opportunities to increase his industry's revenues at the expense of its indirect competitors. Here are some examples:

Manufacturers of audiotape cassettes compete directly with each other and indirectly with producers of tape cartridges and records. In the early 1960s, cassettes were making slow progress against records because each brand could be used only on a few kinds of equipment. Then in 1963, a manufacturer of audiocassettes in the Netherlands made the specifications for its product available without royalties. This move helped to standardize cassette design worldwide and has been credited for

much of the revenue that audiophiles directed away from cartridges and records to cassettes.

Diamonds compete indirectly with Rolls Royces and Ha-
waiian vacations. The deBeers long-running "Diamonds are
forever" advertising campaign increases consumer awareness of
diamonds as an alternative to other luxuries. Similar institutional advertising promotes electric (flameless) heating versus gas,
and wool and cotton versus synthetics.

In summary, your examination of ways to expand the market
by shifting your indirect competitors' revenues to your industry
should give you a second set of options for expanding your own
revenue-growth potential. Again, you should estimate the revenue increase associated with each option.

Tapping New Sources of Revenue

The option of tapping new sources of revenue can be visualized as "expanding the entire rectangle" you assembled earlier
in the chapter, as shown in Exhibit 4C.

You can do this in two ways: You can find new customers,
or you can help cutomers to spend more on your product.

Finding New Customers Finding new customers requires increasing the value of your product to noncustomers. For example, a producer of waterproof rubber membranes used to line
artificial ponds discovered that, with some modification, this
same membrane could be used as a commercial roofing product. As a result, a significant number of noncustomers turned
into customers, and a product with current sales of several million dollars became a product with potential sales of hundreds
of millions of dollars. To turn noncustomers into customers, you
must carefully examine each aspect of product value and cre-
atively seek to serve a need outside your current customer base.

Helping Customers To Spend More To increase customer
spending, ask, "What aspect of product value can I change so
that my customers can afford to purchase more?"

For example, the way the purchase price is accounted for can
make a big difference in the customer's ability to afford the
product. As Peter Drucker has pointed out,[1] a major construc-

---

[1] Peter Drucker, *Managing for Results* (New York: Harper & Row, 1964), pp.
102–3.

tion materials company once found that public bodies could afford more of its products if they were considered operating expenses whereas private businesses could afford more if the products were considered capital assets. The solution was to charge for the same product in two ways: Public bodies were offered a 10-year rental in which the investment was paid off as an annual charge; private businesses were offered a capital asset at a price that included 10 years of free maintenance.

Once you have estimated the potential revenue increase that you might obtain through the kinds of changes discussed above—gaining market share, expanding your market, and tapping new sources of revenue—there remains one final step: deciding whether the cost of making the changes will outweigh the additional revenues.

MINIMIZING YOUR COST

The third task in industry and competitive analysis is an examination of how you can minimize the cost of producing the values you must provide in order to attract customers' spending to your product. This determination defines the limits of your product's profit potential.

As a CFO, you are no stranger to the subject of cost minimization. Almost certainly, you and your staff are already contributing significantly to your company's cost-effectiveness by scrutinizing your internal environment, spotting opportunities for eliminating wasteful activities, weeding out unprofitable customers, reducing the cost of purchased goods and services, lowering the level of assets needed in the business, and minimizing the cost of financing.

An industry and competitive analysis can help you to learn about additional cost minimization opportunities from sources outside your own company. This process requires four steps:

1. Choosing the right cost standard.
2. Correctly allocating costs to the four generic product benefits.
3. Comparing your cost-effectiveness with the competition's.
4. Identifying opportunities for improving your cost-effectiveness.

Choosing the Standard

The standard against which you must gauge your cost-effectiveness is not any internal measure, such as your costs last year, or some arbitrary ratio of cost to revenue, or even your industrial engineers' standard cost targets. Rather, the standard is external: It is the cost-effectiveness of your competitor(s). Here's why: Competitive success in any marketplace is a function of the customers' perception that your product offers a better value—that is, a better benefit/price combination—than your competitor's product. Maintaining this perception requires expenditures to make your product perform properly, to deliver it, to render ancillary services, and to provide exposure. The lower you can keep your expenditures, the lower you can keep your price or the more benefits you can provide and still make an acceptable profit.

Thus, regardless of whether the competitive battle is waged on price or on benefits or both, your cost-effectiveness compared with your competitors' will decide who ultimately wins the battle.

Allocating Costs to Benefits

Adjusting your financial information flow so that you can allocate all your costs to your product benefits is necessary so that you can quickly and accurately determine the true cost of changes in your benefit levels that may be needed to increase your product's competitive advantage.

This will require you to assign all costs, including overhead and cost of capital, to the four generic benefits (performance, delivery, ancillary services, and exposure) and, where appropriate, to the components of these generic benefits. For example:

> *Performance* cost would include most of the costs of research, design, engineering, and production. It would also include applicable overhead and capital costs allocated on a true, value-added basis rather than spread on the basis of revenue or head count, which may or may not reflect the true cost of producing the benefits.

Delivery cost would include the costs of distribution for each channel your product uses, plus the applicable part of overhead and capital costs.

Ancillary services cost would include all the costs of fulfilling guarantees, offering repair service, consulting with customers on the use of your product, and the like.

Exposure cost would include the cost of your sales force, much of your marketing effort, advertising, promotion, and so on.

The results of adjusting your financial information flow can be depicted as shown in Exhibit 6.

Such an analysis will enable you, the CFO, to determine which

Exhibit 6
Cost of Providing Product Benefits

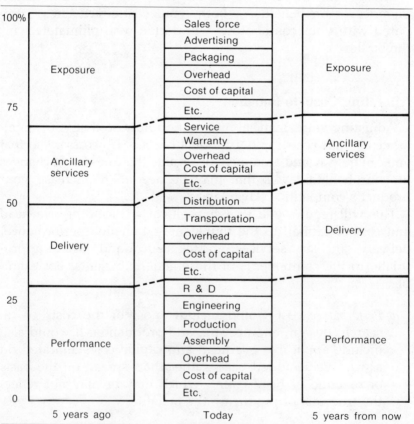

| 5 years ago | Today | 5 years from now |

benefit components represent your most important costs and, over time, which ones are growing or diminishing in importance. As a result, you will be able to advise your chief executive on the relative attractiveness of opportunities proposed by line management for strengthening the competitive advantage of your product. It will also assist greatly in the next step of measuring your company's cost-effectiveness in producing benefits.

Comparing Cost Effectiveness

Comparing your competitors' cost-effectiveness with your own, especially if you build up year-by-year data and can therefore project trends, will give you a good idea of who is ahead in the competitive battle now, and who is likely to gain ground in the future.

For example, if you notice that a competitor's cost-effectiveness is getting better than yours, you will have advance warning that, unless he simply converts this advantage into increased profitability, he will soon either underprice you, or make his product benefits better than yours, or both. In fact, that is just what the Japanese did to U.S. automobile manufacturers during the 1970s. Forewarning operating management of such developments is one of the greatest contributions a CFO can make.

Even more valuable is a benefit-by-benefit comparison of cost-effectiveness, for that enables the CFO to advise operating management precisely where to take action. If, as in the case of Exhibit 6, you have determined that delivery will become a more and more important element in your total cost structure, and if you find that your delivery performance is less cost-effective than that of your competitor, you can help operating managers pinpoint where their cost management efforts will produce the greatest payoff.

Information about competitors' overall cost-effectiveness can be gleaned from their annual reports, speeches by their company officers, industry and trade association data, and analysts' newsletters. Benefit-by-benefit comparisons are more difficult to make—so difficult, in fact, that few companies attempt them. However, there are some good sources. One of the most accessible is your own work force. For example, the best person to

Exhibit 7
Comparative Trends in Cost of Benefits

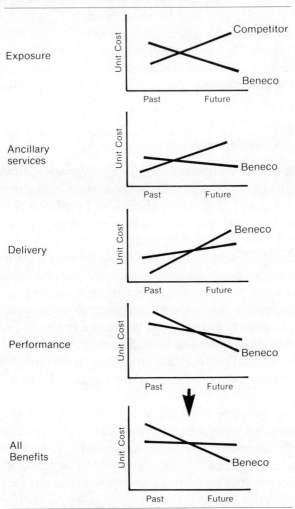

assess the cost-effectiveness of your plant versus your competitors' is probably your own plant manager.

An evaluation of competition should also include a review of the competitors' *potential* cost position and product benefits, as well as an analysis of their strengths and weaknesses, resources, and probable intentions.

It takes effort to tap all available sources, but the result can enable the CFO to make an exceptional contribution to operating management's effectiveness in improving the company's competitive position.

The result of a benefit-by-benefit analysis can be summarized as shown in Exhibit 7.

Identifying Cost Reduction Opportunities

Once you have completed your benefit-by-benefit analysis, you can start searching for opportunities to reduce your costs compared with competition. Even if you are already the low-cost producer, constant vigilance is essential to maintaining your cost-effectiveness lead over competition. Industry and competitive analysis can assist you in tapping two external sources for cost-reduction ideas: your customers and your competitors.

Learning from Your Customers CFOs have developed methods of learning about customers through analyzing company records to a high point. Industry and competitive analysis can enhance the value of this internal analysis still further by adding the insights that can be gained only from direct contacts with customers.

Not long ago, such external research enabled Insucorp (a fictitious name for a real insurance company) to cut its claims-auditing costs in half. Insucorp sells sickness and accident insurance to large corporations that have their own staffs to process claims before submitting them to the insurance company.

At the time of engaging Insucorp, most employee benefit managers request a monthly tally of their own employees' claim-processing error rate. Determining the precise error rate takes a lot of effort, and, in the past, this requirement forced Insucorp to maintain a large auditing staff.

When Insucorp interviewed the employee benefit managers of a wide spectrum of insured corporations, however, it found that most of them lost interest in the precise error rate after about a year. All they really wanted to know was whether Insucorp employees were at least meeting an acceptable standard of accuracy. Insucorp could provide this assurance with very little effort.

On the basis of this new insight into how its customers' information needs changed over time, Insucorp cut its claims-auditing activity for old policyholders by over 50 percent. This saved substantial costs without in any way harming the company's reputation for service.

Learning from Your Competitors Your competitors' successful practices are an equally good source of cost reduction ideas. Tracking these practices is essential to protecting your competitive position.

In the mid-1970s, during a routine scan of competitive activity, a supplier of research services learned that a competitor was about to automate a data-gathering procedure that his own company was still performing manually. Recognizing that this would put the competitor far ahead of him in the cost-effectiveness race, he accelerated his own plans to automate and thereby closed the gap.

By examining the most successful practices outside your company, you can turn up a wealth of opportunities for reducing your own costs. The same sources of information you used to measure your comparative cost-effectiveness will serve you well in this respect.

* * *

After you have completed the analytic steps outlined in this chapter, you are likely to have a final question: "How do I know when to stop?" When, in other words, is an industry and competitive analysis finished?

The answer is: An industry and competitive analysis is finished when you know enough about your customers, your competitors, and your capabilities to understand the full growth and profitability potential of your product and to develop a sound strategy for achieving that potential. That strategy will comprise two plans:

1. A plan for maximizing revenues by adjusting the level of your product benefits and your price in accordance with your new understanding of the preferences of your customers and the capabilities of your competitors.
2. A plan for minimizing the expenditures required to generate that revenue in accordance with your new understanding of your cost-effectiveness compared with that of your competitors.

However, such onetime plans will not give you full value for your effort. Even the soundest strategy needs revising as customers change their preferences and competitors change their capabilities. To get full value for your analytic effort, you should use it as a starting point for developing an ongoing process for gathering information about your customers and your competitors. With that information, you can continue to find new opportunities to improve your product value and your cost-effectiveness compared with competition.

3

Corporate Financial Goals

Hubert D. Vos and Alfred J. Battaglia

Corporate financial goals are an important part of the overall goals of a corporation. They should be determined in coordination with the formulation of other goals. The total system of corporate goals must be linked and supportive, one of the other. Strategic goals begin the process by defining businesses to be in, competitors, market share, and so on. Financial goals must relate to strategic goals by enhancing the likelihood of attaining strategic goals and by being realistic in terms of the resources available to the firm.

Financial goals at the corporate level must integrate well with the financial goals of the operating divisions within the company. The financial concepts and nomenclature used must be applicable and easily understood at both the operating and corporate levels. The sum of the financial goals of the operating

Hubert D. Vos became president of Stonington Capital Corporation in 1984. Prior to that, he had been CFO of Becton Dickinson and Company, Norton Simon, Inc., Commercial Credit Co., and Smith Kline & French Laboratories. Alfred J. Battaglia is president of the Vacutainer Systems Division of Becton Dickinson and Company, and was formerly vice president and controller, and vice president-treasurer of the company.

divisions must relate to the overall financial goals of the company.

The approach presented in this chapter accomplishes the desired integration between strategic and financial goals, and between operating division and corporate financial goals. Operating management relates well to return on net asset analysis and its components—return on sales and asset turnover. They appreciate the fact that the financial goals relate to what is under their control, to the assets they manage, and to what they accomplish with them. They also like the flexibility in the approach which allows different goals for each operating unit and for any one operating unit over time.

Corporate management appreciates the fact that they can deal with each operating unit separately, and yet easily sum up the company as a whole, and compare the results to the near- and long-term strategic objectives of the company. The approach incorporates the impact of taxes, debt financing, and dividend policy, so that a total corporate system is achieved.

FINANCIAL GOALS AND OVERALL STRATEGIC GOALS

To formulate financial goals, one should have a clear understanding of the operating framework of the organization. A company may be structured in many ways; for example, centralized, decentralized with separate subsidiaries, decentralized with operating divisions, and so on. Our company is structured by operating division, and each division is comprised of one or more strategic business units (SBUs). We define an SBU as an independent business with its own unique set of products, competitors, competitive positions, strategies, and objectives. In the setting of financial goals and in the subsequent analysis of performance against goals, the division level acts as the interface between SBU and corporate management.

The process is both "bottoms up" and "top down." There is a strong effort to make it as much bottoms up as is possible. This is in order to have direct imputs from those closest to the marketplace and in order to encourage responsibility and motivation at the local level. Inevitably, however, there are some aspects in both the initiation and review process which have to be top down.

At the corporate level, the process begins with a broad corporate strategy. Derived from the corporate strategy is a set of corporate financial goals which are also broad in scope and which identify the desired financial performance of the corporation. From there, several overall strategic and financial goals for each operating division are preliminarily defined.

At the division level, the work begins within the SBUs. It is important that the business of each SBU be carefully reviewed and understood before beginning the process of formulating strategic objectives and financial goals. A division's financial goals are essentially the sum of the objectives of each of its SBUs after a review process to ensure compatibility with overall division goals.

There usually are several areas of incompatibility between the sum of the financial goals of the divisions and those of the company. It is then necessary to engage in a detailed review of strategic and financial goals at corporate, divisional, and SBU levels to determine what changes need to be made and where so that a total, compatible system of strategic and financial goals for the company, each division, and SBU can be arrived at.

To handle this process of modifying and resolving conflicts in operating and corporate financial goals, we needed a uniform system of financial goals and measurements that operates well at all levels and allows us to see the interrelationships that exist so that we can visualize what effect the modification of one specific goal has on the company as a whole. Some examples of the natural conflicts that arise are:

1. SBUs often require increased funds to deploy against competitors in order to achieve their strategic objectives. These funds may be expense funds or capital funds. The total level of funds requested may not be compatible with the financial goals of the division and the company or with the available financial resources of the company.

    Recognition of such a conflict does not imply a subordination of business strategy to financial goals. It merely highlights the issue for review. The resolution may well be a modification of the financial goals, a financial restructuring, a share issue, and so on.

2. Although shareholder expectations differ, many shareholders want either dividends today or the likelihood of a stream

of capital appreciation in the future. This is their financial return, and it is reflected in a need for increased earnings per share. There may be a conflict with aggressive market penetration strategies that would result in lower earnings for several years.

3. Corporate management wants to maintain a capital structure supportive of the needs of its shareholders and its operating divisions, but it also wants to ensure sufficient financial strength to meet unexpected adverse events, as well as the unforeseen favorable opportunities which may arise. Corporate management wants some resources readily available in cash, cash availability (excess debt capacity), or in other assets readily convertible into cash.

We sought to have a system of financial goals which would permit the analysis and resolution of such conflicts and the many others which continually arise. The system had to be one where all the financial goals were closely interrelated. To accomplish this, it was necessary to pick one overall financial goal and to relate all others to it.

The selection of the overall financial goal was not easy. A number of financial concepts came to mind. One was the maximization of shareholder value. Although a most desirable objective, it proved nebulous in its analysis and most difficult to measure and hold steady over a period of time because of share value fluctuations and the like. We never lost sight of the fact that we needed a system that we could communicate with clarity and ease to a large number of managers, both in the United States and overseas. We did not want an overall financial goal that would cause endless discussions as to its definition and measurement. We needed a goal that was of central importance, easily measured, easily explainable, and readily accepted by managers throughout the company.

We decided to pick the growth rate of earnings as the anchor for our total system of financial goals. Earnings growth is a top financial goal in most companies. It is an important element in stock valuation and in shareholder value. It is easily understood by managers who have been working with it for years, and it is regularly measured on a routine basis in accounting reports.

Finally, we wanted a formula to express the interrelationships between earnings growth and the other financial goals. In the age of microcomputers, a formula was desirable so that our managers would model a number of different financial strategies. The emphasis was on the growth rate of earnings, as opposed to actual earnings in a given period, as this gave the desired long-term focus. Accordingly, we selected a "sustainable earnings growth formula."

THE SUSTAINABLE GROWTH FORMULA

The concept of sustainable earnings growth rate (hereafter sometimes referred to as SGR) has been around for quite a few years and has been developed in different ways by a number of academics and practitioners. A number of formulas have been published to calculate a company's sustainable growth rate. Each formula departs from the same basic concept that a company having no debt, paying no dividends, and having a constant rate of return on equity would have a sustainable growth rate equal to its rate of return on equity. The formulas then adjust for the fact that companies have debt and pay dividends and that their rates of return on equity fluctuate. Some of the formulas have been developed in great detail into quite complex, computer-based models. Others have taken on a fundamentally treasury-management bias by emphasizing funding needs to the exclusion of the measurement of operating profitability. Each of these formulas suits a specific purpose and is valid.

We have selected a formula which is relatively simple, easy to communicate, and relates well to the needs of both operating and corporate management. The formula is:

$$SGR = \left(\frac{NIi}{S} \times \frac{S}{NA}\right)(1-D)(1+R_1+R_2)\left(1-\frac{i}{NIi}\right)$$

Definitions of each symbol in the formula are as follows:

S = Sales for current year.

NIi = Net Income before interest expense but after taxes for current year.

NA = Net assets employed at beginning of year.

   —Total assets less cash and short-term investments less all current liabilities, except any short-term debt.

D = Fraction of earnings paid out in dividends.

R_1 = Allowable debt to equity ratio.

R_2 = Deferred taxes to equity ratio.
i = Interest expense after taxes.

Analysis of the formula and the example shows that a company's SGR is improved by:

- An increase in return on sales.
- An increase in asset turnover.
- A decrease in the dividend payout ratio.
- An increase in the debt to equity ratio.
- An increase in the deferred taxes to equity ratio.
- A decrease in the ratio of interest expense to net income.

The SGR formula is applied to the company as a whole as is illustrated in the example in Exhibit 1.

If the resulting SGR is not adequate in terms of the company's strategic goals, analyses are performed to see what changes are required for each of the components of the formula so that a satisfactory SGR develops. Because of the nature of the formula, there are a variety of sets of goals for each component which yield the desired SGR. However, much more is involved than a simple numbers exercise. One has to go into the business realities behind each component to discover what is feasible, and what the consequences of any change are on the ability of the business to meet its strategic goals.

Exhibit 1

Income Statement Information		Balance Sheet Information		Other Information	
Sales	$200,000	Debt	$ 36,000	Dividend payout	25%
Net income before interest expense	30,000	Deferred taxes	4,500	Allowable debt to equity ratio	.3
		Equity	121,500		
		Total net assets	$162,000	Deferred taxes to equity ratio	.037
Interest expense after tax	2,160				

$$SGR = \left(\frac{30,000}{200,000} \times \frac{200,000}{162,000}\right)(1 - .25)(1 + .3 + .037)\left(1 - \frac{2,160}{30,000}\right)$$

$$SGR = (.15 \times 1.23)(.75)(1.337)(.928)$$

$$SGR = 17\%$$

We conduct this process from the bottom up by first focusing on the goals of the strategic business units and then by consolidating at the corporate level where the final compromises and trade-offs take place.

RETURN ON NET ASSETS (RONA)

At the operating level, we concentrate on the first bracket of the sustainable growth formula $(NIi/S \times S/NA = \text{RONA})$.

Return on net assets, or RONA as it is referred to, has become the key financial measurement of our operating divisions. It only includes the net income items and the net assets that are under each division's control. We also use the average of beginning-of-year and end-of-year net assets as this relates better to operations. At the corporate level, we make numerical adjustments to bring us back to beginning-of-year net assets as is specified by our SGR formula. Since we exclude interest expense and debt from operating RONA, it represents a division's unleveraged return on net operating assets.

Each SBU has a specific RONA goal which is a function of its industry maturity, competitive position, and strategic goals. It is anticipated, for example, that an SBU in an embryonic industry might have a very low RONA or even a negative RONA goal for several years. Other SBUs in mature industries might be expected to have higher than average RONA objectives. The division's overall RONA objective represents a combination of the portfolio of its SBUs. The array of specific SBU RONAs as they are influenced by strategic factors can be presented as in the example in Exhibit 2.

1. An SBU with a strong competitive position in a mature industry would have a high RONA, for example, 25 percent.

Exhibit 2
SBU RONA Objectives

Competitive Positions	Industry Maturities		
	Embryonic	Growth	Mature
Strong	15%	20%	25%
Favorable	6	12	15
Tenable	3	8	10

An SBU with a weaker competitive position in an industry with an earlier stage of maturity would have a somewhat lower RONA objective, for example, 6 percent.

2. After objectives are set, it is possible to use such a matrix to summarize and monitor actual RONAs. SBUs with RONAs that are inconsistent with out expectations are subject to further analysis.

Division management has primary responsibility for developing and monitoring SBU RONA objectives. This is done by analyzing the components of RONA, return on sales ($NIi/S = ROS$), and asset turnover ($S/NA = $ A.T.).

Return on sales is analyzed by focusing on the components of sales, gross profit, expenses, and taxes. Asset turnover is evaluated by studying receivables, inventories, property, plant and equipment, other assets, and trade liabilities. For each such category, past historical performance is analyzed and specific goals are set for each of the next five years, as well as an "objective at maturity." Exhibit 3 illustrates the schedule on which such information is summarized for an SBU. Maturity represents the point at which an SBU has reached its fundamental market penetration goals and is therefore in a state of market equilibrium. In a developing SBU, the RONA targets at maturity tend to be higher and therefore represent the financial goals that the SBU management is reaching for as they develop this business. The RONA at maturity must be realistic yet attractive from a corporate point of view, or questions are raised as to the need to be in this particular business. The number of years taken to reach maturity is also analyzed.

For each of the components of return on sales and asset turnover, great care is taken in setting quantified goals.

RONA represents the product of multiplying return on sales ($NIi/S = ROS$) and asset turnover ($S/NA = $ A.T.). Exhibit 3 represents a RONA summary for a specific SBU or an operating unit for an eight-year period of time. Also, note that the final column represents individual objectives at maturity as previously discussed.

This document is an excellent summary of division management's thinking as respects their individual SBUs. Much can be learned by carefully studying and discussing this document with operating management. A similar document is filled out during

Exhibit 3
Business Plan Return on Net Asset Summary

Division X

Operating Unit

Industry Maturity

Mature

Strong

SBU XY

SBU

Competitive Position

Maintain aggressively

Strategic Role Assignment

Date Issued

	Percent X per yr.	1981 Act	1982 Act	1983 Est.	1984 Plan	1985 Plan	1986 Plan	1987 Plan	1988 Plan	Obj. at mat.*
Return on sales:										
Gross profit	%S	45.6	44.5	45.5	45.9	47.2	48.4	49.0	49.9	50.0
Total Expenses	%S	24.5	23.0	22.9	22.8	22.9	23.0	23.0	22.9	23.0
Income tax rate	%Nii	50.0	50.0	50.0	50.0	50.0	50.0	50.0	50.0	50.0
Return on sales (Nii/S)	%S	10.6	10.7	11.3	11.6	12.1	12.7	13.0	13.5	13.5
Asset turnover:[+]										
Trade receivables	%S	11.2	10.8	10.5	10.5	10.5	10.4	10.3	10.3	10.4
Total inventories	%S	16.4	13.3	10.5	10.3	9.7	9.1	8.5	8.1	8.0
Net PP&E	%S	26.8	32.1	35.8	35.3	33.7	31.7	30.1	27.9	28.0
Other assets	%S	.5	.4	1.2	1.6	1.2	.8	.7	.6	.5
Less: Trade liabilities	%S	9.7	10.4	10.1	9.7	9.8	9.8	9.7	9.3	9.5
Asset turnover (S/NA)[+]	X per yr.	2.22	2.16	2.09	2.08	2.21	2.37	2.50	2.65	2.67
Return on net Assets (Nii/NA)[+]	%NA	23.4	23.3	23.6	24.1	26.8	30.0	32.6	35.8	36.1

* Objective at maturity.

[+] All ratios are based on average (beginning of year and end of year) asset balances.

the annual budget cycle. The budget document has columns for the three previous years, this year's plan, this year's estimate, and next year's plan.

We will refer to the individual components of return on sales and asset turnover as we discuss each in more detail. As can be seen in the example in Exhibit 3, the components of return on sales are expressed as a percentage of sales. The components of asset turnover are also analyzed as a percentage of sales, but asset turnover itself is expressed as the ratio that net sales are to average net assets.

This method of presentation has proved highly useful in communicating the relative value of the components of RONA. This schedule is usually prepared with nine columns: three past years, the year being planned, the following four years, and the objectives at maturity. When filled out, it gives a clear picture of what changes in specific goals are required for the desired RONA at maturity to be progressively achieved. The comparison to past years is helpful in showing whether the forward goals appear realistic. If a major year-to-year change in a goal is indicated for the forward years, a question is immediately raised as to what change in the operations of the business is going to produce such a result.

The fact that for RONA purposes we express receivables and inventories as a percentage of sales does not imply that we do not use the more traditional measurements for daily operating control of these items.

Days sales outstanding are routinely used for control of receivables and for number of months supply for inventories.

When submitted, Exhibit 3 represents the best thinking of operating management on the specific financial goals they can meet. Each goal is carefully analyzed.

RETURN ON SALES

Return on sales at SBU and divisional level is based on operating income after tax. Operating units are not charged interest expense because debt management is centralized at the corporate level and is therefore not under the control of division presidents. However, we do charge specific tax rates to operating divisions. This is because we are a multinational company operating in a number of countries where incentive tax rates exist. We have been successful in significantly lowering our over-all corporate tax rate by having our operating divisions take taxes into consideration when positioning their operations. Other companies could decide that pretax income is more meaningful to them at the operating level and would simply adjust their SGR formula accordingly.

SALES

One of the most important goals is sales or revenue growth. Sales and marketing management normally take the lead in for-mulating sales goals. Financial management participates in their development because these objectives oftentimes are key to de-termining operating expense, capital investment, working cap-ital, and other financial goals. Specific sales goals by SBU are developed through careful consideration of factors, such as market share, competitive position, inflation, pricing trends, and so on.

Sales goals must be realistic. Nonetheless, a stretch element often appears in divisional sales goals so that at the corporate level the corporate sales goal is the sum of divisional sales ob-jectives less a discount factor based on historical experience.

GROSS PROFIT

Gross profit equals sales less cost of goods (or services) sold. This financial measurement is considered very important. It is where price-cost-volume relationships are analyzed, modeled, and challenged many times over before a specific goal for gross profit is agreed upon.

EXPENSES

Another component determining return on sales is identified as "total expenses." These expenses are basically shipping, general and administrative, marketing, sales, research, and de-velopment. It is important to understand the past and current performance of each item. Specific industry characteristics also play a role.

Expense levels have to be realistic in terms of the gross profit generated on sales. Marketing expenses have an influence on the volume of sales and on selling prices, so considerable modeling is required to arrive at an expense goal that is congruent with the sales growth and gross profit goal.

TAXES

In our company, a third important component of return on sales is the income tax rate applicable to particular operating units. Operating managements consider taking advantage of various tax abatement environments, such as Ireland and Puerto Rico. Of course, this may not be an appropriate strategy for every business. Nonfinancial factors, such as political stability, transportation, availability of labor, and the like, should be taken into consideration. Where such opportunities can be properly taken advantage of, dramatic improvements in ROS can be achieved.

We allocate tax benefits to operating divisions. Since the active cooperation of operating management is always needed to implement tax-saving programs, this procedure rewards divisions which have been active in seeking tax abatements. They are able to see the benefits reflected in their operating results. Examples of tax benefits which can be allocated are ITC, and R&D credits and job credits.

ASSET TURNOVER

Asset turnover is calculated by dividing sales by the average net assets used in a business. In today's economic and competitive environment, with volatile inflation and interest rates, as well as more and more pressure for productivity improvements, it is important that management focus on this important financial measurement. As reflected in Exhibit 3, we analyze the following components of asset turnover.

Receivables

The financial goals for receivables go beyond ensuring that good credit and collection policies are followed. Credit terms can be visualized as key tools to be used to help in the attainment of strategic objectives, particularly in the marketing area. In some cases, an extension of credit terms may be worth the cost of the additional investment in receivables that results. Financial management must weigh carefully the marketing benefits versus costs in arriving at the specific receivable goals for each SBU. To tie into our SGR formula, the receivable goals are expressed as a percentage of sales.

Inventories

Specific financial goals are also set for average inventories as a percentage of annual sales. In high-growth SBUs where market penetration is a key strategy, a higher investment in inventories may be allowed than in a mature SBU where holding down asset costs is essential. This is one more case where operating management and financial management must work together to arrive at mutually acceptable goals. If 99 percent customer service satisfaction is required, then inventory goals are going to have to be high, and this will increase investment and reduce RONA for the SBU. Can higher prices be obtained to offset the cost? These discussions take place at planning time and are fruitful in deepening the understanding of the market dynamics of each business.

Plant and Equipment

We try to identify plant and equipment by specific business or SBU. In multiproduct plants this is difficult at times, and some allocations are necessary. It is important to know the investment in plant and equipment supporting each SBU and to know how it affects the RONA calculation for each SBU. In recent years, we have had a number of interesting situations. Some old, established SBUs had grown to the point that plant additions were required. When the RONA schedules for the next five-year period were developed for these SBUs, it was seen that asset turnover was negatively affected by the significant increase in plant and equipment. This was due to the higher cost of a new plant at today's higher replacement cost compared to the depreciated old plant at much lower dollar values. We then looked at the return on sales portion of the RONA schedule to see whether there was adequate compensation in terms of higher gross profit percentages. To an extent there was as a result of the improved productivity of the new plant, but the improvement was not sufficient to affect the negative effect on RONA of the much higher percentage of sales now represented by plant and equipment. In the planning process for the next five years, operating management decided to focus on a combination of strategies involving pricing goals, volume goals, productivity goals to progressively reestablish RONA levels to satisfactory levels. What is important in the RONA analysis is the interaction of the separate components of return on sales and asset turnover to arrive at a given RONA objective.

Other Assets

It is important to be aware of hidden assets, such as investments in leased equipment, prepaid royalties, goodwill, and so on. To the extent possible, we assign such assets directly to SBUs where they are identifiable. We do not, however, allocate corporate assets such as headquarters buildings, corporate research center, or others to operating units. Corporate management is responsible for these assets. To ensure that "operating" assets are not carried at the corporate level, wherever possible, operating assets are recorded and accounted for at the operating division level.

Trade Liabilities

We subtract trade and other current liabilities from operating assets as a way of encouraging our operating management to make effective use of credit. It is not illogical to expect our accounting department to take full advantage of offered terms, including cash discounts. Further, purchasing management plays an important role in aggressively negotiating favorable terms from vendors.

Analytical Process (RONA)

The goal is to attain a level of RONA that is satisfactory for a business unit given its stage of development. The emphasis is not on maximizing either return on sales or asset turnover. What is important is to determine the mix of financial goals that will best accomplish the strategic objectives of the business and yield the desired RONA level. In principle, a business which returns 3 percent on sales with an asset turnover of eight times is as attractive as a business which returns 4 percent with an asset turnover of six times. A gross profit level of 50 percent with an expense ratio of 30 percent is as attractive as a gross profit level of 30 percent with an expense level of 10 percent. A high inventory level with low receivables matches a low inventory level with high receivables. The possible trade-offs are many. Make or buy decisions are included. A reduction in net plant (asset turnover) can fully offset a lower gross profit (return on sales).

In order to arrive at the specific financial goals for each item, it is necessary to understand the history of the business. Some changes are not feasible given the specific nature of a business. It is only within the context of a deep understanding of past performance and current environment, that realistic, consistent, and supportive goals can be established.

In the preceding paragraphs we have applied RONA analysis to operating divisions and SBUs. For inclusion in the sustainable growth formula, we need to develop the corporate RONA. Theoretically, the corporate RONA should be the sum of the division RONAs. In practice there are a few adjustments that are made.

The SGR formula uses net assets "at the beginning of the year." We have found it more meaningful at the operating division level to use the average of beginning-of-year and end-of-year net assets. We make an adjustment for this in calculating corporate RONA.

At the corporate level we have some items of net income that do not pertain to operating divisions (joint venture income, dividends received, and the like) and some assets that are of a corporate nature. We include them in the corporate RONA.

Finally, it is sometimes appropriate to allow a challenge factor to appear in the RONA goals of the operating divisions. This stretch element, if it is reasonable, can be conducive to improved performance. When we judge that this is the case, we apply a discount factor in arriving at corporate RONA.

Corporate RONA in and of itself is a meaningful measure. It represents the unleveraged return on the net assets employed in the company whereas return on equity represents the leveraged return. We focus on the elements of return on sales for the company as a whole, and on turnover of assets. In recent years, we have had meaningful discussions relating to the setting of specific goals at the corporate level for sales growth, gross profit percentage, total expense percentage, inventory levels, and investment in plant and equipment. These have been summarized into overall annual targets for return on sales and asset turnover.

When the sum of the operating division RONAs, after adjustments, does not meet the target for the corporate RONA, then we have to go back to operating division and SBU plans to see where operating strategies or portfolio mix an be altered.

EARNINGS RETENTION (1 − D)

The payment of dividends has an effect on the ability of a company to grow. If a company pays all its earnings out as dividends, it has no increase in its equity base; therefore, no increase is possible in its net assets. Unless the basic profitability (RONA) of the company increases, it is impossible for it to increase its earnings per share. At the other extreme if a company pays no dividends, it makes large increases to its equity each year through retained earnings. This permits increased operating assets and, if they are invested at the same rate of profitability (RONA) as in the past, the result is accelerated earnings growth. This impact of dividends has brought into use the concept of "earnings retention." The greater the earnings retention, the greater the company will have an ability to support higher earnings growth. The lower its earnings retention, the less it will be able to grow.

This relationship is clearly shown in our SGR formula. As can be seen, SGR is affected by the factor $(1 − D)$ which is the equivalent of earnings retention. If a company pays out 50 percent of its earnings as dividends, then the factor $(1 − D)$ would be equal to .5. This would have the effect of halving the long-term rate of growth of a company as compared to the rate at which it could grow if the dividend were zero and, therefore, the $(1 − D)$ factor were 1.

This corresponds to the well-known strategy that dividends should be de-emphasized in high-growth companies and emphasized in low-growth companies. High-growth companies need to be able to financially sustain that high rate of growth, and, therefore, they need all of the factors in our formula to be as large as possible. This means getting the $(1 − D)$ factor to be as close to 1 as possible. In a mature, low-growth company, a low rate of dividend simply results in the accumulation of cash. These funds might be better employed by the individual share-holders if they are dispersed to the shareholders as dividends and if the shareholders can then decide where to invest them for greater profit.

It should be emphasized, however, that dividend policy is also a question of historical trend, of overall corporate strategy, of the stock profile one wishes to have, and of the relationships that the corporation has had with its principal shareholders over the years. It is desirable from a shareholder point of view to have dividend policy as stable as possible.

LEVERAGE AND COST OF DEBT $(1 + R_1 + R_2) \times (1 - i/NIi)$

Leverage is another factor which affects the sustainable growth rate. There are two components: the amount of debt and the cost of debt. The amount of debt includes two factors. The first is the allowable debt to equity ratio (R_1). This is the company's targeted rate of debt relative to equity that management has set as a long-term standard for itself. The second amount is the de-ferred taxes to equity ratio (R_2). In many corporations, deferred taxes increase from year to year. Deferred taxes are, in effect, an interest-free loan from the government. They perform the same role as debt funds, except that there is no interest ex-pense charged for them.

As the formula shows, by increasing the debt to equity ratio or the deferred taxes to equity ratio, one increases the sustain-able growth rate. In other words, leverage enhances the ability of a corporation to grow. However, this needs to be modified by the second factor, the cost of debt. This factor takes into consideration interest expense in its proportion to net income before interest expense. Obviously, if a company's interest ex-pense were as large or larger than its net income before inter-est, the factor would be zero, and there would be no opportu-nity for the corporation to grow. Similarly, if interest expense is very small relative to net income before interest, then the fac-tor will only slightly decrease the benefits obtained from lever-age.

The total leverage benefit is the product of the two factors with respect to leverage amount and cost of debt. If, for example, the leverage amount factor totals 1.65 and if the cost of debt factor totals .9, then the effect of overall leverage on the sustainable growth rate is $1.65 \times .9$ or 1.485. Thus, for whatever level of RONA and earnings retention, leverage has the effect of increasing the SGR by 48.5 percent.

The power of leverage is, therefore, considerable. However, most companies that go into bankruptcy do so because they are unable to pay their debts. Debt management must stem from a clear understanding of the cyclicality of each business, its exposure to sudden surprises, its internal cash flow, and its strategic plans. There is for each business a range of acceptable debt levels. To be above the range exposes the corporation to undue risk. To be below the range may indicate lost opportunity. The formula uses the allowable debt to equity ratio rather than the actual debt to equity ratio because it is understood that in a typical company issuance of debt will be affected by market factors. There may be times when the company is somewhat underleveraged and times when it is somewhat overleveraged. What is important is the target and the long-term adherence to that target. Flexibility in financing is important, and there is no suggestion that the allowable debt to equity ratio must be met at all times, or even in most years.

In determining the appropriate amounts of leverage, cash flow is analyzed in detail. If a company is heading for trouble, typically, interest divided by net income before interest will be increasing. This is a clear signal of deterioration in the company's cash flow. In the reverse case, with the fraction decreasing, it can be a signal that the company may be able to assume more leverage. However, one should be wary of short-term fluctuations due to changing interest rates which have little long-term validity.

Leverage is not only a method of financially accelerating a company's sustainable growth rate; it can also be used as an element of corporate strategy by improving the competitive positions of the company. In a growth company, properly financed debt funds are less costly to earnings per share than are equity funds. For a given amount of capital to be deployed against competitors, a properly leveraged competitor has a lower cost of capital than his unleveraged competitor and, therefore, may have a significant overall cost advantage.

In many companies, the allowable debt to equity ratio is not reached. There is an unutilized balance. This can be effective in corporate strategy if it is consciously highlighted as a reserve that the company can use at any time to enhance its strategic objectives. There is considerable power in having that kind of flexibility.

Also, many companies have as a major corporate financial goal a specific return on equity. Our SGR formula is compatible with such a goal. It will readily be seen that return on equity is equal to the product of corporate RONA, leverage factor, and cost of debt factor.

INTEGRATED FINANCIAL GOALS

Use of the sustainable growth rate formula and application of its return on net assets component to all the operating units of the company permits the integration of the many financial goals in the company. The final focus is the most important measure, the sustainable earnings growth rate for the total company.

In implementing such a program, one should be aware of some of the technical aspects of the system that define some of its limitations.

The sustainable growth rate formula is a "funding" formula. It states what level of earnings growth a company is able to fund or financially support given the financial measurements of RONA, the earnings retention, the leverage, and the cost of debt. It does not by itself create growth. Growth is created by obtaining sales orders and by producing and shipping against those sales orders.

The SGR formula is a long-term formula. It indicates the level of growth that the company can expect to sustain over the long term if its financial measurements remain at a given level. When first applying the SGR formula, one can find that it results in a growth rate quite different from the rate being experienced in any one year. The distinction between reported earnings growth and sustainable growth is important. We refer to the factors making up the difference as the "nonsustainable" factors. The financial staff should identify such factors in analyzing past results and future projections. These factors may mislead a company in terms of what its real long-term growth rate is. If there are a number of positive nonsustainable factors, the company may delude itself that its underlying growth rate is greater than it really is. Similarly, if there are a number of adverse nonsustainable factors, the company and financial analysts may have the impression that the company has no ability to grow when, in reality, a high underlying growth rate exists. Examples of nonsustainable items are capital gains or losses from sales of assets, one-time write-offs, earnings increases because of the effect of a spurt of inflation on pricing relative to the cost of inventories on hand, and so on.

Another factor to be taken into account is that an initial significant change in any one factor in the RONA formula can cause a major change in earnings for the year. For example, year-to-year changes in the rate of sales growth, gross profit margins, expenses, or tax rate can have a dramatic impact on the reported rate of earnings growth. This is equally true of leverage. If a company starts out being substantially underleveraged and increases its leverage year to year until it reaches its allowable leverage goal, it can report major earnings gains in the transition years. However, these gains are nonsustainable, and when allowable leverage is reached, there will be no more extraordinary earnings gains from this factor.

The formula does not take into account the effects of issuing new shares of stock or of repurchasing shares presently outstanding. These are valid financial strategies which can have considerable impact on a company. For purposes of simplicity, we have not added this feature to the formula. However, it can readily be done, and any company desirous of doing share issuance or repurchase transactions should include these as an extension of the formula.

The SGR formula is really a systems approach for handling the task of integrating financial goals. It is not a pat answer to the problem. The advantage is that one can interrelate through the formula all of the many financial goals which affect the growth of the business. These require understanding and analysis before goals can be arrived at. The benefits are in the application of the system to the setting of precise measurements for the components of return on sales and asset turnover for each SBU, division, and the total corporation, and relating these to dividend policy, debt management policy, and the rate of earnings growth.

4

Capital Structure

Jerry K. Myers and John L. Carl

The objective of the business enterprise is to enhance the wealth of its owners. This objective for incorporated businesses is accomplished through the payment of cash dividends and the appreciation in value of its outstanding shares. While privately held companies may be used principally to generate tax benefits for shareholders, this chapter will deal with the public company as its model.

One element of shareholder value, cash dividends, is subject to the direct influence and control of managers/directors. The second, market value of shares, is not subject to the direct control of corporate managers. Therefore, managers must concern themselves with making decisions and taking actions which, over the long term, are designed to increase the market's appraisal of worth. This chapter deals with capital structure and its role in that process.

Jerry K. Myers is currently executive vice president and chief administrative and CFO of American Hospital Supply Corporation. In his fourteen years with American, he has had extensive experience in finance, planning, and operations. John L. Carl joined American Hospital Supply Corporation in 1972. He is vice president and controller of American's hospital sector.

CAPITAL STRUCTURE SHOULD BE A PRODUCT OF CORPORATE POSITION AND STRATEGY

Chief financial officers are often faced with questions such as:

- What is the optimum amount of financial leverage?
- Should we take greater advantage of financial leverage?
- Is it important to maintain a specific debt/equity ratio?
- What is financial flexibility all about? Is it important? Do we have too much or too little

There are no right or wrong answers to these questions. They can't be answered in black or white, but only in shades of gray. Furthermore, developing answers to these questions should not be the exclusive domain of the financial function but of the entire top management of the company.

What comes first, financial policy or corporate strategy? Fortunately, this is not a "chicken or the egg" dilemma. Establishing appropriate financial policies should be done in response to the development of overall strategic direction for the company. Unfortunately, many companies do the opposite. They establish financial policies, such as a 20/80 debt/equity ratio, maintenance of a double A bond rating, or 35 percent dividend payout ratio, and "cast them in concrete." Development of strategy then becomes subservient to these constraints.

If capital structure is developed without considering the various factors influencing it, then we can expect the resulting structure to be less than adequate in supporting the company's planning objectives. Capital structure should be developed recognizing the importance of the following:

- Nature of the business and its industry.
- Strategic plan of the business.
- Relationship between planned growth and sustainable growth.
- Current and past capital structure.

Let's examine each.

Nature of the Business and Its Industry

Capital structure should take into account the type of assets being financed. Ideally, short-term debt should be used to finance short-term assets, and long-term debt and equity should be used to finance long-term assets. Otherwise, a mismatch develops between the time of debt repayment and the asset's generation of returns for the business. This mismatch introduces an element of risk that requires careful management. The risk is comprised of interest rate movements and market receptivity at the time a refinancing is required.

Generally, the greater the capital intensity of a firm, the greater its reliance on long-term debt and equity. Of course, not all short-term assets need to be financed with short-term debt. For example, an expanding nonseasonal and noncyclical business may regard its investments in certain current assets, such as inventories and accounts receivables, as taking on the characteristics of permanent investments. There is a degree of "fungibility" between current and fixed assets for financing purposes.

If a business is seasonal in nature, it may need the flexibility provided by funding a significant proportion of its capital needs at seasonal peaks with short-term debt. Although variations in the national economy have little impact on some businesses, swings in the economy can significantly affect others, for example, construction and capital goods. The risk of financial leverage is increased for businesses subject to large cyclical variations. Businesses subject to such cyclical variations need a capital structure that can buffer the risks associated with such swings. Maneuverability is at a premium during times of contraction.

Another consideration is the degree of competition the business faces. The greater the competition and the lower the barriers to entry, the greater the risk of revenue and earnings fluctuations. As the risk of earnings fluctuation increases, safety is improved by having more weight placed on equity financing. Declining levels of competition and increasing barriers to entry generally mean decreasing fluctuations in revenue/income streams and an opportunity to safely and profitably increase financial leverage.

The risk of economic or technological obsolescence should also be appraised when considering capital structure. Obsolescence can occur in products, manufacturing processes, material components, and even marketing. Excessive leverage could severly limit a firm's ability to respond during a period of crisis triggered by "obsolescence." Consider the increasing cost of energy after the oil embargo in the early 1970s. Some firms suffered economic obsolescence because their cost structures became uncompetitive. Lacking financial maneuverability, they were unable to weather the deterioration in operating performance. The challenge is to properly assess the key factors that could lead to economic or technological obsolescence. If the risks are great, then the financial structure can be built conservatively, or strategic decisions can be made to minimize the risk.

Product or business life cycle is another consideration in developing capital structure. At the venture stage, risk is high. The risk of failure will be high and, as a result, risk equity capital is usually the primary source of funds. The speculative nature of the venture cannot justify the additional risks of financial leverage, and lenders are scarce unless given equity participation as compensation. During the growth stage, risk of failure decreases and emphasis shifts from debt markets to finance growth in the most cost-effective manner. As growth slows, any seasonality or cyclicality will become more apparent. As the business reaches maturation, leverage is likely to decline as cash flows accelerate.

Strategic Plan of the Business

The strategic plan is the single most important determinant in establishing appropriate capital structure. Strategic business needs should dictate financial strategy.

One of the first steps in the planning process is a careful analysis of the growth of served markets. Growth rates have different implications for the type of organization, approach to marketing, facility investments, and overall capital intensity. Generally, the more rapid growth projected, the more flexibility in capital structure needed. Rapid growth generally signals significant opportunities, and requires large sums of new capital to fuel the growth. To sustain the growth, a large percentage of debt may be warranted in the capital structure. However, periodic additions to the equity base are imperative. This is particularly true when the expected growth rate of the business is above the sustainable growth rate—even at high debt to equity levels. In fact, if growth results in a market valuation of common stock well above market medians (as measured in price/earnings and price/book value terms), then the opportunity should be seized to raise equity capital to cover future as well as current needs.

Contracting markets may indicate a need to move away from

debt. Or, strategic decisions may be reached to change market emphasis or the markets being served. Analysis of market growth rates does not lead directly to decisions about appropriate capital structure. Rather, it leads to strategy decisions on how best to take advantage of the current/future environment. The most appropriate capital structure will be the one which most closely supports the strategic direction of the business with the least cost and at an agreed upon level of risk.

Relationship between Planned Growth and Sustainable Growth

Chapter 3 discusses the integration of corporate financial goals with overall corporate strategic goals. A key element is the determination of the firm's sustainable growth rate. Capital structure is an important determinant of the sustainable growth rate of a business. Strategic plans may reflect a growth rate at variance with the current sustainable growth rate. To achieve the planned growth rate, changes may be required in return on sales, asset turnover, dividend rate, or capital structure. If strategic plans are to be realistic, the interrelationship of these factors must be in balance. If they aren't, then achievement of the plan is jeopardized.

Current and Past Capital Structure

Capital structure is, in large part, determined by past events. Prior financing decisions, dividend policy, acquisitions, and other investment decisions create a base which may be difficult to change quickly. Capital structure can be changed by altering dividend payout practices (See Chapter 13), changing the return on sales, changing asset turnover, issuing debt to retire equity, issuing equity or debt not proportionate to the current structure, or by a change in the growth rate of the business.

Because events of the past have placed retrictions on today's capital structure, remember that today's decisions have a similar bearing on future capital structure.

MINIMIZING THE COST OF CAPITAL

Every CFO's objective is to provide capital at the lowest possible cost to his firm. Selection of the appropriate capital structure can minimize that cost.

Step one is to determine cost of capital with the present capital structure and then to measure how it changes with a given range of alternative structures. Knowing the cost of capital is also important because it is the benchmark against which all investment decisions need to be made.

Determining the cost of capital is subject to some imprecision. It is a function of the cost of debt, the cost of equity, and the debt/equity ratio. All three are subject to continual change, so the cost of capital is a moving target. Calculating the cost of debt is easy and fairly precise—not so with equity.

Theories abound on the proper measurement of equity's cost. The starting point for most methodologies is the equity market. The rationale is that securities markets are efficient and that market prices provide the best proxy of cost to the company. In other words the return demanded by investors in the marketplace (as expressed in the price of the stock) is the cost to the company of its equity.

One popular approach in calculating investors' return requirement is the Capital Asset Pricing Model (CAPM). According to this model, the cost of equity is comprised of three factors:

- Risk-free rate.
- General market equity risk rate.
- Individual company risk rate.

The risk-free rate generally used is the yield of U.S. Treasury bills. Historically, the T-bill rate has approximated the rate of inflation. Inflation or, more appropriately, the anticipated rate of inflation is the thermostat that moves the stock market up or down and is an important determinant of your cost of capital.

The general market equity risk rate is more difficult to determine. One way is to assume that investors will demand the same return premium over the risk-free rate when investing in equities that they have required in the past. From 1926–78, the risk premium on Standard & Poor's 500 Stock Index averaged 8.9 percent.[1] This figure is skewed by the depression years. Research focusing on the 1960–80 period puts the risk premium in the 3 to 5 percent range.

---

[1] See Roger G. Ibbotson and Rex A. Sinquefeld, *Stocks, Bonds, Bills, and Inflation: Historical Returns (1926–1978)*, 2d ed (Charlottesville, Va: Financial Analysts Research Foundation, 1979).

Beta is the standard CAPM measure of the individual company risk rate. Beta is a proxy for the price volatility of a company's shares as compared to a broad market index, such as the S&P 500. Stocks with a beta greater than 1.00 rise and fall by a greater percentage than the market and, therefore, have a higher level of risk. Stocks that are less sensitive to market swings have betas below 1.00. The vast majority of companies have betas which range from 0.5 to 1.8 with most clustering between 0.8 and 1.2.

The CAPM formula multiples the individual company beta times the general market equity risk rate and adds the result to the risk-free rate to arrive at cost of equity.

A second approach to determine cost of equity is to discount future cash flows. This requires a projection from the company's strategic plan of net cash flows (before a payment of dividends) for at least 10 years.

These cash flows, plus net book value at the end of the projection period, are discounted at the rate required to equal current market value. This discount rate is the proxy for the current cost of equity.

Regardless of the technique, we've found that the answer (cost of capital) for most companies falls into a rather narrow range of 12 percent to 16 percent—except, of course, when inflation moves into double-digit territory.

HOW MUCH LEVERAGE IS DESIRABLE?

There may be an optimum debt/equity ratio for every company. Unfortunately, no one will be able to tell you exactly what it is for *your* company. Your debt/equity ratio is likely to be heavily influenced by your management's propensity to assume risk. Another influence is sure to be the degree of leverage exercised by your competitors. While these influences are real, they shouldn't rule the day. The overriding objective should be to minimize cost of capital and to enhance sustainable growth.

The tax deductibility of interest gives debt an enormous cost advantage to profit-making corporations. Up to a point, the greater the leverage, the lower the cost of capital. The trick is to determine where that *point* lies. Within some range, increased leverage will not change perceived financial risk or investor return requirements and should have no adverse effect on the price-to-earnings ratio (P/E). It may even produce a P/E ratio benefit if additional leverage is viewed as management's commitment to run the firm more aggressively for its shareholders' benefit.

The threat of bankruptcy establishes the ultimate limitation on leverage. Even the anticipation of financial stress can have a very real effect on the decisions of management and the decisions of creditors. There is some practical limit to the total amount of debt which can be obtained by any firm. Beyond that limit, the tax savings of incremental debt financing will be offset by an increased interest rate demanded by creditors who insist on greater compensation for their increased risk.

At some point shareholders and prospective shareholders will also react negatively to increased leverage. The growing perception of the possibility of bankruptcy will lead to a reduction in the market price of shares. Equity financing becomes impossible or, at a minimum, much more expensive.

In summary, there is a broad range of leverage possibilities for every company. Environmental and fundamental considerations play a role in setting the limits. While there definitely is a benefit to the use of leverage, there is a maximum limit on the amount of leverage which can or should be employed. The effect that leverage has on the stock price is based on investors' perceptions of permissible amounts determined in light of the firm's business.

MARKET TIMING AND THE DEBT/EQUITY DECISION

If one could accurately predict whether a firm's current share price is high or low relative to future values, an obvious step would be to continually alter the debt/equity mix to optimize capital costs. Equity would be substituted for debt when stock prices were judged to be "high", and the opposite substitution would occur when interest rates on debt were "low." However, problems exist with the strategy, not the least of which is the ability to predict future price movements.

Interest rates and stock prices (the returns to debt and equity-holders) have historically been correlated. That is, when equity prices have been rising, interest rates have been falling. Therefore, the relative costs of the two financing methods generally don't change significantly.

During the times of declining equity prices, many firms have been reluctant to issue equity under the belief that prices would rebound soon. However, the decade of the 1970s (and up until the bull market emerged in August 1982) illustrated the difficulty of determining whether "today's" prices are high or low relative to future prices. In the late 1970s, many firms were reluctantly forced to tap the equity market after waiting unsuccessfully for their share prices to return to the highs of 1968 or 1972. The idea that the firm's current share price approximates its true intrinsic value has been supported by 20 years of empirical research by both the academic and professional financial communities.

The likelihood of consistently outguessing the market with respect to equity price movements is not great. And, as in making the maturity structure decision, the costs of making the debt/equity decision on this basis may be great. In addition to the transaction costs of frequent alterations to the debt/equity mix, other costs include lost financial flexibility and a significant increase in interest rate if leverage rises too far above the optimal level. On the other hand, the tax benefits of leverage are sacrificed if the firm's debt is allowed to fall below the target level. Thus, optimum debt/equity mix rather than market timing should be the principal consideration in executing financing decisions.

However, opportunism should not be ignored. While no one can predict equity price and interest rate movements consistently, you do have an advantage. You have a detailed knowledge of your markets, your competition, and your company's plans. You also have instinct developed from years of experience. This instinct can be used, along with the analytical tools at your disposal, to make market judgments.

5

Mergers, Acquisitions, and Divestitures

Roger T. Briggs and Jay F. Higgins

INTRODUCTION[1]

In recent years, merger, acquisition, and divestiture transactions have become accepted instruments of corporate strategy and increasingly important management tools for the achievement of long-term corporate objectives.

Companies engage in mergers, acquisitions, and divestitures (collectively M&A) to achieve a wide variety of goals: to expand an existing business, to enter an attractive new business, or to withdraw from a less attractive old one and either reinvest the proceeds internally, reduce liabilities, or make acquisitions. Through this process of asset reconfiguration and redeploy-

---

[1]This chapter examines mergers, acquisitions, and divestitures as management tools in order to achieve strategic corporate objectives. It should be recognized that an important catalyst in many M&A transactions (which makes them "doable" as opposed to hypothetical) is a change in motivation of a corporation's shareholder base or management team.

Roger T. Briggs retired in 1984 as vice chairman and a director of Esmark Inc. He is currently a partner in the financial consulting firm of Kelly Briggs & Associates. Jay F. Higgins joined Salomon Brothers in 1970 and became a general partner in 1979. He has been head of the mergers and acquisitions department since 1978.

ment, a corporation can make important changes in its geographic presence, product mix, operations, structure, and financial results. It can, among other things, acquire additional management talent and technological know-how, alter or hedge its tax position, reduce its exposure to currency fluctuations and political risk, or access new distribution channels. Mergers, acquisitions, and divestitures can be used to achieve virtually any stated corporate objective other than a static course of "steady as she goes." From the perspective of a chief financial officer, M&A transactions should not be viewed as singular corporate events designed to produce a collection of paperweights but rather as critical elements in a dynamic process capable of producing fundamental change and dramatic enhancement of shareholder wealth.

Whether contemplating a major acquisition or divestiture program or evaluating a single transaction, a corporation must first identify and define the objectives to be achieved. This demands an honest self-appraisal of the company's existing business and future prospects. What aspects of the existing business are successful? Why? Where is the company weak or vulnerable? Why? If the senior management of the corporation could transform the firm into a totally different company overnight, what would that new company look like? Such a process of self-examination should lead to the identification of both the strengths and weaknesses of the company, and it is from this point that specific strategic objectives can be formulated. With this foundation, management can then address the question of whether there are acquisition possibilities that might assist the company in achieving its objectives. Will an acquisition yield new economies of scale, result in beneficial vertical or horizontal integration, or provide access to new markets? Management may choose to explore the acquisition of businesses complementary to existing operations which may add a measure of counter-cyclicality. Where existing businesses have underperformed and where it is impractical to develop these businesses to their maximum potential, it may be appropriate to consider a divestiture.

Whatever particular strategy develops, a candid self-analysis of a company's existing businesses with an honest appraisal of strengths and weaknesses is an indispensable first step. If this self-analysis does not precede the evaluation of a specific acquisition or divestiture opportunity, a corporation runs the very real risk that the transaction will ultimately be deemed a failure regardless of the price paid or received. If this process of self-analysis is done simultaneously with the financial and tactical evaluation of a specific acquisition opportunity, it is most likely that both jobs will be done poorly while the acquisition opportunity which sparked the exercise evaporates. Each acquisition opportunity has a life of its own, and few deals stand still for very long. In mergers, as in life, chance favors the prepared mind.

THE ACQUISITION TEAM

Any significant M&A program will require the attention of a group of senior management who will devote a significant amount of their time to the project. This group, which should include representatives of the legal, financial, and strategic planning functions, must have the confidence of the chief executive officer and key board members, a clear understanding of the company's acquisition and divestiture objectives, and sufficient authority and expertise to evaluate and execute a transaction.

The more significant the program being considered, the more likely it is that outside experts will be able to make a meaningful contribution toward its accomplishment. Business consultants can provide valuable assistance in developing a corporation's strategic plan, evaluating current operating deficiencies, and identifying those areas where internal remedies may be least effective and where acquisitions may offer the best solution. Investment bankers can assist in several different ways. Their contribution can be narrowly focused or quite broad, involving the development of acquisition criteria, the identification and evaluation of specific industries and targets within those industries, and the structuring, negotiation, and implementation of a specific transaction. An experienced investment banker often brings more transaction experience to the assignment than all the other members of the team combined and is most often relied on as a "quarterback," the senior agent of the corporation with responsibility for the successful execution of the assignment. Experienced lawyers can provide invaluable assistance in analyzing the legal, banking, regulatory, and tax considerations unique to a transaction. Accountants can provide assistance in evaluating the financial reporting and tax aspects of various transaction structures. And finally, public relations firms can assist in the drafting of press releases and in dealings with the media and the financial community. It is very important to have a talented, coordinated team, and it is critically important that the key members of the teams be fully informed of all major developments, particularly when a transaction is in progress. Transactions have been irretrievably lost as the result of mistakes in this area.

CONDUCTING AN ACQUISITION SEARCH

Corporate managements occasionally know from the outset precisely what company they would like to acquire and are reluctant to consider other possibilities. However, the inescapable reality is that the particular company that may be most attractive in the eye of the corporate suitor is rarely for sale at that moment in time and may never be available at economically justifiable prices. It is often a wiser course to identify what it is about a particular target that makes it so attractive and then take a broader look at not only that company but also others with similar characteristics. Maybe there isn't any other company quite like good old XYZ, but you will never know unless you take a serious look.

Thanks to the reporting requirements of the Securities and Exchange Commission, voluminous information is readily available on public companies. Identifying and gathering information about privately held companies, including subsidiaries of public companies, is far more difficult. Not only is it difficult to obtain comprehensive financial information on a private company but, without a public market in its common stock, valuation analysis can be problematic and price negotiations potentially more difficult. Without a willing seller, it is virtually impossible to study a private company in depth from the outside.

The type of information concerning the target company and members of its peer group that should be reviewed includes: historical operating, financial, and stock market data for the last five years; annual reports to shareholders and SEC filings, including reports on 10–K, 10–Q, and 8–K forms and registration statements; any current analysts' reports on the company; the book, replacement, and market values of both on- and off-balance sheet assets and liabilities; capital structure, including the interest rate, prepayment provisions and other terms of outstanding indebtedness and preferred stock; and prices paid in recent acquisitions of similar companies. In addition to looking at the numbers, the acquisition team must compare and contrast the various products, services, and market shares of these companies. How do they differentiate themselves? Are they successful? Who will succeed in the environments of the future? Why? Who is the low-cost producer in this industry, and does it matter? If the target participates in a regulated business, what are the specific regulations? Will they prohibit or delay an acquisition and, assuming the acquisition can be consummated, can you live with the regulations going forward? Are the regulations likely to change? In addition, after assessing a target's strengths, weaknesses, and prospects, what specific synergies might result from a business combination with you, and are you confident about them?

If this examination produces growing interest, the acquisition team must, in the case of a public company, also review the target's most recent proxy statement, its certificate of incorporation and bylaws, and all Schedule 13–Ds filed by its 5 percent shareholders. What is the composition of the shareholder base and is there reason to anticipate that any major shareholders might be interested in the sale of their shares? Is it realistic to suspect that one might be able to acquire the candidate?

This information must be evaluated in order to answer four critical questions: First, if the company were ever available, would you want it? This is not a "how much will you pay" question. If you would like to acquire it, is it your first choice, or is it one of several you find attractive? It is important to ask and answer these questions because you will be looking at other companies and because you may ultimately be negotiating a deal with one of the candidates. If that happens, you will almost certainly find yourself stretching your mind, pocket, and patience before the deal is closed, and it is a good discipline to remember how things got started. Second, using traditional investment analysis methodologies, what is the highest price which you can justify for the acquisition candidate? Third, what is the likelihood that the candidate can be acquired by you at a price that you can support? And fourth, realistically, does your company possess the financial resources and capabilities to effect an acquisition of this size?

Countless books have been written on innumerable methodologies to determine the "value" of a business. Several of the most commonly referred to are book, market, investment, and liquidation values. Book value should be calculated both on a gross basis and also net of intangibles. Book value is an important accounting benchmark, but since it is based on historical cost, it should never be used as the sole criterion of value. In some cases, book value will have limited significance, but it can become quite important in certain industries, in low multiple transactions, or in any transaction requiring secured borrowing, such as a leveraged buyout.

The market value of a publicly held corporation is an extremely important reference point since it is the current yardstick with which the target must measure any acquisition proposal. Many acquisition proposals have lain dormant in the face of frothy stock markets. An offer to merge at a price below market is never worth making, and it is generally difficult for a target to endorse an offer at a price less than a level at which it has recently traded. Investment value is that value obtained by "normalizing" the target's expected future earnings and by applying some investment multiple to those normalized earnings.

Liquidation value is that value obtained by either an orderly total liquidation of the company or the orderly sale of the company's component businesses on a "bust-up" basis. One of the assumptions upon which this chapter is based is that acquisitions are made by corporations to fulfill strategic objectives. In the real world, that means buying assets to run them, not liquidate them. An acquiror may, however, plan on divesting one or more of the target's businesses, either because the businesses do not fit with strategic plans or to provide a source of cash to pay for the acquisition. If there are such plans, liquidation values will clearly be important. Even if no divestitures are planned, however, it is a mistake for an acquiror to ignore the liquidation value of the target. The management and shareholders of the target will be keenly aware of potential liquidation values and, if they differ significantly from the value of the business on an ongoing basis, serious hurdles can very easily and quickly arise which may make any transaction difficult, particularly taxable ones. Furthermore, a potential acquiror should always consider the target's value to competing bidders, and even if a particular acquiror does not plan on disposing of any target businesses, other potential bidders (including so-called bust-up artists) may consider liquidation values of prime importance.

In addition to the more commonly referred to valuation measures, another important one is often called the "intrinsic value" of the company. This is based on a discounted cash-flow analysis of projected results, taking into account any cost savings and synergies which are expected to result from a combination of the two companies. This analysis is an important one and must definitely be done by the acquisition team. It is, however, very easy to get carried away and ultimately lost in a complicated analysis of a company's future earnings and cash flows with multiple discount rates and terminal values. One must always remember that those projections are simply someone's best guess, albeit a sophisticated one, of what the future holds. When you introduce a wide range of discount rates and terminal value price-to-earnings ratios (P/Es), the numbers, not surprisingly, start moving all over the lot. This analytical exercise is usually one of the best, but at the end of the day, it is important to remember that assets and companies are worth what people are willing to pay for them, not what certain calculations say they ought to be worth.

The likelihood that an acquisition candidate can be acquired at a price no greater than its intrinsic value depends upon many things, such as (in the case of public companies) the premium of the acquisition price to market value; the relationship of the proposed transaction price to other prices paid in comparable transactions; the shareholder profile of the target company; the existence of any controlling or other substantial shareholders and their attitude toward the offer; the attitudes and motivations of management and of the board of directors; the existence or absence of a competitive bid situation, regulatory approval requirements, and any structural impediments which the target may have in place, such as supermajority or "fair price" provisions for mergers; staggered terms for directors; separate classes of stock with disproportionate voting rights; or any of the variations of "poison pill" securities. Whether an acquiror has the resources to effectuate an acquisition depends not only on the financial strength of the buyer but also on the structure of the transaction, the financial characteristics of the target, and the resolve of the parties. The resolve of the buyer to effectuate the acquisition and the resolve of the target either to effectuate or to prevent the acquisition, depending on the circumstances. The recent wave of leveraged buyouts has demonstrated that an acquiror need not possess substantial assets to make a major acquisition.

STRUCTURING

"Structuring" an acquisition involves a determination of the amount of consideration to be paid (the price), the form of that consideration (generally cash, equity securities, debt securities, or a combination), and the form of the transaction from a legal, tax, and accounting standpoint. These structural choices are, of course, interrelated. For example, the tax implications of a transaction will often affect the price at which each party is willing to strike an agreement. A potential acquiror should remain flexible regarding structure because, as more is learned about the acquisition candidate and the interests of its shareholders, it may be advisable to reconsider any preliminary decisions. Among other things, different structures may have different implications at different price levels. For example, the creation of goodwill and resulting earnings dilution may be acceptable to an acquiror at some price levels but not at higher levels. Similarly, a seller's view of the tax consequences of a transaction may vary somewhat depending on price.

Some of the factors that often influence the structure of an acquisition include: whether the target is a publicly held or a private company; whether it operates in a regulated industry; the likelihood of a competing bid for the target; the time frame in which the acquiror desires to accomplish the acquisition; the relative sizes of the acquiror and the target; the historical tax and accounting attributes of the two companies and the pro forma accounting and cash flow effects of alternative structures; the identity, tax basis, and financial objectives of the sellers; the relationship (if any) between management of the two companies and the need or willingness of the acquiror to retain key employees of the target company; the existence of any controlling shareholders of the acquiror and their attitude toward dilution of their ownership position; the attitude of the acquiror's management and directors as to the existing market valuation of the acquiror's outstanding common stock and on the relevant importance of balance sheet strength and earnings per share; and the covenants contained in both parties' debt instruments.

The price offered in an acquisition must be formulated after consideration of the intrinsic value of the target, of the competitive realities of the situation, and of the level at which the shareholders or management of the target company will be inclined to sell or at least negotiate. Of course, the final price will generally reflect the relative perceived negotiating strength of the buyer and the seller. In the case of a hostile tender offer, success or failure at any given price will depend largely on market reaction, the defenses available to the target, the levels of determination of the bidder and the target, and the actions of potential competing bidders.

Basic Structures There are three basic structures for acquisitions—a purchase of stock, a purchase of assets, or a merger—although the structures can be combined in a variety of ways. The acquisition of a privately held business, including a division or subsidiary of a public company, can be effected through any of these techniques. Even an unincorporated division can be acquired through a merger or stock purchase if the appropriate assets and liabilities are first dropped into a new subsidiary. Whatever the form of the transaction, a nonpublic business obviously can be acquired only in a negotiated transaction with its owner or owners.

The structural considerations in the acquisition of a public company are somewhat different. To acquire a company through merger requires approval of both its board of directors and a majority (or, depending on applicable state law and the company's certificate of incorporation, sometimes a higher percentage) of its shareholders. Similarly, the acquisition of substantially all the assets of a public corporation requires both board and shareholder approval. (Acquisition of a lesser portion of its assets may only require board approval.) While acquisition of stock directly from a public corporation requires board approval, the acquisition of the stock of a public company from existing shareholders can be effected without board approval. Such purchases can be made through open-market purchases, negotiated purchases from major shareholders, a tender offer, or a combination of these techniques. While tender offers were originally used primarily in "hostile" bids, a tender offer is also now often used in a friendly, negotiated transaction because of its speed which, among other things, helps reduce the risk of a competitive bid.

Since even the most successful tender offer (friendly or hostile) will not result in the purchase of 100 percent of a large company's outstanding stock, it is normally followed by a "second-step" merger after the acquiror has taken control. The price and form of consideration may, but need not, be the same as in the tender offer. For example, many negotiated transactions involve a cash tender offer for slightly less than one half of the target's outstanding stock followed by a tax-free merger in which target shareholders receive acquiror common stock. Other combined structures are also possible; for example, a merger can be combined with a divestiture or a spin-off (including a spin-off by the target to its shareholders immediately prior to the merger) to permit acquisition of less than the entire entity.

ACCOUNTING TREATMENT

Acquisition transactions are accounted for as either a "pooling" of interests or as a "purchase" of stock or assets.

In a pooling transaction, the balance sheets of the acquiror and the target are simply added together. Since the book basis for all assets and liabilities is unchanged, no goodwill is created. In addition, because assets are not written up to fair market value (if the acquiror pays more than book), there will be no increase in future depreciation charges against those assets that would result in lower earnings. The same treatment applies to the combined company's income statement, except that the earnings per share calculation will be based on the outstanding common shares of the surviving entity.

To qualify for pooling accounting treatment, (1) at least 90 percent of the consideration paid by the acquiror must be in the form of common stock of the acquiror or its parent, and (2) 100 percent of the target's voting shares must be acquired in the transaction. Among the additional requirements in order to qualify for pooling treatment are that the surviving company must not have repurchased significant amounts of its common stock in the two years prior to the acquisition, nor may it do so in the subsequent two years, and that it may not intend to sell off a significant portion of its assets within two years other than in the ordinary course of business or in order to eliminate duplicative facilities or excess capacity. Because of these rather strict requirements, it is only appropriate to consider a pooling structure in the event of a "friendly" merger transaction, and it may be rejected even then because it can only be accomplished through the process of a proxy solicitation, which takes substantially more time to achieve than a tender offer.

All other mergers and acquisitions are accounted for as a purchase of stock or assets. Therefore, any combination and form of cash, securities, and assets may be used as consideration. In a purchase transaction, the target company's assets and liabilities are added to the acquiring company's balance sheet at their fair market values. If the total purchase price (defined as the sum of the fair market of the consideration paid and the liabilities assumed) exceeds the fair market value of the assets acquired, the excess is recorded as goodwill. Goodwill is amortized as a noncash, nontax deductible charge over a period not to exceed 40 years. If the total purchase price is less than the fair market value of the assets (negative goodwill), the difference is allocated to the target company's nonmonetary assets.

In evaluating acquisition opportunities under alternative prices and transaction structures, it is critical that detailed pro forma financial statements be carefully prepared and reviewed. These pro forma financial statements should be prepared on both a historical basis and going forward, based on a range of projections as to future results. The pro forma financial statements will show, among other things, what effect alternative structures and prices will have on earnings per share, capital structure, and fixed-charge coverage of the combined entity. Investment bankers and accountants can provide valuable assistance in this regard, but it is critical that senior management of the acquiror focus on these issues as well for they will have important financial and operational consequences.

TAX CONSIDERATIONS

The principal tax considerations in the acquisition of the stock or assets of a target are (1) whether the transaction is taxable to the target or its shareholders at the time it occurs; (2) whether the tax basis of the acquired stock or assets in the hands of the acquiror (which in turn determines the acquiror's gain or loss on their subsequent sale and, in the case of depreciable assets, the amount of depreciation deductions to which the acquiror is entitled for such assets) remains the same as their tax basis in the hands of the target or its shareholders or equals the purchase price; and (3) whether certain other tax attributes of the target at the time of the acquisition, such as net operating loss carryovers, are preserved.

Many of these tax consequences of an acquisition depend on whether the transaction satisfies the definition of a "reorganization" found in the Internal Revenue Code. Acquisitions that do not satisfy this definition are referred to as "taxable acquisitions."

In general, an acquisition can be structured as a reorganization if it is structured as a merger of the target into the acquiror or its subsidiary and if over 50 percent of the consideration paid for the target company is in the form of equity securities of the acquiror. These equity securities can be voting or nonvoting, and common or preferred. Thus, transactions that qualify for pooling treatment from an accounting standpoint are generally treated as tax-free reorganizations. However, because tax-free reorganizations can involve a significant amount of cash, the converse is not necessarily true—that is, tax-free reorganizations do not necessarily qualify for pooling treatment. Stock-for-stock exchanges, asset acquisitions, and reverse subsidiary mergers (in which a subsidiary of the acquiror is merged into the target) can also be structured as tax-free reorganizations, but the standards are more stringent in those cases.

If a transaction qualifies as a tax-free reorganization, shareholders of the target company who receive equity securities of the acquiror do not recognize any taxable income as a result of the exchange of securities. A target shareholder will, however, take the acquiror's securities with a tax basis equal to that of the target stock that he has given up in the exchange. Thus, any gain on the exchange will be, in effect, deferred until the eventual disposition of the acquiror stock received by that shareholder. In addition, if the shareholder receives any cash or other nonstock consideration in the exchange, that consideration will be taxable to the extent of the gain that would have been recognized by the shareholder had the transaction not been a tax-free reorganization. Depending on the circumstances, that gain may be taxed as capital gain or as ordinary dividend income. Because of this possibility, that gain may under some circumstances be treated for tax purposes as a dividend and taxed an ordinary income. Tax-free reorganizations are often structured as "cash election" mergers, giving each selling shareholder the option to receive only equity securities, or to receive sufficient cash so as to assure himself of capital gain treatment.

Debt securities received by target company shareholders in a tax-free reorganization generally are treated like cash consideration. In certain limited circumstances, however, the debt securities may be structured to permit target shareholders to defer the recognition of gain pursuant to the installment sales provisions of the Internal Revenue Code.

As a general matter, if a transaction qualifies as a tax-free reorganization, neither the acquiror nor the target company will incur any tax liability as a result of the transaction even if part of the consideration is taxable to target shareholders (because, for example, some cash is used in the acquisition). However, the tax basis of the assets of the target company will remain the same as that basis that had been in the hands of the target. Thus, the acquiring company will not be entitled to increase the depreciation write-off for tax purposes with respect to those assets even if the price that it paid for those assets in the acquisition was higher than their tax basis. For financial accounting purposes, however, unless the transaction qualifies for pooling treatment, the book value of the target's assets will be adjusted to their fair market value. Because depreciation of those assets will now increase for financial accounting purposes but not for tax purposes, a further adjustment will be made to reflect the fact that those increases in book depreciation will not reduce the surviving company's tax expense.

Under current law, unused loss carryovers and other tax benefits available to the target will generally be available to the acquiring corporation following a tax-free reorganization, provided that the former target shareholders maintain a 20 percent interest in the surviving corporation after the reorganization. New, more stringent standards are currently scheduled to go into effect that would affect reorganizations that take place after December 31, 1985. There is considerable doubt, however, as to whether those provisions will go into effect as scheduled or whether legislation will be enacted that will either postpone their effective date or substitute a new legislative scheme dealing with the carryover of a corporation's tax attributes following its acquisition.

If an acquisition does *not* qualify as a tax-free reorganization, the consequences of the transaction will depend on whether it is structured as a sale by the target of its assets or by target shareholders of their stock in the target. In the case of an asset sale, the target corporation will generally be taxed on the excess of the proceeds of the sale received over the target's tax basis (that is, cost adjusted for any depreciation deductions previously taken with respect to those assets) in the assets sold. While the gain recognized by the target corporation on the sale of assets that are used in its trade or business will generally qualify as capital gain, the corporation will be subject to "recapture" (that is, the recognition of ordinary income with respect to certain depreciated assets and a tax liability with respect to certain previously claimed investment tax credits). Typically, however, a sale by a corporation of all of its assets will be structured as of a so-called Section 337 liquidation: The corporation adopts a plan of liquidation, then sells its assets and liquidates within a one-year period. In that case, a tax is imposed only on the shareholders and not on the selling corporation, with exceptions for certain recapture items. The tax imposed on the shareholders will be measured by the excess of the proceeds of the liquidation received by each shareholder over that shareholder's basis in his stock in the liquidated corporation. The gain recognized by the shareholders will generally be treated as capital gain.

Following a taxable acquisition of assets from a target (whether or not structured as a Section 337 liquidation), the corporate tax attributes of the target, including any loss carryovers and investment tax credit carryovers, do not carry over to the acquiror, and the acquiror's tax basis in the target's assets will equal the purchase price of the assets allocated on a fair market value basis among all the assets purchased.

If an acquisition of a corporation is structured as a sale of stock rather than as an asset sale, the selling shareholders will recognize gain, generally treated as capital gain and measured by the excess of the proceeds of the sale received by each shareholder over the tax basis of that holder in the stock that he has sold. The target corporation will not recognize any gain or loss because of the sale, and the acquiror will not be permitted to step up the basis of the assets held by the target.

Under current law, an acquiror of the stock of a company that has loss carryovers or other favorable tax attributes may benefit from those carryovers if it files a consolidated return with the acquired company after the acquisition and provided, in general, that the acquired company continues to operate the same businesses as it had conducted prior to the acquisition. While legislation that is scheduled to come into effect in 1986 will reduce or eliminate the carryover of a target's tax benefits in the case of a taxable acquisition of the stock of that company, the fate of that legislation is uncertain, as discussed above with respect to tax-free reorganizations.

The Internal Revenue Code provides a mechanism (generally referred to as a Section 338 election) under which a transaction that is structured as stock sale and that is treated as such by the selling shareholders, may, in effect, be treated as an asset acquisition by the acquiror. Under Section 338 of the Internal Revenue Code, a corporation that purchases 80 percent or more of the stock of a target may elect to treat the purchase of stock as if it were the purchase of assets, thereby obtaining a stepped-up basis for those assets to the extent that the price paid for the target stock exceeds the target's net tax basis in its assets. This stepped-up election triggers recapture just as if the assets of the target rather than its stock had been sold. The acquiror, therefore, must take the potential liability for recapture items into account in determining whether to make the election and in establishing the price it is willing to pay for the stock. Tax attributes of the target will not survive the Section 338 election. Selling shareholders, however, will not be affected by the election.

Whether it is advantageous for a transaction to be structured as a stock purchase or an asset purchase (either a "straight" asset purchase or a stock purchase followed by a Section 338 election) for tax purposes depends in part on the relationship of the purchase price paid by the acquiror to the target's tax basis in its assets. If the purchase price is higher, it is also important to determine the period over which any step-up in tax basis can be recovered through deductions or reduced taxable income, and to compare the present value of those benefits to any upfront recapture tax costs that would be triggered by an asset acquisition (or a stock purchase followed by a Section 338 election).

LEGAL AND REGULATORY CONSIDERATIONS

Any acquisition must be structured to comply with applicable laws and regulations. While certain of the legal issues (for example, antitrust considerations) are the same whether the acquisition candidate is public or private, acquisitions of public companies generally raise many more legal considerations. In any case, it is crucial to have experienced counsel examine and review with senior management all legal and regulatory issues early in the process of considering any significant M&A transaction.

The law of the target's state of incorporation will establish whether a particular transaction requires a shareholder vote and, if so, the requisite vote. While most states required the vote of either a majority or two thirds of the outstanding stock in order to approve a merger or a sale of substantially all of a company's assets, a number of states have recently enacted supermajority voting requirements for such transactions if the merger is with one of the company's substantial shareholders unless certain statutory "fairness" standards are met. In addition to examining state law, a potential acquiror must examine the target's certificate of incorporation and bylaws because, as permitted in most states, many companies have adopted supermajority voting requirements for some or all acquisition transactions or have adopted other "anti-takeover" provisions.

Similarly, state law will determine whether a particular type of transaction gives shareholders the right to "dissent" and obtain a judicial "appraisal" of the value of their shares, which appraised value must be paid in cash by the acquiror to such dissenting shareholders. Certain transactions (for example, transactions in which the consideration received by controlling and public shareholders is different) may also raise fiduciary duty and "fundamental fairness" issues under state law.

The law of the state of the acquiror's incorporation will determine whether it needs shareholder approval for an acquisition. Generally, no approval is required except if the transaction is structured as a parent-level merger (as opposed to a merger between the target and a subsidiary of the acquiror). In some states, however, the acquiror needs to obtain the approval of its shareholders for any acquisition that will result in a substantial (for example, 20 percent) increase in the number of outstanding shares. Similarly, if the acquiror is listed on the New York Stock Exchange, shareholder approval is required for an acquisition involving the issuance of shares representing (1.) more than 18½ percent of the currently outstanding shares or (2.) more than 5 percent of the currently outstanding shares if the total value of the deal represents more than 18½ percent of the acquiror's current market capitalization. Failure to comply with such a stock exchange requirement will not invalidate a transaction, but it could result in delisting.

Another body of law that must be examined is antitrust. The government, the target company (in a hostile tender offer), a competitor, a customer, or a supplier can bring legal action to enjoin consummation or an acquisition on antitrust grounds. Legal actions can also be brought even after consummation of a transaction, either seeking to require it to be unwound or, more likely, seeking treble damages. An acquisition will violate the antitrust laws if "in any line of commerce in any section of the country, the effect of such acquisition may be substantially to lessen competition or tend to create a monopoly." The interpretation and application of the quoted words and other potentially applicable antitrust provisions is for the lawyers; for the purposes of this chapter it is enough merely to note the importance of having an antitrust review early in the planning process and, if appropriate, for the review to be updated as additional information is obtained regarding the acquisition candidate's business.

In order to give the government an opportunity to review acquisitions from an antitrust perspective prior to their consummation, Congress enacted the Hart-Scott-Rodino Antitrust Improvement Act (the HSR Act) which establishes prenotification and waiting period requirements. As a rough guideline, the HSR Act applies if (1) one of the parties to a transaction has $100 million or more of assets or annual net sales and the other party has at least $10 million of assets or sales and (2) the transaction involves the acquisition of assets or voting securities with a value of at least $15 million. Thus, the HSR Act will generally apply to open market purchases aggregating more than $15 million, except that there is an exemption if less than 10 percent of the stock is acquired and if the purchases are being made solely for investment.

An acquisition subject to the HSR Act requires both parties to submit detailed filings to the Antitrust Division of the Department of Justice and to the Federal Trade Commission. The transaction cannot be consummated (except on a government grant of early termination) for 30 days (15 days in the case of cash tender offers). If during that period the Justice Department or FTC request additional information, the waiting period is extended until 20 days (10 days in case of a cash tender offer) after such information is furnished. Once the waiting period expires the parties are free to consummate the transaction unless the Justice Department or FTC has obtained an injunction

A merger or other transaction requiring shareholder approval will require the preparation of a proxy statement complying with the Securities and Exchange Commission's proxy rules under the Securities Exchange Act of 1934 (the 1934 Act). If the transaction involves the issuance of securities by the acquiror, a registration statement under the Securities Act of 1933 will also be required. Usually a combination proxy statement-prospectus is prepared and filed as part of a Registration Statement on Form S-4 (which replaces prior Form S-14).

Open market purchase programs and tender offers involve the Williams Act provisions of the 1934 Act (and sometimes state "takeover" statutes). There are many potential legal and strategic missteps possible in this area, and the value of expert legal and financial advisors cannot be overstated.

While there are no limitations on the percentage of a publicly traded company's stock that can be accumulated through unsolicited open market purchases, once a purchaser owns 5 percent or more of the outstanding stock of any class, it is required to file a Schedule 13-D with the SEC within 10 days and to furnish a copy to the issuer. That schedule requires disclosure of information about the purchaser and its affiliates, the purchases, the source of funds used to make the purchases, and the purchaser's future intentions with respect to the issuer. An amendment must be filed promptly if there are any material changes in the information in the schedule, including an increase or decrease of more than 1 percent in the purchaser's holdings.

Tender offers are made through the preparation of an "offer to purchase" which is furnished to the target company's shareholders. A filing with the SEC on Schedule 14D–1 is also required on the commencement date, and the offer to purchase must include substantially the same information as is contained in the Schedule 14D–1.

Under SEC rules, a tender offer must be commenced within five business days after announcement of the principal terms of a planned offer. The offer must be kept open for at least 20 business days. Tendering shareholders have the right to withdraw their tenders for the first 15 business days of the offer. In the event of a competing bid, shareholders also have withdrawal rights for 10 business days unless the shares have already been purchased. During the first 15 business day withdrawal period and any other period of withdrawal rights, the bidder cannot purchase tendered shares.

In the case of a tender offer for fewer than all the shares, the bidder must purchase all tendered shares on a pro rata basis. Accordingly, in such a partial offer the bidder cannot purchase any shares until the offer expires; in offers for all outstanding shares, purchases can be made prior to expiration as soon as withdrawal rights expire. Any price increase during a tender offer must be paid for all shares purchased in the offer, regardless of whether tendered or purchased.

As a result of these timing rules, a tender offer can be an expeditious way to acquire control of a company. In the absence of a request by the government for additional information under the HSR Act, a bidder can purchase shares after 15 business days (20 business days in the case of a partial offer).

COMPETITIVE BID SITUATIONS

Ideally, all acquisitions would be negotiated and completed on a friendly basis with no interference from meddlesome third parties who may have the audacity to feel that certain assets are worth more to them than they are to you. Alas, this is often not the case. Competition has become increasingly prevalent in all types of acquisitions, friendly or otherwise. Companies seeking to be sold often conduct formal or informal auctions with the single objective of creating a competitive market for themselves in the expectation of maximizing their price tags. Targets of unsolicited tender offers always seek improved terms from more friendly "white knights," and our free capital market system will create an auction for the company all by itself.

It is an axiom in the world of M&A that a friendly deal is far preferable to an acquiror than a hostile one, but unsolicited third-party bids are occasionally made even in the face of negotiated, signed, announced transactions. Any acquisition of a public company takes considerable time. Even if the fastest acquisition structure—a tender offer—is used, it will take almost a month for the acquiror to take control. During the period, the acquisition is subject to interference by a third party's competing bid. The risk of such an unsolicited third-party competing bid can be reduced, though not eliminated, through the use of so-called lock-up devices.

If the target has a small group of shareholders owning a substantial block of the stock, the advance purchase of those shares or (more often, because of the waiting period under the HSR Act) entering into a contract to purchase those shares at a fixed price can be a very effective lockup. If a majority of the outstanding shares can be so locked up before the transaction is announced, the bidder has effectively foreclosed competition. Even a lockup of 10–20 percent of the outstanding shares can sometimes significantly reduce the likelihood of a competing bid.

In the absence of a lockup of a majority of the outstanding shares, the two most popular lockups are options granted by the target to the friendly bidder, permitting it to purchase a substantial amount of the target's authorized but unissued common stock (usually only up to 18½ percent of the outstanding shares in order to continue to comply with New York Stock Exchange listing requirements) and/or to purchase an attractive asset (a so-called crown jewel) at a fixed price. These lockups make the target less attractive to prospective third-party bidders either by making a competing bid more expensive or by eliminating the possibility of acquiring a particular asset. Generally, these lockups do not literally "lock up" a deal. But they often give the acquiror a substantial leg up against competing bids and help protect the deal. Lockups granted by the target are generally justified as inducements to encourage the bidder to enter the fray and thus obtain a beneficial transaction for the target's shareholders even if the lockups theoretically may reduce the chance of an even better acquisition offer.

DIVESTITURE TRANSACTIONS

There are several reasons why companies decide to divest assets or subsidiaries. Often, a divestiture results from an assessment by management that a business unit has not performed up to expectations or that financial and management resources can be employed more profitably elsewhere. A somewhat related reason is an assessment by management that a particular business unit is worth more to another company than it is to itself. Examples of this might be a company that has substantial mineral reserves but lacks the capital or expertise to develop them, or a company which feels that a new owner may be able to negotiate more favorable labor agreements.

From an economic standpoint, divestiture candidates should be evaluated in the same manner as acquisition opportunities. The seller must first decide what value it places on the divestiture candidate and then attempt to determine what price a prospective buyer might be induced to pay.

In order to sell a business unit, it must be readily separable from the company's other operations. Moreover, prospective purchasers must have a good sense of the divestiture candidate's financial performance and position as a stand-alone company. This can be difficult when the divestiture candidate is not a subsidiary and has had significant intercompany transactions. The more carefully a divestiture candidate is "packaged" from both a business description and a financial disclosure standpoint, the more comfortable prospective buyers are likely to be. And greater comfort will usually result in a higher purchase price. One potential purchaser to be kept in mind is the management of the business unit. In some cases, the best price can be obtained in a leveraged buyout by management, together with other investors.

Like an acquisition, a divestiture can be structured as a sale of stock or of assets or as a merger (of the divested subsidiary with the acquiror or one of its subsidiaries). In a stock sale or merger, the purchaser assumes all of the assets and liabilities that accompany ownership of the divested company as a going concern (unless, of course, the seller agrees first to purchase selected assets or to assume certain liabilities). In a sale of assets, the purchaser acquires only specific assets and liabilities. Under either structure, the seller will be asked to provide certain representations and warranties as to the condition of the business or assets sold. The extensiveness of these representations, warranties, and related indemnification is an important element to be resolved in the negotiation of terms.

One last method of divestiture is a spin-off of the stock of a subsidiary to the parent company's shareholders. Such a spin-off is sometimes appropriate when there is a subsidiary engaged in a business unrelated to the rest of the company and which has the necessary financial and managerial resources to be a viable, independent, public company.

In structuring a divestiture, it is again critical to consider the resulting tax consequences. When a parent company sells the stock of a subsidiary, then (unless the sale qualifies as a tax-free reorganization) the seller generally will recognize capital gain or loss equal to the difference between the value of consideration received and the seller's tax basis in the stock sold. In a sale of assets, the total consideration received would be allocated to the various assets sold, and each asset would be taxed accordingly. Gain recognized by the divesting corporation with respect to the sale of assets used in its trade or business generally would be capital gain, except with respect to sales of inventory and to previously claimed depreciation deductions that may result in ordinary income under the recapture rules. As a general matter, the sale of a subsidiary's assets, followed by the subsidiary's liquidation, cannot qualify as a Section 337 liquidation. However, gain is generally not recognized on the liquidation of a subsidiary.

Thus, a corporate parent selling a subsidiary generally has a choice between selling stock of the subsidiary (and recognizing capital gain or loss on that stock sale), or causing the subsidiary to sell its assets and liquidate (thus recognizing gain or loss at the subsidiary asset level). Of course, a corporate purchaser of stock can, in effect, transform that purchase into the economic equivalent of an asset purchase by making a Section 338 stepped-up election. In such a case, the depreciation and other recapture taxes triggered by the Section 338 election would be borne by the subsidiary and hence, as an economic matter, by the subsidiary's new owner.

In an asset sale, the buyer's and seller's interests with regard to allocation of the purchase price often will be in conflict. The seller will generally prefer that as much of the purchase price as possible be allocated away from inventory and other assets that would result in the recognition of ordinary income, and to goodwill and other capital assets that would generally be taxed at capital gain rates. The buyer, on the other hand, would prefer that less of its basis in the purchased assets be allocated to nondepreciable good-will and that a greater portion be allocated to depreciable assets and inventory (thus increasing its depreciation deductions and reducing the ordinary income that it will recognize on the sale of that inventory). In such a case, where the interests of the buyer and seller are tax-adverse, the Internal Revenue Service will generally honor an allocation of the purchase price made by them. If they are not in a tax-adverse posture (for example, one of the parties is not a taxpayer because of substantial loss carryovers), then that allocation will carry less weight.

If the divestiture is structured as a tax-free reorganization in which the only consideration received by the seller consists of stock in the acquiror, the seller will not recognize gain on the divestiture, but it will take the stock of the acquiror that it receives with a basis equal to its basis in the stock in its subsidiary or assets that it has given up in the exchange.

PLANNING FOR AND RESPONDING TO AN UNSOLICITED TAKEOVER OFFER

The uninvited takeover of a number of billion dollar companies in recent years has highlighted the fact that few, if any, corporations are invulnerable to unsolicited tender offers. Similarly, few companies are exempt from the "greenmail" phenomenon or troublesome proxy fights. Nevertheless, an ounce of prevention can pay substantial dividends in forestalling these possibilities or in increasing the chances that the most favorable possible terms will be achieved if the company is eventually acquired.

A company should start by conducting an audit of its vulnerability to an unsolicited offer or proxy fight. Red flags include recent acquisitions of similar companies, a stock price that fails to reflect the true value of the company, excess cash or borrowing power, and large shareholdings by investors with a very short-term perspective.

The company should carefully review the law of its state of

incorporation, as well as its certificate of incorporation and by-laws and, if it operates in a regulated industry, the applicable regulatory provisions, in order to determine the extent to which it may be vulnerable to various third-party actions that may not be in the best interests of the company and its shareholders. This review is best undertaken with the assistance of your investment banker and outside legal counsel in order to ensure that consideration is given both to the latest innovations in aggressive activities by bidders and insurgent stockholders and to any new defensive responses. Since the M&A area is dynamic and changing, this review should be updated annually.

Following this review, the company should consider the possibility of adopting various amendments to its certificate of incorporation and bylaws (often called shark repellant provisions). In most states, certain bylaw provisions can be enacted by board action without the need for shareholder approval. Most of the most significant shark repellant provisions, however, require shareholder approval. Before proposing any such provisions, the company should carefully evaluate its shareholder makeup in order to determine the likelihood that the necessary approval will be obtained. No company wishes to be in a position of proposing antitakeover provisions to its shareholders and of having the shareholders reject the provisions. Not only does the company then fail to gain the protection it sought, but it suffers publicity, reflecting its perceived vulnerability to aggressive actions. Normally, an experienced proxy solicitor and an investment banker with proxy war experience can provide substantial assistance to the company in evaluating the likelihood that any particular proposal will be approved by *its* shareholders.

Among the charter and bylaw provisions that the board of directors should consider adopting or proposing to shareholders, to the extent not already in place, are: classification of the board into three classes of directors with staggered terms of three years each; limitation on the right of shareholders to call special meetings or to act by written consent without a shareholder meeting; eliminating any right of shareholders to remove directors without cause or to increase the size of the board and then pack it (either of which devices can be used to avoid classified board provisions); elimination of cumulative voting (since cumulative voting can allow an insurgent to force his way into the board room when acting solely in his own interests rather than the interests of all shareholders); and reasonable advance notice provisions with respect to the intention of third parties to solicit proxies at an annual meeting (in order to make sure that the board of directors has adequate time to tell its story). A company should also make sure it has sufficient authorized but unissued shares of common stock and "blank check" preferred stock that it can use for various purposes, including financing, acquisitions, or hostile takeover threats. Finally, in order to avoid shareholders being pressured to tender their shares into coercive, two-tiered tender offers (for example, a tender offer for 51 percent of the stock at a substantial premium with a stated intention, if the offer is successful, to then seek to consummate a second-step merger in which remaining shares would be converted into securities worth substantially less than the tender offer price), the board of directors may wish to ask shareholders to approve fair price/super-majority provisions which are intended to assure that in any such second-step transaction shareholders are not forced to accept consideration with a lower value than what was paid by the acquiror to obtain control (and thus to assure that shareholders are not coerced to tender into a partial tender offer because of the fear of such an unfair second-step merger). Another alternative that may be appropriate for consideration is reincorporation in a state with more favorable laws. Finally, a few companies have recently asked shareholders to enact an "antigreenmail" provision that prohibits the company from repurchasing any of its shares from a substantial shareholder. The theory of such a provision is that it will deter certain stock accumulation programs by eliminating one of the incentives for certain investors; on the other hand, the board may have tied its hands if, despite such a provision, an investor takes actions not in the interests of the company, and it might otherwise be appropriate to repurchase his shares quickly without shareholder approval to terminate disruptive actions. One other defensive technique that has recently been used and is currently being tested in the courts is the distribution to shareholders of warrants (sometimes called "poison pills") or similar securities which prevent certain mergers unless they are converted into the right to purchase acquiror stock on highly favorable terms.

While none of the charter or bylaw provisions referred to above will likely have much effect on a well-financed, determined bidder prepared to make a cash tender offer for 100 percent of the company's stock, some of them will tend to deter other bidders and certain potential greenmailers. Furthermore, to the extent that bids are not deterred, certain of these provisions may give the board of directors more bargaining strength in connection with obtaining the best price for its shareholders or may otherwise help assure that a tender offer is structured in a non-coercive manner.

The company, with the assistance of its investment bankers, should also evaluate other alternatives, such as placing a block of common stock or voting preferred stock in "friendly" hands. The company and its investment bankers should also consider on a preliminary basis the company's financial alternatives in the event of a hostile takeover. For example, the company should be in a position to put together on a highly expedited basis a "black book" of important information that might be given to potential "white knight" acquirors in the event it became appropriate.

In the event that the company actually receives an unsolicited takeover offer, the board of directors and management are required to act in good faith and exercise their business judgment as to what is in the best interests of the company and its shareholders. The board may also take into account the interests of other constituent groups, such as employees, customers, and the communities in which it does business. It should be emphasized that the board of directors is not under any obligation to sell a company merely because some third-party offers to acquire it at a price above the prevailing market price. For example, the premium may be inadequate for a sale-of-control transaction, or it may be structured in an unfair way, or it may simply be a bad time to sell the company to maximize shareholder values.

In the event, however, that somebody makes such an offer and makes it directly to shareholders through a tender offer, the mere opposition of the board of directors will not normally prevent its success. If the board determines that the tender offer is not in the best interests of the company and its shareholders, it can, however, take steps intended to prevent the success of the tender offer. These steps can include litigation if the tender offer raises antitrust, securities, and regulatory laws or other issues. It can also take the form of issuing stock to a friendly investor, repurchasing stock in the open market or through an issuer tender offer, tendering for shares of the hostile bidder (a "pacman" or reverse tender), the selling of one or more divisions or subsidiaries, or the purchasing of a business. The company can also seek to obtain acquisition proposals from other potential acquirors (which can include investor groups, generally including key members of management interested in a leveraged buyout of the company). Where the initial bidder has adequate financial reserves and is fully determined, the various defenses are rarely effective. Thus, in many cases the company's choices unfortunately come down to selling the company to the highest bidder, which sometimes is the original bidder at a negotiated, higher price.

The issue of vulnerability is a critical one for every publicly owned company. What steps might be taken to ensure that a company's common stock price better reflects the economic value of the company and which of the various antitakeover instruments might be most appropriate depend on a host of variables, and many corporate actions are easier to effectuate if they are done in the absence of an unsolicited takeover effort. Accordingly, it is imperative that experienced investment bankers and legal counsel be brought on board sooner rather than later for those companies who feel particularly vulnerable. And remember, when a CEO and CFO are wrestling with issues which relate to a corporation's very existence, it is wise to be sure that your advisors are ones with whom you share boundless trust. When asking the advice of outsiders on whether you should buy a company or sell one, it's nice to know they respect you for your mind and not just your body.

PART TWO

Determining
Financial Policies

6

Capital Expenditure Analysis

Bruce Paul Bedford

INTRODUCTION

The techniques of capital expenditure analysis are well developed and widespread among industry. They focus on the economics of a capital expenditure commitment by creating a measurement which indicates the value of the decision to the corporation as a result of a cash investment in the near term for future economic benefits. A usual type of analysis would determine the discounted value of a project's future cash flow streams and compare that value with the cost of making the investment. This basic analytic process is subject to various refinements or adjustments which take into effect risks, the type of investment, and the investment's purpose as an integral portion of the business operations.

The evaluation and management of the capital expenditure analysis process is a CFO responsibility. Over time, the deci-

Bruce Paul Bedford spent 20 years in finance and general management at the Mead Corporation with his last positions as president of their Financial Services Group and vice president–financial affairs. In a 1984 management buyout from Mead he became chairman of Flagship Financial, an investment management and merchant banking organization.

sions that result from the process can restructure the company's facilities and product lines which, in turn, may determine the direction and success of the business. But a CFO who sees the process as simply the quantification of economic and market factors in order to make an investment decision is not perceiving the process for what it truly is. The process is the means by which management allocates resources to various business activities and, therefore, it must involve the entire management team. They will be interested not only in the economics of resource allocation decisions, but also in how these decisions may affect strategic business alternatives and the attainment of personal career objectives. The CFO must coordinate these varied interests, along with the hopefully logical, quantitative analysis, to reach appropriate conclusions, no matter what other internal processes exist for strategic decision making and capital budgeting.

OBJECTIVE OF THE PROCESS

The process of capital expenditure analysis and approval appears on its surface to be logical, straightforward, and subject to rational economic decision making. However, the reality of the process within an organization is usually far different, more involved, and less straightforward no matter how structured its procedures are. The CFO must keep the organization aware of the fact that the principal objectives of the capital expenditure analysis process are to:

1. Assemble and analyze the business fact base regarding the project.
2. Quantify the expected financial results of making the expenditure.
3. Gain organizational support of the final decision.
4. Provide an economic basis for evaluating and selecting among alternatives.
5. Provide a benchmark for future performance evaluation.
6. Provide a documented, decision-making process.

The Business Fact Base

The analysis process starts with establishing the appropriate fact base and assumptions regarding a project. It requires the project analyst to work with a project team, first creating an overall descriptive framework of the project concept and then building piece by piece the detailed facts and assumptions behind the concept. As the facts are gathered, the analyst documents them and builds a financial model of both the aggregate project and the component subsystems.

- Market research.
- Competitive analysis.
- Product design and pricing.
- Technology and process design.
- Plant and equipment specification.
- Manning structure.
- Raw material and energy requirements.
- Production rates and productivity.
- Distribution.
- Sales and marketing.
- Working capital requirement.

With this broad spectrum of inputs, it is clear in any major project that the analyst must work with a number of financial areas and serve as an integrator rather than as a creator of the project fact base. As the project subcomponents are documented and modeled by the analyst, they should be fed back to the project team so there is an interactive process of analysis, review, and tentative decision making that can work to improve the project's attractiveness and to assure that the project team agrees with the critical facts and assumptions.

The project analysis process should go into a final documentation and presentation mode when the project team is satisfied with all the inputs, and successive interactions of the financial model show little change. This "locked-up" analysis is then the basis for moving the project through the capital expenditure budgeting and approval process.

Quantification

The process of capital expenditure analysis is essentially a process of quantifying and documenting a myriad of assumptions, forecasts, projections, and technical analyses. The objective is to translate these items into the common language of accounting, cash flows, balance sheets, and "bottom-line" business impact. The project cash flows are then examined in terms of amounts and timing to determine a measure of their economic value. Typically, the responsibility for this falls to someone within the CFO's functional area of responsibility. In any case, the CFO has the responsibility for assuring the existence of a consistent and logical analytical framework for the institutionalized process.

Organizational Support

Given the need for integrating and organizing information in various segments and at different levels of a company, the capital expenditure analysis process draws information from various parts of the organization and helps to focus attention on a project and gain commitment to it. Every capital expenditure analysis process should require the analysis team both to (1) interact in its information-gathering processes with the rest of management and (2) solicit documented assumptions and estimates from the various involved areas of the business. Typically, this would include marketing, sales, manufacturing, engineering, and research. With this focus in the information-gathering and preliminary analysis stages, the process helps create internal discipline for reaching mutually acceptable valuations and an understanding of the basic assumptions upon which the project analysis is built.

Selection among Alternatives

Management is frequently confronted with a number of project proposals which exceeds the company's financial capacity or with several alternatives to reach the same business objective. One objective of the capital expenditure analysis process is to establish a system for decision making and selection among the various alternatives. The choice between these alternatives requires the use of both traditional capital expenditure analysis evaluation tools, such as discounted cash flow rate of return, and a broader group of decision-making criteria with which to rate the business risks and rewards present in the basic technical, marketing, and engineering areas. It is critical in this phase of a capital expenditure analysis to consider comments and suggestions from several segments of the organization and to use the process as a way to get a fuller understanding of the alternatives.

Post Evaluation Benchmark

After a thorough documentation of the assumptions and cash flow aspects of the project, the process should include the establishment of a standard against which actual performance can be measured and evaluated. When these measurements are part of the process, participants will be more concerned about the realism and accuracy of their assumptions and estimates. Knowing that project results will be checked helps to focus subsequent analysis on the critical success factors which varied from their earlier assumptions.

Documentation

As stewards of the shareholders' investment, it is almost always necessary (and particularly essential for major projects) to provide a structured and documented summary of a project's expected financial results. Later, if necessary, this helps management explain its position or contention that there was a logical and prudent investment process followed prior to the project's approval and that both management and the directors were acting in the shareholders' interests in making the project decision. While this aspect of the control of the capital expenditure process is normally not needed when a project subsequently meets or exceeds its initial expectations, it should not be overlooked.

CFO RESPONSIBILITY

Regardless of the formal responsibility assignments, the CFO must assume the responsibility for the integrity of the capital expenditure analysis process. The requirement for a structured analytical process is so fundamental to the allocation of corporate resources that it needs an advocate and protector in executive management. The CFO also has the responsibility for assuring that there is in place a documented procedure and capital expenditure analysis process that forms the basis of the decision-making process and provides a uniform, orderly means for moving proposed projects through the organization to executive management.

In its broadest perspective, the formal process for capital expenditure analysis and evaluation should include a system for moving recommendations up through the organization and a way of organizing and presenting information so that it assists both executive management and the board of directors in its resource allocation process. The process should be developed with recognition that there is a fundamental responsibility of management to assure that a solid economic basis exists for major decisions. It must be demonstrable that the process really does enhance strategic resource allocation decisions and the shareholders' wealth.

Policies and Procedures

The CFO has the responsibility to establish and implement policies and procedures for the evaluation and selection of capital expenditure alternatives. In this process, the CFO has principally a mechanical responsibility to assure that there is developed, accepted, understood, and put in place a standardized approach which is both narrow enough to provide for routine cost benefit analyses, and broad enough to take into consideration elements of product, market, technological, and competitive strategies. At the analysis level, the procedures should specify as a minimum the need for the following types of information and, in certain cases, standardized formats.

- Basic economic assumptions.
- Product and market research.
- Project description.
- Facilities design and costs.
- Manning levels and costs.
- Raw material input quantities and prices.
- Production rates over time.
- Sales and price projections.
- Risk analysis.
- Pro forma cash flow and financial statements.
- Profitability measurements.
- Business rationale.

At executive committee and board approval levels, much of this information would be used as backup support information for a more concise presentation of the relevant project considerations.

Cost of Capital

Fundamental to the capital expenditure analysis process is the simple concept of assuring that the project has an economic return which is equal to, or in excess of, the firm's cost of capital. Any management decision which authorizes investments that will not return at least the cost of capital reduces the value of the corporation. Thus, on a recurring basis, the CFO must define the cost of capital for the corporation and disseminate this information throughout the organization so that management clearly knows the minimum acceptable level of economic return for projects. In doing so, there probably should be recognition in this goal-setting process that each and every project may not meet this goal, but that in the aggregate the portfolio of projects must meet it.

While the cost of capital is the overall requirement for economic justification, there are times when other standards of measurements also impact upon the selection and viability of projects. Each capital expenditure project has a different impact upon corporate earnings, cash flow, liquidity, and strategic direction, and each must be considered in light of various needs of the corporation. Thus, standards and measurements other than the cost of capital also become basic components of the process and, at times, may even become primary factors in accepting, rejecting, or prioritizing specific projects.

EVALUATION TECHNIQUES

The essence of the capital expenditure analysis process is quantifying the expected financial results of a project. The objective of quantifying expected financial results is to answer the following questions:

- What is the value of the project?
- Is the project worthwhile?
- How does this project rank compared to other investment alternatives?

Project Analysis

The value of a project is best estimated by determining the future incremental effect it will have on revenues and expenses and by expressing that incremental effect in terms of an internal rate of return or present value. At the heart of the analysis methodology is the project cash flow as they provide the basis for evaluation and ranking. If the basic project cash flows are incorrectly structured or inaccurately estimated, then even a sophisticated profitability measurement can lead to a poor investment decision.

Thus, care and attention must be given throughout a company to the quality and thoroughness with which its capital expenditure analysis is performed. Each step of the process must be meticulously done so as to build confidence in the process and its results by the final decision makers.

Measurement Tools

Given proper analysis and a project modeled with its complete income and cash flow ramifications, it is then necessary to measure its value and economic worth. Management's initial question will typically be "How profitable is the project?" In response, the analysis process must provide a straightforward answer. While several measurement tools have been developed over the years, not all of them give a useful evaluation of economic worth. The CFO must be sure to educate management about these measurements and to make sure that they are properly used. The most frequently used measurement tools are:

Payback Period A measurement of the length of time the project requires to recover its initial investment. While it is widely used because of its simplicity, it is not a real indicator of a project's economic value. It is more an indicator of the amount of cash still at risk. Those who prefer this measurement would give top priority to projects with very high early cash returns regardless of the timing of subsequent cash flows or the ultimate value of the project.

Return on Investment (ROI) A method of generating an easily communicated accounting rate of return, which is the result of dividing the project's average annual return before interest expense by its investment. It is usually compared to the company's cost of capital and, if higher, the project probably would be considered worthwhile. Unfortunately, ROI fails to consider the time value of the cash flows and can lead to an erroneous decision.

Net Present Value (NPV) A measurement that considers the time value of money and thus provides a sound basis for evaluating a project's present economic value. The process involves the discounting of the project's cash flows by a factor which represents the time value of those flows taken at the company's cost of capital. If the present value of cash flows exceeds the cost of capital, the project should enhance shareholder values.

Discounted Cash Flow Rate of Return (DCF) Through a trial-and-error process, this popular tool calculates the discount rate (internal rate of return) for the project which generates a net present value of zero. That is, a rate which, when applied to the project's cash flow, generates a net present value that is exactly equal to the initial investment.

PROJECT CLASSIFICATION

After the capital expenditure analysis process has determined a project's value, it is still incumbent upon the CFO to devise a means of ranking various projects and matching them with the company's business opportunities and financial constraints. This typically involves systems of classifying projects into ranked subgroupings. A typical type of budgeting classification structure might be to sort out all the capital expenditure projects for a business in the following manner:

Mandated. Required by law for environmental, health, and/or safety reasons.

Maintenance. Repair and replacement items needed just to keep the current facilities operational.

Cost saving. Low-risk opportunities for improving profits by reducing product costs or enhancing productivity.

Growth. Opportunities for increased market penetration with current products or for developing new products.

Within these classifications, projects are typically arrayed in order of their financial desirability, probably showing cash investments and returns by year. While classification systems such as this help give structure to the preliminary budgeting and approval process, projects ultimately have to stand on their own and meet or surpass a company's investment policy guidelines.

Project Ranking

With a detailed and structured cash flow analysis, ranking projects in order of their discounted cash flow rates of return is simple. What is difficult for the CFO, however, is blending the subjective factors of a project into the process.

To deal with the subjective elements, managements typically adjust their hurdle rates for the perceived riskiness and uncertainty of projects. Thus, a project with a barely acceptable rate of return and with little risk or uncertainty may be ranked ahead of a high-risk project with substantial business risk and uncertainty in its cash flows.

Nevertheless, ranking the criteria for management approval is a necessary exercise. The objectives of the ranking process are to:

1. Select the best alternative among alternative projects to accomplish the same end goal.
2. Discriminate between desirable and undesirable projects.
3. Prioritize a list of desirable, but different, projects.

Companies typically set a mixture of financial return and risk guidelines for approval depending on the nature of the business and its financial situation. These guidelines usually change over time as a company's financial position, business strategy, and competitive environment change. In all situations, however, for discretionary projects, only those which exceed the company's hurdle rate and guidelines are considered eligible for the ranking process. Thus, the following policy guidelines are typical of those which the CFO might recommend when the indicated circumstances exist:

Tight cash position Defer mandatory spending as much as possible, and fund only essential maintenance and fast payback, cost-saving projects.

Normal operations Fund a reasonable level of mandatory and maintenance expenditures, but emphasize cost-saving and growth projects.

Excess cash availability Focus excess cash on key growth projects, acquisitions, and creative ways to reduce costs, and improve productivity or generally increase shareholders' return on investment.

SPECIAL ANALYSIS SITUATIONS

While a majority of capital expenditure proposals can flow smoothly through the analysis process, there are certain categories of situations which require special attention by both the CFO and his analysis team. In these situations, additional questions need to be asked, and the normal analysis process needs either to be augmented or to incorporate some additional procedures. The "special analysis situations" a CFO typically encounters are:

1. "Bet your company" projects.
2. Projects with major "what if" decision points.
3. International investment projects with currency and political risks.
4. Investments in time of inflation.

While these situations may pose problems for the CFO who initially encounters them, they are subject to some generalized analytical procedures which will clarify the issues, quantify their impact, and facilitate in the decision-making process.

"Bet Your Company" Proposals

At certain, critical turning points in a company's development, there may be capital expenditure proposals which are tantamount to a "bet your company" situation. This is when a single project requires a financial commitment in excess of 50 percent of the company's equity. The project may be the development of a new product, a major facility expansion, or a diversification move. In any case, the project's success is fundamental to the company's success, and it requires extra analysis and thoughtful consideration by all of management.

In such a "bet your company" situation, the project itself requires the highest level of documented and detailed fact-finding, financial modeling, and considered analysis. The elements of projects like this are no different than those of any other proposal. However, when the project analysis team has completed its work, it is prudent to assemble another small group of experts and form a "challenge and review" team. This team should undertake an independent review of all facets of the project, including markets, competition, pricing costs, facilities, technology, and so on. Their objective is both to identify differences in assumptions and expectations and to quantify the project in the same manner as was done by the project team.

In addition, the challenge and review team needs to examine the project from a broader corporate perspective. Critical to this analysis is the defining of major alternate success or failure scenarios and the measuring of their impact on and implications to the company. Some key questions are:

- What is the timing and magnitude of potential cash outflow?
- Can we survive and fund adverse cash flows?
- What happens to the corporate pro forma balance sheet?
- What is the timing and accounting treatment of any earnings impact?
- Given our financial structure and business strategy, is it prudent to undertake the project?

The role of the CFO in this process is critical. He has to push the team to examine and evaluate the unpopular downside risks. More importantly, in the end he has to take a position as to its prudence and clearly articulate the rationale for that conclusion to the rest of management and the board of directors. The risks to the shareowners are high, and failure can irreparably harm the corporate entity in such a "bet your company" situation. Proceed with caution!

"What If" Projects

One of the usual difficulties of the capital expenditure analysis process is that it typically focuses on a single, successful scenario and incorporates the consensus set of assumptions. In both smaller and low-risk projects, this problem can be handled with sensitivity analysis and with review of the project's key performance measurements. However, for larger and/or higher risk projects, it is best also to look at the project under alternative "what if" scenarios.

The alternative scenario process involves an examination of the project's "what ifs" happenings. Procedurely, the process is to:

- Identify major "what ifs" that could potentially impact the project and its timing.
- Define management's probable response to these "what ifs."
- Quantify the impact and response in terms of both time and cash flow.
- Classify the events into several distinct scenarios and lay out an "event tree."
- Summarize each major scenario in terms of the project's performance measures.

This technique is extremely helpful in understanding and communicating the risk/reward trade-offs. Particularly, there may be some "go"/"no go" aspects to the project, such as developing a technological application, penetrating a new market and distribution channel, or achieving key product performance standards.

Key questions that the CFO must then ask are:

- How sure are we of identifying that we're off track and of triggering an appropriate management response?
- What happens to our maximum cash outflow level and timing?
- How probable are each of the scenarios, and what is their expected economic worth?

This analysis and these conclusions then need to be incorporated in the report prepared for consideration by those who must approve or reject the project. It helps to make a clearer presentation of the project's risks when a "what if" becomes an "it's happened!"

International Investment Projects

The long-term commitment of a company's funds on an international basis brings with it new management concerns which do not have to be dealt with when a company is investing on a simple domestic basis. These new concerns focus on three key areas:

1. Political risk.
2. Currency exchange rate fluctuations.
3. Funding and repatriation.

These concerns are then sometimes made more complex to nonfinancial management by the way generally accepted accounting practices deal with international reporting.

For example, it is clear that companies vary in their international treatment of:

- Equity versus full consolidation of international entities.
- Selection of base "functional" currency for financial reporting.
- Taxation.
- Inflation-adjusted accounting.
- Fixed versus current assets.

Thus, the CFO must not only be able to explain the impact of the project on the company's financial results and condition, but also clearly portray the impact of both accounting practices and currency fluctuations in analyzing the project.

Fluctuations in currency exchange rates need to be dealt with explicitly in the capital expenditure analysis process. While the process is relatively straightforward, it requires a high level of expertise and judgment to assure that the possible and probable impact is identified.

In its simplest application, the analysis must incorporate the effect of translating project cash flows into functional and then the domestic currency of the investing company. This requires the development of an explicit set of exchange rates over time and the application of them to the project's cash flows which are assumed to be translated and/or repatriated. Currency control problems can be handled by delaying the repatriation of funds for several years. However, delays in repatriation will have an impact on the project's worthiness. Naturally, by evaluating the project at two levels, its value can be segmented into:

1. Its inherent value in the international environment.
2. The probable effect of foreign exchange fluctuations and currency controls.

Of course, given the highly subjective basis of the exchange rate forecasts, the sensitivity analysis should be done under substantially different exchange rates in order to determine whether adverse consequences are tolerable.

The next level of analytical complexity involves both the financial and legal aspects of international projects. This occurs when a project is funded either partially or wholly with foreign or locally borrowed funds. The analytic process then has to deal with the source and allocation of the project's net cash flows, and whether, under conditions of economic adversity, the parent has an obligation to fund the project's liabilities. In this situation, project cash flows need to be allocated to debt service on a priority basis, and then the residual repatriated or reinvested.

In summary, a CFO can best handle the complexity of investing in an international project by:

1. Having the basic project analysis done first in the indigenous currency of the project.
2. Allocating project net cash flows to service debt and then parent company requirements.
3. Translating parent company and lenders' foreign currency cash flows into the appropriate functional currency.
4. Segmenting the project evaluation into: (a) the international project, and (b) the financial impact of currency fluctuations and controls on the parent company.
5. Performing a sensitivity analysis on the effect of currency rate fluctuations.

Inflation

The outcome of the capital expenditure analysis process is affected greatly by inflation or changes in purchasing power on the project cash flows. Typically a project analysis implicitly assumes a "steady state" of inflation—that is, no further reductions in purchasing power of the dollar. Such an assumption can lead to an erroneous conclusion. To deal with the impact of inflation on a project, price level factors have to be isolated and adjusted for the expected ravages of inflation.

The initial step in this analysis process is to identify the historical prices of major components on products and restate them, establishing a constant, real dollar cost or price trend. It is these trends that are then used in the project financial model to give effect to the probable rate of inflation. Estimating the rate of inflation is a critical part of the analysis process. Estimates not only have to be made with regard to the levels and changes in the general economic rate of inflation, but also with respect to major components of the project. For example, escalation of basic energy or equipment costs may outpace the escalation of general wage levels. In any case, logically consistent assumptions about the compounding impact of inflation need to be made for every cost or price component.

Of course, in looking at the desirability of a project, the analyst must recognize that inflation affects not only a project's cash flow, but also changes a company's inflation-adjusted cost of capital. Thus, the standard discounted cash flow rate of return, which is the standard for a project, needs to be carefully reconsidered to include the effects of inflation.

7

Working Capital Management

Alfred M. Bertocchi

INTRODUCTION

Managing working capital is of critical importance to the success of the corporation. Working capital simply defined is "current assets minus current liabilities." Investment in working capital is often the largest investment a company has.

Good working capital management is good business. It is essential as an element in maintaining daily liquidity. Sound working capital management also affects the ability to finance. The current ratio is one of the most important criteria of financial health, and influences prospective investors and creditors who provide long-term financing.

An approach to the subject of working capital management can take two entirely separate paths. On the one hand, significant contributions to efficiency and the improvement of yield on investment can be made by careful technical analysis and management of the "micro" aspects of working capital: the cash,

Alfred M. Bertocchi retired in 1985 as senior vice president finance and administration for Digital Equipment Corp. He currently is a consultant serving on several corporate boards. He gratefully acknowledges the assistance given by his staff in writing this chapter.

125

accounts receivable, inventories, and other current asset accounts. Optimal management of each of these individual asset categories requires a full-time, professionally managed staff, dedicated to the implementation of cost-effective, analytical, and procedural techniques. This managerial focus on the elements of working capital as individual assets (each requiring specific, frequently unrelated, management techniques) is vital to the effective tactical (or micro) management of working capital.

In the first section, we will attempt to outline some of the processes and procedures that should be reviewed in evaluating the adequacy of micro working capital management within any firm. Attention to the concepts, techniques, and procedures offered for each major asset category should form the basis for review of the management of that individual asset.

The operating divisions of a firm spend and require working capital. Because decisions of line managers affect cash needs and inventory levels, there is an interrelationship between business decisions and the efficient management of individual assets. Optimizing that relationship through "macro" working capital management is discussed in the second section.

MICRO WORKING CAPITAL MANAGEMENT

Cash

Cash—whether in the form of coin/currency, demand deposits in banks, or income earning marketable securities—represents the short-term financial assets of a company. Excess cash is that portion of cash not currently required to meet today's needs.

Theoretically, a profit-maximizing company would hold exactly enough cash to fund its daily cash requirements. Such a firm would hold no excess cash in the form of marketable securities unless the income earned on these investments exceeded the cost of capital. Since the return on operating assets is usually greater than the return on financial assets, any financing assets held above those necessary to fund today's disbursements would decrease that firm's return on assets (ROA).

Practically speaking, the level of cash and marketables that a company chooses to maintain is a function of its financing philosophies, business risk, asset size, financial strength, growth plans, and its ability to forecast cash flows (especially in the short term). However, nonincome-producing cash balances should be targeted to meet the minimum balance requirements agreed upon with a bank as remuneration for certain services. All additional cash should be invested in income-producing securities with maturities structured to provide necessary liquidity.

Financing philosophies and goals should be clearly defined so that financial management can design cash management systems to effect these goals. For example, a firm in a high-growth industry exposed to technological risk could choose to adopt a more conservative financing philosophy that would allow it to take more operating risks than a company in a mature or declining industry. In such a case, the high tech company could choose to keep more cash on hand from the proceeds of equity or long-term debt offerings to weather unforeseen operating circumstances or changes in the financial markets. A company in a mature or declining industry could choose a minimum of cash on hand with short-term cash requirements met through short-term borrowing.

Companies that have a strong financial position and are capable of borrowing at favorable rates in most markets can afford to maintain a lower level of cash and cash equivalents than firms that are more leveraged or are perceived as weaker credit risks.

The more centralized a cash management system is, the easier it is to minimize idle cash in the system and to maximize the cash available for investment or disbursement. An effective cash management system should be designed to integrate as much as possible all the cash flows of the company, including its subsidiaries, divisions, and decentralized sites, both domestic and international. This integration should also work to achieve the most efficient use of the available cash in the total corporate systems, avoiding idle balances and instances where one entity is borrowing externally while another is investing excess cash without a financial benefit to the company as a whole.

Cash management policy is the issue. Efficient cash management includes concentration of all balances daily and centralized control of the processes of investment, disbursement, collection, lock box, and so forth.

In conducting a review of a company's cash management practices, the following areas should be examined.

Bank Accounts The number of corporate bank accounts should be kept to the absolute minimum necessary to economically transact the company's business. Obviously, the more accounts the firm operates, the higher the risk that there will be idle cash in the system. The company should maintain a central corporate account. When balances in other accounts reach prescribed trigger levels, their additional balances should be transferred to the central corporate account.

The accounts should be funded so that balances and transaction costs are minimized. There are trade-offs between "compensating balances" and fees for services. Bank balances should be equal to any balances required for bank compensation. The corporation should minimize costs by using lock boxes, negotiable bank services, and concentration accounts.

Bank Relations Most banks prefer to be compensated for services in balances. These balances are usually more expensive to a company than if the same services were paid for in fees. The use and amount of compensating balances should be reviewed frequently to determine if payment in balances is more costly to the company than other uses for company cash. If compensating balances are too costly, they should be renegotiated with the bank.

Collection and Disbursements Incoming receipts need to be captured and made available for corporate use as quickly as makes economic sense. While cash is defined at first glance as currency and deposits available for current disbursements, at second glance we can see that the cash cycle begins when a payment is initiated by a customer or debtor and enters the collection system. By minimizing the collection period of these funds, the corporation speeds the cash available for investment or disbursement and reduces the opportunity cost of those uncollected funds.

The company should study carefully where to place its lock boxes. Locating lock boxes in cities of major customer concentration in the United States can cause cash to be credited two to five days faster than might currently occur. A worldwide system of lock boxes can have a still greater impact on speeding the receipt of collections.

Disbursements clearly must be made when due or in time to take advantage of meaningful discounts. Where opportunity for a meaningful discount does not exist, disbursements need to be made so as to maximize the collection time within the bounds of good business practice. There are numerous ways to increase the amount of time between initiating a payment and actually funding it out of cash balances. Many of these techniques, however, are considered poor business practice and should be avoided.

Intracompany Payment Terms Intracompany payment terms should be set to maximize the use of the available cash throughout the entire company within the bounds of applicable tax laws and fiscal policies, as well as sound business practice. By making cash available to cash-using entities from the cash-generating areas of a company, borrowing can be kept to a minimum and balances available for investment maximized.

One effective technique is to net foreign currency payments among subsidiaries or branches. This eliminates the costly necessity of currency conversion and reduces float time between operations.

Cash Forecasting The company's cash forecasting should produce reliable information on which to make short-term investment or debt decisions. Enhancements or improvement to the cash forecast accuracy must be cost justifiable. An amount of excess cash or short-term debt capacity should be kept on hand to cover forecasting errors.

The above are some of the issues that need to be addressed in order to determine just how effective a firm's cash management policies really are.

Accounts Receivable

Accounts receivable represent the extension of credit on open account terms by a firm to its customers. Credit is normally extended as a courtesy to qualified customers in order to facilitate the flow of goods. Since accounts receivable usually represent a large portion of the current assets of most firms, it is essential that they be managed properly and efficiently.

Management of accounts receivable consists of three discrete functions: granting credit, monitoring receivable balances, and collecting balances when due. The first of these controls the creation of the asset; the second maintains it during its lifetime; and the third ends the asset's life.

In many companies, these three functions are blended in one

department, frequently being performed by one individual. However, to ensure effective management of the asset, each function should periodically be examined separately.

The credit function has the critical role of defining the criteria for creating a receivable. Although authority to create accounts is frequently shared with other functions, the credit function coordinates the activity and is responsible for seeing that receivables are created within the guidelines of company policy.

The criteria for creation of a receivable include terms of sale, customer creditworthiness, and revenue recognition for account purposes.

Terms of sale will specify how long any receivable is on the books, and therefore how large the total receivables asset should be. Credit limits should be established to contain the size of receivables available to customers. The cost of carrying a receivable is therefore a critical element in setting the terms of sale. The firm should be aware of how this carrying cost impacts the firm's return on assets (ROA), as well as its aftertax profits. This cost should also be an element in the pricing decision; thus, it can influence sales volume. Pressures from the sales or marketing functions to liberalize the terms of sale should therefore be traded off against price levels. Ensuring that such a balancing process takes place is an important element of asset management.

A similar trade-off takes place in the setting of credit standards. In addition to the increased cost of carrying receivables that may take longer to collect, there may be increased bad debt expense. These costs need to be related to projected incremental revenues. Interestingly, this formula also works in reverse, and the absence of measurable bad debts could be an indicator that credit standards are unreasonably restricting sales.

Accounts receivable, if properly managed, can also avoid excessive carrying cost for cutomer credit if a customer has a history of extended payment or if the receivable is expected to be extended for more than a "normal" period. This separation of receivables allows the responsible individuals to concentrate (and be measured) on active accounts and to earn interest income on the delay in collections.

The policy for revenue recognition determines the earliest point at which a receivable can be created and is an important element of receivables management. While the credit function is usually not authorized to independently determine a company's revenue recognition policy, it should ensure that the process to do so has included the trade-offs relating to good accounts receivable management. In this case, these relate primarily to collectability of an account.

The computer industry provides a good example of the importance of this issue. The general practice of the industry is to recognize revenue at the point of shipment, but the general practice of customers is to pay after the equipment has been successfully installed and tested. The credit function needs to ensure that this issue is addressed, particularly if the equipment is complex or if the installation applies to billing practices under a computer contract. Advance billings should be weighed against the possibility that customers will only pay after the service period has elapsed.

The administration function of accounts receivable management is charged with maintaining accurate files and providing timely information. The accuracy and timeliness of the data are critical to the credit and collection functions, which depend on it to manage each customer's account effectively. Automated systems are available and widely used to increase efficiency. As a result, the most frequent problem area relates to adjustments to the files due to discounts, returns, and write-offs. These areas should be monitored carefully.

The most efficient collection function usually also serves as an effective customer assistance organization. While in some cases the collection of a doubtful account will require a tough attitude on the part of the collector, most collection problems are the result of a dispute over merchandise or service. Collection departments need to be equipped to track down and resolve a variety of these issues in order to be effective.

It is important to view accounts receivable management within the overall framework of managing a corporation. For example, the collection cycle is impacted by virtually every organization within the firm. It reflects the firm's ability to design, produce, and ship a quality product; to install it quickly (if necessary); to generate paperwork that is acceptable to the customers; and to provide for the prompt collection of payments.

Accounts receivable goals, such as days sales outstanding, should be incorporated into operating management's performance measures. This is the only way to ensure that an area as critical to a firm's success as accounts receivable management receives the necessary support and attention of a firm's key mangers, its operating management.

Managing the distinction between recognition of revenue for tax purposes and revenue for book purposes is a crucial function. Working capital management in these areas could mean millions of dollars of "free" cash if exploited properly. For instance, installment notes may be considered revenue when booked, but for tax purposes the income would not have to be taxable profit until such notes are paid, which would usually be in annual or periodic installments. Further, transfer of title could be changed (in the case of capital goods) from the date of shipment until the later of customer acceptance or final payment. In both cases, revenue recognition need not be changed, but tax benefits would accrue through improved working capital management.

Inventories

The other major investment which a firm makes is its investment in inventories. There is probably no other area in which there is more potential for gain or loss than the area of inventory management.

In general, there are three types of "classes" of inventories:
Raw material inventory—This consists of material purchased and inventoried in its purchased form in anticipation of consumption in the manufacturing process. In general, this also includes "safety stock", which is extra inventory purchased as a hedge against late delivery, rejections of raw material, and other fluctuations in production schedules.
Work-in-process inventory—This is material in the production cycle to which value has been added in the form of labor.
Finished goods inventory—This consists of final/completed products from production that are ready for sale to customers.

Each of these classes of inventories is generally controlled by a different group within a company. For example, raw material inventories are significantly impacted by the policies of the corporation's purchasing group. The level of work-in-process inventory will largely depend on a company's production processes. However, the level of finished goods inventories will be a function of a firm's production schedules, the quality of its sales forecasts, and its management's decision regarding the level of finished goods inventory needed to support its sales forecasts.

Coordination of the three types of inventory is essential to effective cash management. "Safety stock" alone can tie up funds at all three levels of inventory.

In Japan, the "Kan Ban" system has helped reduce inventory levels. The partnership between manufacturer and supplier is so strong that levels of inventory are reduced because of supplier integrity to ship "just-in-time," allowing the manufacturer to schedule with confidence in both reliability and quality.

Raw Material Inventories Manufacturing firms usually feel it necessary to carry significant inventory to hedge against supplier failure to deliver acceptable parts on time. However, this should be weighted against the lost savings. Such a hedge can consists of 4 to 12 weeks of unnecessary inventory, with the resulting commitment of that amount of working capital on a virtually permanent basis. Firms may find that they cannot afford such an expensive idling of resources. A way to reduce this excessive level of inventories is to work actively with one's suppliers in this area. A concept that invariably helps to conserve working capital through reduced inventories is the notion of a "partnership" with a firm's suppliers.

Partnership does not mean that a firm buys a financial stake in its suppliers. Rather, it means that the firm fosters an attitude of mutual planning and cooperation. Some of the problems which a partnership approach can solve are:

- Expensive and unnecessary hedging of raw material inventories against supplier failure to ship on time.
- Inability of suppliers to respond quickly to increases in purchaser demand.
- Steadily accelerating purchase prices.
- Delivery of parts that do not meet specifications and are of unacceptable quality.

The above list is by no means exhaustive, but it illustrates how levels of raw material inventories can be reduced. In addition, it suggests how a firm's production processes can be favorably impacted by the partnership concept.

When embarking on a partnership, manufacturers and suppliers should mutually agree upon certain goals that are capable of being measured. Examples of such goals are:

- Meeting of delivery commitments within acceptable tolerances.
- Realization of a quality level that is 100 percent to specifications. For the manufacturer, this would mean zero inspection and the ability to take parts directly from the receiving docks to the production areas.
- Commitment by the firm to lead times of 15 days for orders of regularly purchased materials after which no rescheduling or cancellation is allowed.

These types of goals can significantly lower inventory levels, and consequently, the firm's overall level of working capital.

Work-In-Process and Finished Goods Inventories These types of inventories also need to be scrutinized. However, the focus here shifts away from a firm's purchasing function to its manufacturing processes and controls. Significant reductions can also be realized in these inventories through effective control programs with scheduling to match customer demand.

Other Assets

Although generally not significant in terms of amount, other assets, such as prepaid expenses and deferred income tax charges, do nevertheless form part of a firm's investment in working capital. Consequently, these need to be managed in their own right as separate components of working capital.

Current Liabilities

Turning now to the liabilities side of the balance sheet, one can focus on one of the methods of financing a firm's investment in current assets, namely, a firm's current liabilities. In general, there are three main categories of current liabilities: short-term debt, accounts payable, and other current liabilities.

Short-Term Debt

There are many forms of short-term debt available to a company. The most common are bank borrowings and issuance of commercial paper. By definition, short-term debt has a maturity of less than one year.

Historically, although not in recent years, short-term debt has been less costly than long-term debt. It does, however, carry more risk for the company and the stockholder. Reliance on short-term financing makes company earnings more sensitive to interest rate fluctuations and focuses attention on the ability to repay or to roll over the principal balances in the near term. Companies that use only long-term debt or equity to finance their requirements need not be concerned with short-term fluctuations in earnings or interest rates but rather with their longer term performance.

Generally, the term of debt chosen to finance a company's requirements should be consistent with the length of the requirement and corporate financing philosophies. Long-term growth or the purchase of fixed assets should be financed with longer dated debt or equity, while cyclical or short-term liquidity requirements are better matched with short-term instruments.

Accounts Payable

The firm's payables to its suppliers should not be viewed as a means of providing financing although technically it does provide funds during the period between receipt and payment. This source of short-term financing needs to be monitored carefully as it can be extremely expensive through the loss of early payment discounts. Further, the issues of equity and fairness also need to be made visible. A deliberate policy of delaying payments to suppliers not only is unfair but can be counterproductive in the long run by resulting in higher prices from vendors. A bad relationship with one's supplier is not a good base on which to build a partnership of the type described earlier in the section on inventories.

Critical to the proper management of accounts payable are management reports that depict days to pay, lost discounts, aged debit balances, and aged unpaid invoices. These basic tools allow management to focus quickly on problem areas and to take appropriate action to maintain the company's standing in the eyes of its vendors. It is also good practice to establish measurable goals by which financial managers who are responsible for accounts payable can be judged.

Other Current Liabilities

Other current liabilities, such as accrued expenses, should not be overlooked. Although the amounts are relatively small, they also form part of a company's working capital.

MACRO WORKING CAPITAL MANAGEMENT

Now that some of the procedures necessary for the effective management of working capital as individual asset categories have been described, it is important to consider how the management of these assets and liabilities can be integrated into broad corporate decision-making processes. This is the concept of macro working capital management: a process which attempts to ensure complete consideration within the business decision-making process of future impacts on "net" working capital. Such planning is undertaken by a senior staff finance manager who does not necessarily represent or supervise the professional staffs responsible for micro working capital management activities. The final goal, in fact, of a program of macro working capital management is to thoroughly acquaint line management with the impacts and interrelationships of working capital management alternatives so that macro working capital management becomes an integral part of routine line decision-making processes.

One area where an understanding of working capital management can be a vital, competitive tool is in the structuring of manufacturing processes. Manufacturing and production management are frequently offered opportunities to reduce product cost or to increase quality, responsiveness, or capacity through adoption of new technologies, processes, or practices. Yet only by integrating a full marginal analysis of the working capital impact of any proposed decision (primarily on inventories) can the validity and desirability of the proposal be gauged. It does little good to consider in retrospect why inventories have jumped substantially, perhaps requiring infusions of additional capital *after* a major manufacturing process decision has been made.

Much attention is usually given to the consideration of additional *capital* spending in manufacturing environments. An equal amount of consideration should be given to the marginal increase in working capital requirements that may result from the acceptance of each proposal.

A major variable in the marketing equation is the selection of distribution channels for a given product family. Much consideration is given to the subject of discount structures, price elasticity, cross-channel competition, and likely volumes.

Equal consideration should be given to the working capital implications of a given channel proposal. A simple change in terms and conditions may result in legal passage of title at a point much later in the sales cycle, resulting in significantly increased "pipeline" inventories all of which must be financed. While the impact of an extension in payment terms is widely understood to be negative, a full analysis of the actual impacts on receivables balances and the subsequent increases in working capital needs is frequently lacking. Such a relatively elementary calculation should be mandatory and should be considered an integral part of the business review of any marketing proposal.

Working capital management might be the furthest thing from the mind of an engineer involved in new product design. Efficient use of financial assets is seldom critical to the functionality and salability of a product; nevertheless, it can significantly affect the ultimate yield which that investment will earn for its company. This is a special problem for manufactured products that require some degree of installation, debugging, and acceptance and subsequently, field maintenance. Such products are relatively diverse: nuclear power plants, threshing machines, computers, drop forges, and fire protection systems. For each of these products, installability and maintainability expectations are built into the design decision-making process. These decisions are frequently a trade-off of functionality, manufacturing ease and cost, product cost, and field engineering capability.

An additional factor that should be considered is the time interval during which accounts receivable must be carried while installation problems are resolved, systems debugged, and customer satisfaction achieved. The terms of the invoice may read "net 30 days," but the customer will pay 30 days from acceptance, not from invoice date. While this may seem trivial to the design engineer, the question which the CFO must ask is, "What is the marginal effort required by the design engineer to reduce days sales outstanding versus the marginal effort required by his credit and collections organization?" The answer may be that such a feat is impossible for the credit and collections organization and a minor additional cost (in terms of time and inconvenience) for the product designer.

Physical distribution offers another opportunity to integrate macro working capital management with line decision-making processes. Strategies to reduce physical distribution costs may increase inventory balances or receivable balances. (For example, centralized warehousing may require lengthy transportation times to distant customers.) Once again, the opportunity is not to minimize working capital balances but to optimize the cost and responsiveness of physical distribution, along with the costs of acquiring and managing the necessary working capital balances.

In each of these cases, we have seen the need for an effective business plan review process to ensure that the impact of line business decisions on working capital balances is understood and integrated into plans and proposals. To achieve greater productivity, U.S. firms often face the high costs of factory automation. This can require sizable fixed investment, and yet can be necessary for competitiveness in world markets. Usually, the least expensive way for manufacturers to finance this requirement is through improved macro working capital management. This concept of macro working capital management requires a presence and coordination well outside the corporate finance department. It requires an active role during the formative stages of business planning throughout the company.

In conclusion, working capital management is an area of critical importance to a firm from both a micro and a macro viewpoint. We have seen how the effective management of the individual components of working capital can reduce the firm's overall investment in assets and consequently its financing costs. However, we have also seen how concepts of working capital management can enhance decision making in other key areas of the firm, such as product design. This last point cannot be stressed too much.

The key to maximizing this benefit lies in integrating working capital management with the operating decision processes of the company as a whole.

8

Measuring and Rewarding Operating Performance

Bernard H. Semler

Effective performance measurement of business activity requires the identification of the *one* person responsible for each item of income, expense, and investment. Clear-cut identification of responsibility then permits the establishment of meaningful and measurable goals and objectives. Management by objectives (MBO) can thus become an integral part of the management process. A key ingredient is a high degree of flexibility that permits the shifting of emphasis between short- and long-term goals to meet changing conditions.

Effective performance measurement provides a solid base for rewarding the participants in the management organization for their achievements. Performance recognition and incentive compensation are the keys to putting dynamics into the business management process.

Bernard H. Semler, with nine years in public accounting and extensive experience in finance and general management, joined Abbott Laboratories as CFO in 1969 and retired as executive vice president—finance, and a director in 1982. He is chairman and president of Semler Associates, Inc., consultants to management.

BASIC CONCEPTS AND POLICIES

Successful implementation and operation of effective systems for measuring and rewarding operating performance are dependent on rigid adherence to basic concepts and policies relating to the following:

The philosophy of management organization.

The role of the finance function.

The matching of accounting/financial control with responsibility.

The design and operation of business systems.

Philosophy of Management Organization

The basic philosophy of management organization must be one of delegation. Top management must provide the environment and the clear-cut understandings of the basic philosophy of its management organization. The degree of so-called centralization or decentralization will vary between business organizations—and even within certain areas of the same company. Varying degrees of centralization or decentralization are not in conflict with the basic objectives of performance measurement. The key is in the necessity to understand fully the philosophy of the management organization structure and the identification of responsibilities within that organization.

While the definition of the philosophy of management organization must come from the chief executive officer, primary responsibility for translation of this philosophy into business systems that properly measure and control operating performance rests with the chief financial officer.

Role of the Finance Function

A critical factor in the achievement of effective performance measurement is the role of the finance function within the organization. The basic responsibility for positioning the financial organization to support operating management rests with the chief financial officer. He must create and maintain not only the financial organization but, more important, the environment for providing effective support for operating management. The finance function serves many masters (including meeting the many external requirements), but none is as important to the success of the business enterprise as the support which can and must be provided to operating management.

Operating management is responsible for making decisions and meeting objectives. The finance function can and must provide the analysis, interpretation, critiquing, and measurement that supports operating performance.

Matching of Accounting/Financial Control with Responsibility

The basic objective of management accounting must be the identification of the *one* person responsible for each item of income, expense, and investment within the business activities. This becomes a rather difficult and challenging task within a highly complex business environment. However, it must be done in order to develop goals and objectives that all members of the organization can truly feel are within their control to accomplish.

One of the most misused and overused words in accounting terminology is the word *allocation.* The word has a connotation of being an arbitrary distribution, which thus is in direct conflict with identified and traceable responsibility. The primary fault rests with the accountants themselves who use the term without regard to the disciplined requirements of responsibility accounting. Operating management also attaches a definition to the word that removes their sense of responsibility for any elements of financial reporting that are identified with this terminology.

Accountants need to approach the administration of responsibility accounting with a conviction that there is no such word as *allocation*—rather, the word is *charge.* There must then be a determined effort to develop sound bases for *charging* the costs of functions and services to the revenue generating activities. The activity level of all support and service functions should reflect the level required by the end users or beneficiaries. The key is to identify the sources of these requirements and then provide an equitable basis for reflecting responsibility for the costs incurred in their behalf.

It should be strongly emphasized that arbitrary allocations of costs or investment result in a loss of management accountability and hence control. Disagreements between managers, if kept on a business-like basis, are a healthy benefit that flows from the attempt to assign cost/service responsibilities properly. Arbitrary approaches with the intent of avoiding conflicts only add to the loss of control. For central or common support services, an effective ingredient to good relationships and mutual respect is an environment that permits users of services the option of providing their own services (that is, a "make or buy" option) under defined evaluation guidelines. Care must be exercised to be sure that these evaluations are based upon comparable levels of service and full cost. The objective should be to have managers deal with each other as they would with third-party suppliers/customers.

If there are certain elements that, after sound judgment, are considered not to be appropriate applications of the charge concept, then the word *assign* is far more descriptive than allocation. The word *assign* is also generally more appropriate for the identification of responsibility for the various elements of investment.

Design and Operation of Business Systems

Business systems are the vehicle for the recording of and the reporting on business activity. Properly designed and operated, business systems are the essence of the measurement process. Detailed coverage of business systems planning and control is beyond the scope of this chapter. This chapter would be deficient, however, without reference to the following key concepts:

> Systems requirements must be clearly *defined* before they can be properly designed and implemented.
>
> Business systems should fully utilize the concepts of integrated data processing and multiple use of integrated data base management.
>
> Each separable element of the various business systems should be clearly identified with a single "owner" who has full responsibility for control over the definitions and modifications to the respective systems.

The use of common or shared systems is not in conflict with identifying responsibilities.

Responsibility reporting implies the preparation of reports tailored specifically to the accountability of the respective areas of operating management. This reporting structure and format should be as simple as possible and oriented to the needs of the users. A high degree of uniformity is desirable, but standard formats for the sake of standardization should not have a place in the design of responsibility reporting.

The first priority in the generation of reports from the accounting system should be to satisfy the needs fo operating management. Accountants should have the skills to convert the appropriate data into the required accounting formats to meet external requirements. This should be a by-product of the management reporting system but still an integral part of the total reporting structure. Too often the reverse is the case, and conventional accounting classifications and external reporting requirements dictate the format and content of management reports. Accounting is not an end in itself; it is only the means to effective business management.

A key ingredient in responsibility reporting is the utilization of specific indices of performance, such as ratios, percentages and so on. It is not necessary or desirable that all of these control factors be in dollars. In many instances, references to units of activity or volume are far more definitive.

EVALUATING PERFORMANCE

The word *measurement* implies the need for a comparison with some standard. Thus, it is essential in order to measure operating performance that there be a predetermined basis of comparison.

One of the best analogies illustrating the measurement process is found in the game of golf. By very careful analysis and evaluation of external and human factors, golf courses are designed so that the best achievable performance is related to a standard or par score of 72. Comparison of actual performance against par provides a means of calculating handicaps—the built-in allowances to meet the specific abilities of the individuals. The gap between the handicap and par is always know, which then identifies the potentials for further improvement, that is, productivity. The rules of the game allow for the impact of external factors and thus include such things as winter rules, penalties, free-drops, and so on. Similarly, the objective in the management process is the development of the "par target" and the identification of the allowances and/or penalties necessary to provide a sound basis for monitoring performance and stimulating improvement.

Establishing Standards for Evaluation

The principal source for development of standards of measurement/evaluation should be the budget or profit planning process as an integral part of the total business management system. An essential aspect of the measurement process must be a full understanding and agreement on the standards of measurement by the individual being measured. This requires that the budgets or profit plans be developed with the full participation of the operating organization. Too often, budget preparation is left to the finance personnel with little or no involvement of operating management. The result is not a budget but merely a financial forecast reflecting the judgments of the financial organization. This obviously cannot become the standard of measurement and control of operating performance.

Since measurement requires an identified standard, it then follows that *a* standard is better than *no* standard at all. Effective use of the measurement process results in making any deficiencies in the accuracy of standards self-correcting. Continuing attention to analyzing the reasons for variances from the established standards provides for a fine tuning of the standard itself. This highlights another very significant aspect of the responsibilities of the finance function, that is, variance analysis.

Effective management reporting must provide sharp analysis of the variances between actual results and the established standards. Thus, we have the basis for determining whether the actual results are, in fact, *good* or *bad*. A sharp analysis of variances is one of the most important contributions that can be made by the finance function. This analysis should specifically identify the reasons for the variances and the extent to which they signal future performance trends. If a manager knows exactly what is happening, he at least has some chance to make improvements or to take corrective actions. In reporting these variances to higher levels of management, the content of the report should also communicate the corrective actions being taken. This must be a communication from the operating managers as to their intended actions, not the presumptions of the financial representative preparing the report.

The planning and control system reflects the integration of a very complex set of measurements. The results of each area of operations should be measured against standards that truly relate to their respective area of responsibility and control. The consolidation and pyramiding of these comparisons results in an effective system of performance measurement for the entire business.

The best example of establishing solid measurement standards is in the full utilization of standard cost accounting systems based upon tightly engineered factors. There is a long history of successful application of these concepts to the control of production costs and improvements in productivity. Unfortunately, there are still far too many instances where standard costs are used primarily by financial personnel as a basis for inventory valuation, with the standards they set based on historical performance rather than industrial engineering techniques.

The basic concepts and techniques of engineered standards can also be effectively applied to many other areas of business activity. As in the case of manufacturing costs, the application should be an integral part of the planning process. The approach to the utilization of these concepts should be without predetermined limitations. It should also be emphasized that it is the concept of an engineering or carefully analyzed approach to the setting of the standards that is most important, not the mechanics of the system or even the use of professional industrial engineers.

Illustrations of the potential applications of this concept include such areas as work measurement of clerical functions; productivity and performance of sales forces; project control for engineering, research, and computer applications; quality/cost specifications, and so forth.

The use of standards for measurement of performance should extend to nonfinancial factors that have a significant impact on the success of the business. These would include customer service levels, back orders, computer response time, the timing for release of financial reports, and so on.

The application should also extend to management's investment responsibilities, particularly, significant areas of working capital, such as accounts receivable and inventories. Accounts receivable are generally measured in terms of days' sales outstanding or turnover, with standards or targets established on the basis of historical performance. Accounts receivable balances are a reflection of the terms established as part of the marketing strategy and of the effectiveness of the credit and collection function. Given the established credit terms, it should be possible to develop a solid basis for determining the required level of investment in accounts receivable and for measuring the performance of the credit and collection function. This index of measurement also then provides a basis for evaluating the impact on the required investment from possible changes in established credit terms.

Inventories are also measured on a turnover ratio and generally reflect a comparison with the past. The application of computer technology and use of material requirement planning (MRP) systems provides a means of accurately determining what the required level of inventory *should be* to optimize the relationship between customer service, production costs, and inventory carrying costs. This also provides a solid basis for identifying and measuring inventory responsibilities as well as a means of evaluating alternative strategies.

Measuring Financial Responsibility

The ultimate objective of the business enterprise is the achievement of a satisfactory return on investment. Thus, the ultimate overall measurement of management performance should be expressed in those terms. There are a number of methods and approaches for defining the investment and calculating the return including, for example, return on shareholders equity. The subject of this chapter, however, is measuring *operating* performance, and thus the formula for the operating level of performance should be based on the defined investment responsibility.

While taxes on income are recognized as a cost of doing business, the many corporate decisions affecting the final overall effective tax rate makes it more desirable that operating performance reflect a measurement before taxes on income.

The same should be true for the treatment of interest expense. There are those who believe that interest should be considered as a cost and included in the charges to operations. Interest, however, is one element in the cost of capital supporting the investment responsibility and not a direct operating cost. Operating management should have the responsibility for producing the desired rate of return on the investment being used. They should not be responsible for the sources and hence the cost of capital used to fund those investments. This is a corporate responsibility controlled by corporate management and the board of directors. Thus, the performance of operating management should be measured on the basis of the return on investment responsibility, reflecting operating earnings before interest and taxes. Making a few comparative sensitivity calculations of return on investment (ROI), with and without interest as an expense, should help demonstrate the abnormal distortions that can result when the measurement of ROI has the income reduced by a charge for interest.

It should be recognized that ROI responsibility is a rather broad calculation and therefore is not particularly sensitive to what might otherwise be significant variances in short-term performance. This is one of the arguments used for including interest as a charge. An effective technique for emphasizing to management the impact from variations in investment levels is using a memo calculation of a "capital charge" computed by applying an assumed capital cost to the actual level of investment. The projected impact on the ROI calculation can be determined by comparing the dollar variation in the "memo" capital charge with the dollar variation in operating earnings.

Return on investment is the product of the percentage margin on sales times the turnover of investment. It also reflects what has been popularly known as the Du Pont formula which is expressed in equation form as:

$$\text{ROI} = \frac{\text{Margin (operating earnings)}}{\text{Sales}} \times \frac{\text{Sales}}{\text{Investment (as defined)}}$$

It is important that management fully understand the components of this calculation and the leverage for improving ROI that results from improving the turnover of investment. In periods of high interest costs and tight money, corporations are prompted to direct increased attention to the management of their investment responsibility. This attention should not be so directed only in times of crisis or lack of available capital. It should be part of the continuing responsibility of good management performance. The targeted performance level for ROI should be sufficiently high to provide a continuing challenge to management to control tightly the level of required investment.

In demonstrating the dynamics of the control over investment, it is very effective to break the investment responsibility into its major components, which generally are accounts receivable, inventory, and property. Establishing turnover targets for each of these elements as a part of the measurement process adds increased emphasis on optimizing the return on investment. The word *optimize* rather than *maximize* is a deliberate choice. While improvement in ROI is a very desirable objective, there comes a time when maintaining the desired level of ROI is a far more beneficial objective. The ROI target should reflect the overall cost of capital, the risk, and the possible return from alternate uses of the capital by the company or its shareholders.

There is often much debate and confusion on the basis of valuation to be used in measuring the investment responsibility, (that is, LIFO versus FIFO for inventories; cost or replacement cost on a gross or net basis for properties). Remember that the objective of the measurement process is a comparison of actual with a predetermined target. Do not expect to establish a single desired level of ROI for all divisions within a company or an ability to make accurate comparisons of one company or division with another. Any such comparisons should be made at the time of establishing the plan targets. The important thing is that the objectives clearly reflect the desired level of performance and that the comparisons with actual be made on a consistent basis. It is the variation in performance that should be emphasized—not an absolute mathematical calculation. Thus, investment valuation using either LIFO or FIFO, gross or net properties can be equally effective in performance measurement.

Management by Objectives

Extensive discussion of the concepts of management by objectives (MBO) is beyond the scope of this chapter. There is, however, a high degree of interdependence between the successful administration of MBO and the subject of this chapter. Proper integration provides for a highly effective total business management process.

There are two key areas of interrelationship that deserve special emphasis, namely:

The setting of goals and objectives that are sharply measurable in financial or other definitive terms.

The tie-in of goal achievements with compensation programs.

One of the most critical requirements for a successful MBO system is in the setting of measurable goals that clearly reflect achievement. This is one of the most difficult aspects and a principal reason for failure of many MBO systems to be really effective. Too often, goals are set in general terms instead of specifically measurable targets; for instance:

A goal of reducing manufacturing costs versus specific dollar goals for various elements in the manufacturing process.

A goal of increasing sales versus specific targets for individual products.

It is not intended or implied that all of the MBO goals should be in measurable financial terms. They can and should also be established in tightly measurable, nonfinancial terms; for example:

Quantifiable goals for improvement in employee turnover.

A specific date for issuance of financial reports.

A specific lapsed time for processing a customer order.

The setting of specific goals through the MBO process provides a very effective means for delegation and involvement of all levels of management (as well as nonmanagement employees), thus resulting in a very effective total management team.

Many attempts at the application of MBO techniques fail in their installation or deteriorate over time because of the lack of continuing motivation. The participation of employees in the goal setting process and the administration by management of the total system can deteriorate into a paper-processing exercise if not part of an action-oriented environment. An effective means to continue a high level of interest and application is to tie the goals and objectives of the MBO process into the compensation systems. This also provides an effective linkage between MBO and the financial control systems.

REWARDING PERFORMANCE

The final element of an effective system for optimizing operating performance is the rewarding of individuals for their achievements and their contributions to meeting the overall objectives of the company. Rewards to individuals for their achievements fall into the following two broad classifications.

Recognition.   Recognition with or without monetary consideration is a very essential part of any reward. Individuals take pride in accomplishment and are stimulated and encouraged by others recognizing their accomplishments. Athletes compete for recognition as the most valuable player. Not too long ago I saw a very large plaque in the hall of a major industrial company containing pictures of the housekeeping department's employee of the month.

Compensation. Providing monetary rewards for performance generally involves multiple programs that must be carefully integrated into a comprehensive program. Elements of such compensation programs can include: base compensation, merit adjustments, profit sharing plans, suggestion awards, presidential awards, bonus and incentive plans, stock option plans, and so on. They should all be looked upon as possible elements of a comprehensive program for reflecting a competitive and equitable recognition of each individual's performance.

Rewarding for Short-Term versus Long-Term Performance

One of the major concerns, and sometimes criticisms, of incentive compensation programs is that they place too much emphasis on short-term goals at the expense of the long-term growth of the company. This is a very valid concern and the principal reason why there should be a balanced and comprehensive program rather than just one single plan or formula.

There are two basic elements to a balanced emphasis on the

short-term versus long-term factors for *measuring* and *rewarding* operating performance:

The first relates to the methods of measurement.

The second relates to the methods of rewarding.

Method of Measurement The key to effective integration of short-term and long-term goals and objectives is in the administration of the profit planning process. The achievement of long-term objectives doesn't just happen but is made to happen and, therefore, must be planned. The planning process should provide for the integration of short-term budgets and long-term plans, with specific identification of significant elements that are considered necessary to the achievement of the long-term objectives. The clear identification of these specific elements within the planning process then provides the opportunity for top management review and agreement on the required level of investment spending necessary to support the long-term growth objectives.

If these elements are clearly identified in the current year's budget, they can also become the basis for monitoring the degree to which there is any attempt to reduce the commitment for the future in order to make the current year's target. For example, the plans should provide for the required level of expenditures for such items as research and development, new product introduction, advertising, personnel development and staffing, as well as the capital investments considered necessary to achieve the planned results in future years. Incentive formulas for rewarding performance can be designed so that no credit is given to the participants for failing to spend the budgeted amount for these items without specifically demonstrating the achievement of the objectives for which they were established. Putting it another way, current year budgets, and the tracking of actual results, should be sufficiently detailed to clearly identify and measure the performance related to factors that are intended to impact the future.

This is particularly important for incentive plans at the division/subsidiary level. Key members of division/subsidiary management generally represent individuals with high potential to be promoted to larger divisions and/or corporate responsibilities. Thus, it becomes very difficult, if not impossible, to structure incentive programs that are based upon meeting long-term objectives, since in most instances individuals will not expect to be a part of that management at the future measurement date. The emphasis, therefore, must be on measuring and rewarding those managers for their performance on identified long-term factors included in the current year's budget. It is top management's responsibility to be sure that the long-range strategies are consistently reflected in the detailed budgets, irrespective of the changes in local management.

Generally, the greater degree of permanency in corporate management provides the opportunity for building long-term goals and objectives into that measurement process. Having an effective strategic or long-range planning committee, which includes representation from the outside members of the board of directors, can add assurance that members of top management are also taking a balanced approach to the administration of their responsibilities.

Methods of Rewarding

The most effective method of providing management with incentives to concentrate on long-term performance is through the granting of stock options. The Economic Recovery Act of 1981 placed renewed emphasis of the value of this form of incentive compensation. Granting stock options places the employee in exactly the same position as shareholders in being able to benefit from the long-term performance of the company. While the market value of stocks is subject to significant variations as a result of overall economic and market conditions, over the long term, a solid track record of earnings growth is bound to be reflected in the market value of the stock. Stock options that expire 10 years after the date of grant generally should provide ample time to ride out the fluctuations in market prices resulting from business cycles. An additional means of offsetting market fluctuations is through a program of annual option grants.

As previously indicated, at the corporate level, it should be possible to develop long-term objectives and methods of rewarding the key management for their accomplishments. Such programs generally take the form of a long-range target for such overall measures as return on shareholders equity or earnings per share. Individuals are granted "units" of participation with a payout on either a cash or deferred basis.

Design of Incentive Compensation Plans

As indicated throughout this chapter, the systems for measuring and rewarding operating performance should be specifically designed to fit the needs of the company. There is no one best plan or formula that can be applied to all companies. There are, however, certain basic concepts that should apply to the design of all incentive compensation plans. These fall into two major categories:

> Those relating to the development of the amount of the incentive fund (or pool).
>
> Those relating to the basis of participation.

Development of Incentive Fund (Pool) Incentive plans are generally not intended to be a part of, or made contingent on, an employee's regular salary; they are additional compensation for achieving a targeted level of performance. Thus, the development of an incentive fund (or pool) should be based upon a formula that recognizes the achievement of the desired performance level. General guidelines for the development of an incentive formula should include the following:

> The measurement should be as comprehensive as possible and, therefore, would generally be related to return on investment.
>
> The factors reflected in the formula should be only those that are in the control of the respective participants.
>
> Nonperformance-related factors should be excluded in the determination of the actual funds to be available.
>
> The formula should provide for a sufficient range to stimulate over-achievement of the targeted objectives.
>
> There should be a maximum or "cap" to avoid possible windfalls or excessive and inequitable awards.

Basis of Participation Rewarding members of management for their performance should be tied as closely as possible to their measurable achievements. As previously indicated, this requires that management control systems be geared to measure the achievement of specific goals and objectives. General guidelines for developing the basis of participation should include the following:

The level and basis of participation should be clearly defined at the beginning of the measurement period.

Participants should clearly understand their basis of participation and the extent to which they can influence their rewards.

Participation should reflect a balance between individual goal accomplishment and recognition of the contribution to the total team effort.

9

Sustainable Growth during Inflation

Gary L. Wilson and Mark D. Beasman

Chapter 3 presented a discussion of the concept of sustainable growth and its application in corporate financial decisions. Subsequent chapters dealt with specific elements of the sustainable growth formula: capital structure, investment analysis, and working capital management. This chapter will review the elements of sustainable growth and address how, through value-based analysis, inflation can be properly viewed within the context of financial strategy. As will be shown, the concept of cash flow is fundamental to value-based financial decisions. Accordingly, this chapter will also serve as a bridge to the next section on managing cash flows.

A discussion of growth, inflation, and financial policy is both timely and relevant. The U.S. economy has emerged from one of the most severe economic recessions since the Great Depression—one which many economists believe reflects a fundamen-

---

Gary L. Wilson joined Marriott Corporation in 1974 and currently serves as executive vice president and CFO. He is responsible for hotel development and acquisitions, finance, corporate planning and Marriott's worldwide airline catering operations. Mark D. Beasman joined Marriott in 1981 and is currently director—operations planning and control.

tal change in previously accepted structures and assumptions. Such changes include the move away from smokestack industries towards services and information management, the rise of foreign competition, and the burgeoning of the federal deficit. Another structural change of particular interest to financial executives is that which has occurred in the direction of inflationary growth and its impact on the cost of labor, materials, and capital. Unfortunately, most decision tools used in financial planning are either too simplistic, misunderstood, or impractical for dealing effectively with the reality of inflation in the 1980s.

Current inflation rates are lower than in the recent past, but inflation forecasts have become increasingly volatile due to the economic uncertainty arising from these structural changes. Indeed, it is this volatility of inflation expectations more than the level of inflation itself that can cause problems to profitability. A project funded in the past with high fixed-interest rates may have looked fine on paper under the assumption that pro forma prices would track 10 percent annual inflation. Today, however, that project would have problems funding debt service if prices followed the lower inflation that actually occurred. This increased volatility not only makes forecasting more difficult, it also can contribute to continued high rates of interest. In effect, a premium for inflation risk is believed to be incorporated in real interest rates, keeping the cost of capital high in a time of generally lower inflation.

Because of changes in the general purchasing power of the dollar over time, inflation can mask true operating performance. Through changes in reporting, efforts have been made to better reflect the impact of inflation on earnings and assets, specifically in footnote treatment under Statement of Financial Accounting Standards number 33. However, these endeavors focus on historical reporting and are arguably inadequate for making prospective decisions. Furthermore, the simple adjustments to historical costs in these restatements can distort operating economics in certain capital-intensive industries. A real estate based asset, such as an office building or hotel, may require less annual capital reinvestment than is indicated by historical cost depreciation. The true annual *economic* cost of maintaining a facility may be lower than is implied by adjusted depreciation shown in income under FAS 33.

Many believe we have come a long way in wringing near-term

inflation out of the economy. However, uncertainty over long-term inflation is likely to remain a factor for financial decision makers, whether through forecasted increases in overall price levels or the influence of inflationary risk factors in real interest rates. Understanding how inflation impacts the financial decisions and policies discussed throughout this book will therefore remain an important consideration.

This chapter will demonstrate that the key to sustaining profitable corporate growth lies in the consistent application of a "value-based approach" to financial decisions. By focusing at all times on the economic value of decisions, a company can better respond to changes in expected inflation and pursue strategies which maximize the benefit of growth and shareholder return. In the following sections, we will review this value-based approach by describing the underlying conceptual elements and outlining how they can be deployed within a value-based planning system.

Value-based planning has formed the cornerstone of financial analysis within our company for several years. Although most of the concepts, such as discounted cash flow, are in everyday use today, their broad application to financial plans and policies across all levels of the corporation is probably less common. Hopefully, this chapter will yield new insights into how these concepts can become powerful tools when applied in a comprehensive financial planning and control process.

CONCEPTUAL ELEMENTS OF VALUE–BASED APPROACH

Value-based planning is a systematic approach to financial and business strategies in which all decisions are assessed in terms of their impact on corporate value. The key to using a value-based approach is to have a thorough understanding of several underlying concepts.

First, the basic premise of the value-based approach to planning is a simple one: The goal of the public corporation is to create shareholder wealth. Shareholder wealth is created when returns to shareholders, either through dividends or stock appreciation, exceed the return that they would generally require of investments with comparable risk. Compounding these returns with company growth further enhances value.

Second, the stock market values a company on the basis of its return and growth prospects. The value of individual business strategies together yield an overall corporate value. To the extent these strategies are understood and believed by the investor community, their value will be reflected in the company's stock price. Investor requirements with regard to value creation can therefore be translated back into specific return and growth targets for individual business strategies.

Third, value-based planning recognizes that the expected return and growth of a particular strategy must be sustainable over the long term. Return and growth are not independent but together are governed by external market factors and internal management policies.

Fourth, the use of cash flow instead of accrual-based accounting income is necessary for correctly valuing strategy decisions. In particular, "discretionary" cash flow is the means by which inflation is embodied in the process.

Finally, a process of planning and control based on these concepts will ensure that decisions are consistently linked by the common thread of economic value creation. The following sections will expand upon the concepts cited above and will discuss how such a system can be used:

- Value determinants: return and growth.
- Value and shareholder expectations.
- Value and sustainable growth.
- Value and discretionary cash flow.
- Implications for developing a value-based approach to financial decisions.

The Determinants of Value The first determinant of value is the cash return obtained from invested capital. For providers of capital, this value is a function of the degree to which their returns exceed their minimum return expectations. This minimum required return is the firm's cost of capital. When a firm can generate returns on incremental capital investments in excess of this overall cost of capital, value is created for the company. If returns are below the minimum, the firm's value is diminished.

A familiar application of this concept is found in typical capital budgeting analyses. Discounting a project's future cash flows back to the present, using the cost of capital appropriate to that project's risk, generates a present value. The net present value (present value less investment or NPV) is the amount of value created. An investment which is break-even in value yields an internal rate of return equal to the cost of capital. Alternatively, one which generates returns below the cost of capital will have a present value below the investment cost. The NPV in this case is negative, and value will be lost if the investment is made.

Growth is the second determinant of value. As viewed in this context, growth arises when a company reinvests a portion of its returns in new or existing businesses. If this reinvested capital itself generates returns in excess of capital cost, value is compounded. This way, growth acts to magnify the value impact of a company's investment decisions.

It is important to note at this point that growth doesn't always increase value. If the returns on new capital investments just equal the required cost of capital, value is not created on the incremental investments, and growth does little to enhance company value. In fact, if returns are below the requirements of those providing capital, growth destroys value. Thus, a company that continues to grow by investing capital in projects that yield returns below the cost of capital will decline in value. If publicly held, the stock market can be expected to react accordingly and keep share prices low despite continued growth in reported earnings per share.

The Links to Market Value

Just as an individual capital project can be viewed as creating value, so too can the investment in a product line, a division, a strategic business unit (SBU), or an entire company.

In his book *Financial Strategy: Studies in The Creation, Transfer, and Destruction of Shareholder Value*,[1] William Fruhan corroborated the relationship between corporate value, returns, and growth. Using stock market data, Fruhan showed that the market's valuation of individual companies, indicated by the ratio of stock price to inflation-adjusted book equity per share, correlated directly with their growth prospects and the ratio of their

---

[1] William E. Fruhan, Jr., *Financial Strategy: Studies in the Creation, Transfer, and Destruction of Shareholder Value* (Homewood, Ill. Richard D. Irwin, 1979).

Return On Equity (ROE) relative to their cost of equity. Companies whose equity returns exceeded their cost of equity had market to adjusted book ratios greater than one. Among these same companies, those with higher growth had market to book ratios greater than those with lower growth. In contrast, companies that generated returns below their cost of equity generally had market-to-adjusted book ratios below one. Interestingly, those companies that generated returns close to their cost of capital had market-to-book ratios close to one regardless of their growth.

A mathematical relationship between value, growth, and return can be derived from a constant dividend growth model under simplifying assumptions of reinvestment and leverage. Share value relative to book investment (adjusted for inflation and noncapitalized expenditures) is related to ROE, cost of equity, and growth as follows:

$$\frac{\text{Shareholder Market Value}}{\text{Adjusted Book Value}} = \frac{\text{ROE}^* - \text{Growth}}{\text{Cost of equity} - \text{Growth}}$$

*Incremental.

According to this relationship, a company which generates returns greater than equity cost creates value and should carry a market-to-book ratio greater than one. If incremental ROE equals the cost of equity capital, value is neither created nor destroyed, and the market-to-book ratio is one.

For our purposes, the key insight to be taken from this relationship is that value can be derived from a range of return/growth combinations. For instance, a company with a cost of equity of 17 percent will create value at a 1.5 market-to-book ratio with an ROE of 18 percent and growth of 15 percent. This return/growth combination might be typical of a high growth company in a capital-intensive industry. Alternatively, the same value can be created by a company that grows at a slower 9 percent but returns 21 percent on incremental equity. Two companies can, therefore, have the same value-creating potential even though they maintain different return/growth combinations:

$$1.5 = \frac{18 \text{ percent} - 15 \text{ percent}}{17 \text{percent} - 15 \text{ percent}} \qquad 1.5 = \frac{21 \text{ percent} - 9 \text{ percent}}{17 \text{ percent} - 9 \text{ percent}}$$

The concept of value-based planning views the corporation as a portfolio of business units and their attendant strategies. Each strategic business unit (SBU) bears a different level of business risk and an ability to support debt. These differences in risk and leverage produce different costs of capital for investments made in these SBUs. As in the case of an individual project, an SBU's contribution to overall corporate value is a function of its ability to generate cash returns in excess of its cost of capital. The value of a corporation, in turn, is the aggregate value of its constituent SBUs. As we shall see, the portfolio approach can be applied to developing and selecting a mix of SBU strategies which maximize corporate value.

Value Creation and Sustainable Growth

The return/growth combination that a company pursues will be determined by a variety of factors, both external and internal. The external factors include, among others, industry structure, market growth, competitive position, and the overall state of the economy. Internal factors include management ability, strategy, and financial policies.

Within the constraints imposed by the external factors, management can influence the internal factors to achieve the return/growth combination that maximizes value. However, return and growth are not wholly independent. As discussed in Chapter 3, only a certain level of growth is sustainable over the long term for a given return and set of financial policies.

The sustainable growth formula presents a succinct framework for tying together returns and financial policy variables. Used in many forms, the sustainable growth equation is based on the idea that the level of growth a company can sustain is a function of its ability to generate returns on invested capital and its reinvestment policy. That is:

growth = (returns on incremental capital invested) ×
(earnings reinvestment rate)

By incorporating policies regarding leverage and use of non-interest-bearing liabilities (deferred taxes, payables, and so on), the formula can be expanded to:

$$\text{growth} = \text{ROE}^* \times \text{earnings retention}$$
$$= \text{Return on Assets}^*$$
$$\times \left(1 + \frac{\text{Debt}}{\text{Equity}} + \frac{\text{Interest Free Liabilities}}{\text{Equity}}\right)$$
$$\times (1 - \text{Dividend Payout Rate})$$

*Incremental returns after interest and taxes.

According to this formula, growth could be increased by simply changing financial policies. Assume for the moment that a company's return on incremental investments is above the cost of capital but cannot be increased because of competitive pressure. Management, in this case, could conceivably enhance growth by increasing earnings retention (that is, decreased dividend payout). Alternatively, management could increase the amount of debt or interest free payables relative to equity. Both actions would yield more cash for investment. If this cash is reinvested and continues to generate similar incremental returns, the level of growth will increase. The amount of debt and payables will be limited by factors, such as the need for liquidity, exposure to risk, and so on. Such considerations are presumably included in the debt/equity and payables/equity targets set by management.

In a world of no inflation, this sustainable growth relationship is valid. Debt and equity will be measured in the same nominal dollars, and debt/equity targets will continue to reflect economic reality. However, with inflation, debt-to-equity targets stated in typical accounting terms distort the true capacity of the company to support these obligations. Reported monetary liabilities which may be denominated in relatively "current dollars" will not be comparable to reported equity balances denominated in largely "historical dollars." As a result, inflation will cause an understatement in debt capacity when targets are based on reported balance sheet statistics. As will be discussed later, a company which sets debt capacity based on cash-flow coverage of interest will avoid the problem of inflation and will ensure sufficient investment capacity exists to pursue growth opportunities.

Value and Discretionary Cash Flow The fundamental advantage of the value-based approach to planning is that decisions are made on the basis of future economic value. Unfortunately, current accounting methods, for reasons of objectivity, are biased towards historical actions. For this reason, inflation's impact is not fully taken into account in most reported figures. Adjustments under FAS 33 do cover some of these shortcomings, but the results do not lend themselves to forward-looking financial decisions. Therefore, the value-based approach relies upon another measure of income undistorted by historical-based accounting–discretionary cash flow.

Discretionary cash flow represents the amount of cash generated by a business after tax and after reinvestment of the minimum capital required to keep the business running. The reinvestment, so defined, reflects the true economic depreciation of an asset and not an accounting convention. An accurate measure of economic income, discretionary cash flow is defined as:

Operating profit
    Less: Book taxes
    Plus: Book depreciation and other noncash charges,
             Change in deferred tax balance
    Less: Minimum required renewal capital,
             Increase in required working capital
    Equals: Discretionary cash flow

Discretionary cash flow represents the amount of cash generated by a business which is available for deployment elsewhere. Its use in a portfolio planning environment enables management to exploit growth opportunities and to avoid potential cash traps. It also provides the flexibility to deal with changes in inflation and over time.

As shown on page 164, the discretionary cash flow generated by a company can be used four ways: reinvest in current businesses, acquire or develop new businesses, repurchase stock, or pay out dividends.

The first two options are feasible as long as incremental investments in current or new businesses are expected to generate positive returns net of capital costs. The stock repurchase option is appropriate in situations where the stock market undervalues the company's plans. This alternative is approached opportunistically with careful consideration given to the merit of internal forecasts and desired capital structure. The last op-

Exhibit 1

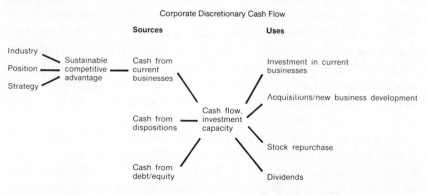

Corporate Discretionary Cash Flow

tion, dividend payout, is pursued if management feels share-holders would have greater use of the funds outside of the company. A high payout policy is appropriate for high-return, low-growth companies.

Three sources of cash—operations, dispositions, and financial—contribute to investment capacity. Prudent management of investment capacity is the key to sustaining growth during inflation. One means of accommodating inflation is inherent in the process for allocating investment capital. In the value-based approach, the present value of future discretionary cash flows is the primary criterion for assessing the economic worth of proposed investments. Investment hurdle rates and cash-flow forecasts which consistently incorporate inflation will yield results that correctly reflect inflation's impact. Periodically updating the hurdle rate and inflation forecast assumptions will also keep the plans responsive to changes in inflation.

Another way to incorporate inflation is to employ a debt policy that is based on income coverage of interest. As previously noted, book debt-to-equity targets may understate a firm's debt capacity in times of inflation. A truer picture of the capacity to support debt is obtained by examining the volatility of a company's or SBU's cash flows over time.

A business with highly volatile cash flows would be less able to cover interest costs on a reliable basis. The business would be assigned a relatively high interest coverage target and consequently would bear a lower amount of debt. The reverse is true for businesses with relatively stable cash flows. This inflation-sensitive debt policy can even be extended to assess recommended levels of floating- and fixed-rate debt in the capital structure. To the extent that changes in a business's cash flows correlate with inflation and interest rates, that business can be funded with variable rate debt which is generally lower in cost. Investments in a business having cash flows which do not correlate with inflation would be better off with fixed-rate financing.

Implications for Value-based Planning System The above discussion has described the conceptual foundation for several key features of the value-based approach to financial decisions.

- All investment decisions are based upon a discounted cash-flow methodology to ensure that the economic value is maximized.

- The cost of capital applied to a specific decision incorporates, to the extent possible, the minimum required return which is consistent with the investment's level of risk. This discount rate is ultimately tied to shareholder-required return.

- The corporation is viewed as a set of individual business units which compete at various sustainable levels of growth and return. Strategies governing these business units are developed from among alternatives and selected on the basis of their maximum-value contribution.

- Valuations based on nominal dollars include appropriate forecasts of inflation both in the cash-flow projection and discount rate. Failure to keep these assumptions consistent can distort the true economic value of a decision.

- Discretionary cash flow, the common measure for valuing decisions, does not suffer from the problems caused by inflation's impact on historical-based accounting. The value of business decision alternatives can be determined by projecting discretionary cash flows and by discounting by the appropriate hurdle rate. The projections and discount rate will comprehend inflation by way of the inflation premium in the capital costs and the use of an appropriate inflation assumption in the cash-flow projections.

- Use of discretionary cash flow in value-based planning facilitates the allocation of investment capacity to various SBUs and strategies.

The section that follows will outline how these features are integrated into a corporate-level planning and control process.

Particular emphasis will be placed upon how this system incorporates the impact of inflation in financial decisions.

VALUE-BASED PLANNING SYSTEM

The objective of a value-based planning system is to ensure that decisions of the company will enhance shareholder value. To accomplish this objective, the value-based approach relies upon a financially driven process which enables corporate management to quantify and evaluate the economic impact of decision alternatives through a two-phase process of planning and control. Goals and strategies formulated in the planning phase are implemented and monitored in the control phase.

The two-phase, value-based process can be further divided into four sets of activities: formulate corporate objectives, develop and value strategies, allocate capital, and monitor results. As shown below, the activities comprising the process range from defining the business and the "set objectives" stage to preparing budgets in the "monitor" stage.

Set Goals and Objectives Objectives and business definitions are set in the first stage of the planning process. Overall corporate objectives of return and growth which maximize shareholder value form the basis for SBU–specific targets. Generally, this activity is top down although review of individual SBU strategies will entail periodic reassessment of such targets.

Develop and Value Strategies In this set of activities, management develops a range of alternative SBU strategies and corporate policies such as debt level, dividends, and working capital. From among the alternatives, those strategies and policies

Exhibit 2

Value-based planning process

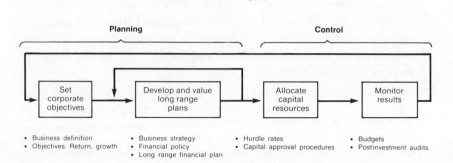

which maximize value are selected. At this point, particular emphasis is placed upon maximizing asset productivity, lowering cost of capital (that is, maximizing "net" return), and identifying growth opportunities in existing and new business. In conjunction with these business strategies, new financing policies may be implemented. Long-range plans are then developed from strategies and valued. In our company, for example, each SBU is valued annually, based upon a 15-year cash flow forecast. The sum of all SBU strategies is the total intrinsic value of the firm and is comparable to the firm's market value. This comparison is important when considering stock repurchases.

Allocating Capital The allocation of capital to specific projects is the means by which plans become actions. Control over strategy implementation begins with the use of stringent capital return hurdles that tie back to shareholder requirements via the cost of capital.

The return hurdle rates vary across SBUs and reflect their respective average cost of capital. The coverage-based debt policy described above is applied at the SBU level to determine levels and cost of debt. Cost of equity is also set for each SBU using the Capital Asset Pricing Model and comparables from other companies in the industry. Updating the hurdle rates on a periodic basis will keep the system responsive to inflation.

Monitoring Results Finally, effective monitoring of strategy results comes by way of annual budgets and postexpenditure audits. Such a system should encourage and reward aggressive asset management. Budgets are based upon the first year of the long-range plan. Management compensation is tied to these budgets to ensure value maximization on an ongoing basis. However, there is a problem of translating value goals into targets against which operations can be managed. Most accounting measures are accrual-based and single-period in orientation. Yet the value of an investment is derived from cash flows generated over time. One way to accommodate this problem is to derive a return on capital target that is based upon the inflation-adjusted cash flow pro formas used to justify investments in the SBU.

PART THREE

Managing Sources and
Uses of Funds

10

Funds from Operations

Raymond H. Alleman and Charles M. Wurst

Expenditures ought not to equal income but should be smaller, so that a surplus will remain for unforeseen contingencies, such as losses that may occur at sea, or, if you are a food merchant, having to sell a certain commodity at a loss because it threatens to spoil. None of this permits the expenses of one day to be measured by the expenses of another day; instead, you must use as a basis of comparison a long period, preferably an entire year. Bad times may follow directly on the heels of good, for receipts which one day are very small may be much larger (or even smaller!) on another day in the same period. And so it is with expenditures; they, too, vary with changing circumstances. Take this advice to heart, and may the Almighty see that you prosper![1]

Mr. Al-Fadl was concerned with the unpredictability of the inflows and outflows of cash, but he nonetheless appreciated the value of examining a period of recent experience as a basis

---

[1] Abu Al-Fadl, "The Delights of Commerce," Damascus, ninth century A.D.

Raymond H. Alleman, CPA, is senior vice president and deputy comptroller of ITT Corporation. He is a member of N.A.A., A.I.C.P.A., and F.E.I. Charles M. Wurst, CMA, is director headquarters A&G and special projects for ITT.

171

for formulating expectations for future periods. In the centuries that have intervened since his time, a more complex, albeit sometimes more confusing, way of describing the commercial enterprise has evolved. Articles written on the same subject today would likely refer to fund flows or funds from operations, but "funds" may be defined in a number of ways. Current alternative definitions of funds include: working capital, net current monetary assets, total assets, total current assets, cash and short-term investments, and cash. The most common practice currently is to equate funds to working capital; however, there is a growing trend of interest in defining funds as cash. The advantages of defining funds as cash, of developing a cash-flow statement on the direct method, and then of modifying the cash-flow schedule to reflect the effects of inflation will be examined in this chapter. A discretionary cash-flow statement will be presented beginning with a traditional cash-flow statement from operations and then adjusting for the effects of inflation and the expenditure of funds which are discretionary in nature or, at least, subject to the determination of management or the board of directors.

The advantage of the working capital concept of funds is that the components of working capital are relatively close to cash, so working capital is deemed to be a close approximation of accessible cash. Also, the amount of working capital is not affected by the timing of the collection of receivables, by the sale or conversion of inventories, or by remittance of payables.

The main disadvantage of working capital as a concept of funds is the likelihood of major differences between working capital flows and actual cash flows. If, for example, increases in receivables and inventories were offset by reductions in cash, these changes would not be readily apparent in a funds statement based on a working capital concept of funds, and yet they might be the indicators of underlying financial problems.

A number of writers have studied the development of W.T. Grant's bankruptcy which occurred in 1975. The bankruptcy was preceded by positive income and working capital from operations from 1966 to 1974. Both the net income and working capital flow tended to obscure the reality of the negative cash flow that was occurring from 1971 to 1974. In this instance, the calculation of working capital provided by operations, which included net income plus depreciation, was a poor indicator of the firm's ability to generate cash, without which bankruptcy was inevitable.

Working capital was the definition of funds used by the majority of firms responding to a survey made in 1980 for the Financial Executives Institute, but according to a follow-up survey made in 1983, better than half of the respondents indicated that they focused on the cash definition of funds. There is an increasing awareness of the inadequacies of using working capital as a surrogate for cash, such as for assessing future cash flows. Expenditures are made in cash, not working capital, and an increase in working capital does not necessarily result in an increase in cash.

PROFITABILITY AND SOLVENCY

The increasing preference for defining funds as cash is related to an increased sensitivity to issues of solvency. However, it must be recognized that goals of profitability have a strong pull and appeal that at times tend to obscure what should be an equally strong concern for solvency.

According to the theory of finance of the firm, the ultimate goal of an enterprise is the maximization of the owner's wealth.

To pursue the maximization of wealth involves management asking these questions: What are the ideal amounts of assets, liabilities, and net worth? What is the ideal relationship of sources and uses of funds for a firm? The limit to the profitable expansion of assets is reached when the cost of finance equals the net returns expected to be obtained from the additional assets.

The goal of maximization of wealth includes two corollary requirements: the maximization of profit and continued solvency (an equally important requirement of ongoing life of the firm). If the firm's management fails to be conscious of the equal importance of these two objectives, it puts the firm at risk. Rapid growth and profitability are strong lures whereas the concern for the solvency objective tends to be drab and unexciting by comparison. The lesson acknowledged in hindsight by those involved with bankruptcies is that a firm can appear to be highly profitable and at the same time become insolvent due to its inability to pay debts and obligations when they fall due. In order to evaluate the success of achieving the two key objectives of profitability and solvency, different types of information are needed for each evaluation.

Solvency is a cash activity, and its evaluation focuses on the risk that a company will not be able to produce enough cash at the time its debts fall due. The information required for the evaluation of solvency concerns the amounts, timing, and uncertainty of a company's future cash receipts and payments.

In the early years of the 20th century, solvency was the central concern of financial reporting. The primary users of financial statements were creditors, particularly bankers. In those years, most bank loans were short-term; they were not for the finance of long-term assets but for what were called self-liquidating purposes. For these short-term purposes, the profitability of the firm was generally not considered relevant in evaluating the risk of the loan. Creditors focused on the firm's current financial position as reflected in its balance sheet. The subsequent shift in focus from servicing creditors to serving the needs of stockholders and investors caused a related change in the emphasis of financial reporting from the evaluation of solvency to a concentration on profitability, and a rise in the importance of the income statement. In recent years, the main focus of financial reporting has been on profitability, and the emphasis of the accounting theorists and accounting standard setters has been on refining income measurement. As a result, the interest in reporting information on a firm's solvency has been significantly diminished, and reporting the timing of cash receipts and payments has been often ignored.

The increased level of sophistication used in determining net income frequently involves numerous subjective allocations that increase the disparity between the reported income and the amount of cash provided by operations. Because of the number of alternative subjective choices, the income reported by different firms faced with identical circumstances can be quite different. Statements of cash receipts and payments do not require arbitrary allocations; cash flows can be measured objectively, making comparisons between firms more meaningful.

It is the noncash items included in earnings that can detract from the reliability of earnings as a proper assessment of current cash-flow performance of the firm.

Yuji Ijiri observed, "Over the years, earnings have become extremely complex and moved further away from the notion of cash flow, since many official pronouncements are concerned with methods of handling noncash items. . . . Unfortunately, the earnings concept is constructed as a residual; after all, cash and noncash items are put together. Noncash items, which are relatively 'soft' and ambiguous, are mixed with cash items, which are relatively 'hard' and objective . . . such a mixture has an effect of reducing the reliability of the resulting figure."[2]

FORMAT OF THE FUNDS STATEMENT

Prior to 1980, the most common format for funds flow statements divided funds flow into two categories: sources and uses of funds. There are two advantages to this format. One is that it summarizes total funds generated and disposed of by the firm during the period; second, it emphasizes the concept that funds flows are fungible and that there does not exist a direct relationship between particular sources and particular uses of funds.

The disadvantage of this format, as expressed by Lloyd C. Heath,[3] is that too many different types of information are included with the result that the format does not facilitate communicating any of the information clearly. Heath's solution is to prepare three separate statements in order to report the different types of information: (1) a statement of cash receipts and payments, (2) a statement of financing activities, and (3) a statement of investment activities.

The arguments in support of presenting a statement of cash receipts and payments include:

1. Funds statements based on a definition of funds as working capital were developed in the 1920s when working capital was the most important measure of debt paying ability. The focus of credit and investment analysis has changed in recent

---

[2]Yuji Ijiri, "Recovery Rate and Cash Flow Accounting," *Financial Executive*, March 1980, p. 54.

[3]Lloyd C. Heath, "Financial Reporting and the Evaluation of Solvency," *AICPA Accounting Research Monograph, no. 3* (New York: AICPA, 1978), pp. 107–8.

years, and there is more concern with the adequacy of cash to pay obligations coming due.

2. In recent years, accrual accounting has become more complex, and refinements in the measurement of income have increased the disparity between reported net income and cash flow.

3. Increased levels of inflation have changed the relationships of reported net income and cash. As prices rise, more cash is required to support receivables and to replace inventory and fixed assets, yet income is calculated on the basis of historical cost. In these situations, net income is not a reliable indicator of cash flow, and a statement of cash flows becomes increasingly important.

The second statement, a statement of financing activity, should disclose the effects of business activities on the capital structure of the company which includes the firm's financing liabilities and the stockholders' equity. Financing activities are defined as changes in capital structure, particularly those transactions which the firm engages in for the purpose of providing financing, distinct from those activities that are a part of the firm's operations. This statement would divide financing activities into two separate components, debt financing and equity financing. Within the section of debt financing, both increases and decreases in each type of debt instrument during the year should be disclosed. Within the equity financing section, changes in the major components in equity are disclosed. The net increase in equity financing ties in with the stockholders' equity section of the balance sheet and reflects the changes in convertible preferred, common stock, capital in excess of par value, and retained earnings. The net change in retained earnings will tie to the details presented in the statement of retained earnings.

The third statement is of investing activities, and it discloses the relatively inflexible, long-term commitments of the firm. This statement should disclose all increases and decreases in long-term investments which include land, plant and equipment, nonmarketable securities, controlled companies, and intangible assets.

These three statements do not require the disclosure of significantly more information than is now required to be disclosed, but their advantage is that they present the information in a clear, understandable way.

The FASB issued a Discussion Memorandum on December 15, 1980, on issues related to "Reporting Funds Flows, Liquidating, and Financial Flexibility." In this Discussion Memorandum, several alternative formats were presented that each offered different aspects of improvement over the common format of sources and uses. Included here is a reproduction of one of the suggested formats for a Report of Cash Transactions in Exhibit 1. This particular format offers the clarity that Heath was recommending in his proposal of three separate statements.

The most common practice in funds statements is to derive sources of cash by the indirect method of analyzing the differences between income and cash flow. This method begins with net income and adds back depreciation, increases in deferred liabilities, increases in deferred income tax, increases in reserves, and then deducts the equity in the undistributed earnings of investments accounted for on the equity method.

There are drawbacks to this approach, one of them being the misleading impression that income and depreciation are sources of cash. Income is neither cash nor a source of cash: Cash comes from customers, and under no circumstances is depreciation a source of cash. Another drawback is that as accrual accounting has become more sophisticated, there are variable acceptable alternatives for measuring the effects of a given transaction; more subjective judgment is reflected in the reported income, and comparability between companies is reduced. The indirect method ends up essentially as being a set of worksheet adjustments instead of an explanation of how operating activities affect cash, although firms are trying to correct this with the "Activity" format which categorizes funds activities as "operating," "investing," and "financing." A more understandable method of presenting cash is the direct method which shows clearly that cash comes from customers and is paid out for merchandise and labor for administrative expenses, selling expenses, taxes, and so on (particularly because readers of financial statements are interested in the past experience of cash receipts and payments as being a useful basis for estimating future cash receipts and payments). A drawback is that it is more difficult for readers to reconcile between the income statement and the balance sheet with the direct method.

Exhibit 1
Report of Cash Transactions

Cash receipts from operations:		
Cash inflow from customers	+	
Interest income	+	
Dividends received from affiliates	+_____	
Cash payments to suppliers		(_____)
Selling, general, and administrative		
expenses	( )	
Interest paid	( )	
Income taxes paid	(_____)	
Cash provided by operations		(_____)
Dividends:		
Preferred	( )	
Common	(_____)	
Cash provided by operations retained		(_____)
in the business		
Investment transactions		
Disposal of investments		
Proceeds from sale of:		
Land	+	
Building	+_____	
Collection of notes receivable	+	
Sale of marketable securities	+_____	
Acquisition of investments	_____	
Purchases of:		
Land	( )	
Buildings	( )	
Equipment	( )	
	(_____)	
Investment in marketable securities	( )	
Increases in advances to affiliates	(_____)	
Net cash used by investing activities	(_____)	_____
Financing transactions		
New financing:		
Notes payable to bank	+	
Long-term borrowings	+	
Sale of common stock	+_____	
Financing discharges:		
Notes payable to bank, repaid	( )	
Repayment of long term debt	( )	
Purchase of treasury stock	(_____)	
Net proceeds from financing activities	(_____)	_____
Increase in cash		_____

FORECASTING FUNDS (CASH FLOW)

The three most important concepts to be incorporated into the process of forecasting cash flow are articulation, realism, and flexibility.

Articulation concerns the logical relationship of the elements of the forecast and a tight causative relationship between the elements on the income statement, balance sheet, and cash-flow statement.

Forecasting cash flow is more a result of the whole forecasting process of the enterprise than an individual exercise in itself. The emphasis in forecasting is usually on profit planning, and thus the focus is usually the income statement. An income statement can be forecast at varying levels of simplicity, and there is likely to be an inverse relationship between the simplicity and the reliability of the resultant forecast. To improve the reliability requires greater depth of analysis and consideration of more facets of articulation between the elements of the forecast. When the elements articulate, then the resultant forecast of cash flow will be a reflection of the net effect of all of the assumptions in the forecast. Budgeting is a systematic approach to profit planning and coordination of all of the factors of the business enterprise that can be measured in financial terms. A sophisticated budgeting program is a total system concept and integrates all of the functional and operational factors of a business, such as sales forecasting, capital budgeting, cost-volume-profit analysis, production planning and control, inventory control, manpower planning, administrative and general cost control, and cash-flow analysis.

In actual practice, whereas management can only directly manipulate the controllable variables of input and output, they also have the decision-making responsibility for taking advantage of the noncontrollable variables that affect sales, costs, and profits. Noncontrollable variables include factors such as the health of the national economy, the sales levels of the industry, and the actions taken by competitors. These and other noncontrollable variables must be accommodated in the business plan to take advantage of the possible favorable variances and to minimize the effects of the unfavorable events.

From the starting point of a sales forecast to a completed budget, the most important principle to be followed is that of articulation. While most financial managers can make the budgeted income statement relate to the budgeted balance sheet and to a cash-flow statement, the relationship can be more apparent than real because they are made on the basis of assumptions. A meaningful articulation requires a detailed explosion of all of the functional factors of the budget. The sales forecast should be expressed in numbers of units of product in order to develop the production plan, the forecast of purchased material, the inventory plan, the manpower plan, and the capital budget. On the basis of this detail, a meaningful balance sheet budget and a related cash-flow budget can be generated. The more extensive the articulation, the more meaningful will be the resultant budget statements. For instance, receivables might simply be forecast as a percentage of forecasted sales, but there are other factors that should be reflected in the forecast, such as bad debt assumptions, collection times, and assumptions on marketing strategy associated with the sales level. If the forecast sales are for new products or if they reflect an assumption of increasing market share, those sales would most likely require a higher level of receivables to support them. It is critical that receivables tactics be in synchronization with the marketing strategy to provide a realistic forecast for the cash-flow budget. Inventories might simply be forecast as a percentage of sales, but a more accurate approach requires an analysis of all related forecasts. The cost of sales includes an estimate of cost of purchased parts, but is the unit cost for the purchased parts based upon lot quantities that relate to the sales level and inventory level? The lowest purchased part cost is likely to require quantity purchases that would result in increased levels of inventory, causing a resultant higher requirement for funds.

If the concept of articulation is carefully observed, the flaws in the forecast assumptions will eventually reveal themselves in the cash flow statement.

The second concept of realism is more often a requirement of the financial executive than of the line manager since the former is faced with the ultimate reality of cash requirements. The sales forecast from operating management is likely to reflect a stronger emphasis on goal setting than on accuracy or most probable result. When this goal divergence is present, some adjustment is required to remove the optimistic bias in the sales and income forecast. Various firms handle this in different ways.

In some large companies, the sales and income forecast of the division or of the subsidiary general manager are adjusted with conservatism by the group executive before they are passed on to headquarters (but not changing the division's submitted budget and holding the general manager accountable for this original forecast). In other firms, the controllers's department receives the original division forecast and prepares a "finance forecast" which includes adjustments to the goal-setting forecast of the division to make it a "more probable result" forecast. In these firms, it is only the finance forecast that is passed on to top corporate management. In other firms, the original divisional forecast is presented to top management, but the controller's department adds a hard/soft adjustment schedule which reflects the controller's judgment of specific items which are hard or soft to the operating management forecast. This retains the goal-setting forecast of operating management but also presents a more probable forecast that is required for an accurate forecast of cash flows from operations and debt service requirements.

The third concept is flexibility and refers to planning for alternative actions in the event of changes in the noncontrollable variables of the economic environment. When the cash budget is prepared, it should not simply be on the basis of a single set of assumptions but prepared on several sets of assumptions, including worst case and best case alternatives. On the basis of the range of outcomes, the financial manager can evaluate the business risk of being able to meet the expected fixed charges while maintaining other necessary expenditures. He can thus assess the liquidity of the firm and plan a realistic margin of safety.

DISCRETIONARY CASH

A cash-flow statement prepared using the direct method provides a relatively clear understanding of historical cash flows but does not address the distortions caused by inflation. Interest in reporting the effects of inflation has predominantly been in measuring the effects of inflation on income. FASB Statements 33 and 70 adjust income for the higher usage cost of higher valued assets. By adjusting the cost of sales to reflect the higher cost of replacing inventory and plant and equipment, the resulting income figure is felt to be a more realistic measure of the firm's operations in an inflationary environment. This inflation-adjusted income figure, however, does not necessarily provide a better basis for estimating the firm's future cash requirements. Inflation brings with it not only an income measuring problem but also a solvency problem. This requires analysis of balances and flows not necessarily important in the calculation of income. Rising prices require more cash for the replacement of inventory and fixed assets, and for carrying a higher level of receivables. These higher cash uses are partially offset by corresponding increases in payables. A statement of discretionary cash modifies a cash flow statement to adjust the reported figure for the distortions caused by inflation. The objective is to identify the total amount of funds available to finance a business.

Two main concepts of capital maintenance have been considered in the accounting literature: financial capital maintenance and physical capital maintenance.

Capital is the wealth of an enterprise and is represented by the net amount of assets less liabilities or as the amount of equity.

Comprehensive income is defined in Concepts Statement 3 as:

> Comprehensive income is the change in equity (net assets) of an entity during a period from transactions and other events and circumstances from nonowner sources. It includes all changes in equity during a period except those resulting from investments by owners and distributions to owners[4]

Concepts Statement 3 (paragraph 57) discusses the concepts of capital maintenance:

> A concept of maintenance of capital or recovery of cost is a prerequisite for separating return *on* capital from return *of* capital because only inflows in excess of the amount needed to maintain capital are a return *on* equity. Two major concepts of capital maintenance exist, both of which can be measured in units of either money or constant purchasing power: the financial capital concept and the physical capital concept (which is often expressed in terms of maintaining operating capability, that is, maintaining the capacity of an enterprise to provide a constant

---

[4]FASB, *Statement of Financial Accounting Concepts No. 3,"* "Element of Financial Statements of Business Enterprises" (Stanford, Conn., 1980).

supply of goods or services). The major difference between them involves the effects of price changes on assets held and liabilities owed during a period.

Under the financial capital concept, if the effects of those price changes are recognized, they are called *holding gains and losses* and are included in return on capital. Under the physical capital concept, those changes are recognized but are called *capital maintenance adjustments* and are included directly in equity and are *not* included in return on capital.[5]

At the time the Financial Accounting Standards Board issued Concepts Statement 3, it had not yet chosen between the financial and physical capital maintenance concepts, but by the time the board issued the exposure draft for the Proposed Statement of Financial Accounting Concepts—"Reporting Income, Cash Flows, and Financial Position of Business Enterprises"—in November 1981, it had adopted the financial capital maintenance concept.

Financial capital maintenance regards capital as a financial phenomenon. The worth of assets to a business is in their ability to enhance the cash flows of the business. The financial capital maintenance concept views all changes during a period in the net assets (excluding those resulting from transactions with owners) as an integral part of enterprise performance. An increase in the price of an asset held by an enterprise is reflected in comprehensive income because it is thought to provide some indication of an increase in future cash flows.

In times when the tempo of technological change is quick, the declines of heavy industries and the shift of investment interest to high technology products accentuate the aura of inflexibility surrounding the physical capital maintenance concept and its concerns with maintaining the capacity of an enterprise to provide a constant supply of goods or services.

Alert executives are continually looking for opportunities to shift capital investments out of less profitable operations into operations, products, and markets promising greater profit potential. In this perspective of a propensity to shift capital investment to pursue the greater profit potentials, the financial capital concept appears to be the better conceptual fit.

Under the physical capital maintenance concept, the histori-

---

[5] Ibid.

cal value of inventory, plant, and equipment is adjusted to current cost by the use of current market price, appraisal value, or specific indexes. However, under the financial capital maintenance concept, there is no assumption that the presently existing capital assets will be replaced; in fact, there is likely to be considerable uncertainty as to the direction of future reinvestment. In this state of uncertainty, it is more appropriate to use a general index that reflects the inflation characteristic of the whole economy, such as the consumer price index or the gross national product price deflator. Thus, under financial capital maintenance, the historical value of inventory, plant, and equipment would be adjusted to constant dollar values.

The constant dollar valuations of plant and equipment are the basis of calculating the constant dollar depreciation, and the constant dollar value of inventories provides the basis for the constant dollar adjustment for the inventory component of the cost of sales.

The constant dollar depreciation and cost of sales adjustment are the means of recognizing the effects of inflation in the modification of cash flow schedule to construct a schedule of distributable cash.

Alfred Rappaport introduced the concept of business capacity maintenance in his article "Measuring Company Growth Capacity During Inflation." According to Rappaport, "This concept is based on the idea that a going concern has distributable funds available only after it makes provisions to maintain that portion of its operating capability financed by equity."[6] He defines distributable funds as "the maximum amount that the company can distribute to its stockholders during a period without impairing its business capacity." According to Rappaport, the maintenance of business capacity includes establishing a target level of financial risk—the risk associated with different levels of debt in relation to the company's equity. Beyond the debt/equity ratio, other factors that affect a company's debt capacity are total interest coverage, cash flows to total debt ratios, the strength of the collateral, the strength of the company's management, and the outlook for the industry.

Rappaport includes the changes in debt level in determining

---

[6]Alfred Rappaport, "Measuring Company Growth Capacity During Inflation," *Harvard Business Review*, January–February 1979, pp. 91–100.

distributable funds on the basis that maintaining acceptable levels of financial risk is an essential element of maintaining any specific level of business capacity.

The section of a discretionary cash schedule on financing transactions would be comprised of three basic categories of new financing—notes payable to banks, long-term borrowings, and sale of capital stock—plus the comparable three categories of financing discharged to provide the subtotal which is labeled net proceeds from financing activities.

A suggested format for a statement of discretionary cash is included in Exhibit 2. The major sections discussed so far include:

> Cash from operations.
>
> Less: adjustments for inflation.
>
> Plus: net proceeds from financing.
>
> Distributable cash.

This subtotal of distributable cash represents the cash available to distribute as dividends or to be otherwise used at the discretion of management. After the levels of dividends to stockholders are determined, what remains is cash that can be invested in new growth of the firm. This investment can be for the purchase of land, buildings or equipment; for advances to affiliates; for investment in research and development, advertising, and sales promotion; or for increases in working capital. As a business expands, a firm's working capital requirements may increase for a number of reasons, including, of course, higher sales volume but also including changes in product mix or changes in credit or inventory policies. In projecting increased working capital requirements for inventory and accounts receivable, using balance sheet amounts as a basis for projections may be misleading for two reasons: First, the year-end balances may not reflect the normal needs of the business during the year as special year-end efforts may have been exerted to reduce receivable and inventory balances. Second, using the total amounts for inventories and receivables would overstate the requirement for increased working capital as it is only the variable costs of inventories and receivables that will require additional working capital.

The variables that can affect the amount of discretionary funds

Exhibit 2
Statement of Discretionary Cash

Cash receipts from operations:		
Cash inflow from customers	+	
Interest income	+	
Dividends received from affiliates	+_____	
Cash payments to suppliers		
Selling, general and administrative expenses	( )	
Interest paid	( )	
Income taxes paid	(_____)	
Cash provided by operations		
Maintenance of financial capital		
Depreciation in constant purchasing power	( )	
Constant purchasing power adjustment to cost of sales	(_____)	
Financing transactions:		
New financing:		
Notes payable to bank	+	
Long-term borrowing	+	
Sale of common stock	+_____	
Financing discharged:		
Notes payable to bank, repaid	( )	
Repayment of long term debt	( )	
Purchase of treasury stock	(_____)	
Net proceeds from financing activities		+
Distributable cash		
Dividends:		
Common	( )	
Preferred	( )	
Discretionary cash		
Investment in new growth		
Purchase of:		
Land	( )	
Building	( )	
Equipment	( )	
Increase in advances to affiliates	( )	
Increases in R&D	( )	
Increase in working capital	(_____)	
Net cash increase (deficiency)		

are sales volume, return on sales, inflation rate, debt/equity ratio, financial risk, and dividend payout ratio.

The interplay between each of these variables will change the amount of discretionary cash available for investment in new growth. An analysis of discretionary cash provides a method of probing the financial viability of a company operating in an inflationary environment. It brings into sharp focus developing problems of insolvency. It can be used as an analytical tool in the budgeting process to test the coherence of the assumptions utilized in building the budget. When the budget assumptions for each of the variables affecting discretionary funds are reflected in the discretionary cash schedule, any inconsistencies in assumptions, such as between sales volume, return on sales, inflation rate, and dividend payout ratio, will appear as reduced or negative discretionary cash.

A schedule of discretionary cash is a means of presenting to management and to the outside financial audience the effects and interrelationships of the complex factors that bear on the funds from operations.

11

Capital Requirements

Karl F. Slacik

INTRODUCTION

Developing a capital requirements system is a fundamental task of managing the sources and uses of funds. The system should encompass tactical and strategic planning, execution of daily operations, and an evaluation process to measure results. The purpose of this chapter is to examine these components of a capital requirements system. The chapter begins with a discussion of the planning process and proceeds through the daily operational requirements, consisting of working capital and fixed-asset management, and concludes with a review of key financial ratios.

PLANNING FOR CAPITAL REQUIREMENTS

Planning is the key to an effective capital requirements system. Planning not only sets the course for daily financial oper-

Karl F. Slacik joined Levi Strauss & Co. in 1978 as vice president of financial operations. In 1980 he was promoted to senior vice president and CFO and elected a director of the company. Formerly, he was vice president, CFO, and a director of Echlin, Inc. He has also held financial positions with ITT and Mobil Oil.

ations, but it also plays a key role in attaining a firm's growth, profitability, and capital structure objectives.

The chief financial officer makes the pivotal decisions in allocating a company's available resources to attain long-term objectives. The planning process aids in determining the steps and the sequence in which they must be taken to allocate resources in an optimal manner. An unhappy example of poor planning is the decision to expand production capacity based on current market demand followed by a drop in sales that negates the need for the new plant. In this instance, the company suffers on two counts: Resources are committed to the unnecessary plant, and the opportunity to use these funds for a more productive project is lost.

The planning process established should enable the financial executive to adapt to changes in the business environment. A key strength of any company lies in its responsiveness to change and its flexibility in dealing with adversity. This can only be achieved through a thoughtfully planned strategy. The CFO's role in establishing this strategy includes: (1) developing a planning system which takes into account company objectives and the capability to achieve those objectives, and (2) defining capital requirements and identifying matching capital resources, thereby optimizing the capital structure of the company. These two areas will be discussed in detail.

Planning Process as a Management Tool

There are several formal and informal models which can be used for planning capital requirements. The "model" used in this chapter consists of three major elements: objectives, operating performance, and financial position. (For an overview of this model, as well as the detailed components of each of the elements, refer to Exhibit 1.)

It is important to note the interrelationship among these elements. For example, the financial position of a firm is largely dependent on its operating performance. Furthermore, the financial executive must constantly evaluate both the financial position and the operating performance of the company to determine the viability of the first element, company objectives. Company objectives and the related capital requirements which cannot be funded internally (that is, through current operating

Exhibit 1
Capital Requirements Planning

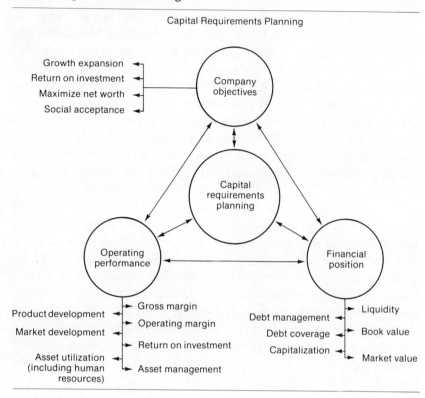

Capital Requirements Planning

performance) will require external financing. In that case, the interdependency among the three elements should be viewed even more critically through the watchful eye of outside parties.

In the discussion that follows, each of the planning elements and their interrelationships will be reviewed in detail.

Company Objectives Many books and periodicals have espoused the benefits of setting company objectives. This brief chapter cannot begin to do justice to that literature. Instead, this discussion will focus on just a few of the most common objectives and their role in determining capital requirements.

Increasing shareholders' wealth is the primary objective for all corporations. At a minimum, a company should generate a return equal to what a shareholder could reasonably expect to earn on a comparable investment. To achieve this goal, the company must increase its earning power and maximize its net worth. Both factors are heavily dependent on operating performance. However, a company's financial policies and strategies also play an important role in optimizing its profitability.

Growth in shareholders' wealth is not always commensurate with sales growth. In fact, the opposite can well be true. In the latter case, retrenchment may be imperative in order to discard certain unprofitable segments of the business. Nevertheless, growth is usually an important corporate objective. Depending on its size, products, markets, profitability, and capital availability, a firm's growth objectives might range from stability to rapid expansion.

Stability is an important, yet very difficult, goal to achieve even for a company which has matured in its life cycle. Erosion of market share, for example, is possible in any business. Its probability is accentuated in industries which are particularly vulnerable to rapid technological development, fashion changes, or noncompetitive labor rates.

The business machine industry exemplifies the changes wrought by technology. For example, the market for the basic typewriter is still fairly robust, but the demand for word processing equipment has clearly affected the product and its sales and profitability. Achieving stability for typewriters in today's marketplace would be very difficult. Maintaining current production levels (that is, survival) becomes the more important goal unless the firm is prepared to shift along with the market.

In fashion-related industries the failure to anticipate or to move with new styles, materials, or designs can raise havoc with market penetration. Two classic examples of industries damaged by the cost of labor are the shoe and automobile industries. In both cases, high wage rates in the United States have contributed significantly to market share impairment.

Growth for a large, stable company can be achieved through product line expansion, market expansion, diversification, or even by increasing market share. Another method of achieving growth is through acquisition. This type of growth may, however, require expertise in a field unrelated to the company's current business. Furthermore, acquisition of publicly listed companies, as a general rule, requires paying a premium over the current market value. The acquiring company must be able to add value to the acquired property in order to receive sufficient value from it to compensate for the premium.

Another objective that companies commonly strive for is social acceptance. Corporate responsibilities in the social arena include compliance with government regulations, the accommodation of demands by private groups (for example, consumers, environmentalists, or church organizations), and adherence to self-imposed codes of business ethics. Issues such as the environment and consumer safety are more visible today than ever before, and the enforcement of the stringent rules and standards has become a fait accompli for many industries, for example, nuclear energy, oil and gas, automotive, and chemical. This has dramatically impacted the cost of compliance.

Identification of public issues with significant potential impact and the determination of possible business exposure must also be considered in planning for capital requirements, for example, possible litigation and its impact in terms of direct cost, as well as damage to corporate image.

Operating Performance The second major element in the planning model is operating performance. Obviously, a company's most important source of capital is its operations. This is true not only for generating cash internally but also for debt and equity, since operating results play a major role in investors' decisions. Operating performance is measured at the product level by several criteria (see Exhibit 1), but particular emphasis should be placed on the gross margin. Is it in line with other companies in the same industry? How are other companies striving to increase their margins? The evaluation of a company's gross margins also requires an examination of pricing structure: Are prices too low? If prices were raised, would sales be sustained?

An examination of the manufacturing cost is even more important: Are there ways of reducing cost and streamlining activities which would expand the gross margin yet still achieve a quality product? This requires creativity and innovation throughout the company. The chief financial officer's role in this entire process as an assessor, as well as a planner, remains essential.

Another area in which the financial executive's assessment of operating performance is necessary is in evaluating the characteristics of the company's products. Is there an additional share of the existing market to be attained? Can expansion be achieved in different markets? On the other hand, are the company's products stable? Can new uses of the products be found through research and development?

Questions such as these assist in evaluating the versatility of the company's product lines. But, at the company level, performance should be measured in terms of shareholders' expectations. A company should generate a return on equity which justifies the use of investors' funds, that is a return above the cost of equity.

Financial Position The last of the planning elements—the financial position of the company—plays an important role in sustaining the operating performance. Financial position is also one of the most visible attributes on which investors target their attention. As a result, a firm's credit worthiness is greatly dependent on its financial position.

As with operating performance, several ratios can be used to evaluate the financial strength of a company. Financial ratios which are used by lenders and shareholders must be closely scrutinized to ensure that the company's financial position and, more importantly, its credit rating are not jeopardized by hasty decisions. (See Exhibit 2 and the discussion on key financial ratios later in this chapter.)

Awareness of creditors' expectations is also important. The primary criteria among many is the firm's ability to repay its debt. On a short-term basis, however, a lender's emphasis may be on pretax interest coverage. Foresight on the part of management can help lead to decisions which maximize cash flow from operations and enhance the firm's credit rating.

Another area of lender interest is the firm's leverage position. The effect on the debt/equity ratio of business decisions, such as acquisitions, must be carefully assessed on a pro forma basis before the final execution of a decision. Using the pro forma assessment, the financial executive can chart the maximum investment which can be financed through external funding while maintaining targeted credit criteria. The assessment also provides the level of financial strength needed to maintain/increase market share and to service the debt.

While the three major elements in planning for capital requirements represent internal factors which can be controlled to varying degrees, there are a myriad of external forces which must also be taken into consideration.

Certainly no chief financial officer can fail to recognize the enormous impact of public sector budgets, especially those of the U.S. government. Fiscal and monetary policy can trigger high interest rates, restrain the economy and/or alter inflationary expectations. Furthermore, the value of the U.S. dollar in the international currency markets can cause economic distortions and stimulate or retard business activity in various countries. Currency exchange rates also impact translation exposure and the firm's ability to compete in both domestic and international markets. Other, though less obvious, external factors include tax legislation, technological developments, international indebtedness, labor legislation, and import/export regulations.

The role of the financial executive is not limited to planning for capital requirements. He must continue to participate in the postplanning phases which generally include implementation, evaluation, and plan modification. These phases are not restricted to capital requirements activities. Indeed, they represent the sequences of many business decision-making processes and are the subject of several of the chapters in this handbook.

Requirements and Resources of the Business

For a business to define its requirements or resources, the objectives of the company must first be determined. For example, if the company's goal is expansion, a onetime capital requirement may possibly fund such a development. On the other hand, capital required to sustain operating expenses and to support a level of working capital sufficient to meet projected sales is of an ongoing nature and therefore more crucial to the survival of the company.

In defining resources, it is important for the financial executive to distinguish between those that are internal and those that are external. Also important is the formulation of a strategy to match short-term resources with short-term requirements.

For any healthy company, working capital generated from operations should be the primary source of funding short-term requirements, such as operating expenses. For labor-intensive companies, payroll represents the major short-term expense whereas in a capital intensive company this will more likely involve equipment maintenance or research and development. Generally, it would be inappropriate to finance these expenses with long-term obligations. However, without adequate planning, such a mismatch and financial dislocation can result.

Meeting all capital requirements through internal operations, especially those needed for expansion, is a luxury not enjoyed by many corporations. That is why most companies also require outside resources. Whether internal or external alternatives are under consideration, certain timing characteristics (short-term, long-term, cyclical, and seasonal) must be carefully defined and reviewed in the planning phase of capital requirements.

Short-term capital requirements cover current liabilities, including the short-term portions of long-term obligations. Cash may also be needed to pay a dividend. An ongoing budgeting and forecasting process should determine whether operating revenues will cover short-term obligations. Other internal resources that should be regularly evaluated may include: factoring accounts receivable, tax reduction or deferral strategies, divestiture of marginal or unprofitable segments of the business, and increasing sales prices.

If internal resources are not available to meet current needs, short-term borrowing may be considered. Issuing commercial paper, utilizing lines of credit, and negotiating short-term loans are a few of the many techniques which can accomplish this type of borrowing.

Long-term capital requirements, on the other hand, include expenditures for capital equipment, internal business expansion, and acquisitions. These requirements often necessitate pursuing external resources, such as the issuance of equity or debt. These may include such special instruments as Eurodollar and industrial revenue bonds. Other long-term options may include leasing versus purchasing capital assets and interest rate or currency swaps in association with long-term debt obligations. Finally, large sums of capital for long-term requirements may be raised internally through sale, spin-off, or trade of certain segments of the company.

Seasonal capital requirements are particularly noteworthy due to their volatility. These fluctuations are usually industry specific and can be identified by historical experience. For example, companies in the apparel industry generally gear their sales to Back to School, Christmas and Spring seasons, each of which corresponds to heavy consumer spending. During these peak seasons, the accounts receivable level is usually far higher than any other time of the year, thereby requiring additional working capital. Working capital may also increase during periods immediately preceding these peak seasons because high inventory levels are created to meet anticipated demand.

The important point is that working capital requirements for many industries change by season. Proper matching of working capital resources, particularly of the short-term debt variety, is essential if the company is to operate successfully on a year-round basis.

Cyclical patterns represent the last of the time-related parameters of capital requirements. Many factors, internal as well as external, affect cyclicality, and these factors vary between industries. Residential housing is one of several industries which must remain abreast of cyclical factors. Demand for housing has historically been inversely proportional to the level of interest rates. The chief financial officer for a property development firm who fails to preplan for interest rate fluctuations and their relationship to other cyclical market trends can seriously compromise the company's future operations.

Another cyclical occurrence is demonstrated by shifts in the general population. One example is the maturing children of the baby boom of the 1950s who, as adults, are now responsible for the increased birth rate in the 1980s. The new "echo boom" will undoubtedly disrupt buying patterns established over the last 30 years. This will impact industries as diverse as insurance, food products, and apparel. The performance of a company in a cyclical industry is dependent on its ability to sustain its operations during less favorable periods and to expand them when the upswing begins. In other words, it must be able to adjust to a "peak and valley" environment. In such a situation, planning is not just required to maximize profits but may also be a key to survival.

In these circumstances, reliable forecasting techniques, both short-term and long-term, are also essential for an effective strategy.

Identifying internal and external funding resources should be an ongoing process. The flexibility a company enjoys through an optimum mix of capital resources may determine its success during periods of adversity, as well as prosperity. Many companies, for example, have unused lines of credit which represent an important security blanket, especially when money supply is restricted.

The financial executive, as a planning strategist, determines how capital requirements will be funded. Moreover, as the architect of the firm's capital requirement plan, he has the unique opportunity, and indeed the responsibility, to blend the operational and financial planning processes.

The remainder of this chapter will explore how the chief financial officer executes this role in the course of his daily responsibilities.

WORKING CAPITAL MANAGEMENT

Working capital, as the lifeblood of the firm, not only funds daily operations but can also provide the capital for future investment. While in most firms the treasurer and controller oversee the various working capital accounts on a daily basis, the chief financial officer charts the course for working capital management and objectives. The underlying objectives of the financial executive's goal setting and strategy is to maximize the return on the working capital investment.

As part of developing a process for working capital management, the financial executive sets forth the controls which facilitate an optimal investment in inventories and receivables. These controls must also be consistent with the achievement of future financial goals.

Although working capital consists of various components, this discussion will be limited to inventories and trade receivables, as these two assets usually represent the largest investment block.

The basic question is: What levels of inventory and receivables are consistent with the competitive environment and good management control?

Inventories

The financial executive's contribution to inventory management is more strategic than tactical. Monitoring such operational aspects as the level of raw materials, work-in-process, and finished goods is important. This, however, is the responsibility of the corporate controller and is not discussed in this chapter, which is limited to the chief financial officer's role in inventory management and how that role relates to capital requirements.

The optimal investment in inventory varies among industries and can also vary among the firms within a given industry. It is important to note that inventory, as a component of working capital, represents a cost which has already been incurred.

Conversion of inventory to accounts receivable will directly increase working capital by an amount equal to gross profit. Thus, the higher the gross profit margin, the greater the increase in working capital. Therefore, the most important and beneficial way to increase working capital is through the sale of inventory.

There are several factors related to managing the investment in and conversion of inventories. These factors include production and sales cycles, sales volume, profit margins, customer service objectives, sales patterns, trends by product line, and, above all, the availability of capital.

The relationship between the production cycle and the sales cycle is one of the most important factors affecting inventory turnover. Long production cycles typical of such industries as coal, oil, and wine lead to a greater investment in inventories. On the other hand, firms producing perishable products, such as meat (for which the famous industry slogan "sell it or smell it" is appropriately descriptive) tend to have higher inventory turnover and thus a lower capital requirement for each dollar of sale.

Whatever the level of a firm's inventory, the underlying objective is to optimize its investment, that is, to attain maximum sales with minimum inventory levels. To do so, it is imperative that inventory levels be closely aligned with the selling cycle.

This is not simple, especially since the objectives of production personnel may be in conflict with those of the sales force or the financial managers. For example, financial management may attempt to minimize the investment in inventories; at the same time, sales management will want to build inventory levels to provide greater flexibility.

Production management may also favor high inventory levels. The standard justification for a bloated inventory is the desire to reduce production costs through longer production runs. However, much of the work-in-process (WIP) inventory and consequently much of the cycle time has a different explanation. It is caused by managers who want to have a hedge against possible nondelivery from the previous production phase. Therefore, a high WIP inventory can signal weaknesses or problems in the production process, and forcefully lowering the inventory can bring these weaknesses into view and facilitate correction. Thus, an active program to reduce WIP inventory via reduction in cycle time has the dual benefit of reducing the inventory investment and improving the production process.

Unless the parochial views of the various functions within a company are held in check, the situation can result in excessive inventory and higher risk of product obsolescence and markdowns. On the other hand, all departmental perspectives must be considered. Optimizing the investment in inventory can only be attained by balancing financial constraints and production capabilities with marketing goals, needs, and desires. It is the chief financial officer's responsibility to promote optimal levels of communication and cooperation among various organizations within the firm, and thus maximize inventory utilization while minimizing the drain on working capital.

In smaller companies, the financial executive can also help establish an inventory and production planning function which will play a key role in solving and, to a great extent, avoiding the above types of conflicts. This function can serve as a catalyst in coordinating inventory, production, and sales information. It can also evaluate this data through the use of certain control tools, such as the following simple equation:

Beginning Inventory (Actual) + Planned Production =
Projected Sales + Desired Ending Inventory.

When and how often the above analysis should be performed is dependent on the type of industry and the length of the production cycle. Clearly, the chief financial officer should provide direct input in setting parameters, that is, inventory turnover ratio, based on his investment objective. However, his expertise and input is also valuable in working with the operating executives in determining the parameters for the other two elements of the equation, projected sales and anticipated production.

Projected sales should be based on a merchandising/sales forecast and determined through historical sales data, as well as future projections by knowledgeable marketing executives. The achievement of investment objectives depends upon accurate (or reasonable) numbers. An invalid sales forecast can lead to high inventory levels and resultant markdowns. Worse yet, it can result in obsolescence and write-offs on the one hand, and low inventory and lost sales on the other. In each case, the result is a deterioration of profit margin and a capital drain. Therefore, sales forecasts must be tested and scrutinized by experienced financial managers.

Anticipated production should also be carefully scrutinized to safeguard against inventory obsolescence and to achieve customer service objectives. A crucial aspect of production is the lead time, which should be determined through careful research and analysis. The lead time process should include the time requirements for all elements of production, including ordering and receiving of raw materials. The chief financial officer's direct or indirect involvement in this process is imperative to ensure that the established controls are operating effectively.

The above points represent a rather simple but useful set of inventory management aids. More complex models, such as economic order quantity (EOQ), also exist, and their widespread use has helped firms in identifying optimal investment levels.

Returning to capital requirements and resources, it should be noted that there are other ways to extract funds from inventories in addition to outright sales. Short-term financing, using inventory as collateral, is one of them. Indeed, the purchase of inventory can also provide a short-term source of funds if a firm takes full advantage of payment terms and bank float. These practices vary from one industry to another and pose certain inherent risks, such as a deterioration of vendor relations, when payment terms are abused. The risks and benefits must be carefully evaluated by the financial executive before formalizing a disbursement policy.

In any analysis of inventories, it is important to understand the relationship between inventories and receivables. The rapid depletion of inventory, for example, may signal an uncontrolled growth in receivables. This may, in turn, result in a higher incidence of doubtful accounts. It is imperative, therefore, that inventories and receivables be managed in tandem.

Trade Accounts Receivable

A firm's accounts receivable is directly affected by its level of sales and type of credit policy. Credit policy generally has a direct impact on both the current level of sales and long-term sales growth. Therefore, establishing an appropriate credit policy is of paramount importance. The financial executive's task is to coordinate a credit and receivable policy that is consistent with industry standards and that finely balances opportunity and risk. The discussion below addresses some of the issues which should be considered when developing such a policy.

First, a firm's credit policy must be developed in conjunction with the sales and marketing strategy to ensure the optimal balance between sales and bad debt losses. Lack of common goals and proper coordination between various groups will invariably result in conflicting philosophies and objectives. The objective of the financial executive is to coordinate the development of a credit policy which maximizes earnings over the long run.

Industry practices also greatly influence the development of a firm's policy. Longer receivable terms may be typical of the industries in which products are sold in advance of retail selling seasons, for example, swim suits. This allows the retail merchant to order and take delivery early but to pay for the merchandise when the product is offered for sale or actually sold. On the other hand, in an industry such as flowers, either the payment is due on delivery or short terms are negotiated.

Centralization versus decentralization is another issue affecting the development of a credit policy in multinational and/or multidivisional corporations. Sales and payment terms vary greatly in the international environment, and what may be a norm in the United States is not necessarily practicable or even advisable in Europe or Latin America. Also, in many countries payment is made through a promissory note which must be discounted if the funds are to be received in a reasonable time.

Trade-offs between sales growth and receivables control must be continually sought when reviewing the policy. Flexibility is also important to ensure that exceptions can be made in unusual circumstances. While it is not ordinarily a firm's objective to serve as a customer's banker, it may be necessary to extend special terms in certain instances. This might well be true, for example, when the firm is seeking to dispose of inventory which might be excessive or on the verge of obsolescence. It should be noted, however, that in order to make effective decisions in a situation such as this, accurate inventory cost information (variable, fixed, carrying, and financing costs) must be available.

Accounts receivable statistics (for example, days sales outstanding, aging standards, and past due criteria) are also very important to consider when developing a credit policy. These measures define a firm's credit granting objectives and should therefore be used to influence the credit policy. The financial executive's role in this area is to set the standards that are consistent with overall company objectives and industry practices. He must also ensure that adequate information systems are implemented to help monitor progress against the objectives.

Perhaps the chief financial officer's greatest responsibility regarding receivables is to convince both the sales force and the customers that the terms of sale stated on the invoice are to be seriously respected. Any deviation from those terms should be accompanied by an interest charge that covers the cost of money and the additional risk inherent in delayed payments.

Finally, it should be noted that short-term cash requirements should rarely, if ever, be a consideration in determining credit terms. Establishing tight credit terms just to raise needed cash may adversely affect sales volume and customer relations. However, satisfying short-term cash needs through trade receivables may be accomplished by factoring the accounts. But this process has an inherent disadvantage: the loss of control. For example, by assigning its receivables, a firm may have to disclose proprietary information to outsiders. The firm must also rely on outsiders to judge the collectibility, discount fees, and the various terms of the factoring agreement.

The advantages and disadvantages of taking this avenue must be carefully weighed by the chief financial officer and his marketing counterpart.

FIXED ASSETS

The next section of this chapter addresses some of the issues affecting fixed-asset investments and the financial executive's role in the related decision-making process. Fixed-asset decisions have a direct effect on the future course of a business. Therefore, a sound capital expenditure budgeting system must be in place in order to analyze and prioritize fixed asset requirements.

The chief financial officer plays a central part in the planning and decision-making process related to the selection and disposal of fixed assets. It is incumbent upon him to aggressively exercise this responsibility in order to ensure maximum asset utilization and to safeguard against waste, misuse, or misappropriation of company funds.

Fixed Asset Requirements

The nature of fixed asset requirements varies among industries. For example, "heavy" industries require enormous amounts of fixed asset investments while service industries, such as insurance and banking, require relatively few fixed assets. The importance of planning, evaluation, and controls in all of these industries varies according to the magnitude of the fixed assets.

When evaluating the capital requirements for fixed assets, the chief financial officer should first review the firm's objectives. The most important of these involves ensuring that fixed assets are meeting the operational needs of the company with maximum efficiency and minimum cost. Many factors must be considered in order to strike this critical equilibrium. Among the more common are: future marketing strategies, potential technological developments, cost versus benefit of research and development, and asset replacement versus asset rehabilitation.

Long-Range Marketing and Manufacturing Plans represent an important, and perhaps the most important, element of the system. The careful alignment of fixed asset plans with marketing strategies will obviously assure the availability of production support to meet market demand. The firm's stage of maturity plays a major role in this process. As a general rule, a new company will require a great deal more capital to sustain initial growth than would one that is well established. Product life cycle also plays an important role. Established, mature products with a strong hold on market share may impose less frequent demands for the expansion or replacement of production capacity. In the case of a new product, however, prudence dictates that elaborate manufacturing facilities be deferred until the product has profitably established itself in the marketplace. Subcontracting production in the initial stages may be an alternative way to minimize the risks attendant with product failure.

Technological developments can alter the course of the firm's manufacturing and distribution functions. Lack of careful planning and foresight in this area can render fixed assets prematurely obsolete. Industry practices generally dictate the need for, and direction of, research and development expenditures. In the chemical and pharmaceutical industries, for example, a large portion of a company's capital is dedicated to fixed assets. Therefore, the bulk of nonproduct research and development is directed towards improving asset utilization and productivity. In "light" or labor intensive industries, such as apparel, fixed assets are lower. Capital resources are therefore devoted to improving the production process in order to reduce the product's labor content.

Research and development expenditures have an important mission, namely establishing new products and/or improving existing ones. Nowhere is this more apparent than in high technology companies. Industry leaders, such as IBM in the computer field, have a clear advantage because their size and enormous asset base allows them to make significant investments in research without unduly threatening cash flow. Smaller firms may not be able to afford that luxury and may therefore choose to forego the leadership role. In evaluating proposed research and development investments, the cost versus benefits analysis should be similar to that used to evaluate other capital expenditure decisions. The objectives of research and development programs, as well as the criteria for measuring progress, should be clear and part of the overall process.

The replacement versus rehabilitation alternative should be a major component of the capital budgeting system. One of the important tasks of the financial executive is to maintain a control mechanism which measures the productivity of machinery and equipment. Machinery that produces a large number of rejects or that is in constant need of repair is a drain on the productivity and the quality of the finished product. It is incumbent upon the financial executive and his subordinates to identify the need for replacement based on the overall benefit to earnings. The evaluation process could include a review of overhead costs, downtime, product rejects, scrap, overall cost per unit, and other factors common to the particular industry. In conjunction with operations managers, a periodic assessment of fixed assets should be conducted to identify obsolete and/or deteriorated equipment.

Fixed Asset Decision Analysis

Other components of the budgeting system should include after tax return on investment and payback criteria. Since fixed assets are expected to provide cash flow in future years, evaluation should be made using the discounting process, that is, by discounting the future cash flows to determine their present value. Also, it is important to evaluate the future cash flow from alternative investments. It should be noted that the principle of wealth maximization is equally as important to fixed asset acquisition as it is to the acquisition of an entire company. In other words, the acquired asset must recover its investment and add a value equal to or greater than alternate investment opportunities.

Operational factors, such as productivity, repair costs, downtime, and product quality, must be quantified to provide sound support for the decision. In summary, fixed asset management and control is critical to the profitability of the firm. Efficient utilization of fixed assets directly affects the viability and financial strength of the firm which are, of course, the key concerns of the chief financial officer.

FINANCIAL ANALYSIS

The corporation's financial statements report on the results of operations and on the financial position of the firm. These statements, plus other information contained in the annual report and similar public documents, are used by investors to judge past performance. They are also used to form expectations about future earnings and dividends, as well as to assess the risks attached to the business. Financial statement analysis is even more important to management. It not only assists in understanding current conditions, but it also serves as a starting point in planning actions that will influence the future course of events, an activity the chief financial officer must constantly lead. One basic tool of financial analysis involves the review of financial ratios. While the number and the type vary from one industry to another, the following section discusses key financial ratios which apply to a cross section of industries.

Key Financial Ratios

A financial ratio measures the balance or spread between interrelated financial or operational factors in a concise and demonstrable manner. Ratios can be categorized into five groups:

- Liquidity.
- Asset management.
- Debt management.
- Profitability.
- Market value.

Detailed components, as well as the function, of each type of ratio are highlighted in Exhibit 2.

Financial statistics provide benchmarks that are useful in internal studies and for external comparisons. It is important to analyze trends in ratios, as well as their absolute levels. The true

Exhibit 2
Capital Requirements Key Financial Ratios/Criteria

Group	Description	Function
I. Liquidity	Current radio Quick (acid test) ratio Liquidity trend	Measure ability to meet short-term obligations.

II. Asset Manage-ment	Inventory turnover
	Days' sales outstanding in
	  receivables (average
	  collection period).
	Days' supply of inventory
	Asset utilization
		Measure the appropriateness
		of the assets vis-a-vis
		current and projected
		operating levels.

III. Debt	Debt/equity ratio Debt/capitalization ratio Debt as percent of cash flow Interest coverage Fixed charge coverage	Measure the capitalization components and the ability to service debt.
IV. Profitability	Gross profit margin Net income margin	Measure price/cost relationship.
	Return on invested capital Return on equity Return on total investment	Measure the adequacy of return.
V. Market Value	Price/earnings ratio Market price/book ratio Stock price trends Dividend payment Dividend/CPI Stock yield Total return (yield plus appreciation) Cash flow per share	Indicate investors' view of performance and future prospects.

value of financial statistics can only be determined by evaluating their relationships to industry standards. The ratio alone does not tell a full story. When compared to the general economic climate, industry standards, and other firms, however, the ratios do bring into focus the financial position of the firm and allow for a more meaningful evaluation.

The external use of financial statistics is of great interest to most managements since it affects stock prices, credit ratings, and the ability to borrow at advantageous rates. The financial executive can rarely change the ratios, but he can coordinate management efforts to ensure results that reflect the true financial strength of his firm.

CONCLUSION

This chapter has discussed a key business activity, evaluating capital requirements. The system to manage this activity should encompass planning, a strategy to execute the plan, and a process to evaluate the results. The objectives of the capital requirement system are to provide (1) a guide in establishing overall objectives, (2) a framework for developing and executing plans and strategies, and (3) a tool for measuring the impact on operations and the financial position of a company.

Expressed more simply, the objective of the capital requirement system is to provide the necessary cash to keep the wheels of the business rolling. The most important function of the chief financial officer is to ensure that the system continually meets this crucial objective. A chief financial officer can commit no greater sin than to allow his company to run out of cash. While this statement is an age-old truism, the paths to bankruptcy and insolvency are littered with the evidence of many forms of poor financial management and the broken careers of too many CFOs.

Material covered in this chapter should provoke ideas which will protect the chief financial officer from committing capital requirement blunders either through errors of commission or errors of omission.

12

Debt Financing

John T. Hickey and Garth L. Milne

The subject of debt financing involves consideration of long-term strategic questions, as well as specific short-term, tactical decisions. High interest rates, high inflation, and the proliferation of debt over the last several years have meant that the rate of change in financing and in development of new financing methods has greatly accelerated. This chapter is divided into five sections in order to cover the total subject of debt financing as broadly as possible: (1) integrating debt financing into financial goals and capital structure, (2) considerations in using financial service institutions, (3) new financing tools and trends, (4) short-term funding, and (5) long-term funding.

John T. Hickey has served Motorola Inc. since 1948 as salesman, division general manager and corporate staff executive. He became CFO in 1970 and executive vice president and a director in 1984. Garth L. Milne has held various treasury managerial and executive positions at Chrysler (1973–79) and Motorola (1979–present) and in 1984 was named vice president and director of treasury of Motorola.

INTEGRATING DEBT FINANCING INTO FINANCIAL GOALS AND CAPITAL STRUCTURE

The cost of debt, as viewed on an individual transaction basis, will almost always be less than the cost of equity because of the tax deductibility of interest and because of investor demands for higher returns on equity due to more risk and volatility. However, for any company there is an appropriate limit to the amount of debt it should incur because of the inherent financial risks to the company and its shareholders. The amount and type of debt should bear a proper relationship to the nature of the business and its capital structure strategy.

The business considerations that should be evaluated when determining a firm's capital structure and debt policy include:

1. The nature of assets and their inherent risk. High quality receivables and general purpose assets, such as railroad cars, would allow higher debt ratios. The lives of such assets also impact on maturities.

2. The cyclicality of the business. The more stable the business, the higher the debt that may be supported, all other factors being equal. The cyclicality of the business could also significantly impact on the desire for fixed-rate debt and/or the maturity of debt. At a cyclical business low point, when credit might be unavailable or only available at very high premiums, having long-term, fixed-rate debt could be quite important.

3. The potential for extraordinary expenditures. The possibility of major unforeseen expenditures, such as acquisitions or settlements of legal suits, could result in a desire to keep significant, unused debt capacity available.

4. Technological obsolescence. The degree of technological risk inherent in the business may lead to a conservative financial structure since the combination of high business risk and financing risk could prove fatal.

5. Foreign risk. The degree of foreign competitive risk or exposure to significant foreign exchange risks in the revenue or cost structure of the company.

6. Individual company risk attitude. Possibly the most important point is the "culture" of the company as far as the de-

gree of risk, either business and financial or just financial, that the company is willing to assume.

Once the above and any other appropriate business considerations are reviewed, a company should formulate guidelines or strategies regarding debt financing. Besides stating the overall amount or proportion of debt, these guidelines should also address the following other factors:

1. The credit rating targets appropriate to provide the desired degree of cost and access to financial markets.
2. The degrees of financial flexibility and ability to respond quickly to financing opportunities which are appropriate. Besides being related to the credit rating, these considerations also will impact upon internal staffing decisions, establishment of financing vehicles, and decisions whether to consider using certain markets that tend to require flexibility and speed. The recent dramatic increase in interest rate volatility means that financial flexibility, in not being forced to issue debt or equity at a particular time and in having access to most markets, is more important than ever.
3. Structure of debt appropriate, to include both maturities and fixed versus floating rates. Some lower-cost financing vehicles used in the past few years require large "balloon" payments or maturities. The traditional concept of short-term, floating-rate debt on one hand and long-term, fixed-rate debt on the other hand has been supplemented by numerous financing alternatives that are floating-rate, long-term instruments.
4. The complexity of the capital structure. Does the company want senior and subordinated debt, secured and unsecured debt, finance companies and leasing companies, or other "off balance sheet" financing, project financing, and so on?
5. Tax considerations. What is the tax position of the company, and how much tax risk is acceptable?
6. The amount and frequency of capital requirements which can impact on the need for flexibility, strength of financial structure, access to markets desired, and the like.
7. The international risks of the company, including its foreign exchange position, foreign tax credit position, tolerance for currency exposure risk, desire to finance in foreign currencies, and so on.

8. Whether to arbitrage outstanding debt with marketable securities either on or off the balance sheet and to what extent.

CONSIDERATIONS IN USING FINANCIAL SERVICE INSTITUTIONS

Over the last several years there has been a dramatic change, which will probably continue, in the services and capabilities offered by the various types of financial service institutions. There have been a series of mergers and acquisitions, as well as changes in certain regulations, such as the deregulation of interest rates paid to smaller depositors. Many of these changes have also been motivated by basic economic forces, such as high inflation, high and volatile interest rates, and changes in the patterns of savings and insurance by individuals. For example, money market funds have attracted about $200 billion of assets over only a few years.

The nature of some entire financial industries has changed, possibly the most publicized of which have been the dramatic changes in the savings and loan (S&L) industry. The very large mismatch between long-term, fixed-rate assets (mainly mortgages) and short-term deposits caused virtually all S&Ls to have significant losses when interest rates were high, particularly in 1981 and in early 1982. As a result, there have been numerous mergers and changes in regulations to permit S&Ls to make commercial loans. Also, there has been a significant move away from long-term, fixed-rate mortgages, the establishment of national markets for packaged mortgages (to allow S&Ls to sell off some of their assets), and moves by S&Ls to try to increase the amount of their fixed-rate debt which has included many interest rate swaps. Some of the other changes that impact on debt financing have been the changes in the life insurance industry whereby companies have decreased the terms of their loans because of mismatches between the maturities of their assets and liabilities and policy loans. In addition, new insurance policies and the mix of insurance sales have resulted in increased short-term investing by the insurance companies as standard whole-life policies have become less prevalent.

In the long-term, tax-exempt market, both banks and casualty insurance firms have recently been smaller buyers because of their reduced need to shelter income, in turn caused by poorer profits.

There has been a significant increase in the size of some sources of capital, such as money market funds, tax-exempt bond funds, and pension funds. A few of these have begun to make some direct loans, such as master notes and mortgages. The significant expansion of the Eurodollar markets has meant that some institutions with the capability of lending and/or underwriting Eurodollars/Eurocurrencies have become relatively more important for several years. Because of the withholding tax on interest payments to foreigners through mid-1984, which most corporations have managed to avoid through Netherlands Antilles subsidiaries, intermediate-term interest rates for higher quality U.S. corporate issuers were often significantly lower over the last few years in Europe than in the domestic market. Incidentally, the U.S. government, as a borrower, was not able to avoid the aforementioned withholding tax on interest payments to non-U.S. investors. Now that withholding taxes have been eliminated, the ability to issue bearer bonds and the greater degree of privacy for Eurodollar lenders has often meant continued lower interest rates in the Eurodollar market although not as much lower as in the past.

The use of SEC Rule 415, on shelf registration, allowing faster placement of domestic public debt, has led to more business for the highly capitalized and larger investment banking firms. Another major development has been the growing role of the major U.S. commercial banks. Although the regulations prohibiting banks from underwriting U.S. public securities still prevail, several banks have emphasized their "Capital Markets Groups" and have become significant competitive forces in areas such as currency swaps, interest rate swaps, the Eurobond market, and private placements.

Over the last few years there have been numerous mergers of brokerage and investment banking firms that have changed their relative competitive strengths. In addition, there has been the entrance of major firms, such as Sears, Prudential Insurance, and American Express, with large capital bases that have enabled them to acquire brokerage and investment banking firms, and thereby become credible competitors in other sectors of the financial markets. As a result, the relative capabilities of the different investment banking firms have changed considerably, and the capabilities of these institutions have begun to overlap. Thus, there has been increased turnover of people in many such firms as these changes have caused certain firms to recruit more experienced people to get fast starts into new businesses.

These changes have broadened the number of financial institutions and the types of relationships available. The questions of whether a company should directly issue its own commercial paper, directly sell long-term debt and/or use an investment banker as merely an arranger and not an underwriter on long-term debt arise with increasing frequency. In some cases, such patterns have not been pursued because of the limited frequency and amounts of debt issuance by the company. Added internal staffing and a different interface with financial service institutions would be required, compared to the present system which has continued to serve them well. But, for well-known, highly rated companies with large and frequent financing needs, the changes of the past few years mean that it is now possible to place public debt directly in the form of short-term debt, master notes, commercial paper, or long-term debt. It is also possible to implement other debt-related transactions directly, such as calling bonds, buying bonds for sinking fund purposes, and so on. Also, the private placement debt market has broadened to include some foreign entities, pension funds, and others compared to past years when only banks or insurance companies participated.

Another judgment that a company must make is whether to seek open bids on each financing transaction or to develop a close and continuing relationship with one or a few financial service institutions, combining both financing and significant financial advice. The changing nature of many financial service institutions and the increased turnover of people are important considerations in this judgment. This decision must also be related to the size of the company's treasury staff since dealing with many financial institutions and on a bid type basis does require more people. Some believe that there is value in long-standing relationships, particularly because understanding a company's particular financing strategy, financial needs, attitudes toward flexibility, tax position, corporate "culture", and the like is important. However, any company must be reasonably demanding for price and service, and it must still be willing to look at and act on new and good ideas from whatever source. The rapid rate of new financing innovations is such that no one or two institutions can be expected to develop and present all such new ideas.

It is also important to match the financial services institutions' capabilities and culture to the company's needs and culture. This should include domestic versus international considerations, a short-term transaction orientation versus a long-term service orientation, strengths and weaknesses in various market sectors, such as commercial paper, tax-exempt financings, swaps, international financings, and strength with small individual investors versus large institutional investors (all compared to the needs and characteristics of the company itself).

NEW FINANCING TRENDS AND TOOLS

The dramatic increase in new financing trends and tools has been spurred by high interest rates and high inflation, the changes in the financial services institutions, the growing internationalization of markets, deregulations, the changes in exchange controls, the changes in tax laws, the development of some new financing tools which have then spurred the development of other related financing methods, the increased total debt of companies, and the growing acceptance of some new methods by corporate financial officers. High and volatile interest rates have meant that asset and debt mismatches in terms of maturity, or fixed versus floating rates, such as in the S&L industry or some banks, are bigger problems than ever before and, in fact, have been fatal for some such institutions. This has spurred the development of even more new financing tools. In the future, we believe changes in tax laws, in governmental regulations in the United States and abroad, and in market considerations will continue to result in the creation of new financing vehicles and the elimination of other financing vehicles. It is mandatory to remain up to date with the changes in the financial market.

There is not space here to discuss all of these financing techniques or even any of them in great detail. Nevertheless, we will try to summarize the characteristics that motivate many of these new financing methods and the parameters we believe necessary to look at while evaluating them, and we will also briefly discuss some of the more important of these financing tools. The specific financial tools discussed may change over time, but the characteristics that motivate them and the parameters to evaluate them are more constant.

It is important to try to understand what causes new financing tools to appear since such knowledge sometimes helps to identify risks, such as tax risk or the required giving up of some financing flexibility. If there is such a thing as a significant absolute "free lunch" in financing available to companies, it almost always seems to get arbitraged, regulated, legislated away, or at least minimized over time. This also means that sometimes a company must make decisions and be able to act very quickly. Generally, changes in regulations and legislation have not been made retroactive. It is also important to understand cash flows each year and to calculate their present values, not just look at the short-term impact on reported earnings. One should be skeptical if a new financing tool seems to "manufacture" short-term reported earnings.

Many new financing tools relate to the tax laws and changes therein. Several of the major financial services institutions seem to have assigned some key people solely to study and monitor the tax code and to devise new financing tools to capitalize on its provisions. Several of the resultant new tools have been devised to take advantage of the U.S. tax rules on the timing of interest deductions versus the payment of cash for interest payments. Still others have been related to avoiding taxable gains upon retirement of old debt or sale of assets. Others have been related to taking advantage of foreign tax laws. Often, the tax code seems to have been written to favor the government and to have uniform impact upon the buyer and seller, assuming both are taxable entities. However, with the emergence of tax-exempt institutions, such as pension funds and foreign buyers, the government has perceived itself to be the frequent loser since the seller can deduct expenses rapidly and the buyer may not be taxable. The window for use of some such tax-driven types of financings is often quite short, particularly if their use becomes widespread, if they are "too abusive," if they do not cause some "social good," such as helping build equity, or if they lack a strong political constituency supporting them. An example of a widely used type of financing that had its benefits dramatically curtailed after only a short time is the Original Issue Discount Bond. In 1984, there was a modification in the tax laws directed at correcting many such abuses (in the opinion of the IRS) in the past few years. We would expect this effort to continue and to adversely impact many of the "now you see it, now you don't" financing schemes.

Several other new financing tools involve the use of options, futures, forwards, and other such recently developed markets in order to lock in spreads versus Treasury bond rates but defer actual issuance of debt and, therefore, the setting of fixed rates on long-term debt up to a specified period of time or even indefinitely. Options, futures, forwards, and so on have also been used to establish interest rate ceilings. There have been options to do some of the above, including options on options.

Another area where there has been a recent expansion of activity has been in the use of options on both future defined debt and equity, partial pay bonds, convertible bonds, giving up call provisions, and other means of the issuer giving up some of his flexibility and/or giving potential security holders a "gamble" or "leveraged gamble" on the course of future interest rates, currency movements, or equity prices. A few bonds have even had their interest rates tied to oil or precious metals prices. These financing techniques have facilitated issuance and have lowered coupon interest rates. The long-term value to the issuer can only be determined in light of its total financing needs and strategy, as well as the anticipated course of future interest rates, currency values, and equity prices. However, there has undoubtedly been some advantageous financing of this type as investors have been able to leverage their forecasts (also in light of their local tax situations) and pay accordingly for securities. From time to time, with hindsight, there seem to have been some speculative excesses on the part of buyers of these types of securities that have also resulted in lower cost financings for issuers.

The usage of tax-exempt financing by corporations has expanded significantly in recent years. There has been a trend to take advantage of the current and strong historical pattern for short-term, tax-exempt interest rates to be significantly lower than long-term, tax-exempt interest rates in order for the tax-exempt yield curve to have a strong positive slope. As a result, there has been a series of either floating-rate, tax-exempt bonds or bonds where the rate is reset periodically at the option of the issuer and where the holder then has an option to redeem the bonds after the rate has been reset. Without getting into all the details of the IRS regulations and local government rules on tax-exempt financing, the current general pattern requires prior approval by the local governmental authority, capital expenditures of less than $10 million over six years in the locality unless expenditures are for certain specified purposes, such as pollution control, the utilization of slower depreciation if tax-exempt financing is used, and financing only for the life of the asset. The savings have often been 3 percent or more per annum in interest rates and in some states the elimination or reduction of sales taxes and property taxes. In 1984 (and possibly in the future), changes in the tax laws imposed further limitations, such as a maximum dollar amount per company, a per capita maximum dollar amount per state, inclusion of common-wealths (for example, Puerto Rico and Guam) under these rules, and elimination of arbitrage profits.

The emergence and widespread use of currency swaps and interest rate swaps in recent years have provided new tools to move efficiently and/or at lower cost to meet certain financial needs. Interest rate swaps capitalize upon inefficiencies between markets, particularly for certain types of borrowers. As a result, a borrower who might have access to low-cost, fixed-rate financing in the Eurodollar market can utilize that ability to obtain lower cost, floating-rate debt costs in the United States by doing an interest rate swap with an entity that doesn't have that Eurodollar market access but needs fixed-rate dollar debt, such as an S&L. Another borrower might have access to lower cost floating-rate debt, such as the U.S. commercial paper market, and through an interest rate swap can translate this into lower cost, fixed-rate dollars. A bank or financial institution can obtain lower cost, floating-rate debt by being the counterparty. Sometimes a financial institution will stand in the middle of an interest rate swap in order to satisfy the credit concerns of both parties. Currency swaps also capitalize on inefficiencies between markets (sometimes caused by governmental regulations), allow certain financing needs to be met at overall lower costs, or allow otherwise unavailable access to certain markets or currencies. For example, a particular borrower may not be known in a foreign market or may have excessively utilized that market or may not be allowed to use that foreign market due to governmental regulations. Through currency swaps, that borrower may be able to better access such a market. The other party may be able to gain a lower cost financing by a currency swap through using his ability to access that market. As in interest rate swaps, a financial institution may stand in the middle of the transaction to satisfy the credit concerns of the two parties. Since interest rate swaps and currency swaps do not involve registration, governmental approval (usually), syndicates, or the like, they can often be tailored to meet the needs of the parties. Some large financial institutions will take positions themselves on currency or interest rate swaps either to meet their own financial need or until they can find counterparties. It is also possible to use currency swaps and interest rate swaps together so that a borrowing can be made, for example, in fixed-rate Swiss francs and the net obligation converted into floating-rate U.S. dollars.

The usage of extendable debt has also become fairly widespread for companies that have continuing financing needs and are generally of high credit quality. In this manner, they can reduce the time and expense of many issues while staying short on the yield curve initially which they believe will save them money.

The usage of equity-linked securities has also become more widespread, particularly for higher quality issuers, whereas at one time such transactions might have been considered appropriate only for lower quality companies. In our opinion, however, equity-linked securities like convertible bonds (at least those of a type generally issued in the United States) should be considered to be just a delayed issue of common stock at a price above the current level. The usual 20- or 25-year convertible bond should be converted since with any kind of inflation and/or company performance the stock should rise by more than the 20 percent plus the premium normally required to induce conversion.

The usage of defeasance as a financing tool has recently become more widespread. Since defeasance usually generates instant "booked profits," it has a great appeal to some companies. It can also capture gains on low-coupon debt and not be taxable whereas retiring the debt would usually be a taxable event. Defeasance can also be effective for a company seeking to overcome the impact of a person or institution attempting to acquire enough of the outstanding bonds to force the company to pay higher prices for sinking fund purchases. Defeasance has also been used to lock in an arbitrage profit while keeping the debt "off the books." We believe the possibility of additional booked profits should mean that the arguments against defeasance, such as creating a lower yielding treasury portfolio, should be examined carefully before deciding on defeasance since the "profit" could distort proper judgment. However, it would seem prudent to include defeasance enabling provisions in all new indentures.

The use of leasing has expanded significantly in the last several years as companies have sought to expand their apparent debt capacity by off-balance sheet financing. Also, leasing has allowed firms to obtain total overall lower cost financing when they cannot use all the tax deductions and tax credits associated with the assets in a timely manner. This factor has been very important for many companies, such as where significant consumer financing of depreciable equipment is involved, or in certain foreign countries, such as the United Kingdom. The lower corporate tax rates of the last few years have accelerated this trend as has the overall increase in corporate debt.

A suggested word of caution: We strongly believe that it is very important for financial management not to delude itself in considering leasing and the other available types of off balance sheet financing. No matter what the accounting rules provide, debt is debt, whether owed to a lender via a debt instrument or to a lessor via a lease. Earlier in this chapter, we mentioned the need for a company to determine its total debt capacity, considering risk, financing flexibility, and a variety of other considerations. Leasing uses debt capacity as much as borrowing and, given proper concern for overall debt capacity, the accounting convenience of off balance sheet financing should not be allowed to support the rationalization of excessive debt.

When reviewing the various new financing tools and trends (and there will undoubtedly be more), we believe it is important to consider what happens if interest rates should go up or down, what are the tax considerations and might they change in the near future, how much financing flexibility is given up or gained, what might happen under the various options, such as puts and calls, as interest rates vary, how does any particular financing tool or proposal fit into a company's intermediate-term financing needs and strategy, what are the exact cash flows and timing thereof, and how do all these considerations fit the company's other policies. In addition, from a manpower and timing standpoint, a company must prepare and staff itself to utilize these tools, especially some of the newer and/or more complex ones.

SHORT-TERM FUNDING

Years ago, it could be argued that the major reasons for short-term debt were to finance the seasonal needs of a business and as interim financing of major capital expenditures until enough such expenditures had been made to justify permanent long-term financing in an economically issuable amount. Over the last decade or two, there has been a well documented and significant increase in the percentage of total debt outstanding that is short-term debt. Part of the reason has undoubtedly been a reluctance to issue long-term debt, given the high interest rates over recent years. In addition, there seem to be several other reasons for philosophies that have contributed to the increase in short-term debt. A philosophy of always having a moderate amount of total debt in short-term form seems more widespread. Many companies seem to carry short-term debt to arbitrage short-term investments or floating-rate-type investments, such as floating-rate preferred stock or tax-free portfolios in possessions' corporations. Another significant factor seems to be more companies borrowing short because of the positive shape of the yield curve.

In making comments on the sources of short-term debt, we will not cover all possible procedures for borrowing short-term but will mention only the major sources, which are:

1. Commercial paper. The use of this increased dramatically in recent years to about $200 billion now outstanding so that it rivals bank loans in size and is the major source of short-term funding for higher rated companies. The increase in commercial paper usage is because, for these higher rated and larger companies, it is usually the lowest cost source of short-term debt. The credit rating agencies require backup bank lines of credit or equivalents thereto, usually at 100 percent of peak commercial paper outstanding. A recent innovation has been the usage of commercial paper and foreign exchange con-

tracts as a method of obtaining lower cost foreign currency debt than bank borrowings in foreign currency.

2. Bank Loans. Pricing for bank loans has changed significantly to where they are not only at or related to the prime rate as was the case about a decade ago. For high quality borrowers, banks will quote rates related to various money market rates and often below prime. Many short-term credit arrangements will provide for borrowings related to certificates of deposit, federal funds, or Eurodollar rates. Often the pricing choice will be that of the borrower. One consideration that higher quality borrowers should keep in mind, particularly as regards certain foreign countries, such as Japan and France, is the question of the continuity of relationships with banks if sufficient borrowings are not made.

3. Master notes. The use of master notes, which are essentially call borrowing agreements directly with a lender, have expanded from the traditional bank trust departments to money market funds.

4. Bankers acceptances.

5. Accounts receivable financings. Factoring where credit risk and collection is passed to the financial institution has become less widespread than formerly because of its high cost. The use of captive finance companies has expanded significantly as a way of segregating assets and thereby obtaining increased total entity leverage with consequent lower total entity financing costs. The sale of receivables with or without collection administration has become more widespread with the frequent use of hold backs, reserves, and the like, to mitigate the financial institution's risk. A recent innovation has been finance companies jointly owned by a manufacturer and a financial institution and/or a third-party investor.

6. Inventory loans.

LONG-TERM FUNDING

The motivation for long-term debt has progressed from financing fixed assets to also financing increased amounts of permament additions to working capital largely caused by high inflation. Long-term debt pricing is now essentially related to the Treasury bond yield curve. Before briefly listing and commenting on the major sources of long-term debt, it is appropriate to outline factors that should be considered in making a long-term debt decision.

Due to the dramatically higher interest rate volatility of the last few years, it is generally desirable to plan so that quick response can be made to financing opportunities, such as obtaining a shelf registration under SEC Rule 415, and having appropriate (faster) internal approval and documentation procedures. A policy needs to be established regarding fixed-versus floating-rate debt since availability of funds can be locked up but the rate allowed to float. A company's present and expected tax position can have a major impact on long-term debt decisions since leasing, for example, can be used to get lower financing costs in many cases if a company is not in a taxpaying position by "passing on" depreciation and/or investment tax credits to the customer or provider of funds. As mentioned earlier, many of the financing innovations of the last few years have been closely related to tax rules.

Another issue that must be considered is the degree of financing flexibility desired or which might be given up in issuing long-term debt. By giving warrants which provide lenders the right to require the issuance of further debt, giving up call provisions, giving lenders put options, using zero coupon or deeply discounted debt which essentially gives up call provisions, or other vehicles a borrower can obtain lower coupons (or initial effective interest cost) on its long-term debt. The different markets to which a company has access should be reviewed since they can vary in terms of cost, covenants, or availability. For example, the Eurodollar market has often been lower cost for higher quality borrowers in the last few years but at other times has been almost "closed." We believe it is desirable to keep covenants as flexible as possible due to the rapid changes in the financial world. It is therefore appropriate to have a financial executive, along with a lawyer, negotiate covenants because a full understanding of financial trends and procedures is required.

There has also been an increased use of letters of credit and other forms of credit substitution in order to access markets or reduce interest costs. The increased use of collateralized mortgage obligations or similar instruments by many companies shows in the issuance of $0.4 billion in 1982, $4.0 billion in 1983, and over $4 billion in only the first quarter of 1984 out of total United States corporate public debt offerings of approximately $40 to $50 billion per year.

The major sources of long-term debt and some brief comments related thereto are as follows:

1. Real estate mortgages. Historically, these have usually been private placements. However, recently the dramatic increase in collateralized mortgage obligation financing has provided a new public financing source.
2. Mortgage bonds.
3. Tax-free bonds. The large increase in the issuance of tax-free bonds has occurred in several categories, such as pollution control, industrial development revenue bonds, possessions corporations, and various other permitted purposes. There has been a trend toward floating interest rates or periodic rate adjustments because of the strong tendency of the municipal yield curve to remain positively sloped.
4. Private placements. Banks have reduced sharply their term loans somewhat and shortened maturities. Insurance companies have also shortened maturities. Pension funds have started making some direct loans. Some major foreign institutions, such as the Saudi Arabian Monetary Authority, have been significant lenders from time to time.
5. Debentures. These unsecured, flexible long-term debt instruments are usually thought of as being public issues but can be used for private placements.
6. Equipment trust certificates. These debt instruments secured by personal property are often the lowest cost, long-term financing for all except high credit-rated issuers but are limited to general purpose, usually moveable, "commodity-type" equipment, such as railcars.
7. Project financing. This type of financing, tied to specific projects, has become more widespread, particularly in certain industries such as energy where expenditures may be large, where joint ventures are used, and where projects are self-contained.
8. Extendible debt. This new type of financing avoids the time

and expense of repeated issues for frequent issuers and also results in lower initial rates when the slope of the yield curve is positive.

9. Zero coupon or original issue discount debt. The major tax advantages associated with such debt have been eliminated, but lower interest rates may still be available due to effective lack of callability and foreign tax laws.

10. Subordinated debentures. These issues are often private placements and for relatively smaller amounts. Financial institutions have used them most frequently to increase overall leverage, a pattern which the credit rating agencies are currently reviewing.

11. Capital notes. Such debt is usually to banks or where regulations count them as equity capital because the debt is subordinated to all but the banks' equity capital.

12. Equity-linked debt. Such debt is usually subordinated and is convertible into the company's or parent's stock or even convertible into another company's stock. It should be expected that the bond will convert into equity given the usual 20- to 25-year maturities in the United States although often in Europe shorter maturities (and smaller premiums) make conversion less certain. Convertible bonds are usable mainly by companies with reasonably good growth prospects and lower dividend yields, so they can, in effect, sell stock at a premium if events occur as expected.

13. Supplier financing.

14. Customer financing.

15. Governmental (state, federal, or foreign) incentives, loans, or guarantees. This type of funding can result in low-cost financing through one or a combination of grants, in low interest rate loans, and/or in tax relief.

16. Export financing. Export financing can be used either as a source of low-cost financing or to reduce certain foreign-country or foreign-currency risks. Some countries offer better export financing programs than others, but they may be somewhat restricted for foreign corporations doing business in that country. Some of the lesser developed countries have had particularly attractive export financing programs.

17. Foreign-currency long-term debt. Such debt tends to be available (other than for some types of export financing) only in a limited number of countries, particularly on the fixed-rate basis. In making a foreign-currency financing decision, a company should balance its assets in that country, specifically those assets exposed to currency valuation change, the interest rate involved, the potential for currency revaluation or devaluation, the availability and cost of currency swaps, and the company's policy on neutralizing currency exposure. For example, a six-year Swiss franc borrowing (not hedged by a currency swap) at a low coupon from 1972–78 would have proven very expensive whereas a similar six-year borrowing from 1978–84 would have been very low-cost financing for a dollar reporting borrower. The recent expansion of the European Currency Unit (ECU) debt market has provided the opportunity to effectively get a "mix" of foreign currency fixed-rate debt in one issue at a good interest rate, in relatively small amounts per currency, and in some currencies where fixed-rate debt is not generally available.

18. Currency swaps. As discussed earlier, currency swaps can be used by themselves or in connection with interest rate swaps. Currency swaps can result in lower cost financing in the desired currency by exploiting inefficiencies between different currency markets for different borrowers.

19. Interest rate swaps. As also discussed earlier, interest rate swaps can result in lower cost financing, either fixed-rate or floating-rate, by exploiting inefficiencies between different markets for different borrowers.

20. Leasing. Leasing has boomed over the last few years both for cash-flow and reported profit reasons. The pros and cons of leasing and the arguments as to whether leasing provides incremental financing and should be evaluated related to the cost of debt or the total cost of capital are far too numerous and complex to discuss here. Leasing is also sensitive to tax laws which are prone to change from time to time and from country to country as recently (1984) occurred in the United Kingdom. Leasing can offer some definite advantages, such as the ability to acquire small quantities of assets like office space, the flexibility in use of assets

(albeit perhaps at a high cost), the 100 percent financing, and the ability to lower financing costs in cases where a company's tax position makes it such that some other entity can better use the tax benefits of ownership (depreciation and investment tax credit).

In evaluating a lease proposal, the cash flows must be looked at on an aftertax basis versus ownership, including the tax implications of both leasing and ownership. Two difficult assumptions pertain to the residual risk assumed and the rate at which to discount cash flows. We tend to take the conservative approach in looking at leasing as a debt alternative, and we use discount rates appropriate to debt financing. The residual risk question can vary greatly depending upon the type of asset, the country, the particular tax law applicable at the time, and the impact of renewal options, ground leases, or other factors which impact the residual value. The proposed "Finance Lease" law in the United States which was to have become effective in 1984 and is now being deferred or eliminated would have allowed the residual value to be stipulated in a leasing contract. Other changes in the laws affecting leasing are also possible. The negative considerations in leasing usually relate to the cost (particularly if discounted at the cost of debt) and the ability to "control" the asset sufficiently for a long enough period of time. The cost of leasing has almost invariably been higher than the cost of debt on a long-term basis if a discount rate for debt is used. We believe the reason for this is that the lessor must earn a profit and that the lessor takes a residual value risk for which he must be compensated, but the lessee operates the asset and usually better understands its risks, so the lessor must price accordingly. If an aftertax discount rate at approximately the cost of equity is used, leasing probably will seem less expensive than ownership.

13

Dividend Policy and Equity Financing

*John S. Wadsworth, Jr.**

This chapter will look at the right-hand side of a company's balance sheet and consider financing strategy—the trade-offs between different financing alternatives. In particular, it will consider whether a firm should reinvest most of its earnings in the business or should pay them out as dividends (through cash dividends or share repurchase) and, if a company needs more money, when equity financing is the appropriate vehicle. It will also consider both the choice of distribution of equity financing or method of share repurchase and the choice of an investment bank.

FRAMEWORK FOR EVALUATION

As a framework for evaluation, let us first isolate dividend policy from other problems of financial management. In order

---

*The author would like to thank Maurine M. Murtagh of Morgan Stanley for her contributions to this chapter.

John S. Wadsworth joined Morgan Stanley in 1978 and is currently a managing director in the investment banking division. Previously, he was executive vice president and a member of the board of directors of The First Boston Corporation, having joined that firm in 1963.

to do this, let us make two simplifying assumptions. The first, and most important of these, is that the firm's investment decision is fixed. This makes dividend policy a residual decision. Second, let us assume for simplicity's sake that the firm's borrowing decisions are also given.

Given these two assumptions, the financing of dividends must come either from retained earnings or equity financing. Thus, dividend policy may be viewed as the trade-off between retaining earnings on the one hand and paying out dividends and issuing new shares on the other.

Some companies may restrict dividends to avoid equity financing while others may pay dividends and raise equity as needed. In either case, the company is facing the dividend policy trade-off.

Should the chief financial officer of a company care about this trade-off? Clearly, if investors value firms that pay dividends more highly than those that don't, paying dividends and raising equity as needed is probably the preferred alternative. Similarly, if high dividend payout improves a company's value, the attractiveness of an investment project will depend on how it is funded. Therefore, as a CFO, one should be interested in the impact, if any, which dividends have on the value of the firm.

Since the early 1960s, there has been much debate on this issue. Three basic schools of thought have emerged: Dividends are irrelevant to the firm's value; increases in dividends increase the value of the firm; and increases in dividends lower the value of the firm.

These three opposing views will be evaluated, citing data and specific cases where relevant. Then an attempt will be made to determine where the controversy over dividend policy leaves one as a CFO in formulating the firm's strategy both as to dividend payments and the financing of those payments.

DIVIDEND IRRELEVANCY

The argument for dividend irrelevancy began with a seminal paper in 1961 by Franco Modigliani and Merton Miller (MM) who argued that the value of a firm is not affected by its dividend policy in a world with no taxes and no transaction costs (or other market imperfections).

Since the MM argument went against the conventional wisdom at the time, the paper was met with skepticism from both the business and academic communities. The nonbelievers argued that MM ignored a multitude of real world considerations including risk, market imperfections (especially taxes), and the signals that dividends provide to the market.

DIVIDEND INCREASES MEAN INCREASED FIRM VALUE

Many of the MM critics argued that the market places a higher value on dividends because of their relative certainty versus the relative uncertainty regarding the firm's ability to reinvest those funds so as to provide higher future dividends. This has become known as the "bird in hand" argument.

But is it the higher dividend payments that in some way affect the market's perception of the risk of a company's stock, or is it the riskiness of a company's operations that influences the level of dividends? It seems that companies in riskier operations do consciously choose to limit their dividend payouts— that is, these tend to be growth companies. Thus, the line of causation is from higher risk to lower dividends and not the reverse. Thus, the "bird in hand" proponents have made the error of confusing investment and dividend policies. Companies, especially growth companies, paying lower dividends tend to have riskier investments or greater uncertainty surrounding future investment decisions. For this reason, the market tends to discount the earnings of low-dividend companies at higher required rates of return.

DIVIDEND INCREASES MEAN DECREASED FIRM VALUE

By the beginning of the 1970s, the consensus of academic researchers was that no strong conclusion about dividends and stock prices could be drawn from existing studies. Ten years after its inception, therefore, the MM "irrelevancy" argument was without empirical support but, on the other hand, had not been refuted by rigorous testing. Attention during the 1970s, therefore, turned to tests related to market imperfections that do exist in the real world and might cause dividend policy to affect stock prices. More specifically, attention focused on the potential tax effect of dividends on firm value. It is also interesting to note that this represented a shift in focus of the dividend controversy itself—from a disagreement between those who were prodividend versus those who felt dividends were irrelevant to irrelevancy versus those who were antidividend.

The substance of the tax argument is as follows: The higher marginal tax rate (for most individuals) on dividends relative to capital gains has a negative impact on stock prices. The retention of earnings, however, results in capital gains equal (on a pretax basis) to the dividends that could otherwise have been distributed. Capital gains have two apparent tax advantages over ordinary income for individual investors: 60 percent of long-term capital gains is tax-exempt, thus reducing the maximum effective tax rate to 20 percent (40 percent times 50 percent); and capital gains are taxed only when realized, thus allowing for the use of tax-deferred and timing strategies. To the extent that the investor never intends to realize holding gains, they are tax-free indefinitely.

There are two exceptions to this. The first is financial institutions (for example, pension funds and most foreign investors), many of which have tax-exempt status and therefore have no reason to prefer capital gains to dividends. Corporations, on the other hand, have a tax reason to prefer dividends as they pay corporate income tax on only 15 percent of any dividends received; the effective tax rate is then 15 percent of 46 percent or 6.9 percent.

The structure of the present U.S. tax system would mean, then, that taxpaying investors might pay more for stocks with low dividend yield—that is, they should accept a lower *pretax* rate of return from securities paying returns in terms of capital gains rather than dividends.

A series of studies was done which seemed to indicate that investors did require additional pretax return for high dividend paying stocks and that there was a "clientele" effect—that is, effective segmentation of security holdings according to investors' tax brackets. This evidence would imply that companies could substantially increase their share values by *reducing* dividends.

It should be noted, however, that the president's Tax Reform Plan for 1986 would dramatically reduce the differential between ordinary income and capital gains. Therefore, in the future, investors would be less will to accept a lower pretax rate of return from securities with a relatively low dividend yield.

DIVIDEND IRRELEVANCY REVISITED

Despite the findings of these previous studies, there were those who continued to maintain that a company's value is not affected by its dividend policy. For example, in the mid-1970s Fischer Black and Myron Scholes did a study that purported to show the irrelevancy of dividend policy in a world *with* taxes and transactions costs. The result of the paper in a nutshell is that it is *not* possible to demonstrate empirically that the expected returns on high-yield common stocks differ from the expected returns on low-yield common stocks either before or after taxes.

Black and Scholes conclude that this might be true for the following reasons:

> *Supply effect*—Companies will adjust their dividend policies to supply the level of yield that is most in demand at a particular time so that supply will equal demand at each yield level. Therefore, the corporation will be unable to affect its share price by changing its dividend policy.
>
> *Tax effect*—The existence of differential taxes on income and capital gains seems to suggest that the shares of corporations that pay low dividends would be more desirable.
>
> *Diversification effect*—There are systematic differences between high and low yield stocks that ensure that an investor who concentrates his portfolio in high- or low-yield stocks will hold a portfolio that is not as well diversified as a portfolio constructed containing both.

But despite the evidence that would suggest that many individuals would prefer capital gains, we see corporations paying dividends. Black and Scholes suggest that the reason for this may be what they term the *uncertainty effect*. There is great uncertainty as to the effects of dividend yield on stock returns. If this is so great that investors act as if dividend yield is not important in constructing their portfolios (because they don't know how to take it into account), changes in dividend yield will not affect their portfolio decisions and stock prices. Thus, corporations could ignore the effect of their dividend policy.

Most recently, attention in the dividend controversy has centered on the notion that dividends may have an informational content that serves a useful role for investors. Proponents of this view argue that dividend declarations provide a signal to investors about the future prospects of a company. To the extent that this provides information not already known by the investor, the investor may buy or sell shares of the company and thereby improve his situation and, of course, impact the value of the firm. There are some who feel that the potential informational content of dividends provides a substantive, though not necessarily complete, explanation for the prevalence and persistence of positive dividend policies.

GUIDELINES FOR THE CFO

Is the situation one where "the harder we look at the dividend picture, the more it seems like a puzzle, with pieces that just don't fit together"?

Let's take stock of the theory for a moment. If one holds a company's investment policy fixed, dividend policy is a trade-off between cash dividends (or dividends through share repurchase) and the issue of common stock. Should firms retain whatever earnings are necessary to finance growth and payout any residual as cash dividends? Or should companies increase dividends and then (sooner or later) issue stock to make up for the shortfall of equity capital? Or should they reduce dividends below the "residual" level and use the released cash to repurchase stock?

If one lived in that world of perfect capital markets that MM describe, the choice would be a simple one for, whatever the decision, there would be no effect on the market value of the firm. However, since in the real world there are market imperfections, the dividend controversy has blossomed.

A common view in the investment community is that high payout enhances share price and that there is a natural clientele for high payout stocks. But it seems difficult to explain a general preference for dividends other than in terms of irrational prejudice. While the case for "liberal dividends" seems to depend largely on tradition but very little, if any, on statistical evidence.

The most obvious and serious market imperfection, on which much research has focused, is the differential tax treatment afforded dividends and capital gains. The view that investors in high-yield stocks would require a higher before-tax return has a respectable theoretical basis. It is further supported by some indirect evidence that investors are influenced by the tax treatment of dividends and by some direct evidence that gross returns have, on average, reflected the tax differential. But its strongest opposition is the sheer empirical evidence that most companies continue to distribute such large sums in the form of dividends.

A third view of dividend policy suggests the fact that companies pay substantial dividends as the best evidence that investors want them. The theoretical and empirical support for this is lacking, however.

While the theories considered are probably still too incomplete and the evidence too sensitive to even minor changes in assumptions to warrant a definitive answer on the dividend question, some guidelines are still possible:

1. First, there seems to be ample evidence that sudden shifts in dividend policy can cause abrupt changes in stock price. The primary reason is the information that investors read into the company's actions—that is, the signaling impact of dividends. Given this, there is a clear case to be made for defining the firm's target payout and making relatively slow adjustments toward it.
2. On the other hand, if it is necessary to make an unanticipated change in the dividend payout, the company should provide as much forewarning as possible and take considerable care to ensure that the action is not misinterpreted.
3. It may be prudent to adopt a target payout that is sufficiently low so as to minimize the company's reliance on external financing.
4. It should be recognized that surplus funds available after meeting the target payout can be used to repurchase the company's stock, which effectively provides a dividend to shareholders that is tax-advantaged since it is taxed at the capital gains rate.

EQUITY FINANCING—INTRODUCTION

For most companies, whether or not they pay dividends, there will come a time when there is a need for financing. This financing decision usually consists of a choice between equity (through new issues of shares or through retained earnings) and debt (including "hybrid" debt). Once the choice of equity financing has been made, the choice of the method of distributing shares becomes important. In addition, the choice of an investment bank becomes important.

METHODOLOGY AND SIZE

The extent to which a firm chooses equity financing depends on its optimal capital structure which, in turn, depends on the objective of the firm and the extent to which imperfections, such as taxes and transactions costs, exist in the market. But in any event, the objective of the financing mix should be to maximize the market value of the firm which is given by the sum of the value of its debt and equity.

In the real world, this is a difficult objective to achieve with great precision. Due to the tax deductibility of interest on debt, which reduces the tax liability of the firm and therefore increases its value, firms would like to increase their leverage. This reduces the firm's taxes and increases the aggregate amount the firm can pay out to its stockholders and creditors. However, there is a practical limit to the use of debt since it is clear that 100 percent debt in a firm's capital structure would result in situations where the firm would be unable to meet its interest obligations and where it would incur bankruptcy costs, including the costs of reorganization, liquidation, and the like.

Therefore, in theory, the optimal capital structure is determined by the trade-off between the tax benefits of issuing debt and the possibility of incurring bankruptcy costs. Such an optimum is reached when the present value of the tax shield due to additional borrowing is just offset by increases in the present value of the expected costs of financial distress.

While this determines the choice between debt and equity, equity can be obtained either through external financing or retained earnings. Retained earnings will be the source of equity funding if, based on inside information, the firm believes its share price does not reflect the true value of its assets. In addition, retained earnings may be the preferred choice if transactions costs are high for external financing. In fact, the choice of the size of a given equity financing (or share repurchase plan) or the choice between the use of retained earnings or a new issue of equity depends on:

1. The type and extent of transactions costs.
2. The differences in information possessed by managers and shareholders as they relate to the underpricing or overpricing of equity.
3. Dividend policy.

The existence of transactions costs influences the size of new issues of shares and also influences the choice of dividend policy and the retention of earnings. To the extent the retention of earnings is consistent with the firm's dividend policy, this will be the type of financing used in the presence of transactions costs.

In conclusion, the choice of equity financing or share repurchase will depend upon the optimal capital structure of the firm. The source of equity funding (internal funds or new issues) will depend on transactions costs and differences in information possessed by managers and stockholders. Finally, the size of any particular new issue will also depend upon the transactions costs associated with new issues.

CHOICE OF TYPE OF DISTRIBUTION

The sale of equity, once the decision has been made to issue it, is one of the most important financing decisions management can undertake in terms of cost, visibility, and long-term impact on stock price. Therefore, it is critical that a company make intelligent decisions regarding the choice of distribution of its equity securities.

Basically, a company can choose one of four methods of distribution:

1. Broad syndication.
2. Limited distribution.
3. Sole distribution.
4. Dribble out.

An additional method of distributing equity is through the use of dividend reinvestment plans. Since this method differs in its

basic nature from those listed above, it will be considered separately.

Since broad syndication is the method most frequently employed by companies in raising equity, let us consider its advantages and disadvantages first and relate the other methods
of distribution to it.

Broad Syndication Given the importance of an equity financing, it is critical that management maintain its prerogatives in
supervising and achieving an offering's objectives. A broadly
syndicated offering allows the issuer the largest measure of
control over the distribution process, thereby giving the highest
probability of the highest net price. This is because an organized marketing effort is associated with a traditional syndicated issue. In this process, the issue manager has tools to impact the success of the issue, such as orderly development of a
presale book, creation of scarcity value, the designation process, syndicate stabilization, and an overallotment option.

Moreover, a broadly syndicated offering achieves for a company the sponsorship of the financial community. It provides a
unique opportunity to communicate a favorable message to
would-be buyers in the market and therefore enhance the image of the company. This enables the company to attract the
focus and attention of the securities market, including the research community, and to develop net additional buying power
for its stock.

A broadly syndicated offering also gives the company an opportunity to impact the composition of purchasers for its stock—
for example, institutions versus retail customers. It also fosters
the development of sales to the least price-sensitive buyers.

Against these advantages, there are several disadvantages to
a broadly syndicated equity offering. These are:

1. Highest nominal transaction cost (underwriting spread and
   issuance costs) which may not lead to highest net proceeds
   to the issuer.
2. Some possibility that the speed of execution *may* be compromised.

Limited Distribution While a limited distribution overcomes
some of the disadvantages of a broadly syndicated offering—
for example, by allowing a lower nominal transaction cost, fa-

cilitating quicker execution, and allowing for easier control of the distribution process—it has its own disadvantages. Limited distribution of an equity offering can result in a situation where there is a failure to reach important buyers, both institutional and retail. It also offers less opportunity for the issue manager to create value and provide price leadership. Finally, large concentration of shares in a few dealers' hands raises the probability of large, unsold positions of the company's shares, causing a negative impact on the offering price.

Sole Distribution The sole distribution of an equity offering by a single underwriter may have the advantage of lowering the nominal cost of an issue below that achievable with either a broad or limited syndication. It also has the advantage of allowing for quick institutional distribution.

However, sole distribution does not permit the organized marketing effort associated with a more traditional syndicated issue. No syndicate tools are brought to bear. In addition, sole distribution tends to compromise an issuer's prerogative to exercise control over the distribution process and impact the composition of purchasers for its stock. Finally, sole distribution can limit both the size and price obtainable in an equity offering.

Dribble Out It is possible for a company to periodically sell its common stock off a shelf registration statement through SEC Rule 415's "dribble-out" provisions. However, generally speaking, this method of raising equity has been used only by utilities and not by industrial companies. This is due to the significant costs associated with this type of sale relative to its benefits.

The advantages of dribbling-out stock are that the nominal cost per share to the issuer may be the lowest. It enables the company to sell stock at an average price over some time period. Finally, dribble-out may be the quietest method of common stock issuance as it allows sales to occur intermittently off a block trading desk as demand originates and with less visibility than a traditional publicly announced offering.

The disadvantages of a dribble out are, however, significant. For example, dribbling out stock diminishes management's ability to maximize the proceeds of an offering by optimizing the timing of the sale. Dribbling stock out also means that the company loses the sponsorship of the financial community which would otherwise be possible in a broadly syndicated offering. This method of sale favors development of the biggest buyers and not necessarily the most price-insensitive buyers. Moreover, there is strong evidence that the registration of common shares for periodic sale has the effect of depressing a company's stock price. This is due to the introduction into the market of a sustained, visible supply of an issuer's stock which thereby alters the existing balance of supply and demand for the issuer's security. As a result of registering a large piece of equity in this manner, institutions are likely to withdraw their bids in the secondary market in anticipation of an upcoming offering or possibly even becoming a seller. This occurs in a more traditional equity filing as well, but with the organized marketing effort a traditional deal entails, the negative effect is mitigated.

These disadvantages have been compelling enough to preclude most firms other than utilities from attempting a dribble-out program. In general, most companies will find their interests are best served by financing through an underwritten, broadly syndicated public offering.

Dividend Reinvestment Plans For a variety of industries, dividend reinvestment plans (DRPs) have proven to be an effective method of raising equity capital. This has been particularly true for the capital-intensive public utilities. These plans, which allow stockholders to purchase additional shares with quarterly cash dividends, have helped relieve utilities' financing burdens and have provided stockholders an attractive investment opportunity.

Under the typical DRP program, the companies issue new shares for purchase with the reinvested dividends (some companies buy outstanding shares in the marketplace), absorbing all brokerage commissions and administrative expenses. Many companies offer a discount from market price on reinvested dividends. Often, this discount is as much as 5 percent. The discount makes the plan especially appealing since an immediate profit can be realized if the shares are sold. In addition, regular cash purchases of varying amounts of stock are often permitted.

Since 1982, DRPs have benefitted from the extra stimulus of the tax-deferred treatment accorded reinvested dividends under the Economic Recovery Tax Act of 1981 (ERTA). It allows individual investors to defer public utility common and preferred stock dividends from taxable income if they are reinvested in the company's "original issue" common stock. Such stock is treated on a zero-cost basis; it is taxable at the investor's capital gains rate if the shares are held for a maximum of 12 months and one day or at the ordinary personal income tax rate if sold sooner. This offers annual tax deferrals up to $750 for individuals and $1,500 for joint returns.

Dividend reinvestment plans have been an effective method of equity financing for many companies. The passage of ERTA provided added incentive for the use of DRPs. The proposed tax reforms for 1986, including the proposal to reduce the net capital gains tax exclusion and the proposal to reduce the marginal income tax rate and allow a corporate deduction for only 10 percent of dividends paid may eliminate some of the tax incentives to DRPs from both the issuer's and shareholder's perspective.

COMMON STOCK REPURCHASE—INTRODUCTION

As mentioned earlier, a company may also choose, either in connection with its dividend policy or capital structure decisions, to repurchase its own shares. The increasing number of repurchase programs indicates that companies are more actively pursuing this method of managing its equity position. In the first ten months of 1984, for example, there were $18.8 billion of nonmerger-related stock repurchase transactions versus $6.2 billion in 1981, which was the next most active period.

There are four basic methods of repurchasing stock:

1. Open market purchase.
2. Fixed price self-tender offer.
3. "Dutch auction" self-tender offer.
4. Private repurchase.

Open Market Purchase Under this method, the company hires an investment bank to act as its agent to purchase its shares in the open market from time to time at prevailing prices. Under this method, the company is subject to market risk for the period of the repurchase. This period can last for as long as it takes to acquire the requisite number of shares at acceptable prices.

The size of an open market purchase program is a function of the average daily trading volume of the stock, the proportion of that volume which the company expects to buy, and the length of time for which the company is willing to be in the market. Acquiring 25 to 30 percent of daily volume is probably a reasonable expectation.

There is no SEC disclosure under this share repurchase methodology. However, companies must notify the New York Stock Exchange (NYSE) and must issue a press release announcing the intended size of the repurchase.

Fixed Price Self-Tender Offer Under this method of share repurchase, the company hires an investment bank as a soliciting dealer to assist it in buying a specified number of shares at a fixed price. The soliciting dealer either purchases stock from sellers and tenders these to the company or convinces a seller to tender directly. The self-tender must be open to investors for a minimum trading period of 15 days.

The size of a fixed price self-tender is determined by the company and will be a function of the premium paid. Historically, companies have purchased 10 to 20 percent of their outstanding shares.

The SEC requires that a tender offer document be distributed to all shareholders. The company must also disclose the number of shares tendered and the number of shares repurchased.

"Dutch Auction" Self-Tender Offer Under this method of share repurchase, the company commits to purchase a specified number of shares at a specified maximum price. Sellers are then requested to offer their shares at various prices. The soliciting dealer performs the same role as in a self-tender and, as in a self-tender, the dutch auction must be open to investors for a minimum period of 15 days. The dutch auction forces holders to bid to sell shares to the company, thus giving them incentive to offer to sell at the lowest price acceptable to each. This should result in a lower average price paid relative to a conventional tender offer.

Like a self-tender, the size of the share repurchase is determined by the company and will be a function of the premium paid. The size of the dutch auction tender is approximately the same as for self-tenders.

Disclosure requirements are also the same as for self-tenders.

Private Repurchase Under private share repurchase, the company negotiates the purchase of a privately held block(s) of stock directly with the holder(s). An investment bank will act as advisor to the company by setting offering price and negotiating with the seller(s).

The size of a private repurchase depends on the availability of large blocks of stock. These transactions may be accomplished in a short time as they are a function of private negotiation.

There is no SEC disclosure required on private share repurchase transactions.

THE CHOICE OF AN INVESTMENT BANK

Once the decision is reached to do external equity financing, a company should choose an investment bank to execute the transaction.

In selecting an investment bank, one should look for:

- Execution capability at the best price.
- Execution capability in size.
- Good institutional and retail distribution.
- Good geographic distribution.
- Good after-market performance.
- Happy investors/shareholders.
- Low spread.
- Good secondary market capabilities.

The importance of secondary market expertise should be emphasized. A company should be concerned with an investment bank's market judgment. This judgment enables the bank to provide accurate views of prospective issues, that is, expertise regarding what buyers want and don't want, where and when the market can be lead, and where it cannot.

Secondary market expertise also involves the ability of the investment bank to provide active issue management, that is, knowing what is happening to a company's stock and doing something about it and providing after-market sponsorship both through research coverage and trading.

In the longer term, an investment bank's secondary market ability should include product development capabilities, the identification of specific market opportunities for the company, and the willingness and ability to commit its capital.

Similarly, once the decision has been reached to enter into a share repurchase program, the company should choose an investment bank to execute the transaction.

The factors to consider when choosing an agent to represent the company are:

- Knowledge of corporate repurchase rules.
- Equity trading capability.
- Knowledge of the company and its industry.
- Strong operations department.
- Competitive commission rate per share.
- Position in the capital markets generally and in the company's industry specifically.

PART FOUR

International Financial Management

14

International Risk Assessment and Management

Edward H. Schwallie and Hernando Madero

INTRODUCTION

International risk is significantly more complex than typical business risk when only one country is involved. All types of risk involve uncertainty, but the uncertainty of business risks can be compounded several times when the international dimension is added. Though they are more complex and quite awesome in some cases, international risks can be manageable. Some of the most successful businesses are in countries which most U.S. executives consider very risky. It just takes a full understanding of the risks and an ability to anticipate and remain flexible.

Each company can and should define and evaluate its own unique risks. For example, a capital-intensive company, operating in a hyperinflationary country with an unpredictable devaluation record (such as Mexico), would have entirely differ-

Edward H. Schwallie joined Booz Allen in 1966 and has been an officer since 1969. He is currently a senior vice president of Booz Allen and president of Booz Allen acquisition services. Hernando Madero joined Booz Allen in 1975 and has been an officer since 1976. He is currently a vice president of Booz Allen International.

ent risks than a less capital-intensive consumer goods company or a company that relies heavily on imports. Also, where a company is in its growth cycle, it is important to anticipate exposures at future volume and mix levels.

The technological content and uniqueness of a company's product are also important, particularly if there can be substitutes of national origin or ownership.

One way to look at the potential of a product if to ask:

- How important is this specific product to the national interest of this country and its people?
- How many people are employed because of our business here?
- How significant is this employment to the local, national interest?
- Do we have a monopoly (which can create additional risk) in this country?
- Do we have a perceived influence on the government or certain branches of government?

Remember that a multinational is a guest in a host country and is welcome as long as it is contributing something of value to the country and its people. When you are important to the country and welcomed rather than feared, your risks are likely to be less.

WHAT RISK MEANS TO A COMPANY

Risks vary by country, by industry, and by specific company. Companies may be quite willing to assume high risk because of strong profit potential. The degree of flexibility (to move in or out of a country situation) will probably affect the amount of risk a company is willing to accept.

The bottom line in risk taking is the concern that management has on exposure involving: (1) profits and cash (present and future), (2) ability to control its destiny (for expansion, contraction, or exit), and (3) protection of the crown jewels (reputation, technologies, brand names, and the like). Business risks may be significantly different for each country. Change in degree of risk may be due to shifts in governments, social and economic trends, changes in political alliances, or modification of national goals.

Some companies are impacted by such country risks more than others. This can be due to the political sensitivity of the company's operations in the local economy (for example, necessities, such as food; natural resources, such as petroleum; or value-added processes that utilize local labor). The degree of cooperation (or threat) provided by a country to a multinational can be significant depending on the real or perceived importance of the company's operations to the national interest of the host country. The risks can differ further based on how the company's businesses are structured within a given country (e.g., local ownership, special agreements by subsidiaries with the local or federal government of the host country, and the like).

What this all means is that risk should be defined by each company, taking into account how current and anticipated future political trends will impact that company's profitability. It is not sufficient to review overall country assessments or ratings by banks. Risk assessment must be customized against each company's strategic goals.

When a company evaluates risk on a country-by-country basis, it should consider both current risks and the flexibility to change (or get out) when risks increase or decrease over time. The need for flexibility involves, among other things, the ability to transfer capital, to pay dividends, to introduce new products or technologies, to control operations (to improve productivity or establish competitive advantages), to set policies, and to remain healthy and prosperous even when conditions change.

It is essential to examine both risk and flexibility when setting profit objectives.

An analysis of a company's current profile might indicate a less than optimum balance between risk, profit potential, and flexibility. This point is illustrated in Exhibit 1 where risk and flexibility vary considerably by country.

Risk represents the exposure resulting from factors impacting the company's business within a particular country. The flexibility axis is intended to show variation between (1) low flexibility (for example, high commitment to fixed assets [brick and mortar], repatriation restrictions, and difficult termination laws) and (2) high flexibility (for example, modest fixed asset commitment, nonrestrictive regulations, ease of moving in or out of a country).

As shown in the Exhibit, the business in Country D is the

Exhibit 1
Risk/Flexibility Profile by Country

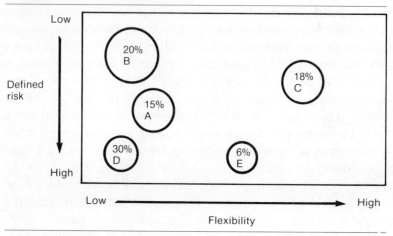

Note: The size of the circles represents the current annual volume. The percents indicate return on investment.

most profitable (30 percent ROI), but it is in a high risk country where the company has low flexibility to modify its actions as conditions shift.

Country B also shows relatively high profitability (20 percent ROI), but with low risk, the low flexibility of B may be less sig-

Exhibit 2
ROI Targets Based on Risk/Flexibility Profile

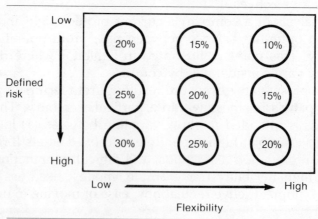

These targets would serve as benchmarks. The next step would be to identify and evaluate risks.

nificant because in a low risk country there may be no need for flexibility to modify investment or exit.

The businesses in Country E are not very profitable (6 percent ROI), and the risk is high. With reasonable flexibility indicated, the company should develop a strategy to either improve profitability or to exit the country.

A more ideal matrix would be one where profitability should increase with the degree of risk involved, modified by the level of flexibility available for the company's specific operations within a given country.

Minimum profitability targets might be established by balancing defined risk and flexibility, as shown in Exhibit 2.

IDENTIFYING AND EVALUATING A COMPANY'S RISKS

Before developing a risk strategy, there are three major interrelated categories of risk factors that must be assessed.

- Political.
- Legal/regulatory.
- Economic base.

Political risk factors could impact the protection of a company's assets or recovery of investment. They include:

- Abrupt changes in the policy of the ruling party in government or a change in the government itself.
- Physical damage due to civil disorder or armed conflict.
- Anticapitalist or anti-U.S. activities and alliances.

National goals or policies are obviously dependent on political factors and have some impact on the legal and regulatory guidelines used in governing the country.

Current apparent political stability can still include investment risk.

Legal/regulatory risk factors include those that may discriminate against foreign business or limit flexibility. The following are examples of what should be evaluated:

- Discrimination against foreign business, such as the degree of foreign ownership limitations; local content requirements; tariff barriers; repatriation restrictions; currency conversion restrictions; or favoritism toward local businesses (subsidies, that is, low cost loans).

- Factors limiting business flexibility would include language/business culture differences, weak business law (protection), degree of corruption, administrative controls (red tape) and delays, unionization and labor flexibility, environmental regulations, price restrictions, tax structure and systems, and local capital availability.

Economic base risk factors should be evaluated to address both the strength of the country's economy and the quality of its infrastructure.

- Strength of the economy can be judged on the basis of past and current inflation rates, underlying causes of the country's inflation (and possible changes), history of devaluation (and its relation to historical inflation), likelihood of recession, GNP (absolute and per capita), growth in GNP, export/import balance, export as a percent of GNP, manufacturing diversification, and natural resources.
- Quality of industrial infrastructure depends significantly upon communications and utilities; labor quality, availability, and flexibility; strike history; and technological base, (both production and service).

The relative importance of each of the above factors varies among industries and companies based on (1.) products and services, (2.) stages of value added, (3.) magnitude of exposure, and (4.) the structure of the particular business. The balance between fixed commitment and degree of flexibility is also important when evaluating risk.

MANAGEMENT OF RISK

Management of risk should be embedded in a company's strategic management process. Sources of competitive advantage and consequently economic performance can be drastically altered by policies of foreign governments. To cope with these complex and uncertain influences on international business, traditional concepts of corporate planning must be augmented. A systematic approach can be used to assess future political risks to international business and to contribute to strategic planning in an international environment.

The concept upon which this analysis technique is based is

that the international operating strategies adopted by multinational corporations to maximize competitive advantage worldwide may conflict with goals of governments in countries in which the companies operate. Such conflicts lead to government-imposed changes in the business environment and thus to political risks. These risks must be managed strategically.

Four basic international operating strategies may be employed by companies doing business internationally.

> *Export.* Raw materials sourcing and all stages of production are located in the company's home country.
>
> Finished products are exported to foreign countries.
>
> *Locally Integrated.* Production is vertically integrated completely within each market country.
>
> There are no cross-border flows of intermediate or finished goods.
>
> *Multicountry Integrated.* Raw materials sourcing and stages of production are located in different countries.
>
> Raw materials and intermediate products are imported, and intermediate and finished products are exported.
>
> *Licensing.* Foreign firms are licensed to produce and market the company's product.
>
> No cross-border flows of the company's intermediate or finished products.

Without risk of government actions, traditional strategic planning techniques can be used to develop the optimal mix of operating strategies for a company. However, an international risk strategy analysis procedure, such as the one illustrated in Exhibit 3, can be used to augment traditional techniques in the real world of uncertain government policies that affect business conditions.

The following paragraphs describe each of the steps suggested by Exhibit 3 as this approach would apply to a single-product company or division. Forms can be developed to record information for comparative purposes, but it should be kept in mind that analyses cannot be carried out from a corporate office: The analysis should be done by those who know the environment and the people and who can talk to government officials and "test the waters."

Throughout this section, the need for knowledge about com-

Exhibit 3
International Risk Strategy Analysis Procedure

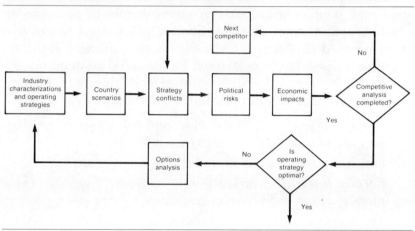

petitors' actions is implicit. There are many possible sources of bits of information which must be combined very much like the "mosaic" theory which financial analysts use in piecing together information about a company. Obvious information sources include, but are not limited to, annual reports and 10–K filings, trade and business papers and magazines, attendance at industry meetings and conventions, and reports from salespeople who call on common customers.

An analysis must be made to define both business and government strategies, to identify the conflicts and resulting political risks, and to estimate the economic impact on the business and its competitive situation. The output of this analysis will be an assessment of the impacts of political risks, compared with their effects on competitors, over a future period (say five years) and a strategy that minimizes such risks.

Describe Industry Characteristics and Operating Strategies and Forecast Future Government Goals

The first two steps of the international risk analysis procedure provide the basis for assessing conflicts between business and government strategies.

Industry characteristics can be defined by identifying markets for the company's products. Market information can be analyzed in terms of size, importance of product to the local economy, import substitution, life cycle, status of the local industry, political strength of competitors, and unemployment rate in the industry.

The *operating strategies* employed by the company and its major competitors should be summarized and compared. Among factors considered for competitors in each major market country, the following should be included:

- Products sold.
- Multinational association (if any) and share of ownership.
- Basic operating strategy, such as degree of vertical integration, raw material sources, licensing (if any), local versus import sourcing and estimated value added.
- Other relevant factors, such as degree of technology transfer, local content, and probable net trade impact.

The next step is to generate scenarios of political and economic developments and resulting government goals over a five-year period in each major market country and countries where critical materials are available and/or sourced. The scenarios should address various country goal/policies related to GNP, employment, balance of trade, foreign exchange, protection of local industry, and trade controls.

More than one scenario should be developed for each country in order to estimate uncertainty involved in the forecasts. Each scenario should consider the varied impact of each country's goal/policy.

Match the Host Government's Goals and Policies against the Company's Desired Product Characteristics to Identify Risks

It will be necessary to evaluate areas of conflict between the company's desired business strategy and the government's desired policies and goals for each country under the alternative scenarios.

Examples of points of conflict between government goals and the desired business strategy might include:

- A high ownership share of the local subsidiary by a multinational which conflicts with a major government policy of increasing political and economic independence.
- The multinational's presence in a market with politically active local competition which conflicts with a government independence goal.

Note that not all characteristics of business strategies conflict with government goals. Minor conflicts could occur without resulting in political risks.

The alternative scenarios may lead to the same or different sets of conflicts.

Political risks to the company likely to result from conflicts with government policies should be identified. Such risks might involve local ownership requirements, technology transfer, nationalization, entry controls, taxes, and subsidies.

More specific descriptions of high or low political risks relevant to the company can then be developed. For example, if technology transfer is already high, new restrictions on technology transfer are not likely to impact the company.

It will be important to:

- Determine the *possible* range of change from the present regulations and requirements (for example, if local content requirements are currently 90 percent for the industry, only an increase to 100 percent is possible).
- Estimate by *how much* regulations are likely to change within this possible range according to (1) the amount of potential change in political and economic factors; and (2) the number of conflicts between the government's goals and the company's strategy. (A forecast increase in the trade deficit of 20 percent may result in local content requirements being raised from 80 percent to 85 percent while a 50 percent increase in the deficit could result in a 95 percent local content requirement.)

Also identify political risks to *all industries* due to forecast changes in government goals and policies. Some government policies that do not conflict with specific company strategies may still change business conditions for all industries. For example, greater emphasis on combating inflation may result in stricter wage and price controls even though the company's operations are not in conflict with this government goal.

Estimate the Economic Impacts of Likely Political Risks on the Company

This is the last step in the basic procedure of international risk strategy analysis. The output of this step is the estimated net impact on costs for the company in each country and on the price and profitability in the market country due to probable political risks.

Such risks, both in the market country and each major country in which production stages and resources are located, might relate to such requirements as:

• An increase in local content requirements to 95 percent.
• Local majority ownership of subsidiaries.

The types of economic impacts from such political risks might include:

• Higher variable costs due to barriers to trade, local content requirements, production requirements, and exchange rate fluctuations.
• Higher capital costs due to local financing requirements, barriers to financial flows, and production requirements.
• Reduced margins due to price controls and taxes.
• Reduced market share and sales growth due to technology transfer requirements, entry controls, taxes and subsidies, and higher costs.
• Loss of return on investment due to barriers to financial flows, local ownership requirements, and nationalization.

Use the production, distribution, marketing, and financing economics of the company's operations to estimate the change in costs associated with each probable specific political risk at each stage of production.

The impact of probable specific political risks on the company's sales, earnings, and return on investment should be estimated after similar international strategy analyses are performed for each major competitor.

Assess the Political Risks and Impacts on Competitors in Each Market Country

The complete analysis of the impacts of probable political risks on the company's performance requires a similar analysis of risks and impacts for competitors. Since competitors often have differing sourcing and production strategies and cost structures, changes in business conditions will not affect all companies the same way.

Estimation of the economic impact of likely political risks on competitors is difficult, but approximations can be made from available intelligence on costs.

The outputs of these analyses are net impacts on competitors' prices in the market country and likely specific risks that affect sales growth.

Estimate the Overall Impact on Political Risks on the Company in Each Market Country

The results of the company and competitor analyses of political risks and cost impacts can be used to estimate the net impact on the company for each market country under each scenario. Use traditional methods to forecast probable changes in the company's sales, earnings, and return on investment due to possible changes in competitors' costs and prices. Summarize these estimates for all market countries.

Develop and Evaluate Alternative Operating Strategies

The previous five steps of international risk strategy analysis provide a systematic method for assessing the impact of political changes on the company's current operating strategy. An important application of the procedure is to aid in the development of an optimal, risk-minimizing operating strategy.

The current company product and production characteristics that conflict with likely future government policies can be identified. Alternative operating strategies can be formulated to reduce such conflicts. For example:

- If a market is served by export from the home country, conflicts with balance of trade and economic development goals can be reduced by establishing production facilities in the host country.
- Conflict with government policies to increase economic independence and to promote GNP growth can be reduced by increasing local content of production.

The effect of alternative operating strategies on probable political risks, and the economics of the company's operations can be estimated. When the total net economic impact on the company for each alternative operating strategy has been developed, the optimal operating strategy can then be identified.

Optimal strategies for entering foreign markets can also be developed using the same analytic procedure.

IMPLICATIONS FOR THE FINANCIAL EXECUTIVE

On balance, a company can manage and customize its risk-minimization strategies for important, high-risk country operations consistent with its global requirements. The common strategies can include:

- *Avoidance*—not investing because projected profit is not worth the risk as reflected in the potential reduction of profits by the potential costs associated with each risk element.
- *Insurance*—using a blend of government and private insurance coverage to protect against such things as expropriation, war, revolution, insurrection, inconvertibility of assets, contract repudiation, embargo contingencies, restrictions on foreign imports, and political kidnapping.
- *Transfer*—sharing the risk with host country governments, local industry, or other foreign investors.
- *Retention*—quantifying financial exposure and creating reserves from the profit stream before calculating the rate of return.
- *Diversification*—spreading risk by business segments, by type of risk, or by country; in essence, using a portfolio approach comparable to a stock investment portfolio.

Beyond the basic strategies, executives should build a risk-minimization philosophy around their own situation. The CFO, in anticipation of exchange controls or devaluation, may, for example: (1) minimize funds held in countries identified as high risk, (2) increase exports to generate convertible currency, (3) use local financing, (4) hedge local currency markets or in some cases local dollar denominated paper, (5) hedge in world currency markets, and (6), in some circumstances, negotiate for exemption.

In building corporate working relationships with a host coun-

try, the country general manager may select from an array of
business strategies. For example:

- Use every opportunity to underscore the importance of private and foreign investment in the host country's national
  development and in the investor's support of these goals and
  contribution to the economy. Some form of social cost/benefit
  analysis may be appropriate.
- Avoid partisan political involvement, and maintain a low
  profile (to the extent practical.)
- Be informed on political, legal, regulatory, and economic
  events that may affect the investor's business.
- Develop a strong set of local suppliers, customers, employees, and indigenous management, and encourage local investment participation by leading business institutions.
- Seek to maintain a technology base and R&D effort offshore,
  and stay technologically ahead of indigenous competitors.

Unrealistic rates of return should not be targeted merely because a country is judged to have high, uncertain risk. Sophisticated business executives and their financial staff should determine, to the best of their ability, the financial consequences
of dealing with each risk factor and, within the resulting cash
flow projections, seek a satisfactory return on investment.

Not all risks can be quantified the way we would like. An example might be an unanticipated change in corporate tax rates
or closing a border to imported products. When a host government has a track record of behaving this way, a higher (but realistic) return might be targeted, or it might be prudent to provide reserves against such capricious actions. Reserving
techniques can create a responsible method of managing exposure and of understanding the true economic cost of international business operations.

Country-specific risk management strategies may have global
implications for a corporation. If, for example, a company operates on a worldwide, integrated basis with various stages of
production spread among several countries, disruption within
one country (for example, import/export rules or ownership requirements) could have a major impact on worldwide operations.

Identifying and managing risk have been described in the

previous sections. Here, we share some lessons learned through extensive experience, and by living and working in countries considered high risk by many multinational executives (including Argentina, Brazil, Chile, Colombia, Mexico, Spain, and Venezuela). These are examples of actions taken by multinationals who have successfully managed risk internationally.

- *Negotiate a special contract with the government geared to assure recovery of new investment.* In this case, the company (which had a very large investment in the country already) negotiated a contract that provided for specific cash flow over an unspecified period of time. Because the selling price was determined by international market conditions, it was difficult to predict annual cash flow; thus, the agreement covered an absolute cash flow number rather than a time period.

- *Adjust depreciation schedules to meet local laws.* In this situation, the company had stringent depreciation rules geared to U.S. IRS allowable schedules. However, the local tax laws provided for substantial acceleration for tax purposes. The company appropriately allowed for a deviation from policy to generate the cash flow that would result from special acceleration.

- *Support alternative sources of supply.* Another company was concerned about the availability of materials needed to support its operations. It provided incentives (and a market) for others to develop feeder industries even though this was somewhat of a subsidy during periods of abundant supply. The company pursued this approach (although very low key) as a form of insurance.

- *Renegotiate situations during the time the company is in the strongest bargaining position.* Many companies have used very senior (and well-known) local executives to handle government relationships, being prepared to defend company position (when necessary) and to be receptive to government programs (for example, improvements in worker housing or health conditions). Such handling avoids negative worker conditions and possible unfavorable government action.

In summary, the successful companies:

- Assure that the economic prospects are sufficiently greater than a comparable U.S. investment to warrant the risk.

- When in a good bargaining position, attempt to get government "guarantees" or contracts to minimize the downside.
- Maintain continuing sensitivity to local issues and government policies.
- Put the right people in the job (local where possible).
- Keep a low profile without getting involved with controversial issues (except those dealing with their own divisions).
- And continually plan for and manage international risk as any other major factor in the strategic management process. This chapter has described how that process might be applied.

The process of realizing successful foreign investment is increasingly complex and demanding; it requires statesmanship, sound business ethics, and realism.

15

Controlling Foreign Operations

James M. Cornelius and Michael Grobstein

INTRODUCTION

Dollar's Rise, a Boon for Many, Also Hurts Major U.S. Industries

—The Wall Street Journal, February 22, 1985.

Rekindling Is Seen of Latin Debt Crises

—New York Times, February 26, 1985.

Strong Dollar Has Led U.S. Firms to Transfer Production Overseas

—The Wall Street Journal, April 9, 1985.

Global Economic System Faces Serious Challenges

—Reuters, April 21, 1981.

As experience clearly indicates, the international business arena is dynamic, complex, and challenging. Larger multinational

---

James Cornelius joined Eli Lilly and Company in 1967 as a financial analyst. He was appointed CFO in January, 1983, after serving as corporate treasurer during 1982. Michael Grobstein is vice chairman—accounting and auditing services in Ernst & Whinney's national office in Cleveland, Ohio. He is responsible for the firm's acccounting and auditing standards, audit-related services, audit quality control, and training.

companies and companies establishing new foreign operations must cope with, among other matters, volatility in the movement of foreign exchange rates, changes in individual countries' restrictions on the flow of funds, hyperinflationary economies, devaluations, and political uncertainties. Increasingly, multinational companies face the tough question: What is the best control strategy to minimize the risks in our international operations in view of our financial and business objectives?

Achieving effective control over international operations requires a recognition that the international environment is different from the U.S. environment—that is, what works in the United States will not necessarily work in foreign operations. Determining the nature and extent of control necessary for an operation outside the United States requires an analysis of pertinent environmental factors. The identification and assessment of these factors for different types and sizes of operations provides a basis for measuring risk and for establishing appropriate and cost-effective controls.

The CFO of a multinational company works with a portfolio of business units operating in a variety of political, economic, and cultural environments. The risks of doing business and of earning targeted returns varies significantly in each of these environments. In addition, international political, economic, and cultural forces are dynamic, so CFOs must continually monitor these forces and measure their potential impact on operations. The CFO, in turn, must make or recommend appropriate adjustments that will cause the operating strategy to be responsive to the changing environment. These adjustments might include modifying the terms of doing business, hedging currencies, reorganizing international banking relationships, centralizing certain international financial activities, or changing the focus of the international audit function.

Ultimately, the CFO's role is to provide the expertise and judgment in the financial arena necessary to support line management in achieving corporate goals. The CFO does this by influencing operating, as well as financial, decisions with objective analysis of risks and potential rewards. The CFO's overall corporate perspective and basic understanding of critical economic variables provides the opportunity to combine this objective analysis with practical suggestions for dealing with investment and financing decisions in foreign operations.

International financial management may be effectively di-

Exhibit 1
Financial Management Functions

Treasury
    Cash management
    Foreign exchange exposure management
    Monitoring environmental risk (political/economic/cultural)
    International banking
    Resource allocation (investments/borrowing/capital structure)
    Corporate risk management
    Other (credit policies/pensions/investor relations)

Controllership
    Financial reporting
    General accounting
    Cost accounting
    Income taxes
    Financial planning and analysis
    Capital budgeting (facilities planning)
    Profitability and performance reporting

Audit
    Internal audit
    External audit

vided into three functions: treasury, controllership, and audit. Exhibit 1 lists the typical responsibilities under each function. In this chapter, we will discuss the following:

The use of environmental risk analysis to develop a control strategy.

The case for centralized treasury management.

The focus of the controllership function—designing financial reporting systems and analyzing operating results.

The role of internal audit and ideas for effective coordination with external audit.

The critical need for good communication.

ENVIRONMENTAL RISK ANALYSIS

Defining Risk Factors

The country in which an operation is located is the primary consideration in determining the degree of control necessary for foreign operations. To assess objectively the potential risks for a given location, the CFO should examine the political, economic, and cultural factors that will impact operations. Infla-

Exhibit 2
Environmental Risk Analysis

Location Characteristics	Lower Risk and Stable Location	Higher Risk Location	Vulnerable and Very High Risk Location
Economic:			
Inflation rates	Consistently single digit	Double digit	Reaching triple digit
Interest rates	Single digit	Double digit	Extremely high—triple digit and difficult to obtain local financing for operations
Foreign exchange rates	Moderate changes	Not predictable	Volatile
Exchange controls	None	Some restrictions	Very difficult to remit funds to parent company
Economic growth rate	Median or above	Below median	Negative
Unemployment and termination costs	Low	Average	High
Political:			
Exports	Many incentives	Some incentives	Few incentives
Import duties	None or low	Reasonable rates	Very high rates
Foreign investment incentives	Many	Few	None
Foreign ownership	Not restricted	Few restrictions	100 percent or even 51 percent ownership not allowed
Expropriation	Not likely	Some risk	High risk
Accounting and statutory reporting requirements	Similar to United States	Different from United States, but not onerous	Onerous
Taxes on income	Foreign investor treated the same—favorable tax treaties with United States	Some additional taxes and/or higher rates	High rates on foreign employees and investors
Product pricing	Not restricted	Few restrictions on certain commodities	Government controlled product pricing
Cultural:			
Productivity rate	Median or above	Slightly below median	Static or declining
Management practices	Similar to United States	Different, but not a problem	Difficult adjustment
Language	Similar	Different, but manageable	Difficult to master and assimilate

tion and interest rates, exchange and pricing controls, foreign investment incentives, and management practices are some of the specific factors that should be carefully reviewed. The assessment of the risks associated with these environmental factors, coupled with a definition of the size and scope of operations, provides the basis for structuring control strategy.

Exhibit 2 summarizes the key environmental factors that should be identified and analyzed to assess the degree of risk. In reality, the distinctions between political, economic, and cultural factors tend to be blurred; nonetheless, Exhibit 2 provides a useful checklist and analytical tool.

Clearly, individual countries around the world present varying degrees of environmental risk to a multinational company trying to generate profits. But the political, economic, and cultural factors that cause these risks create a crosscurrent of problems and opportunities (the balance depending on the area of the world being analyzed). Third World countries (including much of Latin America) and communist nations present the highest risks. While Japan, Western Europe, and Canada present lower risks, these countries are certainly not without significant challenge. Exhibit 3 depicts the overall level of environmental risk associated with various countries and the effect of

Exhibit 3
Relative Risk versus Financial Control

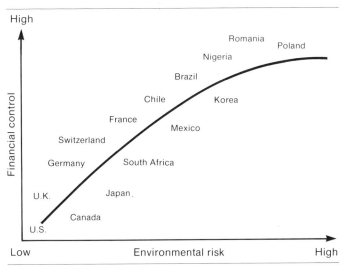

that risk on control requirements. For a further discussion of this topic, refer to Chapter 14.

Effect of Size and Scope of Operations

Once the degree of risk has been assessed, the next step is to define the level of investment and scope of activities to be controlled. For example, a small foreign operation may be selling—perhaps on letter of credit—to a distributor. This operating commitment may evolve from a three-employee sales branch, to a full-scale branch, to an assembly operation with sales support, and to an integrated manufacturing and marketing operation that employs hundreds or thousands of people dealing in a number of different currencies. The key point is that as the operation evolves, so do the control requirements.

While few structural changes may be necessary in the initial stages of entering foreign markets, the need for controls increases significantly as a company expands to more than one country and to full service branches or subsidiaries. The CFO should have a plan to adapt the control strategy to changes in the scope of activity and environmental risks that are inherent in an evolving foreign operation. Exhibit 4 depicts how the level of investment—or scope of operations—impacts control re-

Exhibit 4
Level of Investment versus Financial Control

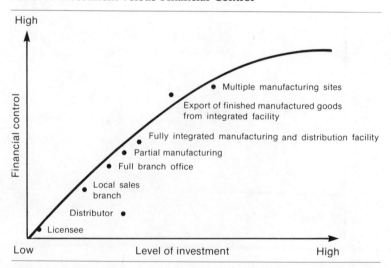

quirements. The control strategy should address organizational considerations, as well as financial systems and procedures. Developing and maintaining the plan is essential to the long-term success of the multinational company. The plan should provide for structuring the financial organization and related systems and controls to (1) facilitate the monitoring of changing political and economic conditions and (2) provide the information and decision framework needed to facilitate timely and informed management actions.

Once the environmental factors have been evaluated and the size and scope of activities defined, the degree of risk can be assessed, and decisions can be made about the organizational and financial systems necessary for controlling individual operations.

THE CASE FOR CENTRALIZED TREASURY MANAGEMENT

Organizational Factors

One of the principal concerns of the CFO of a U.S. multinational company is how to design and maintain a financial control strategy that minimizes the risks associated with doing business in foreign currencies and yet allows line management the freedom to pursue profitable business opportunities in international markets. The advent of floating exchange rates in 1973 and the oil crisis of 1979, coupled with the increasing potential for a world monetary crisis, has significantly increased the volatility of currency rate fluctuations. In this environment, the appropriate financial control strategy is difficult to define.

To meet the challenge of international financial control, many companies have appointed an international treasurer (in an assistant treasurer capacity) to take on the day-to-day responsibility for managing individual foreign entity cash flow, capital structure, and working capital—through an existing network of local or regional treasurers—in a manner that reduces the negative impact of foreign currency fluctuations on overall corporate earnings. The international treasurer has the responsibility to evaluate the potential risk of adverse currency movement against the cost-effectiveness of strategies to protect against that risk. Centralizing the treasury responsibility benefits a worldwide organization in various ways.

1. Centralized cash management will result in maximizing cash flows and minimizing borrowing costs and unfavorable tax effects.
2. Centralized foreign exchange management will help avoid losses. Uncoordinated efforts to minimize losses from fluctuations in exchange rates will, at a minimum, increase the costs of covering exposures, and may well result in inadvertently creating exposures. Stated another way, effective foreign exchange management requires *(a.)* centralized consolidation of exposures and *(b.)* a level of expertise that the local operation may not have or be able to afford.
3. Improved communications between corporate financial management and operating unit financial management will facilitate *(a.)* coordination of various related financial management functions and *(b.)* more effective implementation of operating strategies.
4. The consolidation of operating unit treasury functions may provide opportunities for eliminating redundant tasks and positions. Integrating common activities, along with more efficient automation, can lead to significant cost savings.
5. Local management will be relieved of certain administrative responsibilities and can concentrate on manufacturing and marketing efforts.

Centralizing the treasury functions listed in Exhibit 1 provides necessary corporate oversight and helps minimize the cost of duplicating the specialized talent and experience necessary to carry out these functions in each country. However, some level of local or regional treasury management also is essential since cash must be collected and deposited efficiently and bills and taxes must be paid on a timely basis. In addition, maintaining local banking relationships will help reduce the cost of short-term, seasonal financing.

Ideas for Managing Exchange Risk

The following list of strategic objectives and treasury programs is not meant to be all inclusive, but it does illustrate the actions that a multinational company can take to deal with the risks inherent in doing business in international markets.

Strategic Objective	*Treasury Program*
1. Reduce banking costs of foreign currency conversions through intercompany netting of payables and receivables.	Coordinating cross-currency flows between affiliated companies with a multilateral netting system will reduce the amount of currency conversion and enable the company to receive same-day value of transactions. Leads and lags also can be used to manage financing and/or currency exposure and to set intercompany terms for the same purpose within the exchange control regulations and tax rules of each country.
2. Hedge specific local entity or corporate cash transactions with foreign exchange contracts.	The international treasurer determines when transactions may be hedged and by what entity. The gross amount will be based on the net hedge requirement after considering expenses and tax effects. Transactions that might be hedged include recorded and future foreign currency obligations, such as royalties, dividends, intercompany and third-party obligations.
3. Use "proxy currency" to hedge anticipated currency exposure where appropriate foreign exchange market coverage is not available.	Proxy currencies may be used to cover exposure in closely controlled currencies and in near-term dollar denominated liabilities. For example, a Greek drachma exposure could be covered with deutsche marks or with other EMS currencies that generally move in tandem with the dollar.
4. Obtain insurance coverage to protect high risk monetary or nonmonetary assets in politically sensitive countries.	The corporate risk manager may use insurance policies to protect company assets from political risk, including expropriation of assets and/or currency inconvertibility. One example is the federal government's Overseas Private Investment Corporation (OPIC) program for lesser developed countries. Another option is to utilize relatively new commercial insurance policies that cover the same two risks globally or on a country-by-country basis.

Strategic Objective

Treasury Program

5. Lock in lower interest costs on medium term debt and ensure credit availability in a specific country by executing a currency swap. (Usually a financial intermediary is necessary to match the parties.)

Significant arbitrage gains can be realized by swapping the strong financial reputation of a multinational in one country for the favorable reputation of a multinational in another country. For example, a U.S. company might deposit $5 million at 8 percent for five years in the U.S. branch of an Italian bank and receive a preferential 15 percent borrowing rate on an equivalent amount of lire in Italy. The Italian bank would then lend the U.S. dollars to an Italian customer in the United States who has excess lire in Italy, allowing each party to realize an overall interest rate saving.

6. Use multicurrency credit lines and investments to hedge local exposure or to reduce global borrowing costs.

Affiliate working capital requirements can be met by a multicurrency borrowing strategy. For example, Swiss francs might be borrowed by a Canadian affiliate because of a lower interest cost associated with the Swiss currency. However, the new exposure to the Swiss franc must be watched closely and hedged if the risk becomes too large.[1]

When foreign exchange management is centralized as part of the international treasury function and placed under the control of experienced executives, it can potentially save a multinational company millions of dollars. An important caution: Management must establish parameters that eliminate speculation. There must be a real economic risk that merits the foreign exchange transaction. In addition, the authorization process for entering into foreign exchange contracts should be clearly established.

Exchange rate risk and inflation tend to be linked. In addition, political factors have a bearing on exchange rate risk. One

---

[1]Note: Taking advantage of interest differentials in borrowing is viable only if the company has offsetting cash flows expected in the currencies in which the debt must be repaid. Otherwise, current savings in interest costs could be more than offset by future exchange losses.

can predict inflation's impact on the Argentine peso in normal times, but political and military upheavals create uncertainty as the Falkland Islands incident made clear. No one can predict the impact of such confrontations on exchange rates. And no one can control exchange rates; they can only control their exposure level by managing their foreign exchange risk.

THE FOCUS OF CONTROLLERSHIP

The benefits of centralizing virtually all treasury functions and of establishing operating guidelines for local and/or regional treasurers are clear. On the other hand, controllership functions cannot always be centralized to the same degree. The controllership functions listed in Exhibit 1 require extensive attention on a local basis. The local finance director does, however, need direction from corporate financial management so that worldwide consistency can be achieved. Guidelines for general and cost accounting practices and the basis for performance measurement, along with a structure for financial reporting, are key areas where such direction is required. In this section, we will provide some suggestions on (1) how to design a financial reporting system and (2) key measures in monitoring and evaluating performance.

Designing Financial Reporting Systems

There are three common pitfalls in financial systems designed for international operations.

1. *The system is not decision oriented.* Although significant effort is directed toward developing information for corporate and regional management, it is more important that major systems be designed to provide information for planning, controlling, and improving the individual operations. The system should highlight areas that are not within the range of budgets or other expectations, and these out-of-line conditions should trigger action. An effective decision-support system is in sharp contrast to a system that is designed merely to maintain the books and records and report results up the line.

2. *The system does not address the unique aspects of international operations.* The following usually warrant special consideration in the system design:

Joint ventures/minority interests.
Exports/imports.
Local requirements for accounting/reporting/tax.
Consolidation needs for multicurrency operations.

3. *The system is too complex for the size of the operation.* The standard corporate package may not be appropriate for all overseas operations. If the operation is a simple one, it does not need a sophisticated system. In most cases, it will be beneficial to consider overall system needs for the various operations within a country or region. This analysis will help determine automation strategy, as well as where systems can be consolidated. Centralizing accounting and reporting systems for all operations within a country or region will eliminate the administrative burden from marketing and production operations, especially for those that are too small to justify the resources.

Exhibit 5 outlines the steps required to avoid these pitfalls. Maintaining control over international operations depends, in large part, on the effectiveness of the reporting systems in place. It is unlikely that too much emphasis could be placed on designing the appropriate system.

Exhibit 5
An Action Plan for Designing a Financial Reporting System for International Operations

1. Visit key locations and discuss with users.
2. Define user needs and related system requirements.
3. Develop general specifications.
4. Review with users.
5. Obtain local management input and concurrence.
6. Develop detail specifications.
7. Pilot test in one country.
8. Make revisions based on pilot test.
9. Finalize design and testing.
10. Implement the system.

Analyzing Operating Results

Monitoring trends and flagging problems in a foreign operation require analysis that goes beyond net income. Because of the exposures to inflation and exchange fluctuations, the focus should be on cash flow and working capital with emphasis on intercompany accounts above prescribed limits. In measuring performance, the following are particularly useful for international operations:

Asset turnover. High turnover helps minimize risk of loss from inflation or currency devaluations.

Sales per employee. Monitoring headcount to control personnel additions will keep the operation efficient. If the operation experiences a downturn, it also will protect against the significant termination costs that are required in many foreign countries.

Net cash flow. Relating cash flows to intercompany account balances will highlight how effectively local managers manage their liquidity, as well as inventory and receivable balances.

Return on investment. Meaningful evaluation of ROI requires adjustments for environmental risks and cost of capital.

The analysis of operations should consider who has responsibility for setting intercompany prices and making various financial decisions. Of course, when responsibility is changed, so should accountability. Local managers should not be rewarded or penalized for matters over which they have no control. For example, if the local manager is not responsible for the capitalization of the operation or managing foreign exchange risk, then interest charges and the effect of foreign exchange gains and losses should be eliminated from profit and loss calculations that are used to measure performance. Other methods must then be established to control working capital movement and capital expenditures.

AUDIT ROLE IN INTERNATIONAL CONTROL

Cost/Benefit Considerations

Internal audit can perform an important role in the control of overseas operations. However, a company should make a cost/benefit analysis to determine whether it makes sense to have internal auditors travel overseas from their U.S. headquarters or to establish an internal audit function at a regional location (for example, London) to handle certain overseas operations.

If operations are decentralized, it becomes more important for internal auditors to have an ongoing program of review that covers these operations. On the other hand, if control is centralized, it becomes questionable as to whether internal audit involvement can be cost justified. A company should assess the likelihood that internal audits (both financial and operational) will result in suggestions for efficiencies that could lead to significant cost savings. If the primary role of internal audit is viewed as one to identify potential cost savings, then a regional overseas base or ongoing overseas travel by a U.S.-based internal audit group may well be justified.

Many corporate directors, as well as chief financial officers, believe that internal auditors should focus on control effectiveness rather than operating efficiencies. In this case, integration with the efforts of the external auditors becomes important. If the internal and external auditors are using the same audit methodology to conduct their audits, external auditors can realize the benefit of the internal audit efforts and minimize the work they would otherwise be required to perform.

The extent to which external auditors can rely on internal auditors in overseas operations is, in most cases, more limited than the extent to which they may be able to rely on them in domestic operations. This is because of the separate statutory audit reports required of subsidiaries in many countries outside the United States. The audit of a subsidiary in the United States ordinarily has no separate audit report requirements, so less than a full audit can be performed. Some of these limited audits can often be handled by internal auditors with only a review required by the external auditors to meet their professional standards. However, for operations outside the United States, the external auditor can delegate only a small portion of his work to the internal auditors because of the need to have separate audit opinions expressed on the subsidiaries' financial statements.

Nonetheless, there are significant benefits to be gained from integration of audit efforts at operations outside the United States. The following should be considered:

1. Internal auditors based in the United States who travel overseas will have a difficult time abroad because of language difficulties and a lack of understanding of local business customs. Some public accounting firms will provide their personnel to function as internal auditors and to accomplish the objectives of the internal audit assignment without experiencing the language problems, along with the high travel costs, that are obviously associated with this type of assignment.

2. International accounting firms can offer an English-speaking staff person based abroad to work with the visiting U.S. internal auditors to help with language translation and to help explain local business customs.

3. Internal auditors could have personnel from one of the company's other overseas operations temporarily assigned to internal audit. This person should have a financial background and appropriate language capability.

4. Internal audit personnel should meet with the local external audit executives serving the company's overseas operations to review problems noted in the previous audit and to discuss any other areas of concern. These meetings assist in directing internal audit emphasis and help provide early resolution of accounting issues.

5. To avoid duplication of effort and facilitate the internal auditor's work, internal audit should seek access to the external auditors' work papers. Similarly, the external auditor also should receive any internal audit reports relating to the company's overseas operations, as well as have an opportunity to review related work papers, to identify important accounting issues that may require their follow-up.

6. If the company follows a program of internal control evaluation that is consistent with the methodology used by their external auditors, there are opportunities for further efficiencies.

Many companies believe that the benefits of maintaining an audit function to develop personnel and to provide additional opportunities in order to identify operating efficiencies and control weaknesses more than justify the cost. However, other companies are challenging the cost-effectiveness of maintaining an internal audit function, and some have concluded that their external auditors may be able to do the job for less. Recently, N. V. Philips, the Dutch electronics multinational, eliminated most of its internal audit group to reduce costs. The internal audit role will be assumed largely by their external auditor.

Setting Audit Priorities

Once a decision is made for internal audit to become involved in audits of operations outside the United States, the next step is to set priorities. Some type of risk analysis methodology should be used so that resources can be effectively allocated. A structured approach to setting priorities also will facilitate responding to questions from management and audit committees about the extent of audit coverage and the reasons why some locations are being visited and others are not.

Exhibit 6 is an audit program decision diagram that is an example of one way to summarize the impact of using a type of risk analysis.

To determine whether a location should be classified as A, B, or C, some type of quantitative analysis should be made con-

Exhibit 6
Audit Program Decision Diagram

		B—Moderate priority locations	A—Key locations
Exposure	High	• Specific procedures in selected areas of higher exposure	• Extensive audit procedures annually
		C—Low priority locations	B—Moderate priority locations
	Low	• Analytical review and ongoing monitoring procedures	• Specific procedures in selected areas of higher risk
		Low	High
		Risk	

sidering the various risk factors, as well as the exposure (materiality) of the operation. The risk factors should include (1) environmental risks, (2) overall quality of internal control, (3) management's ability to make accurate estimates, (4) complexity of operations (including extent of EDP), and (5) recent changes in key personnel and information systems. Multiple factors might also be used to measure materiality (for example, sales, assets, operating expenses, and head count).

Attaching weights to these various risk factors, as well as considering the materiality of each location, will provide a basis for (1) a quantitative assessment of each operation and (2) listing the operations in order of their risk and exposure. For example, those operations that exceed a certain point of total would be classified as A, key locations. Extensive audit procedures would be performed at these locations on an annual basis. The extent of internal audit procedures would depend on the involvement of external audit and cost-effectiveness of providing the service. B locations would require less extensive procedures, and areas of audit emphasis would be rotated. For example, there may be a policy that would require internal audit to perform some procedures at least every two years. C locations—the low priority ones—would require only analytical review procedures annually and ongoing monitoring of results. Visits by internal audit would depend on (1) whether external auditors provide full statutory audit procedures and (2) the results of the ongoing financial analysis. Depending on the results of these factors, internal audit might plan to visit these C locations on a 24-to 28-month rotation program.

Regardless of the methodology that is used to set priorities, corporate operating management should provide input to the planning process. This involvement is essential for several reasons:

1. It provides an opportunity for internal audit to get up to date insight into management concerns. This information can then be used to modify the results of the quantitative analysis to respond to current risks.
2. It provides for a mutual understanding of audit objectives and improved cooperation with local managers.
3. It sets the stage for an increased interest in audit results and corrective actions.

GOOD COMMUNICATIONS ARE CRITICAL

Effective communication between corporate headquarters and the company's overseas operations is particularly important. A good example of the need for effective communications took place recently when a large United States multinational acquired a company in the United Kingdom. The financial manager of the acquired company had never met face to face with financial management of the acquirer, so he was not familiar with the parent company's stated policy against accumulating funds at the local level. When he accumulated funds and invested them at a favorable interest rate, he thought he was performing in the parent's best interests. Unfortunately, the value of the pound dropped against the dollar, and several hundred thousand dollars were lost.

If the local financial manager had been aware of the policy against accumulating funds at local operating companies, he would have avoided the loss by forwarding the funds to corporate and reducing the intercompany balance. The problem was a direct result of poor communications.

Maintaining effective communications in a multinational environment is not an easy task. One way to help make sure all financial managers are "hearing the same message" is to conduct annual financial conferences. These provide an excellent open forum to discuss operating developments and to review corporate policies. These conferences also provide an opportunity for the CFO to emphasize to local financial managers the importance of (1) maintaining effective internal controls and (2) keeping open lines of communication with corporate headquarters. The cost of these conferences is more than offset by the improved lines of communication.

SUMMARY

Controlling foreign operations to achieve desired profits while maintaining risks within acceptable levels is a challenge to every CFO who operates in the international arena. It requires establishing controls proportionate to the risk and investment involved. Risk can be measured by identifying and assessing pertinent political, economic, and cultural factors.

The degree of risk and level of investment have a direct bearing on how a company should be organized. The higher the risk and related investment, the greater the need for centralization. In particular, centralization of treasury functions provides a variety of benefits that help minimize the risk, as well as the cost, of doing business outside the United States. Most controllership functions require ongoing attention at the local level; however, corporate financial management needs to provide the direction and structure for fulfilling these functions.

The key point to remember when considering internal audit as an element of control over international operations is the cost-effectiveness of the function. A CFO should look at the opportunities for identifying areas for operating efficiency, as well as the need to oversee the effectiveness of the local operation's internal controls. Whether overall control is centralized or decentralized will influence this decision. And it is essential that the internal audit effort be integrated with that of the external auditors to avoid duplication of effort and to achieve maximum cost-effectiveness.

Ultimately, however, thoughtful planning and good communication are the keys to an effective financial control strategy.

16

International Capital Markets

Lewis L. Glucksman, Jacques Gelardin, and Bruce D. Fraser

INTRODUCTION

During the past 20 years, financial practitioners—corporate executives as well as their financial advisors—have had to learn to manage and plan the finances of commercial enterprises in ways responsive to the problems posed by high inflation, interest rate volatility, foreign currency exchange rate instability, and massive funding requirements. Complicating this task has been the element of surprise posed by often-changing and unpredictable governmental regulation and taxation policies.

One rather major development occurring during all of this, attributable to both the circumstances as well as managements' responses, has been the rapidly increasing internationalization of the world's capital markets. This has involved not only the closer "linkage" of the principal domestic capital markets but, in fact, the creation of a truly "supernational" or international market for both issuers and investors in money market, debt, and equity securities. Modern telecommunications technology,

---

Mr. Glucksman was formerly Chairman of Lehman Brothers Kuhn Loeb, Inc. Mr. Gelardin is currently a Managing Director of Shearson Lehman Brothers International, Inc. Mr. Fraser was formerly a Director of Lehman Brothers Kuhn Loeb International Inc.

together with the continuing global "sprawl" of financial service institutions, now permits a 24-hour, worldwide trading day wherein the "book" of buy and sell orders is simply transferred from financial center to financial center as the day progresses. The takers and providers of investment capital are now faced with a wide array of alternatives and, subject to exchange control and taxation policies, constantly seek out and evaluate the best terms available on a global basis, and not just those within their own domestic market.

The implications of these rapid developments have been profound for corporate financial management. Faced with the threat of "crowding out," the pressure to finance during so-called windows, and the R&D new products of modern-day banking's financial "engineers," the chief financial officer has had to change the way he thinks and acts about financing transactions and banking relationships. Market "reconnaissance" and continuous monitoring have become required elements of the financial function as decision times have been compressed and the competition for funds increased.

This chapter will attempt to describe a broad mosaic of this new international financing landscape, explaining why it is important and how it can be used to a company's advantage. Not unlike all other areas of today's modern financial arena, changes in international financing techniques occur rapidly and in unexpected ways. In this regard, it should be noted that some of the discussion which follows could very well be out of date in a short period of time. Nonetheless, despite this natural evolutionary process, the reader will hopefully come away with an understanding of the basic role and importance of the international markets to the enterprises's financial objectives and progress. The international arena, perhaps more than any other area of the financial function, offers characteristics of vital importance to modern financial management: speed, flexibility, and creativity.

BACKGROUND

A Brief History

The history of the development of international money and capital markets follows closely the patterns of international trade, economic development, and war. Examples of cross-border financing can be traced back through the centuries as the needs of financing trade, capital investment, and armed conflict exceeded the local (domestic) supply of savings capital.

The genesis of today's international capital markets is closely linked to the configuration of economic development of the principal European colonial powers during the 18th, 19th, and early 20th centuries. A large amount of capital was exported from Europe, raised by a growing group of financial intermediaries principally from wealthy individuals, and structured initially as loans and later as bond issues. A number of today's better-known U.S. and European investment banking firms trace their origin to this period of industrial and trade expansion and to the role Europe played in its financing.

These earlier patterns of international finance were really structured as bilateral transactions wherein investable savings of one country were directed, in one form or another, to an investment project or debtor of another sovereign nation. As such, using today's financial nomenclature, this activity was essentially "foreign" or "cross-border" financing without the truly global scope of today's "international" capital markets.

The rapid "internationalization" of the financial marketplace is more closely related to the post-World War II economic acceleration of the United States and the displacement of the pound sterling by the U.S. dollar as the leading international reserve, trading, and investment currency. The substantial growth during the 1950s and early 1960s of the U.S. economy, together with a rapid increase in overseas investment by U.S. corporations, led to large and expanding balance of payments and capital account deficits for the United States. This growing pool of dollar holdings which was owned by foreign, private, or government institutions became known as Eurodollars, and transactions in these funds constituted the Eurodollar market. Centered principally in London, interbank deposit and loan activity in Eurodollars grew steadily as it was not under the control of any national authority, allowing the banks relative freedom from exchange control and other regulations. Today, the term Eurodollar broadly includes all global activity in offshore dollars whether or not such activity is conducted in London, New York, Bahrain, Singapore, or wherever. Exhibit 1 depicts the rapid growth of the total Eurocurrency market.

Throughout this period, the U.S. capital-outflow problem was

Exhibit 1
Eurocurrency Market (All Eurocurrencies,
U.S. $ billion equivalent)

	Gross Market Size	Net Market Size
1964	20	14
1965	24	17
1966	29	21
1967	36	25
1968	50	34
1969	85	50
1970	110	65
1971	150	85
1972	205	110
1973	310	160
1974	390	215
1975	480	250
1976	595	281
1977	740	361
1978	949	471
1979	1,233	655
1980	1,524	819
1981	1,861	1,002
1982	2,057	1,125
1983	2,144	1,153
1984	2,380	1,275

Source: Morgan Guaranty Trust Company of New York.

made worse by a growing level of borrowing by foreign (principally European) entities in the U.S. capital market known as the "Yankee" market. As part of an effort to reduce the capital outflow, the U.S. government imposed in 1963 an Interest Equalization Tax (IET) which had the effect of closing the New York market to foreign borrowers (there were some exceptions). Given their continuing requirement for funds, these borrowers were thereby forced to turn to Europe and other non-U.S. sources for their financing. The substantial pool of Eurodollars, which had been the source of a large amount of bank lending and interbank deposit activity, became additionally a natural base of new investment in bond issues. The first true "Eurobond" issue was completed in 1963 for an Italian state agency and had all the principal characteristics of what has now come to be generally referred to as a Eurobond. The issue was underwritten by an international syndicate of banks, sold principally outside of the country of the issuer and into countries other than the country of the currency in which the issue was denominated, and was offered in bearer security form free of withholding taxes or other taxes at source.

Following the imposition of at first voluntary (1965) and later mandatory (1968) controls by the U.S. government on foreign investment and loan activity by U.S. corporations and banks (the Office of Foreign Direct Investment [OFDI] programs), U.S. issuers were forced as well to turn to this growing international Eurobond market for financing their overseas expansion.

A significant portion of the overall level of funds raised by U.S. corporations in this market during the existence of the OFDI controls was in the form of bonds convertible into common stock (the strength of the U.S. stock market during this period helped make such securities of appeal to non-U.S. investors), and the entry of U.S. borrowers to this market added substantially to the market's growth and appeal during those still-formative years.

While the Eurobond market's origins are linked rather directly to the imposition by the U.S. government of these controls programs aimed at stemming the dollar outflow, the market's demise did not occur, as was widely predicted, when the controls were lifted in the mid-1970s. While subsequently threatened by dollar devaluation and floating exchange rates, high interest rates and negative yield curves, and a global energy crisis which triggered a tremendous transfer of financial wealth, the market's growth and maturation nonetheless continued as a wider array of issuers, and investors became attracted to the market. These attractions included speed and flexibility (to issuers), anonymity and freedom from withholding taxes (to investors), a growing choice of currency denomination, and the absence of governmental regulation and interference. Moreover, the active involvement in, and commitment to, the market by a growing range and type of financial intermediaries helped enhance the market's ability to innovate and to structure new instruments and techniques to meet the needs of borrowers and investors alike at any point in time. This market's ability to adapt during such periods of volatility is perhaps the strongest of reasons for its size and legitimacy today.

The Importance of International Capital Markets

While perhaps of interest earlier to only the highest rated sovereign and corporate issuers, the international marketplace today is of major significance to a broad and diverse array (in terms of type, size, and credit standing) of borrowers. The attractive features of the market, together with a growing universe of investors interested in the internationalization of their expanding investment portfolios, have resulted in a market and financing mechanisms which clearly competes with the New York-based U.S. capital market.

The market plays a major role in the overall worldwide flows of capital and savings and is thereby of substantial political and economic significance. In 1984 alone, over $107 billion was raised in the international capital markets (of which nearly $80 billion

Exhibit 2
1974–1984 Volume of International Bond Financing and Eurobond Financing (All issuers)

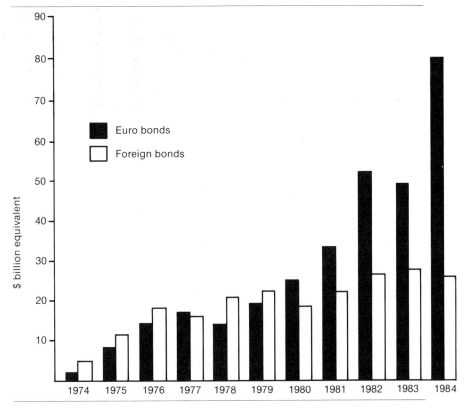

Note: A *Eurobond* issue is one underwritten by an international syndicate and sold principally in countries other than the country of the currency in which the issue is denominated. A *foreign bond* issue is one underwritten by a syndicate composed of members from one country, sold principally in that country, and denominated in the currency of that country.

Source: Morgan Guaranty Trust Company of New York.

Exhibit 3
1974–1984 Volume of International and Eurobond Financing (U.S. issuers only)

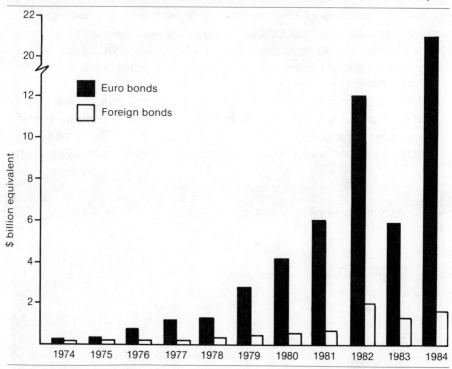

Source: Morgan Guaranty Trust Company of New York.

was in the Eurobond market). Between 1963 and 1984, over $550 billion was raised in total, of which nearly $320 billion was in the Eurobond market alone.

The market is obviously an enormously important source of capital for borrowers of all types and nationalities. In particular, however, U.S. corporations have become frequent and important issuers; today, over 800 Eurobonds of U.S. issuers (including convertible bonds and floating rate notes) are traded in the market, and U.S. issuers raised nearly $50 billion in the international markets in the 1981–84 period alone (of which approximately $45 billion was in the Eurobond market).

The principal attraction to these borrowers, including the U.S. issuers, has been the availability of capital on terms (including maturity, amount, currency, and all-in cost) which compare favorably with alternative sources of funding. In fact, the question of availability per se has at times been the motivating factor in the decision to raise funds in the international market. A major, ongoing objective of many issuers of all credit ratings has been to broaden and diversify the sources from which they may raise future funds.

Over the past several years, changes have occurred in the Euromarkets and in the U.S. market that have had the effect of blurring a number of the relative advantages or disadvantages (for U.S. issuers) of the two respective markets. For instance, prior to the adoption in the United States of Rule 415 by the Securities and Exchange Commission, Europe offered a very definite advantage in terms of the speed with which a financing could be arranged and the cost established. This advantage, while now diminished, would still exist for many companies not willing or able to avail themselves of shelf-registration procedures in the United States. Similarly, the relative advantage of Europe in terms of an issuer being able to arrange a financing with easier, or more relaxed, restrictive covenants than would be required in a U.S. offering has been somewhat diminished. While lower rated companies can still realize some benefits in this area, the spirit in the marketplace today among underwriters is one of providing international investors with the same quality of "protection" as would be provided to U.S. investors.

Comparability of covenants is certainly more commonplace for higher rated issuers although for them such covenants are rather limited in any event. It should be noted here also that the increasing use in the Euromarkets of a fiscal agency agreement structure, rather than an indenture, by definition provides the international investor with a somewhat more difficult mechanism with which to seek any remedies.

For some period of time, one of the relative disadvantages of the international market was the somewhat limited size in which issues could be done. At times when $100 million or more could be accomplished in the U.S. public market, only $50 or $60 million was viewed as the optimum amount to be raised in the Eurobond market. These size constraints and the resultant reduced liquidity of the issues diminished at times the appeal of the market, particularly in terms of pricing. Today, this disparity has disappeared to a large degree. An issue size of $100 million has become rather standard in the Eurobond market, and transactions in larger amounts occur quite frequently. In fact, the European Economic Community in 1983 and again in 1985 successfully completed $1.8 billion floating-rate note issues. It would probably be safe to suggest, however, that in many cases (despite the $1.5 billion raised in two convertible issues for Texaco in early 1984) the Euromarket is still unable to compete with the New York market in terms of size for convertible bond offerings, which are largely directed at equity investors rather than fixed-income investors.

Additionally, the nondollar sectors of the Eurobond market (for example, deutsche mark, pound sterling, dutch guilder, and European Currency Unit [ECU] and the foreign capital markets (for example, Switzerland and the domestic U.K. bulldog market) are accustomed to issue sizes smaller than that obtainable in the United States. Exhibit 4 displays the history of average issue size in the Eurobond market.

Another relative disadvantage of the Euromarkets has historically been the fact that the market was limited for fixed-rate issues to intermediate maturities, although in its very early years the market often absorbed issues in excess of 15 years. Until the inflation and interest rate crisis of the early 1970s, maturities of 10 to 15 years were quite common. Since then, however, the

Exhibit 4
Average Issue Size in The Eurobond Market 1963–1983

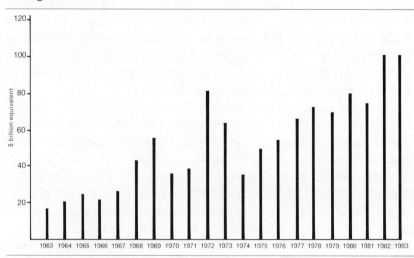

Source: Datastream International Limited.

Exhibit 5
Average Weighted Maturity for New Issues in the Eurobond Market
1963–1983

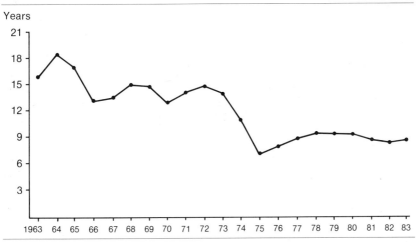

Source: Datasteam International Limited.

market has essentially become a 5- to 10-year market with the emphasis within that range at any point in time depending on overall market conditions and investor sentiment.

While the U.S. market was similarly restricted to the intermediate sector during the recent periods of extremely high interest rates, today it does once again offer maturities as far out as 30 years for fixed-rate issues. Exhibit 5 displays the history of the weighted average maturity of new issues in the Eurobond market.

Other than the advantages and features which have been discussed above, American issuers have at times been largely compelled to turn to the international markets on purely the basis of relative cost of funds for the desired (and available) maturity. Due to the fact that U.S. securities (that is, securities bought in New York) are in registered form and until recently were subject to a withholding tax (of up to 30 percent) on interest payments to nonresidents, foreign investors have demonstrated a large demand for the securities of well-known or high-grade U.S. companies offered in the Eurobond market. These issues are sold in bearer form and in such a way (prior to the removal of U.S. withholding tax, such issues were structured through Netherlands Antilles finance subsidiaries or domestic 80/20 finance companies) as to be free of withholding tax.

This appetite for U.S. issuers has been additionally fueled by (1) investors' "flight to quality" during a period of international turbulence and tension marked by energy crisis, Third World debt crisis, and concern for the credit quality of the international banking sector and (2) investors' desire to own dollar-denominated investments during the last several years of dollar strength. Since for many international investors U.S. Treasury securities were subject to withholding tax and/or information reporting requirements, U.S. corporate issues in the Eurobond or foreign bond markets have been the most attractive alternative. As a result, U.S. corporate issuers have been able generally to raise intermediate-term debt at an all-in cost substantially below, often by as much as 25 to 50 basis points or more, the cost obtainable in the domestic bond market. While gross underwriting commissions are higher in this market, this cost is mitigated by the fact that interest payments on fixed-rate bonds are made annually rather than semiannually.

While this result often applied to issues in the straight, "pure vanilla" Eurobond market, the relative savings have often been realized, and at times to even a greater extent, as a result of the market's ability to design and absorb novel structures and terms. Interest rate swaps, currency swaps, dual-currency issues, partly-paid issues, debt warrants, "drop lock" bonds, "bought" deals, and zero-coupon issues are all examples of the market's flexibility and ability to create instruments designed, at any point in time, to meet the needs and objectives of issuers and particular investor sectors alike. The Euromarkets have been at the forefront of change and innovation in financing structures and offering mechanisms.

Recent years provide clear evidence of the innovative qualities and resilience of the international capital markets. Of course, another factor which has sustained new issue activity has been the growing level of refinancing activity in the marketplace as older issues have been repaid or partially retired through the operation of sinking funds or repurchase programs. Not only must these repayment streams be refinanced, but also investors have often been inclined to reinvest these cash flows into new issues. The size of these funds "reflows" has now reached substantial proportions and suggests a self-perpetuating quality to the markets. The chart on page 292 depicts a forecast of funds reflows during the period 1985–1994, including interest and scheduled principal repayments.

The significance and relevance of the international capital markets are clear to both the providers and users of capital throughout the world. The markets' aggregate size, diversity, and characteristic features are of substantial importance to modern corporate financial management concerned with the cost and availability of an ever-growing need for capital.

The pace of change and the need for creativity are unlikely to abate in the future. There is little doubt that the international markets will continue to be a leading and active arena for those developments.

The Role of the Banker

For the financial management of a corporate issuer, the role of the banker in this rapidly changing international market is both a traditional one and one which has undergone substantial changes in recent years. Not surprisingly, the relationship between the two has also been altered.

Obviously, there are differences between the principal roles played by commercial bankers and investment bankers (or merchant bankers) although the distinctions have significantly blurred over the past 10 years as banking and securities laws and regulations have been dismantled, revised, or reinterpreted. Commercial banks still are in the business of lending money, and investment banks essentially engage in the underwriting of securities or the private arrangement of financing. Both types of financial institutions act in the capacity of financial advisors to their clients, assisting in the evaluation of financing strategies and structures.

However, where previously corporate management often concerned itself with the proper management of operational activities and results of the company and turned to traditional outside financial advisors and intermediaries for information and expertise when the time came to consider external financing, today's financial management is often as well informed and sophisticated with respect to the financial markets as the advisors. Given this level of financial understanding, together with the complexities, pace of change and range of alternatives char-

Exhibit 6
Scheduled International Capital Market Reflows 1985–1994

($ millions)

	1985	1986	1987	1988	1989	1990	1991	1992	1993	1994
Eurobonds	37,119	41,796	47,514	43,436	51,512	40,813	34,638	29,960	22,184	25,245
Foreign Bonds	15,268	16,169	18,068	17,437	16,894	12,187	12,795	12,699	8,811	6,210
Total International Bonds	52,387	57,965	65,582	60,873	68,406	53,000	47,433	42,659	30,995	31,455

Based on information as of 12/31/84.
Source: Orion Royal Bank Ltd.

acteristic of the financial markets, corporate management now feels comfortable, in many cases, in dealing with a broad spectrum of financial institutions far beyond "traditional" relationships. Bankers have by no means been innocent "victims" of this process; indeed, they have encouraged it. In today's environment, a client of one firm is viewed without hesitation as fair game by many other institutions. The ability to create and bring new ideas to a company is now considered the principal battleground of competition among banks of all stripes. In a worldwide financial marketplace characterized by volatile market conditions and ever-changing tax laws and regulations, the financial institutions have really been the leading creative force in the new product R&D process, and it has been competitively incumbent for them to convey these new ideas as quickly as possible to as wide a list of corporate managements as possible. Once a new idea has actually evolved into a financial transaction for all to see, it is no longer a new idea, and everyone will have seized upon it.

To financial management, therefore, the financial community has become both the development-engineering department, as well as the market research department—the "eyes and ears" into the marketplace. Managements have increasingly come to appreciate this process and recognize the importance of listening to much wider channels of financial information and advice. The key is still for management to ferret through all of this input, which is often conflicting, and to choose an appropriate course of action or financial strategy, and to implement it with financial institutions whose advice is sound, whose execution capabilities are evident, and with whom management feels comfortable and confident. This task can be particularly confusing and difficult in the international context where there are so many aspects and alternatives to consider, where changes occur so rapidly, and where such a large number of views are being offered by firms which appear to be equally capable and persuasive. It is of obvious importance for management to distinguish and understand the differences between the financial intermediaries and to select the firm or firms who are really well suited to contribute "value added" to not only a particular financial exercise but also to the achievement of long-term international financial objectives.

The selection process should consider a number of factors beyond just that of "pricing." In the international market, in particular, the awarding of mandates based solely on price competitiveness can often adversely affect the future ability of the company to access the market on favorable terms.

In connection with international bond issues, a company has a greater ability to involve a larger number of financial institutions in a meaningful role since co-management groups (of new issues) have traditionally been much larger than is the case in the domestic U.S. market. The careful selection of these additional firms to play an important role in a financing can thereby bring to a transaction the respective skills those firms possess, such as placement (selling) strength with specific investor sectors or market-making commitment. In a marketplace now widely characterized as being "transactional," it remains clear that sound and trusted financial relationships, with perhaps a larger group of institutions than was previously considered necessary but nonetheless still based on continuous and thoughtful client service, remain integral to the company's long-term success.

FOREIGN CAPITAL MARKETS—A BRIEF DESCRIPTION

The Eurobond Market

Previous portions of this chapter have described the history, size, and significance of the Eurobond market and a number of its features which have so clearly accounted for its growth and appeal. While the Eurobond market is only one sector of the overall international capital market structure, it is by far the most important and is accessible to the widest array of issuers and investors.

This market sector is clearly of the greatest relevance to a broad spectrum of U.S. issuers (industrial corporations, public utilities, banks, and other financial service companies covering a broad spectrum of size and credit rating) who have principally been interested in borrowing dollars although they have at times tapped a number of foreign capital markets. Since the dollar has traditionally been the dominant sector of the market, this section will principally deal with Eurodollar bond market although much of the generic discussion will apply to the other Eurocurrency sectors as well.

Regulatory Considerations As has been already described, the

Exhibit 7
Proportion of Eurobond Market Represented by U.S. Dollar New Issues 1974–1984

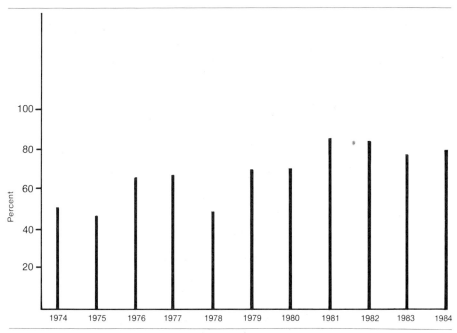

Source: Morgan Guaranty Trust Company of New York.

creation and early development of the Eurobond market was attributable to a great extent to a series of U.S. governmental regulations designed to halt the substantial outflow of dollars. The market's continued growth and maturation, however, has been largely due to its lack of regulation.

In contrast to most other Euromarket currency sectors, there is very little governmental regulation of the Eurodollar bond market. What regulation that does exist is essentially a matter of self-regulation as exercised by the Association of International Bond Dealers (AIBD), a body comprised of the market's principal participating banks and securities firms. A Eurodollar bond financing does not require the filing of a registration statement with the Securities and Exchange Commission, nor does any European regulatory authority review the financing and related documentation in a comparable manner.

Eurodollar bonds are placed by international underwriting syndicates in a manner which does not subject them directly to national regulations. These bonds are distributed directly in those countries, such as West Germany or the Netherlands, which do not regulate public offerings of foreign currency obligations. Elsewhere, such as in the United Kingdom, Eurodollar bonds are distributed consistent with local private placement standards which generally limit purchasers to professional investors or institutions in the business of buying and selling securities. Such mechanisms permit the placing of bonds in discretionary accounts or by way of sale to customers as long as there is no public solicitation or advertising. With respect to the United States, Eurobonds cannot be sold to the U.S. public during the initial (90 day) distribution process unless the offering documentation permits the sale of the securities by the lead manager (or others) on a private placement or restricted basis to a limited number of institutions. Naturally, exchange controls can at times limit the purchase of Eurodollar bonds in any given country.

Virtually all Eurobond offerings are listed on the Luxembourg or London stock exchanges. Listings are "required" because certain countries allow their citizens to purchase foreign currency securities only if they are listed on a recognized stock exchange and because many European insurance companies and mutual funds can only acquire bonds listed on an exchange. While an offering circular (prospectus) in a Eurodollar offering is not subject to any governmental regulation, it is subject to the requirements of the exchange on which the bonds will be listed. The regulations of the exchanges are to some degree similar to the disclosure requirements of the U.S. securities laws although they do not require the same amount of detail. In addition, prospective purchasers of Eurobonds have come to expect a level of disclosure in the offering circular similar to that provided to investors in a U.S. public offering. Full disclosure gains the confidence of potential investors. While there are few court precedents, it is widely accepted that issuers and underwriting syndicates may be held liable for providing inaccurate or incomplete information on which investment decisions are made.

Tax Considerations As a general principle, it is essential that payments of principal and interest on Eurobonds be free of any taxes imposed by the country of the issuer. In this regard, U.S. corporations in the past traditionally used finance subsidiaries to borrow money abroad to eliminate any applicable U.S. withholding tax imposed on the payment of interest to nonresidents.

If the proceeds of a Eurobond issue were to be reloaned to U.S. affiliates of the finance subsidiary, a Netherlands Antilles corporation was customarily used (due to a favorable network of tax treaties). On the other hand, if most of the proceeds were to be invested in foreign affiliates, it was possible to use a separate domestic (U.S.) finance subsidiary.

The documentation required the finance subsidiary and its parent-guarantor to agree to pay any withholding tax that may be imposed so that bondholders would receive the stated interest net of any deductions. On the other hand, the issuer was typically permitted to redeem the bonds at par in the event that withholding tax was imposed or there developed a substantial probability that interest payments would become subject to such tax.

During the summer of 1984, however, the United States enacted legislation (the Tax Reform Act of 1984) which removed the withholding tax on interest paid to foreign investors. The legislation itself, together with supplemental regulations and interpretations, is rather complex and deals with a number of withholding tax related issues, such as backup withholding and information reporting requirements, bearer versus registered securities, recharacterization of foreign source income/interest rules, and required characteristics of an offshore finance subsidiary.

Generally speaking, U.S. corporate borrowers can now directly issue Eurobonds in bearer form without the necessity of using a separate finance subsidiary. While (Netherland Antilles) finance subsidiaries can still be used as the issuing vehicles, a change in foreign tax credit rules would, in most cases, make such a structure uneconomic. Although the removal of withholding tax simplifies the structural arrangements attendant to a Eurobond financing, market practice *allows* corporate issuers to still be able to redeem an outstanding issue without penalty if such tax were to be subsequently imposed, and *requires* the issuer to, in the event of an imposition of regulations requiring the identification of bondholders, redeem such bonds at par and/or gross up interest and principal payments to the extent of any backup withholding tax which would be imposed if investors' identities were not disclosed. Eurobond issues can be offered in bearer form so long as certain, well-established offering procedures are followed. Outstanding Eurobond issues (those issued prior to June 22, 1984) structured by way of Netherlands Antilles finance subsidiaries were exempted from any imposition of withholding tax through a "grandfather" clause in the legislation so long as certain capitalization standards are complied with.

Eurobond Investors Ownership of Eurobonds cannot be traced directly because they have traditionally been issued in bearer form. Indeed, the anonymity of ownership is a principal attraction for a large sector of investors.

Because the ownership of Eurobonds is not known, it is necessary to rely on informed judgment regarding the potential purchasers of Eurobonds. It is estimated that a majority of Eurobonds, including Eurodollar bonds, are purchased by banks, especially in Switzerland, London, and Luxembourg, for the accounts of nonresident, individual investors in Europe, the Middle East, the Far East, and Latin America. These banks also purchase Eurobonds for bank-managed investment funds whose shares are held by the same type of investors.

Institutional investors, such as insurance companies, pension funds, and central banks, while of increasing importance to the market, play a less dominant role in the Eurobond market than in the domestic, U.S. bond market because many of them are subject to legal investment restrictions which affect the amount of foreign securities they may hold and the minimum credit rating for issues in which they may invest.

International investors, particularly individuals, are motivated by different investment criteria than are investors in the United States. Most Euromarket portfolios are nondollar based, and, therefore, volatility in foreign exchange markets often means that currency selection is the most important determinant of total portfolio return. These investors also face a wide variety of national regulatory and tax constraints. Changes in exchange control regulations or tax treatment can dramatically alter international investment patterns.

Because individual investors' transactions costs are relatively high compared to the size of investment, most retail investors prefer to hold to maturity rather than trade their investments.

Therefore, retail investors often evaluate the attractiveness of a security very differently than do institutional investors.

The primary new issue market is generally affected by these differences. In the U.S. institutionally dominated market, an issuer is categorized by its credit rating, which in turn determines its securities' spread over the rate on U.S. Treasury issues. In the Eurobond market, each issue is a unique story with its success depending not as much on its rating as on the issuer's name recognition with investors, the history of its previous offerings, prevailing currency rates and expectations, the new issue calendar or dealer "overhang," the political climate, and how the issue is syndicated. Additionally, the name recognition factor can often be influenced by the degree to which the issuer's common stock is followed by international equity investors. In this regard, listing of the issuer's common stock on foreign stock exchanges, particularly in Switzerland, can have ancillary benefits when undertaking a debt financing in the international market.

While it is widely thought that the Eurobond investor is less sophisticated, it would be more correct to view the market as simply different, in key ways, than the rating-conscious, institutionally orientated, U.S. market. A careful understanding of these different and changing criteria and motivations is important for both issuers and intermediaries alike when considering the timing and structure of a financing in this market.

Offering Techniques and Considerations As with other aspects of the Eurobond market, issuing techniques and procedures have evolved in response to changed market conditions and the needs of both issuers and investors.

There are two principal marketing methods employed in Eurodollar offerings: (1) the underwriting method similar to that traditionally employed in the U.S. corporate bond market where the final terms of the issue are established at the end of the marketing period, and (2) the "bought deal" or "firm bid" method where an underwriter or group of underwriters enter into a binding (although at the outset unwritten) agreement with an issuer setting forth the final terms of the issue and agreeing to underwrite such issue prior to the marketing period. The bought deal method has become the predominant form of offering in the Eurodollar market (other than for convertible debt) and no doubt contributed to the adoption by the SEC of the Rule 415 shelf-registration procedures in the United States. Initiated during a period of extreme market volatility and brief market windows, this marketing method has both advantages and disadvantages for issuers and underwriters alike. If rates deteriorate subsequent to the launching of a fixed-price issue, underwriters can face heavy losses on their unsold positions and issue prices can be discounted rapidly in the when-issued market, an outcome which can adversely affect the pricing on future issues for that borrower.

On the other hand, if rates improve following the announcement of a new issue, the borrower foregoes the ability to realize any additional rate savings which otherwise would have been obtainable using an open-pricing procedure. However, issuers' desire to "lock-in" the cost of a financing in a market fraught with rate, spread, and currency risks has become in the end the compelling consideration.

The Euromarket, in addition, has two other features relating to offering procedures which distinguish it from the domestic U.S. market. The underwriting/selling commission structure is substantially higher in Europe due to the higher cost of servicing the important demand from individual investors through banks' retail branch networks, with gross spreads for fixed-rate issues typically ranging from 1½ to 2 percent or more. Additionally, there is a much longer period of time between the "launch" of an issue (that is, the unwritten agreement between the issuer and the lead manager or management group as to the offering terms) and the actual signing of an underwriting agreement and the allotment of securities to the underwriting group. These factors, together with the fact that there exists no fixed-price reoffering requirements (as exist in the U.S. market), leaves great room for "grey-market" (preissue) trading in an issue at somewhat uncontrollable discount prices. So many new-issue Eurobonds immediately trade very poorly in the grey market due to overly aggressive underwriter bids in order to win lead-manager mandates from issuers, and the fact that too many weak comanagers are often included in the management group who are able to rather anonymously unload their commitments at discounts in the grey market.

As a result, it is important for issuers to carefully select and structure the management group for a new issue and to decide (with the advice of the lead-manager) whether to include a broad underwriting group. Since the lead-manager and, in turn, the comanagement group have the primary underwriting commitment until such time as a sub-underwriting group can be formed, it is important to structure a well-balanced management group which is orientated to reaching desirable or targeted investor sectors. An overweighting of investment bank/merchant bank participants, who are essentially geared to institutional investors, runs the risk of encouraging destabilizing price competition during the offering process since they are likely to all cover a large proportion of the same institutional accounts. Given the importance of the retail investor to the market, particularly in the case of fixed-rate issues, a management group should appropriately include geographically diverse firms able to reach this key sector of the market. Individual investors, since they tend to buy and hold to maturity, are less price sensitive and, together with the firms which are good at placing bonds with them, less likely to sell out their investment (or position) simply because Treasury bonds traded off that day in New York. This investor base should be considered, as well, when determining whether to include a large sub-underwriting group in the offering structure.

Timing, too, is an important element of the financing process and much has been written about market windows and the pressures to finance when they occur. Experience, however, would seem to suggest that once a window has been widely identified, it will often be too late for an issuer to proceed with a successful financing. There is a rather steady and constant cash flow available for investment in the Euromarket, and oversaturation can occur quickly. Unless there has been a fundamental change in interest rate or exchange rate expectations and views (thereby triggering substantial shifts in portfolio mix or speculation), trying to follow other issuers through a window can seriously jeopardize the ability to conclude a well-received offering. With the markets now more-or-less continuously suffering from all kinds of uncertainty, and assuming a borrower is satisfied with absolute rate levels, it is best to try to finance at a time when there is not a great deal of competition in the new-issues market for available investor funds. The chances for a successful transaction are enhanced, and the issuer's ability to bring future issues at appropriate and competitive prices will have been preserved.

Types of Issues Traditionally, the Eurobond market has been principally one of medium-term, fixed-rate issues. However, many U.S. corporations have also issued convertible Eurobonds, particularly corporations that do not have domestic convertible issues outstanding.

Because the Euro-convertible transaction is restricted (at least initially) to another capital market, the pressure on the domestic price of the issuer's common stock is somewhat diminished since domestic U.S. investors will not sell the common stock in order to buy a newly offered convertible Eurobond. Euro-convertibles establish a financial presence in international capital markets that provides an important alternative to the U.S. markets for future capital needs as well as heightened international interest in the company's common stock. In terms of equity-linked securities, the convertible bond form has been much more widely used than structures featuring debt with equity warrants attached.

A recent phenomenon has been the explosive growth in the Eurodollar (as well as sterling) floating rate note (FRN) market. Although the first FRN dates back to 1970, it has only been in the past several years that the market has really grown and developed. While industrial corporations occasionally have been issuers in this market, the trend has been strongly toward banks and sovereign governments and their agencies. Priced at margins relative to London Inter Bank Offered Rates (LIBOR), these floating-rate securities have been attractive to issuers who either do not have access to the U.S. commercial paper market, which offers lower rates, or to those who have LIBOR-indexed assets, such as banks. With a scarcity of new activity in the syndicated loan market, banks have turned increasingly to the securities markets as an avenue to build asset growth. Banks have been both the principal borrowers and investors in the FRN market where over $34 billion was raised in 1984 on terms which improved considerably during the course of the year.

The FRN market became an appealing alternative to the traditional money markets as investors became increasingly comfortable with the degree of liquidity characterizing the market. The rapidly expanding demand for new issues has allowed issue sizes to increase, maturities to lengthen (perpetual or un-dated issues have even been concluded), and spreads (over LIBOR) to narrow.

The Euromarkets, as mentioned previously, have been the creative laboratory for a wide range of innovative financing structures, including zero coupon bonds, partly-paid issues, drop-lock bonds, and debt warrants. These new structures, which have gone through cycles of both popularity and disfavor as interest rate expectations change, have been designed in response to both difficult market conditions wherein borrower and investor needs are hard to match together and to the (institutional) market's appetite for securities offering greater volatility and leverage. Fixed-rate bond offerings with warrants to buy additional fixed-rate bonds demonstrate the speculative dimension of the market for both the issuer and the investor. The issuer is speculating that interest rates will not decline; for if they do, the warrants will be exercised, and the issuer will have additional higher coupon debt outstanding than would have been the case had he waited to do a second tranche of financing. The investor, on the other hand, is speculating that rates will decline and that, therefore, the value of the warrants will increase and/or he will be able to own additional above (then) market rate debt.

While the issuer is able to realize value for selling this option and since this value is often viewed as having served to reduce the cost of the original tranche of debt, the sale of that option entails financing risks of which the true costs will not be known until much later when the warrants are either exercised or expire. Techniques have developed, however, using "contingent" interest rate swaps, the future markets, or "host" bond call features which serve to reduce or eliminate the risk if outstanding warrants are exercised.

Currency Denomination While the dollar sector of the Eurobond market has traditionally been the largest, reflecting the dollar's role as the leading investment and reserve currency, other Eurocurrency sectors have also been of importance to international investors and issuers. U.S. borrowers, in particular, have recently become more active in tapping these other markets either as a means of hedging currency exposure or as part of interest rate/currency swap exercises designed to obtain below-market dollar financing. However, these other currency sectors of the Eurobond market, as well as the various foreign bond markets, have generally not been able to digest issues as large as the dollar bond market.

Because of its role as an important international currency which has traditionally been characterized by relative strength and low inflation and low interest rates, the deutsche mark sector of the market has consistently ranked second only to the dollar.

While there is little distinction between deutsche mark Eurobonds and deutsche mark foreign bonds, financing in this currency has been typically undertaken by international borrowers as Euromarket transactions. Although such issues were historically required to be lead-managed by a German bank and are listed on a German exchange, the underwriting syndicates are international in scope and are aimed at reaching a broad international distribution. Since the removal of withholding tax regulations at the end of 1984, international and German investors are free to invest in either the domestic bond market or the Eurocurrency market.

While the deutsche mark market has attracted international borrowers due to its size, relatively low interest rates, and general ease of access (except in late 1980 and early 1981 when the authorities suspended most new international issues), the market was nonetheless subject to self-regulation by the Central Capital Market Subcommittee whose principal role was to monitor and schedule new deutsche mark issues. The German central bank, the Bundesbank, has now liberalized the issuing procedures for this market, including now allowing a wider range of types of securities and currency swaps. There is also a large and active private placement market for international deutsche mark issues which are generally smaller in size but can be appropriate for issuers new to the deutsche mark sector.

The pound sterling sector of the Eurobond market has also seen periods of increased issuing activity since the first issue was arranged in 1972 and particularly since U.K. exchange controls were removed in 1979. Activity in this sector has been volatile and, perhaps more than is the case for other currency segments, subject to changing interest rate levels and exchange rates.

Since the Eurosterling market is orientated to international investors, maturities of issues have been comparable to the Eurodollar sector (that is intermediate) whereas the domestic sterling market for foreign issuers has typically been much longer in term. Domestic U.K. investors are generally institutional since individual investors have only for a short period of time been able to invest in international securities. Issuing procedures in Eurosterling bonds are also similar to the dollar sector although the Bank of England has had historically somewhat complicated rules regarding who can lead or co-lead a sterling issue.

Another sector of the market which has experienced recent rapid growth is the European Currency Unit (ECU). The ECU is a composite currency created in 1978 as a unit of account for the European Monetary System and whose value is tied to a basket of European currencies. Most ECU bond issues are sold principally within Belgium and Luxembourg by the branch networks of the big three Belgium commercial banks and the Luxembourg banks, although sales are made to other international investors, notably in Germany and the Netherlands.

While the volume of new issues has increased dramatically, access to the market is informally controlled by the big three Belgian banks, and the market's depth is still more limited than other markets. U.S. corporate activity or interest in this market has been very limited to date and has been related to swap transactions.

Activity in other currency sectors of the Eurobond market, notably the Canadian dollar, Japanese yen, French franc, Dutch guilder, Kuwaiti dinar, and Australian dollar, has been spasmodic and rather limited as a result of either currency weakness and/or governmental restrictions.

Other Foreign Capital Markets

While the predominance of international capital market financing by U.S. corporations has been undertaken in the Eurobond market, other foreign capital markets are accessible to selected issuers and have been of increasing importance for international borrowers of all kinds.

By far the most notable and substantial of these is the Swiss franc market, which has been accessible for foreign issuers almost continuously since the early 1960s. In fact, in most years a greater volume of finance is raised by foreign borrowers in the Swiss market than by domestic borrowers. The market's appeal has included low interest rates, an increasing ability to do issues in size, and the ability to swap the proceeds into other currencies.

Given the Swiss authorities' concern for the control of the currency, Euro-Swiss issues have not been permitted since the initial and only issue in 1963, and the Swiss National Bank has until very recently exercised close control over the number, size, and timing of foreign issues in the Swiss capital market. Previously subject to a queuing system similar to that applied in other markets, the Swiss authorities in late 1983 relaxed the scheduling procedures, thereby making the market more quickly and readily available.

Financing in the Swiss market is achieved either through public bond issues (minimum maturity of nine years) or private placements (maturities of from three to eight years) managed or arranged by resident Swiss banks or securities firms. Swiss foreign exchange and capital market regulations change from time to time and can limit the level of investment in Swiss franc securities by nonresident investors.

The Swiss market has also been an arena of innovative financing techniques, particularly convertible securities and dual-currency issues. Although aimed at a rather narrow segment of investors, a growing number of dual-currency issues have been completed which have resulted in fully hedged dollar finance being achieved at below-market rates. Because the market is either directly or indirectly (through fiduciary or investment accounts) orientated mainly toward the relatively conservative individual investor, access has generally been limited to only higher rated or well-known issuers.

The other principal foreign bond markets, notably the United Kingdom and Japan, have been experiencing growth as exchange or capital controls have been relaxed, but they have generally been accessible (with a few exceptions) only for sovereign, quasi-governmental, or well-known bank issuers. With respect to the United Kingdom in particular, U.S. corporate issuers have not found the bulldog market to be of great appeal due to the long-term maturities (25 to 40 years) characteristic of the market, the inability to hedge sterling liabilities out that far, and the historically high interest rates in effect (relative to dollars, deutsche marks, or Swiss francs). While Japanese investors are important elements of demand in the overall Eurobond market, greater opportunities for financing in yen are now available for highly-rated corporate borrowers following the recent liberalization of the market by Japan's Ministry of Finance. The "Yankee" bond market (that is, the New York-based market for issues of non-U.S. borrowers), is a substantial market but one which (due to the SEC registration, disclosure, and accounting requirements) has been seldom used by foreign corporate issuers.

One other capital market which deserves at least historical comment is the private placement market with the Saudi Arabian Monetary Authority. Since loans to governments and very high-grade corporate borrowers were made in dollars, sterling, and some other currencies, these transactions were rather like "Euro-private placements." While competitively priced with a borrower's financing alternatives, the market was tapped by large "AA" or better borrowers essentially wishing to diversify the sources of intermediate funds. With the collapse of the worldwide energy markets and the reversal of balance of payments positions, this source of funding has all but dried up.

The other major source of intermediate-term financing for borrowers of all types and quality has been the Eurocurrency (principally Eurodollars) syndicated loan market. This market grew substantially as a result of the need to recycle "petro-dollars" following the oil shocks of the 1970s. Tied to floating rates and at margins over LIBOR, this is also a very large and flexible market whose lending participants include a wide and diverse array of international banks and financial institutions. From a U.S. corporate perspective, this market's appeal has generally been one of providing low-cost (in terms of commitment fees), standby commitment used to support U.S. commercial paper programs. Other borrowers have included banks (who have LIBOR-based assets) or companies whose size of borrowing levels suggest funding source diversification irrespective of the relative costs of Eurodollars versus alternative markets. While generally not providing fixed-rate funding, the market does offer great flexibility in terms of the timing of drawdowns, repayments, term, and selection of currency.

Given investors' increasing penchant for liquidity and borrowers' desire for cheaper sourcing of floating rate funds, many borrowers have turned increasingly to the Euronote issuance facility structure as the means of raising such finance. While being as flexible as the more traditional syndicated loan format, these structures offer a cheaper cost of funding and/or standby commitments for a wide array of borrowers.

A group of banks still provide the essential standby funding commitments, essentially acting as "underwriters", but the actual funding is contemplated through the issuance of short-term promissory notes either through a dealer or by way of a competitive tender panel bidding process. Euronotes and floating rate note issues, together with other developing hybrid structures, are causing the bank and capital markets to become even more integrated over time, and the short-term Euromarkets are increasingly competitive with the U.S. commercial paper market.

RECENT DEVELOPMENTS AND CONCLUSIONS

As detailed above, the international capital markets are dynamic and subject to change in unpredictable ways. With the passage of time, the markets have become more closely linked, and investors and issuers have become more "internationalized" in their thinking and patterns of action. While this perspective is fairly well developed within the money and fixed-income sectors of the market, the process is still at a rather early stage in terms of equity issuance and investment. Increasingly, however, portfolio managers are considering international economic and political risk diversification, as well as currency opportunities. Similarly, multinational corporations are demonstrating greater interest in expanding their equity shareholder base beyond that of their own home market. As this process continues, a substantially greater volume of cross-border or international equity flows will occur.

The money market, currency exchange market, and futures market are also becoming increasingly related as investors and borrowers become more analytically sophisticated as well as more concerned with the cost-effective hedging of risks and the enhancement of returns. While still at an early stage of development, the London International Financial Futures Exchange (LIFFE) has promise of expanding the use of futures as a hedging device for Euromarket participants concerned with the "basis" risk which presently exists when using U.S. futures instruments to hedge Euromarket positions. While the degree of appreciation and use of futures may never reach that which exists in the U.S. market, it will clearly continue to expand substantially as will the use of new instruments, such as foreign currency commercial paper, Eurocommercial paper, currency options, and others.

The international interest rate and/or currency swap market is another recent example of the innovativeness of the marketplace. Much like international trade patterns which are predicated on relative advantages and disadvantages, the swap market developed as a result of relative advantages which different borrowers enjoy (in terms of cost of funds) in different markets. Two borrowers of diverse credit standing and with different relative costs (for example, in the Euro fixed-rate market versus the syndicated loan market) can take advantage of those differences to respectively obtain (indirectly) fixed-rate or floating-rate funds at a cheaper cost than if they directly sourced the market of choice. This is accomplished by having the two parties enter into an interest rate exchange agreement wherein interest payment streams, not principal, are made to one another.

The market initially developed when banks, desiring floating-rate funds but enjoying a relative rate advantage in the Eurobond market, were put together through a financial intermediary with lower rated industrial companies who desired fixed-rate finance but enjoyed a relative (not absolute) advantage in the floating-rate loan market. As a result, both parties obtained the desired type of financing at costs below that which were available from alternative sources. Once the nature of these relative advantages were more fully understood, and the "spread" differentials between different types of instruments in different markets were more closely analyzed, the swap market grew rapidly. As more intermediaries and borrowers became involved, the market developed into a substantial, discreet sector of the international marketplace. More and more permutations on the same theme have been created, including asset-based swaps, currency swaps, floating-to-floating swaps, and others, and the expectation is that the scope, size, and nature of the market will continue to expand and change. In 1984 alone, the interest swap and "long-term" currency swap market is estimated to have approached $70 billion in size.

One of the most important recent developments relates to the recent removal of the U.S. withholding tax on interest pay-

ments to foreign investors. This issue has been a very complicated and emotional one, and there have developed many points
of view regarding its eventual impact.

Some observers have been of the view that the elimination of
the tax will make it easier for U.S. investors to access the Euromarkets without having to go through all the "gymnastics"
and costs of using an offshore finance subsidiary. Other observers, however, have been of the view that the relative rate
advantage which many U.S. issuers have enjoyed will disappear as the yield levels of the two markets come together through
market arbitrage and as international investors are able to buy
U.S. Treasury securities free of withholding tax.

In the relatively brief time since the tax was removed, a large
number of U.S. corporate borrowers have raised money directly in the Euromarkets through traditional Eurobond distribution structures at rates which, in most cases, compared favorably with domestic, U.S. alternative costs. Despite the fact
that some observers predicted that U.S. Treasuries would become the benchmark of the market above which all other issues
would scale in price and that a New York-based "global" market would emerge, it should be recognized that not all international investors will naturally or automatically turn to Treasury
securities as the preferred investment vehicle; Treasuries are issued in registered form, except for certain specially targeted issues, and the mechanisms can easily be established for U.S.
companies to offer (even for SEC-registered issues) bearer securities for international investors. The ability of U.S. corporate
issuers to issue truly bearer securities and their willingness to
provide investors with the indemnification from future changes
in identification requirements would suggest that the markets
will remain distinct.

Moreover, well-established and familiar channels of distribution exist overseas for reaching a substantial number of investors, particularly individual investors, who will be willing to accept a lower rate of interest in return for these characteristics of
U.S. corporate Eurobonds.

This important investor group would not be expected to simply buy U.S. securities in New York. While most, if not all, offerings for U.S. companies could again be registered with the
SEC, the nature and structure of management groups and underwriting syndicates and procedures would have to change

radically to reflect the need to reach a global array of investors. These same SEC registration requirements will also continue to cause non-U.S. issuers to utilize the Euromarkets. The Euromarket may become more closely integrated with New York, but predictions of its demise, as has been true during previous periods of disruption or change, are no doubt premature.

In summary, the international marketplace has continued to demonstrate strengths of resilence and creative adaptability. Techniques may change, new securities structures may be engineered, and the financial services industry may be rendered totally unrecognizable as compared to today. But the existence and importance of the international financial market will remain if not increase. This point should not be lost upon corporate financial management.

17

Managing Currency Exposure

Alastair I. Hunter-Henderson

Since the world's currency system was released from the gold standard in November 1971, there has been a high degree of volatility in the relative value of major world currencies. The dramatic changes in the value of the British pound sterling which has risen and fallen several times in the last 12 years is a good example of this volatility. Using the dollar as a relative measure, the following table illustrates some of the major changes in the value of the major investment country currencies over this time period.

For companies which often rely on foreign currency earnings for 40 to 60 percent of their business, annual movements in relative exchange rates create a particularly vulnerable earnings risk. This chapter will outline some of the policy implications of operating in today's volatile international exchange rate environ-

Alastair I. Hunter-Henderson, a vice president of Morgan Guaranty Trust Company of New York, is head of the bank's international money management group in the treasurer's division. A native of Great Britain, he holds degrees from Imperial College and London University School of Economics, and a Ph.D. from New York University Graduate School of Business Administration, where he is an adjunct professor.

Fluctuations in World Currency Values (Amount of currency per U.S. dollar, 1971–1984)

Country	Currency	November 1971	November 1984	Percent Increase
Canada	C$	1.00	1.32	32%
France	FF	5.55	9.19	65%
Germany	DM	3.33	2.99	(10%)
Italy	Lira	612.74	1,863.10	204%
Japan	Yen	328.40	243.60	(26%)
Switzerland	SF	3.98	2.47	(38%)
United Kingdom	£	0.40	0.81	101%

ment and suggest various approaches for addressing these issues.

BASIC CONCEPTS

Exposure, or vulnerability to foreign exchange risk, can be viewed as two separate problems in currency management: how to protect the value of an *investment* in a foreign currency, and how to optimize the corporation's *sourcing* strategy in light of its business and competitive position. These two problems are often confused by focussing on their accounting and noneconomic implications rather than the fundamental business issues involved. This discussion will focus on the fundamental issues, using a U.S. multinational company with overseas operations and competitors of different nationalities as a prototypical model.

Protecting the Value of a Foreign Investment Companies seeking to exploit the business potential of their products will sooner or later consider making overseas investments in order to develop new markets. Each investment will be expected to generate a foreign currency cash flow which, with certain currency expectations, will justify the investment decision. When an unexpected currency movement takes place, the anticipated return to the investor of that investment will change until or unless the company can alter its pricing to compensate for the erosion of the value of currency.

If we assume that the present value of expected foreign currency earnings is at least equal to the value of the equity invested, the present value of the foreign currency impact could well be consistent with the equity adjustment determined by the accountants. However, the concern of senior management should focus on ensuring that operating management has the maximum flexibility to react to these currency changes in the basic business. Protecting the accounting adjustment, which will not influence the cash flow of the business, should be a secondary concern. Ways to protect the value of this investment are discussed below under the heading "Managing Investment Exposures."

Optimizing Sourcing Strategy The second concern in exposure management is how to optimize the corporation's sourcing strategy. Even without an overseas investment, a company can source a product or component in a currency that is different from the currency of revenue generation. A movement in exchange rate between the currency of revenue generation and the currency of expense will impact the business margin of the product. The economics of this situation are complex since the flexibility to react is largely a function of a company's competitive position. If major competitors have a different sourcing pattern, the economics of that market will be influenced by the company with the most favorable cost structure. Hence, in considering sourcing exposure, senior management should be primarily concerned about the business economics and only secondarily concerned about the currency mismatch since there are often market techniques for managing this.

The Functional Currency Concept The concept of functional currency is that each individual company has a currency which best represents the economics of its business. This useful concept became widely used after it was incorporated into the Financial Accounting Statement 52 in 1981.

To illustrate the concept of the functional currency consider the example of a U.S. multinational company with a subsidiary in the United Kingdom. This subsidiary manufacturers, sources, and sells its product in pounds sterling. Hence all transactions, except for one ingredient, are priced in pounds. The exception is a foreign ingredient which is priced in deutsche marks. This situation is illustrated in Exhibit 1.

Functional Currency Definition Since the British company operates in pounds sterling, the economics of the business can best be measured and understood in sterling terms. Hence, in this example, the functional currency of this subsidiary company would be the British pound.

Exhibit 1
Definition of Functional Currency (U.K. subsidiary of U.S. multinational)

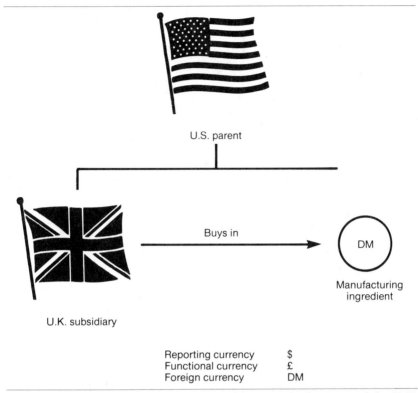

The *functional currency* is the British pound because the business of the U.K. subsidiary can best be described in terms of the local economy. The *reporting currency* is the U.S. dollar since the owners of the company will evaluate its performance in dollars.

Investment Exposure Definition The cash flow generated by the subsidiary is in pounds, and yet its parent company functions in U.S. dollars. To the extent that the value of the pound changes in U.S. dollar terms, the value of the U.S. company's investment in its British subsidiary will fluctuate. Thus, the company has an investment exposure in pounds and in this example is long pounds (the functional currency of the subsidiary) against the U.S. dollar (the functional currency of the parent). This relationship is illustrated in Exhibit 2, next page.

Sourcing Exposure Definition Since the British company functions in pounds, it considers all revenues and expenses in other currencies to be exposed. This example, the only cash flow

Exhibit 2
Definition of Investment Exposure (U.K. subsidiary of U.S. multinational)

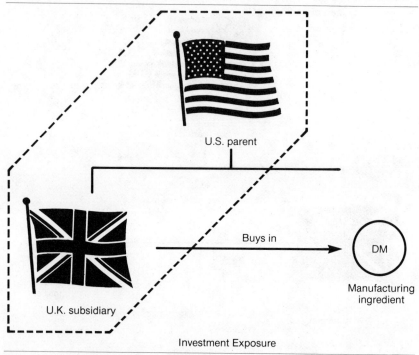

U.S. parent

Buys in

DM

Manufacturing
ingredient

U.K. subsidiary

Investment Exposure

This chart shows the effect of movements of the functional currency against the reporting currency on the value of the parent company. The *investment exposure* of the subsidiary is that the company is long British pounds against the dollar since the reporting currency is the U.S. dollar.

not in pounds, is the ingredient sourced in deutsche marks. Hence, this subsidiary has a short deutsche mark sourcing exposure against its functional currency the pound. This is illustrated in Exhibit 3.

Since the functional currency is determined by the business economics of the situation rather than by where a company is located, management should consider the following factors in order to understand currency economics of their business:

1. *The underlying cash-flow currency.* For example, many oil companies view themselves to have dollar functional currencies worldwide due to the predominance of that currency in their international payments.

2. *The economics of the market.* This is particularly relevant for commodity companies where the currency in which the

Exhibit 3
Definition of Sourcing Exposure (U.K. subsidiary of U.S. multinational)

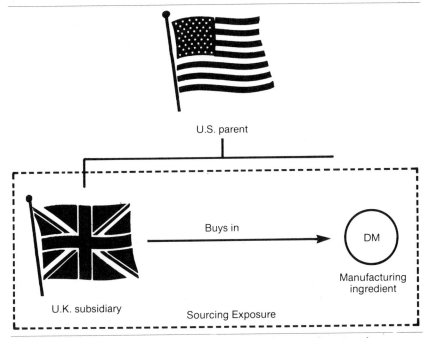

U.S. parent

Buys in

DM

Manufacturing
ingredient

U.K. subsidiary

Sourcing Exposure

This chart shows the exposure due to cash flows not in functional currency. The *sourcing exposure* of the U.K. subsidiary is (that it is short deutsche marks) against the pound.

commodity is traded (often £ or $) does not represent the best measure of their exposure.

3. *The sales price.* Many companies often find themselves exposed to the pricing currency of the largest competitor regardless of their actual sourcing pattern.

4. *The predominant expenses.* A good example would be the airline industry, which due to the level and currency of its asset financing and of their petroleum expenses frequently finds its useful to consider itself to have a dollar functional currency.

5. *Special purpose companies.* Often, special purpose companies (finance companies, reinvoicing companies, or captive insurance companies) will need special consideration, which should be based on the function of the company.

6. *The level of intercompany international trade.* Companies that benefit from economies of scale of production and centralize

their production often have significant intercompany flows across national bounderies. For these companies, a regional approach may be more appropriate when choosing a functional currency. It is possible that the E.C.U. could be the most appropriate unit of account.

Management will wish to review the following questions before deciding whether the local currency is indeed the functional currency.

1. What is the currency of the underlying cash flow?
2. What are the economics of the market?
3. How is the sales price determined?
4. Does the company have any predominant expenses?
5. What is the business purpose of the company?
6. Is there a significant amount of intercompany trade?

Accounting Implications There are often significant differences between the economic and accounting impacts of currency movements. Thus far these changes have been analyzed in economic terms through the concepts of investment and sourcing exposure. However, both of these concepts have accounting parallels which are, respectively, translation exposure (parallel to investment exposure) and transaction exposure (parallel to sourcing exposure).

Translation Exposure: Parallel for Investment Exposure

Description:	Translating a foreign balance sheet from its functional currency into the company's reporting currency will result in a foreign currency gain or loss.
Treatment:	These gains and losses are recorded directly in a special Cumulative Translation Adjustment account and do *not* pass through the income statement.

Translation Exposure: Parallel for Sourcing Exposure

Description:	Holding assets and liabilities (usually receivables and payables) in foreign currencies will result in gains and losses when remeasured in the functional currency.

Treatment: Since these gains and losses directly affect the cash flow of the company they are reported in the income statement as a foreign exchange income or expense.

It should be noted that the actual U.S. accounting treatment of foreign currency items is fairly complex and recognizes special situations such as high inflation economics, therefore the above description should be used as a guide only.

The key difference between an economic exposure and its accounting recognition results from the historic perspective necessary in accounting practice. A strict accounting perspective on managing foreign currencies can dangerously underestimate the severity of a situation. For example, a company that sources in dollars and sells in Europe will only record its outstanding accounts receivable as being exposed. This represents maybe 60 days of exposure. Unless the company has significant pricing flexibility, its sourcing exposure will usually impact its earnings for a period many times greater than this. To manage the receivables already recorded will do little to assist the more fundamental problem of the company's sourcing exposure. In the following sections both economic and accounting strategies are suggested for management.

MANAGING INVESTMENT EXPOSURE

Once the functional currency implications of an overseas investment are understood, senior management must make sure that the investment is being managed to keep pace with the appropriate market conditions. Exhibit 4, page 320, illustrates the movements of the Italian lira and the Italian price index against comparable currency and price indexes of its trading partners. Although Italy typically has a weakening currency when compared with its trading partners, this weakness has gone a long way towards offsetting the higher inflation rate experienced. Management should be aware that a subsidiary operating in a weaker economy will have to make a higher return to compensate for local economic conditions if the value of the investment is to be maintained. Under these conditions, the balance sheet will show a consistent loss in the cumulative translation adjustment account which should be compensated for with higher

Exhibit 4
Inflation and Exchange Rate Indexes: Italy 1970–84

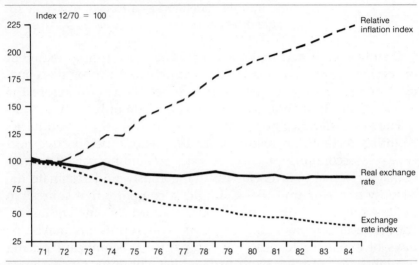

earnings. To manage this exposure effectively, the long-term earnings implications must be considered first and accounting policy concerns later.

Managing Earnings Senior management must make sure that overseas business units are managing their earnings against the economies of their respective functional currencies. Unless higher returns are generated in weaker economies, there is nothing that senior management can do to protect the integrity of the company. Once the overseas units are generating the appropriate return, financial management can manage the cash flow to protect the company from sudden earnings volatility. The five policy issues which need to be addressed to when managing the investment exposure of a subsidiary are:

1. Determination of the correct allocation of responsibility for the management of foreign exchange between treasury and operations.

    Historically, many companies gave local management the responsibility for managing earnings exposure because it was already charged with producing dollar earnings. Recent movements in the exchange markets have been so material that most companies have decided that this approach is im-

Exhibit 5
Allocation of Responsibility for Managing Exchange Exposure—
Italy Example

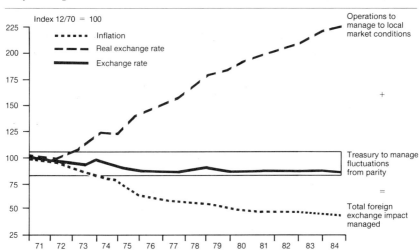

practical. The evolving approach is one of responsibility allocation, having operating management charged with producing adequate returns in the local (functional) economy and treasury responsible for protecting the value of these earnings once generated. The philosophy behind this approach is illustrated in Exhibit 5.

2. Development of the appropriate criteria for evaluating overseas operations.

   Here, management has three choices: to use a local return on investment (ROI), to charge earnings for the higher local cost of money, or to adjust earnings for inflation. All three approaches reflect the results of improved asset management.

   Conceptually, use of a local ROI is the easiest approach to understand. Given that businesses in weaker economies need to generate higher returns, many companies simply adjust their ROI criteria by the interest rate differential (or forward market premium/discount if it exists) to arrive at a local currency target.

   The second approach involves applying an asset charge to the local currency operating earnings before converting them to dollars. The asset charge is the sum of the net working investment employed times the local short-term borrowing rate. Thus, the cost of financing the working investment is charged to the units regardless of the actual financial structure of the business unit. This, in turn, affords financial management greater flexibility to restructure the actual debt of the company as the market permits.

The third approach requires a price adjustment to local earnings for local inflation. Real earnings are then comparable with other units when converted into dollars. This approach is preferred by companies in consumer markets that are heavily price sensitive.

These approaches allow for a decentralized operating structure which, with the flexibility to develop centralized financial management, is an important consideration for many companies.

3. Development of pricing flexibility when possible and appropriate.

Since the vulnerability to currency erosion lasts until pricing decisions can be made to regain operating margins, the weaker the functional currency, the more pricing flexibility that is desirable. Thus although a U.S. company may strive for price stability, a foreign company operating in a high inflation environment must achieve pricing flexibility.

4. A match between financing and the underlying cash flow.

Senior management should set capital structure objectives which provide reasonable protection against foreign currency movements at an acceptable cost. Assuming that operating margins are able to keep pace with inflationary pressures, the discipline of local currency finance expense provides an additional degree of protection against sudden currency movements. As long as adequate local currency financing is available, senior management should expect higher leverage in riskier countries and lower leverage in stronger economies.

5. Creation of a dividend policy that creates cash-flow flexibility.

A dividend standard, set by senior management, is necessary if excess cash is not to unnecessarily inflate the company's investment exposure. A dividend policy should allow for both real growth and also working asset inflation. However, senior management should not be encouraged to leave funds overseas simply to save the additional tax burden of repatriating profits. The cost of economic risk, coupled with the investment opportunity foregone, is frequently much greater than the one-time repatriation cost.

Protecting the Balance Sheet Although accounting considerations are secondary to business economies in effective exposure management, they are still important. The size of the Cumulative Translation Adjustment (CTA) experienced by many major international companies in the first four years following the introduction of the Financial Accounting Statement 52 has been large. Exhibits 6 and 7 show the foreign currency erosion in 1984 as reported in the published annual reports. Fortunately, there is no requirement to include these adjustments in net income. The effect of the 1981 through 1984 CTA accounts would have been material for most companies and without an extensive explanation would not have added much to the understanding of performance.

Since these CTA accounts are not included in net income and only reflect the revaluation of the company's overseas investments rather than the underlying cash flow, they do not affect the earnings criteria by which senior management often manage earnings. However, the CTA account does impact the valuation of shareholder's wealth, and this adjustment could put

Exhibit 6
FAS 52 Cumulative Translation Adjustments: Some 1984 Examples
($ millions)

Company	Total Equity	Cumulative Translation Adjustment	C.T.A as percent of Equity
Exxon	28,851	1,818	6.3%
IBM	26,489	2,948	11.1%
Ford	9,838	1,365	13.9%
ITT	6,032	943	15.6%
Xerox	4,543	537	11.8%
United Technologies	4,169	268	6.4%
Burroughs	2,297	263	11.4%
Upjohn	1,134	126	11.1%

Source: 1984 Annual Reports.

Exhibit 7
FAS 52 Equity Adjustments: Some 1984 Examples
($ millions)

Company	Net Income	Equity Adjustment	Adjustment as % of Net Income
Exxon	5,528	748	13.5%
IBM	6,582	878	13.3%
Ford	2,907	366	12.6%
ITT	448	203	45.3%
Xerox	291	135	46.4%
United Technologies	645	69	10.7%
Burroughs	245	54	22.0%
Upjohn	173	29	16.8%

Source: 1984 Annual Reports.

a company's financial ratios in breach of lending covenants. For these reasons, the CTA account cannot be ignored and a policy should be set for managing translation exposures.

To manage translation exposure, financial objectives must be set for both minimum acceptable net worth and leverage ratios. The only method of minimizing equity exposure is to minimize overseas equity. This is often impractical. To minimize the impact of foreign currency movements on a company's financial ratios, the company should have a capitalization policy which standardizes the debt-to-equity ratio in each country. In this situation, the ratio of the consolidated accounts will always be the same regardless of currency movements. Therefore, the optimal financial strategy will be to have a standard capital structure as a benchmark which closely resembles that of the consolidated company. Financial management should then be given the flexibility to manage from this guideline in order to increase debt in riskier situations.

A centralized corporate finance group can take a consolidated approach to managing translation exposure. Foreign currency debt does not have to be incurred in the exposed legal entity or even in the country involved. The evolution of the Eurodebt markets and the development of the long-date foreign exchange markets allow management the flexibility to match exposures on a global basis in situations where the local company may not be able to support the required debt burden.

In addition, the U.S. accounting standards permit a foreign

currency borrowing to be designated as a hedge of another investment in the same or related currency. Hence, current accounting practices encourage financial management to look through the actual legal entities and take a centralized approach to managing investment exposures.

PROTECTING CROSS-BORDER CASH FLOW

Sourcing exposure, unlike investment exposure, can have a direct effect on the size of the operating margins. Hence, the price adjustment flexibility required to compensate for currency erosion for overseas sales is even more critical than for domestically produced products. The two key policy issues raised by sourcing exposure are: What is treasury's role in managing these exposures, and what is the best location for management? Each question has to be considered in light of the size of the cross-border flows of the company and its competitive position.

Determining Treasury's Role Once a sourcing strategy has been agreed upon and an exposure has been created, the only ultimate recourse to changing margins is through the pricing policy of the company. Treasury's role is one of stabilizing exchange rates for limited periods of time. The length of the appropriate hedging period must be determined by considering both the business context of the company's competitive position and the degree of risk involved. Once the hedging period is determined, both pricing and currency of billing criteria can be set to centralize the exposure in the appropriate location for management. A company that has a high degree of pricing flexibility should consider billing in the manufacturing or sourcing currency. Currency fluctuations would then automatically be passed on to the cost or benefit of the customer. In this case, treasury has minimized its role.

More often than not, operating management is forced to commit to a price structure in order to meet competitive pressures. Understanding the nature of this pricing commitment is the first step to determining treasury's role. Financial management then has to decide whether a fully hedged strategy is appropriate. Both the certainty of the underlying cash flow and the degree of currency risk involved must be considered. Fortunately, the developing currency options market may provide treasury greater flexibility to guarantee prices in situations where both the volume of sales is uncertain and where the ability to take advantage of favorable exchange rate changes is important. Clearly, the additional cost of entering into options will balance out the advantages in the longer term. However, the management flexibility created by this market technique makes it a valuable treasury tool.

Determine the Management Structure Once the appropriate exposure management horizon and the hedging philosophy have been decided, senior management should place the exposures in the appropriate location. There are three alternatives: the sales or importing companies, the manufacturing companies or exporting companies, or a special purpose treasury management company.

Sales Companies Centralizing exposures in the sales companies is achieved through changing the billing currencies. Billing in the manufacturer's currency shifts the exposure to the selling companies. This is probably the most common practice for international companies, and it has the advantage of making the marketing units responsible for managing their pricing to meet changing costs. From a treasury perspective, the exposures are disbursed and a centralized exposure management strategy requires that a sophisticated information system be developed.

Manufacturing Units The second alternative, centralizing exposures in the manufacturing units, can be achieved by billing the sales companies in their local currencies. The cost of a multicurrency invoicing system has to be weighed against the management benefits achieved. In addition, there are transfer pricing issues to be resolved. Billing in local currencies is more defensible under a resale price minus transfer pricing system whereas billing in the manufacturing currency lends itself to a cost-plus pricing system. Recently, there has been increased interest in multicurrency invoicing due to the desire of many companies to centralize their expsoures and the development of more advanced computer invoicing capability.

Special Purpose Companies The third alternative, which should be considered only by companies with a large number of manufacturing and selling locations and a significant amount of intercompany trade, is the creation of a special purpose treasury management company that would manage the exposures in one place. The three most common examples are the currency clearing center, the factoring company, and the reinvoicing center.

Currency Clearing Centers A currency clearing center is based

upon a netting system. Many multinational companies have established multilateral netting systems in order to minimize the
cost of funds movement. The cost reduction results from centralizing all foreign exchange transactions in one location where
float can be minimized, exchange costs can be reduced, and
transfer commissions can be optimized. The currency clearing
center is managed by a coordinator who is responsible for ensuring that the individual companies participate in the clearing
and that any issues are resolved before the netting date.

For the company that has a regional treasurer, the currency
clearing center can be used to implement exposure management decisions. The regional treasurer has access to all of the
cross-border flows and can manage the exposures for the price
adjustment period. Thus, he would have the necessary information to take advantage of matching possibilities. He can also
take the necessary hedging decisions in the name of the center
and independently from the local companies. The results of his
actions would be recorded separately, and the benefits would
be allocated back through a management adjustment system.

In a simple example, suppose three subsidiary companies
regularly trade with each other and generate the following annual flows.

Exhibit 8
Trade without Currency Center

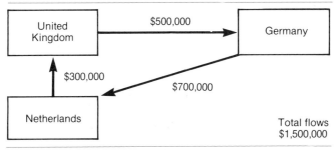

A currency clearing center or simple netting system would
reduce these flows and the resultant exchange costs by 73 percent. The net flows would be made as shown in Exhibit 9.

The clearing center would receive and pay $400,000, as shown
in Exhibit 10.

In this example, foreign exchange cost would be saved on
$1,100,000 or 73 percent of the flow.

Exhibit 9
Trade with Currency Center

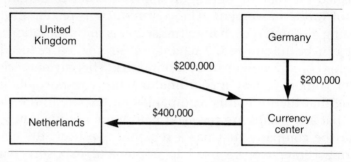

Exhibit 10

Without Currency Center			With Currency Center		
Buy	**Sell**	**Amount**	**Buy**	**Sell**	**Amount**
Guilders	Marks	$700,000	Guilders	Pounds	$200,000
Marks	Pounds	500,000	Guilders	Marks	200,000
Pounds	Guilders	300,000			$400,000
		$1,500,000			

Factoring Company There are several types of captive finance companies that purchase export receivables (with or without recourse) from operating units. The attraction of this evolving type of exposure management vehicle lies in its ability to separate treasury from operating concerns. Also, by including third-party customers in the factoring system, the factoring operation is in a position to centralize credit and accounts receivable control for the company as a whole.

The exchange exposure is centralized when the exporting company invoices its customers in their local currencies. This may require changing the invoicing system to bill in multicurrencies. The effect of this is to centralize the exposures in the exporting companies.

Exhibit 11
Trade without Factoring Company

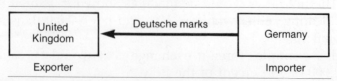

Exhibit 12
Trade with Factoring Company

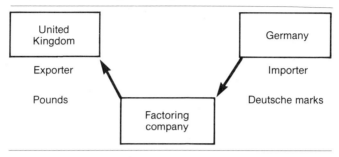

The factoring company then purchases this receivable using a deutsche mark discount rate and provides pounds to the exporting company.

Thus, the factoring concept is useful for companies that (1) have a trade financing need, (2) can bill in multicurrencies, (3) wish to centralize collection services.

Reinvoicing Centers A reinvoicing company is an intermediary company which acts as a centralized purchasing company. All importing companies place their orders on the reinvoicing company in local currency at guaranteed local prices and credit terms. The reinvoicing company then directs the order to the manufacturing or exporting company with instructions to ship the goods directly to the importer. Since the manufacturer receives the order in his currency on his trade terms, it is possible to centralize the exposure management and related trade financing in the reinvoicing company. The mechanics are illustrated in the following Exhibits.

By centralizing trade flows into one company, treasury has the maximum flexibility to manage its cross-border exchange exposure. Management time and expertise will be efficiently applied, and the results of hedging actions can be clearly iden-

Exhibit 13
Trade without Reinvoicing Company

Exporter has Deutsche mark exposure

Exhibit 14
Reinvoicing Company Assumes Exposure

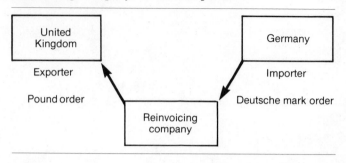

Exhibit 15
Reinvoicing Company Provides Trade Finance

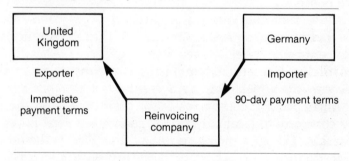

tified and evaluated. Since all intercompany flows will be centralized, transactions can be kept to a minimum. Trade financing can be selectively offered to the importing companies as required. The reinvoicing technique is most often applied when:

1. Company has significant intercompany flows and has followed a policy of centralizing its manufacturing in a few key manufacturing locations,
2. Advantages might accure from centralizing purchasing activity for a number of manufacturing sites that use the same commodity or raw material, or
3. A number of subsidiaries export to the same foreign customers and benefits can be obtained from centralizing credit and collections.

Protecting the cross-border cash flow of a company can be particularly difficult when a company is competing in international markets with foreign suppliers. The ability to protect prices in local currency terms and to maintain operating margins can be a challenging task for treasury.

Senior management, when designing a strategy for managing sourcing exposure should (1) locate the exposures in the most favorable location for management, (2) use standard market techniques to provide adequate protection for operating companies, (3) provide an adequate system for allocating the results of the hedging program to offset the impact of the underlying cash-flow exposure.

SUMMARY

In summary, the following checklist is provided for the chief financial officer wishing to review his exposure-management policy:

1. Does the policy differentiate between economic and accounting exposures and determine the appropriate guidelines for each?
2. Does the company separately identify investment and sourcing exposure and set criteria for managing each?
3. Does corporate policy clearly define treasury responsibilities and operating responsibilities for managing exposures?
4. Are there guidelines for determining the appropriate operating margins in different economic environments, and how can these be applied to the budgeting process?
5. Are there capital structure objectives for the overseas units and, what flexibility does treasury have in order to manage foreign currency debt?
6. Is there a dividend policy for the company, and does this take into account the need to reinvest a greater proportion of earnings in weaker economies?
7. How are sourcing patterns determined, and what flexibility does the company have to adjust them as economic conditions change?
8. What is the implicit price stability period required on cross-border sourcing and intercompany trade?
9. Does the company have a policy that sets hedging stan-

dards and objectives for protecting cross-border flows against currency movements?

10. Does the company have a transfer pricing policy, and is it consistent with the exposure management and tax management strategies?

11. Has the company reviewed all of the available structures for managing its cross-border flows?

12. Does the company evaluate the performance of financial management in managing exposures, and is this consistent with corporate objectives?

The answers to the above questions should determine where the company is most vulnerable in managing its foreign currency exposures.

18

Employee Compensation Outside the United States

Rennie Roberts and James A. Reid

Everyone who works knows what compensation is, just as everyone who eats knows what food is. While both notions enjoy a degree of universal acceptance, each varies considerably by geographic region. Generally speaking, cash payments are an internationally honored form of compensation; rice enjoys comparable acceptance as food. Certain types of compensation and food, however, are viewed quite differently from one part of the world to another. For example, Swedish labor law prescribes up to nine months state-paid leave for fathers of newborn children as a valid and valuable form of compensation. In societies where male and female roles remain more traditional, such as in Japan and Latin America, the idea would be considered absurd.

The key objective of this chapter is to consider the extraordi-

Rennie Roberts joined American Express Company in 1976 and is currently senior vice president–corporate human resources. Previously she held positions at Chase Manhattan Bank and Fleet National Corp. James A. Reid joined Associates for International Research, Inc. (AIRINC) in 1973. He is currently vice president and the firm's senior consultant to the financial and high technology industries.

nary variety in compensation practices around the world and to suggest ways for a company to evaluate the total cost of an international work force. The material will:

- Identify the employee groups in an international work force, the reasons behind employment of these groups, and the ways they are compensated.
- Provide guidance in estimating the total costs associated with these different work forces.
- Identify specific techniques for cost-effective compensation within and among these groups.
- Discuss why compensation costs can fluctuate rapidly in an international arena.

The definition of compensation varies widely, depending on one's perspective. A business executive's dictionary might read, "that which is given as equitable return for something rendered, usually services." The IRS and its international peers might define it as "anything of value which is given by an employer to an employee, and therefore subject to consideration for tax." An employee might say, "what I get to live on in return for working, usually less than what I need to live on." A company's accountants might suggest, "the direct cost of providing one of the resources which the company needs—people." Each of these views must be considered in order to design an effective compensation program which can then be integrated into the company's overall financial plan.

To achieve this goal, it is important to understand how the *selection* of the international work force affects compensation costs. Any truly international work force will contain employees of diverse national origin. They may be working in their respective home countries or in foreign lands. They will be compensated in very different ways, depending upon local custom, tax codes, and social legislation.

THE INTERNATIONAL WORK FORCE

The work forces of most international companies are made up of local nationals and expatriates. These are simply defined as employees who *are* and *are not* citizens of their country of employment, respectively.

Although a company may employ expatriates of many nationalities, their compensation usually has, within a company, a common conceptual thread. On the other hand, compensation of local nationals in different countries usually has little or no common ground.

U.S. corporations employ basically three kinds of expatriates in managerial positions.

> *U.S. expatriates*—Employees who originate in the company's base country (United States) and/or U.S. citizens who work in a country other than the United States, for example, U.S. nationals working in France.
>
> *Reverse transfers*—Employees who work in the company base country (U.S.) and who are not U.S. citizens, for example, German nationals working in the United States.
>
> *Third country nationals (TCNs)*—Employees of a U.S.-based company who originate in a country other than the United States and who work outside of their home country but not in the United States, for example, British nationals working in Singapore.

The table below summarizes the advantages and disadvantages of employing expatriates and local nationals.

	Expatriates	**Local Nationals**
Why?	Special technical or managerial expertise which may not be available locally.	Knowledge of country, political, business, social trends and customs, and language.
	Control from headquarters to reinforce corporate attitudes and objectives.	Their employment helpful to a foreign company's acceptance in a location.
	Flexibility to move from country to country as needed.	Generally less expensive than expatriates. No moving or incentive payments are required.

	Expatriates	Local Nationals
Why Not?	Costs generally much higher than those for local nationals, ranging from an additional 100 to 200 percent of cash compensation.	If the company wants to close down a business, termination indemnity payments can be significant.
	Not easily integrated into the local work force.	May not have the broad, corporate perspective desired for key management positions.

The compensation packages for the two groups are very different and are discussed below.

EXPATRIATE COMPENSATION

Most expatriates begin life as local Nationals. Prior to expatriation, they receive compensation in their country of origin consistent with local practice. This compensation yields a combination of purchasing power and savings ability to which, by definition, they have become accustomed. This combination is commonly called the living standard. The cost to "purchase" this living standard varies throughout the world. The living standard implicit in a predetermined amount of compensation shall be called, for this chapter's purpose, its *value*.

If the foreign compensation package suggests a reduction in living standard, it is difficult to recruit expatriates. As a result, most conventional expatriate compensation programs are designed so that the compensation received at the work country is equal or greater in *value* to that received by peers *in the home country*. These are called *home country based (HCB) compensation programs*, using the "Balance Sheet" approach.

The "Expatriate Balance Sheet" sorts home country compensation into its various elements, for example, salary is divided among income taxes, spendable income (to purchase goods and services), housing costs, and savings. It then adds or subtracts separately identified amounts of money so that each element is adjusted to be equal in *value* at the foreign location to what it was in the home country. The identification and reestablishment of compensation *value* on an element-by-element basis is the basic concept of the balance sheet.

With the balance sheet approach, the expatriate compensation package produced is unrelated to the compensation of local national peers in the work country. The expatriate on a HCB program is provided with a living standard that is equivalent to that enjoyed by his peers back in the home country.

HCB programs are the foundation of the vast majority of all U.S. expatriate compensation programs, a growing minority (30 to 40 percent) of all third country national programs, and a small but reluctantly growing minority (10 percent) of reverse transfer compensation programs. (This approach has been rarely used when bringing non-U.S. citizens to the United States on assignment because typical expatriate allowances are highly visible to home office employees. To reduce visibility, necessary allowances can be camouflaged in upfront payments made before the executive begins the assignment.)

The company cost to compensate expatriates will be very different than the cost to compensate them in their home country. Using the balance sheet approach, this variation is caused by four general factors:

1. The income taxes of the home and work countries.
    a. The rates at which earned income is taxed varies greatly from one country to another, due to widely differing procedures for determining taxable income from gross income, and the tax rate schedules themselves. For example, the maximum marginal tax rate in Hong Kong is 15 percent; in Denmark, it is 70 percent.
    b. Any difference in taxes for expatriates vis-a-vis local nationals will affect the company's cost to provide the compensation to expatriates. These differences may take the form of straight exclusions of part of income, such as have existed in the United Kingdom and in Belgium. Alternatively, they may allow imputing value to noncash compensation which is lower than its true market value, such as company leased housing in Japan. Naturally, this type of difference helps to reduce the company's cost to deliver a prescribed amount of net income.

2. The living cost factors of the two countries.
   a. If the cost to purchase normal consumer items is greater in the foreign country than in the home, this difference is measured as excess cost. This excess cost is normally covered with a cost-of-living differential.
   b. Changes in living patterns may also create excess cost for the expatriate. For example, in many developing countries, use of full-time domestic help is necessary to offset the lack of modern conveniences, to ensure security and so on.
   c. The absence of a financial history and/or the inability to speak the local language could require adjustments with cost consequences.

3. The incentive factor.
   a. This rewards the expatriate for uprooting his/her family and going on assignment far from home. If the country has less than adequate health, social and physical safety factors (a "hardship" post), the incentive payment will have to be significantly higher than for a modern Western European assignment. Also, more frequent rest and recreation trips will be needed, adding further to the "incentive" cost.

4. Relocation and other miscellaneous costs.
   a. At the beginning and end of the assignment, there are additional expenses, such as language training for the family, temporary housing costs, and moving of the family and household good to and from the location.

Economic and social disparity between the home and foreign location are the root of the compensation differences which are measured by the Balance Sheet. While it is difficult to generalize, it can be said that if the home country has low taxes and low living costs while the work country has high taxes, high living costs, and is a hardship post, the company cost will be much greater for an expatriate than for a home country peer. If the transfer is from a high tax, high cost country to a low tax, low cost, equally desirable country, then company cost for an expatriate could be less than that for a home country peer.

THE COMPENSATION ELEMENTS OF A HCB PROGRAM

The various elements of typical HCB systems are described below. First, annual ongoing costs are shown, next, costs to start and finish an expatriate assignment are shown. Exhibit 1, page 350 shows the range of costs based on these elements for a U.S. expatriate family of four in London, Tokyo, Rio de Janiero, and Saudi Arabia.

Annual Ongoing Costs

Program element/definition

Foreign service premium (incentive to leave the home country).

Commonly computed by formula as a percent of base salary with a cap. Usually the same for all foreign assignments in a company although it may vary according to compensation custom by country of employee origin, that is, U.S. and U.K. employees might have a different formula.

The range of premiums paid is broad and varies by industry.

Low: Zero.

Typical: 10 to 15 percent of salary; maximums $5,000 to $10,000.

High: 20 percent; maximums $10,000 to $15,000.

An alternative to this allowance is the mobility premium, paid in two lump sums at the start and completion of assignment.

Hardship premium (incentive for working in undesirable locations).

Commonly computed as a percent of base salary with a cap. Sometimes computed as a lump sum independent of salary, or a combination of percent and lump sum. Usually determined exclusively on the desirability of the work location.

The U.S. State Department pays its employees hardship premiums and publishes its structure which is the common reference. Allowances range from a minimum of zero for many developed countries to a maximum of 25 percent of salary for developing countries with high health risk and social/psychological isolation.

Low: Slightly less than State Department levels.

Typical: Equal to or slightly higher than State Department levels.

High: 150 to 200 percent of State Department levels.

Cost-of-living adjustors (offset higher living costs in country of assignment relative to country of origin; generally paid with monthly salary).

Most companies rely on outside services to compare living costs between home and foreign locations. Most services conduct continuing research on living costs on a global basis and provide recommendations to fit company requirements.

Moderate variation in recommendations from different services, leading to moderate variation in company practices. Small to moderate variation among industry groups.

Housing/utilities subsidy (full or partial compensation for housing at the country of assignment).

The difference between home and foreign housing costs is determined. *Home cost* usually determined from standard cost tables with homeownership assumed. *Foreign cost* determined either from standard tables or as actual cost incurred by employee, usually based on local rental. Information on foreign costs provided by outside services and/or foreign local management. When program operates on actual foreign cost incurred, a mechanism for cost approval *prior* to lease signing is usually established. Considerable variation among industry groups. Moderate variation among companies within an industry group. Foreign rental housing costs and payment procedures *vary enormously* around the world; costs in some areas can approach U.S. $100,000 per year.

Low: Tightly controlled subsidies based on actual cost incurred. Multiple sources of information and centralized approval mechanism usually associated with program.

Typical: Statistically determined subsidies based on information provided by outside services.

High: Actual cost incurred determines subsidy with few (if any) outside cost limits.

Home retention assistance (to help expatriate retain principal residence in home country and simplify repatriation).

Based on actual costs incurred. Small variation among industry groups and among companies:

Low: Verbal encouragement.

Typical: Reimbursement of property management fees associated with renting home while on assignment.

High: Additional reimbursement to cover difference (if any) between carrying costs and rent received.

Tax protection/ equalization

(to offset changes in income tax liabilities which exist between home and foreign countries).

Computed as difference between *hypothetical* home country income tax if expatriate had stayed home and if any *actual* income tax incurred while on assignment.

Tax Protection reimburses difference if *actual* taxes exceed *hypothetical*. If *actual* tax is less than *hypothetical*, companies rarely make any adjustment.

Tax Equalization deducts *hypothetical* from compensation and fully reimburses foreign taxes and actual home taxes (if any).

Most companies use Tax Equalization; a small minority has no formal program.

Low: Tax Equalization with a high hypothetical tax by design in selecting assumptions regarding its computation.

Typical: Tax Equalization with a hypothetical tax that is slightly less than would be indicated by pure statistical analysis.

High: Tax Equalization with low hypothetical tax.

Education subsidy

(for private education equivalent to that available in the normal public sector in home country).

Use actual costs incurred for tuition, fees, room, and board (if necessary). In each foreign location, maximum reimbursed costs are based on pre-selected, international schools.

Minimal variation among companies.

Low: No reimbursement.

Typical:	Use standard international schools to set maximum reimbursement.
High:	Allow full or partial additional reimbursement for higher cost schools.

Home leave
(annual visit for all family members to country of origin).

Computed as cost of round-trip airfares from foreign location to expatriate's point of origin plus transit costs (if any).

Small variation among companies.

Low:	Provided less frequently than annually, that is, two home leaves in a three year assignment. Coach class travel.
Typical:	Annual provision with vacation time set as greater of four weeks or normal expatriate vacation entitlement. Coach or business class travel.
High:	Pay computed value as cash whether employee returns to home country or not. Business or first class travel.

R&R (rest and relaxation)
(limited to expatriates in high hardship areas-such as Arab States, certain African countries).

Computed as actual cost incurred from foreign location to R&R site plus hotel expenses there. The number of annual R&Rs determined specifically for each area.

Moderate variation among industry groups. Small variation among companies within an industry group.

Low:	Limited to very high hardship areas. One or two R&Rs per year for a week's duration.

	Typical:	Limited to high hardship areas. Number of annual R&Rs determined by formula from hardship premium level.
	High:	Given in any location with a hardship premium. Number determined by formula from hardship premium level. Rarely exceeds three R&Rs per year.

Perquisites
(these vary by country, but could include servants' allowances, car, and so on).

Cost incurred or as a cash allowance to provide perquisites not received in home country but judged necessary under foreign conditions.

Considerable variation among industry groups. Moderate variation among companies within an industry group. Foreign conditions often dictate moderate variation among expatriates of one company.

Low:	Only those required by foreign law. Possibly offset in another component of pay package.
Typical:	Only those by legal obligation and strong, local precedent. Partial offset in other pay components.
High:	All legal and socially dictated perquisites. No offset in other pay components.

"Start and Finish Costs"

Orientation
(a support package ranging from language lessons to instructions in business and social customs).

Cost incurred.

Moderate variation among industry groups and among companies within an industry group.

Low:	In-house orientation briefings.

Typical: Foreign language instruction for expatriate and spouse. In-house orientation with multiple facets.

High: As above plus orientation package from professional service outside company.

Shipment of household effects.

Cost incurred to ship household/personal effects that are deemed by company to be required at foreign location.

Minimal variation among companies in concept. Wide variation based on foreign location.

Low: Only personal effects, with storage provision for furniture, and so on.

Typical: Excludes only items of unusual value or size. Personal effects by airfreight. Household by land or seafreight as necessary.

High: No common practice.

Temporary housing costs (paid until permanent housing is available).

Costs incurred or paid as a cash per diem. Usually limited by number of days with extensions available (if necessary).

Moderate variation among industry groups and companies within an industry group.

Low: Costs incurred for less than 30 days.

Typical: Costs incurred or per diem for 30 days.

High: Per diem for 30 days with routine extensions.

Transport over/back.

Cost incurred. Usually as provision of actual tickets for travel.

Minimal variation among industry

groups and among companies within an industry group.

Low: Coach class travel with direct routing.

Typical: Coach or business travel with extra transit day for large distances.

High: Business or first class travel with extra transit day for large distances.

Preassignment visit.

Cost incurred for travel and on-site expenses.

Considerable variation among industry groups. Moderate variation among companies within an industry group. Often limited within a company to higher job level expatriates.

Low: No provision.

Typical: Expatriate only and in conjunction with other business.

High: Expatriate and spouse with minimal business obligations and local support in viewing location.

Household setup allowance.

Cost incurred or paid as a lump sum allowance, computed as percent of salary up to prescribed limit, for example, $5,000.

Moderate variation among industry groups and among companies within an industry group.

Low: Costs incurred with limit determined as percentage of salary, usually one month's salary.

Typical: cash relocation allowance of one to two month's salary.

High: cash relocation allowance of

	two month's salary or costs incurred for large-scale refurbishing.
Visa/medical checks.	Cost incurred. Minimal variation among companies.
Auto Sale.	Guaranteed price on forced sale of private auto(s) just prior to transfer. Minimal variation among companies.
	Low: No provision.
	Typical: Referenced to standard auto value charts, that is Red book, Blue book, and so on, limited to two automobiles.
	High: No common practice.
Auto purchase.	Difference between foreign cost and home cost of "equivalent" new automobiles. Paid as lump sum with pro rata company ownership on sale. Loan may be provided to assist with employee share.
	Moderate variation among industry groups and among companies within an industry group.
	Low: Limited to one automobile, no loan assistance.
	Typical: One or two automobiles. Eligibility based on expatriate family size and foreign auto requirements. Low to moderate interest loan assistance.
	High: Two automobiles for families, interest free loan.

A Word about Salary and Benefits First, most expatriates' salary increases while on assignment are linked back to their home country salary program.

And, second, most expatriates also remain in their home country benefit plans if it is expected that they will return there following assignment. For others who are destined to move from one foreign assignment to another, companies often establish special programs to assure group insurance, pension, and other coverages.

Alternatives to the HCB Approach

The most common alternative is to structure expatriate compensation on practices in the country of assignment. Since expatriates normally expect something more than local nationals receive, the compensation package is often just that. Commonly called a *Country of Assignment* system, expatriates are given a compensation package identical to that of local nationals with something extra. The *extras* are usually some of the elements found in the HCB approach. Most commonly, incentive payments and housing subsidies *are* used; cost-of-living adjustors and tax equalizers, if used, are quite limited.

A commonly stated advantage to this approach is that a large part of the expatriate's compensation is geared to the local economy. This portion is adjusted in the same way that local national pay is adjusted. The extras are usually clearly associated with the temporary status of the expatriate. The overall effect is to make the expatriate's total pay package more understandable and acceptable to key local nationals. This type of approach is most commonly used for expatriate assignments where the transfer is within a geographic region, that is, TCNs on intra-European assignments, TCNs on intra-Latin America assignments, and for transfers between the United States and Canada.

Managing Expatriate Program Costs

The cost of maintaining expatriates overseas ranges from an additional 100 to 200 percent of salary. Despite this investment, expatriates are often unhappy with their compensation levels. Plan administrators who would like to control the costs frequently feel that, given the complaints often heard from expatriates, they cannot prune back or reshape programs to contain costs.

There are four primary ways, however, that expatriate compensation costs can be effectively reduced with a minimum of pain.

1. *Prudent tax planning* to minimize expatriate income taxes can often reduce costs without reducing compensation value to the expatriate. This can be achieved by paying compensation in forms other than cash. Foreign governments have widely varying views on imputing value for tax purposes to non-cash perquisites. In Japan, housing subsidies for expatriates will be fully taxed if paid in cash. However, if the company secures the lease and "provides" housing to the expatriate, the value imputed will be about 10 percent of the actual cost of the lease. Since housing costs and tax rates are very high in Japan, this is significant. Similar tax benefits occur in many other countries and can be associated with automobiles, social club memberships, company contracting for domestic help (drivers, home security guards, gardeners, and so on), as well as for housing. By providing some of these benefits in kind and equally reducing cash compensation, considerable tax savings can be achieved.

   The exclusion on foreign income up to $85,000 (in tax year 1984) provided by the 1981 Economic Tax Recovery Act also helps shelter some allowances from U.S. tax.

2. A *periodic review* of the package is vital and can result in cost savings. Are all its elements really needed? Value provided is often greater than necessary and can be reduced.

   Virtually every expatriate compensation package in existence contains incentive—either explicitly as in Foreign Service and hardship premiums or implicitly as in the subsidy of luxury housing accommodations, reduced tax obligations, increased vacation entitlement, and so on. A curious but understandable aspect of administration is that it is easier to add new incentive pieces than to eliminate or reduce old ones. There are some experienced administrators who feel that reducing incentives is "effectively" impossible since management often negotiates individual deals which exceed current policy. Over time, incentive pieces tend to accumulate in the expatriate compensation package. Any expatriate compensation system that has grown "organically" as a series of consecutive, isolated decisions rather than by design probably contains more incentive than is really needed.

   A regular review of the expatriate compensation program's objectives and elements can identify any excess amounts. Once identified, they can be controlled, reduced, or eventually eliminated.

3. *Keeping current on all international legislation* and treaties which could affect expatriate cost. The various treaties currently being negotiated which eliminate double Social Security taxation will help to lower costs.

4. *Controlling expatriate head count* and assignment length may be the most important system control of all. Use the Human Resources Management group to evaluate the need for expatriates in light of their cost. Assignment length is a two-sided issue. It is less costly to have one expatriate on a four-year assignment than to have two expatriates for two years each, simply by avoiding one set of start/finish costs. However, assignments which are longer than fruitful are needlessly costly. Where the long-range intent is to replace expatriates with local nationals, it may be appropriate to institutionalize in the review process the annual progress made toward this end, thereby encouraging timely assignment completion.

Exhibit 1
Cost of Mainstream United States Expatriate Overbase Compensation Package in Four Locations—Early 1980s

I *Ongoing Annual Costs*—Base Salary $40,000; Married with Two Children—(U.S.$ per year)

	London	Tokyo	Rio de Janeiro	Saudi Arabia
Foreign service premium				
Typical:	5,000	5,000	5,000	5,000
Range:	4–6,000	4–6,000	4–6,000	4–6,000
Hardship premium				
Typical:	0	0	0	8,000
Range:	0	0–2,000	0–4,000	6–12,000
Cost-of-living adjustors				
Typical:	5,000	12,000	4,000	10,000
Range:	3–8,000	10–15,000	2–6,000	8–12,000
Housing/utilities subsidy				
Typical:	18,000	25,000	12,000	35,000
Range:	15–25,000	20–30,000	10–15,000	30–40,000
Home retention assistance				
Typical:	1,000	1,000	1,000	1,000
Range:	500–1,500	500–1,500	500–1,500	500–1,500

Exhibit 1 (*continued*)

	London	Tokyo	Rio de Janeiro	Saudi Arabia
Tax protection/equalization				
Typical:	17,000	50,000	48,000	1,000
Range:	15–20,000	40–60,000	45–50,000	0–2,000
Education subsidy (2 children)				
Typical:	9,000	11,000	6,000	9,000
Range:	8–11,000	10–12,000	5–7,000	8–10,000
Home leave				
Typical:	4,000	7,000	6,000	7,000
Range:	3–5,000	6–8,000	5–7,000	6–8,000
R&R (rest & relaxation)				
Typical:	0	0	0	10,000
Range:	0	0	0–8,000	5–15,000
Furniture storage				
Typical:	1,500	1,500	1,500	1,500
Range:	1–2,000	1–2,000	1–2,000	1–2,000
New perquisites				
Typical:	3,000	2,000	3,000	4,000
Range:	1–5,000	1–4,000	1–5,000	2–6,000
Total ongoing annual costs				
Typical:	63,500	114,500	86,500	91,500
Total annual overbase as percent of base salary				
Typical:	159	286	217	229

II *Start/Finish Costs*—Base Salary $40,000; Married with Two Children (U.S.$)

	London	Tokyo	Rio de Janeiro	Saudi Arabia
Orientation				
Typical:	1,500	3,000	3,000	4,000
Range:	1–2,000	2–4,000	2–4,000	3–5,000
Shipment of household (both directions)				
Typical:	15,000	20,000	20,000	20,000
Range:	10–20,000	15–30,000	15–30,000	15–30,000
Temporary housing				
Typical:	5,500	5,000	4,000	6,000
Range:	3–10,000	3–10,000	2–8,000	3–12,000
Auto sale				
Typical:	1,000	1,000	1,000	1,000
Range:	0–2,000	0–2,000	0–2,000	0–2,000
Auto purchase				
Typical:	7,000	3,000	3,000	1,000
Range:	5–10,000	0–5,000	2–5,000	0–3,000
Mobility premium				
Typical:	Interchangeable in Cost with Foreign Service			
Range:	Premium and/or Hardship Premium			

Exhibit 1 (*concluded*)

	London	Tokyo	Rio de Janeiro	Saudi Arabia
Transport over/back				
Typical:	4,000	7,000	6,000	7,000
Range:	3–5,000	6–8,000	5–7,000	6–8,000
Preassignment visit (employees and spouse)				
Typical:	5,500	8,500	7,500	8,500
Range:	4–7,000	7–9,000	6–9,000	7–10,000
Household setup				
Typical:	4,000	4,000	4,000	4,000
Range:	3–6,000	3–6,000	3–6,000	3–6,000
Visa/medical checks				
Typical:	2,000	2,000	2,000	2,000
Range:	1–3,000	1–3,000	1–3,000	1–3,000
Total start/finish costs				
Typical:	45,500	53,500	50,500	53,500
Amortized over 3 year assignment				
Typical:	15,200	17,800	16,800	17,800

III Total annualized costs in addition to base salary, bonus, and normal home country benefits for a U.S. expatriate (salary $40,000; married with two children) on a three-year assignment. (Annual Ongoing Costs + Start/Finish Costs)

	London	Tokyo	Rio de Janeiro	Saudi Arabia
Typical (U.S.$):	78,700	132,300	103,300	109,300
Typical (as percent of base salary):	197	331	258	273

Many of the costs shown on the preceding Exhibits would be significantly reduced for expatriates without families. As an approximate measure, the last line is repeated for single status.

IV Total Annualized Costs in addition to base salary, bonus, and normal home country benefits for a U.S. expatriate (salary $40,000; single) on a three-year assignment. (Annual Ongoing Costs + Start/Finish Costs)

	London	Tokyo	Rio de Janeiro	Saudi Arabia
Typical (U.S.$):	42,700	73,500	57,700	58,500
Typical (as percent of base salary):	107	184	144	146

LOCAL NATIONAL COMPENSATION

The compensation of locals in any country results from its social and economic history. The overall productivity of a country's economy plays a large role in determining its general wage levels and living standards. The relative shortage or abundance of specific labor skills sort out this general level. Its social attitudes, as enforced by government (primarily through the tax structure), affect the way this total wealth is distributed. No two countries are identical in these areas at present. As a result, the variety of compensation elements found around the world is dramatic. There are only two constants—all local nationals are paid a salary and, in almost all countries, taxes on personal income must be paid. The size of the tax bite often determines the other elements in the local national package.

Base Salary The primary component of compensation in most countries is established in the currency of that country. By selecting exchange rates and converting the salaries of local nationals to a common currency, it becomes apparent that considerable variation exists.

Typical salaries for local nationals at two management job levels in 18 countries are shown on Exhibit 2 as an approximate guide to relative pay levels. The salary amounts shown are typical annual base compensation and include not only "conventional" salary but also the numerous "bonuses" which are legally mandated or effectively institutionalized by years of precedent, such as vacation bonuses, Christmas bonuses, 13th month's pay, 14th month's pay, and so on. The amounts shown on the chart include these common bonuses as part of annual compensation but exclude discretionary management bonuses. The salaries are shown in U.S. dollars (exchange rate noted) and as an index with the United States having a salary index of 100.

Exhibit 2 was created from 1983 local national salaries which were expressed in local currency, that is, £, DM, FF, and so on, and converted using 1983 exchange rates. The local currency salary amounts will change based on wage movement in each country which is not uniform. Secondly, exchange rate fluctuation will alter the relationships. The purpose of Exhibit 2 is simply to demonstrate the variation in salary levels, not to suggest a fixed relationship among countries.

A Note of Caution When examining what appear to be in-

Exhibit 2
Local Nationals—Comparative Salary Levels Early 1980s (1983), Annual Salary plus Mandatory Bonuses

		Job A		Job B	
	Exchange 1 U.S.$=	U.S.$	Salary Index	U.S.$	Salary Index
United States	$1.00	$40,000	100	$60,000	100
Australia	A$1.10	27,000	68	45,000	75
Belgium	BF50	38,000	95	60,000	100
Brazil	CR450	29,000	73	46,000	77
Canada	C$1.20	35,000	88	54,000	90
Egypt	E£0.8	14,000	35	25,000	42
France	FF7,00	33,000	83	54,000	90
Germany	DM2.40	41,000	103	63,000	105
Hong Kong	HK$6.75	28,000	70	45,000	75
India	RP9.9	20,000	50	35,000	58
Indonesia	RP965	16,000	40	30,000	50
Italy	LIT1400	24,000	60	38,000	63
Japan	Y235	30,000	75	43,000	72
Singapore	S$2.10	31,000	78	52,000	87
Sweden	SK7.40	23,000	58	41,000	68
Switzerland	SF2.00	50,000	125	77,000	128
United Kingdom	£.60	28,000	70	44,000	73
Venezuela	B4.30	44,000	110	68,000	113

ternational salaries stated in weekly or monthly terms, remember that the annual salaries may not be the amounts shown times 52 or 12, respectively. Even annual salaries are occasionally quoted in some countries without including the mandatory bonus amounts of the 13th or 14th month, for example.

Taxes on Income

Almost anyone who earns money pays taxes. Even in Saudi Arabia, there is a Social Security Tax. Just as the basic salary amount varies greatly from country to country, so does the amount of income tax associated with a fixed amount of income. Exhibit 3 shows the total income tax at two management salary levels in 18 countries. Each set of columns represents a fixed amount of income, not a common job level, and its normal income tax liability for a family of four. The income tax amounts shown are as a percent of income and as an index with the United States as the reference point (100). The relationships vàry from one income level to the other, reflecting the range of variation in the ways that the tax rate schedules progress. Also, the relative tax on single individuals vis-a-vis large families with equal income also varies greatly from country to country.

From a company standpoint, the income tax rates are important for at least two reasons.

1. The company's ability to reward higher level employees with cash compensation is strongly affected by high marginal tax rates. For example, a senior employee in Sweden may be in a marginal tax bracket of 85 percent. Increased cash of the Swedish kroner equivalent of U.S. $10,000 would yield only U.S. $1,500 to the employee. Alternatives to cash are clearly desirable, especially alternatives with preferential tax treatment.

2. High tax rates may indicate that certain fringe benefits are provided by the government and reduce or eliminate the need

Exhibit 3
Local Nationals—Total Income Tax Liability (Effective rate), Family of Four
1982

	Exchange 1 U.S.$=	Income Tax on Salary= U.S.$30,000		Income Tax on Salary= U.S.$60,000	
		Percent	Index	Percent	Index
United States	$1.00	20	100	25	100
Australia	A$1.10	27	133	43	168
Belgium	BF50	39	192	53	207
Brazil	CR450	33	163	39	154
Canada	C$1.20	17	83	27	105
Egypt	E£0.8	24	121	28	111
France	FF7,00	13	64	20	78
Germany	DM2.40	27	135	34	134
Hong Kong	HK$6.75	15	74	15	59
India	RP9.9	40	200	53	211
Indonesia	RP965	31	154	38	151
Italy	LIT1400	29	143	38	148
Japan	Y235	21	105	31	121
Singapore	S$2.10	26	132	29	115
Sweden	SK7.40	41	206	55	218
Switzerland	SF2.00	12	59	24	96
United Kingdom	£.60	22	111	30	120
Venezuela	B4.30	8	38	9	37

for private programs. The high tax rates in most Scandinavian countries reflect a well developed government program for assuring the financial security of retired workers. Private programs to supplement this are unnecessary for the vast majority of Swedish employees. By contrast, U.S. employers fund separate retirement programs for their employees, encouraged by the government to do so by tax incentives for the employer and employee.

The number and types of income taxes which exist in different countries can provide opportunity for extended study. In the United States, a worker may pay five or more separate income taxes (federal, state, county or city, FICA, unemployment, and so on) which in total make the United States a low to moderate income tax country by international standards. In Australia, there is only a national income tax from which all government activity is funded; Australia's one tax makes it a high tax country by international standards. The income tax liabilities shown on Exhibit 3 include all income taxes regardless of name or collection point.

Other Compensation Elements

The typical local national compensation program will include many of the programs described below. The number and the importance of each element will vary greatly by country. Each has important cost implications for doing business.

Benefits

Retirement/Pension Most U.S. companies fund private programs which provide benefits in addition to, and frequently integrated with, the U.S. Social Security program. Local national employees' retirement benefits are frequently provided via locally established plans if Social Security benefits are not sufficient to provide adequate retirement income after a full career.

Where the population is too small to warrant a plan, a company might include employees of many countries in one plan intended to offer some level of retirement income protection. These plans are usually established at headquarters.

Typically, local plans are funded by annual contributions to a trust, an insurance contract, or a book reserve. The amounts contributed or booked are usually determined by actuarial judgments about the future and current benefits provided and investment performance.

Many "socialized" countries arrange for retirement security through state funding and make private funding unnecessary or minimal. In some developing countries, however, companies must establish private programs to attract skilled workers or local management level employees. Because of the relative economic instability of these governments, the offering of substantive long-term financial security may be the most important type of compensation offered to qualified local employees.

The company's pension cost may occur in two ways:

1. It may be fully or partially buried in gross cash compensation (funded by income taxes).
2. Additional company contributions may be required to supplement the amounts contributed by employees through their income taxes or fully funded private programs.

Medical Insurance Governments frequently participate in the provision of medical services. Funds are collected through income taxes and used to subsidize a wide range of medical programs, including hospitals, medical centers, doctors' fees, medicines, and so on. Cost to the user ranges from zero to modest.

In countries such as the United States, where government involvement is minimal, companies commonly fund private programs of medical insurance that provide a similarly wide range of subsidization. Private plans may also be provided to senior staff in countries where government programs are overcrowded or are judged inadequate to meet a high level of expectation as in the United Kingdom.

Life Insurance Life insurance tends to be a universal benefit, but amounts of coverage vary greatly by country. In addition, employee eligibility may depend on service or job rank requirements. These criteria for participation appear more frequently in foreign plans than in the United States where coverage in some multiple of salary generally applies to all.

In a few countries, life insurance coverage is not an effective benefit because the beneficiary is heavily taxed on the proceeds.

Perquisites

Company Automobiles One of the most famous noncash perquisites in the world is the company car. In the United States, cars are usually provided only to employees whose jobs require use of a car or to very senior executives. If a car is provided for purely personal use, the value of that perquisite must be reported as income and is taxed fully in the United States.

Company cars are used in many countries, however, as a noncash perquisite. They usually are provided to employees of certain job levels and are often given preferential tax treatment. In England, most companies provide cars to all employees above a particular job level; the job grade chosen is probably best described as middle management or one that would carry an annual salary of approximately U.S. $35,000 in the United States. The income attributed for tax purposes to the provision of a company car is much lower than its real cost. As income tax rates have decreased in England, however, the value imputed by the Inland Revenue Service to company cars has increased.

In some countries, a cash amount is paid as a transportation allowance instead of providing a company car. This payment, where common, often receives comparable preferential tax treatment.

Subsidized Loans Another common, noncash perquisite is permitting employees to borrow from the company at interest rates significantly below regular bank rates. The most important use is in home mortgages, which is particularly common in the banking industry. In many countries in Western Europe, employees of banks may borrow amounts up to predetermined multipliers on their salary at very low interest rates. Being an employee in good standing may be all that is necessary to qualify. Personal loans with lower limits are very common. This benefit is rarely taxed.

Subsidized Meals Company subsidized cafeterias are common in the United States and pervasive in other parts of the world. When the company does not have a cafeteria on premise, a voucher program may be used to obtain meals at private restaurants near the company.

Social Clubs/Entertainment Allowances Company paid memberships in sports and social clubs are common perquisites for high level management in many countries. In Australia, a tax-free entertainment allowance of approximately A$3,000 per year is paid to managers. The company credit card is also a valuable form of compensation for senior managers in many countries.

Vacation In the United States, typical vacation entitlements for most employees is two to three weeks per year. Four weeks or more usually comes only with considerable seniority or service. In Europe, however, four weeks is common for all employees, and senior executives generally receive even more.

Holidays These are defined as predetermined or floating days on which the entire work force is paid to stay home. Those who work are paid at premium rates.

The number of paid holidays in the United States is typically ten, with additional personal days available. Internationally, it ranges from ten to fifteen.

Termination Indemnity A major cost factor often forgotten when looking at local national compensation stems from termination indemnity. A termination indemnity is an amount of money usually based on service that must be paid to an employee upon leaving the company. Events which trigger payments vary by country. In some, it is considered an acquired right and is payable on retirement, death, disability, and, in certain instances, resignation, for example, India and Greece. In other countries, a payment is made only on a dismissal; sometimes a mandatory retirement is considered a dismissal, and a payment must be made. In some countries, termination indemnities aren't legally required but are prevalent practice. In these cases, the indemnity is frequently part of a labor contract or an employment contract, for example, Germany. As a result, closing down an operation can be extraordinarily expensive.

Depending on the country, the additional company cost for local national compensation can range from as little as an additional 20% to near 100% of gross salary. The United States is a good example of a low "additional cost" country while Japan and the Scandinavian countries are examples of high additional cost countries.

VOLATILITY

In 1973, one U.S. dollar was routinely exchanged into ten Argentine pesos. In 1983, one U.S. dollar was routinely exchanged into ten Argentine "new" pesos. The difference between the 1983 new pesos and the 1973 pesos was the simple mathematical factor of 10,000. Only the renaming of the pesos occurred suddenly; the peso's value dropped in bumps and spurts throughout the 10 year span. This massive devaluation was accompanied by price inflation of comparable magnitude in Argentina. Because the currency devaluation and the internal inflation rates were not always synchronized, Argentina showed a level of volatility that fully frustrated forecasters.

In 1973, Buenos Aires was (and today is) a moderately inexpensive city by international standards. In the intervening years, it was alternatively extremely inexpensive and extremely expensive. The cost to compensate expatriates in Buenos Aires rose and fell in dramatic fashion as unsynchronized inflation and devaluation ran their 10,000-fold courses. Cost-of-living indexes for U.S. expatriates in Buenos Aires wandered up and down a range from 65 to over 200. When measured in U.S. dollars, compensation costs for local nationals were equally volatile. The salaries for Argentine nationals, when compared to salaries of U.S. peers, ranged from roughly one half to two and a half times the U.S. salary scale for equivalent positions. While Argentina is an extreme example, the point is that compensation costs vary rapidly in most developing countries. The potentially volatile combination of high general inflation and soft currency exists in most countries in Latin America and in Africa.

Rapid change may also occur in countries where international business is rapidly expanding. When increasing numbers of expatriates enter an area with a limited supply of good quality housing, local landlords respond quickly. High housing costs in Asia and in the Middle East reflect the influx of foreign business more than any other factor.

Though generally of lesser concern, the costs for expatriates will be affected by changes in tax laws or local living conditions. Changes in the taxation of expatriates may stem from changes in statute, in interpretation of existing statutes, or in new home country "tax effective" programs. For example, the granting of incentive stock options to U.S. expatriates who then exercise those options while overseas can significantly increase equalization costs. The gain attracts local tax which in certain countries will be significant. Since most expatriates are compensated relative to their home country counterparts, any adverse local tax changes would normally increase the company's expense. A deterioration of local living conditions would normally require an increase in incentive payments to expatriates.

Clearly, the establishment and administration of compensation programs for an international work force is a very complex task. Its complexity results largely from the need to deal with the financial complications of multiple currencies and differing rates of inflation while being constrained by multiple and disparate customs, laws, and employee expectations.

The importance of planning, constant monitoring, and realistic administration cannot be overstated. In the international environment, many line managers balk at what they view as cumbersome administration, preferring a "seat-of-the-pants" approach with its associated "hands-on" intuitive grasp and quick response opportunities. While this approach can be successful, it is narrowly focussed, viewing compensation issues as ones to be quickly decided in order to get on with the important business. It can result in the haphazard and unnecessarily expensive use of expatriates. Such an approach usually fails to contain compensation costs over long periods of time and often creates precedents which have expensive long-term implications.

In recent years, the concept of "cafeteria" benefit plans has gained popularity in the United States. Whatever the value of the offerings in the world's different "cafeterias," the notion is useful in considering the design of international compensation packages. From a broad menu of compensation "edibles," the company can select and offer "foodstuffs" in the proper portions to satisfy the appetites of expatriates and local nationals while keeping a close watch on the company's waistline.

PART FIVE

Public Reporting
and Relationships

19

Meeting Public Disclosure Requirements

Joseph E. Connor

Charged with the primary responsibility of ensuring the organization's compliance with public disclosure requirements, the CFO is confronted with a formidable array of regulatory and professional requirements—rules which specify how much, when, and in what format information about the company's financial affairs is to be disclosed.

Since the modern era of financial reporting was spawned by the passage of the Securities Acts in the early 1930s, the laws and regulations enacted by the public sector and the accounting standards initiated by the private sector have consistently expanded and seldom contracted the body of financial information available to the public. Corporate options to select accounting methods are dwindling as accounting rule makers, in a move to promote uniformity, have prescribed specific methods for treating more and more types of business events and transactions. Regulatory authorities responsible for oversight exert a

Joseph E. Connor is chairman and senior partner of Price Waterhouse. He has written widely on public policy issues, has served on several presidential councils, and is involved in numerous business and civic activities.

strong continuing influence on the accounting and reporting process.

The purpose of this chapter is to present an overview of existing requirements and emerging trends which indicate possible future directions. It describes the fundamentals of the U.S. financial disclosure system, discusses the more important recent expansions in disclosure requirements, and examines several specific unresolved issues. The final section briefly describes movements toward international accounting standards. As an exhaustive treatment of many of the topics addressed here would require entire volumes, the discussion of each is necessarily limited to a brief summary, intended to highlight key features and explain their significance.

THE DISCLOSURE SYSTEM

Public Sector/Private Sector Roles

Unlike many other jurisdictions, the United States does not have a federally mandated financial disclosure system. Instead, public disclosure of corporate financial information is governed by a unique structure in which the Securities and Exchange Commission, the Financial Accounting Standards Board and the public accounting profession each play important roles.

The Securities and Exchange Commission (SEC) has broad statutory authority to prescribe the form and content of filings under the acts that it administers, and the commission also has the responsibility to ensure that investors are provided with adequate information. Comprehensive sets of commission rules govern the form and content of, and requirements for, financial statements filed in compliance with the acts. Over the years, the commission has published views and interpretations relating to financial reporting in Accounting Series Releases (ASRs), Financial Reporting Releases (FRs), and Staff Accounting Bulletins (SABs). But, historically, the commission, as a matter of policy, has looked to the private sector to establish and improve accounting standards.

Since its formation in 1973, the seven-member, full-time Financial Accounting Standards Board (FASB) has been the designated organization in the private sector for establishing financial accounting and reporting standards. These standards, the principal component of generally accepted accounting principles (GAAP), are developed through an often extensive process of research and analysis and are issued pursuant to prescribed due process procedures.

The corporations which must comply with standards established by the FASB are among the groups comprising the FASB's constituency. Through the mechanisms provided in the FASB structure, they provide financial support and contribute their views about standards under consideration. This active support fosters voluntary compliance with the standards issued.

In the absence of voluntary compliance, two formal mechanisms act to compel public companies to comply with board standards. First, Rule 4–01 of SEC Regulation S–X requires the use of GAAP in SEC filings. Second, the Code of Professional Ethics of the American Institute of Certified Public Accountants (AICPA) provides that, except in very unusual circumstances, auditors must follow FASB pronouncements in reporting on client financial statements. The latter rule acts to make the audited financial statements of nonpublic companies subject to FASB standards.

Attorneys and underwriters also have important roles in ensuring compliance with mandated public disclosure requirements. Filings with the SEC are legal documents requiring expert legal advice on compliance with often complex requirements. Underwriters are subject to civil liability under Section 11 of the 1933 Act if they knowingly distribute securities covered by a false or misleading registration statement. Accordingly, they have a legitimate interest in the contents of documents prepared as part of the registration process and exert influence on that process in various ways.

Despite its stated reliance on the private sector to establish standards, the SEC exerts substantial influence on the FASB's actions. A close working relationship between the commission and the FASB ensures that final standards are consistent with SEC views. On one occasion, the SEC overruled the board; it rejected an FASB standard for reporting by oil and gas producing companies and embarked on an attempt, later aborted, to develop an alternative system.

SEC concurrence with an FASB standard is often exhibited by withdrawal of the commission's regulations in the subject area. If, however, experience shows that a new FASB standard is not producing a satisfactory level of disclosure, the commission may act to remedy the situation by regulation. The commission's perception that current reporting problems warrant timely attention also may be the source of regulatory action.

Chapter 20 discusses relationships with the SEC and FASB in greater detail.

Broad Objectives

The central objective underlying SEC rules and regulations in the disclosure area is described in the commission's 48th annual report to Congress as follows: "The Commission's full disclosure system insures that full and accurate material information about publicly traded companies is available to investors."

FASB's focus on financial disclosure is somewhat broader. Its user orientation extends to creditors and numerous other users of financial information, including those interested in the reports of nonpublic companies, as well as investors. Although the FASB uses such terms as "relevance" and "reliability" to describe the characteristics of financial information, the essential goal is full and accurate disclosure.

Decisions on the specific types of information necessary to meet these objectives are the prerogatives of the SEC and FASB. The underlying thrust of disclosure objectives is, however, of paramount importance to preparers who have the ultimate responsibility for providing the information that will reach investors and other users. The words "full," "accurate" and "material" in the SEC description are particularly important to preparer decisions.

Rule 4–01 of Regulation S–X makes it clear that full disclosure for preparers goes beyond specific prescriptions. It states, in part: "The information required . . . shall be furnished as a minimum requirement to which shall be added such further material information as is necessary to make the required statements, in the light of the circumstances under which they are made, not misleading."

The word "material" appears repeatedly in SEC regulations and FASB statements are issued with the proviso that they need not be applied to immaterial items.

Rule 1–02 (n) of Regulation S–X defines "material" as follows: "The term "material," when used to qualify a requirement for the furnishing of information as to any subject, limits the information required to those matters about which an average, prudent investor ought reasonably to be informed."

Compliance with the spirit, not merely the letter, of disclosure rules requires judgment in determining the nebulous lines separating what is material from what is not and in evaluating the facts and circumstances to ensure that statements made are not misleading through either misstatement or omission.

The Foreign Corrupt Practices Act (FCPA)

That the information furnished to investors be reliable and contain no material misleading statements has been a cornerstone of the public disclosure system since the passage of the securities acts. The accounting provisions of the Foreign Corrupt Practices Act (FCPA), enacted in 1977, look beyond the information reported to the internal mechanisms that affect its preparation.

Hastily enacted in response to the questionable payments revelations of the early 1970s, FCPA carries a dual-pronged fix— a direct attack on the perceived problem in the antibribery provisions and the far broader solution sponsored by the SEC in the accounting provisions. The latter requirements lift record keeping and internal control system considerations from the private domain of management and make them matters of law.

FCPA, technically Section 13(b)(2) of the Securities Exchange Act of 1934, requires public companies to:

- Keep financial records which, in "reasonable" detail, accurately and fairly reflect transactions and asset dispositions.
- Maintain a system of internal accounting control sufficient to provide reasonable assurance that certain stated objectives are met. Among the objectives drawn directly from professional auditing standards, to ensure preparation of financial statements in accordance with GAAP and to maintain accountability for assets.

FCPA's accounting provisions have been widely criticized for their lack of clarity. For example, there is no specific reference to materiality or to the cost/benefit determinations necessary to establish "reasonable assurance." There is no guidance on what constitutes a violation and no amplification of the "reasonable detail" and "accurately and fairly reflect" criteria applicable to financial records.

Spurred primarily by perceived unfavorable effects of the antibribery provisions on U.S. foreign trade, legislation to amend FCPA has been under consideration for some time. A bill passed by the Senate in 1981 would have clarified the act's accounting provisions and eased some of the penalties for noncompliance but would not have changed the act's principal message: A reasonably sound internal accounting control system is required. Substantially similar bills have been introduced in Congress several times, the latest in 1985.

The proposed clarifying changes, whether eventually enacted or not, strongly support the pragmatic approach taken by most managements in undertaking an FCPA compliance program. Such programs involve four basic steps:

- Evaluate and document the existing system, identifying any material weaknesses.
- Use cost/benefit analysis to determine the disposition of identified weaknesses, documenting the action taken and, if applicable, the reasons why correction was not considered practical.
- Provide for continuous monitoring of compliance with the system.
- Provide mechanisms to ensure that control procedures are revised as necessary when operating conditions change and that system documentation is updated.

Viewing FCPA compliance as a continuing obligation is extremely important. The accounting provisions are a part of the SEC's arsenal and have been invoked in a number of actions (in all cases, however, in tandem with assertions of noncompliance with other provisions of the securities acts). Documentation that is badly outdated in the face of changed conditions would be unlikely to be persuasive in the event the company's compliance with FCPA were challenged. Current documentation is also critical if management elects, as discussed in the next section, to report publicly on the status of its internal control system.

Management Reports on Internal Controls

The issuance of a formal management report accompanying an entity's published financial statements is a recent phenomenon based entirely on voluntary action.

Although management reports appeared earlier in the annual reports of a few leading-edge companies, the concept first received widespread attention with the publication in 1977 of the tentative conclusions of the Commission on Auditors' Responsibilities (Cohen Commission), an independent study group commissioned by the AICPA. Endorsements issued a short time later by the Financial Executives Institute and by a special AICPA advisory committee were soon followed by a significant increase in the number of companies publishing management reports.

SEC interest has made the status of the internal accounting control system a focal point of management reports, but that topic is only one of several originally suggested for coverage and frequently found in practice. Other subjects include:

- Acknowledgement of management's responsibility for preparation of the financial statements and other reported financial information.
- Assurances that the statements have been prepared in accordance with GAAP and that all material uncertainties have been addressed properly.
- Descriptions of the work of the company's audit committee and internal auditors.
- Discussions of codes of ethics.

In April 1979, the SEC issued proposed rules[1] which would have required the inclusion of a statement of management on internal accounting control in annual reports to shareholders and in reports on Form 10–K. After a one-year, phase-in period, an examination and report on such statements by independent auditors also would have been required. Clearly a derivative of FCPA, the release stated that such reporting "may be necessary to enable investors to better evaluate management's performance of its stewardship responsibilities and the reliability of interim financial statements and other unaudited financial information generated from the accounting system."

These proposals evoked a flood of comment letters, and, in June 1980, the SEC formally withdrew them but stated that it would continue to monitor voluntary developments in the private sector. The monitoring phase came to an end in a January

---

[1] *Release No. 34–15772 Securities Exchange Act of 1934*, April 30, 1979.

1982 release[2] which concluded: "Although the importance to companies of effective systems of internal accounting control has not diminished, the Commission now believes that there is no need for a regulatory requirement for disclosure about such systems."

With the threat of regulatory intervention thus removed, managements were free to decide the management report question on its own merits, but some strings remain. The SEC's decision was based on tangible evidence of significant private sector initiatives in the subject area. If later events indicate that industry has failed to keep its own house in order, regulatory action to correct the perceived deficiency will almost certainly follow.

Whether management reports attesting to the reliability of financial statements and the control systems which support them add measurably to investor confidence is an important unknown. Many such reports have become mechanistic recitations which, like the standard auditors' report, might be more noticed by the average investor if absent than if present.

Quite possibly, the report itself is accessorial—a prod to ensure that the structure behind the report language is firmly in place. Because public reporting automatically adds to management exposure, knowledgeable CFOs understand clearly that failure to ensure that statements made are supported by underlying facts is playing with fire. Consequently, the matters reported upon tend to receive closer attention than they otherwise might. If the movement toward voluntary public reporting continues, the result over the long term will have been a significant improvement in the overall reliability level of the public disclosure system.

EXPANDED DISCLOSURE REQUIREMENTS

During the past decade the real or perceived needs of the users of financial information have become the central focus of the accounting standards-setting process. Users are seen as no longer satisfied with the presentation once a year of financial statements containing a record of past events. They are seen as de-

---

[2] *SEC Accounting Series Release No. 305,* January 28, 1982.

manding more frequent information that sheds some light on a company's prospects in the future.

This user focus is unquestionably proper, simple recognition that financial reporting has a central purpose. It is also the source of expanded disclosure requirements—an expansion which is checked, at least in part, by recognition of preparer considerations. The legitimate needs of users for information about a company's affairs must be balanced against preparer capability to supply reliable information of the type perceived as desirable and to do so cost-effectively and without harm to the interests of the business.

Recognition of user interest is changing the character of financial statements. The more pronounced effects of this focus are evident in the macro view of financial reporting developed to accommodate numerous collateral forms of financial disclosure outside the formal financial statements.

This section examines recent expansions in disclosure requirements: disaggregated information, more timely information, interpretive information, continuous reporting, and supplementary information. Some of these concepts are well developed; others are the initial phases of emerging trends. Those which are not solely SEC requirements are directly traceable to SEC influence on the standards-setting process.

Disaggregated Information—Segment Reporting

The differences in such factors as rates of profitability, risk, and opportunities for growth that may exist among the various industry segments and geographic areas of operations of an enterprise are the source of views that investors need disaggregated information as well as consolidated financial information or information presented on a total-enterprise basis.

When Statement of Financial Accounting Standards No. 14, *Financial Reporting for Segments of a Business Enterprise* (FAS 14),[3] became effective for fiscal years beginning after December 15, 1976, line-of-business reporting was already required in filings with the commission and shareholder reports of SEC registrants. And, based on the notion that "most foreign assets stand

---

[3]FASB *Statement of Financial Accounting Standards No. 14*, (Stamford, Conn., December 1976).

in some degree of jeopardy," specified disclosures about foreign operations had been required by authoritative accounting pronouncements for over thirty years.[4]

FAS 14 requires that, where its provisions apply, consolidated financial information be disaggregated to show summary indicators of performance in industries and in geographic areas which meet specified materiality criteria. Disaggregated information on revenue, operating profit or loss or, for geographic segments, an alternative measure of profitability, and identifiable assets is required to be reported in a format showing the reconciliation to the corresponding total-enterprise aggregates. Intersegment sales must be shown separately, and the basis of pricing such sales must be described. Export sales and sales to any single customer, including a government, that meets specified materiality criteria must also be disclosed.

FAS 14, as amended, applies when complete sets of financial statements for annual fiscal periods are presented by publicly held companies. FAS 24, *Reporting Segment Information in Financial Statements That Are Presented in Another Enterprise's Financial Report*,[5] requires that segment data be presented in some of the named circumstances but not in others.

The SEC has conformed its requirements in most respects with FAS 14, as amended. It requires that segment data accompany the financial statements for each period for which an audited income statement is presented and requires three-year presentations as a part of the description of business requirements covered by Item 101 of Regulation S–K. Although a FAS 14 requirement for segment data in complete interim financial statements has been removed by amendment, the SEC may conclude, in given circumstances, that some segment data is necessary for a fair and reasonable understanding and appraisal of interim reports. A 1984 SEC proposal, if adopted, would require inclusion of certain segment data in quarterly filings with the Commission.[6]

---

[4] AICPA *Accounting Research Bulletin No. 4*, "Foreign Operations and Foreign Exchange," (New York, December 1939) paragraphs 4–6 which were incorporated without substantial change in *Accounting Research Bulletin No. 43*, "Restatement and Revision of Accounting Research Bulletins," June 1953, chapter 12, paragraphs 6 and 9. These requirements are still in effect.

[5] FASB *Statement of Financial Accounting Standards No. 24*, (Stamford, Conn.), December 1978.

[6] *Securities Exchange Act of 1934 Release No. 34N-20657*, February 15, 1984.

Industry segment determination has been one of the principal problems in applying FAS 14. Although suggesting various means of grouping products and services, the statement acknowledges that the determination depends to a considerable extent on management judgment. Problems encountered in practice led the SEC to issue the guidance now incorporated in *Codification of Financial Reporting Policies*, Section 503.03.

Appendix D of FAS 14 discusses three factors to be considered in determining industry segments: nature of the product, nature of the productive process, and markets and marketing methods. For purposes of combining countries for reporting by geographic area, paragraph 34 states that the factors to be considered include proximity, economic affinity, similarities in business environments, and the nature, scale, and degree of interrelationship of the enterprise's operations. In both cases, the goal is to report segments which are homogeneous in terms of rates of profitability, opportunities for growth, and degrees and types of risks.

Most subject companies have accumulated experience in applying FAS 14. It is, however, important to recognize that the tests specified must be applied separately for each new fiscal year and that each new year may bring implementation questions that have not been previously addressed.

Segment reporting is deeply ingrained in SEC requirements, as well as the subject of a definitive professional standard. There is little question that it is a permanent extension of financial reporting necessary to an understanding of the activities of today's complex business organizations.

Timely Information—Interim Reporting

Periodic interim financial reporting meets a perceived investor need for more up-to-date information than that provided by annual financial reports.

The relatively longstanding practice of issuing interim financial reports to shareholders has evolved from management recognition of the merits of this type of disclosure. Although the SEC encourages companies "to publish readable, understandable quarterly reports to shareholders,"[7] there are no mandatory rules requiring such action.

---

[7] *SEC Codification of Financial Reporting Policies*, Section 301.06.

Most public companies must file quarterly reports on Form 10–Q with the commission and, where appropriate, interim financial data is required to be made available in 1933 Act filings. Companies meeting specified criteria must include selected quarterly earnings data in annual shareholder reports and in certain commission filings. In addition, specified, significant events must be reported currently on Form 8–K. Listing agreements of the New York and American stock exchanges require that selected quarterly earnings data be furnished to the exchanges and to the financial press.

Authoritative professional guidance directed specifically to interim financial reporting is less developed than that pertaining to reporting for annual periods. For example, the basic question of whether an interim financial reporting period should be considered as a discrete period that stands alone or as an integral part of the annual reporting period has never been resolved. This distinction is critical to determining how interim income should be measured.

Following the SEC's direction that quarterly data submitted on Form 10–Q should be prepared in accordance with GAAP, the FASB's predecessor, the Accounting Principles Board (APB), issued Opinion No. 28[8] establishing accounting principles for interim periods and specifying disclosure levels for summarized interim financial data issued by publicly traded companies. The FASB has issued guidance on the treatment in interim reports of accounting changes, income taxes, and prior period adjustments.[9] A major project addressing the full gamut of interim reporting issues on FASB's agenda at one time was later removed on the grounds of low priority in relation to other projects.

The SEC's interim reporting requirements are consistent with a view of interim reporting as an updating mechanism. The data may be condensed and need not be audited. On the grounds

---

[8]AICPA *APB Opinion No. 28,* "Interim Financial Reporting" (New York, May 1973).

[9]FASB *Statement of Financial Accounting Standards No. 3,* "Reporting Accounting Changes in Interim Financial Statements" (Stamford, Conn., December 1974); *FASB Interpretation No. 18,* "Accounting for Income Taxes in Interim Periods," (New York, March 1977) FASB *Statement of Financial Accounting Standards No. 16,* "Prior Period Adjustments" (Stamford, Conn., June 1977), paragraphs 13–15.

that users are presumed to have access to previously issued annual financial statements, certain disclosures may be omitted. While disclosure should be sufficient to make the interim information presented not misleading, the focus should be on significant changes since the end of the most recently completed fiscal year. The required management's discussion and analysis is also expected to focus on significant changes in the matters required to be covered.

In the future, interim reporting requirements could be refined or expanded in a number of ways. A 1984 proposal, if adopted, would expand the SEC's interim reporting requirements.[10] Interim reports to shareholders could be required. The presently optional auditor involvement with interim data could be expanded. At some future date, the FASB might reinstate its abandoned interim reporting project and issue a final standard that could change present practice significantly.

Interpretive Information—Management's Discussion and Analysis

Statement of Financial Accounting Concepts No. 1 acknowledges that "financial reporting should include explanations and interpretations to help users understand financial information provided."[11] Few direct derivatives of this concept are found in authoritative professional standards, but the SEC has made interpretive information an integral part of the financial disclosure package.

As a part of its integrated disclosure program, the SEC introduced an entirely restructured Management's Discussion and Analysis of Financial Condition and Results of Operations (MDA) which is required to be presented in annual shareholder reports, in most SEC filings requiring annual financial statements, and (in the context of material changes) in interim financial reports.

The commentary provided in MDA is to cover financial condition, changes in financial condition, and results of operations; such commentary must include specified information on liquid-

---

[10] *Securities Exchange Act of 1934 Release No. 34-20657*, February 15, 1984.

[11] FASB, *Statement of Financial Accounting Concepts No. 1*, "Objectives of Financial Reporting by Business Enterprises" (Stamford, Conn. November 1978), paragraph 54.

ity, capital resources, and results of operations. Registrants are instructed to focus specifically on material events and uncertainties known to management that would cause reported financial information not to be necessarily indicative of future operating results or of future financial condition.

The thrust of both the governing rules and the SEC's public comments on the expected content of MDA is toward "known material trends, favorable or unfavorable," "unusual or infrequent events or transactions," "significant economic changes" with material effect, "commitments," and "uncertainties." MDA requirements, contained in Regulation S–K, Item 303, are intentionally general and nonspecific in order to encourage registrants to discuss those matters most significant in individual circumstances.

The SEC encourages, but does not require, the presentation of forward-looking information in MDA and provides safe harbor rules for those who do so. A distinction is made between such "forward-looking information" as management forecasts of future revenues and earnings and presently known information which will impact future operations. Known data, such as future increases in the cost of labor or materials, may be required to be disclosed.

Since MDA was restructured in September 1980, the SEC has devoted considerable attention to encouraging compliance with the spirit of the rules. Studies of MDAs submitted have been followed by interpretive releases containing the SEC's views on areas requiring improvement. They also have served as a springboard for speeches by commission representatives calling for improved MDA disclosures.

Further, MDA seems to have become a repository of most qualitative and quantitative disclosures deemed important by the SEC but not required by GAAP. Because the formal MDA requirements are general and subjective, MDA is a convenient medium for implementing SEC changes in emphasis without the need to comply with the formal rule-making process. Changes in the SEC's perception of business and economic factors that should be highlighted or of perceived deficiencies in the level of disclosure required by professional standards could well be followed by formal releases imposing further disclosures or shifts in emphasis in MDA.

Continuous Reporting—Integrated Disclosure

In September 1980, the SEC introduced the first elements in a major overhaul of its disclosure and reporting requirements. The stated objectives of the integrated disclosure program were to simplify disclosure requirements, reduce reporting burdens, encourage integration of formal and informal shareholder communications, and enhance the value of quarterly and interim information disclosed to investors and shareholders. The commission often refers to integrated disclosure as a program to ensure the "continuous flow" of meaningful current information to shareholders and to the trading markets.

The integrated disclosure system provides a single comprehensive set of rules governing reporting under both the 1933 and 1934 securities acts. Annual shareholder reports and most SEC filings requiring annual financial statements are required to contain a basic information package designed to capture the key financial attributes of the registrant. This package consists of audited financial statements, management's discussion and analysis, and a summary of selected financial data appropriate for trend analysis. Uniform rules are also provided for other data elements commonly required in SEC filings.

The rules governing interim reporting were restructured to emphasize the role of interim reports as an updating mechanism in a continuous reporting process. Preparers of interim financial reports are instructed to "presume that users of the interim financial information have read or have access to the audited financial statements for the preceding fiscal year."[12]

With uniformity, periodic reports required under the 1934 act can be used to fill many of the requirements for 1933 act registration statements. For qualifying companies, a 1933 act filing precedent to the sale of securities may be little more than a shell—a cover wrapped around a list of references to annual and quarterly filings previously made available. The information conveyed through the annual reporting pipeline has become the centerpiece of the entire disclosure system.

It is important to recognize this shift in emphasis. If deregulation has indeed simplified and reduced reporting require-

---

[12] *SEC Regulation S–X*, Article 10, Rule 10–01 (a)(5).

ments, it has also brought increased management responsibility. Compliance with periodic reporting requirements can no longer be approached in isolation; each required report must be viewed in the context of its place in the entire reporting chain. Failure to do so may be accompanied by penalties. For example, the use of certain abbreviated registration forms is contingent upon the registrant's having filed, on a timely basis, all required reports for the 12 calendar months and any portion of a month preceding the filing of the registration statement. In addition, the use of a single report to fill the requirements of both the 1933 and 1934 securities acts brings that report under the liability provisions of both acts. Corporate disclosure policies should ensure that procedures are in place to promote prompt disclosure of major corporate developments and full compliance with the enterprise's periodic reporting obligations.

Supplementary Information

Supplementary information is information that is required to be presented as a part of the financial reporting package but not as part of the financial statements. Both the SEC and FASB have used the medium to supply information believed to be of interest to users but lacking the necessary characteristics, usually reliability, for inclusion in the financial statements. From a cost standpoint, presentation outside the financial statements is an advantage: The information is subject to prescribed limited review procedures but not the full scope audit procedures that would be required if covered by the audit report.

A proposed Concepts Statement, *Reporting Income, Cash Flows, and Financial Position of Business Enterprises*, now superseded, discussed the role of supplementary information in the reporting process. It stated: "Supplementary information . . . may include information that has a different perspective from that adopted in the financial statements, including information that is highly relevant but low in reliability or information that is helpful but not essential." The section also includes interpretive information supplied by management (previously discussed) within the parameters of supplementary information.[13]

---

[13]FASB *Proposed Statement of Financial Accounting Concepts* (Stamford, Conn., November 1981), paragraph 42.

The FASB presently requires the presentation of supplementary information in two instances; the changing prices information required on an experimental basis by FAS 33, as amended, and the disclosures about oil- and gas-producing activities required by FAS 69. The first is an example of information presented from a different perspective—current cost rather than historical cost; both the relevance and reliability of FAS 33 data have been challenged by some observers. Clearly in the low reliability category, parts of the mandated oil and gas disclosures, in the opinion of some, also fail the relevance test.

It can be conceded that the supplementary information device is an appropriate vehicle for short-term experimentation and that compelling reasons might justify its use in some other circumstances. Its prescription, however, should be weighed carefully. Information that is not essential or not necessarily reliable adds length to an already voluminous reporting package. If information is not essential, business should not be required to supply it. If information is not reliable, the risk that it will mislead users may overshadow any perceivable benefits.

POTENTIAL FINANCIAL STATEMENT CHANGES

Just as focusing on user needs has prompted the expansion of the financial reporting package in the ways discussed in the previous section, the accounting conventions which control the preparation of financial statements are being reexamined from a user-oriented viewpoint. This section discusses the FASB's conceptual framework intended to provide criteria for determining the future direction of accounting standards, and several specific issues which may be the source of changes in present practice.

Conceptual Framework

Shortly after its formation, the FASB began work on a major, multiphase project to develop a conceptual framework for financial accounting and reporting. Completed as to business enterprises in late 1984, the conceptual framework is described as "a coherent system of interrelated objectives and fundamentals that prescribes the nature, function, and limits of financial accounting and reporting." Its purpose is to provide a basis for consistent conclusions on all future standards.

The conceptual framework for business enterprises comprises four Statements of Financial Accounting Concepts, each building on those that precede:

- No. 1—*Objectives of Financial Reporting by Business Enterprises*
- No. 2—*Qualitative Characteristics of Accounting Information*
- No. 3—*Elements of Financial Statements of Business Enterprises*
- No. 5—*Recognition and Measurement in Financial Statements of Business Enterprises*

Other Concepts Statements (one issued and another nearing completion) apply to not-for-profit enterprises.

Concepts statements do not establish financial accounting standards and may, in some instances, be inconsistent with existing practice. Their importance lies in their potential for influencing Board determinations on specific accounting and reporting issues considered in the standards-setting process.

Concepts Statement No. 1 adopts decision usefulness as the central focus of financial reporting: "Financial reporting should provide information that is useful to present and potential investors and creditors and other users in making rational investment, credit, and similar decisions." Among other things, the information reported should help users "assess the amounts, timing, and uncertainty of prospective net cash inflows" to the enterprise.

Concepts Statement No. 2 ranks a number of qualities of financial information in a hierarchy which shows relevance and reliability as primary qualities, both of which must be present to some degree if financial information is to be useful. A third quality, comparability, is also ranked as important but given somewhat less weight than relevance and reliability. The precise definitions given in the statement are not substantially different from the common meanings of the terms.

Concepts Statement No. 3 contains definitions of ten "elements" of financial statements—broad classes such as assets, liabilities, revenues, and expenses—that are relevant to financial reporting. Drawn very broadly, as they must be if they are true fundamentals and if they are to endure, these definitions establish points of reference for judging whether proposed items qualify for inclusion in financial statements.

Following a lengthy discussion of the role of various financial statements in meeting the objectives of financial reporting, Concepts Statement No. 5 deals with recognition criteria, guidance on what and when information should be incorporated into financial statements, and certain measurement issues that are closely related to recognition.

The concepts of "earnings" and "comprehensive income," introduced in Concepts Statement No. 3, are a major topic of Concepts Statement No. 5. "Earnings" is similar—but not identical—to net income in current practice. The broader concept, "comprehensive income," includes earnings and all other changes in equity during the period except transactions with owners. Items now shown in shareholders' equity that are considered part of comprehensive income include foreign currency translation adjustments and changes in market value of investments, both pursuant to *Marketable Securities* standard FAS 12 and the specialized accounting practices followed by certain financial services industries.

As the end of the road in the much-touted conceptual framework project, Concepts Statement No. 5 was a disappointment to many constituents. It presents only those concepts on which board members could agree. Such contentious issues as selection of a measurement "attribute,"—historical cost, current cost, and the like—are not addressed. The Statement does not call for major changes in present accounting but leaves room for evolutionary change that may occur through application of the concepts at the standards level rather than through further direct consideration of concepts.

Reference to the concepts embodied in the framework has become a normal element of board deliberations on individual issues. The conceptual framework's long-term impact will depend importantly on how closely the board adheres to its provisions and on how it interprets them. The concepts adopted can be interpreted as supporting broad segments of present practice or be used to support the implementation of untested theories. The statement in the introduction to Concepts Statement No. 5 that the "Board intends future change to occur in the gradual, evolutionary way that has characterized past change," however, is reassuring.

The Effects of Inflation versus Changing Prices

Before this chapter is printed, a second-generation pronouncement dealing with changing prices likely will have been adopted. Released as an exposure draft in December 1984 and scheduled to be published in final form in the third quarter of 1985, *Financial Reporting and Changing Prices: Current Cost Information* combines the requirements of ten existing pronouncements in the subject area. With one exception—elimination of an option to express constant purchasing power in terms of a base year—the exposure draft, if adopted as proposed, will continue changing prices disclosure requirements in effect at the end of 1984.

Statement of Financial Accounting Standards No. 33, *Financial Reporting and Changing Prices,* was issued in 1979 as an experiment expressly subject to review within five years. Under its provisions, large public enterprises meeting a size test were required to disclose as supplementary information selected financial data calculated by two methods: historical cost/constant dollar (terminology later changed to historical cost/constant purchasing power) accounting and current cost/constant purchasing power accounting.

Historical cost/constant purchasing power accounting is simply the expression of financial statement elements in units, say dollars, each of which has the same general purchasing power. Restatement is accomplished by applying an index to amounts recorded using the traditional historical cost model.

Current cost accounting is a method of measuring and reporting assets and expenses associated with the use or sale of assets at their current cost or lower recoverable amount at the balance sheet date or at the date of use or sale. Current cost is defined as the "cost of acquiring the same service potential as embodied by the asset owned." Current cost/constant purchasing power accounting comprises the conversion, by use of an index, of current cost amounts stated in nominal units to units of constant purchasing power.

The requirement to present historical cost/constant purchasing power information was removed for certain multinational enterprises by FAS 70, issued in December 1982 to conform FAS 33 requirements with the concepts adopted in Statement No. 52, *Foreign Currency Translation.* Statement No. 82, *Financial Reporting and Changing Prices: Elimination of Certain Disclosures,* issued in November 1984 incident to the board's reexamination of all changing prices issues, eliminated dual-method reporting requirements for all companies. Historical cost/constant purchasing power information, while no longer required, may, however, continue to be substituted for current cost amounts in defined circumstances—for example, by companies with specialized assets that are impractical to measure on a current cost basis.

Present minimum requirements specify restatement only for inventories, cost of sales, property, plant and equipment, and depreciation expense. Restated income from continuing operations is the result of restating cost of sales and depreciation and of factoring all other components, including income taxes, into the computation at the historical cost amounts reported in the primary income statement.

Although the amount of purchasing power gains or losses on net monetary items is required to be calculated and disclosed, including such gains or losses in the calculation of income from continuing operations is expressly prohibited. This prohibition is not, however, always observed in practice. Similarly, the increases or decreases in current cost amounts of inventory and property, plant and equipment (often called holding gains or losses) are required to be reported both before and after eliminating the effects of general inflation, but are not to be included in income from continuing operations. Where applicable, a recalculated foreign currency translation adjustment also is required to be disclosed.

It is important that those interested in financial reporting understand the focus of changing prices disclosures. Although measuring and reporting the effects of inflation often is cited as a primary objective in the debate over changing prices issues, the current cost method does not measure inflation, the price spiral that occurs as the purchasing power of the monetary unit declines. As expressed in the titles of the relevant FASB documents, the phenomenon addressed is the broader topic of changing prices.

The concept behind current cost and several similar methods intended to approximate fair value is that any change in prices, regardless of its source, is an event that should be recognized in the determination of income and in the valuation of assets. The method does not distinguish between price changes related to fluctuations in the value of the monetary unit and those which occur because of scarcity, oversupply, or technological

changes in a climate where the value of the monetary unit remains constant or moves in a direction opposite to that of the
specific price change.

Although the use of the current cost method now is limited
to the presentation of partial, supplementary information, extension of the concept to the primary financial statements would
spell the end of the historical cost basis of reporting. The
groundwork is in place in the conceptual framework to recognize price changes—up or down, permanent or temporary—in
the computation of earnings if the FASB is able to discern a
consensus in favor of such action. Instead of reporting a summary of transactions and events recorded at exchange prices
determined in the marketplace, financial statements would be
based on theoretical values, said to represent current cost or some
alternative approximating fair value.

There is little reason, however, to expect near-term abandon-
ment of the historical cost model. Influential business groups
adamantly oppose any shift toward fair value accounting. And
failure of the board, in issuing Concepts Statement No. 5, to
select a measurement attribute, for example, historical cost or
current cost, as some had hoped and others had feared, signals
near-term adherence to the status quo. Concepts Statement No.
5 states: "Items currently reported in financial statements are
measured by different attributes, depending on the nature of
the item and the relevance and reliability of the attribute measured. The Board expects the use of different attributes to continue."

The future outlook for the present experiment with changing
prices disclosure is unclear. In its reexamination of Statement
33, the board considered evidence that the data has not been
widely used to date and weighed assertions by numerous com-
mentators that costs of preparing the information far exceed its
benefits. Nevertheless, the board opted to continue the experimental nature, supplementary status, and limited scope of FAS
33 requirements, as previously amended. Close monitoring and
encouragement of additional research are planned.

The most compelling reason for this action relates to the use
of the data as a surrogate for reporting the effects of inflation.
The board stated: "If Statement 33 disclosures were discontin-
ued today and reinstated in the future should the inflation rate
increase, the cost of redeveloping the data could be high, and

a continuing series of information would not be available to users."

Although the FAS 33 experiment deserves more time, it suffers from important defects.

The presentation of one set of supplementary disclosures rather than the former two should eliminate an important source of confusion. But the stigma of the supplementary label remains. The restated earnings reported by companies complying with FAS 33 show dramatic changes—for example, reported profits cut by half, or more, when calculated on a current cost basis; or ostensible profits are turned into losses. The significance of corrections this massive tends to be obscured when not shown in the primary income statement.

Failure to determine the disposition of purchasing power gains or losses on net monetary items and of holding gains and losses on productive assets is a further defect in present provisions. These two controversial items now are listed separately along with operating income and the translation adjustment previously consigned by the board to shareholders' equity. With aggregation expressly prohibited, interpretation of the possible significance of the items listed is left to the user.

Survival of the present limited level of disclosure almost certainly depends on either a sharp increase in user acceptance or upon the identification of modifications that would significantly increase the data's inherent usefulness. The December 1984 exposure draft, if adopted, will be only an interim solution to changing prices questions—questions sure to reemerge as the subject of future accounting debates.

Foreign Currency Translation

During its first decade, the FASB has tried twice to resolve the controversial problem of how to translate foreign currency financial statements so that they may be consolidated, combined, or reported under the equity method in U.S. dollar financial statements.

Statement No. 8, *Accounting for the Translation of Foreign Currency Transactions and Foreign Currency Financial Statements*, became effective in 1976. It was based on the concept that consolidated results should be measured from a single perspective, a U.S. dollar perspective. The practical effect of the "temporal" translation method adopted was to calculate foreign currency translation gains and losses for monetary accounts but not for nonmonetary accounts. Under FAS 8, foreign currency translation gains and losses were required to be included in income in the periods in which rate changes occurred.

FAS 8 encountered widespread criticism from the beginning. It was said to produce accounting results incompatible with the underlying economic facts, to distort operating margins, and to produce undesirable fluctuations in earnings. In an attempt to correct these perceived deficiencies, the board, after three years of study and public comment, issued Statement No. 52, *Foreign Currency Translation*. FAS 52 became effective in 1983 although many companies adopted it earlier.

The functional currency approach adopted in FAS 52 is a radical departure from earlier standards. It rests on a premise that the individual entities comprising a multinational enterprise operate and generate cash flows in a number of separate economic environments each having a specific functional currency. Since gains and losses arising from exchange rate fluctuations generally are recognized in income only to the extent that these affect each separate economic environment, the effect is to measure consolidated results using multiple measurement bases.

Depending on the facts and circumstances, a foreign unit's functional currency may be the local currency, another foreign currency, or the U.S. dollar. For example, the U.S. dollar generally would be the functional currency for foreign operations that are a direct and integral component or extension of the parent company's operations. Also, the U.S. dollar is the prescribed functional currency for a foreign entity operating in a highly inflationary economy, as defined in the statement.

The determination of each unit's functional currency is extremely important. If the functional currency is determined to be the U.S. dollar, exchange gains and losses arising in the "remeasurement," that is, translation, process are recorded in the income statement nearly the same as under FAS 8. If, however, the functional currency is a foreign subsidiary's local currency, such gains and losses accumulate in a translation adjustment account that is part of shareholders' equity until sale, including partial sale, or liquidation of the investment. Once a functional currency for a foreign unit is determined, the determination may be changed only where warranted by significant changes in the economic facts and circumstances.

The fact that three board members dissented to the issuance of FAS 52 on conceptual grounds casts doubt on whether that standard provides a long-term solution to foreign currency measurement. The board's use in FAS 52 of shareholders' equity for recording translation adjustments, however, sets a possibly important precedent. Similar treatment has been suggested for some aspects of pension accounting and for recording the impact of inflation. The concept of "comprehensive income" introduced in the board's conceptual framework may be viewed as an extension of the same theory.

All-Inclusive Reporting of Obligations

Several unresolved financial reporting issues are concerned, at least in part, with examining the accounting conventions which act to exclude corporate obligations from direct recognition in the statement of financial position. They are the forerunners of a movement to reconcile practice with the broad definitions of assets and liabilities created by the FASB in constructing the conceptual framework.

Concepts Statement No. 3 defines assets as probable future economic benefits obtained as a result of past transactions or events; it defines liabilities as probable future sacrifices of economic benefits arising from past transactions or events. Application of these definitions might exclude from the statement of financial position some items now recognized as assets and, provided that measurement difficulties and legal constraints can be overcome, recognize obligations now customarily disclosed in footnotes or presented as part of net investments.

Unfunded Pension Liabilities An exposure draft, *Employers' Accounting for Pensions*, published by the FASB in March 1985, proposes significant changes in accounting for single-employer defined benefit pension plans.

A successor to a more far-reaching proposal that received widespread objections from constituents, the complex proposal, among other changes, would require corporations to recognize unfunded pension liabilities in their statements of financial position. The "unfunded accumulated benefit obligation" required to be reported would be equal to the excess of the present value of benefits earned to date over the fair value of plan assets. After considering any prepayments or accruals resulting from the recording and funding of period cost, any additional liability recorded would be offset by an intangible asset, to the extent of unrecognized prior service costs, with any excess recorded as a reduction of equity. Plan overfunding would not be recognized as an asset in the financial statements.

In deciding on this proposed solution, the board has concluded that there is a present liability for future benefits to the extent that such benefits have been earned by previous employee service. Because that liability is deemed to meet the Concepts No. 3 definition, it should, in the board's view, be recorded. Others have reservations on both conceptual and pragmatic grounds.

The drive to recognize a "minimum" liability would be accomplished by creating an offsetting intangible asset of doubtful validity and through the prescription of dual measurement methods for a single class of transactions; future compensation levels would be considered in determining period cost but would be excluded in calculating the "unfunded accumulated benefit obligation" reported in the statement of financial position. These pragmatic decisions, among other features of the proposal, are subject to challenge on their conceptual merits.

The practical effect of the board's proposal would be to move conjectural data from the footnotes to the statement of financial position where it would affect financial ratios. This, it may be noted, is the converse of the treatment specified for the similarly "soft" data on changing prices required to be shown as supplemental information. Temporary swings in the fair value of plan assets having no effect on plan ability to discharge obligations when due might nevertheless generate a reportable liability. And perhaps more damaging than the data's questionable reliability, evidence to date suggests that adoption of the proposal might encourage corporations to change the structure of their pension arrangements to avoid the accounting consequences of defined benefit plans.

The major amounts committed under the terms of pension plans make pension accounting a major issue. How it is settled could affect not only the immediate accounting question but set important—possibly undesirable—precedents for unrelated future issues.

Income Tax Accounting Since 1967, accounting for income taxes has been governed by Accounting Principles Board Opinion No. 11 which prescribes comprehensive interperiod tax allocation. SEC requirements for analysis and reconciliation of income tax expense augment GAAP disclosure requirements.

For many companies, the result of following APB 11 has been balance sheets showing increasingly large amounts of deferred income taxes—a trend accelerated by implementation of the accelerated cost recovery system (ACRS) prescribed by the Economic Recovery Tax Act of 1981. Further, the concept of deferred items is not recognized among the FASB's definitions of financial statement elements.

Spurred by such concerns, the FASB has undertaken a major reevaluation of income tax accounting issues and has issued a discussion memorandum and held a public hearing. The central question posed is whether to report income tax expense measured solely by the amount currently payable under tax laws, to continue with comprehensive interperiod allocation, or to adopt a partial allocation approach. The project also embraces numerous collateral issues.

Despite the basic controversiality of the issues, the taxes project has generated less debate than expected. Although present practice has its critics, the demand for a change does not appear to be widespread. In such a climate, the results of the board's reconsideration might be preservation of the status quo, some implementation adjustments, and GAAP disclosure tuned to SEC requirements.

Exclusions from Consolidation Majority-owned investments in such entities as banks, insurance companies, and finance companies are frequently excluded from consolidation on the grounds that these businesses differ too radically from that of the group to make consolidation meaningful. Such exclusions are among the topics to be addressed in a major FASB project dealing with consolidations.

Some contend that subsidiaries which exist wholly or mainly to finance sales of group products are necessary to group operations and should be consolidated. They view exclusion as undesirable because it understates the group's total debt and distorts comparisons between companies that finance their own sales and those which do so through subsidiary companies.

Segment reporting tends to undermine the argument that unrelated enterprises should not be consolidated. In the case of truly diversified enterprises, it is difficult to sustain a position that some classes should be excluded simply because they are different. When, on the other hand, the preponderance of the consolidated group is homogeneous, treatment of a disparate part of the business as an investment accompanied by informative disclosure may constitute the most meaningful reporting.

Joint Venture Accounting Despite their significance in the conduct of business, joint ventures have received little attention from accounting standards setters. A forthcoming FASB project will examine the similarities and differences among such varied forms as corporate joint ventures, general and limited partnerships, undivided interests in unincorporated undertakings, and joint arrangements which are financing devices not investments.

The one-line equity method is prescribed for corporate joint ventures and is sometimes employed through extrapolation to other joint venture arrangements. This method is effective for some situations but deficient for others. Some contend that its use for joint financing arrangements is particularly undesirable because the effect is to underreport obligations that should be shown at face value.

In the petroleum, real estate, and construction industries which carry out substantial parts of the business through joint arrangements, use of the equity method obscures the full scope of the business reported upon in both the income statement and the statement of financial position. Proportionate consolidation for joint arrangements is standard practice in the petroleum industry and is used to some extent in other similar situations.

The board's review should result in better definition of the different classes of arrangements loosely described as joint ventures. Some changes in requirements may ensue—changes which expand the perimeters of the statement of financial position in line with the board's asset and liability definitions and, quite probably, foreclose some present opportunities to conceal debt by net reporting.

INTERNATIONAL ACCOUNTING AND
REPORTING STANDARDS

Although the nomenclature can be found in isolated examples of financial reports prepared abroad, generally accepted international accounting and reporting standards do not exist. The standards followed in preparing financial reports in individual countries are highly diverse, ranging from disclosure systems that approximate U.S. standards to those where formal standards are all but nonexistent.

Uniform international standards have long been recognized as a desirable goal, but until recently there has been little action. Two of several current efforts to promote international or regional standards are discussed briefly below.

International Accounting Standards Committee (IASC) This autonomous body was established in 1973 by agreement among professional accounting bodies from nine founding countries to promulgate international standards. It now has a membership of about 60 organizations from more than 40 countries.

To date, IASC has issued more than two dozen Statements of International Accounting Standards and proposed standards. Although the expressed intention of IASC is to "concentrate on essentials," some of the standards contain details which create immediate exceptions when compared with national standards. Their effect in any given jurisdiction depends entirely on the degree of influence local professional organizations are able to exercise over national standards, many of which are set by statute, and their authority over the actions of their members.

In the United States, there are no reporting, accounting, or disclosure requirements of any kind arising from IASC pronouncements. As a signatory to the agreement that created IASC, the AICPA agreed to support IASC standards and to use its best efforts to ensure that published financial statements comply with the IASC standards or disclose the extent to which they do not. That group, however, has little power to act. Sole authority for setting accounting standards in the private sector in the United States rests with the FASB. Although the AICPA exercises authority over its members through its ethics rules, those rules necessarily recognize the authority of the FASB. Further, the influential organizations other than the AICPA which support the FASB have no structured means of input into the international accounting standards-setting process.

European Economic Community (EEC) The Fourth and Seventh Company Law Directives, which are intended to effect a more consistent approach to financial reporting among the 10 EEC nations, were adopted in 1978 and 1983 respectively.

The Fourth Directive sets minimum disclosure requirements, establishes standard reporting formats, and restricts the use of some alternative accounting principles. It also offers a variety of elective modifications which may be exercised by individual member states at the time they incorporate the directive's provisions into their own company laws as they are required to do under the terms of the basic Common Market treaty. Although the Fourth Directive should have become effective in most of the member states no later than 1982, only six had taken the required action to implement it by late 1984.

The full impact of the Seventh Directive on consolidated financial statements will not be known until member states adopt implementing legislation. The directive, which does not require the production of consolidated financial statements before financial years beginning in 1990, is replete with member state options and cross-references to the provisions of the Fourth Directive. The alternatives provided affect both the determination of the types of entities that will be subject to consolidation and the technicalities of preparing consolidated accounts.

Full implementation of the EEC Directives will be an important step toward establishing international accounting standards. The adoption of standards having at least a measure of uniformity in this internationally important region should foster the development of improved standards in other countries. Although implementation of these directives is likely to result in some basic differences, particularly in disclosure requirements, between individual country standards and U.S. GAAP, on balance, their adoption in many of the EEC countries should tend to narrow rather than broaden such differences.

SUMMARY

This chapter has briefly covered the more important actions and issues which have influenced present requirements for disclosing corporate financial information to the public or which may result in future changes. Financial accounting and reporting standards are established by the FASB, subject to SEC oversight, and are implemented through voluntary compliance, SEC regulations, and the ethics rules of professional auditors. The accounting provisions of the Foreign Corrupt Practices Act foster improved disclosure by mandating the maintenance of the accounting records and internal control systems necessary to prepare reliable information. Up-to-date documentation of internal control systems is important to establish compliance with FCPA and to support the issuance of voluntary public reports on such systems.

In response to real or perceived user needs, disclosure requirements have expanded to include disaggregated information, interpretive information, supplementary information, and more timely information viewed as part of a continuous reporting process. Issues that may be the source of future changes include changing prices, foreign currency translation, and the treatment of corporate obligations. Movements to develop international or regional accounting and reporting standards may have an important future impact but have little effect on present practice.

20

Relations with Regulatory Agencies

Robert C. Thompson and Leonard S. Chaikind

Regulatory agencies and regulations are a part of everyday business activities. This chapter deals with preparing the chief financial officer (CFO) to work more effectively with these agencies on an ongoing basis. It covers the authors' views on regulations and regulatory bodies, as well as on establishing and maintaining effective working relationships with them. Representative agencies, which tend to be important to the CFO, have been chosen for more detailed analysis and to use as examples for describing working relationships.

Throughout the chapter, the authors have drawn on extensive interviews with various companies' senior financial managers and selected personnel in key governmental agencies, as well as their own experiences. Although emphasis is placed primarily on the chosen federal and quasi-official agencies, most of the comments apply equally well to other federal, state, and

Bob Thompson joined the Shell Oil Company in 1953 and retired 30 years later as vice president—finance and CFO. During the 1981–82 period, Bob was chairman of the board of directors of the Financial Executives Institute. Len Chaikind is currently assistant treasurer policy and administration with Shell Oil. He is also chairman of the Financial Executives Institute Committee on Government Liaison.

local regulatory bodies. However, each CFO will have to re-work the analysis to fit his or her specific company's needs and the agencies with which it is most involved.

BACKGROUND

The CFO relates to regulatory agencies both as the head of a company's financial function and as a member of its senior management group. Particularly since the 1930s, with the passage of the Securities Acts, the CFO and financial managers in general have found it necessary to be aware of and to respond to the actions of many regulatory agencies at the federal, state, and local governmental levels. In the 1960s and 1970s, the number of agencies and regulations impacting business accelerated to the point where the economy was affected in a negative way (Exhibit 1). As Murray Weidenbaum so aptly said at the end of this period: "The slowdown of productivity and the pervasiveness of inflationary pressures suffered by the American economy are no mystery. Among the most serious and re-

Exhibit 1
The Growth of Federal Regulatory Agencies

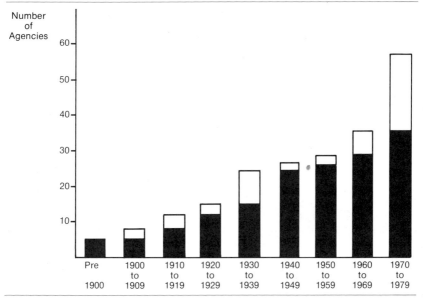

Source: M. L. Weidenbaum, "Public Policy: No Longer a Spectator Sport for Industry."

medial causes of these ailments afflicting the American economy, excessive regulation surely deserves a spotlight."[1]

During the Ford, Carter, and Reagan administrations, there were some significant moves made towards deregulation and regulatory reform, but that momentum has clearly slowed and the number of regulatory agencies has not diminished. Business in general, and the financial executive in particular, will have to continue operating in a highly regulated environment in the foreseeable future.

PERSONAL VIEWS ON REGULATIONS AND REGULATORS

In the authors' opinion, the American economy works most efficiently and the public's interest is best served with a minimum amount of government intervention. Regulations and minimum safety standards are, of course, needed in the areas of environmental, consumer, and worker protection. Also, the various federal, state, and quasi-governmental regulatory agencies have an important role to play in monitoring business activity in order to assure compliance with the many laws of the land. The basic role of the government in these areas, however, should be to encourage competition and the free market system and to provide only those services that society can't provide through the competitive system.

In the past, most federal economic regulations and controls of industries, such as airlines, trucking, railroads, petroleum, and pipelines, have not worked in the broad public interest. This position has been supported by the majority of the economists who have studied the subject.[2] Moreover, the authors believe there can be a tendency for companies operating in a regulative environment to become complacent, less innovative, and less efficient over time.

In some instances, coalitions of government and private interests find it mutually beneficial to perpetuate regulatory situations which may work against the public good. These coalitions, which have been called "iron triangles" or

---

[1]Murray L. Weidenbaum, *The Future of Business Regulation*, 2d ed. (New York: AMACOM 1980).

[2]For example, see Chapters 12, 14, and 15 in A. D. Strickland's book entitled *Government Regulations and Business*.

"subgovernments" by the political scientists,[3] might include agency staffs; congressional staffs; private interests, such as the regulated businesses themselves; related labor unions; and lobbyists.

These subgovernments tend to stifle or slow up any changes that might lessen the existing regulatory environment. The changes that do occur, moreover, usually take significant action primarily by the executive branch and can only be accomplished by continuous pressure for cost-benefit-risk reviews of existing regulations and with strong support from the public, business, and congressional areas.

WORKING WITH REGULATORY AGENCIES

There are many ways that CFOs can establish working relationships with regulatory agencies; for example, through formal meetings, by serving on agency committees and study groups, and by testifying at public hearings or by submitting statements on existing and proposed regulations. Even letters or phone calls directly to agency representatives can start the process going. For those CFOs who do not have the time for direct contacts, another approach to consider is working through other groups, which will be discussed later in this chapter.

From the Perspective of Business

The authors do not share a common public perception of the typical Washington federal employee as "slow moving, resistant to change, and inefficient."[4] Based on their own personal experiences with agency representatives and those of other business people who have had similar dealings, the authors believe that agency professionals, for the most part, are much the same in their work attitudes and endeavors as business professionals; that is, they are generally dedicated, hard working people who make a wide spectrum of real contributions to their organizations. Some recurring comments from CFOs, however, were statements such as: "The government people don't seem

---

[3]For a full description of this concept, see T. B. Clark, "Iron Triangles," *National Journal*, March 28, 1981.

[4]For example, see Joe H. Brinbaum, "Busy Bureaucrat," *The Wall Street Journal*, September 22, 1983, p. 1.

to understand our business," and "They are motivated by a set of objectives and interpretations of laws which are not the same as ours." Business people often view agencies as adversaries who seem unwilling to compromise.

It is important for the CFO to approach the regulatory agency relationship with an open mind and a readiness to listen. Moreover, each side should be willing to compromise to a certain extent in order to get an issue resolved. A mutual educational program can also be very helpful in establishing these relationships although both parties should be careful not to "preach."

If a business person is unsuccessful in getting an adequate or timely hearing directly with an agency, an effective alternative might be to work through the legislator or the staff of a congressional subcommittee which has oversight responsibility for the particular agency. This approach usually works quite well but should be used sparingly since it is not very popular with the agencies.

From the Perspective of the Agency Itself

Some views heard recurringly from the agency representatives were: "Business people don't talk to us, except in panic situations"; "Often they are not prepared for the discussions—they don't do their homework"; and "Business executives don't always have to bring their lawyers with them—things can often be discussed informally."

These comments should be carefully considered by a CFO before contacting an agency. However, some of the comments made about CFOs seem to apply equally to the regulatory representatives themselves. Also, it is important for an agency to start with the assumption that business people are responsible individuals who want to obey the laws. Their interpretations may not necessarily be the same as those of the agencies but could be just as valid.

REGULATORY AGENCIES—EXAMPLES

There are over 60 major federal regulatory agencies described in the United States Government Manual.[5] In addition, there are

---

[5]*The United States Government Manual 1984/85* (Washington, D.C., U.S. Government Printing Office, 1985).

innumerable state and local regulatory bodies. While it is not possible to cover all of the agencies in this chapter, it should be useful to review some representative ones with whom the CFO could have contacts. The specific ones chosen fall into three categories: (1) independent federal agencies, for example, Securities and Exchange Commission and Federal Trade Commission; (2) executive branch/cabinet agencies, for example, Department of Commerce and Department of Energy; and (3) quasi-official agencies, for example, Financial Accounting Standards Board and New York Stock Exchange. Also, a more detailed supplemental case study of the Department of Energy has been developed, based on the authors' own experience in the 1971–81 period.

Securities and Exchange Commission (SEC)

Congress established broad guidelines for business disclosure and created the SEC with the passage of the Securities and Exchange Acts of 1933 and 1934. In general, the 1933 Act deals with disclosure on new security issues while the 1934 Act deals with reporting requirements on existing traded securities. The commission's objective is to provide for full and fair disclosure to the investing public and to protect the interests of the public and investors against malpractices in the securities and financial markets.

The commission is an independent, bipartisan, quasi-judicial agency. It is composed of five members, not more than three of whom may be from the same political party (Exhibit 2). They are appointed by the president of the United States, with the advice and consent of the Senate. The SEC staff includes accountants, engineers, lawyers, security analysts, and other professional and support personnel.

The laws administered by the commission relate in general to the field of securities and finance and seek to provide protection for investors and the public in securities transactions. The SEC is not authorized to judge the merits of securities and, assuming proper disclosure, cannot bar their sale even if they appear to be of questionable investment value.

Programs and Activities Public offerings in interstate commerce or through the mails require that a registration statement containing financial and other pertinent data be filed with the SEC unless otherwise exempted by them. A registration statement may be refused or suspended after a public hearing if it

Exhibit 2
Securities and Exchange Commission

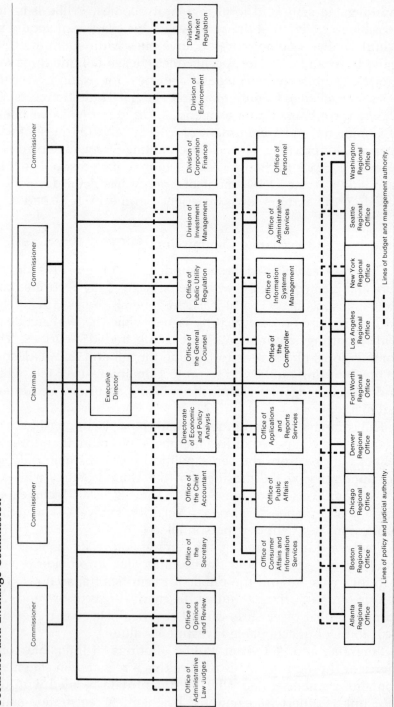

Source: The United States Government Manual 1984/85. U.S. Government Printing Office.

Lines of policy and judicial authority.

Lines of budget and management authority.

contains material misstatements or omissions. Additionally, periodic corporate reporting, as well as registration, is required for companies whose securities are traded on an exchange. Proxy statements and tender offer solicitations are also subject to SEC disclosure requirements.

As described by a major accounting firm, "The SEC has undertaken an extensive program to harmonize the informational requirements of the 1933 Act and the 1934 Act by means of an integrated disclosure system. The common or uniform rules implementing this system consist of the following:

- Regulation C.
- Regulation 12B.
- Regulation S–K.
- Regulation S–X.

Regulation C sets forth the procedural requirements for registration under the 1933 Act; Regulation 12B is the counterpart under the 1934 Act. Regulation S–K sets forth the requirements concerning the content of the nonfinancial statement portions of SEC filings and also applies to certain aspects of annual reports to security holders. Regulation S–X prescribes the form, content, and requirements of the financial statements included in SEC filings and the annual reports to security holders, and of schedules included in SEC filings."[6]

There are several good references that can be used to keep up with changes in SEC regulations and to help in preparing SEC filings. The *Federal Register* and the *SEC Docket* published by Commerce Clearing House, Inc., (CCH) announce matters that are being considered or have been acted on by the commission. The *SEC Compliance Manual* by Prentice-Hall and CCH's *Federal Securities Law Reporter* are practical reference tools that can facilitate SEC securities filings because they offer interpretations and examples, as well as the text of SEC regulations.

Working Relationships The commission has broad powers regarding private sector accounting procedures and works with the Financial Accounting Standards Board in an oversight role. The SEC chief accountant is the principal commission advisor

---

[6]This paragraph comes from a pamphlet describing the SEC reporting system entitled *The SEC's Integrated Disclosure System—Phases One and Two* by Deloitte Haskins & Sells.

regarding accounting and auditing matters and is responsible for policy execution in these areas. This includes examination of financial data filings, accounting and auditing studies, and consultation with such groups as accounting authorities and professional organizations.

The SEC becomes an adversary only in matters of questionable actions or noncompliance with disclosure and registration requirements and in investigations of complaints or other indications of possible securities laws violations. It has consistently had a good image among business people for responsible, fair, and helpful dealings with both the public and other interested parties.

The commission staff is readily accessible by telephone, formal written inquiries, or planned visits. Ideally, such contacts should be a coordinated effort with a firm's public accountants and attorneys experienced in SEC law. The SEC is also willing to give "no action letters"—that is, written confirmation that they will not initiate any action relative to a company's plan for stock options, registration, and so on. These plans should be spelled out in a letter to the SEC.

The SEC would also welcome participation by the CFO in its rule making and interpretation process. This could be done by the CFO speaking at public hearings or by submitting written comments on proposed changes to SEC regulations. Additionally, one could participate in this process by working through other groups, such as the Financial Executives Institute and various trade associations.

Federal Trade Commission (FTC)

As they describe themselves, "The Federal Trade Commission (FTC) is an independent, law enforcement agency charged by Congress with protecting the public—consumers and businessmen alike—against anticompetitive behavior and unfair or deceptive business practices."[7] This rather foreboding statement might well frighten a business person away from ever dealing with the FTC. This is unfortunate since the FTC wants to and can, in many cases, be helpful to CFOs and companies.

The FTC was set up with the enactment of the Federal Trade

---

[7] From a publication on the Federal Trade Commission entitled *Your FTC— What It Is And What It Does.*

Commission Act in 1914 and the Clayton Antitrust Act in 1915. The FTC Act prohibits "unfair methods of competition and unfair or deceptive acts."[8] The Clayton Act outlaws certain specific practices, such as mergers which lessen competition and interlocking directorates. Since the original legislation, there have been many additional laws which have supported the FTC and have spelled out in more detail the FTC's authority and responsibilities. As a result, a significant body of law and guideline decisions have built up over the years.

The FTC is headed by five commissioners appointed by the president of the United States, with the advice and consent of the Senate, for a term of seven years. The commissioners are supported by a large legal, economic, and administrative staff whose key mission has been defined as "maintaining competition and consumer protection."[9] An organization chart is shown as Exhibit 3.

The commission uses various methods to carry out its responsibilities: advisory opinions, industry guides, trade regulation rules, and administrative proceedings. Advisory opinions are issued upon request of a person or corporation which seeks the commission's advice about a proposed course of action. While not binding, they will normally be indicative of the commission's views. Industry guides are issued by the commission to provide guidelines for voluntary action by an industry and relate to specific practices within that industry.

Contacts Contacts for meetings and discussions can easily be made through the FTC's Washington office or through any of its six regional/field offices. A CFO might wish to confer with the FTC staff for guidance or to get informal opinions on such items as: credit practices and disclosure requirements, business reporting to the FTC, and premerger/acquisition notifications. Also, the FTC issues a number of publications on business subjects, economic reports, and general business analyses, all of which a CFO might find useful.

None of this should imply that a CFO should not have legal counsel when dealing with the FTC on legal actions, administrative complaints, or compliance issues. However, the FTC is normally willing and able to confer informally in a number of nonlitigant areas.

[8] Ibid.
[9] The United States Government Manual 1984/85.

Exhibit 3
Federal Trade Commission

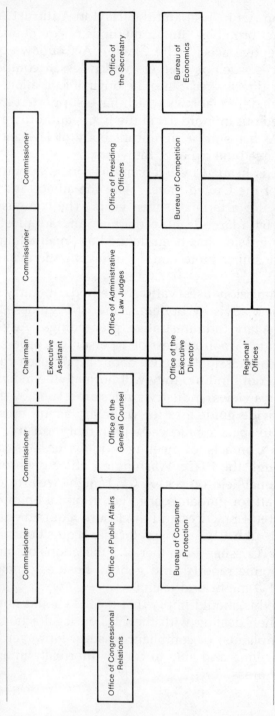

*Located in Atlanta, Boston, Chicago, Cleveland, Dallas, Los Angeles, New York, San Francisco, and Seattle.
Source: The United States Government Manual 1984/85. U.S. Government Printing Office.

Department of Commerce (DOC)

"The Department of Commerce encourages, serves, and promotes the nation's international trade, economic growth, and technological advancement."[10] DOC provides a wide variety of programs including:

- Export assistance and information.
- Unfair foreign trade prevention measures.
- Social and economic statistics.
- Analyses for business and government planners.
- U.S. merchant marine development and maintenance.
- Scientific, engineering, and technical development, research, and support.
- Patents and trademarks.
- Domestic economic development assistance.
- Weather service.
- Oceanic life information, protection, and development.
- Travel and tourism.
- Minority business development.

The Department of Commerce and Labor was established in 1903. A 1913 reorganization transferred all labor activities to a new separate Department of Labor. Over the years, the DOC tasks grew and diversified and now include a number of seemingly unrelated agencies and bureaus within the department (Exhibit 4).

A reorganization of trade functions of the DOC, the Office of the U.S. Trade Representative, and other federal agencies to form a new cabinet level department has been proposed by the Reagan administration. The objective of this new department, which may be called the Department of International Trade and Industry (DITI), would be to consolidate and improve trade policies and to address the nation's increasing trade deficits. Current DOC functions unrelated to trade, such as the National Oceanic and Atmospheric Administration and the Economic Development Administration, would likely be incorporated into other federal agencies or become separate agencies of their own.

Contacts The DOC and its unique blend of varied programs

---

[10]The United States Government Manual 1984/85.

Exhibit 4
Department of Commerce

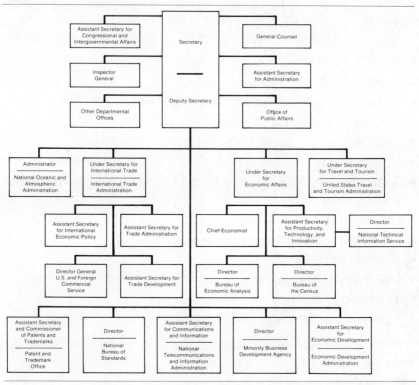

Source: The United States Government Manual 1984/85. U.S. Government Printing Office.

may be categorized as the business community's place in Washington which offers a multitude of services to aid American business. It may not be the first agency a CFO would contact regarding a particular area of interest or problem but possibly the agency of last resort on matters not clearly covered by other agencies. In addition to offices in Washington, a number of DOC functions also have regional offices which can be contacted.

Department of Energy (DOE)

On October 1, 1977, the DOE became the 12th cabinet-level department (Exhibit 5). It assumed the responsibilities of the

Exhibit 5
Department of Energy

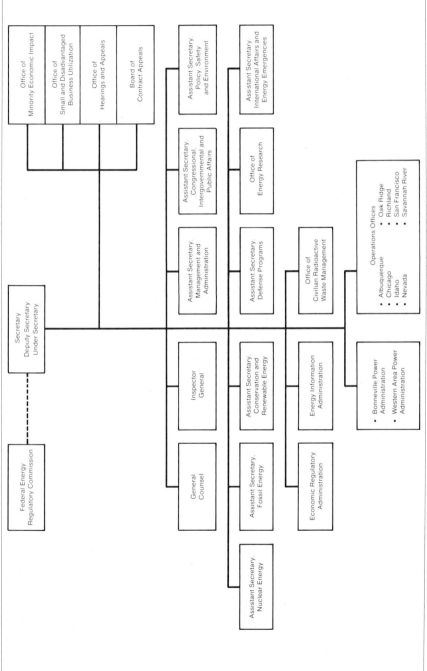

Source: The United States Government Manual 1984/85. U.S. Government Printing Office.

Energy Research and Development Administration, the Federal Energy Administration, and the Federal Power Commission. Also transferred to DOE were certain functions of the Interstate Commerce Commission, the Departments of Commerce, Housing and Urban Development, the Interior, and the Navy. DOE is responsible for long-term fossil fuel and nuclear energy technology research and development; federal power marketing from federal hydroelectric and reservoir projects; energy conservation and renewable energy programs; nuclear weapon research, development, testing, production and surveillance programs; federal emergency preparedness programs; and energy regulatory and information programs.

Energy Regulation The Federal Energy Regulatory Commission (FERC) is an independent, five-member commission within the Department of Energy. It retained many of the functions of the old Federal Power Commission, including natural gas regulation, electric rate setting, and hydroelectric licensing. FERC also assumed the oil pipeline regulatory functions, including pipeline valuation and rate setting from the Interstate Commerce Commission.

The Economic Regulatory Administration (ERA) administers the DOE's regulatory programs, other than those assigned to the Federal Energy Regulatory Commission, along with enforcement programs to assure compliance with ERA regulations. ERA administered the former crude oil and petroleum product price and allocation control programs.

Energy Information The Energy Information Administration (EIA) is responsible for timely and accurate collection, processing, and publication of energy data on reserves, production, demand, consumption, distribution, and technology. EIA administers mandatory reporting programs to satisfy DOE data needs, as well as certain data tasks specifically assigned by Congress. It also provides analyses of energy data to assist government and nongovernment users in understanding energy trends.

Contacts The EIA makes available to the public a variety of reports, guides to reports, and data in machine-readable form. Inquiries about energy data can be made to the National Energy Information Center. Its publication, *Energy Data Contacts*, identifies contact persons by subject area: forecasting and analysis; conservation and consumption programs, and so on.

Working Relationships—a Case Study

The Department of Energy and its predecessor agencies (Cost of Living Council, Federal Energy Office, and Federal Energy Administration) administered economic controls in the petroleum industry for a decade beginning in 1971. During this period, the industry went from an unregulated to a highly controlled status and was faced with crude oil and refined product shortages, spiraling costs, and a decaying public image. The early phases of the economic controls were broad, industrywide wage and price programs which were short-term and temporary. Subsequent controls focused on individual sectors of the economy and the administrative burden increased significantly as separate guidelines applied to each sector.

The petroleum sector control programs included ever-changing price and allocation regulations on crude oil and most petroleum products, as well as energy conservation and coal conversion plans. The programs brought with them many requests for information and new reports—weekly, monthly, quarterly, and annually—directed not only to Washington but also regional (federal) and state energy offices.

Compliance with complex regulations and reporting requirements necessitated frequent interpretation and stringent monitoring efforts throughout the financial, operating, and legal areas of companies. Mistrust of the industry over fuel shortages and agency procedures against hiring knowledgeable industry people contributed to many counterproductive regulations. Also, regulations were often hastily drawn up with a quick-fix approach which later had to be revised to meet new problems, many created by the regulations themselves.

The regulatory control programs continued longer than originally anticipated but were largely eliminated by January 1981. As of this point in time, however, the price of natural gas is still controlled.

The consensus of many economists and other observers is that the oil price and allocation programs were unnecessary, wasteful, and actually made matters worse.[11] The DOE should not

---

[11] For example, refer to M. Elizabeth Sanders, *The Regulation of Natural Gas* (Philadelphia: Temple University Press, 1981) Chapter 1; and Allyn Douglas Strickland, *Government Regulation and Business* (Boston: Houghton Mifflin, 1980) chapter 14.

bear all the responsibility for the regulatory mess, however, since Congress and several presidents were directly responsible for many of these programs.

In retrospect, perhaps the affected companies should have made an even stronger effort to convince both the public and government that the regulatory programs would be counterproductive. Also, greater sensitivity on the part of the industry to the concerns of the public was clearly needed. In addition, once the programs were initiated, more active industry participation with the agency regarding regulatory implications and their effects on both the industry and the public might have contributed to less regulation and reporting.

The agency should have used more personnel with a working knowledge of the petroleum industry and actively sought out greater understanding of the industry. That difficult period would also have worked better had both the industry and the government been able to work together in a mutual trust rather than in a continuous adversary relationship. This is not to imply that a healthy, arm's-length position should have been abandoned but rather that each party should have listened to the other's comments more carefully.

Based on the authors' experience, other suggestions for dealing with "short-term or temporary" agency regulations are as follows:

1. Establish a control group within the company to provide a single contact point for agency information, reports, and audit requests.
2. Maximize the use of existing staff, financial records, computer systems, and internal controls to maintain work quality and experience and to provide auditable records; the costs of setting up entirely new data systems could be horrendous.
3. Use the control group to coordinate reporting and to minimize the financial impact of regulatory requirements and the burden of compliance auditing.
4. Keep the control group as small as possible in order to minimize the risk of self-interest in perpetuating the programs and to facilitate a return to normal work groups when the regulations end.

Financial Accounting Standards Board (FASB)

The FASB is the designated, private sector organization for establishing financial accounting and reporting standards. Those standards govern financial report preparation and are officially recognized as authoritative by the Securities and Exchange Commission (SEC) and the American Institute of Certified Public Accountants. Although the SEC has statutory authority to establish financial accounting and reporting standards, it has always relied on self-regulatory organizations from the private sector to provide this function. The commission still retains its oversight role, however, and could veto FASB actions.

The mission of the FASB is to establish and improve standards of financial accounting and reporting for the guidance and education of the public, including issuers, auditors, and users of financial information. The FASB also develops broad accounting concepts, as well as standards for financial accounting, and provides guidance on the implementation of those standards.

The FASB is the operating part of a tripartite structure (see Exhibit 6). The Financial Accounting Foundation (FAF) is responsible for selecting members of both the FASB and the Advisory Council and for exercising general oversight over FASB activities. The FAF's board of trustees, in turn, is made up of nominees from six sponsoring organizations:

- American Accounting Association.
- American Institute of Certified Public Accountants.
- Financial Analysts Federation.
- Financial Executives Institute.
- National Association of Accountants.
- Securities Industry Association.

The seven FASB members serve full time and must sever all previous business or professional connections prior to joining the board. They are aided by a staff of technical specialists and other support personnel. The staff works directly with the board and various task forces. As such, it conducts research, participates in public hearings, analyzes public comments, and prepares recommendations and draft documents for consideration

Exhibit 6
Financial Accounting Standards Board Relationships and
Composition

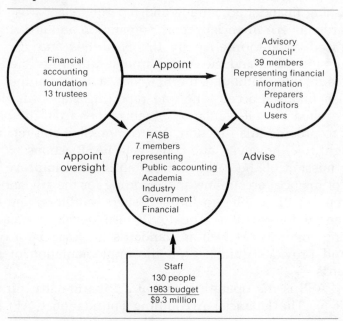

*Financial Accounting Standards Advisory Council.

by the board. Funds for the FASB operations are provided by contributions, largely from business and professional organizations, and by the sale of its publications.

FASB actions affect all public businesses and are the major source of generally accepted accounting principles (GAAP). In general, companies must comply with GAAP in order to receive an auditor's opinion favorable enough to assure acceptance of their financial statements in SEC filings.

Information on current FASB activities is regularly distributed to a mailing list of constituents by the board in "FASB Action Alerts," "FASB Status Reports," and periodically, in "Highlights of Financial Reporting Issues." Other information on the FASB can be found in various publications and periodicals, such as *The Week in Review* by Deloitte Haskins & Sells, *Accounting Events and Trends* by Price Waterhouse & Co., and the *Corporate Accounting Reporter* by Executive Enterprises.

Participation CFOs can participate in this process and, at the same time, bring a business perspective to accounting rules in the following ways:

- Submit written comments on FASB invitations to comment, exposure drafts, and so on.
- Speak in public hearing proceedings.
- Work with professional organizations, such as Financial Executives Institute or the National Association of Accountants, whose positions tend to carry more weight than those of an individual company.
- Work on special committees set up by the FASB or provide staff support to them.

New York Stock Exchange

The New York Stock Exchange (NYSE) is the largest organized securities market in the world and has been in operation for over 190 years. As a quasi-public, self-regulatory institution, it has to both serve and protect the interest of many diverse parties. Its programs and policies are set by a board of directors consisting of 10 public representatives, 10 exchange members, and a full-time chairman and president. The exchange staff, in turn, is responsible for carrying out those programs and objectives.

Descriptive materials and statistics about the NYSE are readily available from its public information or marketing offices at 11 Wall Street, New York, N.Y. 10005. About 1,500 corporations, with assets of about four trillion dollars, had their securities listed with the NYSE as of the end of 1983.

Listing requirements and procedures can be obtained from the Corporate Services Division. Normally, it takes about three months from an initial application to the time an eligible company's securities can be listed on the exchange.

Current Issues While the market value of shares listed on the New York Stock Exchange is many times that of all the other U.S. exchanges combined, the Big Board still faces many issues in the future. For example, competition from the other U.S. and international exchanges, particulary the National Association of Securities Dealers (NASD) over-the-counter market, has been very intense. Continued automation of the floor and trading activities to handle increased business is critical. The exchange also has to keep up with other changes constantly occurring in the securities industry. In order to meet the challenges of the decade ahead, a broad study of the exchange and its future has been going on during 1983 and 1984. The exchange's ability to effectively cope with the problems of the past decade, however, would indicate that it will also be successful in the next one.

Contacts CFOs will probably wish to keep current on trading procedures and practices and on other exchange developments which might affect their companies. This can be accomplished by direct contacts with exchange officials in New York or by participation in Exchange Market Information Programs that are periodically run by the Stock Exchange in major U.S. cities.

Contact should also be made with a company's stock specialist who is an exchange member specially registered for that function. The specialist acts as an agent for other brokers and is accountable to the exchange to maintain a liquid and continuous two-sided auction in a company's securities. There are now about 400 specialists trading on the exchange, and currently they account for about 11 percent of all shares bought and sold.

State Agencies

The increasing importance of state agencies to the CFO, particularly in the tax and environmental areas, should be noted. As the fervor of some of the federal agencies has lessened under recent administrations, there seems to be a growing militancy at the state level. Some CFOs have even indicated that in certain instances they would rather operate under a single federal regulation than under the often chaotic and conflicting multistate regulations.

Companies relate to a number of state agencies in such a wide variety of ways that specific advice cannot really be given. However, the authors believe that their comments about federal agencies should also apply to state agencies. Once the CFOs determine which state agencies are really important to their companies, an effective procedure for working with them can usually be developed.

WORKING THROUGH OTHERS

A CFO may not have the time, the desire, or the skills to deal directly with regulatory agencies. In this situation, a company's Washington office, if one exists, can be very helpful in establishing contacts, monitoring activities, and working with federal agencies. Another way to get involved is by working through other organizations, such as the Financial Executives Institute, the Business Advisory Council on Federal Reports, or the trade association of the company's particular industry segment.

A good first step for a CFO to take would be to join the Financial Executives Institute (FEI). With over 12,000 members representing more than 6,000 corporations, the FEI is the premier association of financial managers in the country. The FEI's mission is to maintain a position of national leadership on issues affecting corporate financial management and to provide services that will meet the professional needs of its members. Through its national staff, technical committees, and area chapters, it serves as an effective financial voice in and for the business community. The FEI frequently presents its position on key financial issues to its membership and selected audiences, such as the FASB, the SEC, U.S. Government Departments and Agencies, Congressional Committees, and the Stock Exchanges.

The Business Advisory Council on Federal Reports (BACFR) was started in 1942. Its mission is "to minimize federal paperwork burden and assure meaningful reporting programs in the public interest." BACFR has worked diligently on both the passage and the implementation of the Paperwork Reduction Act of 1980. It keeps its membership well informed through various ways, such as newsletters, meetings, and seminars. BACFR would welcome interaction with CFOs and their staffs and, of course, new members. Their offices are located at 1625 Eye Street, Washington, D.C.

Working with trade associations and with Washington lawyer-lobbyists are also ways to relate to the regulatory agencies. They can be particularly useful to a CFO whose company does not have a Washington office. There are hundreds of sizable associations with Washington offices, such as the National Association of Manufacturers, the Securities Industry Association, the Investment Company Institute, the American Bankers Association, and the American Petroleum Institute. Two publications that the authors would highly recommend in this area are *Conquering Government Regulations* by M. Stokes (particularly Chapters 1, 5, and 14) and *Getting Your Point Across in Washington* by Price Waterhouse & Co.[12]

The CFO, of course, will have to choose the ones that are most related to his or her own company. For example, the National Association of Manufacturers (NAM), which was founded in 1895, is the nation's oldest trade association representing about 80 percent of the country's industrial capacity and 85 percent of the industrial work force. NAM promotes U.S. foreign trade and represents the industry's views to government on many national and international questions. It maintains numerous committees, including ones on regulatory reform and government organization, taxation, and corporate finance.

REGULATORY IMPROVEMENTS

President Reagan issued Executive Order 12291 in February 1981, directing the Office of Management and Budget and the Presidential Task Force on Regulatory Relief under Vice President Bush to review federal regulations for provisions that were costly, burdensome, and unnecessary. Independent regulatory agencies were not covered by the order. This was a continuation of the process to "streamline" and reduce the detriments of the regulatory process which began under President Ford and was continued by President Carter.

In August 1983, the President's Task Force was terminated, and the process of regulatory review was totally turned over to the Office of Management and Budget. It is estimated that the changes made as a result of the cost/benefit review process will save business, state and local governments, and consumers $150 billion over the next 10 years.[13]

While this effort was moderately successful, the various legislative efforts for regulatory reform, including the independent

---

[12]See bibliography for details on these publications.

[13]A different but related effort is the President's Private Sector Survey on Cost Control under J. Peter Grace. The Grace Commission proposals, which were submitted to the president in the fall of 1983, contain over 2,000 recommendations for potential savings in federal government operations which total over $300 billion.

regulatory agencies, have been a disappointment. One approach under consideration was a legislative veto process which would have given Congress veto power over agency regulations. However, the courts have held one-House legislative veto provisions to be unconstitutional.[14] Also, the proposed Regulatory Reform Act which, among other things, would provide for regulatory analysis of major rules seems to be stalled in Congress and will probably remain so until public pressure on them causes a change.

SOURCES AND MATERIALS

The Office of the Federal Register (National Archives and Records Service–General Services Administration) issues the *Federal Register* (FR) on a daily basis. The *Federal Register* provides a uniform system for making regulations and legal notices issued by federal agencies available to the public. It includes proposed rules, final rules, notices (general interest documents), agency contacts, and schedules of meetings called by the various regulatory agencies.

The *Federal Register* is an excellent source of data for finding out what's going on. Using the information as published in the raw, however, is very time consuming. It is now running about 60,000 small print pages per year. One way to deal with this raw data is through a library service function.[15] In the area of regulations, the librarian has many resources available, such as computerized indexes to the *Federal Register* (FR) and the *Code of Federal Regulations* (CFR).[16]

Keeping current on federal regulations is fairly simple. Commerce Clearing House publishes a wide variety of bulletins, digests, and summaries of governmental activities. There are also

---

[14]Supreme Court decision in *Immigration & Naturalization Service* v. *Chadha,* 103 S. Ct. 2764 (1983).

[15]If a company does not have a library, the consulting service of the Special Libraries Association, 235 Park Avenue South, New York, New York 10003, can put one in touch with a local librarian service. In many locations this service is free or low cost.

[16]Systems Development Corporation (SDC) of Santa Monica, California and DIALOG of Palo Alto, California, offer a computerized index to the FR created by Capitol Services, Inc. Another automated system is Mead Data Corporation which provides full text, rather than just citations, to the FR and the CFR.

numerous periodicals which monitor activities of all branches of the federal government. Some of these are *Congressional Quarterly*, McGraw-Hill's *Inside* newsletters (*Inside Energy*, *Inside FERC*, and the like), and the *National Journal*. In addition, many general interest periodicals provide coverage of regulatory activities. These include *Business Week*, *U.S. News and World Report*, and *The Wall Street Journal*. Most of these periodicals are indexed or included full text in data bases.

In addition, many business or trade associations publish newsletters and magazines on regulatory trends in a particular industry. Several of these associations provide telephone information services which offer the opportunity to talk directly with a subject specialist.

CONCLUSIONS

The conclusions of this chapter are fairly straightforward. Government regulations will be with us for the foreseeable future and will continue to have a significant impact on business and the financial community. Therefore, it is important for CFOs to be involved in the governmental process, particularly in those areas and with those agencies that are most significant to their businesses.

The involvement of CFOs can take many routes—from direct participation in work groups to support of trade associations and professional organizations. The vast majority of the government agency representatives that the authors interviewed both welcomed and encouraged these involvements. It is very clear that the views of individual companies are important to the regulatory bodies. If a CFO is not currently active in these areas, the time to start is now.

BIBLIOGRAPHY

American Enterprise Institute. *Regulation and Regulatory Reform (A Survey of Proposals of the 95th Congress.)* Washington, D.C.: 1979.

Breyer, S. *Regulation and Its Reform.* Cambridge, Mass.: Harvard University Press, 1982.

Price Waterhouse. *Getting Your Point Across in Washington.* New York: 1982.

Sanders, M. E. *The Regulation of Natural Gas.* Philadelphia: Temple University Press, 1981.

Stokes, M. *Conquering Government Regulations.* New York: McGraw-Hill, 1982.

Strickland, A. D. *Government Regulation and Business.* Boston: Houghton Mifflin, 1980.

Vancil, Richard F. *Financial Executive's Handbook.* Homewood, Ill.: Dow Jones-Irwin, 1970.

Weidenbaum, M. L. *The Future of Business Regulation.* New York: AMACOM, 1979.

21

Relations with Equity Investors

Francis A. Stroble and A. Nicholas Filippello

Today, the question of how to maximize shareholder value occupies the time and effort of every chief financial officer in the business world and investment community. One of the ways to manage this concern is through an effective investor relations program.

The basic and overriding purpose of any financial relations effort is to facilitate cost-efficient capital formation. Equity capital is high in cost relative to other financing alternatives, so the intrinsic objective is to minimize the cost of equity capital by enhancing the company's stock price. Therefore, a high level of ongoing communications with equity investors is an essential activity for virtually all publicly held corporations.

It is clear that there are many benefits that can be gained from a fully valued stock. On those occasions when equity capital must be raised, a good market valuation can minimize the dilution of existing shareholders' investments. Additionally, enhanced ac-

Francis A Stroble joined Monsanto Company in 1956 and is currently senior vice president and CFO. He is an advisory director of the company and a member of the Council of Financial Executives. A. Nicholas Filippello is director of financial relations and chief economist at Monsanto.

cess to equity capital generally will be reflected in the improved access and cost of debt capital as well.

On an ongoing basis, good communications with the financial community will enhance the value of the shareholder's investment. More immediately, however, and from a very practical standpoint, favorable stock performance is a particularly effective defense against shareholder dissatisfaction.

If a company is interested in expanding its markets or product portfolio through acquisition, a well-valued stock can reduce the costs and dilutive effects of any exchange of stock for assets. It may, in fact, make an otherwise infeasible acquisition financially attractive. A high stock price relative to earnings generally tends to be associated with a firm's debt capacity and its ability to use internally generated funds.

Favorable stock valuation can also help to discourage takeover threats. By making unfriendly acquisition attempts more costly, management can more effectively do that for which they are being paid rather than maintaining a vigilant eye for prospective pirates.

Finally, and not insignificantly, financial benefits of a good price-to-earnings (P/E) ratio accrue directly to the company's management and employees who may individually own the company stock, own options to purchase the stock, take part in company thrift or profit-sharing plans, or receive shares through Employee Stock Ownership Plans.

This emphasis on the enhancement of stock price, however, should not be misinterpreted. It would be a shortsighted and a potentially damaging error for a financial relations effort to focus too specifically on moving up the stock price. It certainly is within the power of a CEO, CFO, or the investor relations executive to "hype the stock" through unbalanced or overly enthusiastic presentations, or even through misleading statements. Any benefits achieved by such an approach are likely to be only temporary in nature. Furthermore, once the euphoria has worn off and investors and analysts conclude that they have been misled in some way, the credibility of the company will suffer. This will result in a heightened degree of skepticism and uncertainty regarding the company and the statements of its senior executives and spokesmen. The end result then becomes less investor enthusiasm for the company and undervaluation in the marketplace. Once credibility is lost, it is extremely difficult to regain. In addition, of course, legal liabilities might well result from any efforts to deceive the investing public. It is a clear violation of the securities laws for anyone to make untrue or misleading statements about material facts.

The philosophy of corporate investor relations, therefore, should not be to market the stock for near-term gains—as tempting as that approach may often be. Rather, the objectives of the corporation and its long-term needs can best be addressed by striving for *fair* valuation in the marketplace. This means sharing the bad news, openly and candidly, as well as the good news. This is sometimes difficult to do because it may have temporary adverse effects on the stock price. But, over a period of time, the market value of a company's equities will be fairly valued only if there is confidence in management and its credibility. To the extent that financial markets operate in a reasonably efficient manner (and most evidence suggests they do), the best a company can hope for on a sustained basis is a *fair* market valuation which accurately reflects a company's strengths and weaknesses. The job of the investor relations executive is to provide, with the active support of top management, that information which is necessary to minimize deviations from a fair market valuation.

Of course, the law requires that no misleading information be disseminated. It also requires that any material information, including disclosure of financial results or of earnings estimates, be made equally available to all segments of the investment community. Consequently, the effort to provide that information which will aid in the fair market valuation of the stock must be accompanied by diligence in ensuring that no analyst or investor receives an unfair advantage in gaining access to such information.

The investor relations needs for each company are unique. The degree of public ownership, the distribution of that ownership between and among institutions and individuals, the industry or industries in which a company participates, a company's size, the geographical distribution of its customers and suppliers, and the degree to which a company and its products are recognized or identified by consumers all determine the market for the company's securities. Consequently, the approach to communicating a company's message to existing and potential investors depends heavily on individual circumstances.

There are more than 5,000 corporations in the United States competing for the attention of equity investors. Of these, nearly 1,600 are listed on the New York Stock Exchange, nearly 900 on the American Exchange, and more than 3,000 on the NASDAQ over-the-counter market. The 25 largest brokerage firms follow only some 460 companies, and with significant duplication. As a result, half of all publicly held companies are followed by three brokerage firms or less. Obviously, no single financial relations approach will suit the needs of all.

The large Fortune 500-type companies most often have the advantage of being followed by at least several brokerage house ("sell side") analysts and a significant number of institutional ("buy side") analysts and portfolio managers, as well as receiving frequent coverage in the financial press. For these companies, communications with a well-identified group of security analysts and a select group of institutional portfolio managers is the primary vehicle for investor relations. These are the people who make the market for the company's stock.

Smaller companies, in general, have a less broad-based institutional following and, therefore, must aggresively compete for investor attention. Many of these companies have regional followings and limited funds for an investor relations program. Often companies such as these will concentrate their efforts where the company name recognition is greatest—that is, in the area where they are headquartered and in those areas where they operate plants and employ a significant portion of the local population. Also, they may concentrate efforts in major market centers for their products. Finally, a small firm may find it advantageous to employ the services of an investor relations consulting firm. In this way, optimum coverage of potential investors may be attained within the limits of budgets and the available time of corporate officers. In all cases, however, the Investor Relations Program must be tailored to the specific needs of each company.

In general, the market focus of investor relations activities has changed dramatically during the past 20 years. During the early 1960s, more than 60 parcent of the value of public trading on the New York Stock Exchange was accounted for by individual investors, with less than 40 percent accounted for by professional money managers. Since that time the relationship has more than reversed. In recent years, professional money managers have accounted for 70 percent or more of the trading volume. This reflects the new dominance of equity markets by financial institutions and the growth of individuals' indirect participation in equity markets through financial intermediaries, such as pension funds or insurance companies. In recent years, more than half of the more than one-half trillion dollars of institutionally held stock has been controlled by private and public pension and retirement funds. Another 20 percent has been held by insurance companies, ten percent by mutual funds, and fifteen percent by foreign investors.

WHAT INFORMATION MUST BE COMMUNICATED?

If the ultimate purpose of investor relations activities is to facilitate capital formation, the principal objective is to promote investor understanding of the company. There are four general areas which require frequent and ongoing communication between the company and investors:

1. Product portfolio and markets served.
2. Current business conditions and outlook.
3. Corporate strategy.
4. Sources of potential surprise.

Product Portfolio and Markets Served

It is essential that the existing and potential investor understands what the company is all about—that is, what are the key products and product groups of importance to the company and what are the primary end-use and intermediate markets served. Good institutional analysts will be unwilling to rely solely on the company's expectations for its prospects. Rather, they will need to build up sales and profit projections of their own in order to make judgments regarding the company's earning power and potential attractiveness as an investment.

Providing product/market information can be relatively straightforward for a company selling a few products directly into well-defined and readily identified consumer markets. In these cases, simple identification of major products may be sufficient.

For many large, diversified, industrial companies which sell intermediate products (to other companies rather than to consumers), the job requires a much greater degree of education. Here, it is necessary to trace out for the investor the chain of demand, beginning with the end-use markets ultimately served, through the intermediate customer industries served, identification of major competitors, and some degree of information concerning the company's position within those particular markets. While it would be unproductive to disseminate market information in such detail that it can be digested by only the most dedicated analyst, sufficient information should be made available to allow the investor to understand the chain of demand for the company's products. The objective is to give the analyst/investor sufficient information to allow an independent estimate of sales and earnings prospects.

Current Business Conditions and Outlook

Competitive pressures within the institutional investing community place current earnings prospects high on the security analysts' list of priorities. Institutional estimates for the current quarter, the current year, and the following year are constantly being revised and massaged to be as up-to-date as possible. Consequently, a major portion of day-to-day investor relations activities centers on current business conditions and the outlook for principal markets or factors which could affect near-term financial results. In conducting these activities with the investment community, it is crucial to be ever mindful of the basic legal prohibition against divulging any item of material nonpublic information unless and until it has been publicly disclosed by a press release or equivalent public statement.

Major financial institutions employ their own economists who generally work closely with industry analysts in developing projections on which to base independent sales and earnings projections for individual companies. Nevertheless, the typical analyst wants to know how the company views its own business prospects and what kind of assumptions regarding the external business and economic environment are being utilized for internal planning. More importantly, however, the analyst will be critically interested in recent developments in orders, shipments, pricing, and inventories. Where this type of information can be shared without compromising competitive considerations or legal requirements, it is beneficial to do so. It is almost always in the company's best interest to help analysts do their jobs and to "be smart" relative to the company's performance capabilities from ongoing operations.

Corporate Strategy

Oliver Wendell Holmes once said, "The greater thing in this world is not as much where we stand as in what direction we are going." This is an undeniable truth in the valuation of corporate equities. The product and market information previously discussed are essential for investor understanding of where and what a company is today. But a frank and candid communication of strategy tells the investment community where the company intends to go.

A credible discussion of strategy must include an upfront analysis of any problem areas. What areas of the company may be underperforming? What alternatives are available to management? What are the objectives management has set to deal effectively with these problems? There is a natural tendency to want to minimize discussion of problem areas, but astute investors and analysts will know that the problems exist. And management can gain substantial credibility and confidence with the financial community by openly acknowledging their existence, identifying possible solutions, and presenting plans of action.

A discussion of strategy must also include plans associated with ongoing product lines. This might include plans for market share gains, expansions into specific industrial or geographical markets, product improvements or process changes, or even "cash cow" or wasting asset strategies. It might also include a discussion of how the company plans to respond to changes in the competitive, regulatory, or economic environment.

Additionally, a discussion of strategy must focus on new products, areas of planned growth for the future, dividend payout and stock split policy, acquisition/divestiture strategy, areas of planned capital investment, and where research and development will be concentrated. In short, the company should attempt to answer the investors' question, "Where and what does the company want to be 2 years, 5 years, or 10 years from now, and how does it plan to get there?"

Finally, it is critical to integrate a discussion of a growth or product strategy with a consistent financial strategy. Equity analysts will want to know how a growth strategy will be financed. How much can reasonably be financed through internally generated funds? What kind of debt expansion will be required? Is it likely that the company will raise funds in equity markets?

A credible, positive, and well-understood growth and financial strategy can be a key element in building a healthy and sustainable price-earnings multiple.

Sources of Potential Surprise

It is a well-known dictum that the market reacts negatively to uncertainty. While uncertainty often is unavoidable, the company can seek to reduce it by openly discussing sources of potential surprise. If a company creates a reputation for hitting the market with negative surprises or failing to discuss candidly potential liabilities, competitive threats, or adverse product developments, uncertainty will develop regarding the fundamentals of the company's earning power, financial stability, and management capability. Once such a reputation has been developed, market demand for the stock likely will be somewhat less than it otherwise might be if management were viewed more credibly. A natural result is a stock price which is depressed relative to its industry and its own potential.

The price of an equity security generally is considered to represent the discounted present value of the expected future stream of earnings from operations (or return to the investor as represented by dividends plus capital appreciation). That future stream of earnings is discounted to account not only for returns on alternate sources of investments but also for the degree of perceived risk. While the risk factor will be a function of many things, it will include a judgment of the degree of relative predictability associated with the company's reported financial results. The message is clear. To the extent that surprises can be minimized, the long-term valuation of the stock can be enhanced.

Striking the balance between what information investors and analysts want and what is feasible to give them is a constant source of careful decisions on the part of a company's financial management. Of primary importance is consistency. It is improper to give preferential treatment to a few analysts, and it is *illegal* if it is of material significance. The cardinal rule to remember is that information of such significance cannot be selectively disclosed to some analysts and not to others or to analysts and not to the investing public. Anytime it is expected that material, nonpublic information is to be revealed, a press release should be delivered to the financial press and wire services prior to, or concurrently with, the disclosure.

Second only to consistency in importance is credibility. It is necessary to be as open and honest with analysts and investors as legal and competitive considerations will allow and to be willing to talk in bad times as well as good. "No comment" or "trust us" statements in the face of adverse news or developments may simply fuel rumor and uncertainty. The result may well be a more negative stock price reaction than an open discussion of the situation would cause. In fact, talking openly about potential negative developments can actually have a positive long-run impact on the stock price by enhancing the sense of comfort in management's credibility.

HOW TO CARRY OUT COMMUNICATIONS

Financial relations takes many forms, including written communications to shareowners, the annual meeting, and personal communications with the financial community. Each of these is addressed in turn.

Written Communications to Shareholders

The most widely distributed vehicle of financial communication is the annual report. Its principal function is to inform shareholders, within SEC and FASB rulings and guidelines, about the company, its organization, major products, and financial results for the prior year. For many companies, however, the objectives of the annual report go well beyond straightforward shareholder information. Other key audiences include employees, customers, suppliers, universities, potential new employees, and the community at large. The annual report represents the single most widely distributed piece of corporate identity documentation for most companies.

More importantly to the financial relations effort, however, it provides a ready source of information to analysts, lenders, and potential investors. Not only does the document provide basic financial data needed by potential investors, it provides a statement by the company of what it is and where it is going. A good annual report will deliver a clear and direct message to the shareholder and potential investor.

Interim reports in the form of the quarterly financial report are generally used far less than the annual report as a public relations vehicle or even to provide basic information to potential investors. Nevertheless, the quarterly report can be far more than a simple statement of the prior quarter's financial results. It represents a regular opportunity to communicate with shareholders, analysts, and investment managers. As with the annual report, the quarterly report can be most effective if it communicates a straightforward message to shareholders. The report might contain a summary of the annual shareholders meeting, features on topics of current importance to the company, informational pieces on topics of potential interest or concern to shareowners, or discussion of new products, research efforts, or progress toward previously stated goals. Topics can often be addressed which may be more timely than those covered in the annual report. Also, topics can be covered which might otherwise be "out-of-place" as part of the annual report. In short, the quarterly report is a means by which shareholders can be made better aware of their company and developments through the year as they occur.

The needs of most individual shareholders, analysts, and institutional portfolio managers can differ sharply. To provide the individual shareholders routinely with the kind of information required by a professional security analyst as part of the annual or quarterly reports would likely be counterproductive in many cases. The individual investor may be turned off, and the intended message of the report will be lost. On the other hand, the analyst seeks and needs far more detail and information than the average individual shareholder wants or could use.

To meet the needs of the analyst and profesional investor, some companies publish an annual corporate/financial data book and/or periodic institutional investor newsletters or communications. Obviously, for legal reasons, such publications must be available to individual investors on request. Individual shareholders can be made aware of these publications in the annual report. The content and format of these special forms of communication generally are designed specifically to meet the needs of the professional analyst and money manager. The objective is to increase the depth of understanding of the company, its markets, and its management. For example, the data book might include an analysis of information by operating unit, such as total assets, capital expenditures, research and development and depreciation, as well as sales and operating income. Additionally, a summary of markets served, major products, principal competitors, and locations of facilities might be included. These publications are distributed principally to a select list of institutional analysts and investors who follow the company closely and regularly.

Some companies also publish a regular investor newsletter for analysts and selected money managers. A quarterly newsletter can be used to update investors on business conditions, cost and price developments, and significant developments of importance to the company.

In addition to specialized regular publications, many companies also send news releases of quarterly earnings and selected events of special significance to key analysts and investors. Occasionally, the text of a top management presentation will be distributed, as well as occasional special written communications on an important topic where timeliness is a consideration. An example of a special distribution might be a fact sheet on an issue of intense concern to analysts and investors. The objective of such a fact sheet might be to create a sound understanding of the issues, based on fact, thereby minimizing investment decisions which otherwise would be based on incomplete information, rumors, or misinformation.

In recent years, many companies have put substantial effort into written communications with key analysts and investors. The payoff is difficult to measure, but we think that it is a cost-effective endeavor, and one well worth actively pursuing.

The Annual Meeting

The importance of the annual meeting varies from company to company, depending on the ownership base and the geographical distribution of that ownership. Nevertheless, beyond simply satisfying legal requirements, the annual meeting provides the single public forum during the year where the individual shareholder has the opportunity to be heard. Furthermore, it provides management with the opportunity to articulate statements of policy or intent to shareowners, to explain developments, and to answer questions of general interest.

For the most part, annual meetings are of limited interest to institutional analysts. They are viewed primarily as a communications vehicle for the individual investor. This being the case, a company is well advised not to attempt to make the annual meeting all things to all investors. It is properly the individual investor's forum and an opportunity for favorable press coverage.

Communications with Top Management

No investor relations program can reach its potential level of success without the active participation of the corporation's top management. The credibility of a company's message to the investment community is enhanced when the CEO, the CFO, and others who are making policy and making decisions communicate directly with analysts and money managers and respond candidly to questions. Limited, but reasonably frequent, accessibility of principal executives is the cornerstone of a good financial communications program for most institutionally held firms.

These communications should take several forms. Most widely followed companies will be invited to make periodic presentations to security analysts societies, industry splinter groups, and occasional broker-sponsored client meetings. In the principal financial centers of the United States, such as New York, Boston, Chicago, or Los Angeles, the CEO frequently will be called upon to address the full security analyst societies. These generally are major events that receive broad attention far beyond the normal range of close followers of the company. Many companies publish the presentations made at these events and distribute copies to their regular target list of analysts and portfolio managers. Of course, any items of material significance should also be covered in press releases timed to coincide with the initial presentation.

Appearances by the CEO before large groups of this type in major financial centers are best limited in frequency to perhaps no more than once or twice a year. Furthermore, such appearances are best timed, if possible, to coincide with a major announcement or "new" information about the company. Such an approach results in the CEO's appearance as signaling the investment community that the company has a message to convey. Normally, this will generate increased interest and attention in such meetings.

More frequently, a widely followed company will be invited to make presentations to analysts' industry splinter groups or broker-sponsored client meetings in major financial centers. Occasionally, the CEO will make presentations to these groups as well. More often, however, these meetings provide an excellent forum for other senior executives, such as the CFO, the executive vice presidents with major operating responsibilities, or the operating division heads, where there may be substantial focused investor interest in a particular product group.

Periodically, it is useful for the company to sponsor large analyst meetings or field trips where principal analysts and money managers are invited to a concentrated, one- or two-day program. It may make sense to focus these field trips on a specific area of the company and to hold the meetings at appropriate company facilities where the analyst can gain some first-hand knowledge of the operation.

The principal objective of such a field trip is to provide some in-depth "education" on a specific and important (or potentially important) area of the company. A secondary objective is to provide the opportunity for analysts and selected members of management to become better acquainted in a more informal setting. This helps to foster a sense of comfort, understanding, and communication on the part of management, as well as analysts and investors.

Finally, key brokerage firm analysts following the company will occasionally visit headquarters with a small group of analysts or money managers from major investing institutions. Where feasible, it is helpful to enlist the participation of senior level management to talk informally to these groups and answer questions. Often, these visits will concentrate on several specific areas of business as opposed to an overview of the corporation. Where this is the case, operating managers with specific product group responsibilities can be most helpful in answering questions or updating the analysts on business conditions or product strategies.

Financial Communications Abroad

For most U.S. companies, the financial relations effort is concentrated heavily within the United States. A company with substantial foreign operations or a high degree of identifiability outside the United States may be missing a large source of investment funds if it concentrates on the United States to the exclusion of foreign financial communities.

For the most part, institutional investors outside the United States frequently tend to have a longer-term investment horizon than many near-term, results-oriented U.S. institutions. Consequently, they tend to be very concerned with strategy and long-term growth but less concerned with current earnings than their American counterparts. As a result, they generally are anxious to meet with or listen to presentations of the top management of firms in which they may have an interest. Most often, however, they neither need nor want the kind of frequent attention that their U.S. counterparts routinely receive.

Some companies have found it useful to make a series of luncheon presentations to institutional investors in major European and Far Eastern financial centers, with select one-on-one visits, to significant banks and underwriters approximately once every two or three years. In the interim, interested investors receive routine mailings of annual and quarterly reports, financial data books, and investor newsletters. A company may also find it cost-effective to engage in some degree of ongoing, targeted, institutional advertising in order to keep the company's name at the attention of potential investors. It is critical, however, that a member of top management (generally the CEO or CFO) be the principal spokesperson for the company at most presentations made in financial centers outside the United States. European investors, particularly, tend to emphasize the need for *direct* communication from those making long-term dicisions. Furthermore, it is essential to signal to the foreign investor that his or her institution is as important to the company as those in New York, Boston, or elsewhere in the United States.

Since most U.S. companies are less familiar with the participants and customs in financial markets outside the United States, it often is helpful to enlist the help of a third party in setting up luncheon presentations. Investment bankers, "local" brokerage firms, or investor relations consultants are good sources of such assistance. Whatever the method used, the principal goal is to get the company's message to those individuals and institutions which represent the greatest potential source of equity investment. If you are going to make these visits only every other year, you had best do it right!

The Financial Relations Staff

As we have said, the active and enthusiastic participation of top management is essential to an effective program of financial communications. On a day-to-day basis, however, it is the financial relations staff which maintains regular contact with the investment community. This staff is the primary point of contact between the corporation and the investment community. As such, to be effective, the investor relations executive must be privy to information that will facilitate a factual and timely response to the questions of investment analysts.

The investor relations staff can be viewed by the financial community either as a valuable and effective resource or as ineffective and of limited value. Which view is realized depends on the perception of the financial community as to how well that staff is informed on corporate issues and how well they can truly speak for the company in a candid and accurate manner. Consequently, it is essential that the investor relations function be perceived by the financial community as having an important role in the company and that the senior staff executive is seen to hold a sufficiently high position within the company to have a solid understanding of operations and issues, in addition to having some degree of influence with top management.

Next to credibility, the most important characteristics of a financial relations staff are accessibility and responsiveness. In a sense, the staff is there to speak for top management, thereby eliminating the need for the CEO, CFO, and others to spend undue time away from their principal responsibilities. To be effective, however, analysts' inquiries need to be met in as timely and accurate a fashion as practical (obviously within the bounds of legality and established policy). Because it is so important that responses be both proper and prompt, it is helpful to have a set of guidelines, worked out with legal counsel, to follow in making decisions regarding disclosure and dealings with the investment community. This area is a peculiarly sensitive one in which an individual's conduct will typically be judged in hindsight. There has been litigation in the past challenging dealings with financial analysts, and there will be in the future. Such dealings involve inevitable risks and have been described by one court as a "fencing match conducted on a tightrope." The objective of the financial relations staff should be to limit this risk, and appropriate legal counsel can be invaluable to this end.

In order to manage properly the flow and content of information for the sake of consistency and legality, the Investor Relations executive must exercise control of analysts' access to management. Communications normally should be channeled through the investor relations staff, and a member of the staff should generally be present in discussions between analysts and the company's management. Where exceptions exist, it is the responsibility of management to inform the investor relations executive of the circumstances and general content of any such communication. Only through controlled access to management and monitoring of released information can the investor relations staff fulfill its responsibilities to (1) remove top management from the burden of routine analysts' inquiries and (2) maintain consistency and an even flow of information (from the standpoint of equity and legality).

The role of the investor relations staff goes beyond acting as an intermediary between management and the financial community. Often the investor relations executive will act as a company spokesperson as well. Duties normally will include coverage of major financial centers between top management appearances, acting as the principal speaker or spokesperson in smaller financial centers not covered by top management, and one-on-one meetings with key analysts and money managers.

Senior investor relations executives normally will spend a significant portion of their time "on the road." Typical presentations might include appearances before industry analyst splinter groups, security analysts societies in financial centers not covered by top management, company-sponsored, or broker-sponsored luncheons for institutional investors, or focused visits to key institutions—sometimes alone and sometimes with a key brokerage analyst who has a specific interest in the company.

Optimizing investor interest in a company requires dedicated *personal* communication in addition to written material. Furthermore, it requires that personal contact be taken beyond the major financial centers which warrant top management time to other metropolitan areas where significant pension funds, insurance portfolios, mutual funds, or trusts are managed.

CONCLUSION

As stated early in this chapter, the financial relations needs of each company are unique to its situation. Each CFO will want to adopt a customized variation of the approaches discussed that is in keeping with the size and style of his or her company.

It is worth emphasizing that the best financial relations program is of minor importance when compared to how well the company is managed. The best that can be hoped for in the long run is the full valuation of a company's stock. A good communications program can enhance access to capital markets, but it is no substitute for a sound balance sheet, a solid base of earnings, and a favorable outlook for growth that justifies reinvestment.

The investor relations effort is in every sense a marketing effort. But, as in any good long-term marketing plan, the program must concentrate not only on immediate results but on high quality service and continuing investor (that is, customer) attention. This translates into the establishment of the company's equity securities as a perceived sound long-term investment.

22

Relations with Professional Resources

Paul Hines and Robert J. Chrenc

INTRODUCTION

Today, it is possible to find consultants who claim to be expert in nearly every area of corporate endeavor. The purpose of this chapter is not to provide an exhaustive list of those areas where consultants might be most helpful for the chief financial officers, but rather to focus on how the CFO can use them most effectively.

CFOs normally have continuing relationships with their auditing firms as well as with tax and pension consultants and investment and commercial bankers. These relationships generally are historic in nature and are established in order to deal with fairly specific tasks. Most CFOs are well versed and well adept at managing the costs of the services provided by these professionals. This chapter deals with the more ambiguous tasks and more complicated relationships where more room for mis-

Paul Hines manages corporate development, control, and executive development within E.F. Hutton & Company Inc. He is an executive vice president and director of E.F. Hutton & Company Inc. and chairman of the Hutton Insurance Group. Robert J. Chrenc joined the New York office of Arthur Andersen & Co. in 1968 and was admitted to the partnership in 1979. He is a member of the American Institute of Certified Public Accountants and the New York State Society of Certified Public Accountants.

takes exist. There are few senior executives who, in an age of specialization, rapid environmental change and compressed business cycles haven't hired outside consultants and, once having done so, felt out of control.

To make these relationships successful in an increasingly complex business environment requires good communications, strong management, and clear-cut objectives within a framework of trust and openness. The result of a successful relationship can be rewarding both to the CFO and to the organization. Several of the consultants interviewed emphasized that the most productive relationships, in their opinion, were the ones that were sustained over longer periods of time. These relationships have at their core continuing mutually beneficial value added in relation to a diversity of important business opportunities and problems. In such relationships, the consultants have developed a continuity with their clients which greatly enhances their ability to function in an expeditious and cost-effective manner.

WHEN OUTSIDE CONSULTANTS ARE NEEDED

The staff of the typical CFO consists of people who have specific responsibilities and expertise in narrow areas. Thus, when confronted with difficult problems, especially in areas where neither the CFO himself, nor any of his staff, possesses expertise, the organization must look elsewhere for the required specialized competence.

Similarly, a problem may arise that is within the presumed functional expertise of the CFO and his staff but is either of such importance to the firm or so complex that no one in the existing organization has either the time or experience to effectively define an appropriate solution with the required professional level of completed staffwork.

Another reason for using consultants is to establish credibility. Even if you have adequate internal resources, it may be advantageous to use outside consultants whose professional credentials are recognized. The results they produce or the recommendations they suggest have the imprint of outside authority, and, consequently, these results or recommendations may be more acceptable.

Similarly, you may want to use an outside consultant to deal adroitly with special situations or particularly sensitive issues.

By using such a consultant, you can often avoid unnecessary personal confrontations or highly charged emotional situations. One CFO wanted to examine the functions and operations of his company's purchasing department. He believed that the head of purchasing perceived him to be interfering and biased anytime he had conducted even a routine examination. To accomplish his objective, the CFO hired a outside consultant acceptable to the head of purchasing. The CFO got the examination he needed, and the head of purchasing felt that the outside consultant was unbiased and fair.

Perhaps one of the most common uses of outside consultants is to provide an independent, objective point of view. This objectivity can frequently be put to work to review staff work supporting important and complex discussions where the cost of error is large. Review of internally completed staff work by acknowledged outside experts can have a number of benefits where important decisions are at issue. Such reviews can establish the credibility of the internal work and satisfy whatever gnawing feelings exist that the internal staff may have over assumed or under analyzed. Being an outsider, the consultant does not have a client organization's biases, attitudes, or values. Consequently, the consultant brings a perspective that is detached and impartial. Auditors do this, of course, when they audit a company's financial statements. But they also do so, for example, when they review the procedures in an accounting department.

An outside consultant may also be utilized as an intellectual interlocutor. In this capacity, the CFO would be able to freely discuss radical ideas with a respected, impartial mind that won't be threatened. Trust and intellectual integrity are crucial characteristics for a successful consultant.

In these instances, the CFO who has developed a network of relationships with professional resources has an advantage. The obvious advantage is the ability to quickly access the required expertise at an efficient cost and with the assurance that cost-effective solutions to the problem will be proposed.

THE PROFESSIONAL RESOURCE NETWORK

There are several ways to identify professional resources and to inventory them for future use. Professional resources include not only consultants but also peers who have achieved superior performance in areas important to an individual CFO's success. The CFO who has not taken the time and effort to identify and to make himself known to a range of professional resources is at a professional disadvantage. Successful conduct of his responsibilities requires that the CFO have available a broad and extremely competent network of professional resources.

It is well known that the establishment of a resource network is one of the principal benefits of membership and meeting attendance in organizations, such as the Financial Executives Institute. Meeting with appropriate frequency with successful peers to discuss mutual problems is one of the most beneficial support networks available to a CFO or any other executive.

Discussions with CFOs in other industries indicate that the potential benefit of creating a similar resource network with a broad array of consultants is an often overlooked and undeveloped opportunity for performance improvement. The task is one of accumulating an ever-improving resource pool over the course of a career. Consultant sources may be outgrown or "peter out" just as any executive. It is wrong and even dangerous, for example, to assume that the recruiter who was most helpful in staffing departmenthead positions can effectively staff divisionhead positions. That resource pool which is most effective is the one which offers the greatest potential for insight and support in relation to those tasks most critical to the success of the CFO in his job.

These areas of functional expertise are often those with which the CFO is least experienced. Examples include organizational behavior, personnel administration, operations research, and other areas of management and management science. Knowledge of these areas may not have been critical to achieve the CFO position but may be critical to excel in it. A paradox of executive career development is that technical expertise which formed early career success may not be that important to senior executive success. When asked what they wished they were more skilled at, most senior executives desire organizational and human relations skills.

SOURCES

Developing a network of available professional relationships is a process which can be managed. The process involves identifying those professionals with superior functional expertise in areas that matter the most, particularly those with which the CFO is least experienced and knowledgeable. One financial officer actually maintained an active inventory of professional relationships that were carefully cultivated. The list was actively maintained and professionals were added to and deleted from the list when appropriate. When specific expertise was required and a relationship existed, he was able to initiate an engagement with little time or cost expended in search. Assignments with income potential should be awarded with sufficient regularity to maintain a professional's level of interest.

The same executive stated that he conducted ongoing searches for professional expertise. He felt those searches to be as important as searches conducted for the purpose of staff additions. His process was to search out names of candidates from sources such as peers, recruiters, and even periodicals. He would then contact the potential candidates and invite them to his office, to lunch or for dinner, to conduct his interview. Normally there would be enough mutuality of interest such that even the most accomplished professional would succumb to the invitation. Peers who have successfully managed to overcome difficult problems were perceived to be the most effective resources.

The objective is to construct an available support network of world-class professional expertise in those areas where the executive may need help. Most executive careers are a function of the individual executive's ability to perform independently and under stress, as well as his ability to create a superior internal and external support organization. It is a sobering notion that a career is as limited by the quality of the support organization as it is by the ability of the executive. Clearly, the executive capable of building and utilizing both internal and external support organizations optimally is in a far better position than he would be were he to depend only on his own ability. This reality was summed up by an executive who commented that if he were only dependent on his own ability, he would have failed long ago.

BUILDING YOUR OWN NETWORK

The best sources for outside consultants, obviously, are those you previously have used with success. They know your business and understand your organization. You can save both time and money by not having to educate them about your industry and your company. They get straight to the problem without requiring extensive background information.

A second source for outside consultants, mentioned above, is the recommendation of other financial executives. Find out what their experience with various consultants has been, and get names of those they think have performed especially well.

You can also learn about various consultants at meetings of professional societies and trade associations where you have an opportunity to meet them and discuss their qualifications and experience. Speakers may themselves be consultants or be able to recommend ones appropriate to your needs. By-lined articles in professional publications and trade journals may also provide potential leads.

You may want to use consultants with whom you are unfamiliar on a small, limited engagement to observe their performance. Such an engagement allows you to see the consultants in action, requiring only a limited expenditure of time and money. It gives you an opportunity also to observe the personal "chemistry" between you, your staff, and the consultants. Staff feedback is an excellent indication of how well the consultants and their professional staff fit your consulting needs. Because so much consulting work entails organizationally or otherwise sensitive issues, it is important that the consultants behave responsibly in the engagement. If you or your staff are uncomfortable with them, you will probably not be happy with their performance.

Another technique of evaluating the capability of a variety of professional resources is to accept proposals or invite presentations from a group of suitable candidates. This is an opportunity to compare competitors on a level playing field, and it not only provides a forum through which you can determine which consultant to use for an immediate need, but can help in network building. This is true to the extent that you can assess the strengths and weaknesses of each player and store that information away for future use. Often several investment bankers will do presentations for a single proposed transaction even though the firm already has an ongoing investment banking relationship. Their hope is that they can show sufficient skills in financing capabilities to get all or some of the business. Colleges, universities, and business schools can also be excellent sources for consultants.

WHAT TO LOOK FOR IN A CONSULTANT

Once the CFO has established a professional resource network and has identified a specific need, he must decide which consultant to use. The choice is often difficult even when choosing among good alternatives. Although there may be any number of competent consultants available, it is crucial to choose the best one for the particular problem. One should avoid applying the right solution to the wrong problem.

Some of the most often-mentioned attributes of the consummate consultant are:

- Established reputation.
- Technical competence.
- Good professional staff.
- The right "chemistry."
- Industry familiarity.

All of the consultants and professional resources interviewed mentioned the above characteristics as being crucial. However, certain attributes are relatively more important to particular areas of resource need as we identify below.

Auditors

Auditors are the most commonly used consultants by CFOs. The more important reason for this, of course, is the SEC requirement that all publicly held companies must file audited financial statements. Many privately held companies also have their financial statements audited for a variety of reasons. For example, submitting audited financial statements to a bank may help in securing a loan. Auditors can be helpful in a wide variety of areas.

The passage of the Foreign Corrupt Practices Act placed a new emphasis on management responsibility for internal controls. Your auditor can examine your internal controls to make certain that they are functioning adequately and make recommendations to improve their effectiveness. In fact, your auditors can provide an important perspective on your company's overall accounting management. In the course of the audit they will make recommendations that can be very useful to you. It is a mistake to overlook these recommendations as they ultimately will enhance your performance as CFO.

Computer technology has changed rapidly in recent years, and businesses have greatly expanded their use of computers both for information and for processing transactions. But with this increased use has come the increased possibility of computer fraud that can seriously jeopardize a company's assets. Establishing effective computer controls to safeguard these assets is critical. Your auditors can help analyze the adequecy of your firm's EDP controls as well as determine the points at which more controls may be necessary.

Another area in which your audit firm can provide valuable assistance is tax planning and compliance. Careful tax planning can help you maximize profits and improve cash flow. If your company has overseas branches, an analysis of foreign tax laws can indicate which countries may be best from a tax point of view. Likewise, if you are sending U.S. nationals to a foreign country or bringing foreign nationals to the United States, your auditing firm can help with expatriate and inpatriate tax planning.

Many auditors can help design, develop, and implement management information systems. By working with such a consultant who brings not only extensive experience but also an outsider's perspective to your information needs, you can often not only make your systems more effective but less costly as well.

Investment Bankers

Investment bankers are often faced with a different set of problems to solve that require different skills and expertise. Those particular capabilities include:

- The ability and capacity to arrange for outside financing.
- Experience and expertise in mergers and acquisitions.
- Experience and proficency in innovating creative financial products.
- The ability to recommend, structure, and execute a myriad of financial transactions.

It should be clear that although all professional resources must display certain fundamental attributes such as good professional staff and industry familiarity, each particular need requires a unique set of finely honed technical skills and experience. The CFO's array of tasks, already broad, continues to expand in breadth and increase in complexity. For example, new financing instruments are developed with increasing regularity and speed in response to specific financing needs and market opportunities. Zero coupon bonds and adjustable rate preferred stocks are two recent examples. Similarly, new financial instruments will continue to be developed to hedge national and international financial risks. Investment bankers and other financial consultants in these areas require specialized skills only recently available to even the most financially sophisticated CFOs.

WHEN TO USE PROFESSIONAL RESOURCES

Many executives having achieved the CFO position make a classic mistake which a less kind observer might label the "arrogance of ignorance." A common failure, even among experienced executives, is to presume competence in areas where they have neither professional training nor personal experience. Most CFOs have themselves experienced this phenomenon in others in relation to their own tasks. There is a human tendency to underestimate the complexity and value of professionalism and experience in areas of unfamiliarity. This is especially true of the "soft areas," such as personnel, executive development, and other areas of organizational behavior.

A methodology for avoiding the temptation of assuming there are simple solutions for complex problems is to discuss the problem with the right level of experienced professional. Clearly, the executive who has figured out his weaknesses in background and experience and built a competent support network around himself has a compelling advantage compared to the executive who has not.

An example of a situation in which outside experts can often be helpful is in the area of staffing at senior management levels. Senior level hiring decisions involve risk. The risk is usually not one of functional or technical competence but rather one of ability to work successfully with the other senior executives in the organization and within, rather than against, the culture of the organization. Most senior executives, including CFOs, are not able to see beyond functional and technical competence. On the other hand, an organizational consultant with knowledge and experience in working with the internal culture can quickly reduce the risks around whether or not the potential senior executive hire will be able to succeed in the organization and strengthen the CFO's ability to perform effectively.

There are many other instances when it may be beneficial to use an outside professional. There will be times when sensitive issues can best be addressed when identified and presented from objective sources. As an example, one of the CFOs interviewed for this chapter mentioned the use of an independent consulting firm to force domestic functional executives to focus on the need for a strong international leader. This need was obvious not only to some of the internal executives, but also it was the solution employed by many of the more successful international competitors. The internal problem was the strong domestic functional organization which was resisting the loss of prerogatives, responsibility, and power in the international region. This control would have to be given up to accommodate a relatively independent and autonomous international president. In this case, an experienced and independent management consultant was engaged. He thoroughly researched the external environment, including the competition, and became sensitive to the internal corporate culture in the course of his work. The force and logic of his presentation created an opportunity for the firm to make a correct executive decision to install a semiautonomous, independent international president.

Another frequently effective and efficient use of outside professional resources is to assign them to action task forces made up of line managers. In this instance, the broader technical experience, along with more developed skills in working in task forces effectively, can be used as a lever to substantially ratchet up the effectiveness of the task force itself. This ratcheting up occurs when the outside consultant assists in the following:

- That the task force remains focused on the most important issues.
- That the task force concentrates on solutions which are within the capability of the organization and its available resources to implement.
- That the task force is realistic about which solutions can be accomplished in a reasonable period of time.

As you can tell, the author's bias is toward the use of consultants to *cause change*. It is unfortunate when the consulting report purchased at whatever large or small expense is put on the shelf. Rather, the use of consultants is most productive when viewed from the perspective of *"change agents."* Their work is most productively viewed as interventional, which can improve:

- The quality of management's decisions in specific instances.
- The effectiveness of management processes within the firm.
- The productive efficiency of the organization to function with its resources in its environment.

MANAGING PROFESSIONAL RELATIONS

The best external professional resources would, ideally, also be those who manage themselves the best. Unfortunately, such is not always the case. All too often the cobbler's son is barefoot. External professionals capable of great functional insights and contributions are often the worst managers of their own practices. As a result, it can be foolhardy to assume that a competent technical expert is also a competent project manager, especially one acting on your behalf.

The larger the externally managed project, the more important it is that it be *disaggregated* into appropriate bite-sized chunks with stand-alone milestones for review. The best position for a client to be in is one where the project can be stopped at any appropriate point. Projects should always be reviewed in the context of their bona fide alternatives. However, the alternatives of doing nothing or of stopping the project should always be discussed at each level of milestone achievement or lack of achievement. This latter point cannot be overstressed. External consultants, even at the best, are under pressure to produce revenue. No matter how professional they may be, their best interests are not always the client's best interests. It is the client's responsibility to see that projects are managed in their own best interests.

While it is important to *define the scope* of the assignment, and while it is helpful to *limit the scope* of the assignment, it is dangerous to *limit the background* to any assignment. It is not real-

istic to expect a consultant to make a knowledgeable recommendation with imperfect or intentionally biased information.

Also important is the *management of expectations* in relation to
what even the best professional consultants can reasonably
produce. For example, in a culture that is hostile and resistant
to change, it is unreasonable to expect an external consultant to
be able to position the need for change any better or worse than
the internal executive. Expectations in relation to the value of
accomplishment must be reasonable and achievable. The best
consultant projects are those of limited scope and limited duration and which achieve their objectives. All too often, inexperienced executives will hire consultants to perform tasks that they
themselves have failed to achieve over long periods of time.
Despite popular notion, *consultants, even the best of them, are only
human.*

HOW TO BE A GOOD CLIENT

The key question here is: Are you demanding enough? One
of the most effective ways to get the most out of your consultant is by being a good client. An important aspect of the client-
consultant relationship is openness and honesty. One way to
ensure honesty from your consultant is by making an example
of yourself. Make sure you provide them with adequate background information to enable an understanding of "where the
firm is coming from." Additional areas of emphasis are:

- Frequent communication.
- Good documentation.
- Periodic performance evaluation.

All of these items necessitate that the CFOs maintain strong
involvement with their consultants. Once you have engaged a
consultant, you can't simply sit back and wait for a final report.
You must be involved on an ongoing active basis for you and
your organization to get the maximum benefit from their services.

Keep involved in the engagement, and know what is going
on. Don't delegate too much and don't take a hands-off approach. You are the principle contact for the consultant, and your
personal involvement is essential. You should strive for an open
unbiased relationship.

To achieve that kind of relationship you cannot view the consultant as a threat or react defensively. Don't approach an engagement with preconceived opinions. This would lead you to automatically reject positive suggestions and recommendations for which, after all, you are paying.

But this does not mean that you should suppress your critical faculties altogether. Don't be afraid to challenge conclusions that are undocumented or unsupported. Ask for clarification when a point is unclear to you. Sometimes your consultant will offer negative news or opinions. Don't reject it. Instead, look for it because it can help you do your job more effectively. The right information and advice will help you to make the right business decision.

ENGAGEMENT LETTER

An *engagement letter* should be required for all work done by outside consultants. The client can and should insist upon an engagement letter that satisfies his needs for specificity. Global engagement letters which only broadly cover work to be done and make expansive promises for improvement are to be avoided at all costs. Engagement letters should, at a minimum, include specific information on the following items:

- Objective of the assignment.
- Scope of the project.
- Staffing involved.
- Expected duration.
- Significant project milestone achievements and dates.
- Fees.

Engagement letters can range from one paragraph statements of objective, scope, staff, duration, and fees to lengthy legalistic documents. The more costly and complex the projects, the more the need for specificity and detail. Greater initial detail reduces the probability of later misunderstanding and conflict. In many instances, particularly in large complex projects, the engagement letter should be reviewed by a general counsel and bear his imprimatur.

The best consultants are often the most expensive. The issue is whether their utility value exceeds their cost. Frequently, expensive consultants are that way because of their experience and expertise. High qualifications are frequently insurance against mediocre performance. In other words, by and large, you get what you pay for.

Determining what fees are appropriate is not a simple matter. There are no specific guide lines or standard costs. Some consultants charge a per diem plus expenses; others charge on an hourly basis. The rate charged depends on a variety of factors, including:

- Qualifications and experiences of the consultant, as well as the nature of the expertise.
- Complexity of the assignment.
- Support provided to the consultant.
- Changes in the scope in the assignment after it has begun.

In most cases, you should determine both the rate and the manner of billing in writing before the engagement begins. By establishing the fee arrangements before the work begins, you can save yourself misunderstandings, friction, and a poor working relationship.

In addition, it is helpful to explicitly detail the support the firm will provide to the consultant. A CPA firm, for example, that assumes a role of auditor or management consultant without a specific commitment of cooperation from the CFO for his staff, most likely is set for a confrontation regarding access to information.

Investment bankers, on the other hand, often engage in proposals or actual work before specific terms are discussed. As mentioned above, this is an opportunity for the CFO to assess competence, while at the same time providing a marketing tool for the investment banker. In fact, much of the work involved in an investment banking proposal is frequently completed before the transaction is proposed. Although there are times when this causes unrealistic expectations, it is a result of the nature of the industry. Keep in mind that part of maintaining the professional resource network involves developing an awareness of expectations and managing expectations to your long-term benefit.

As mentioned earlier, large projects, especially complex ones, should be broken down into manageable pieces with formal periodic milestone reviews. This will enable the project to be restructured and the fees renegotiated as the project progresses. Often executives forget that some projects may just not be achievable. Consultants, in their enthusiasm and confidence, are prone to overestimate their own qualifications and expertise. Many projects that consultants undertake have not been done by them before. The notion that the project may not be doable for organizational or technical reasons is an idea that only the best consultants confront clients with. It is, therefore, a mutual responsibility to demand and respond to regular, frequent progress evaluations.

Experienced users of consultants all feel that the engagement letter and fee negotiation process are perhaps the most important factors in a successful engagement. They are the most important factors because in the process performance expectations and fee levels are established and are mutually agreed upon. Further, a well-prepared engagement letter should be the basis for periodic project performance review. Clients should be aggressive in insisting upon the most professional and comprehensive engagement letter. They should also be aggressive in holding the consultants to the terms of the engagement letter.

The best consultants not only encourage clients to participate in and challenge their work; they demand it. The first instance that a client feels uneasy about any part of the work in progress is the moment when he should discuss his feelings and uneasiness with the senior engagement manager. Clients who actively and appropriately participate in the engagement management process not only ensure the likelihood of successful project completion but also frequently gain insights that lead to better and more informed executive decisions on their part. Examples include:

- Improving their own project management skills.
- Developing competences at high levels of expertise in areas where they formally were weak.
- Identifying individuals to add to the portfolio of consultant relationships.

SUMMARY AND CONCLUSIONS

One CFO made the interesting comment that the most important personal goal in his life was continuous personal and professional growth. Executives who spend almost all of their waking hours working or thinking about their business must satisfy their needs for professional growth in work-related activities. The executive who strives and is driven to be successful does not stop the work week on Friday afternoon. Most very successful executives think, sometimes obsessively, about business problems when they are shaving or showering and even when they are engaged in leisure and family activities. Pressing and important problems cannot be dropped and forgotten easily.

One way to relieve some of this pressure and also to build in personal and professional growth opportunities is to build a support network of individuals with relevant consulting skills who are available to assist in the process of both relieving some of the pressure of executive life and also providing opportunities for continuing personal and professional growth. Pressure can be relieved when appropriate consultants are engaged and appropriate amounts of the problem-solving staff work is delegated to them. Continuing personal growth is achieved when the work done complements and extends the executive's skills, particularly in those areas which may be necessary to his future success but with which he has neither formal education nor practical experience. The result is that the executive who understands the process of continually shaping and reshaping consultant support as his career evolves has a significant competitive advantage over his peers who lack such a finely honed and ever-evolving professional support and personal growth system.

PART SIX

Managing the Financial
Management Function

23

Organization for Financial Management

Thomas H. Howe and William S. Cashel, Jr.

During the 1960s and 1970s, many significant changes occurred that reshaped the way most corporations conduct their business. The growth of strong government and regulatory pressures affected many companies in very fundamental ways. In others, deregulation became a way of life. Foreign competition created major dislocations in entire business segments, while new opportunities prompted many companies to expand rapidly into foreign markets.

In addition to these external influences, there were significant internal changes. For example, most companies followed a path of continuing decentralization that resulted in new and more complex organizations. Also, goals emphasizing productivity and quality became more prominent as firms strived to maintain or regain competitive positions. The combination of these forces resulted in fundamental changes in almost all aspects of the financial organization.

Typically, financial organizations underwent major changes

Thomas H. Howe is president of Management Analysis Center, Inc., an international general management consulting firm. William S. Cashel recently retired as Vice Chairman and CFO of AT&T. He currently serves as Chairman of the Board of Campbell Soup Co. in Camden, N.J.

to adapt to the changing environment. Such changes included more rigorous and sophisticated accounting systems to meet the demands of the profession as well as of managers at all levels; extensive computer-driven, information-processing systems; strategic planning as a major corporate function; improved cash-management methods; and, recently, new methods to cope with inflation-adjusted data in measuring performance. Changes in approaches to external financing also were required as a result of new financing methods and major fluctuations in interest rates.

Other changes also affected the organization, including an intensified drive to improve efficiency in the face of declining productivity, emphasis on performance measurement, and a recognized need for better overall corporate financial direction and control. To meet these growing demands, the chief financial officer's role has gradually expanded. In many companies, CFO responsibilities now transcend financial matters and the financial organization. The CFO participates in decisions affecting top-level policy, corporate direction, and major operational issues, in addition to meeting traditional responsibilities involving financial matters.

Generally speaking, the role of the CFO today involves 10 major responsibilities, often in varying degrees:

- Serves as a key member of the top management team.
- Promotes financial discipline.
- Is called on to assess the economic impact of major business decisions.
- Is the architect of corporate financial policies.
- Provides stewardship over assets.
- Participates in strategy development.
- Maintains external financial relationships.
- Evaluates performance of operating units.
- Participates in setting financial goals and objectives for the corporation and its subunits.
- Develops a strong financial organization.

The broad nature of these responsibilities requires the CFO to have an effective financial organization—one that includes cross-disciplinary experts who are capable of assuming many delegated responsibilities. This requirement is even more important in view of the significant time CFOs now devote to corporate-level management processes. How financial organizations are structured to meet these responsibilities is the subject of this chapter.

Five Organizational Areas

Five areas should be considered when examining how the financial function is organized:

1. Criteria for organizing the financial function.
2. Support for top-level committees.
3. Alternative organization structures.
4. Functions reporting to the chief financial officer.
5. Relationships with the financial function in divisions and subsidiaries.

CRITERIA FOR ORGANIZING THE FINANCIAL FUNCTION

While every company has unique characteristics and preferences, some common factors influence the organization of the financial function. These factors will require that the organization be adjusted from time to time to accommodate changes in the business and in new internal and external requirements. Such factors include the following:

1. Overall corporate structure:
   a. The overall strategy of a firm determines its corporate structure, and this structure, in turn, helps determine the organization of the financial function. For example, one might consider to what degree the company is centralized or decentralized, and which functions must be centralized and decentralized:
      (1) A holding company structure may require a strong staff focused on financing needs, a strong merger and acquisitions group, and a reporting group that focuses primarily on profitability, ROI, and similar financial measures.
      (2) A decentralized firm requires dedicated support from the financial organization for each profit center.

(3) A more centralized firm would be likely to require a larger corporate staff that demands detailed operating information.

2. Concept of corporate value added:
   a. What functions are most effectively and efficiently provided at corporate as a pooled service for the business units?
      (1) This might include MIS, pension fund management, and taxes.
      (2) Functions such as payroll and accounts receivable can be profitably centralized.

3. Corporate decision support requirements:
   a. What are the support needs of the CEO and other key managers?
      (1) Top-level executives may need to call on various specialists in the financial organization for specific information concerning many different types of business transactions.
      (2) Analytical support may be economically centralized in the financial organization. Support needs can be considerable, for example, when a corporation is pursuing an aggressive acquisition strategy.

4. Financial strategy:
   a. What are the external financing needs of the company?
      (1) Large financing needs or an aggressive financing posture may require more specialized expertise.
   b. How much specialized expertise from either internal or external sources is needed in such areas as leasing, credit and receivables management, or cash management?
      (1) There are almost always concerns that require expert attention either from internal sources or by engaging outside expert advice on an ad hoc basis.

5. Business complexity:
   a. Do some business segments require specialized and sophisticated financial expertise?
      (1) International operations require foreign exchange capabilities and local tax expertise.
      (2) Utilities require regulatory accounting.

6. Size of the company:
   a. Which functions require dedicated resources, and which can be shared?

(1) As size increases, shared functional entities can be economically established as separate organizations.
b. What resources should be bought from outside?
(1) Some services must be acquired from outside sources. An example is accounting services to certify financial statements. Generally, however, there is considerable flexibility in sourcing decisions for many financial services. As size increases, there is greater justification for providing services internally. A good example is the creation of captive insurance units by larger firms.

7. Management systems:
a. What types of financial control and reporting processes are need to be effective?
(1) As new business strategies evolve, which may require different organizational structures and management processes, the financial organization must respond with an appropriate supporting structure to provide effective financial management reporting.

8. Management skills:
a. What is the financial experience, sophistication, and skill of the CEO and other top managers?
(1) When the CEO and other top-level managers do not have backgrounds that include exposure to some of the important financial functions, (which might, for instance, involve regulatory or policy issues), the financial organization must be prepared to provide appropriate support in those areas.
b. What is the experience, sophistication, and skill of the CFO, treasurer, controller, and other financial managers?
(1) Senior members of the financial organization should have enough technical training and experience to meet the special qualifications required for sensitive financial positions. In addition, they must understand the business and the needs of top management so that the financial organization can be fully responsive.

SUPPORT FOR TOP-LEVEL COMMITTEES

The complex and diverse nature of most large corporations today has broadened the decision-making process and placed a considerable burden on top management. As a result, many companies have created senior management committees that play a prominent role in the decision-making process. There are two types of committees that involve the CFO. The first—typically called the management committee—is concerned with overall policy, operating, and resource-allocation decisions. In some companies there is a second committee—usually called the investment committee—that is primarily involved in capital investment decisions.

Because these committees can require a significant amount of time from the CFO, there is a need for highly qualified financial personnel heading up each of the functions reporting to the CFO organization and for a structure that permits these individuals to take increased responsibility for carrying out traditional financial activities. Also, the financial organization increasingly must provide various types of support to the management committees, typically in the form of financial analyses or special studies. These issues will be discussed in detail later in this chapter.

Management Committees

The use of a management committee has fundamental implications for how a company will be run. Some firms use a shared decision process in which the senior managers as a group make all major corporate decisions. Management committees of this type are commonly referred to as operating management committees. In some cases, its members are those executives in the office of the chairman or president. An alternative approach is an executive policy committee which acts as an advisory group to the CEO on major issues. In this case, the committee serves as a top-level forum for discussion and advice.

Operating Management Committees As the primary decision-making body of the corporation, an operating management committee has an overall operating responsibility. The committee functions in a direct line capacity, often meeting several times a week. This approach is frequently used by firms having closely related business units that require coordination. The operating management committee ties the various business entities together so that top management can obtain a complete view of the company.

To encourage a corporatewide perspective rather than to satisfy discrete vested interests, members of operating management committees generally have few if any direct operating responsibilities. The CFO, as a key member of the top management team, is usually a participant on this committee—even if not an official or voting member—and is active at meetings, providing major input to deliberations. Through the financial staff, the CFO provides support to the committee regarding business performance, forecasts of future results, and analyses of alternative courses of action.

Executive Policy Committees In contrast to operating management committees which concern themselves with ongoing operating decisions, executive policy committees tend to focus more on long-term strategic or policy issues. The executive policy committee is more commonly found in diversified firms where a greater number of operating decisions are delegated to line managers.

In order to deal with long-term strategies and policy issues, the committee is usually composed of a mix of line and corporate executives. It generally meets less frequently than operating management committees. The CFO provides an important financial and managerial perspective at meetings of the executive policy committee, and the financial organization is often used to provide support to the committee in the form of special studies and analyses.

Investment Committees

Investment (or finance) committees review and recommend levels of capital expenditure, and review the status of ongoing capital projects. They make recommendations to the management committee, the CEO, and sometimes the finance committee of the board of directors on proposed capital expenditures. The investment committee serves as a forum for in-depth reviews of capital expenditures involving major commitments by the firm. Thus, it plays a key role in the decision process and is an important group, particularly in companies that are capital-intensive.

Typically, the CFO chairs the investment committee. In addition to line executives, other executives on the committee include the director of strategic planning and, occasionally, the treasurer or controller.

ALTERNATIVE ORGANIZATION STRUCTURES

There is no "right" way to organize the financial function under the CFO. The financial organization must serve the business, strategic, and administrative needs of the company, while taking into account the capabilities of the CFO and other senior managers who run the corporation, as well as the capabilities of the various support staffs involved. Three distinct organizational approaches have evolved, however (see Exhibit 1). In this discussion they are called traditional financial functions, the chief of staff approach, and separate financial functions.

In the first approach, traditional financial functions, only those units with a financial orientation report to the CFO. In the second approach, the chief of staff model, the CFO has a variety of functions reporting to him that go beyond the purely traditional financial functions. In the third model, separate financial functions, financial activities are divided between the treasurer and the controller who report separately to the chief executive officer.

Traditional Financial Functions

The traditional financial functions approach follows the classic view of the CFO and his organization in which the functions are strictly financial in nature. In this simple structure, the treasurer and controller work closely with the CFO, and all three may substitute for one another on various committees or at meetings. The CFO's participation on various top management committees and his attendance at regularly scheduled management meetings provide for necessary integration between the financial functions and other staff functions. This approach requires that all specialized financial entities under the CFO be located in either the treasurer or controller organizations. These might include:

- The tax director.
- A financial analysis group, responsible for budgetary review, capital appropriations requests, and business performance.
- The internal audit organization, which is often found in the controller organization (or as a separate unit reporting to the CFO).

Exhibit 1
Three Models for Corporate Financial Management Organizations

A. Traditional Financial Functions

B. Chief of Staff

C. Separate Financial Functions

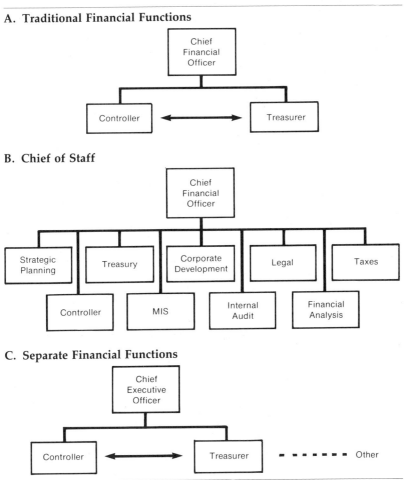

- Pension trust management, if pension funds are managed internally, and pension fund performance monitoring, if they are not.
- Financial manpower development and training, in companies with a strong commitment to training.

Depending on the size of the company and complexity of functions, the tax director (often a vice president) and the internal audit director may report directly to the CFO.

The Chief of Staff Approach

A variety of specialized staff units are under the CFO in the chief of staff approach, such as strategic planning and MIS. This structure facilitates coordination and integration between functions that must work together. Obviously, however, many aspects of these specialized staff units are not strictly financial in nature; thus the CFO must ensure that these types of functions do not become too financially oriented and fail to meet their broader responsibilities.

The chief of staff role may be extended to the point where the CFO also becomes the chief administrative officer. Even human resources and public relations units might be found under the CFO's control in this structure. A major drawback to designating these additional responsibilities is that the CFO's attention is diverted from important financial matters.

Separate Financial Functions

In the third approach—separate financial functions—financial responsibilities are divided between the controller and treasurer, both of whom report directly to the chief executive officer. In this structure, no one has complete responsibility for directing and coordinating the financial organization. Generally, however, the treasurer assumes the title of CFO. This approach separates the treasury functions of financing and asset-liability management from the controller functions of financial reporting and internal control, and it elevates each of these activities to a direct reporting relationship to the CEO. When measurement and analysis of operating performance is viewed as a critical adjunct to top-level decision making or when a company has a continuing need for extensive outside financing, this approach can make sense. However, it is used by only a very few companies today.

FUNCTIONS REPORTING TO THE CHIEF FINANCIAL OFFICER

There are many functions that are or can be carried out within the financial organization of most companies. The basic func-

Exhibit 2
Financial Organizational Functions

Typical Controller Functions	Typical Treasury Functions
General Accounting Services	Cash Management
Financial Reporting	Banking Relationships
Cost Accounting	Credit and Accounts Receivable
Inventory Accounting	Management
Financial MIS	Foreign Exchange
Statutory Accounting	Employee Benefits
Tax	Pension Fund Management
Personnel Accounting	Investor Relations
Operating and Capital Budgets	Financial Community Development
	and Relations
	Risk Management
	Payroll

Other Functions in the Financial Organization
Strategic Planning
Management Information Systems (MIS)
Financial Analysis
Internal Audit
Corporate Development

tions of controller and treasury require only brief elaboration. Several other functions, however, are discussed in some detail either because it is not precisely clear where these activities should fall in the corporate structure, or because they represent important opportunities for increasing management effectiveness (see Exhibit 2).

Controller and Treasury

The corporate controller's organization establishes the accounting policies and practices for the company, maintains the fiscal records, collects and consolidates financial results from operating units, and prepares financial reports. The treasury organization serves as custodian of the company assets, determining the amount and sources of the funds required to meet commitments, and maintaining external financial relationships with banks, shareholders, and other members of the financial community. These functions can, of course, be specified in more detail and, depending on the size and complexity of specific financial activities of the company, the structure of each of these organizations may be subdivided into departments dedicated to narrow specialties.

Strategic Planning

A strategic planning group is sometimes located in the CFO's organization. Usually, however, the strategic planning group reports directly to the CEO or to another executive outside the financial area. By reporting directly to the CEO, it is provided with a measure of independence and is assured high-level involvement and visibility. Because the strategic planning function must respond directly to top management's philosophy and approach to planning, its location in the organization should be governed by how best to meet those requirements.

In some companies, strategic planning consists of a senior executive who, along with a small staff, counsels the CEO on major issues facing the company. In this role, strategic planning is almost a personal staff unit to the CEO. Alternatively, strategic planning can play a broader role, working with and counseling operating units, conducting special studies or analyses, recommending alternative strategies, reviewing business plans submitted to corporate, and administering a multiphase planning process. These two approaches have quite different structural implications because of the size of staff required and the need for regular coordination with many different organizations.

Whether or not to establish the planning function within the CFO organization is best answered by examining how the needs of the CFO and top management can best be met while providing the necessary linkages to the financing and control activities of the company. If positioned under the CFO, care must be taken to assure that line organizations do not feel relieved of their coordinate responsibilities for planning. Clear signals must be sent to line management concerning top management's intentions regarding strategic planning and what this entails.

When strategic planning does not report to the CFO, formal linkages must be established between the strategy and financial organizations. In the annual planning process, this is especially important during the formulation of business financial objectives and in linking the longer term plan with the yearly budget. Within operating units, this linkage is often made by having the controller provide many of the financial projections.

Management Information Systems

The location of the corporate MIS organization varies widely from company to company. Regardless of location, however, the interactions between MIS and the financial organization must be dealt with explicitly. Most financial data are computerized in some fashion, and every financial manager today is highly dependent on the support of information systems.

Some major management information systems, such as those for marketing and manufacturing, may not be financially oriented, so there is no fundamental reason for including the development and maintenance of these systems in the financial organization. In many firms, MIS has become a separate, stand-alone organization serving all who need it in the company. In such cases, the MIS group can become one of the largest corporate staff organizations, often having larger numbers of personnel than the entire controller organization.

MIS has grown rapidly in most companies, with increasingly greater requirements for resources. This growth needs proper management to ensure that it is not wasteful and inappropriately directed, and proper management can be very time consuming. When MIS is in the financial organization, the CFO can expend considerable time on MIS, even though MIS is not necessarily more important than the CFO's other areas of responsibility. In many companies, therefore, the resources and personnel required by MIS may justify its operation as an activity separate from the CFO organization.

The development, enhancement, and maintenance of information and decision support systems needed by managers to examine the performance of operating units is, nevertheless, a continuing concern of the financial management organization. These systems can have significant impacts on other financial management processes, and technological innovations are creating new opportunities to design procedures and systems to gather more and better internal and external data and to make them routinely available. Technological developments in networking, interactive systems, and distributed data processing have created opportunities for more efficient, accurate, and timely reporting and forecasting between operating units and corporate, and such developments have greatly increased the scope and ease of performing many analytical tasks. For these reasons, many CFOs who do not have MIS within their organizations have a small systems planning group dedicated to financial information systems. This group maintains a close relationship with the MIS function and commonly resides in the controller's department.

Financial Analysis

Many companies have found that it makes good sense to have a separate, analytical function to support top-level committees and decision-making groups. While analysis usually involves financial matters, it can also extend to a wide range of issues involving operating units and overall company performance. Often this function is found in the controller's group, but in larger firms there may be a separate group reporting directly to the CFO.

Financial analysis is generally asked to review the analytical work done by other staff departments and by the operating units. The vigorous use of this activity by the CFO (and the CEO) can serve to motivate the operating units to submit complete and accurate analyses to corporate. Typically, financial analysis reviews financial data involving operating performance, capital budget proposals, and business plans that are submitted to top management. In this role, the group ensures that top management has complete and accurate information for making operating and investment decisions.

In a highly decentralized company, operating units have their own financial organizations and analytical groups. Most of the real analysis done in support of major activities, such as the business planning and capital budgeting processes, is carried out in these line groups.

The corporate financial analysis group should set the criteria and standards for analysis throughout the entire organization. These standards guide the operating groups and ensure that consistency and quality criteria are routinely met. The standards should include, as a minimum, methods for calculating rates of return, discounted cash flows, and profitability.

Internal Audit

A variety of approaches are found in the organizational placement of internal audit. Most often, it reports to either the controller or directly to the CFO. Some firms, however, feel that independence from the financial function is essential; in such cases, internal audit may report directly to the CEO, another officer, or even to the board of directors. In many companies the function has been moved over time from one location to another in an effort to find the best location. This experimentation has stemmed from increasing concern over internal control requirements and from external pressures, such as those generated by the Foreign Corrupt Practices Act.

In companies that are highly centralized, it can be argued that it is unwise to locate the audit function in the controller function because it would lack the independence necessary to assure objectivity. In a highly decentralized company, however, this argument may not hold true, and it is very unlikely the argument would be true when placing the audit function under the CFO.

There are important advantages to having the audit function in the financial organization. The most important of these is that the audit function can be properly focused on key financial and control issues that are the responsibility of the CFO. When the audit function is outside the financial organization, there is an increased need for coordination to ensure that important financial subjects receive adequate coordination. For example, outside auditors should minimize their fees by coordinating their efforts with that of the internal audit staff; such coordination is more difficult if the internal auditor reports outside the financial organization.

Corporate Development

Corporate development is an organization dedicated to the evaluation and management of mergers and acquisitions and, in some cases, divestitures. In acquisition-minded companies, the resources and staff dedicated to this effort may be relatively significant. Specialized investment banking knowledge and other similar expertise is needed on a regular basis. In these situations, corporate development is usually a separate organization. In firms where acquisitions are an infrequent activity, required analytical skills are often provided by other groups, such as strategic planning and financial analysis. In this latter case, the financial organization will be directly involved in corporate development activities.

RELATIONSHIPS WITH THE FINANCIAL FUNCTION IN DIVISIONS AND SUBSIDIARIES

A strong relationship between the CFO's organization at corporate and a business unit financial organization, usually headed by a controller, is of considerable importance in meeting the corporatewide responsibilities of the financial organization. The CFO must have the capability to carry out the firm's financial and control policies and to ensure complete, accurate, and timely reporting of financial data from business units. Without a clear mandate and free access throughout the company, the CFO cannot oversee the financial integrity of the company.

Typically, an operating unit controller reports directly to a line general manager while simultaneously maintaining what is commonly known as a "dotted-line" reporting relationship to the corporate financial organization, usually through the corporate controller. Some firms, however, prefer a more control-oriented approach and have the operating unit controllers report directly to corporate while maintaining a dotted line to the line general managers. This latter approach is less common in larger, decentralized companies that delegate broad authority to the managers of decentralized business units. Within the decentralized management concept, a business unit controller is responsible for providing information and reports to corporate, but the controller must balance this role with the role of acting as the line manager's "CFO," which means providing financial services, analytical support, and advice to the line organization.

For most large, decentralized firms, a structure that has operating unit financial managers reporting directly to their line general managers, with a strong dotted line to the CFO at corporate, makes excellent sense. This approach provides the desired responsiveness to the line manager and still allows the CFO to promulgate necessary policies and procedures and to call on a division controller to provide information without having problems with access to data or data credibility. It also aids in meeting the broader CFO responsibility for developing a strong corporatewide financial capability that can be accomplished only

Exhibit 3
Chief Financial Officer Authority Over Financial Personnel
in Operating Units

	Dotted Line	
Solid Line	Strong	Weak
1. Hire and fire	Approve or suggest hires	Little input to hires
	Fire and veto fires	Suggest fire for incompetence
2. Compensation (Input from line manager)	Input to line manager	Limited influence
3. Authority to transfer	Manage career path	Cannot transfer

by providing for necessary human resource development which involves personnel management and training.

It is the strength of the dotted-line reporting relationship between business unit financial organizations and the CFO organization that determines the nature and scope of the CFO's involvement. As summarized in Exhibit 3, firms with strongdotted-line relationships include within their authority the right to approve the hiring of key division financial personnel and the right to fire financial personnel for incompetence, but, importantly, the actions are carried out by line management. The CFO is also given a strong voice in compensation levels of key financial personnel and a major responsibility for managing their career paths corporatewide. Those CFOs with weak dotted-line relationships have much less influence in decisions involving selection, retention, and compensation of financial personnel and much less responsibility for the management development of financial personnel.

Because of the growing role of the financial function and its significance to an effective management process, increasing attention is being given by many CFOs to the development of highly qualified financial personnel. A strong dotted-line relationship give them the authority to assure that key financial positions in operating units are staffed by highly trained and competent individuals possessing a strong professional orientation and sense of esprit de corps. This can be accomplished through regular training programs both at the entry level and as part of a continuing education program. By integrating career path management with training, the CFO can assure that financial managers also obtain the necessary breadth and depth of experience. A program of career development might include both transfers among operating units and corporate staff and rotations between general management and financial positions. This would provide future financial managers with experience in the operating units and develop specialists who can evaluate these operating units effectively later on.

Another mechanism that helps to define the dotted line and tie a company's corporate and operating financial functions together is the use of conferences on an annual or semiannual basis. For instance, the conferences bring together financial personnel from across the firm to discuss complex issues and common problems. They enable a broad base of operating unit financial managers to meet senior personnel and to develop the informal ties that are essential to an effective financial organization.

SUMMARY

The roles of both the CFO and the financial organization have gone through significant changes in most businesses over the past two decades. Typically, the financial organization has been called upon in many ways to assist management in maintaining and improving their ability to complete—both through a deeper understanding of the economic considerations surrounding business decisions and through the efficiencies achieved by internal cost control and seet management. The complexities associated with major environmental pressures and changes have accentuated the need for a more effective financial organization.

In order to meet its growing responsibilities, the financial organization responded with various changes in its organization structure. These changes frequently involved the role and responsibilities of the CFO, as well as the functional activities within the financial organization. Accommodations to the overall needs of the business and its management processes were required, and this resulted in a variety of organizational arrangements, some of which are discussed above.

Looking to the future, there are a number of emerging trends that could bring further changes in the financial organization. The pervasive effects of information technology will be felt increasingly by all of the organizations within a business, and the effects on the financial organization are likely to be of major significance. Also, the contraction of middle management that has taken place in many corporations may require some accommodation by the financial organization. With the development of new tools, more sophisticated methods for carrying out financial functions, and new management processes for directing business activities, it is likely that new organizational arrangements will be needed. How these new needs are met will depend the overall business needs of particular companies. Meeting this challenge could become a major issue for CFOs.

24

Developing Financial Managers

Robert J. Canning and Arthur W. Harrigan

The chief financial officer is a member of the top management group in almost all industrial companies.[1] There are many reasons for this designation, only one of which is pertinent to the subject of this chapter: the CFO's particularly broad responsibility for developing financial personnel with the integrity to carry out management's fiduciary responsibilities and with the skill to develop a financial strategy that facilitates the implementation of the company's overall strategy.

The CFO has the manager's typical responsibility for developing replacements for key personnel in his own organization, including those who may report to him functionally. But the CFO has the additional responsibility for developing replacements for

---

[1]The Conference Board Report No. 821, "Who Is Top Management?" (New York: The Conference Board, 1982).

Robert J. Canning, manager, corporate financial manpower operation, General Electric Company, was involved in the financial personnel development area for over 30 years before retiring in 1983. Arthur W. Harrigan resigned as Western Electric's vice president—finance in 1972 to join International Paper as executive vice president—finance. He retired in 1982 and became clinical professor, management, New York University.

financially oriented key managers elsewhere in the company, some of whom may rise to top management positions.

As a member of the top management group, the CFO is able to identify the management development needs and opportunities for financial personnel; this is especially important because the work of financial personnel gives them a greater exposure to the company's operations than other staff people and thus enhances their potential for general management. Top management membership also helps to alert the CFO to the nonfinancial managers who need some financial developmental experience as they move up the general management ladder to top executive positions. The recent startling increase in the number of course offerings in "Finance for the Nonfinancial Manager" testifies to general manager aspirants' interest in gaining financial knowledge.

The CFO must focus management's attention on the bottom line and other indexes of financial health to be sure the company has the financial flexibility to take advantage of unforeseen opportunities. Today's executives, whatever their functional specialty, recognize the potential of financial personnel to succeed in general and in top management, a potential which develops out of their preoccupation with the activities and strategy for the financial health of the firm. Thus, the CFO's performance in developing financial managers is a critical factor in whether the company has the numbers and quality of skilled financial personnel and financially oriented general management personnel required for its long-term success.

FINANCIAL MANAGEMENT DEVELOPMENT APPROACHES

The conventional wisdom is that most, but not all, management development takes place on the job. Training, both formal and informal, plays a subordinate but a critically important supplemental and supportive role to "real time" experience. There is nothing quite like the meaningful development that comes from the day-to-day activities of problem solving and interacting with associates to work toward the company's objectives; but it is more meaningful and satisfying if it is accompanied by the broadening that results from some planned educational activities.

The finance function is not exempt from the conventional wisdom about on-the-job development. Consciously or not, the development of financial managers moves along with the work as it is processed by the members of the financial organization. Even though an organization is static, having few promotions and rare lateral moves, changes in the external environment—such as new accounting requirements, altered disclosure rules, and the evolution of new financing techniques—will put new dimensions on existing jobs and force the incumbents to develop new skills and different, broader capabilities.

Thus, the CFO's first step in developing financial managers is to recognize the inevitability of the process and to control and guide it. Even though the resources and needs of the organization may preclude a formal development program, the CFO should periodically set aside time to assess the development needs of his or her organization and to consider whether personnel moves could be made to help fill those needs.

The next step is to consider how far to go in pursuing the following successively more sophisticated approaches:

- Identify the promotional potential of finance personnel (personally if there is not a companywide program) and consider the specific developmental-type of jobs to which those with the greatest potential should next be assigned to accelerate their career progress.

- Identify the most suitable developmental types of jobs; that is, those with the scope to challenge the prospective incumbent to a new learning experience and those which report to a manager or which have one or more subordinates who can "carry" the newcomer until he/she has met the challenge of the new job.

- Develop estimates of future year-by-year requirements for financial personnel for replacement and growth in total and for each managerial level by use of a succession planning type of program which pinpoints specific jobs for which there are no (or an inadequate number of) successors fully qualified to advance now or at a specified time in the future.

The most common format of financial management development programs is a series of rotating, on-the-job, practical working assignments in the various subfunctions of accounting and financial work. These should be challenging, meaningful, and monitored; they should also provide truly hands on experience.

To assure the success of a job rotational development program, care should be exercised to structure the assignments in a way which will round out and complement the individual's background and which will build on the work experience of the prior jobs.

Success also depends on instilling in the minds of the participants the concept that advancement and development must be self-directed and self-centered. The program design should encourage individuals to be involved in planning and implementing their own personal and professional growth. It will do them no good to believe they have potential if they do not persuade others of its existence through their interest, their initiative, and their performance in the successively more difficult jobs to which they have been assigned.

Initial assignments should be in such basics as general, cost, and personnel accounting, as well as key treasury functions, with the time spent determined by (1) the individual's prior accounting and financial education and experience; and (2) the individual's job performance. Then, more advanced assignments in auditing, budgeting financing, taxes, and investment and financial analysis, as well as in other line operations, will round out and develop financial specialists, managers, and executives.

Another approach to financial development is "rotation of the work" rather than the job by assigning selected individuals to the internal audit department. Depending on the structure of the company and the scope of the internal audit department, a series of assignments in that organization can provide a broad range of meaningful developmental experience. This is especially true if the organization emphasizes operational auditing.

But there are risks and possible costs to assigning inexperienced personnel to auditing. The individuals so assigned may become frustrated with the time it takes to demonstrate efficiency, or they may become disillusioned if much time is consumed in being a traveling auditor. The higher costs could result from more hours put in by the independent auditors because of less reliance on an inexperienced group on the internal audit staff.

Other companies prefer to consider assignments to auditing work as a second- or third-tier layer of development because of the nature of the work and the need to have auditors who have had an extensive exposure to the company's accounting practices, its financial cycle, and organizational structure.

There are differences among the details of financial management development programs because of company size, structure, the extent to which the treasury and tax organizations have unique skill requirements, and other characteristics which make no two financial organizations identical. But there are two common threads which run through all of them: First, they are all built on "doing" rather than watching because nothing will more quickly kill a college graduate's interest in a job than to have him or her observe rather than do; and, second, all of the programs have the top-down commitment of general and financial management that is so important to their success.

FORMAL TRAINING AS A MANAGEMENT TOOL

Formal training, an important tool for management development, has a wider range of approaches in actual practice than it should have: from "none" to quite rigorous programs of graduate-level quality (MBA) which are offered in university settings, company-operated educational sites, or at the job location on an in- or out-of-hours basis.

There are two versions of "none": the unconditional "none, period"; and the conditional—"none unless business is good and we can afford the (tax deductible) expense." The latter is just as bad as the former since an on again, off again approach has about as much value for employee development as no program. In addition, both versions frequently have unrecognized costs in the form of the higher salaries paid for people trained and developed by other companies. These salaries can easily exceed what it would have cost to hire, train, and develop an entry-level employee (who would also have built up more loyalty than the newcomer).

Between the extremes of no offerings and highly sophisticated programs, numerous training approaches can be adopted depending upon the size of the company (and its financial organization), its resources, and its longer term needs for personnel. The following listing of alternatives makes no distinction between entry-level programs and those intended for mature personnel either because the distinction is obvious or because similar programs can be oriented to either group:

- Coaching is the fine art of counseling and guiding subordinates rather than telling them what to do and an integral part of the supervisor/subordinate relationship; too often it is overlooked as the most basic of training programs and, in the right hands, the most effective.

- Informal get togethers of finance organization personnel to exchange information on the latest developments in the respective areas of the participants—of interest to both the older and newer members of the organization.

- Participation in the Financial Executives Institute activities— area or annual conferences, chapter meetings, and, when offered in the area, the professional development seminars— and participation in whatever opportunities are offered locally for treasurers and other finance people to meet their peers.

- Tuition refund programs—specific courses related to finance or a full course of study leading to a degree.

- Executive programs offered by universities in major cities which require only two days a week (one week day) attendance, many of which lead to an MBA.

- Advanced university programs of three to six weeks in duration (some offered during the summer) which are geared to specific financial areas.

- Specialized financial programs of one to two-years duration generally conducted after hours on the job site for several hours on one or two nights a week; courses are geared to accounting and finance as those functions are carried out at the sponsoring company. Usually it is open only to bachelor degree holders, and the course is frequently viewed as a prerequisite for advancement. Faculty may be in-house supervisory personnel or a mixture of company people and college professors or consultants. General Electric was the first company to establish (in 1919) a program of the type, and its program is currently the largest in existence. It is an ambitious program which other companies can justify as cost-effective over the long term only if they recruit for the long pull and if their annual requirements for entry-level hires are significant; that is, they are a "growth from within" company.

In considering financial type training programs, it is important not to overlook the need for integrating them with the rest of company training programs covering corporate history and the economics of its industry, as well as other functions, such as general, marketing, and manufacturing management.

Top-level commitment to training and to maintenance of whatever level is decided upon is absolutely essential because the absence of training support is much more quickly evident and could encourage outstanding people to leave, as well as discourage prospective recruits.

STAFFING

An obvious need in any training/development program is to determine the "customers"—the number and type of present and prospective staff members who will participate in some aspect of the program both in the immediate future and in the following five or more years.

Determining staffing requirements involves the application of historical average retirement age and rates of terminations for other causes to the age distribution of the present finance population. The year-by-year losses thus calculated, plus a factor for additional personnel needed to support the projected growth of the company, will produce a total hiring requirement. While this measure of the magnitude of your hiring requirements is useful for planning purposes, the total current hiring requirement has to be translated into specific numbers and types of individuals before hiring is possible.

Specific requirements for hiring are developed by preparing a succession list for each key position in the organization, including the growth positions which are not now populated. For each position, the previously prepared potential assessments and career development positions are used to identify the individuals capable of filling the job when it becomes vacant. If there are no, or an insufficient number of, possible successors available, the company will have to decide when and how it will fill the projected vacancy with other potential candidates.

Preparation of succession lists is fully as complicated as it sounds, but it is sufficiently worthwhile for the CFO to undertake the effort even if such a companywide program is not in place. In addition, succession planning is doubly worthwhile as a company program because it stimulates badly needed interdivisional moves.

SOURCES OF FINANCIAL PERSONNEL

Candidates for financial management positions are available at the many levels of educational institutions and from a great variety of other employers. The specific source will depend upon: (1) the requirements of the position being filled and (2) whether a short- or long-range plan exists for further developing and training the talent being sought.

Entry-level personnel usually come from colleges and universities offering business administration, engineering, and liberal arts bachelor degrees and from graduate schools offering the MBA. For certain specialized requirements, a good source is certificate-granting business colleges and specialized schools, such as those which offer computer skill training.

Other employer sources include CPA firms, business and industrial organizations, nonprofit institutions, and government departments, including retiring military service personnel. These sources can be tapped through executive search firms, classified advertising, and current employee referrals.

The biggest source of entry-level financial talent is the college campus. According to the American Institute of Certified Public Accountants (AICPA), there were more than 61,000 accounting majors among the bachelor and masters degrees that colleges estimated they would award in the 1984–85 academic year. Of that group, 28 percent were expected to join public accounting firms according to an AICPA report.[2] In addition, many thousands of graduates with majors in business administration have studied accounting and finance.

Graduates of liberal arts schools who major in mathematics and economics are possible candidates for finance positions; but,

---

[2]Mary McInnes and James H. MacNeill, *The Supply of Accounting Graduates and the Demand for Public Accounting Recruits* (New York: American Institute of Certified Public Accountants, 1985).

to be realistic, they should be hired only when there are entry-level training and development programs geared to the unique needs of individuals with no accounting or finance education. Also, the turnover of these hires may be higher than that of business majors because their lack of special knowledge may lead to disillusionment with some of their initial assignments.

With over 50,000 master's degrees in business administration being awarded annually, the graduate business schools are a great source of personnel. But there is much competition for the best graduates. They are more expensive to hire than those with bachelor degrees, and, based on the higher MBA turnover rates some companies have experienced, their expectations in terms of job challenge and rapidity of promotion are much higher than those of other graduates. As a result, some companies steer away from MBAs, preferring to "train their own" and thus limit their hiring to the bachelor level. Other companies with greater requirements than can be filled at the graduate level hire both MBAs and bachelors. While there may be no intention of letting this result in a two-track training/development program, companies should be aware that the bachelor-level employees may perceive that it exists, particularly if the MBAs move ahead more rapidly.

Rather than conducting a basic entry-level training program for college graduate hires, some companies prefer to hire individuals with two to four years of public accounting experience. If these people come from the company's own auditing firm, the CFO should have had an understanding about such employment with the audit engagement partner.

Companies also look to the outside for highly specialized skills which are more typically developed in the financial services industry. For example, the treasury organization may seek Chartered Financial Analysts (CFAs) or similarly trained people to manage pension and other benefit trust funds or to monitor the performance of external managers of those funds. CFA-trained people might also be the best types to fill requirements if the treasurer's job has a high volume or an unusually complex variety of investment analysis work.

The days when all jobs above the entry level were filled from within may be drawing to a close because the pace of change is so great that the "growth from within" companies find that they can no longer anticipate their specialized needs. Also, there is a philosophy developing that some outside hires above the entry level will keep the "insiders" more on their toes. As a consequence, there has been a lot of growth in executive search firms, some of which have specialized in locating financial personnel for middle management and higher levels. Some of the larger public accounting firms have become involved in executive search, generally through their management consulting component.

COLLEGE RECRUITING—SOME GUIDELINES

These comments are offered regardless of whether financial recruiting is a "go it alone" operation or a part of a coordinated company effort (as it more typically is).

No matter what the size of your college recruiting requirements, there are several key items which must be in place before "operations" commence: The duration and content of the training/development program must be determined; the nature of the entry job has to be specified, and the successive upward progression steps have to be identified and described; the training courses must be firmly in place, and their correlation with job rotation should be thought through. Prospective recruits need to know what they may expect for the first year or two if for no other reason than to compare the opportunity you offer with that offered by the other companies they are considering.

Unless your recruiting requirements are too small to warrant the expense, a recruiting pamphlet should be prepared to give prospects the background of your company, to list the specific opportunities which are available, and to describe the training-development program you offer.

The CFO or one of his key associates should visit the colleges from which they expect to recruit to become acquainted with the placement director and establish rapport with the dean of the business school and head of the accounting department.

It is most desirable to make use of recent college graduates on the CFO's staff to smooth the way of the campus interviewers with a prior campus visit and to go along with the interviewers when they make their recruiting visits.

Other ways to enhance the recruiting environment is to become acquainted with college faculty who are members of the Financial Executives Institute, the American Accounting Association, and National Association of Accountants and to attend regional meetings of those groups. Also, it would be well to seek invitations to speak to various accounting groups, such as Beta Alpha Psi, the National Accounting Honorary Faternity, and the college's accounting or finance club.

Finally, organizations planning to recruit as many as 25 graduates would be well advised to take a listing in the *College Placement Annual*[3] which is distributed to every college senior at most schools in the United States.

CONTINUING EDUCATION

To be sure that their employees are capable of meeting the challenges and complexity of the modern business world, increasing numbers of companies are encouraging continuing education beyond entry-level training and beyond the traditional tuition reimbursement for evening study. In-house education is the trend, with comprehensive financial and accounting skill training the order of the day.

Formal education programs offered by companies range from full-time classes for a number of days to weeks of evening or weekend courses as a supplement to the full-time work experiences. Regardless of the plan adopted, guidelines should be established for the curriculum and length of time required to complete the prescribed program.

The full-time class approach gives decentralized companies the opportunity of bringing people from different locations together to share a common experience and to get to know the other members of the team whose ability to be helpful with particular problems would not necessarily be evident from the box they occupy on the organization chart. In other words, friendships developed at these training sessions can be ever so helpful in resolving future problems.

While a small number of trainees may limit the educational program to specific courses at local schools, in-house education should be used whenever practical since it enables the organization to bring into the classroom its own methodology and the lingo of its systems, procedures, and practices. Even the cases used can be written around the company and perhaps even

---

[3]Published by the College Placement Council, Inc., Bethlehem, Pa. 18017.

written by people who had participated in the issue involved.

Another advantage to in-house education is that the management instructors become more closely acquainted with the students and help to identify their professional needs and their potential for advancement.

Although few companies have the resources to emulate it or the recruiting requirements large enough to justify it, a formidable after-hours, two-year curriculum was developed by General Electric for its financial management program members.

Courses meet weekly for up to 13 weeks and include readings, quizzes, and final examinations. Instructors are company supervisors and managers. The financial courses include principles of accounting, financial reporting, auditing, and business planning. Members also enroll in a seminar which requires utilization of learned skills in a case study format. Finally, G.E program members complete a three-day seminar in developing managerial effectiveness, a 12-week evening course in effective presentation, as well as a 2-day personal computer course.

More and more companies are also encouraging financial employees to earn the Certificate in Management Accounting (CMA) offered by the Institute of Management Accounting.[4] As of mid-1985, more than 5,000 individuals held the CMA, with the number growing 10 percent annually.

To become a CMA, candidates must pass all five parts of a comprehensive examination within a three-year period and complete two years of accounting work experience.

To help their employees to benefit from the CMA approach, a number of large companies have tailored internal programs to fit their own training/development needs. The following summarizes the Du Pont approach which is typical of these tailored programs:

Du Pont's accountants from several of its operating departments use the structure of the CMA exam as an outline to work with professors of corresponding expertise from the University of Delaware to develop a five-segment course with a Du Pont flavor. Participants can choose between two versions of the course: one for those intending to take the exams and the other for professional development only. Students attend one class at

---

[4]The IMA is located at 10 Paragon Drive, P.O. Box 405, Montvale, N.J. 07645 (201) 573–6192.

the university each week and spend about 10 hours a week studying at home. All five areas of the exam are covered in a year. Du Pont estimates that the cost is about equal to enrolling employees in regular college courses and feels the program is effective.

Other professional programs with examination requirements which are used in developing financial managers include those for certified public accountants and chartered financial analysts. The CPA examinations and work experience requirements vary among the individual states; for example, there is a difference among states on whether industrial accounting experience can substitute for work experience with CPA firms. A summary of the requirements of the various states may be obtained from the National Association of State Boards of Accounting.[5]

To become a chartered financial analyst, an individual must pass a different level of examination in each of three years in such subjects as financial accounting, portfolio management, and economics and work for three years as a financial analyst in any of a number of financial areas, some of which are found in the typical financial organization of an industrial company. The only qualification for taking the series of examinations is a bachelor's degree or its equivalent. The Institute of Chartered Financial Analysts is the national body which establishes the standards for the CFA and prepares the examinations.[6] Currently, there are about 5,400 candidates in the three-year examination and work experience cycles.

SUMMARY

Some concluding points to ponder:

● Management development, like machine maintenance, can be deferred, but only at a cost. Because it takes so long to realize the cost of neglecting management development, it is difficult, time-consuming, and costly (perhaps even impossible in the available time) to restore the staff to its former effectiveness.

[5]The NASBA is located at 545 Fifth Ave., New York, N.Y. 10017. (212) 490–3868.

[6]Details about the CFA may be obtained from the ICFA at P.O. Box 3668, Charlottesville, Va. 22903 (804)977–6600.

- The CFO should not neglect his own personal self-development as a professional finance type or general manager. This word of advice is offered not only in his/her own self-interest but also in the interest of showing good example to subordinates.

- The CFO should be careful to view any program for developing financial managers as a part of the company's overall management development program and not create a finance "cult" which isolates his organization from the rest of the company. General management courses are probably the most frequently offered formal training program in industry, and the development programs have the same emphasis. Any programs for finance (job development or training) must be integrated with these mainstream general management programs if they are to do the individuals, the organization, and the company the maximum good.

25

Income Tax Planning

James M. Denny

In this chapter I hope to pass along a philosophy of tax planning, observations on some major pitfalls, and a few comments on how a company might arrange itself to deal with this complex subject and to maximize the opportunities available from intelligent tax planning.

PROLOGUE

There is a consensus, I believe, that taxes are an important item in the normal corporate P&L statement. Using Value Line Industrial Composite statistics for 1982, pretax profit averaged 6.6 percent of sales. At a 50 percent tax rate, taxes would represent 3.3 percent of sales. Three percent of sales equals average aftertax profit and ranks tax expense with administrative and interest expense in impact and importance. It is an issue big enough to spend time worrying about. Like administrative or interest expenses, it is not an uncontrollable item.

Effective tax rates run the gauntlet for American industry,

James M. Denny is executive vice president and chief financial and planning officer of G. D. Searle & Co. and serves on several boards. Prior to joining Searle in 1978, he was treasurer of Firestone Tire & Rubber Company.

ranging from zero to the U.S. statutory rate (and in some cases even higher). An effective tax rate lower than the blend of applicable statutory rates may reflect strategic decisions involving return on investment and operating trade-offs, the residue of prior business misfortune, or intelligent tax planning. This range of effective tax rates and the reasons generating them demonstrate clearly the size of the playing field. I do not recommend that anyone should search out business misfortune. Rather, I suggest that a company arrange itself so that it can evaluate the numerous opportunities to lower its effective tax rate and to avail itself of those with which it is comfortable.

The effective tax rate is an accounting concept. There frequently is a wide discrepancy between the tax provision for book purposes ("the effective tax rate") and the actual cash outlay for taxes. The difference is clearly reflected in the cash-flow statement and represents the divergent approaches of the accounting profession and the tax authorities to issues of recognition of revenue and realization of expense.

The first objective in tax planning is to search for ways to reduce (rather than postpone) tax liability. When this is achieved, both the effective tax rate and the cash outlay for taxes are reduced. If this can be achieved over a period of time, with predictability and without sacrificing the quality of pretax earnings, the company derives a significant benefit. Reducing the effective tax rate under these circumstances increases earnings per share, the company's return on equity, and its aftertax return on assets. These are key factors affecting a company's common stock valuation in the marketplace. A company which is able to register important improvements in these key indicators will improve its relative attractiveness vis-a-vis other investment opportunities.

Companies with low effective tax rates may not have achieved an advantage if the lower effective tax rate results from investment strategies which reduce pretax income. The easiest way to demonstrate this is to contrast investment of surplus cash by Company A in tax-free municipals yielding 7 percent with the investment of surplus cash in fully taxable securities yielding 14 percent by Company B. Company A's tax rate will be zero, but its aftertax rate of return on assets employed within its business will be 7 percent, the same as the aftertax return on assets for Company B which had a tax rate of 50 percent.

Even if the effective tax rate for accounting purposes approximates the statutory rate, there is ample opportunity to reduce the annual cash outflow for payment of taxes. Reducing cash outflow is important and should be achievable by many companies without adversely affecting their reported earnings. The essence of this strategy is tax deferral. The most widely recognized device for tax deferral is utilization of accelerated depreciation of fixed assets for tax return preparation but using straight line depreciation for calculation of pretax accounting earnings. While the favorable differential between these two approaches ultimately turns around and becomes unfavorable, it is, in a growing business, normally more than offset by the purchase of new fixed assets which starts the process over again. The cumulative effect of these deferrals can be significant. Indeed, the accounting profession has considered a proposal to convert generally accepted accounting principles for taxes to a cash-flow approach. One of the arguments advanced was that the current tax accounting conventions result in an understatement of income. Referring again to the Value Line Industrial Composite statistics for 1982, the effective tax rate was 46.2 percent while the cash tax rate was only 37.2 percent. In a recent survey conducted by a leading financial publication, cumulative deferred taxes on the balance sheets of some of the major corporations in the United States amounted to as much as 31 percent of shareholders equity. To the extent these balances are unlikely to shrink because of the reinvestment process discussed above, they actually constitute a form of quasi-equity with which there is no readily identified cost of funds. These accumulated balances, therefore, represent a low-cost source of financing which contribute significantly to the leverage of the firm and its return on equity. These figures clearly demonstrate the importance of tax deferral to U.S. companies.

LIFO inventory accounting is also considered a deferral device. Although it produces cash-flow benefits, it also involves a reduction in pretax income. Accordingly, it is a deferral method which involves a significant accounting price. It should not be eschewed for that reason, but the accounting cost should be recognized—an accounting cost not entailed by most other deferral methods.

Perhaps the best way to put the issue in proper focus is to talk about aftertax rates of return on assets employed in the business. The objective is not simply to reduce the tax rate; that is easy enough to do by utilizing such common techniques as tax-free municipal investments of surplus cash. In this case, the reduced tax rate does not represent a real increase in shareholder wealth since the reduced tax rate merely compensates for the lower before tax return on the assets involved. The real objective is to earn above average before tax returns which are enhanced by intelligent tax planning to yield superior returns on an aftertax basis.

It would be a mistake, of course, to focus only on the asset side of the balance sheet. These comments apply equally to the liability accounts. If effective tax planning can reduce the after-tax cost of borrowed funds and maximize the after-tax contribution of leverage to a company's rate of return on equity, so much the better. Industrial revenue bond financing is an obvious example.

And finally, one should not ignore the possibility of significant savings which may be achievable in seeking to find tax effective means of distributing profits to shareholders. For example, a stock repurchase program which is initiated for legitimate, nontax-associated reasons may coincidentally have significant ancillary tax benefits for the shareholders. The combination of increased earnings per share (EPS) for the remaining shares and possible increase in the applicable price/earnings multiple may produce a higher effective aftertax yield for the remaining shareholders (assuming sale of some of their shares) than would a dividend of the amount expended on the share repurchase.

The opportunities listed above should demonstrate that decisions designed to have an impact upon the tax cost of operating a business or distributing accumulated wealth to shareholders are not spur-of-the-moment decisions. Rather, they must be part and parcel of a company's long-range strategic plan. If I leave you with but one impression in this chapter, I hope it will be that tax planning should be an integral part of your long-range corporate strategy. Involvement of tax planning at this phase of corporate strategy formulation can pay handsome dividends. Among the key performance indicators that can be favorably affected by innovative tax planning are return on equity, return on assets, EPS growth, funds flow, and the company's reinvestment rate.

I do not need to remark on the effect of tax advice regarding the structure of acquisitions, divestitures, or financing decisions. That topic is covered in Chapter 5, and everyone should be aware of the importance of early and careful tax review of these special events.

Finally, a word of caution. All tax plans involve an element of risk. Some tax plans may be aggressive; some may be conservative. Wherever on this spectrum your tax plan lies, the CFO has responsibility to be sure that the CEO and the board of directors understand the degree of risk and the consequences for earnings and the financial condition of the company implicit in the tax plan, including the ability to finance payment of alleged deficiencies and companion interest and penalty charges. The ultimate disservice to the CEO is to deprive him of flexibility because he was unaware of the odds that a well-conceived but high-risk tax strategy may not evolve as originally anticipated.

CFO'S ROLE IN TAX PLANNING

Goals

The most important contribution of the CFO to tax planning is to establish the tax goals of the company. An integral part of this goal setting is the definition of the risk appetite of the company and the degree to which the company is prepared to diminish its flexibility in order to achieve tax savings. By definition, using a new and untested way of doing things is riskier than adopting an established and proven route. The old way involves little risk of challenge and is comfortable. The new way will invite scrutiny by the tax authorities and provoke some anxiety pending determination of its fate. But it may contribute to an increase in aftertax profits and cash flow. No matter how strong the rationale supporting the new approach, some CEOs will be unwilling to gamble on it perhaps because the rewards are not large enough and because the potential aggravation of a dispute outweighs the estimated advantages. On the other hand, some CEOs will endorse the new approach even though the supporting rationale is not free of doubt. The CFO must know and accurately reflect the CEO's attitude toward, and appetite for, this type of risk.

Managing the distinction between taxes provided in the financial statements (and the concomitant effect upon EPS) and taxes paid in the tax return is a critical element in setting these goals. There are occasions where taxes are not currently payable and where the provision for taxes in the company's financial statements is discretionary. A decision not to provide for such taxes will lower, at least temporarily, the effective rate with the corresponding favorable effect on EPS.

A good example is the decision not to provide for the taxes which would be due upon the repatriation of accumulated low-taxed foreign earnings of subsidiaries. A decision not to provide for such taxes is perfectly legitimate if the expectation is that they are permanently invested abroad. If these accumulated earnings, however, are convertible into liquid funds of which the parent company may have need, the benefits of flexibility would appear to recommend systematic provision for some or all of the taxes which would be due upon repatriation. When a crisis arises and the company needs to reach for these funds, it will be an embarrassing moment if the price of such utilization is an unacceptable and unexpected surge in the effective tax rate (and correlative diminution of EPS) necessitated by the provision for several years of taxes which would have been more properly assigned to earlier periods. By systematically providing for the taxes which would be due upon the repatriation of some or all of these accumulated foreign earnings, flexibility is preserved, and the cash benefits of leaving these funds abroad are not foregone.

The lesson to be derived from this example is that reductions in the effective tax rate should only be booked if there is a high degree of assurance that such savings are permanent. If there is a risk that such savings are transitory, prudence would normally appear to dictate that provision be made for the ultimate day of reckoning and that the company be satisfied with the cash savings associated with the deferral of the day upon which payment is due.

Because these decisions may have a material effect upon reported EPS, it is incumbent upon the CFO to ensure that the CEO understands and is willing to accept the risks involved in the company's tax strategy.

Achievement of Goals

Having staked out the parameters of the company's appetite for tax risk, the CFO must ensure that the company has a properly staffed tax department which is a participant in the planning and investment apparatus of the company. One of the keys to the effectiveness of a tax department is the degree to which, and the time at which, it is exposed to contemplated strategic and investment decisions. I have found that one way to achieve full and early involvement of the tax department is to have it report directly to the CFO. This reporting relationship appears to make the most sense given our management organization, our operating philosophy, and the nature and magnitude of our tax issues. Other reporting relationships may work as well or better for other organizations. What I believe is essential is that a knowledgeable tax professional be close enough to the center of corporate thinking to be aware, in the normal course, of ideas under consideration.

The qualifications of the principal tax professional will have a major impact upon the success of the company's tax planning endeavors. He or she must, of course, possess the technical skills and tax knowledge necessary to function in this area. Of equal importance, however, is the financial acumen and experience of this individual. If a company is going to be successful in integrating its tax planning and its strategic planning, the principal tax professional must be a broad-gauged financial executive who understands the role to be played by tax planning and who is capable of advising the CFO with respect to the balancing of the trade-offs between tax, financial, and operating objectives.

Not only must the tax function be an integral part of the strategic planning apparatus in order for tax planning to be effective, there must also be a high degree of integration of the tax function with the company's other finance functions. All too frequently, there is a tendency to view the tax people as separate and distinct, operating in a world all their own. This frame of mind impedes the flow of information into the tax department which diminishes its effectiveness. It is imperative that the CFO prevent this isolation of the tax professionals from the regular flow of financial information within the company.

The interaction between the CFO and the principal tax professional will determine, more than any other factor, the efficacy of the tax planning endeavor. It is incumbent upon the CFO to identify those corporate strategic issues which have tax planning ramifications and to ensure that the principal tax professional is aware of them. Conversely, it is incumbent upon the principal tax professional to identify tax issues which could have ramifications for the corporate strategy and to ensure that the CFO is aware of them. I would venture to say that in most companies the evolution of business plans by operating units which do not involve significant capital expenditures or the purchase or licensing of assets occurs without any awareness by, or input of, the tax professionals of the company. The advantage of a finance organization in which the tax department has access to, and is a regular recipient of, operating information is that important tax-saving opportunities can be identified early on and factored into the operating units' business analysis.

This type of organizational approach requires that tax professionals spend time being educated and thinking about the long-term tax consequences of the business plans of operating units. This takes them away from the preferred task of solving specific problems and, therefore, may be greeted with a certain reluctance. It is here that the effect of having a broad-gauge financial executive as the principal tax professional will be manifested. He must encourage the members of his department to become strategic thinkers so that the company can derive the full benefit of their knowledge and experience.

The interaction between the CFO and the principal tax professional and his department should be regularized and not haphazard. Meaningful intervention points need to be identified and then used. One such possible intervention point is the establishment of an annual and long-range tax plan which runs parallel with the company's annual budget and long-range strategic plan. To be useful, it should be comprehensive and set forth in detail with the key assumptions underlying the projections. For example, it should identify the risk associated with assumptions that net operating loss carryforwards and excess tax credits will not expire unused. A periodic review of the tax plan and long-range strategy will increase the likelihood that the tax department is aware of changes in the company's annual budget or long-range strategic plan which render assumptions used in the tax plan no longer valid.

We have found that utilization of such a tax plan and long-range tax strategy is a very effective device to focus attention on both current and long-range issues which need to be rethought. The role of the CFO in this process is one of communication and understanding. It is not problem solving. I have assumed that the CFO is not a tax professional. On the other hand, he or she must be capable of understanding the basic tax concepts underlying the firm's tax strategy so that he can both assess the risk profile of that tax strategy as well as raise questions regarding the continued relevance of the tax strategy or the relevance of underlying assumptions.

Since the dialogue necessary for the development of a solid and sound business strategy is a two-way street, the CFO must also make sure that the company's line managers and its legal counsel understand the importance of tax planning and are aware at least of the rudimentary concepts. Knowledgeable line managers are the first line of defense, and added dividends can be obtained if they appreciate the value of involving the company's tax professionals in the evolution of their own operational planning exercises.

From time to time, tax proposals are offered in Congress which can affect significantly the tax exposures of the company. The CFO must be sure that the company has in place an intelligence gathering system which will make him aware of these proposals and the ability to diagnose their effect on a timely basis. The decision to attempt to affect the outcome of proposed legislation affecting the company's tax exposure must be made within the context of the company's overall government relations posture and may be implemented by other units within the company. What is important is that the CFO know when an important tax issue is at stake so that he can mobilize the forces of the company, both internal and external, to deal with it.

The last aspect of the operations of the tax department with which the CFO should involve himself is the degree to which the company will use independent tax consultants and what their role will be. The CFO must have a good sense of the strengths and weaknesses of his own tax department and know when it is appropriate to bring in outside resources. When outside resources are engaged, he must be sure that they are properly controlled so that the tax philosophy of the company is reflected in their recommendations and actions.

SPECIAL HAZARDS

In the lives of most companies, management spends its time on the fundamentals of the business—generating increased sales or revenue, introduction of new products, expansion into new markets, control of operating expenses, investment in plant and equipment, and so on. Considerable effort is expended in reviewing and revising organization charts to be sure that the management structure and reporting relationships are those that are required to meet the demands of the business and to implement forward plans. The legal structure of the company is not considered to be nearly as important, and it is frequently assumed that dealing with the legal niceties of the company's structure are matters which will be routinely handled after the fact by the company's treasury, legal, and tax staffs. For many line managers, profits mean operating profits, and it makes little difference whether they are earned in Subsidiary A or Subsidiary B or in Country X or Country Y. The tax laws, however, do not focus on a business in its aggregate; rather, they focus country by country and legal entity by legal entity. The task for the CFO is to arrange his tax and treasury departments so that they will be in a position to shape the legal structure in response to the business needs of the line managers in a way that will have the least tax cost and preserve flexibility.

The consequences of careful tax planning at the time that legal organizations are formed and businesses are assigned to them manifest themselves in a number of ways. Some of the more common are discussed below.

1. One of the most obvious but nevertheless recurring examples is a mismatch between revenues and expenses with the result that expenses occur in a subsidiary where there is insufficient income to cover them and where the possibility of consolidation of the subsidiary with another organization does not exist. The cost of expenses which cannot be tax benefited is a heavy penalty.

2. To the extent separate businesses can be housed in their own legal entities, the task of divesting those businesses in the future is rendered much easier. If separate businesses are comingled in the same legal entity and if it is later desired to divest one of them, the tax cost of carving out the business to be sold may be much higher than it would otherwise have been if such a breakup was not necessary. In this case, flexibility has been compromised.

3. For a company engaged in international business involving the shipment of goods manufactured in one country to an-

other country where they will be sold, the establishment of acceptable transfer prices can have a major effect upon the company's profitability. If a company has attempted to arrange itself so that the bulk of its profit will be earned in the country with the lowest tax rate (both on earned income and on repatriation of earnings to the parent company), it will need to establish transfer prices which accomplish this objective and which the company will be able to justify to the tax authorities of the country which believes it has been shortchanged by the allocation of profits.

4. An area of equal concern to companies engaged in international business is compliance with the regulations issued under Section 861 of the Internal Revenue Code pursuant to which expenses incurred in the United States (such as corporate headquarters stewardship expenses, interest, R&D, and so on) are allocated to foreign earnings, thus diminishing the benefit of the foreign tax credit.

   Since these expenses are frequently not recognized as deductible in the countries to which they would be allocable, the effect is to increase the tax cost of doing business in those countries. Careful tax planning can create opportunities to reduce the adverse affect of Section 861.

5. Bringing profits home from abroad is also an area in which effective tax planning can pay big dividends. If the total tax costs of repatriating foreign earnings produces a tax rate higher than the U.S. statutory rate, it may behoove a company to delay the repatriation of such earnings until it is able to generate sufficient levels of foreign source income which are taxed at rates below the U.S. statutory rate so that the low-taxed foreign earnings will offset the high-taxed earnings when they are repatriated. The delay of the repatriation of earnings, however, may entail separate risks, such as inadequate investment return pending repatriation or exposure to devaluation. On the other hand, earlier repatriation may generate excess foreign tax credits which might expire unused if low-taxed foreign source income cannot be generated on a timely basis. The situation is rendered more difficult by the LIFO rule governing the use of foreign tax credits. All of these considerations raise complex issues of timing which are best addressed at the outset rather than after the

fact. If they are looked at beforehand, they can frequently be resolved or minimized by altering the chain of ownership which links the foreign subsidiary to the U.S. parent, by financing techniques, or by altering the nature or scope of the foreign operations.

A sine qua non of effective legal entity tax planning is maintenance of accurate and current legal entity financial statements. The tax consequences of shifting funds from one legal entity to another are determined by the tax books of the legal entities involved. The retained earnings of a legal entity prepared in accordance with generally accepted accounting principles is a far different number than the accumulated earnings and profits calculated in accordance with the relevant tax code. It can be a costly error to ignore the need to maintain accurate calculations of accumulated earnings and profits for each of the legal entities comprised within a corporate family.

CONCLUSION

We are living in a world characterized by a lack of stability in the tax laws. This lack of certainty offers significant rewards for careful tax planning and significant penalties for the failure to plan. The CFO's responsibility is to see that his financial staff is organized adequately to cope with the situation, manned by competent professionals, and integrated into the day-to-day operations of the company in a way that will maximize the contribution to earnings, cash flow, and return on equity.

26

Pension Fund Management

Eugene L. Schotanus and Jarrod W. Wilcox

INTRODUCTION

The chief financial officer in many corporations is responsible for the oversight of assets often as large as one of the company's major divisions—the trusted employee benefit funds. One may view the pension fund, at one extreme, as a profit center or, at the other, as a social responsibility. But there is no disputing its importance.

Why has the management of the pension fund and other trusteed funds been raised from its former operational status to a matter of strategic concern?

Exhibit 1 plots the market value of U.S. private noninsurance pension fund assets and equity holdings through time. Total U.S. equity market value is shown for comparison. Between 1950 and 1975, both total fund assets and equity holdings grew much more rapidly than did the market value of corporate equity. Since then, the relative growth seems to have stabilized but at a high level.

The figure shows a shift from almost total reliance on bonds

Eugene L. Schotanus is senior vice president—financial services, and CFO for Deere & Company. Jarrod W. Wilcox is senior vice president, Batterymarch Financial Management.

Exhibit 1
Private Noninsured U.S. Pension Funds versus Corporate Equity

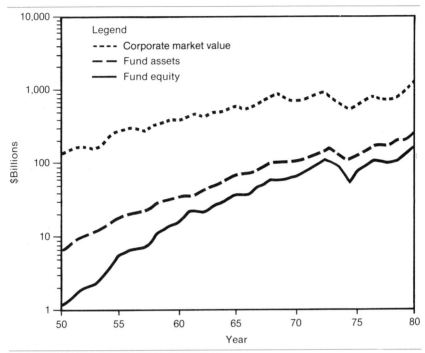

Source: Flow of Funds, Federal Reserve Board.

to a mix of equity and bonds. To a lesser extent, it also demonstrates the growing role of pension funds in the ownership of corporate America. In 1950, noninsured pension funds held less than 1 percent of corporate equity. In 1980, this was at 7 percent. These figures do not include substantial corporate pension funding through insurance company contracts.

Exhibit 2 illustrates the potential eventual magnitude of pension funds relative to operating assets as a successful company matures. The augmented balance sheet, including the pension funds, presents an entirely different perspective than does the normal balance sheet. For General Motors, our example, it shows the pension fund accounting for over one fourth of total assets and almost half of total liabilities.

Trusteed employee benefit funds, which are dominated by pension funds, provide a long-term benefit to the employee and to the employer. But variations in investment performance of such a fund, particularly in the more popular "defined-benefit"

Exhibit 2
Potential Magnitude of Pension Funds Relative
to Operating Assets

GENERAL MOTORS
Augmented Balance Sheet 1983
(billions of dollars)

As Reported

Current assets	20.8	Current liabilities	14.9
Other assets	24.9	Other liabilities	10.0
		Equity	20.8
Total	45.7	Total	45.7

Pension Fund

Trusteed assets*	14.8	Present value of benefits†	21.4
Insured assets	3.3	Unfunded benefits	(3.3)
Total	18.1	Total	18.1

Augmented

Sponsor's assets	45.7	Sponsor's liabilities	24.9
Fund assets	18.1	Present value of benefits	21.4
		Combined equity	17.5
Total	63.8	Total	63.8

*Market value.
†A discount rate of 9 percent was used by GM. The annual report does not state whether the value of benefits includes projected salary and wage increases for the nonvested portion.
Source: Calculated from 1983 Annual Report of General Motors Corporation.

form, can have substantial impact on the employer contributions and thereby on total corporate pretax profit. Exhibit 3 traces the history of U.S. employer contributions to private noninsured pension funds as compared to wages and salaries and also compared to pretax corporate profits. Annual corporate contributions rose from 4 percent of pretax corporate profits in 1950 to approximately 25 percent by 1980!

For the U.S. economy as a whole, corporate pension fund *equity* holdings approximate 70 percent of pretax profit. A usual, annual fluctuation of plus-or-minus 15 percent in equity returns implies, therefore, that a defined-benefit plan might induce a 10 percent typical annual fluctuation in corporate income. This fluctuation is normally dampened by accounting conventions which spread gains and losses over several years, but the true pass-through of risk to the corporation is significant, a risk for which compensation can be rightly expected.

However, offering tax-shielded benefits for employees does not require a defined-benefit plan in which the corporation

Exhibit 3
U.S. Private Pension Contributions versus Pretax Profit and Wages

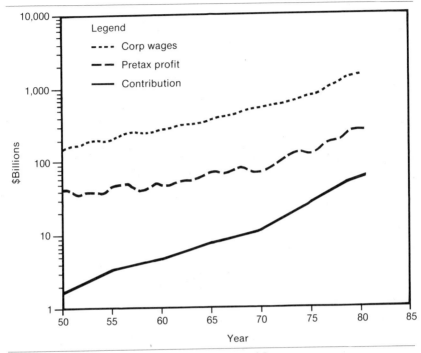

Source: Survey of Current Business, U.S. Department of Commerce.

guarantees a definite benefit according to a formula. Corporations can alternatively transfer all of the investment risk to the employee. Any of the defined-contribution plans (which might be a pension plan, an employee thrift plan, or a self-insured accident and health plan, that is, an IRS 501 C–9 Trust) play this role. In these plans, there is a definite investment but no guarantee as to results. Going further, not only all the investment risk but also a portion of the corporation's own operating risk may be transferred to employees through a profit-sharing plan in which even the size of each year's investment (or contribution) is not guaranteed.

What should be the mission of these various plans, particularly the corporate pension fund? How should the plan administration be organized? What should be investment policy? And what special pitfalls lie in wait, particularly in the area of supervising outside portfolio managers?

CORPORATE FUND MISSION

Trusteed employee benefit funds can be found in as great a variety as the character and circumstances of the companies that sponsor them. The first mission of any CFO is to ascertain why the fund either exists or is proposed and what are its basic objectives.

Fringe benefits, among which trusteed funds fall, are generally designed to serve these objectives: to attract, motivate and retain employees, and to optimize tax treatment of compensation. There also exist a few plans of considerable size for which the sponsors' justification includes capital formation for the company or even capital formation in general.

At least several alternatives exist to meet each of the basic objectives. This offers the CFO a geometrically expanding universe of multiple alternatives to analyze and consider and ultimately to be responsible for.

Obviously the personnel or industrial relations organization has to be a guiding force in the detailed creation, design, and administration of all such plans. It is incumbent, however, upon the CFO to insist that the overall plan remain consistent with original objectives. For example, a profit-sharing plan designed to discourage unionization may be totally obsolete if a union is certified. Even the pension plan itself may diminish in value as IRAs, 401K plans, and other means of deferring income and income taxes evolve. The critical role of the CFO in plan content is to consider original objectives and new alternatives.

Interaction between the CFO and personnel (or industrial relations) management is critical to the design of any plan and ultimately to how it is funded and managed. Frequently, the financial circumstances of a given plan sponsor may differ from trends in compensation practices, which are driven by market forces. To enforce efficiency, one must continually reexamine the original objectives for offering the fringe benefit. While great precision may not be possible, the personnel (or industrial relations) value of any benefit can be expressed quantitatively and compared to the CFO's evaluation of its risk-adjusted cost.

Quantitatively thus armed, the question of circumstances versus objectives can be assessed qualitatively. This is art, not science. An emerging high-technology company with rapid growth might best opt to attract and reward entrepreneurial employees with a high-risk, high-reward profit-sharing plan. The "smokestack America" company with less exciting prospects will probably better achieve its recruiting and other objectives with a defined-benefit plan.

Having determined the objectives of the benefit plan and its most desirable form, the CFO must weigh the cash-flow attributes of the plan or plans. The added value of any tax-qualified benefit plan comes principally from the employee's perception of incremental value compared to the smaller aftertax amount otherwise added to his paycheck. To the plan sponsor, a dollar added to the next paycheck has the same aftertax cash-flow effect as a dollar contributed to a benefit fund, except for relatively minor timing and, in some cases, FICA tax differences.

The current dollar invested in a tax-qualified plan remains intact as it goes into the fund. What it earns over the years while in the fund is similarly untaxed and can compound faster than an individual's own savings aftertax. Ultimately, both contributions and earnings are taxed at individual taxpayer rates, which may presumably be lower at postretirement income levels.

Considered as a unit, the employer-employee partnership is considerably better off from a net present value standpoint. How this tax or cash-flow benefit is divided between employer and employee is a matter of perception, communication, and perhaps bargaining. This is a key challenge to plan administrators, as it is the determining offset to the risk of sponsoring a defined-benefit plan and must, in part, accrue to the risk-bearing sponsor.

Defined Benefit versus Defined Contribution

Defining the contribution versus defining the benefit is no small issue. Historically, most pension plans provided defined benefits. During the late 1970s and early 1980s, by some accounts, 75 percent of all new plans formed primarily by smaller companies were defined contribution. Due to the larger number of small companies, initial funding, and their more rapid growth rates, assets of defined-contribution retirement plans have been estimated to account already for as much as one third of the total pension fund assets.

Trends toward or away from defined-benefit plans will probably be cyclical. The high rates of inflation in the latter 1970s followed by deep recession in the early 1980s obviously squeezed the sponsors of defined-benefit plans. Also, a developing propensity of at least the academic wing of the accounting profession to give pension obligations some form of balance sheet status obviously increases corporate sponsors' concern over the implication of defining benefits. In the short run, earnings and balance sheet pressures can lead corporate sponsors into an unfortunate temptation to lessen funding of the tax-shielding plan. Examples of these include changes in funding policy, actuarial assumptions, and innovative tactics.

A preeminent example of the latter is the "dedicated bond" portfolio in which bond income and liquidation cash flows are matched with planned benefit outflows. The motivation sometimes appears to be the securing of a higher actuarial assumption as to asset returns. For conservatism, actuaries have been willing to certify highly certain bond returns as greater than uncertain, long-term equity returns. By improving *actuarial* return assumptions, the sponsor can reduce current contributions and, in some cases, recover capital from the fund. This factor may cloud the relative investment merits of equity versus bonds.

In facing the issue of whether to define benefits or contributions, the CFO can gain insight from the experience of employee thrift plans. These began with no assumption of risk by the sponsor. Most such plans started as a vehicle for employees to become shareholders of the company. Over time, the plans proved quite volatile in terms of the objective to provide retirement security. In response, sponsors offered participants the opportunity to diversify into bonds or a managed portfolio of other common stocks. These, too, proved to be as volatile as the capital markets, resulting in true hardship for some participants and in a windfall for others, depending only upon timing. As a result, many sponsors, including the very largest, have undertaken to guarantee at least a minimum return to each participant, thus reintroducing the risks and attributes of a defined-benefit plan. Such guarantees may provide only a minimal return of typically 6 percent or so. During the 1970s however, it was not uncommon for the cumulative return for individual accounts to have fallen short of that guarantee. The departing employee then received the value of his share of the securities, plus a cash subsidy from the sponsor. As a result, so-called savings and investment plans can become a form of defined-benefit programs.

ORGANIZATIONAL ISSUES

If it is deemed that a trusteed benefit plan provides some form of advantage to the process of acquiring employee services, a whole host of organizational questions arise. What is the role of the firm's board of directors? What is the role of the actuary? Who should invest the fund's assets and how, etc.? In a pure start-up situation, the board of directors would presumably approve a comprehensive plan contemplating all such organizational detail most likely designed by the CFO together with his personnel counterparts. In the case of older, established plans, an almost infinite variety of organizational forms can be found, ranging from a separate board of trustees to a single "pension executive," with a variety of committee arrangements in between.

The Employee Retirement Income Security Act of 1974 (ERISA) has undoubtedly influenced this matter by defining and allocating fiduciary responsibility. Comprehensive research into the myriad of possible organizational solutions would likely be beyond the resources of the CFO of even very large corporations and is really not necessary. The guidelines of ERISA, supplemented by logic and realism, suggests a central organizational theme. The board of directors is also ultimately responsible for everything else the corporation owes, does, or undertakes. But it cannot cope with the intimate detail of every corporate endeavor.

As a practical matter, the CFO should guide the board in delegating responsibility for plan design, plan administration, funding decisions, and asset supervision. An extension of that same logic suggests that the board regularly review the results of each function that it has delegated to a subordinate level. There is some powerful subtlety here in that many boards of large corporations have had a high propensity to monitor investment performance but ignore plan design or administration, even though the two are so highly interdependent. Again, the CFO needs to reexamine continually the objectives of the plan and help the board reconcile those to the sponsor company's financial circumstances.

A critical juncture is reached when financial management, personnel management, and the board of directors all view employee benefit funds in the larger context of compensation objectives, cost or cash-flow effectiveness, financial reality, and organizational efficiency. From that point, and that point only, the CFO can begin to address the components for delivery of benefits to employees with optimal effectiveness. The latter includes the consideration of the actuarial process, the asset investment process, and reported earnings or shareholder implications.

Actuary and Liability Considerations

The selection of both an actuary and an actuarial philosophy is a powerful determinant of how the benefit plan will evolve, be administered, and in particular, how assets will be deployed. Perhaps more important, however, is one last iteration with the board to identify the likely future course of the benefits promised by the plan's liabilities. There is a vast difference between, for example, the defined-benefit pension plan of a mature company in a mature industry and a new plan in a high-growth sector. The former must obviously concern itself with plan asset liquidity, the latter with growth prospects. In between these obvious extremes are most plan sponsors who are subject to potentially long and extreme cyclical experience of periodically increasing or decreasing employment levels.

In this age of readily constructed simulation models, it is relatively easy to build or access an existing model that replicates the actuary's work and permits sensitivity analyses. What more useful tool could there be for either the CFO or the board than to know whether the fund needs to be invested conservatively with an eye toward liquidity or rather that liquidity is irrelevant and maximum return may be sought?

Such a model need not be excessively complex. It mainly needs to measure sensitivity to differing assumptions regarding wage escalations, level of employment, and investment performance. The parameters identified by this kind of sensitivity analysis can provide invaluable guidance not only toward the plan's investment strategy but to the sponsor's funding policy and even the overall corporate strategy. All of these are, of course, important not only to the CFO but to other members of the management team and the board.

The actual choice of an actuary and, more importantly, an actuarial method is somewhat akin to choosing the independent auditors. There are a number of actuarial firms, including some divisions of the big eight accounting firms. All offer differing levels of auxiliary services but tend to be quite similar in terms of their basic work and to adhere to the quite high standards of the Society of Actuaries. There are a number of actuarial methods which are in generally accepted use, and which may have significant differences in the timing of funding requirements. In addition, management determines such variables as minimum versus maximum funding strategy and, hence, retains a considerable degree of control of, and responsibility for, the fund beyond choice of actuary. Since employee benefits costs, like all other costs, must ultimately be recovered by selling prices, the CFO will want to select an actuarial method which realistically assigns these costs to current production or revenues. If the result is radically different from benefit expenses incurred by competitors, the whole plan probably needs review, not just the actuarial method or assumptions.

Since the passage of ERISA, the actuary's independence has increased. He must now serve at least several constituencies. These include the company or its shareholders, the employees or plan beneficiaries, the government, and, increasingly, the general public. This was not really a profound change in that the interest of these constituencies generally coincided anyway. One area of potential contention, however, is the matter of assumed interest rates or investment return. Prior to ERISA, actuaries tended to accommodate to the plan sponsor's estimate of investment return. They simply adjusted the offsetting assumption about wage escalation to produce a realistic final result. This worked well in that, for the most part, it is the spread between the two which determines contributions and expense.

ERISA charged the actuary with the use of a "realistic" interest or investment assumption. Consequently, the actuary could no longer ignore the existence of double-digit interest rates existing in the late 1970s and early 1980s. Because, as a rough assumption, inflation affects both interest rates and wage inflation similarly over long periods, shifting to such substantially higher interest assumptions was of more interest to the media than it was of substance. Wages, especially those linked to the Consumer Price Index (CPI) were unarguably rising at least the new higher rate of interest, driving the offsetting wage assumption. However, if for some reason long-term interest rates and wage inflation trends continued to diverge as they did in

1980 and 1983, the actuary's imposed realism requirement could begin to really affect funding and expense recognition.

The CFO needs to have a constructive relationship with the actuary, as each must respond to their several constituencies harmoniously. To that end, a gross oversimplification of the actuary's computation, to be used conversationally, is probably useful. Simplistically, the actuary quantifies everything that management has explicitly or implicitly promised employees. He then grosses up this amount by some assumed combination of real wage increases and inflation for as many years as remain the expected lifetime of existing employees, and he arrives at an astronomical potential liability. Then much like the common real estate mortgage tables, he solves mathematically for that combination of straight line infusion of principal, upon which compound interest will be earned at the assumed rate, which would extinguish the ultimate liability.

From such computations which are clearly in the domain of present value, alternative measures can be drawn. These alternatives are the general basis of current accounting disclosure and would be the basis for eventual presentation as balance sheet items. There are several major sources of uncertainty. Diminished numbers give recognition to whether or not promised benefits are vested. More important, however, is the notion of present value. Unlike most other numbers on the balance sheet or income statement, deferred employee benefits are expressed in terms of their present value, thus increasing the importance of realistic assessment of investment or interest rate potential.

Fund Asset Administration and Performance Measurement

If a sponsored plan has substantial assets to invest, the CFO must turn his attention to how those assets will be managed. Again, there exists a wide variety of alternatives. At one extreme, the plan sponsor can, as was historically popular for many years, simply abdicate most of the responsibility to some other institution which will act as overall portfolio manager. At the other extreme, particularly if the fund is large, the plan sponsor might elect to undertake the entire management process.

Before the CFO and the board decided upon an asset management plan, some basic realities must be faced. First and foremost, there is no escaping the reconciliation of investment results with the plan's original objectives. Poor investment performance destroys the efficacy of a defined-contribution plan, and it makes a defined-benefit plan more costly. Even the law (ERISA) suggests that fiduciaries must get rid of an asset manager that can be consistently expected to produce bad results, whether or not it meets the test of prudence. This is a very important concept. However fund management is organized, fiduciary responsibility requires institutional change once the probability of poor investment results become apparent. This suggests that all plan sponsors must face more involvement in the investment process because fiduciary responsibility can never be fully delegated.

Investment Management Administration

The majority of benefit funds are still defined-benefit plans or, as in the case of thrift plans, incorporate features approaching defined benefits. As a result, sponsors have special incentive to respond to the performance issue. Generally, the first step in that process is to engage more than one manager, thereby both diversifying and ostensibly stimulating some performance competition. Logically, the performance-minded sponsor will continually search for investment firms which appear to offer the best performance. Ultimately, this leads to the engagement of specialty type managers: growth stock specialists, fixed-income specialists, real estate managers, and the like. At this stage, the plan sponsor has crossed an important line. By default, the company has become involved in the asset allocation decision. Many believe asset allocation to be actually the most important decision affecting investment performance.

There is nothing inherently wrong with the plan sponsor making the asset allocation decision. It does mean the company must have a rationale for the mix it decides upon, and that implies that some organizational and staffing decisions must be made. A common approach to the allocation decision is to find out what other prudent people (that is, other plan sponsors) do and to copy. This ultimately leads to the appointment of at least one pension investment officer since executives whose principal responsibilities lie elsewhere may not have time to devote to monitoring investment trends. A more rational approach to the allocation decision is obviously to draw upon all the work suggested earlier. The objectives of one particular plan might suggest extreme conservatism while another would call for more aggressive, very long-term investments, such as real estate ownership. Analysis of the liquidity needs of the particular fund or its sensitivity to changes in levels of employment of inflation is even more useful, whether the product of a simulation model or simply discussions with the actuary.

In the normal evaluation of trust fund administration, plan sponsors who have crossed the line into asset allocation or even just multiple managers, and have some staff dedicated to the process, inevitably confront the question of managing some funds "in house." There are good arguments both for and against actually managing some or all of the plan's assets. Too often, the decision whether or not to do so is made for the wrong reasons. Outside directors, for example, are often disproportionately influential in this regard. The presence of one or more directors associated with companies who do manage their own assets can influence a decision to do so prematurely or when the character of the plan is not best served.

If internal administration is under consideration, the CFO must play an important role as he will probably be most responsible for the process after it is undertaken. To succeed, internal administration must be established with clear objectives, be based upon sound economics, and be managed by people with credibility. A complete discussion of those characteristics would itself constitute a rather large book. A few examples of each, however, can be cited briefly.

A sound objective of internal administration, for example, might be to rationalize the diversification. Analysis of the holdings of a fund guided by multiple managers can often yield some real surprises in that one or more unusual companies coincidently appeal to each of the managers and accidentally become the fund's largest holding. An unsound objective would be to outperform the market by a large number of percentage points. The economics of internally managing, particularly a large fund, are generally favorable based upon the avoidance of management fees alone. If this is not true, the notion is probably being considered prematurely. Finally, credibility is perhaps the most difficult issue. It is always possible, of course, to hire well-established investment people from other firms and rely on their reputation. This can be a shocking experience for many industrial companies attempting to fit the required salaries into an established compensation package.

If internal administration is to be undertaken, its organizational form can do much to smooth the issues of rational objectives and credibility. Some experienced investment people should, of course, be recruited. A brief stint at interviewing, incidentally, usually reveals that superstar status is partly dependent upon marketing skills. Competent investment people with less marketing skills, less needed in house, can be found within a realistic price range. An oversight committee, including officers or inside directors, adds immeasurably to the credibility of the effort and provides an indispensable degree of control that is needed anyway.

The existence of an investment staff, whether to actually invest funds or to monitor the performance of outside managers, is often cited as having additional synergy with the rest of the company. This can, of course, be true if the company has other investment portfolios, has a highly active investor relations effort, or is, for other reasons, financial market oriented. More often than not, the converse is true. In fact, it is incumbent upon the CFO to see that trust investment staff are shielded from interested, individual investors from other staff areas, including senior management.

Mechanics of Performance Measurement

However fund assets are ultimately managed, it is obviously necessary to measure the returns being earned. Again, a variety of theories exist as to how performance should be measured. The key to this question is, once measured, what use will be made of the results? Generally, the measures of investment results are used comparatively. They are compared to the actuarially assumed interest rate (although this is questionable), used to compare to alternative investments, and to compare one manager's performance against another. Comparison of past rates of return to the actuarial assumption can be misleading, for example, in the case of a bond portfolio. The portfolio's current yield to maturity is far more germane relative to a future interest rate assumption. The same is true of equity and other investments, but expected returns are more subjective.

The useful numerical rate of return to be used in comparing

alternative investments is called dollar weighted. Simplistically, this is the compound rate of return the portfolio actually earned for the length of time it was invested just as if it were a savings account at a bank. Again, securities are valued at market in the computation.

To compare managers' or individual portfolios' performance, a time weighted return is generally computed. Since individual portfolios nearly always have contained differing amounts of funds for differing periods of time, this seeks the return earned on a dollar continually invested in the portfolio. The computation is similar to mutual fund accounting. Each time funds are added or withdrawn from the account, a new unit value is computed. New cash funds coming in at par buy more or fewer units depending on the current unit value. A compound rate of return is thus computed by comparing the beginning and ending values of one unit.

The behavior of time and dollar weighted rates of return can cause some amount of consternation among users, so the CFO needs to be familiar with their limitations. Anomalies occur surrounding large inflows or outflows, especially when markets are, coincidentally, highly volatile. If a credible organization, that is, professional staff, and a high-level oversight committee exist, the board is really best able to discharge its responsibilities by considering only the dollar weighted return on the entire trust or, at most, on segments by type of investments. If for some reason the board desires to examine more detailed comparison, such as between managers, the wise CFO will have prepared a clear reconciliation between time and dollarweighted results for any individual portfolio.

INVESTMENT MANAGEMENT

Unfortunately, the skills and attitudes useful in running an operating business may not always be readily transferable to managing a pension fund. This may be an uncomfortable proposition for the management team but, once accepted, it enables the corporation to avoid potentially at least three critical investment mistakes.

The fund might buy and sell too frequently, running up transaction costs because the value of management's special insights and information is overestimated.

The fund might fail to diversify away obvious sources of risk uncompensated by any special extra-expected return.

The fund sponsor might underestimate the role played by chance and become overly enamored with the investment vehicles and portfolio manager having the best recent performance.

At the other end of the spectrum, when the fund sponsor hands over too much responsibility to investment professionals (whether external or in-house), other mistakes are made.

The company may forego adequate returns.

It may incur so much periodic discomfort as to disrupt long-term funding or investment programs.

The company may fail to coordinate the risks affecting plan liabilities from inflation or plant closings, for example, with the risks in its investments.

A pattern of any of the foregoing six-problem symptoms, brought on by too close or too distant a relationship between senior management and the fund's investment decisions, ought to trigger policy review.

In leading or supervising such a review, the CFO should have a clear understanding of two strategic concepts against which the detailed recommendations of staff or fund managers must be appraised. These are, first, the efficient market, and second, the portfolio.

The Efficient Market

There may be hundreds of active buyers and sellers for an investment security during a single day. The delay time in changing effective supply or demand in reaction to price changes or any other news is usually no more than a few hours or days as compared to months or years for new capacity for many real products and services. In consequence, no single-market participant, often including the security issuer's own management, has as much information as has already been expressed in the stock price resulting from the transactions among other participants.

On the one hand, there may be no above-average payoff to the investor unless his data or ideas are such as to surpass nearly all other participants. Investment research which duplicates that used by quicker participants has no payoff. This is very unlike ordinary experience where more effort, higher motivation, and a little better idea will usually be rewarding.

The saving grace of this quick incorporation of new information into current prices means, on the other hand, that security purchase decisions based on wrong data or ideas, so long as they allow diversification and do not run up brokerage costs, do about as well as random choice. Again, this is very unlike ordinary business product and service markets where investments based on wrong assumptions end up as disasters.

This concept does not necessarily mean that the fund sponsor cannot expect to "beat the market." But it implies that most of its ideas for doing so have probably already been used by others and are, therefore, already expressed in the price of the security. This efficient market concept puts a premium on investment approaches which avoid the consensus approval of other investors. The efficient market tends to ensure that views of skillful, professional investment managers will often seem contrary to the common sense of their clients. Unfortunately, the implication does not run the other way; mere contrariness does not predict investment skill!

The Portfolio

Portfolio risk is usually measured in terms standard deviation or typical fluctuation in annual total return from a collection of different investments. When securities of different kinds of risks are combined in the same portfolio, the portfolio's risk goes down. This is the principal of insurance. Generally speaking, the more diversification, the more is the reduction of portfolio risk, although at a diminishing rate of reduction. What remains is so-called nondiversifiable risk.

When the investment decision maker evaluates the risk versus expected return of an individual investment, the pertinent risk is its contribution to nondiversifiable risk. The residual independent risk will be offset by fluctuations of other securities within the portfolio.

When the CFO evaluates a portfolio, it is important to ask what available kinds of risk diversification have been omitted. Unless this decision is explicit and represents an intentional, skillful bet against the omitted investment class, it represents loss of opportunity for lower risk, higher expected gain, or both.

Investment Objectives

The major dimensions of investment performance are average return and risk, both judged over a specified time interval.

The first step in intelligently establishing risk and return objectives is to learn what performance is realistic (that is, consistent with history) and what have been the trade-offs between average return and return standard deviation. This should be done over a fairly long historical period, at least several decades if possible, so as to avoid being unduly influenced by temporary trends.

Real returns are arrived at by subtracting average inflation rates. Real returns have averaged about 0 percent for treasury bills, about 1 percent for corporate bonds, about 6 percent from common stocks, and about 9 percent for small stocks, according to widely quoted estimates prepared by Ibbotson & Sinquefield (see Reference). The standard deviation of annual return ranks in the same order, about 3 percent for bills, 6 percent for corporate bonds, 22 percent for stocks, and 37 percent for small stocks. Although these risk-return trade-offs are improved somewhat by portfolios with a diversified mixture of different asset types, they are illustrative. Relatively high long-term real returns are typically attained only through the assumption of risks of substantial year-to-year fluctuations.

These long-term records are suitable maximum return objectives for pension fund management. The prudent CFO may hope for a better than average record, but he will not formally plan for it.

There is no mechanical rule for selecting an appropriate point on the risk-return trade-off. In general, long-term pension fund management should take as much risk as the corporation can stand because to do so has historically resulted in far higher average returns. This assumes that investment policy does not waver and withdraw from more risky investments during market downturns. The key here is a realistic simulation and assessment of how the board is likely to respond in times of negative returns.

An important point to keep in mind is the differing tax situation of a tax-exempt fund and of the senior executives on the management team who are likely to influence its investment policy. Taxable individuals may be unconsciously biased toward "growth" stocks because of favorable capital gains treatment. Tax-exempt funds ordinarily can obtain higher average total returns by giving greater emphasis to securities with greater current income.

Investment Policy—Asset Allocation

It is unlikely that the CFO will want to participate in day-to-day investment decisions. But he should lead in assisting the board to arrive at a consistent long-term investment policy. The most important decision is establishing proportions for asset classes with long-term norms for U.S. equity, bonds, bills, and other newer forms of accepted investments such as real estate, guaranteed investment contracts, or international securities. The critical phenomena to avoid is increasing any one category sharply because of its recent (say five year) performance. Such timing decisions are best confined to relatively small fractions of the portfolio and, in any case, are not policy decisions but tactical ones. The CFO may get more help than he needs from board members who have strong opinions about bonds today and equities tomorrow.

The fund should seek broad diversification by type of asset class to cover different types of risks. For example, real estate will do especially well during periods of accelerating inflation. Foreign securities will benefit from a weak U.S. dollar. The CFO should not allow the corporation's own business experiences with particular types of investment vehicles to color unduly the policies governing its pension funds.

The optimum percentages of equity versus fixed-income securities, a key issue, depends on the time horizon of the fund and how much "heat" the corporate trustees can stand in their pursuit of higher average return. The 60, 40 equity-bond ratio common for many pension funds is probably more appropriate to a five-year horizon than to the 15- to 20-year horizon of the beneficiary. Over such a long period, the portfolio ought to tend to do better with higher proportions of equity or with whatever is deemed to be the higher average compound return asset class.

Setting Limits on Nondiversifiable Risk

What risks remain after a portfolio has been diversified across many different investment vehicles? The chief source of fluctuation in return will be fluctuations in equity prices based on changes in the rate of real profitability. Realistic worst-case scenarios incorporating changes in an unfavorable direction should be explored and the probable impact on corporate contributions and board attitude assessed. This is particularly necessary for companies likely to be experiencing simultaneous corporate cash-flow problems and build-downs in employment levels during such a recession scenario.

Historically, much of the long-term benefit of owning equity is realized during the periods of economic recovery. The primary rationale for ever-owning equity will thus be lost if the plan sponsor is forced to retreat during market declines either through recapturing "overfunding" or switching from equity to fixed-income vehicles. If this kind of scenario is likely, the volatility of the fund should be reduced on a permanent basis whether through emphasizing equities with lower nondiversifiable risk, such as utility stocks, or by increasing the proportion of a variety of short- and long-term, fixed-income securities.

Seeking Out Diversifiable Risk

Risks which potentially might be diversified away according to the insurance principle are taken to seek greater returns, especially when the investment decision maker is supposed to have above-average skill which can be exploited.

This can be done at a variety of levels: individual security selection, industry or group selection, and vehicle type.

At each level, the most fundamental investment decision is whether to make an active or passive selection. An active selection policy intentionally sacrifices some diversification benefit to achieve an expectation of a return greater than that normally available at a given risk level. It assumes market inefficiency—that is, that one knows something not already reflected in the market price. It need not imply frequent trading activity.

Passive investment may be achieved either by purchasing an index fund or by collecting such a large stable of managers of differing styles that all bases are covered. The latter will usually be more conventionally acceptable but at a cost in fees.

The key information to collect for investment policy making is whether the fund has access to skill levels adequate for active selection. If not, does it have any skill in finding fund managers who do have such skills? This is much harder than it would seem. Equity managers who are in the upper quartile during one year are quite likely to be in the bottom quartile the next, particularly if they specialize in a specific stock group or are "market timers."

Who Should Make Tactical Investment Decisions

As noted earlier, as funds grow larger, portions are likely to be brought in house rather than delegated to an independent portfolio manager.

To an extent, this decision is like any other make-or-buy choice faced by the plan sponsor and is influenced by simple economics. But, because the quality of investment decision making is sometimes difficult to assess, the choice will probably be made based on more subjective factors.

The experience and independence of external portfolio managers may increase the chance for superior results over an in-house manager who must win the consensus of corporate executives. Also, external managers are generally easier to hire and fire. But in-house managers may be more open to revealing the bases for their decisions and performance, allowing the plan sponsor to improve investment ability through time.

Continual careful analysis of the ingredients of the overall results is important in either case. And both in-house and independent portfolio managers should be managed so as to make the fund's overall risk and return expectations consistent with longer-term policy. One way to achieve this with minimum interference with individual portfolio managers' natural investment styles is to maintain a portion of investment in a buffer index fund or mutual fund from which rapid withdrawals or additions can be made at low cost.

Role of Timers and Rotational Managers

Those managers who attempt to add value by switching between cash and equity or between utility stocks and technology stocks, for instance, can upset the long-term balance of the portfolio of which they are a part. Rather than viewing their activities as asset allocation, which is a policy-level decision, it may be more useful to consider their timing activity as a source of diversifiable risk. It is obvious that such maneuvers will either need to be restricted in size or offset by other kinds of unrelated risks. An extreme example of the latter would be one portfolio manager buying securities from another portfolio manager for the same fund. In this case, however, although the risk is completely diversified, there is a net loss in transaction costs. This can be limited through the use of a Master Trust in which one manager can "buy" another's holding.

Although the potential rewards of skillful market timing are enormous, the increased risks and transaction costs make it a specialty whose role in the fund's total portfolio should be carefully monitored and controlled.

FURTHER ISSUES

Several further issues should be noted and reemphasized. They are special pitfalls for corporate management and the CFO.

Conflicts of Interest

Corporate management will sometimes be tempted to encourage external portfolio managers to vote stock in takeovers, proxy fights, and so forth in some way not determined by the portfolio manager to be desirable from an investment point of view. Presumably the manager was hired because of the value put on his skill; such interference undermines that value and not only in the case at hand. The manager may well become so concerned with what the client thinks that his future usefulness is impaired.

The corporation pressed for cash may also be tempted to extract funds from the employee benefit funds. The CFO should ask the question: Will money put to work in the company's own business earn more on an aftertax basis, and at a comparable risk, than the same money invested tax-free within the pension fund?

Similarly, the corporation may issue stock to the fund in lieu of a contribution. While there may be occasions when this is justified, it may create problems subsequently if objective investment judgments point to disposition. An alternative would be an off-the-shelf stock issue.

In supervising the trusteed employee benefit fund, the CFO enters a very public arena where even the appearance of conflict of interest is to be strenuously avoided.

Careerism

Most of the participants in the management of a pension fund are agents. The CFO is an agent of the chief executive officer and of the shareholders. Trustees are agents of the plan's beneficiaries. External portfolio managers, often institutions, are agents of the trustees or, more often in reality, of the CFO. The individuals actually managing investments are usually employees who are, in turn, agents of the external portfolio manager as an institution. All agents have in mind not only their client's but their own interest in making their decisions. This is not only apparent in obvious conflicts of interest but more subtly.

One obvious symptom is overconservatism toward short-term risk. Another is spending too much time on peripheral investments with high entertainment or professional challenge content.

The CFO's best encouragement for goal congruence is to be sure that compensation, promotion, fee, and so on is, in fact, based in investment performance as best it can be measured.

More on Performance Appraisal

Unfortunately, it is extremely difficult to separate skill from chance in measuring investment performance. Assessing skill in market timing, for example, may well require several market cycles of at lease a decade and perhaps two.

The CFO will undoubtedly be influenced in his choice of external managers by recent performance numbers. But every effort should be made to get underneath overall figures to find out how much these results can be ascribed to decisions on asset class, market timing, how much to group rotation, how much to individual security selection, and how much to low trading costs or low fees. The former cases may take many years to provide confidence that we are observing skill, the latter only a few months.

Final Thoughts

One of the CFO's most challenging roles is to serve as a bridge between the beliefs and attitudes of experienced corporate operating executives and those of experienced investment managers.

It may be difficult for the corporation's board to imagine that hard work and high motivation will have no investment payoff in an efficient market if it is merely part of the consensus. It may be difficult for investment managers to keep in mind the crosscurrents of often conflicting organizational needs to which the CFO must attend. Both are essential.

A variety of issues periodically arise which are really peripheral to the basic objectives of, and responsibilities for, trusteed benefit plans, such as pensions. These can assume varying degrees of importance depending upon either individual company circumstances or macroeconomic developments. Following a substantial rise in stock prices or a major decline in interest rates, for example, trusteed benefit funds can appear to be more than adequate and tempt the acquisition prone to view them as hidden assets. Conversely, long and severe declines in stock and bond values, such as occurred in the 1970s, stimulated at least as much, if not more, popular conjecture about hidden liabilities.

In the final analysis, the CFO must remind himself, his peers in senior management, and the external constituencies that trusteed benefit funding is a very long-term process. By its nature, the actuarial process is intended to smooth out cycles of even extreme amplitude of duration. It is also natural and proper that compensation consultants, investment bankers, and other entities competing for the company's attention and business will point out cyclical or even momentary opportunities. This is just another form of the efficient market at work. Finding a steady course between these often antagonistic voices represent perhaps the greatest challenge to the CFO who is charged with the stewardship of corporate, as well as trusteed, funds.

REFERENCE

Ibbotson, R. G., and R. A. Sinquefield. *Stocks, Bonds, Bills, and Inflations: The Past and the Future*, 1982 ed. (Charlottesville, Va.: Financial Analysts Research Foundation, 1982).

PART SEVEN

Financial Management in
Diversified Firms

27

Planning in a Diversified Company

Richard W. Miller, Lorian L. Marlantes, and Franklyn A. Caine

INTRODUCTION

Planning within a diversified company has a number of extra dimensions and therefore is more complex than planning in a single-industry company. Moreover, most of the additional complexity involves corporate level financial issues for which the chief financial officer has major responsibility.

The concept of planning for a diversified company is based upon the premise that mere financial opportunism does not maximize the benefits which can arise from corporate size, structure, and synergies. Although examples of 1960s-style, unrelated conglomerates continue to exist, the trend of successful companies is definitely towards a more strategic and systematic approach to diversification. That approach is the subject of this chapter.

Richard W. Miller is executive vice president and CFO of RCA Corporation. Lorian L. Marlantes is vice president—strategic planning and corporate development of The Rockefeller Group. Franklyn A. Caine is staff vice president and assistant treasurer of RCA Corporation. The authors assumed their current positions in 1982, prior to which, they were employed in similar positions at the Penn Central Corporation.

Whether or not the CFO has direct responsibility for the planning function, it is important for him or her to be familiar with the elements of the strategic management process. This discussion is organized into several sections. Within each, special attention is paid to the aspects of the process that are unique to diversified firms.

TYPES OF DIVERSIFIED COMPANIES

At the outset, it may be useful to talk in terms of three categories of diversified companies. This breakdown may be of some use in viewing the alternative management styles that can be used to describe diversified firms and in turn to define the firms' approach to strategic planning.

1. The first category is the financially driven conglomerate. These companies seldom have business strategies per se, but can be viewed as being strategically motivated to construct financially attractive deals which will add to earnings or contribute to financial synergy. Components "fit" only to the extent that they improve the financial balance of the group. Thus, businesses that create tax shelter are linked with taxpayers; cyclical businesses are joined with countercyclical businesses; cash users are matched with cash generators.

2. The next category is the common-theme company whose strategic focus tends to be on diversification within one general business area (such as energy or electronics). In some cases, these companies also adopt a very decentralized management style under which little attempt is made to coordinate across businesses.

3. The final category is where essentially all of the business units are truly integrated and are managed from a common perspective. Although a high degree of diversification may be possible, the separate business units can be perceived to be in the same "industry." From a management perspective, they enjoy less autonomy of operation and are expected to be active in serving a general corporate interest while pursuing their own objectives.

ORGANIZATIONAL ISSUES

In beginning to plan, there are a number of organizational issues that must be handled or the process cannot succeed. The unwavering commitment of the company's CEO is critical. Unless that individual sponsors and actively participates in the planning process, it will quickly degenerate into a sterile exercise in paper shuffling. We have seen planning processes get launched with the consent of the CEO but without his active support. The organization quickly perceives that the CEO is reaching his strategic decisions outside of the formal planning system and immediately turns its energy to those channels. Formal planning will continue to receive lip service—sensible plans may even be created in the process—but the firm's course of action will actually develop with little regard for formal plans.

Assuming that the CEO is fully committed, he should personally become involved in assigning formal responsibility for planning throughout the organization. After the CEO, the key responsibility for planning rests on the operating managers of the various business units, not with "planners." Without the involvement and commitment of operating management (which are easily within the power of the CEO to obtain), the usefulness of the plans and the likelihood of their even being implemented will be dramatically reduced.

For clarity, it would probably be helpful to define a typical organization for a diversified company. Different firms use different nomenclature to describe the structure which is depicted in Exhibit 1. Some refer to "corporate management" as a parent company or a holding company. "Operating groups" are referred to by some as sectors or zones or divisions. "Business planning units" (BPUs) are often strategic planning units or affiliates or operating companies or subsidiaries.

It is important to guard against assigning too much planning responsibility to the operating group level. Most likely the groups exist only as administrative or control units, not as strategic entities. Under such circumstances, it probably makes sense to re-

Exhibit 1
Typical Organization for a Diversified Company

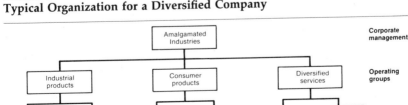

quire formal planning on the operating group level in only one or two cases. One such case would be where the parts of a group relate closely enough to require some integration of their strategies. The other would be where a financially driven conglomerate is willing to give operating group executives the responsibility to build diversified businesses of their own. Outside of those two situations, group executives should be responsible for overseeing the planning efforts of the business planning unit managements that report to them, but they should not waste their time and other valuable corporate resources attempting to construct strategies for groups which have no strategic basis.

At the corporate level, there should be a staff adequate to support the CEO and CFO in the top-down aspects of planning, including goal setting and resource allocation. The staff should also be adequate to assist in physically managing the planning process, as well as in reviewing and analyzing the plans submitted by the BPUs. Finally, the corporate staff can be of help in the sharing of planning tools and resources that cannot be supported by one business unit alone but which could be of value to more than one business planning unit on a shared basis.

There may be cases where a broad-gauged chief financial officer could also act as the chief planning officer. This approach may, in fact, be appropriate in the financially driven conglomerate where financial interrelationships are complex and important. Even in companies with a somewhat more focused diversification, financial standards and measures of performance are key aspects to managing the business portfolio, so it will be important for the chief financial officer to play a leading role in planning.

CONCEPTUAL FRAMEWORK

As with many other fields, there are a number of ways to approach strategic planning. All have their proper place, and all should be employed at some point. We have found it helpful to think in terms of two pairs of complementary methods:

1. Top-down versus bottom-up.
2. Inside-out versus outside-in.

No planning process can be complete unless it encompasses all four of these concepts.

In a top-down planning environment, the business planning units are expected to respond to a master plan established by the corporate management. In the bottom-up approach, each individual BPU sets its own strategic course and establishes its own goals or has the major voice in setting them.

At first glance it may seem that a top-down approach is antithetical to all that is implied by the modern trend towards diversification and decentralization. In almost every conceivable circumstance it is impossible to plan effectively for a diversified company without a strong bottom-up system. At the same time, strict adherence to a bottom-up policy alone can sacrifice a great deal. In all likelihood, only the financially driven conglomerate can afford not to emphasize at least some top-down planning. In all cases, it is the senior corporate management, including the chief financial officer, who must supply the unifying vision for the total enterprise and provide the overall direction for the company. In fact, it is this aspect that should be emphasized in planning for the diversified company.

Inside-out planning concentrates on factors and conditions internal to the firm and attempts to develop a strategy for imposing those strengths on the external environment. The risk in a purely inside-out approach is that external changes which can severely hurt the prospects for a business can go by unnoticed until it is too late.

An outside-in perspective consists of an environmental analysis which can be integrated into the process to help perceive external threats, as well as to uncover opportunities for entering new businesses and developing new products. Providing this outside-in perspective is also a major function of the corporate planning department of the diversified firm.

SETTING CORPORATE GOALS AND OBJECTIVES

In principle, the management philosophy of the firm will dictate the strategic investment objectives of the company—for example, an unrelated conglomerate may be looking only at earnings, growth potential, or return on equity while an integrated conglomerate may ascribe high value to a plan that increases overall integration, internal development, and economies of scale. Too often, strategic planning fails to produce results for senior management primarily because they find themselves with detailed plans for each of their operations but without a way to gauge the value of the strategies to the corporation. Obvious as it may seem, many diversified firms have never managed to plan effectively because they never decided what they wanted to achieve.

Most often in financially driven companies, goals and objectives are stated in purely financial terms. There can be a greater tendency in integrated companies (and to a certain extent, in common-theme companies) to state goals and objectives in *strategic* terms. These range from very tangible characteristics, such as business mix, capital intensity, or exposure to regulatory restraints, to more subjective notions, such as image or social desirability.

It is not uncommon in major diversified companies for objectives to be summarized in terms of a target growth rate or return on investment that corporate management would like to achieve. To be meaningful, these targets cannot be set in a vacuum, rather they must be chosen in the context of what is possible for a given business or a given mix of businesses. They must also be selected with a view to how much risk, both business and financial, the corporate management feels is appropriate. The final step is to test the goals to make certain they are realistic and attainable within the context of the firm's strategic posture.

BUSINESS PLANNING UNIT GOALS AND OBJECTIVES (ROLES)

Once the company's overall financial goals have been established, the intersection of those goals with the strategic plans of the business units allows the corporate management to determine what role is to be played by each of the individual business planning units. Under this approach some business planning units will be managed for growth, to take risks, to develop new products, or to open new markets. Their targets will be set in terms of market share, sales growth, or plant start-ups to mention only a few examples. Other business units will be managed to provide cash, lower the company's overall risk profile, or provide predictable and maintainable earnings. Still other business units will be seen as requiring some sort of strategic breakthrough to make them viable. Absent this breakthrough, their goals should be set to position them for divestiture.

The idea of developing a specific role for each business was one of the key conceptual principles upon which much early thinking in the field of strategic planning was based. Although it has been oversimplified in the hands of some practitioners to the point of becoming a caricature and recently has been subjected to a certain degree of criticism, individual goal setting within an overall strategic context remains a valid concept.

MANAGING THE BOTTOM-UP PLANNING PROCESS

Making the correct choice of which units should do planning can do much to improve the chances of success. They key is to find the largest unit for which it is logical to have a single plan. In most cases, if businesses face the same competitors or share the same facilities, it makes sense to consider them as a single business planning unit irrespective of whether they are organized as a legal entity.

Sometimes it may be difficult to distinguish between a product line and a business planning unit. Indeed, to some extent it will be possible and even desirable for a business planning unit to develop a strategy for each of its product lines. These strategies will contribute to the overall BPU strategy. In a financially driven conglomerate it is generally not appropriate for corporate management to get involved in detailed product line strategies. Even in common theme or more integrated kinds of diversified companies it may not be practical for corporate management to participate in formulating strategies for more than a few key products. Thus, aggregation and planning for business planning units that can be viewed as strategically important by corporate management become keys to a successful planning effort.

A significant, ancillary benefit may be realized in the process of determining the business units which enter the planning process. Inevitably, in a widely diversified company, some units will not fit the mold. Their current size and future prospects do not seem to warrant consideration as a separate strategic unit, yet they do not fit strategically within the umbrella of any other unit either. In all likelihood, these business segments could be sold to raise cash and reduce unnecessary distraction of top management.

In creating an integrated plan, the seemingly trivial activity of determining the way information should be handled can become critically important. Paying proper attention to this activity in the beginning can prevent a variety of problems later on.

The process starts with instructions. These instructions are developed by the corporate planning staff and should clearly state what information is wanted from the business planning units. Forms and formats must be given a good deal of attention. A poorly designed form or a misleading instruction not only can waste time but may actually render a portion of the plan useless. It is usually quite helpful to include numerous examples in the instruction package, and sometimes a workbook to go along with the forms is a good idea.

It is common for different operations within a diversified company to have very different planning needs. Therefore, one's approach to planning must be sufficiently flexible to accommodate those differences but should not be so unstructured that operating divisions are not sure what is being asked of them.

An important element that goes along with the instructions is a common set of planning assumptions. Although business planning units are expected to make their own environmental assessments, there are certain broad areas where every effort should be made to develop companywide consistency. Obviously it makes no sense for some units to plan for an expansionary economy while others plan for a nationwide recession.

The instruction package should also contain a timetable. The milestones will allow the corporate management to monitor progress on the plan. If the corporate culture permits, it will be helpful to set up one or more sessions where the corporate management can get a preview of the BPU plan to enable them to monitor the quality as well as the timing.

ALLOCATING RESOURCES

This chapter will not cover the aspects of corporate strategic planning that involve preparing, reviewing, and critiquing the plans of the individual business planning units. Those aspects of strategic planning are virtually identical to the process of planning for a single-line company, which is discussed in Chapter 3.

Since there are a variety of techniques for pulling business unit plans together into an overall plan, it is helpful to develop a familiarity with the strategic planner's tool kit. Over the years a number of techniques have been developed which can add considerably to the understanding of a corporation's strategic options. Often, more than one of these techniques can be used effectively. However, it is worth noting that they are not a substitute for hard analysis and can lead to some foolish conclusions if followed in a totally mechanical fashion.

1. *Business portfolio analysis* has been in vogue for some time and has many adherents. Additionally, a number of well-known management consultants use these techniques. The technique starts from the premise that a diversified business can be viewed as simply a portfolio of business units. Strategic portfolio analysts typically construct some sort of matrix. On one axis they plot some evaluation of the industry in which a business unit competes, either its growth or overall attractiveness, perhaps based on some combination of factors. On the other axis is some evaluation of the competitive position of the business planning unit. A representative framework for such analysis is depicted below in Exhibit 2.

   The business portfolio of the diversified firm will consist of units which are scattered throughout the matrix. In a nutshell, the idea is to direct resources where they will do the

Exhibit 2
Business Portfolio Analysis

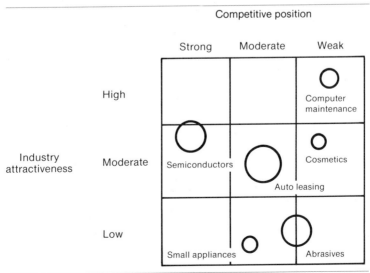

most good and to avoid putting resources into weak companies with unfavorable positions in unattractive industries. Eventually, as divestitures proceed and as new investments are made, the company will achieve a balanced portfolio of mature and growing *businesses* in a mixture of mature and growing *industries*.

2. *Analysis of key variables* can be used to determine the relative positioning of a business planning unit in the portfolio approach. Research in this area has been pioneered by the Strategic Planning Institute. Their PIMS (Profit Impact of Market Strategies) program provides empirical data on the financial and strategic characteristics of successful and unsuccessful businesses. For example, many of the portfolio analysis schemes take market share as a key determinant of a business unit's strength. The PIMS research tends to support that position.

3. *Balancing risk and returns* is another aspect of portfolio analysis that aims at analyzing a portfolio of businesses from a capital market perspective. In this approach, the underlying riskiness of a business or industry is evaluated and compared to the level of return on investment for that particular business. All businesses currently in the firm's portfolio are evaluated on the same basis. Businesses that add materially to risk without providing any compensation in the way of expected return are candidates for additional management attention. The basic diagram relating to this approach is shown in Exhibit 3.

Plotting business units in this way has the strong advantage of forcing management to face up to risk/return trade-offs and explicitly to choose where they, as a company, want to be located on the chart.

4. *Value-added analysis* is a more recently developed technique which combines some of the key variable research mentioned above with stock market valuations and seeks very directly to tailor a corporate portfolio so as to maximize its overall value in the stock market. This approach has been pioneered mostly by management consulting firms who have developed methods to analyze a firm's business planning units for their contribution to (or subtraction from) the firm's

Exhibit 3
Balancing Risk and Returns

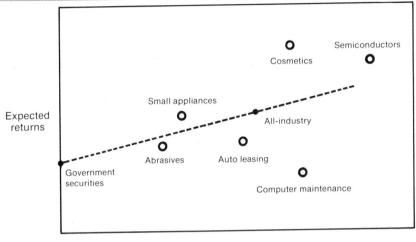

price-earnings multiple or market-to-book ratio. One of the more interesting suggestions which this approach has at least partially documented is the idea that under some circumstances rapid growth can reduce the stock market's valuation of a company while deceleration or divestiture (even of apparently profitable units) can help.

5. *The sustainable growth model* was developed many years ago and is still in use in a number of companies (see Chapter 9). It is not so much a strategic planning technique as a means of helping management dissect their various businesses from a financial point of view. The formula—which expresses return on equity of a business as a function of return on sales, asset turnover, and capitalization ratio—allows management to pinpoint how various aspects of business performance are affecting its financial return and ability to grow.

6. *Strategic analysis of industry structures* is an area that has recently received considerable attention. Unlike many of those mentioned above, it is less of a portfolio analysis technique than a way of viewing the strategic condition of an individual business planning unit vis-a-vis its customers, suppliers, and competitors.

7. *Traditional financial analysis* will always be an important influence on the planning process. However, it is often advisable to delay a formal consideration of financial factors until the firm's underlying strategic options have been explored. Turning too soon to the numbers can result in an early narrowing of scope and limitation of perspective. Long-range strategic plans, annual operating budgets, and capital budgets are not the same and should not be confused. The operating budgets and capital budgets are simply the manifestations of executing the long-range plan. Strategic thinking must eventually be reduced to numbers (and finally to people and products), but it should not get bogged down in numbers. In many cases it will help to keep the long-range planning focused on strategic issues if there is a minimal amount of data requested with the plan. In fact, we have occasionally achieved our best success in developing strategies in cases where no financial projections were initially to be included as part of the long-range plan.

The result of all the reviewing of BPU plans, consideration of the goals and objectives of the company, and of one or more of the methods of portfolio analysis will be that the parent company management will be in a position to reach a few conclusions. Some of these conclusions will involve which business planning units should get scarce resources (including capital and human resources), which units will provide those resources, which units will augment their market positions, which units will shrink, and which units will disappear.

Gradually, a strategic picture of the total enterprise will emerge, and every business planning unit's role can be clearly specified. It is imperative that the conclusions of the analysis be stated very clearly. Business units may originally have formulated a plan on the assumption that certain corporate resources would be available to them or that they would embark on a risky strategy or that they could sacrifice short-term profits to gain market share in their industry. They need to understand if their assumptions are wrong (for example, that capital will be taken from them, not given to them; that they should reduce the corporation's risk, not add to it; or that their industry is not "attractive" and their share should decline, not grow), so they can adjust their plan and play the role that is expected of them in the firm's overall strategy.

THE CFO'S USE OF THE STRATEGIC PLAN

From the perspective of the chief financial officer, it is important to be aware of the planning process, but it is probably more important to have a clear sense of how to use and understand the plans that are prepared by the business planning units. By making good use of the strategic planning process, the CFO can enhance his personal effectiveness and ultimately help improve the results for his company.

Perhaps the most obvious use the CFO can make of the long-range strategic plan is to form the basis for the long-range financial plan. Understanding the pace and direction of the corporation's development, along with any changes in its business mix and degree of risk, will enable the CFO to plan his financial strategy, capital structure, dividend policy, and other activities pertaining mainly to the right-hand side of the balance sheet.

An equally important use of the long-range plan on the part of the CFO is as a consistency check on the annual operating planning and budgeting process. Without a strategic plan, the annual plans will be prepared in a vacuum and, just as bad, evaluated and approved in a vacuum. BPU managers should be made to understand that items should normally not be included in their short-range plans unless they are consistent with the agreed upon long-range plan. Conversely, the annual plans ought to reflect those steps necessary to attaining the planning unit's long-range strategic goals. A good understanding of the long-range plan greatly simplifies the CFO's ability to develop annual operating budgets that are realistic and effective.

Facilities planning or capital budgeting could also potentially be areas of interest to the CFO where the perspective of the strategic plan would be beneficial. Obviously, during the long-range planning process various capital programs required to carry out the approved strategic plans of the operating companies will have been reviewed. Irrespective of how the capital budgeting process works, it will be beneficial to ensure that individual projects, whether previously identified or not, continue to be consistent with the strategic plan.

Planning can make an important contribution to the business analysis function, which is almost invariably under the direction of the CFO. By giving the planning function a role in this process, several benefits can be achieved that go beyond the typical analysis of actual performance against a financial budget. For example, the planning staff will naturally be led to evaluate performance against nonfinancial strategic objectives, such as new product roll-outs, market share improvements, or organizational shifts. Performance against competition will be analyzed, and the performance can be evaluated in the context of various national and international economic parameters. The key concept is to elevate business analysis above a purely financial exercise.

It is important for the chief financial officer to take steps to ensure the long-term credibility of the planning process. Credibility can be assured by making certain that the strategic actions and financial projections that are finally produced are realistic. Nothing can destroy a planning effort more quickly and thoroughly than the perception that the plan is not "in touch with the real world." This adverse perception can be equally damaging whether it comes from factions within the company or from outsiders, such as bankers, other lenders, consultants, or financial advisors. On the other hand, a well-conceived plan that is viewed as realistic and attainable can be of inestimable value as a communications device, both with insiders and outsiders alike.

In this context, communicating the fact that management has a plan which it intends to carry out will go far towards shaping investors' attitudes. In meetings with outsiders, the plan should be presented in enough detail to allow the investment community to develop a sense of comfort with the overall direction being pursued. The planning process provides the raw material for the CEO and CFO when they appear before the various investment analyst groups which are becoming an increasingly effective forum for informing the investment community about the company.

From the point of view of the CFO, the plan can also be an effective means of communicating with the financial institutions who currently (or potentially) are involved in extending credit to the company. A well-conceived, well-documented plan is bound to increase lenders' confidence and to facilitate negotiations involving credit availability and terms.

CORPORATE DEVELOPMENT

The corporate development function can be one of the greatest beneficiaries of long-range planning. In fact, it could even be argued that to have a tactical program of new business development, acquisitions, and divestitures without a strategic plan is to put the cart before the horse.

Under no circumstances should any units below the parent maintain a separate merger and acquisition capability. This is a specialized activity which has complex legal, accounting, and tax implications. Although managers at the business planning units should be allowed (even encouraged) to suggest acquisition opportunities, the actual process of negotiating, structuring, and closing the deal should normally be handled by the corporate staff, with the participation of the business planning unit management, where that is appropriate.

THE USE OF CONSULTANTS

Consultants can often be beneficial, but care should be taken to ensure that the corporation receives full value for what will normally turn out to be a very expensive exercise. Most of the top management consulting firms *start* at a fee of $100,000 for general studies in the strategic planning area, and five- or six-month studies at upwards of $100,000 per month are not uncommon.

The benefits of outside consultants are generally well known:

1. They lend an air of prestige and legitimacy to the planning effort.
2. They can function as an effective sounding board for testing some of management's ideas.
3. They have the capacity to be objective in that they should typically have no preconceived idea of the right answer.
4. They can absorb or deflect political heat in a way that insiders cannot do.
5. Being specialists in strategic planning, they can bring to bear special expertise and direct knowledge of successes and failures in other firms, sometimes in the same industry.
6. They can focus large quantities of intense, high caliber effort on the problem in a short time, obviating the need to recruit a full team.
7. They are not a permanent addition to the corporate staff.

The drawbacks of consultants are equally well known:

1. They often have methodological biases, that is, favorite sets of ideas or rules of thumb which they may attempt to apply.
2. They are usually not familiar with the company that has retained them, and even if familiar with the industry in general, will require an extended learning curve to become familiar with the organizational structure and special attributes of the firm with which they are working.
3. They too often work without a clearly defined target for their effort or a clearly understood expectation regarding the work product they are to deliver.
4. No matter what they say, consultants are not implementers—they will not be around to live with the results of their recommendations.

Because of the learning curve involved, there is a great deal to be said for staying with the same consulting firm and even with the same individuals within the firm. Although independence and objectivity are important and must be maintained, the best results in the long run can be achieved when the consultant becomes so familiar with the firm's problems and challenges that no reeducation is necessary. Remember, however, that consultants are expensive. If they become quasi-permanent members of the planning staff, it may be more cost-effective to explore bringing some of those functions in house.

SOME CONCLUDING THOUGHTS

What we have attempted to do is to focus briefly on a collection of planning topics that we believe to be unique and of primary importance to the CFO of a diversified company who is thinking about creating a planning capability, or who is looking for some additional perspectives from which to review an approach that is already in place.

In that light, we might offer a few concluding comments on planning in a diversified firm:

- Most approaches and techniques are essentially the same as those used in planning for a nondiversified company. However, the diversified firm must develop methods for handling a wide portfolio of businesses.
- The planning approach and planning organization must be designed to fit corporate diversification objectives and the type

of corporate organization that is required to fulfill those objectives.

- The commitment of the CEO is critical.

- Within a diversified firm, business planning units should have clearly defined strategic roles. Moreover, steps should be taken to ensure that those roles are clearly understood.

- The ability to analyze trade-offs at the corporate level is a key to success of the process; in order for that to happen, corporate investment objectives and corporate development policies must be clearly articulated and understood.

- The CFO has an important role to play in most aspects of strategic planning. The strategic planning process, if understood and used intelligently, can make a valuable contribution to the financial management of the diversified firm.

28

Allocating Corporate Resources

Leo W. Yochum and Donald J. Povejsil

INTRODUCTION

This chapter describes a new conceptual approach to the traditional problem of allocating corporate resources among the divisions of a diversified corporation. The concept was introduced in our company in 1981, and it has been the foundation for resource allocation and strategic planning since then. The concept is based on the belief that:

1. Resource allocation among divisions is inextricably linked to the entire process of strategic planning.
2. The present value of the corporation is the sum of the present values of the financial projections for each business.
3. The present value of the corporation, imputed from the val-

Leo W. Yochum joined Westinghouse in 1951. He was elected vice president, finance in 1970, having risen through a succession of controller and treasury positions. He became senior executive vice president, finance in 1978. Donald J. Povejsil joined Westinghouse in 1949. He was elected vice president in 1971. He has had two general manager assignments, (nuclear fuel and large turbine) and was vice president of personnel and administration prior to becoming vice president, corporate planning in 1977.

ues of its parts, is representative of the market value of the stock.

4. Selection of the combination of strategies that maximize the value of each business will maximize the imputed value of the corporation and its stock.

It would be presumptuous to state that the process we have evolved is the final answer or even that it is running perfectly. Like any such process, it needs continuing fine tuning, and it probably always will. However, we have been pleased by the results we have achieved to date and believe this process has potential value for other firms. (For an inflation-oriented discussion of some of the concepts discussed here, please refer to Chapter 9.)

SCOPE OF THE "RESOURCE ALLOCATION PROBLEM"

There are two perceptions of the problem of resource allocation in diversified corporations.

Oliver Twist Model

One perception is that capital availability is limited, and the allocation problem consists of ladling out allotments to the hungry divisions in a way that makes the most effective compromise between their needs and the limited supply in the corporate pot. This might be called the Oliver Twist model.

Exhibit 1
Oliver Twist Model
(Resource allocation)

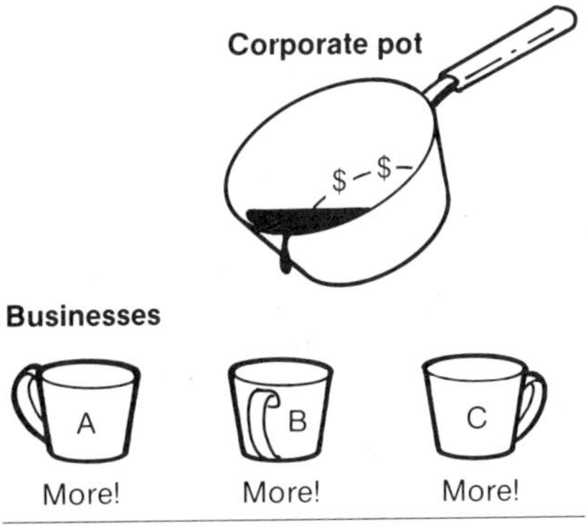

This perception has the inherent problem that giving more to one business means taking it away from another. There is the problem of comparing the risk, return, and impact on the corporate portfolio of multiple projects, each in widely diverse and perhaps noncomparable industries. Further, each business puts its best foot forward in the rate of return promised for its project, injecting enough optimism in the financial assumptions to assure it a share of the "pot." A pattern develops where large businesses justify large resources, based on promised project returns, while small businesses that may have higher growth prospects tend to get small allocations. Experience has shown that a low-return business, getting repeated high-return projects approved, in many cases tends to remain a low-return business.

Simple Business Model

The alternative perception is far broader. This recognizes that there is a vast reservoir of both debt and equity capital available in the world financial markets. This capital is seeking to be employed at competitive rates of return. The resource allocation problem in a diversified corporation is merely a confined case of the continuing process of capital formation. Most corporations have the ability to raise additional capital as they are utilizing only a part of their potential debt leverage and likewise in many cases could issue additional stock. For this reason, their available pot is a variable, not a fixed amount (see Exhibit 2).

Exhibit 2
Simple Business Model (Resource allocation)

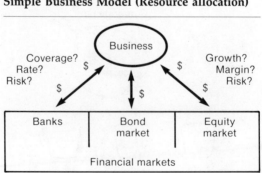

Free capital markets are quick to respond to profitable investment opportunities. Increased price-earnings ratios available for growth potential make sale of stock possible at attractive prices. Consistent cash flow makes possible additional debt funding. The free market is equally quick to downsize the funding potential of companies where future prospects become unattractive.

Financial Intermediary Model

Expanding this perception, the top management of a diversified corporation is really in the position of an intermediary for the free financial market. They can raise capital from the financial market and invest it in the opportunities presented by their individual businesses. They can also disinvest by downsizing or divesting unattractive businesses and returning the capital to the financial markets or by redeploying it to other internal businesses. In this "financial intermediary case," the procedures and judgment of corporate management must provide a substitute for the ultimate wisdom of the outside financial market in making available resources that are related to the future profitability of each individual business (see Exhibit 3).

The Oliver Twist model is inadequate for a modern corpora-

Exhibit 3
Financial Intermediary Model
(Resource allocation)

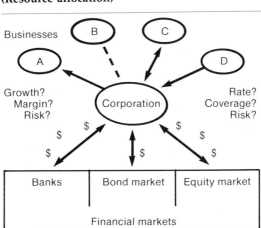

tion. Recognition of the financial intermediary role of corporate management ties in with a broader vision of the entire strategic planning process. This has provided a starting point for combining resource allocation with the strategic planning process. The following pages describe the thinking and process that were developed.

RESOURCE ALLOCATION AND SHAREHOLDER VALUE

The process that evolved was built on a foundation of the following simple facts. The ultimate purpose of a corporation is to increase the value for its shareholders. This is achieved by a combination of operational excellence and optimization of strategy. Resource allocation, or the control of investment decisions, is the primary control possessed by corporate management for determining the present strategy and future nature of the corporation. In this way, the resource allocation problem is directly coupled with the concept of shareholder value.

It is demonstrable that the investment community values all stocks on the same basis regardless of the industry, cycle, profitability, or growth. In general terms, the valuation is based on a measure of profitability today and what is projected for the future. "Profitability" in this case means return on equity relative to the cost of equity (see Exhibit 4).

The appendix summarizes the algebraic expression for profitability that has been found to be most accurate; this has been derived from classic finance textbooks. In simple terms, the "value" of a business can be expressed as the present value of future cash flows plus the present value of a terminal or residual value, each discounted at the current cost of equity. Empirical analysis shows that the value derived on this basis is closely approximated by market value, resulting from informed judgments made by real-world investors on the stock exchange.

As background for the combined judgment of the equity markets in setting market prices that approximate the calculated value of corporations, the investment community has developed and is continually refining its ability to sense the *future* profitability (and therefore the value) of each *piece* of major diversified corporations. Professional investment analysts have developed an uncanny ability to know not only which divisions

Exhibit 4
Dow Jones Industrials (Spring 1985)

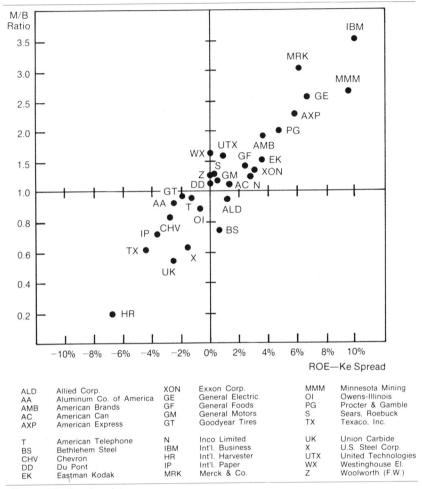

ALD	Allied Corp.	XON	Exxon Corp.	MMM	Minnesota Mining
AA	Aluminum Co. of America	GE	General Electric	OI	Owens-Illinois
AMB	American Brands	GF	General Foods	PG	Procter & Gamble
AC	American Can	GM	General Motors	S	Sears, Roebuck
AXP	American Express	GT	Goodyear Tires	TX	Texaco, Inc.
T	American Telephone	N	Inco Limited	UK	Union Carbide
BS	Bethlehem Steel	IBM	Int'l. Business	X	U.S. Steel Corp.
CHV	Chevron	HR	Int'l. Harvester	UTX	United Technologies
DD	Du Pont	IP	Int'l. Paper	WX	Westinghouse El.
EK	Eastman Kodak	MRK	Merck & Co.	Z	Woolworth (F.W.)

Source: Marakon Associates.

are profitable and which are not, but to approximate the present and future earnings capability of each. This leads to the basic belief that the corporate shell is transparent, and the market value of the whole (expressed by the stock price) is the sum of the imputed values of the pieces as seen by the investment community. This value concept has been validated empirically by calculating the imputed value for many companies based on Value Line forecasts and by matching the total of these values with the market value of the stock. There has been a surprisingly close match. The same kind of calculation can be made to determine the value of a corporation by adding the value of its individual businesses.

RESOURCE ALLOCATION PROBLEM TRANSFORMED

Recognition of the above makes possible a complete transformation of the resource allocation problem. Instead of the complex problem of dividing a resource pot between many claimants for capital, the task can be changed to one of developing a strategy for each business that will maximize its value as it would be seen by the market if it were a freestanding business. In simple terms, this can be done by developing reasonable alternative strategies for each business, calculating the value for each strategy alternative based on financial projections for each strategy and then implementing the strategy that maximizes the value of each piece of the business.

This approach makes use of the "financial intermediary" concept, which states that there is more capital available from the financial market if a good enough opportunity exists. This could be realized by accepting more debt leverage or sale of more stock. The opposite is also true; a business with poor future prospects will tend to show that its best value is realized from a strategy alternate of downsizing or divestment. The net effect is self-limiting; there is enough to fund the best strategy of each business. The strategic planning process is iterative; the evaluation of the resource requirements of the most valuable strategy of each business provides information to shape the corporate capital requirements and debt leverage.

EMPIRICAL EVIDENCE: IT WORKS

This process has been in effect for several years, and experience with it can be summarized as follows.

1. A capital investment project must be really good to produce an increased value for the business.
2. Looking at the value of plans in this way creates a much increased level of financial understanding at the division manager level in the organization.

3. This process enhances recognition of the true deleterious effect of marginally profitable businesses (measured conventionally) on the overall value of the company.

4. Evaluating plans on a present value basis in this way puts appropriate emphasis on near-term results. It normalizes the "blue sky" that tends to be present in the distant years in many financial plans.

5. The consideration of different degrees of risk inherent in different businesses can be integrated on a consistent basis when it is recognized that risky or cyclical businesses have a higher cost of capital.

6. Downsizing or divestment of a marginally profitable business will usually show a higher value than a strategy of continued new investment.

7. The value process automatically balances the resource needs of value-maximization strategies with the corporate resources available, providing that the leverage and cost of equity assumptions used for each business are properly matched to the corporate balance sheet.

8. People working with the process are uneasy at first because they are forced to make judgments in an area of unknowns and feed these into a precise-appearing calculation. However, with experience the comfort factor increases as they realize that they are only comparing their own alternatives and that their value is not being compared with other businesses. Furthermore, the discounting of future years minimizes the impact of the more uncertain distant years.

ADMINISTRATION

The above description of the value process has been described in very simplified form. Obviously, it is more complex, and seating it in our decentralized organization required a great deal of careful education and process refinement. Workshops or classes were necessary to teach the principles to many business unit and corporate-level people, many of whom were not finance specialists. A standard computer program was developed for the value calculation and made available with variations usable on Apple, TRS, and IBM microcomputers. Extensive effort was necessary at the corporate level to tailor debt leverage and cost of equity factors for each business and to conform them to the total for the corporation.

In administration, the value calculations in the "preferred" strategy are not accepted blindly. There is a continuing need for corporate management judgment to interpret the results and to approve the final strategy selection decision.

An additional concept has been important to this process. This is the recognition that investments should be regarded as investments in the *entire business* of the division, and not as free-standing projects to be justified individually. Experience has shown that all too often repeated *project* investments, each promising a 20 percent return, have no beneficial effect on the total ROI of a division that has a poor earnings history because of a weak strategic position or its participation in a sick industry. The value calculation for an investment should measure the alternative values of the *total* business with and without the proposed increment and compare these with other strategies for the individual business.

Approval of the preferred strategy by corporate management is an implicit agreement to the entire financial projection that it represents. This includes revenue and profit projections, as well as working capital changes and capital expenditures. Obviously, this commitment is a two-way street and is subject to continuing review as conditions change. It may need fine tuning, especially in regard to the timing of major capital expenditures to conform to annual corporate capital budgets. But the process provides a credible basis for agreement between corporate and business unit management on the strategy to be followed for each business and on the resources that will be available to it. As a result, it provides continued integration of these two aspects of the planning process.

APPENDIX: MATHEMATICAL BACKGROUND

The calculation of the value of a business follows conventional finance theory. A computer program can be developed for personal computers to make the necessary calculations conveniently. This makes it possible to calculate value as a function of the following inputs:

C = Equity cash flow for each future year 1 through n

K_e = Cost of equity capital for the business today

IAT = Income after tax projected for year n

g = Earnings growth rate $\left.\right\}$ estimated steady state levels for years following year n

ROE = Return on Equity

$$\text{Value} = \frac{C_1}{1+K_e} + \frac{C_2}{(1+K_e)^2} + \cdots \frac{C_n + \text{Terminal value}}{(1+K_e)^n}$$

$$\text{Terminal value} = \frac{IAT_n\,(1+g)\left(1 - \dfrac{g}{K_e + \text{Spread}}\right)}{K_e - g}$$

$\text{Spread} = ROE - K_e$

Where ROE is estimated for years after n

Recognize that divisions of a diversified company each experience different conditions of cyclicality, risk, cost structure and profitability. If they were freestanding, independent businesses, they would each have a unique debt capacity, determined by the ability to cover interest charges from likely average cash flow. In addition, each would have a unique cost of equity, K_e. This is determined by the expression

$$K_e = K_f + \beta(K_m - K_f)$$

Where K_f = risk free rate today, that is, long-term, U.S. government bonds

K_m = average return on stocks today
(Note: Historic average for $(K_m - K_f)$ is .057)

β = Beta; "Market Risk" the average relative variability of earnings (or stock price) to the variability of the average company

Division Betas can be estimated by comparison to published Betas for similar listed companies

Some benefit could be obtained by using a single corporate debt leverage and cost of equity for all divisions. However, to make the analysis more realistic, individualized K_e's and leverage ratios should be derived for each business in such a way that the aggregate matches the corporate totals.

29

Budgeting

*August Umlauf, Edward H. Gross
and Mary V. Litle*

Budgeting is often used as a catch-all word to encompass the three separate and distinct bottom-up phases of the planning process. These three phases are the strategic plan, the tactical plan, and the annual budget which will be the focus of this chapter. However, before discussing the annual budget, it is important to relate all three bottom-up phases to the overall top-down planning activities carried out by diversified companies.

The top-down activities in a diversified organization generally include definition of organizational structure, firm policy or strategy statements, resource allocations, and monitoring. The interrelationships of these top-down and the aforementioned bottom-up activities are depicted in Exhibit 1.

Once the applicable portions of the top-down activities have

August Umlauf is president of The Baker & Taylor Division of W. R. Grace & Co. with whom he has been associated for 10 years. Prior to that he was in public accounting both in the U.S. and Brazil. Edward H. Gross has 17 years of diversified financial experience and is vice president—finance and CFO for Baker & Taylor. Mary V. Litle, an assistant treasurer with W. R. Grace & Co., has been with the company five years, prior to which she spent several years in the banking industry.

Exhibit 1
Budgeting and Planning Top-down/Bottom-up Interrelationships

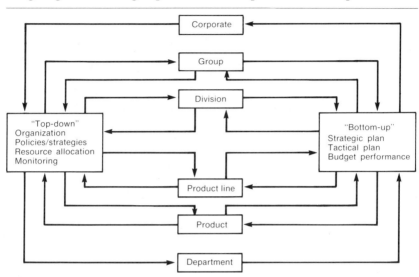

been clearly defined and communicated to all levels of management, individual business unit[1] managers can commence the bottom-up process which, as stated, consists of the strategic plan, the tactical plan, and the budget.

Strategic Plan

The unit strategic plan, prepared within the parameters of overall top-down corporate objectives, takes into consideration the historical performance of the business unit, its present market position, and the environment in which the business unit is expected to operate. From that base, alternative approaches to the future (from 2 to 10 years out) are evaluated and a long-range strategy is developed for each business unit. This long-range strategy is then communicated to top management for their acceptance and approval.

---

[1] A business unit for purposes of this chapter can be a product line, an entire division, an entire corporation, or a new business venture.

Tactical Plan

After top management has approved the long-range unit strategy, tactical plans are developed. These plans consist of the action programs necessary to achieve the long-range strategic goals and should be specific in nature, including timetables, required resources, and expected results for each function involved in the long-range plan. Examples might include the need for a new plant, a targeted acquisition, additional research and development requirements, the move of a product line from one locale to another, new financing, or manpower and training necessary to launch a new product. These tactical plans must reflect the degree of complexity presented by the business unit and serve as the base from which the short-term budget and the longer term forecast are created.

Budgets

Budgets and forecasts are quantitative predictions of performance expected in the future, usually one year in the case of a budget and from two to five years in the case of a forecast. Therefore, the budget and forecast become the yardsticks against which actual progress is measured in order to focus on new opportunities as they occur or to take corrective action if necessary.

While it is axiomatic that the consolidated budget in a diversified firm is nothing more than a compendium of each of the smallest product or departmental budgets, caution should be exercised in two specific areas of consolidating and interpreting the budget.

First, the "life and death" factors affecting each business unit need to be specifically stated and interrelated among the various diversified business units to be sure that the final corporate budget is an accurate reflection of expected results. For example, an optimistic forecast by a unit engaged in marketing alternative home-energy sources may be in direct conflict with a unit expressing severe pessimism concerning the near-term profitability of its contract drilling and oil field service business.

The second caution in the bottom-up approach to budgeting in a diversified company is that each successive layer of management review and approval may have a tendency to add some "fat" to the budget in order to "give them (the next higher authority) what they want" rather than what is achievable. This may not seem to be much of a problem when dealing with the lowest denominator product line or department. It could have a major impact on expected results, however, when a multitude of individual budgets are added together to form a whole. The opposite situation can also be true. Some managers are inherently pessimistic about the future in the mistaken belief that the worst thing that can happen is "to miss the budget." Both situations, adding fat or low-balling the budget, can have a serious impact on the company, as in the case of installing new equipment in the face of over optimism or as in the case of missing opportunities because of too conservative a view of the marketplace.

Even if the various elements of pessimism and optimism were to cancel one another, the net result would be of limited value in tracking what actually occurs in comparison with what was thought would occur. An effective means of dealing with and resolving the conflict presented by differing management views of the future is through the judicious use of contingency factors which will be more fully explained in the following section of this chapter.

WHY BUDGET

While it is recognized that the development of a meaningful budget is a time-consuming and difficult task requiring communication among all levels of management, there are substantive benefits to be gained by the process. A carefully conceived and executed budget motivates managers to take actions consistent with company/unit goals and provides a systematic and quantifiable basis for evaluation of both management and strategies.

Communication

The overview of the planning process at the beginning of this chapter indicated that, while the corporate policy and strategy statements must be a directive from senior management, the development of a feasible strategic plan, tactical plan, and budget must all be from the bottom up. In order to achieve congruence of goals throughout the organization, it is imperative that the firm have an effective system for communicating and examining past performance, as well as for the upward and downward communication of goals and objectives to and through each level of responsibility. For instance, if the head of a division issues a clear statement of the division's goals to department heads, then they, in turn, are more apt to develop workable budgets for their departments.

The communication back and forth among levels of management during the budgeting process creates a consensus of objectives and formalizes programs for their achievement. The budget then becomes a useful tool for resource allocation, staffing changes, production scheduling, and the overall operation of the unit.

Motivation

By using a bottom-up approach to budgeting, the manager at each level in the organization shares in the responsibility for its adoption. This responsibilitity provides the framework for unit management to plan for growth, to implement stated strategies, and to allocate resources effectively.

While the bottom-up approach provides motivation toward achieving a common set of goals, it may also create an environment in which budgets are set above or below achievable performance levels. There are many methods that can and have been employed by succeeding levels of management to sift out the bias inherent in the budgeting process. One which is effective is the contingency concept. Under this concept the unit is not required to change its budget and is held responsible for actual performance in comparison therewith. However, as this budget and other unit budgets are combined for presentation to the next level of management, contingencies are added *or* subtracted from the summed totals for sales, profits, invested capital, returns on investment, cash flow, and so on. In this manner the integrity of the unit budget is maintained while the next level of management is held responsible for its view of how the combined operations will perform. In the case of an overly optimistic unit budget, the unit manager is on notice that actual performance will be measured against the aggressive budget, but the aggressive budget is pared back before being passed on to the next level of authority. On the other hand, a unit manager submitting a low-ball budget is on notice that there are higher expectations for that unit and compensation could be tied to achieving these higher levels of expectation.

Evaluation

Detailed budgeting provides not only the motivation to achieve certain goals but also the yardstick by which achievement can be measured. The budget establishes a base for predicting performance over a specified period of time. Having developed this base, one can then compare actual performance to this preestablished yardstick. The more complex the organization, the more valuable becomes this ability to review performance at intervals during the budget cycle.

Operating performance reviews should involve the managers of all the responsible areas. This ensures a full range of discussion of relevant factors and, as a result, an early warning system with respect to problems and/or opportunities, be they internally or externally generated.

ORGANIZING FOR THE BUDGET PROCESS

Having determined in the prior section of this chapter that there are good reasons to enter the time-consuming budget process, it is important to focus on how to organize to get the job completed.

Commitment

One of the reasons most often cited for the failure of a planning/budgeting system is the lack of support and involvement by top management. In order for managers throughout the organization to take budgeting seriously, a strong commitment by senior management is necessary. This support may be communicated in various forms ranging from issuance of a policy statement to annual face-to-face strategy and budget reviews with senior management; but, however established, it is a mandatory prerequisite to effective budgeting. The best results are obtained when top management actively participates in key decision points in the planning process. This ensures their understanding of the base against which actual results are later measured.

A second prerequisite is an area previously discussed, the involvement of operating management. The overall objectives and the final approval of a budget may be the prerogative of senior management, but the detailed operational plan to achieve those objectives must originate from those closest to the business. This is especially true in a diversified company where responsibility for the operating units has been delegated.

Organization

The budget serves as a basis for comparison of actual results, with the ultimate goal being the highlighting of problems or opportunities in a timely and accurate fashion. The organizational structure from which the budget flows must, therefore, be related to, and supportive of, the general demands of the business unit's strategy. In a diversified firm the structure of individual operating units differs due to variations in the business characteristics of the units. These variations may take the form of one unit being driven by retail selling considerations, while another's focal point is manufacturing for sale to other manufacturers and a third might be people and service oriented. In order that the budgeting process maintain its validity and effectiveness, it is important to recognize these variations and take them into consideration in structurally organizing the operating unit as well as in structuring the budgeting process.

Responsibility

Given that management support has been established and an organizational structure that reflects monitoring needs is in place, budget responsibilities must be formulated. Administration of the budgeting process is a function that is critical to the smooth operation of the organization. Just as it is essential that business managers have well-defined areas of responsibility and commensurate authority to carry out those responsibilities, so must the responsibilities of the budget participants be clearly defined, assigned, and supported. As the budgeting activity often falls within the purview of the financial staffs of the various management levels, communication links among these levels and with operating managers are critical and must be established.

A corporate financial staff is usually responsible for the issuance of budget guidelines and/or instructions. For the budget process to work smoothly, these guidelines must be as clear and as inclusive as possible. As this is the starting point of the actual budgeting process, vague or ambiguous instructions can lead to an inefficient use of time and energy and to bad feelings among the managers.

The guidelines should be comprised of several distinct parts. The first is a statement of the purpose and value of budgeting. As the budget process provides a discipline to complex organizations and contributes to systematic management, this statement of purpose and value can be very important in communicating senior management's commitment to the process. This statement should emphasize that budgeting is a part of every manager's responsibility and that their ability to manage against their respective budgets will be taken into consideration in the evaluation of their performance.

Procedures

This overall statement should then be followed by a detailed procedural guide explaining how to prepare each of the components of the budget. This should include an explanation of any specific criteria to be used in the development of the overall budget (that is, economic factors, compensation guidelines, and so on), specifically what is required and why, and in what format such information is to be communicated. Because budget requirements usually follow existing financial reporting formats, the mechanics should provide no major surprises. An exception is intracompany activities which require synchronization when consolidating.

In a diversified corporation, such instructions must take into account variations in the types of business units being managed. This may lead to differences in what individual business units are required to report. Any variations must be carefully defined and justified. Alterations in business unit reporting requirements should be kept to a minimal level, as the presentation of budgets to senior management is less confusing if a level of consistency in reporting is maintained.

Timetable

The third part of the guidelines should be a schedule of when and to whom information is to be submitted for compilation, review, and approval. In a large organization, setting realistic timetables and ensuring adherence to them is a key to a smooth budgetary process. Leaving time for review, revisions, assimilation, and consolidation may therefore require that the budgeting process begin as early as July or August if budget adoption is expected prior to the end of December for a calendar-year firm.

WHAT TO BUDGET

Having reviewed why the preparation of a budget is a worthwhile exercise and how to organize for the process itself, it is now important to review what should be budgeted. As stated earlier, the budget is a quantitative representation of the following year's plan that serves the purpose of measuring progress toward longer range objectives. For this quantitative representation to be used as a measurement and evaluation tool at multiple management levels, it needs to be developed and committed to from the bottom up. The budgetary process starts, therefore, at the least divisible level, that is, a specific product, product line, or department. The process of budgeting converts operating plans for business units into actual profit and loss and balance sheet items, which, when aggregated, represent an integrated month-by-month financial model for the organization. In its perfect form the completed budget will show the monthly sales and profit levels of each product line and/or profit center and the monthly spending plans of every department and cost center.

Build Up

The budget should be a building process starting at the product level and building to the business unit and the consolidated corporation. The structure of each budget level must keep in mind the authority level of the person being held responsible for meeting that budget, and each must be consistent with goals set by succeedingly higher organizational levels.

The budget is intended as a tool to communicate, motivate,

and evaluate; the person responsible for meeting the budget should also have the authority to do so, and the budget should be comprehensive and consistent among departments. For instance, the sales manager cannot be expected to increase sales by 10 percent without having the authority to do so within certain sales force and advertising expense limitations. With respect to conflicting goals, the sales manager needs to know that the production department will provide sufficient product to meet sales volume goals.

Special Situations

In order to meet corporate and business unit goals, there often arise special budgeting situations involving potential acquisitions, divestitures, and the addition or deletion of products or product lines. Such situations may be handled in various ways, but most often are evaluated separately and then integrated back into the budget as separate and distinct items.

In order to maintain employee motivation, divestitures or product line deletions may be incorporated into the unit budget in their totality with elimination taking place at a level beyond the direct operating unit level. The uncertainty of special situations makes them important in the overall development of the budget and in directing the company toward meeting its longer range goals.

ECONOMIC/ENVIRONMENTAL CONSIDERATIONS

For a budget to be meaningful, basic assumptions must be set forth concerning anticipated economic conditions and how these conditions are expected to affect volume, prices, and costs (and resulting profits) of the unit's product(s) or service(s). Most businesses today operate in multiple environments and it is necessary that one understand and apply both the macroeconomic, as well as the microeconomic, factors which have an effect on the health of the organization. Certainly the basic business assumptions of two firms selling a similar product would be widely divergent if Firm A were located in Detroit and sold its product in the United States and Western Europe, while Competitor B had its plant in Belgium and sold only in Belgium and the United States.

External Factors

Before annual or monthly projections can be stated meaningfully, there must be general agreement as to the expected operating environment (1) where the business is located (2) where it purchases its raw materials, and (3) where it is expected to deliver its product(s). This knowledge will impact the extent to which selling prices can be changed, whether labor, material, and operating costs will fluctuate, and ultimately whether or not the firm will be able to earn the desired profit. Anticipated changes in the interrelationship of foreign currencies (as discussed in Chapter 17) are important as these can and do have a major impact upon the profitability of an organization. Therefore, forecasted changes among rates need to be addressed and factored into a unit's budget.

Inflation rates, capital availability, interest rates, and the cost and availability of energy, labor, and raw materials will all affect the earnings of the business in the periods ahead; therefore, the more that can be stated in the underlying budget assumptions, the more sound the budget will be. As will be noted later, even if certain assumptions turn out to be incorrect, the unit will still be in a better position to explain the variances from budget and to understand *why* the budget was not accurate—as long as the ground rules are clearly set forth at the outset.

Some budget assumptions may be developed at the corporate level and disseminated to each unit in a multiunit firm, while other assumptions are generated at the unit level. Examples of the former might involve the general inflation rate, limits on salary increases, or U.S. interest rates, while the latter could involve raw material prices, anticipated labor rate increases, and energy prices. Regardless of who in the organization develops the information, key items must be summarized so that the assumptions are clear to all who are concerned with the budget setting and approving process.

Market Data

Market share estimates are the key to the preparation of a sound budget as these estimates lead to volume and price estimates which result in defined action plans and expected levels of profitability. Therefore, in addition to stating the underlying economic assumptions which are anticipated to affect volumes and prices, it is also necessary that the unit garner reliable market and competitive data which will lead to market share estimates. Market share estimates will be affected by government policies and regulations, technological advances, and competitors' entry into or exit from the marketplace.

Unfortunately, market and competitive data are rarely available in usable form and are generally developed and refined over a period of years using information provided by trade associations, ongoing internal market research/intelligence gathering, publications of banking institutions and government agencies, and consultants specifically hired for that purpose. Regardless of the initial degree of reliability, estimates of market share are of primary importance in estimating how profitably the unit is expected to perform.

TYPES OF BUDGETS

Just as a diverse company is made up of many individual product lines (and variations of size and specification even within product lines), the firm's budget is made up of many subbudgets—from the components of an operating budget by marketing territory and cost center, to the components of the balance sheet which result in a forecast of working capital and cash required (or which will be generated) and to the capital budget, which defines projects required to support both the immediate operating budget as well as the longer range objectives set forth in the strategic plan.

Operating Budget

Key components of the operating budget will likely be sales, cost of sales, operating expenses (selling, general, administrative, research and development), and taxes. Since many income statement accounts (such as cost of goods sold, commissions, and other selling expenses) vary in direct proportion to changes in sales volume or dollars, the sales forecast is key to the generation of a meaningful unit budget.

Therefore, the sales budget should be built up by product line (or subproduct line) and by sales region or territory, with volumes and unit prices clearly set forth. The total sales budget for the unit would then simply be the compilation of many subsets of numbers. In measuring actual performance, as will be discussed later, it is definitely necessary to have sales data available at the product line or subproduct line level.

Development of a realistic sales budget in a manufacturing concern is also required before the organization can begin to develop a realistic manufacturing department budget. Based upon volume assumptions, there may be capacity constraints (or excess capacity) which the unit needs to address. On the other hand, available capacity may be appropriate for a given level of expected sales activity, but manufacturing may require different shift or manning levels to achieve forecasted production which once again changes the assumption with respect to costs. Without close coordination of these budgeting activities, an imbalance in actual practice can be costly at best, or disastrous in the extreme if the company is unable to meet its commitments in a timely fashion at quoted prices.

The manufacturing budget should be prepared for each stage of the manufacturing process setting forth capacities, estimated changes in inventory quantities, materials and supplies required, available supply and cost of utilities, and probable availability and cost of labor. Capacity levels, inventory changes, and manpower requirements will further correlate to capital budgets, working capital/cash needs, and manpower budgets, as discussed later.

Other departmental budgets relating to the profit and loss or operating statement will also be required, such as those for general and administrative expenses, selling costs, and R&D expenditures. Unfortunately, these expenses tend to be "fixed" in nature with each budget period's cost looking much like the prior period's cost with an inflation factor tagged on. These areas of costs, which should be analyzed by department (and by cost components, such as salary, fringes, travel, equipment, communications, and the like), should be reviewed as vigorously as the other components of the operating budget. While it is not a popular notion to cut back on overhead departments, a zero-based budget approach to these cost elements could result in major profit improvement for many firms. This is particularly true as business conditions, competitive constraints, and government regulations change, thereby obsoleting some overhead functions. Other new costs may be required, of course, but these should individually stand the critical eye of management review.

The foregoing has dealt generally with the firm's budget in total; but, as stated at the outset, to make the best use of the budgeting process, key product lines or subproduct lines should be budgeted individually from sales volume to profit after tax. This procedure will likely entail the allocation of expenses from one department to another as much of the overhead costs and, in many instances, manufacturing and production costs will be shared. While certain product lines may not show much (or any) profit when viewed after cost allocations, these product lines may, in fact, complement the overall business and cannot simply be dropped in order to improve overall profits. Profits may actually decrease if nonvariable costs must be absorbed by other product lines. On the other hand, use of product line budgets will point out areas that produce the greatest and the least share of a firm's overall profits. This information should lead to an in-depth review of the long-range viability of the weakest of the product offerings with a view toward weeding out those which have a limited future.

There may be other profit and loss components which need to be budgeted separately, such as interest, other income or expense, and items particular to a specific business (royalties, investment income, and so on). These items, while adding or detracting from the overall profitability of the firm, are usually not as critical to the strategic plan as are the other operating budget components.

As everyone is aware, one or more government entity will take its share of pretax profits. It is important, therefore, that with a tax rate of about 50 percent (combined federal, state, and foreign), the firm fully address the various tax-planning alternatives available to it when preparing the budget.

Balance Sheet Budgets

While the absolute level of profit is often the most visible sign of a product line's or business unit's success, it is important not to lose sight of the fact that capital is required to support all facets of the business, including capital required for fixed assets relating to office space and/or production facilities, as well as capital needed for increases in receivables, inventories, and so on.

While we are dealing primarily in this chapter with short-range budgets, one must plan cash needs over a longer span of time to ensure that sufficient liquidity exists through cash flow from operations and/or from external sources (borrowings, equity infusions) to support the projected growth of the firm. In the short run, however, regular monthly cash needs must be provided for; and these can be forecast considering the balance sheet as it stands at the beginning of a period plus-or-minus the changes that are expected to occur over the budget period based on the results reflected in the operating budget.

As in the case of the operating budget, the use of product line breakouts is important in budgeting cash and other working capital needs for it is through the product line analysis that individual levels of inventories, receivables, and payables can be projected. Once again there is a need for allocations as it may be difficult to identify separately cash, receivables, and payables by product line. Nevertheless, this procedure should be followed as a prerequisite to the preparation of product line statements of sources and applications of funds. These data are required by product line if the firm is to understand which product lines are users of cash and which are cash generators.

The preparation of a source and application of funds budget by product line will begin by using the profitability arrived at in the product line operating budget and will add back those benefits of income statement expenses which did not actually use cash, such as depreciation and amortization. Assumptions set forth in the operating budget as to inventory levels plus estimates of increases/decreases in receivables and accounts payable are then factored into this budget and are usually developed by estimating days or months on hand for each product line.

In addition to the budgeted increase/(decrease) in working capital, the firm needs to estimate the increase/(decrease) in fixed assets and other long-term assets and liabilities that will be required to operate the business, and these are then factored into the budget.

All the sources and uses of funds thus budgeted will result in a net amount of funds generated or required by the product line before financing. If the product line is a cash user, direct financing may be required, or a cash allocation should be made from another product line. In either case, the cash user should be allotted its pro rata share of all financing costs, and these should be included in its operating budget.

Capital Budget

While the purpose of this section is not to discuss capital resource allocation, the capital budget (whether fixed assets are purchased or leased and capitalized on the balance sheet) has important ramifications on what capacities will be available and what will be needed for cost reduction projects, replacement of existing assets, pollution control, and the like. Although the greatest effects of major projects will likely be felt in periods beyond the budget year, the capital budget is, nevertheless, closely linked with the operating budget.

Each year's capital budget will therefore need to focus on both authorizations and expenditures (since there could be long lead times for certain projects with spending taking place over several years). While firms will have widely differing policies on how capital projects are evaluated and approved, we suggest that detailed justification for projects not be prepared coincident with the operating budget, but that these take place during the course of the succeeding year sufficiently in advance of the time when approval to begin a project is required. This does not mean that major projects should not be considered in detail prior to finalizing a capital budget (or operating budget since there will probably be effects on manufacturing and operating costs as well as depreciation), but that the formal approval take place separately when projects can be evaluated individually and in depth (or in groups if there are related projects or commitments).

Operating management will probably be unable to undertake all capital projects identified during the finalization of the budget. These projects will depend on the results of ongoing research and development studies, marketing research, or cost reduction studies. To help a business entity or unit of a diversified firm avoid planning and budgeting for *all* possible projects (and therefore overstate actual capital needs), a probability concept can be utilized. Using this approach, a list of likely projects is set forth with the capital required to carry out each. This is followed by a subjective percentage probability as to whether the project will actually be undertaken. Exhibit 2 gives an example of how such information can be summarized:

For the major projects considered extremely probable, a 100 percent likelihood is used. After this group, there may be several projects with, say, a 70 percent chance of being proposed/approved and a few more perhaps at 50 percent. If one anticipates capital needs and depreciation expense based on the net amount after probability reductions, the overall amounts anticipated to be carried in the balance sheet and operating

Exhibit 2
EG Industries, Inc.
19X4 Capital Budget

Line No.	Project Title	(1) Authorization Amount	(2) Probability of Approval	(3) Net Amount Carried in 19X4 Budget*
	Projects Over $1,000,000			
(1)	Project A– New Projection Facility–CA	$5,000,000	80%	$4,000,000
(2)	Project B– New Warehouse–NJ Plant	2,500,000	60	1,500,000
(3)	Project C– Pollution Control Equipment	1,000,000	100	1,000,000
(4)	Total Projects Over $1,000,000			6,500,000
	Projects $100,000–$1,000,000			
(5)	Project D– Land Purchase—TX	800,000	50	400,000
(6)	Project E– Modernization Project Line R	400,000	100	400,000
(7)	Project F–Truck Replacements	200,000	100	200,000
(8)	Project G–Laboratory Equipment	150,000	10	15,000
(9)	Total Projects $100,000–$1,000,000			1,015,000
	Capital Projects Under $100,000			
(10)	Total Only			350,000†
(11)	Total Capital Budget (4)+(9)+(10)			$7,865,000

*A separate schedule or added columns to this schedule would be needed to indicate over what time periods (yearly or quarterly) expected spending would take place.
†This can be broken out individually by department, for example, on supplementary worksheets, in much the same manner as tiers 1 and 2 above.

budget will more likely reflect reality than if *all* the projects were incorporated. Conversely, this procedure prevents projects from being eliminated from the budget prematurely because they do not seem 100 percent likely. The objective here, of course, is to reflect adequately the capital needs of the business and whether these needs can be met via internal sources or whether external financing is required. A comparison of past approvals with capital budgets and the amount of spending on planned projects (actual versus forecast) in prior periods would help determine whether the above procedures would be beneficial.

Manpower Budget

One of the key assumptions underlying the operating budget is the availability and attendant cost of manpower. Thus, manpower should be budgeted in detail, by category of personnel, to facilitate an understanding of what is needed to accomplish the operating goals. A detailed manpower budget will be useful in explaining variances from actual to budget, as discussed below.

A breakdown by category of personnel might be as follows: direct production or manufacturing (by product line); factory overhead by department; administrative, clerical, and research by department; and selling by product line or territory. Each category should be tailored to each specific business and should acknowledge highs and lows due to seasonality or other operating factors. Further, the unit should assess whether full-time employee equivalents are a better measure than is the total number of part-time employees in those instances where part-time employment is a big factor.

BUDGET MONITORING

An important benefit of having prepared a budget is to be able to monitor actual performance versus projected results in order to identify and analyze why there are variances. Some variances depicting overbudget costs may be reasonable if sales are also higher, so not all unfavorable variances from budget are necessarily undesirable. However, this monitoring activity should lead to either an affirmation of adopted strategies or to an adjustment of those strategies if the original objectives are still valid.

Once the underlying budget assumptions have been set forth and detailed budgets by product line have been prepared, the firm should be in a position to report against these in the coming year. To do this, the annual product line budget needs to be reduced to a monthly basis taking seasonal trends into account. For example, two operating units with identical sales projections and similar cost structures could, nevertheless, have vastly different monthly budgets if their production capacities were dissimilar. In addition, each department or cost center should have its own budget, and actual costs should be captured in a manner which enables them to be charged against the appropriate department or cost center for comparison against the budget.

"Waterfall" Concept

Prior to management's acceptance of the annual budget, however, and before monthly breakdowns are completed, it may be useful to have historical annual actual results compared with prior periods' annual budgeted and forecasted results as an indicator of built-in budget bias. To do this, we would like to offer as a tool a concept, developed at W. R. Grace & Co., which may be useful in helping management assess the bias attendant in most budgets and forecasts. This tool consists of a chart designed to present how unit management's prior years' budget and forecast data compared with actual results. This concept is called a "waterfall" (because a continuing flow of new information reflecting each succeeding year's view of projected results is compared to each year's actual performance) and is particularly useful where forecasts are made for both the budget and future years although it can also be adapted to a single-year budget format. Exhibit 3 is an example of a completed waterfall chart for a business which has regularly prepared a budget and a five-year forecast:

To read the waterfall chart, Line 1 indicates that management of Product Line A budgeted that it would sell 34,554,000 units in 19X0 and forecast that it would sell an increasing number of units through 19X4 rising to 39,941,000 (Line 1, Column 5). However, actual sales in 19X0 came in at 32,149,000 units for a 7.0 percent shortfall (Lines 5 and 6, Column 1). Management backed off its rosy outlook and budgeted only 34,021,000 units in 19X1 but with continuing increases throughout the new forecast period ending in 19X5 (Line 2). Unfortunately, Product Line A was again unable to meet its budget in 19X1 and came in with a 7.3 percent shortfall (Line 7, Column 2). This decreasing sense of optimism and consistent inability to meet lowered targets continued in each of 19X2 and 19X3. If you were reviewing the Product Line A budgeted 19X4 volume of 28,720,000 units (Line 5, Column 5) and its forecast of 32,000,000 units shown in Line 5, Column 9, how confident would you be that management will achieve these sales levels given the brackets shown in the second tier, Lines 6 through 9?

The preceding waterfall serves to point to the fact that Product Line A management consistently had rosier expectations of its sales volume than actually turned out to be the case (although unit selling prices were generally conservatively stated). In evaluating a unit's budget and performance, the waterfall provides a graphic presentation of how accurately results were forecast in the past. While a close correlation will not ensure success in coming periods and since some businesses are inherently more volatile than others, this method can be used to point to areas requiring deeper analysis before the new budget is approved.

While the example depicted in the foregoing waterfall covered sales volume, sales dollars and average selling price, the waterfall concept can be applied to any element capable of being budgeted and forecast. Without attempting to limit the imagination of the reader, the following are some of the items which the authors have seen waterfalled:

Industry and market share data.	Capacity utilization.
Manufacturing cost elements.	Balance sheet components.
Capital expenditures.	Exchange rates.
Gross profit.	Employees.
Net income.	Raw material supply.
Capital employed.	Utility costs.
Operating expenses.	Wage rates.

While the concept looks detailed and complicated, a rather simple time-sharing or internal computer program can be writ-

Exhibit 3
EG Industries Product Line A
Sales Volume/Net Sales
Waterfall

	(1)	(2)	(3)	(4)	(5)	(6)	(7)	(8)	(9)
	19X0	19X1	19X2	19X3	19X4	19X5	19X6	19X7	19X8
	Comparison Between Prior Years/Current Forecast and Actual Results								
Total Product Line A Volume (000's)									
(1) 19X0 budget and forecast	34,554	36,905	38,605	39,317	39,941	—	—	—	—
(2) 19X1 budget and forecast		34,021	35,235	37,785	38,485	39,485	—	—	—
(3) 19X2 budget and forecast		—	31,500	32,755	33,490	35,025	35,665	—	—
(4) 19X3 budget and forecast		—	—	28,220	29,950	30,750	32,350	33,200	—
(5) Actual/19X4 budget and forecast	32,149	31,543	27,675	27,810	28,720	29,470	30,500	31,400	32,000
Percent Actual/19X4 Forecast Favorable/(Unfavorable) versus:									
(6) 19X0 budget and forecast	(7.0)%	(14.5)%	(28.3)%	(29.3)%	(28.1)%	—%	—%	—%	—%
(7) 19X1 budget and forecast		(7.3)	(21.5)	(26.4)	(25.4)	(25.4)	—	—	—
(8) 19X2 budget and forecast		—	(12.1)	(15.1)	(14.2)	(15.9)	(14.5)	—	—
(9) 19X3 budget and forecast		—	—	(1.5)	(4.1)	(4.2)	(5.7)	(5.4)	—
Total Net Sales ($000's)									
(10) 19X0 budget and forecast	$36,516	$41,182	$45,750	$49,309	$52,964	$ —	$ —	$ —	$ —
(11) 19X1 budget and forecast		37,070	39,262	43,447	45,225	47,752	—	—	—
(12) 19X2 budget and forecast		—	38,371	43,049	45,402	48,948	51,444	—	—
(13) 19X3 budget and forecast		—	—	39,716	43,836	46,826	51,234	54,702	—
(14) Actual/19X4 budget and forecast	33,853	35,649	35,013	40,603	47,064	50,627	54,804	59,004	62,841

Percent Actual/1984 Forecast
Favorable/(Unfavorable)
versus:

(15) 19X0 budget and forecast	(7.3)%	(13.4)%	(23.5)%	(17.7)%	(11.1%)	—%	—%	—%	—%
(16) 19X1 budget and forecast	—	(3.8)	(10.8)	(6.5)	4.1	6.0	—	—	—
(17) 19X2 budget and forecast	—	—	(8.8)	(5.7)	3.7	3.4	6.5	—	—
(18) 19X3 budget and forecast	—	—	—	2.2	7.4	8.1	7.0	7.9	—

Average Unit Selling
Price

(19) 19X0 budget and forecast	$1.06	$1.12	$1.19	$1.25	$1.33	$ —	$ —	$ —	$ —
(20) 19X1 budget and forecast	—	1.09	1.11	1.15	1.18	1.21	—	—	—
(21) 19X2 budget and forecast	—	—	1.22	1.31	1.36	1.40	1.44	—	—
(22) 19X3 budget and forecast	—	—	—	1.41	1.46	1.52	1.58	1.65	—
(23) Actual/19X4 budget and forecast	1.05	1.13	1.27	1.46	1.64	1.72	1.80	1.88	1.96

Percent Actual/1984 Forecast
Favorite/(Unfavorable)
versus:

(24) 19X0 budget and forecast	(0.9)%	0.9%	6.7%	16.8%	23.3%	—%	—%	—%	—%
(25) 19X1 budget and forecast	—	3.7	14.4	27.0	39.0	42.1	—	—	—
(26) 19X2 budget and forecast	—	—	4.1	11.5	20.6	22.9	25.0	—	—
(27) 19X3 budget and forecast	—	—	—	3.5	12.3	13.2	13.9	13.9	—

ten quickly to produce a waterfall, assuming the data to be reviewed is available.

Variance Analysis

Once monthly breakdowns are established, product line and departmental analysis can and should be made throughout the budget year comparing the actual results with both budget and the prior year for reference. Exhibit 4 gives a suggested format for presenting the monthly data of a product line:

While the preceding table was presented in summary fashion for the current month activity of a single product line, additional backup analysis would also generally be prepared for each caption of the statement, including volume, selling prices, personnel, raw material costs, capacity utilization, and the like. Separate analysis for each department or territory would also normally be prepared. In addition, year-to-date actual comparisons versus budget and prior year will be helpful as there usually are month-to-month timing differences which affect individual departments or cost centers in any given month. These should balance out over the course of a few months, and this should be confirmed in a year-to-date analysis.

The purpose of the variance analysis is not simply to point out unfavorable comparisons to budget that may require corrective action but also to highlight opportunities where the unit may be able to capitalize on favorable trends in the current business climate. In any case, all variances need to be analyzed in sufficient detail to assure that major budget components are not being masked because one component's favorable result offsets another's unfavorable result. One example of a detailed analysis is the price/volume/mix concept which can be applied to sales and costs of sales. Efficiency, rate, and usage analysis in the cost area is another example (with many more to be found) in standard accounting and financial texts.

In addition to P&L variance analyses versus budget and prior year, information on balance sheet components will also be useful in evaluating performance. A comparison of the beginning of each year with the balance in major accounts at the end of each month (actual/budget/prior year) provides a good summary. This analysis might also include key statistics, such as inventories and receivables months or days on hand, capital spending, loans, working capital ratios, return on investment, and so on.

Exhibit 4
EG Industries, Inc.
Current Month P&L Data

	(1)	(2)	(3)	(4)	(5)	(6)	(7)	(8)	(9)	(10)
	Statement of Income			Variance Favorable/(Unfavorable) Actual versus				Percent of Sales		
				Amount		Percent				
February 28, 19X3 ($000)	Actual	Budget	Last Year	Budget	Last Year	Budget	Last Year	Actual	Budget	Last Year
(1) Net sales and revenues	$3,737	$3,491	$3,792	$ 246	$ (55)	7.0%	(1.5)%	100.0%	100.0%	100.0%
(2) Cost of sales before depreciation	1,251	1,241	1,104	(10)	(147)	(0.8)	(13.3)	33.5	35.5	29.1
(3) Depreciation	99	62	50	(37)	(49)	(59.7)	(98.0)	2.6	1.8	1.3
(4) Gross profit	2,387	2,188	2,638	199	(251)	9.1	(9.5)	63.9	62.7	69.6
Operating expenses:										
(5) Selling	1,602	1,431	1,302	(171)	(300)	(11.9)	(23.0)	42.9	41.0	34.4
(6) General and administrative	312	321	239	9	(73)	2.8	(30.5)	8.4	9.2	6.3
(7) Research and development	263	273	215	10	(48)	3.7	(22.3)	7.0	7.8	5.7
(8) Other	87	84	77	(3)	(10)	(3.6)	(13.0)	2.3	2.4	2.0
(9) Total operating expenses	2,264	2,109	1,833	(155)	(431)	(7.3)	(23.5)	60.6	60.4	48.4
(10) Operating income (loss)	123	79	805	44	(682)	55.7	(84.7)	3.3	2.3	21.2
(11) Other income (expense)	26	37	27	(11)	1	(29.7)	(3.7)	0.7	1.0	0.7
(12) Income (loss) before taxes	149	116	832	33	(683)	28.4	(82.1)	4.0	3.3	21.9
(13) U.S. federal and foreign tax (Net of investment tax credit)	74	57	371	(17)	297	(29.8)	80.1	2.0	1.6	9.8
(14) Income (loss) after taxes	$ 75	$ 59	$ 461	$ 16	$(386)	27.1%	(83.7)%	2.0%	1.7%	12.1%

Reassess Assumptions

While there is a school of thought which believes that the annual budget should be recast to reflect significant changes in conditions, we do not believe a budget, once approved, should be changed during the course of a year.

We do believe, however, that major changes in budget assumptions should be communicated to all levels of management, and this can be accomplished through the medium of periodic operating reports or meetings. If the outlook changes significantly even after one month, individual business units should be required to communicate this to top-level management.

Typically, business conditions are such that many budget assumptions will prove invalid during the course of the year. Examples include exchange rate fluctuations, gain or loss of a significant customer, volatile swings in raw material costs, and plant shutdowns. Therefore, a somewhat detailed review of the latest projection of the year's results after perhaps four or five months and again after eight or nine months may be beneficial. This type of review can be formal but less detailed than the budget review process and would not be calendarized or supersede the approved budget. This form of update will not require the unit to look back over prior years as the exercise is a current reassessment of where the unit will be heading vis-a-vis the approved budget. Furthermore, the update after eight or nine months serves as an excellent springboard to preparing for the ensuing year's business planning cycle.

SUMMARY

This chapter on budgeting in a diversified firm commenced with a comparison of the top-down activities of the corporate office to the bottom-up approach proposed for the budgeting process. This same theme has been iterated throughout each subsequent section of the chapter, and we added to it a discussion concerning the importance of communication before, during, and after the process.

We followed these thoughts with our opinion with respect to

(1) The importance of budgeting.
(2) The need to organize for the process.

(3) The level to which the organization should be dissembled for budget purposes.
(4) The factors to be considered in the budget process.
(5) The types of budgets which should be prepared.
(6) Budget monitoring.

To restate the obvious: The budget process is a waste of time, effort, and resources if it takes place in an vacuum or does not have the 100 percent commitment of all levels of management from the CEO to the department manager.

30

Approving Capital Expenditures

William J. Ledbetter

The process for reviewing and approving capital expenditure proposals within a diversified firm is affected by the degree of business unit dissimilarities and the separation of operating and strategic decision-making authorities. Since these factors can lead to the presence of conflicting goals within an organization, the capital investment process should be directly linked to long-range corporate plans and reflected in executive compensation policies in order to ensure that everyone is working in concert.

Differences among corporate cultures, organization structures, and current needs suggest that every company must tailor its capital expenditure approval process to fit its own requirements. To the extent that a corporation's investment policy is not consistent with its goals, objectives, and inherent limitations, poor capital allocation decisions may result. In addition to watching for signs of possible problems, management should periodically evaluate the effectiveness of its procedure for re-

William J. Ledbetter practiced law on Wall Street and served in various legal, financial, and general management positions before joining Textron Inc. as vice president—finance in 1974. His current position is senior executive vice president—administration and planning.

viewing and approving investment projects with a view toward its long-range goals.

DECISION-MAKING CONTEXT

The set of traits which distinguish diversified firms from highly concentrated, single-product, single-market, or single-technology businesses have important implications for the capital expenditure approval process. These implications, which arise from the very nature of the organization, can be better understood by examining two key traits: product-market-industry dissimilarities and the apportionment of authority.

Product-Market-Industry Dissimilarities

Diversification complicates decision making within a firm by introducing a wide variety of environmental and business factors which must be monitored and evaluated. Consider for a moment the possible impact of a very simple form of diversification—the offering of a new product or service. This action may require that a firm deal with new customers, competitors, or suppliers. Different marketing tactics and distribution channels may be necessary. The rate and pattern of market growth may be unlike anything previously encountered. Product and process technology may be significantly different. In addition, the risks taken and the rewards received may vary substantially from prior circumstances.

Within a widely diversified firm, the complexity of issues facing corporate management can be tremendous. The characteristics of each business unit can vary enormously with respect to such things as:

- Growth potential.
- Length and volatility of business cycle.
- Product life cycle.
- Competitive situation.
- Capital intensity.
- Resources required.
- Degree of integration.
- Rate of change in product and process technologies.

- Barriers to entry or exit.
- Synergy with other operations.
- Long-term goals.

In effect, a diversified firm consists of large numbers of business units, having different sizes and competing in different markets and industries, each simultaneously attempting to optimize its performance through an allocation of corporate funds tilted in their favor.

In addition, each business unit also varies in its degree of political power and importance to the corporate parent and exhibits unique risk/return characteristics arising from its particular situation. In order to direct funds to those businesses offering the highest returns or of the greatest strategic importance, corporate management must have a clear understanding of these varied operations and the trade-offs inherent in providing or denying capital to each of them.

Apportionment of authority

Within many diversified firms, authority and responsibility for day-to-day operations is delegated to the various business units or divisions while authority over strategic matters is retained by corporate management. The reason for doing so is directly related to the complexity and variety of business units. Only local managers have the information, understanding, and proximity necessary to efficiently control their operations in a real-time environment. Likewise, only corporate management can properly assess which actions and investments will enable the entire firm to meet its long-run objectives. Unfortunately, this logical division of authority is not always well suited to the capital expenditure approval process.

Capital investment proposals, which are usually initiated and developed by individual operating units, represent different *strategic* options for the firm. For example, if limited funds are available, a situation can easily arise where investments which would maximize the potential of any one unit may not be in the best interest of the company as a whole. From the corporate perspective, other investment opportunities may be more attractive if they generate a higher return, provide a comparable return with less risk, or position the company in a new growth area.

IMPLICATIONS FOR THE APPROVAL PROCESS

Given the attributes of diversified firms just discussed, three factors emerge as being critical to the design of any capital investment approval process if a corporation, as a whole, is to achieve its long-range objectives. These are:

1. The linkage between long-range strategic plans and capital expenditures.
2. The structure of compensation plans.
3. The adequacy of reporting and control systems.

Linkage between Plans and Capital Expenditure Approval

The capital expenditure approval process is probably the most important tool corporate management has to ensure that the operating units are implementing their approved strategic plans. It provides a direct link between day-to-day operations and the planning process. To the extent this linkage does not exist, plans do not get implemented, and poor investments are likely to be made.

In fact, investment plans should be driven by strategic plans. That is, once a decision has been made concerning business strategy, all spending projects should be consistent with that strategy. For example, a strategic plan to enter a new market with a new product must be supported with funds not only for R&D and marketing expenses but also for any necessary equipment, tooling, or capacity expansion. Similarly, although new equipment might be justified on the basis of replacement, if the operating unit's strategy calls for phasing out the product line which is manufactured with that equipment, the investment would appear to be a poor one.

The approval process should also allow corporate management to compare internally available projects with external investment opportunities, such as acquisitions or joint ventures. For this purpose, the approval process should view the entire spectrum of investment opportunities available to management. A diversified company which reviews its business units' capital investment proposals individually (for example, based only on the ROI of the project itself) and without regard for other possible opportunities would certainly have difficulty allocating funds in a rational fashion.

Structure of Compensation Plans

The compensation policies adopted by a firm will determine the actions of its employees, becoming the de facto strategic plan. All other things being equal, people act to maximize their total compensation. Thus, compensation plans should be designed to reinforce approved business strategies. Otherwise, there is the risk that investment recommendations and decisions will be based on personal rather than business considerations. For example, a policy which rewards the maximization of return on investment will usually result in fewer projects being submitted, often the minimum required to keep the business going without regard to building to grow or gain future competitive advantage. The effect is to minimize the investment base. This type of compensation policy may be appropriate for businesses with harvest-type strategies or for businesses which are directed to maximize short-run cash flow. However, the same incentive system would be totally inappropriate for a manager whose business unit has a high growth strategy since return on investment is usually kept low to maximize growth. In this case, a compensation policy rewarding swift growth would be more desirable, resulting in a greater number of project submissions and increased cash requirements.

Severe morale problems can arise where unit-level management is evaluated against a set of standards which are inconsistent with the strategy imposed on the business unit by corporate management. This would be the case if unit management was held responsible for deteriorating business performance following the rejection of proposed capital investments that they believed were imperative for adequate performance. Again, consistency with respect to strategic plans, capital expenditures, and incentive compensation is required if corporate management objectives are to be achieved.

Adequacy of Information and Control Systems

Corporate officers and staff within a diversified firm are unlikely to be personally familiar with or have a strong understanding of all the corporation's varied activites. For this reason, formal information and control systems play a crucial role in the capital expenditure approval process. Accurate and timely information must be gathered from the divisions or operating units on a continual basis. For example, major changes in competitor strategies, recent legal decisions, large contract awards, or rapid deterioration in business unit performance may suggest the need for a significant reordering of the corporation's investment priorities. Poorly designed or poorly implemented information systems will probably lead to improper investment decisions.

One element of the corporation's information system which demands special attention is the mechanism for gathering information on projects which have previously been approved. Meaningful feedback on the results of prior decisions is necessary to ensure that inadequate assumptions or analyses are revealed and mistakes will not be repeated. While many investment decisions cannot be reversed, projects which require the continued infusion of cash over time can always be altered or terminated. Since a large, ongoing investment program usually entails the commitment of considerable funds, continued review of project results is imperative.

DESIGN OF THE APPROVAL PROCESS

The design and characteristics of a corporation's process for approving capital expenditures must reflect the firm's culture, organization structure, and needs in order to be successful. In the same way that different business units require distinctive strategies, different companies require individualized approval processes. The tight system of controls adopted by an established manufacturer in a stable industry may be far too slow and cumbersome for a high growth firm facing a swiftly changing environment.

Control, however, should not be confused with paperwork and procedures. Control is really control over the *outcome* of projects. Corporations routinely commit large amounts of money to an array of projects, businesses, or strategies in hopes of producing superior returns. However, actual performance is often subpar, or the payoff never materializes at all. In most cases, actual performance falls short of forecasted returns for more reasons than merely sloppy project analysis, which is usually blamed. In truth, it is very hard to accurately forecast the risk and amount of cash flow that will be generated by a new project.

Managers must be asked and given incentives to propose

projects that are consistent with strategic objectives and that are accompanied by realistic forecasts. The only way to overcome the problems associated with the capital allocation process is to meet them at their origin—that is, to develop better strategic and operational planning supported by consistent capital budgets and complementary capital requests. Projects submitted without regard to a capital budget tied directly to a viable strategic plan are often not accompanied by any strategic justification. Approval of such projects could take the company in an undesirable direction and might preclude a more attractive option.

Some of the points which need to be addressed in the capital budgeting/approval process are as follows:

- Forecasts should take into account competitive and environmental factors. If market conditions or competitor responses are not taken into account, a project's projected return will not reflect the probable actual economic return to the business.
- Projects should be evaluated for their "strategic" compatibility.
- Strategic plans should provide a sound basis for capital allocation decisions by including an unambiguous picture of how the business will be managed. Unfortunately, plans often contain overly optimistic earnings projections, understate investment programs, and lack the supporting data necessary to judge their credibility. Moreover, they may not show how different growth and investment scenarios might alter the expected return.

By combining a thorough project analysis with realistic forecasting and a tighter integration between strategic and operating goals and compensation policies, a company has an excellent chance to achieve its projected payoff.

In designing an approval process, decisions must also be made concerning a number of important elements, such as whose approvals are necessary and in what order, information to be submitted with the capital project request, minimum financial return criteria, and even the definition of a capital project. In setting these "rules," the elements of the approval process could fall anywhere along a range from very tight controls to relatively loose controls. At one end of the spectrum, operating units might be required to submit annual capital budgets in support of their alternative operating and strategic plans. Once corporate management has reviewed its alternatives and approves specific plans, the units would be responsible for spending the funds as agreed upon, but would not be required to submit individual project analyses. At the other end of the spectrum, the project request process might be totally divorced from the planning process. In this case, individual projects would be submitted and approved without strategic justification so long as the project was projected to meet a minimum financial rate of return.

Indicators of Potential Problems

Realistically, few managers feel compelled to assess the adequacy of their firm's capital expenditure approval process unless there are indications that it results in poor investment decisions. Given this observation, it is very important to watch for signs of process failure or breakdown. Indicators of possible approval process problems can be found at a "macro" level by examining division or corporate performance and at a "micro" level by reviewing certain aspects of the approval process itself.

Deterioration in broad-based indicators of corporate and division performance, while not entirely conclusive, suggest that procedures for approving capital expenditures are not working properly. Since the allocation of resources is the primary method of implementing strategy within a diversified firm, a deteriorating performance suggests that either the strategy(ies) are not working or that resources are not being properly committed to achieve the corporation's objectives. Important symptoms to look for at the macro level include:

- Steady declines in return on investment.
- Substantial sales growth or increases in market share followed by declining profitability.
- A lack of profitable growth.
- Deteriorating competitive positions.
- Increasing evidence of missed opportunities.
- Pro rata funding across all business units.

Potential problems at the micro level are often revealed in the way proposals have been submitted and processed. For example:

- Were there lengthy delays between the time a proposal was submitted and the time a decision was rendered?
- Were projects ever approved with little or no accompanying justification?
- Have projects been split into many pieces to avoid review by higher-level management?
- Were all required forms filled out appropriately? Were supporting documents included?

The presence of these conditions or others that indicate a circumvention of the approval process are symptoms of a procedure gone awry. Even a perfectly designed process will fail if it is ignored. Management must recognize that the formal approval procedure may not correspond to the way in which investment proposals are actually reviewed. While the enforcement of corporate procedures is beyond the scope of this chapter, differences between prescribed and actual behavior cannot be ignored. Since no one process can be absolutely correct for all firms, management should evaluate the adequacy of its own process from time to time.

Framework for Evaluation

The acceptability of a particular capital expenditure approval process can be determined by testing whether the logical effects of that process are consistent with the company's goals, objectives, and limitations. This type of analysis can be broken down into four distinct phases: identification of key process elements; exploration of the implications of each key element; test of the actual results of the process versus stated objectives and actual limitations; and finally, an examination of possible modifications or alternative procedures.

Identification of the key process elements is often the most difficult of the four phases listed above. While management should use any methodology they feel comfortable with, situation analysis techniques which utilize simple questions can be quite effective. For example, in the case of capital investment decisions, representative questions might include the following:

- Who participates in the approval process—from origination to final approval?

- What information must be considered or presented—from business and financial justification to engineering specifications, bids, and alternative courses of action?
- What are the criteria for project acceptance or rejection?
- When, where, and by whom are proposals to be submitted, evaluated, and returned?

Obviously, only some of the process elements identified by asking these questions will significantly affect the structure of the approval process. Once a group of key elements has been agreed upon, the implications of each should be considered.

The exploration of the implications of each of the process elements is nothing more than looking at the logical consequences associated with each element. For example, assume that proposals are individually submitted and approved based on their expected ROI without regard to a long-range strategic plan or a previously set budget authority. This process implies that business units are treated as equals and corporate control is minimal. In addition, since no room is allowed for the simultaneous consideration of alternate investment opportunities, the investment strategy of the corporation is simply the sum of whatever is approved. Unit strategies are not coordinated.

Once the possible effects resulting from current procedures have been detailed, they should be compared to the firm's goals, objectives, and limitations. Continuing with our example in the previous paragraph, suppose that the firm whose approval process involves individual submissions is a true conglomerate and has no interest in directly controlling its operations. In this case, as long as the various units continue to meet the level of return their parent desires, this element of the procedure for handling capital expenditures is probably adequate. Conversely, imagine that the company in question is a diversified operating company which desires to maximize its long-term potential in total by rapidly growing select businesses in opportune areas while maintaining its position in its more mature markets. A process which reviews individual investment proposals on their stand-alone, financial merits will likely not satisfy this set of conditions.

At this juncture, firms which have uncovered inconsistent process elements can begin to examine possible alternatives. These alternatives should then be examined for implications and consequences in the same manner as the existing process to determine if they are compatible with company goals, objectives, and constraints.

ROLE OF THE CORPORATE FINANCE ORGANIZATION

Although the process for studying and approving capital expenditure proposals is often managed by a company's finance organization, responsibility and authority over final approval is generally shared by operating, strategic, and financial managers. The finance organization, therefore, has two distinct roles to play: on the one hand, it is a facilitator and manager of the process; on the other, it is a direct participant and decision maker.

As a process manager, the corporate finance staff within a diversified (or undiversified) firm has one basic responsibility—to ensure that all appropriate parties have received a clearly documented procedure for reviewing and approving capital expenditure proposals. The procedure itself, if properly specified, becomes the process manager. Instructions, relationships, forms, and requirements should all be incorporated in the document. While all eventualities cannot be anticipated, the finance organization should only need to worry about unusual cases that arise.

As a participant and decision maker, the corporate finance staff can contribute in a number of ways. Aside from verifying the acceptability of the financial analysis of large projects, the corporate staff can establish minimum financial requirements, suggest dollar approval levels, determine the availability of funds, and explore tax considerations and financing vehicles which the operating units may not be aware of. In addition, the corporate finance staff could track business unit progress on multiphase projects and also facilitate postcompletion project reviews. Finally, the finance organization might advise top management on the ranking and timing of various projects.

31

Internal Auditing

John H. Kennedy and William M. Laughlin

OVERVIEW

The final process of all financial management is the auditing of results. Although, on a consolidated basis, these are generally examined by independent, outside accountants, the audit process used by the modern public accounting firm is not designed to contribute significantly to management's knowledge of the effectiveness, accuracy, or operations of financial or other information systems. Their stated purpose is to perform an examination of financial statements in accordance with generally accepted auditing standards. But corporation managements, at all levels of the organization, still need to know that the financial and other information systems are functioning as intended or perceived. And this has been a primary determinant in the decision of so many companies to establish an internal audit department.

John H. Kennedy is senior vice president, CFO, director, and member of the executive committee of Alco Standard Corporation. He is also president of the Pennsylvania Institute of Certified Public Accountants. William M. Laughlin, previously a partner of Touche Ross & Co., joined Alco Standard Corporation as director of internal audit in 1982.

Since there are no mandated professional or legal requirements governing the establishment or operation of an internal audit function, there is a wide divergence among companies in the size, composition, mission, and approach of their audit group. A professional society, the Institute of Internal Auditors, Inc., has published "Standards for the Professional Practice of Internal Auditing" and codes of ethics, but compliance is required only of members of the institute. Corporate management is therefore free to do whatever it desires. In other words, internal auditing may be whatever you want it to be in your organization. But at its best, it will be the catalyst for causing improvement in controls and a valued contributor to overall corporate profitability.

Although internal auditors can wear many hats, it appears that their basic activities will fall into the following categories:

1. Financial Compliance Audits—(a) to evaluate the effectiveness of the system of internal controls in place to safeguard company assets; (b) to assure reliable financial information; (c) to determine adherence to applicable laws, regulations, and company policies.

2. EDP Audits—to provide assurance that controls over electronic data processing operations effectively prevent unauthorized processing or manipulation of data.

3. Assistance to the outside accountants in the annual opinion audit of the financial statements.

4. Operational auditing which can range far afield from the financial arena.

5. Special assignments including investigations into employee fraud and dishonesty, single-purpose assignments, and assistance to the operating financial staffs.

To say the least, the above comprises a full plate of responsibility, and the relationships involved and skills required of internal auditors to perform the tasks is the theme of this chapter.

Auditing, particularly internal auditing, has been with us a very long time. Substitute the word "checker" for auditor and we can see tracings back to Babylonian times. In our own day the complexity of business systems necessitates that an organized professional auditing effort be made to determine that the mission of the corporation and of its multitude of subsets has been properly and correctly carried out.

Internal auditors traditionally did not enjoy the highest status, probably because they were perceived as nonimplementors. But this perception was on its way to being outdated when the Foreign Corrupt Practices Act (FCPA) of 1977 was enacted. The Act placed additional responsibility and an exceptional need for expertise on internal auditors. In addition to their focus on compliance with company policies and practices, they were put into the role of reviewing and evaluating the adequacy and effectiveness of the entire system of internal control within the corporation. And with this redefinition of role, the enhancement of the auditor's status has been a natural outcome. No longer the checker reporting to another upper middle management employee, but rather one involved in an integral corporate function reporting to members of the board of directors and to the highest level of financial management within the company.

ORGANIZATION

Structure

In order for tasks mandated by the audit committee of the board of directors, senior financial management, and not least of all, the overview of the Foreign Corrupt Practices Act, a well-defined, cohesive internal audit organization must carry the first priority.

No two companies are organized the same way and no two are quite alike in their management philosophy and style. Some organizations of immense size are still highly centralized and staff relations with operating units are very closely entwined. In other organizations there is a high degree of operating autonomy, generally surrounded by self-sustaining functional units. In the centralized environment, the structure of an audit department is primarily related to its technical capacity to audit the standard systems of the corporation. In a multidivisional, multi-industry organization, the audit function, in effect, takes on a number of "clients." In this latter case the various operations, be they divisions or subsidiaries, foreign or domestic, tend to have differing systems and procedures stemming from the fact that they manufacture or distribute different products, may have come to the corporation through acquisition as opposed to internal establishment and may, in most all respects, be largely independent of each other.

In any organization the size of the staff must be based on the nature of the company and its businesses, the number of locations, and the organizational mold which is in place. In a centralized structure, the internal auditor and assistants work through their function with perhaps not too much interplay with the operating units of the company. In the diversified environment the function must be organized with its clientele in mind. And in this latter environment, the role model for corporate internal audit can well be the organizational structure of a firm of public accountants. The internal audit manager and assistants have a parallelism with the partners, managers, seniors, and assistants found in the public firms.

Location

In a diversified, multilocation environment, corporate management must also consider the geographic location of its internal audit function and weigh the relative merits of centralization versus decentralization on a cost/benefit basis.

From experience, it appears that a central location audit department provides for greater overall control of the function, including enforcement of uniform standards, training, and audit approach. It has the additional advantage of greater administrative support and provides for easier, corporatewide, evaluation of resource allocation. In short, a single department location provides better control over the attainment of the mission and the efficiency of the function.

However, if a company cannot provide a clear career path, a unitary location for a geographically dispersed company can pose the greatest single obstacle to attracting good people—incessant travel. All but the least attractive candidates will shy away from a job that requires more than 50 to 60 percent travel unless compensation rates are set at unreasonably high levels. Even under the conditions of higher pay rates for excessive travel, there is the probable experience of burnout as the staff memorizes airline schedules.

Travel for an auditor is inefficient.

A decentralized audit function reduces travel-related staff inefficiencies and the substantial costs of travel. But while it results in more productive staff time, it does require redundant administrative effort and reduces the likelihood of uniform quality of work product.

As a guide, in a geographically dispersed audit department, each unit must be large enough to be a free-standing organization in itself so that high standards and staff development can be accomplished. Unfortunately, a decentralized audit department is probably feasible only in the largest of companies.

Frequency of Examination

The internal auditors must be in a position to provide the board of directors and all levels of management with an assessment of the probable degree of risk of loss and recommendations to minimize the chance of loss from financial misinformation, weak internal controls, irregularities, and operational inefficiencies. Their schedule of audits must be based on this objective. The frequency of audit is a function of risk, audit scope, and staff size. Like every other area of corporate activity, cost/benefit decisions have to be made.

Certainly, more frequent audit visits are in order for problem locations or functions, but there can be no fixed guidelines except that audit coverage must be sufficient to provide management with the information needed to make decisions concerning financial and other information systems. A sound approach could include visiting high-risk locations every year (month, quarter, or whatever period is deemed appropriate) and lower risk locations on a rotating basis.

The risk assessment process entails a combination of mechanical computations, including distribution of assets and income, together with subjective factors, including auditor instinct. The most important risk to a particular company is probably determined by the dollar amount of potential losses, but other things, such as damage to corporate image or reputation, can well be equally important.

The risk assessment thought process is relatively simple. You need only to ask (1) what can go wrong, and (2) does it matter.

If the impact of a particular error or weakness is not significant, there is no need to deal with the risk of such happening.

The ability to ascertain what can go wrong and determine whether it matters must be based on a sound understanding of the audited company's business and environment. Without such an understanding, the auditor can overlook the things that really matter and dwell on meaningless side issues.

Selection of Staff

There is a great deal of benefit to be gained from modeling the audit department after a firm of public accountants. This approach is particularly useful in the selection of the audit staff. Competent accountants with public experience are highly adaptable to a client approach to internal auditing and their recruitment assures the department of well-trained, professional auditors who, secondarily, can become a pool of management talent. While clearly not all staff members need to have come from public accounting, the concept of professionalism and independence stressed by those firms becomes highly useful in the corporate environment.

There are two different philosophies on the selection of internal audit staff members. The first, and probably most practical in a start-up situation, is the hiring of experienced people from public accounting firms. This approach avoids an initial investment of time and talent in training entry-level people to be good auditors of systems and statements.

While this approach can ensure a well-trained, professional audit staff, it has some practical disadvantages. One of these is reducing leverage because all staff would be above the entry level, that is, recent graduates, and earning higher than entry-level salaries. Further, bright young auditors with two- or three-years experience in public accounting don't want to (and are being underutilized if they have to) count petty cash or foot computer printouts no matter how well compensated they are.

Another problem may be the training time required for the transition from public accounting to the internal audit environment where financial statement presentation and external reporting take a back seat to operational systems auditing. But in the final analysis, competent accountants with public accounting experience are readily adaptable to a client approach to internal auditing.

In a larger organization, once an internal audit function has matured, entry-level hiring is both necessary and desirable. Competition for good entry-level candidates is very intense from public accounting firms, and the effort is further impeded by the tendency of business schools to steer their best people toward public accounting firms. The internal audit recruiter must be prepared to overcome a conditioned bias toward public accounting.

The approach to entry-level candidate selection should be more thoughtful and deliberate than may be required in an innate environment of high staff turnover. Since an internal audit function is generally hiring far fewer people at one time than the large or medium size CPA firms, it can less afford to make employment mistakes. Candidates must be evaluated in terms of long-term career objectives and compatibility because wholesale turnover is disruptive and cripples continuity. But the realities of a dynamic corporate environment, in practice, means that the internal audit organization will forever be called upon to supply financial and accounting talent to the operating, as well as staff sides, of the corporation. It is probable, therefore, that a combination of entry-level hiring supplemented by bringing in experienced personnel is the practical method of departmental staffing.

The screening and selection process should be only the beginning in the home growing of good internal auditors. To be successful, the function must offer a carefully designed career path geared to professional development and must operate in an atmosphere that challenges the pursuit of personal excellence.

Operational Independence

From the outset it should be made clear that the auditing function performs best when it is clearly divorced from participation in company operations. If the internal audit function is watered down to permit its members to be fed into operating crises on other than a very infrequent basis, cohesiveness will be lost, and the mission of the auditor (that is, the evaluation of the adequacy of the corporation's policies and procedures for the safeguarding of assets and ensuring proper financial controls) will have been greatly weakened.

Training

As to staff selected from public accounting firms, the tendency will be to assume that not only are they well trained, but they will remain so. This is wishful thinking. Just as the outside auditing firms annually put their personnel through 40 to 50 hours of formal training and refresher courses, the corporate auditor, home grown or experienced, must have the same opportunities for continuing professional education.

Basic auditing procedures are very similar in both internal auditing and public accounting, but management should, and generally does, have differing expectations of internal and outside auditors. The role of the internal auditor is to evaluate financial and other information systems and to provide management with data relating to the operations of systems and internal controls. Since the final work product of each group is different, the training of the internal auditors must be different. Specifically, it should be more heavily oriented toward operational considerations and other matters that are of narrow corporate interest. For example, it is more important for an internal auditor to be aware of profit-making/cost-saving opportunities to the corporation than his or her counterpart in public accounting because the internal auditor has been placed into work assignments to do just that.

A sound approach to staff development and continuing professional education utilizes a combination of externally developed programs, together with topics of immediate corporate importance, for which in-house expertise exists.

For outside training, many professional organizations, including the Institute of Internal Auditors, the American Institute, and state societies of CPAs, as well as local colleges and universities, have excellent programs. Individual CPA firms will also present pre-prepared courses or develop training programs to your specifications.

For internal programs to be effective, they must be prepared and presented with the same degree of professionalism as outside programs. As a gauge of the quality of an internal program, you may be able to have them evaluated and accepted by a state board of examiners of public accountants, or its counterpart, as meeting professional standards for a course in continuing professional education. An outstanding and recognized training program is an excellent selling tool in the recruiting effort.

Pool of Talent

We have commented on the department as a provider of financial management talent. Since the auditor has the opportunity to travel, to investigate, and to become known by different units of the organization, his or her outlook may broaden more quickly and effectively than the counterpart initially assigned to some other financial department. In-depth knowledge of the workings of a corporation, of its culture, and of its philosophy generally can become known only by working in the varying environments that make it up. The auditor clearly has a ringside seat and the opportunity to delve into all of the various areas of the company and of being in a position to learn and yet still be an "outside" observer.

Career Path

The career path for internal auditors is dependent upon the needs and requirements of the organization. While a total career in internal audit is possible and available in many companies, there is a tendency among young candidates to shy away from a permanent career in internal audit. Invariably during an interview, a candidate will ask what career possibilities are with the company and how long they will have to stay in internal audit.

Those companies that use their internal audit department as a stepping stone into other areas of corporate activity are usually successful at recruiting outstanding staff members. It may pose administrative problems for the director of internal audit, but the recruitment of the best people demands continually pushing the best audit people out to operating environments. A good departmental middle ground is to have a combination of both career and shorter term internal auditors. Many organizations have career positions in management of internal audit for some and use a stepping stone philosophy for other staff. Stability at the management level of the department provides for continuity and consistency of approach but carries with it the danger of growing stale on recurring assignments.

Conclusion

The organization of the internal audit function can be summed up as follows: Staff it with those of a professional outlook and probably with a professional background; provide staff training on a continuing basis to enhance technical competence; motivate staff with the knowledge that they represent the senior financial managers of the future and that auditing need not be the final purpose in their careers.

APPROACHING THE CONSTITUENCY

There is a natural bias on the part of the auditee to be wary of the auditor. No one has ever enjoyed being checked. It is therefore extremely important in all audit engagements that there be dialogue beforehand. Before work is undertaken, senior management of the location or operation to be audited should be made aware of the timing and personnel involved by making a broad outline of the scope of audit work and special areas where the auditor may need the assistance of local employees. In planning the work, the auditor needs to pay close attention to his staffing requirements. Time budgets should be prepared in detail in order to monitor efficiency and completeness. Work programs themselves, to the fullest extent, should be developed to bring out the unique characteristics of the operating entity being examined.

During the course of the work, supervisory audit personnel should visit the location to review the progress of the work and to mediate discussions between the field staff and operating unit personnel. At the same time, the supervisor should get to know his "client" so as to better understand the background development of existing systems and procedures and to be alert early on to problems of valuation or control.

At the completion of the work there must be a closing conference, considered an integral part of the engagement, to enable all audit points developed to be thoroughly reviewed with the operating personnel involved. The conference itself provides a forum for open discussion with the constituency. In this way the subsequent written report will contain no surprises. The attendees at the conference should be selected so that the even-handed aspect is stressed. For example, the unit president or general manager and the controller should represent one side; the most senior audit department representative available should represent the other. People senior to either of these levels should not be involved although lesser staff on both sides should attend to provide their special knowledge of points at issue. Let it be a meeting of peers for the purpose of an exchange of views.

Frequently during the closing conference an existing weakness will be acknowledged and the response made that corrective action has already been taken. Since this is the case, the unspoken request is to delete it from the list of findings. The fact that a situation has been corrected should not be a reason for it not to be in the report, albeit with the comment that correction has taken place. It is only by putting points in writing that independent observers have an opportunity to assess the quality of the systems in place, had an audit not taken place. At the closing conference it should be agreed what matters will be included in the report. It is then most important that the report be promptly issued.

Reporting the results of an internal audit must be done in such a way that the significant findings are communicated to the appropriate individuals for timely, remedial action to be considered. Questions as to length of the report, format, and even the number of copies to be issued must all be considered with the audience in mind.

Some organizations believe that a two-tier report method is best. With this method, an overall summary of findings, highlighting only the more significant exceptions or recommendations, is issued to senior corporate management and members of the audit committee. This summary form of report is seen as an effective method of highlighting operating problems and opportunities. In addition to the high-level summary report, the auditors would also prepare a more comprehensive report on all audit findings for action consideration by management of the location or function.

A more convenient and effective approach is to create a single, comprehensive audit report, expressing an overall opinion and including all findings. The report cover letter will enumerate the more significant points giving an overview to senior management, while at the same time permitting the opportunity to review findings in detail. This type of report is also easier to deal with administratively since it is all inclusive.

But regardless of which report method is used, the internal auditor must remember that, as in all written communication, brevity is a virtue. The need to be sure that significant findings are appropriately considered should not require verbosity. Final decision on the points to be included in the report should be made only after the audit closing conference. On occasion an internal control weakness that is seemingly easy to correct in the mind of the internal auditor has significant operational ramifications to local management. The closing conference is, in reality, the preliminary draft of the report.

In an autonomous environment, only the more obvious cost/benefit trade-offs should be considered by the internal auditors in deciding which recommendations to make in the report. Their responsibility is to be sure that management has sufficient information to make thoughtful risk evaluations in determining which control recommendations to implement. The decisions on cost/benefit should rest with the profit center manager who has ultimate responsibility for the location. In a centralized or uniformly controlled decentralized environment, cost benefit decisions will more likely be made on a global basis with input from the internal auditors. In summation, final decisions must be made by those responsible for profitability—operating management.

It is proper procedure for the operation reported upon to respond in writing to the points made, indicating corrective action to be taken or why it is thought no action is required. At this juncture the audit team may find itself in a quandry. The point was valid and serious enough to be put in the report and yet not so great a control weakness as to demand correction. It is here that the negotiating skill of the audit manager comes into play with the operational personnel so that both sides feel comfortable with whatever course of action ultimately transpires. There must also be a mechanism for ensuring that corrections agreed to are, in fact, made. There is a frequent tendency to acknowledge shortcomings but to dismiss the imperative to change. Unless follow-up procedures exist, the same condition may be found two years later on a return visit.

While the report is addressed to the senior person at the location audited, the question arises as to who else is copied. If the contents are clearly embarrassing, the auditor is asked to be discreet; conversely, if the report is laudatory, everyone should know about it. The solution to this is to have published distribution policy so that before the audit everyone involved will know who will be receiving a copy. Conceptually, since the audit committee of the board of directors carries a degree of ultimate responsibility, a copy of reports should be sent directly to them, and they would also receive the operation's response to comments. Since audit reports can tend to be voluminous, the fact that they are sent to board members, of itself, will improve the organization, content, and clarity of the report. Such distribution will also ensure a thoughtful and serious response on the part of the auditee.

REPORTING RELATIONSHIPS

The role of the internal auditor leads to ongoing reporting relationships, including:

1. Senior financial and other management personnel of the organization.
2. The audit committee of the board of directors.
3. The independent accountants.

Relationships with Senior Management

Part of the reason for the auditor's visibility and the reliance placed on his work is that senior management depends on the audit group to act as an early warning that things are not going well (or an assurance that they are) or, unfortunately, as a confirmation that the shortages, unintentional or not, uncovered in the accounts are real enough. The best outcome of the audit function occurs when the auditors report to very senior officers. In the past, the most senior person overseeing the audit function would be the corporate controller. Today the more common practice is for the auditor to report to the chief financial officer, executive vice president, or even president of the organization. It is the visibility and status given the auditor that permits him to influence the constituency to address those weaknesses outlined in his report. The fact that the auditor is responsible to the highest levels of the corporation is not lost on the audit subject. It should, in turn, impress the auditor with the necessity for his technical competence, diplomacy, and, above all, evenhandedness.

Above the level of the chief financial officer, the auditor must be prepared for a certain lack of ease with technical control considerations on the part of his listeners. At times there may be outright annoyance at nit-picking. The successful auditor must take reasonable precautions that he does not end up exasperating the very people who are depending upon him. And this brings us to whom should the audit department report. As is suggested above, the chief financial officer may be the senior who better understands the mind set of the auditor and is in the best position to oversee the function and to assist in the advocacy of recommendations. A cohesive, well-run internal audit group can be a real and positive force to provide a CFO or his designate with a large measure of "sleep insurance."

In any event, the internal auditor must report to someone high enough up in the organization who can assure his independence, in fact as well as in appearance. This means that the audit function must report to those above the level of the function he is auditing.

Relationship with the Audit Committee of the Board

The formalization of board of director audit committees was mandated by the 1977 action of the New York Stock Exchange, requiring listed companies to establish such committees made up of directors independent of management. The audit committee then becomes the link between the internal audit department and the board of directors. Now the internal auditor has a forum where he can voice his concerns and put forth his point of view. The relationship of the auditor to the audit committee reinforces the role of both. The board of directors does not conduct day-to-day operations; it does, however, have an oversight role in the overall performance of the enterprise. This requires a responsibility to review financial results and prospects. And, since directors and senior management cannot guarantee lawful conduct on the part of responsible employees in a large organization, there must be policies and procedures and internal controls designed to promote compliance. It is logical that the committee delegate to the internal auditor the field work necessary to provide the committee with such assurances. Members of the audit committee and the internal audit group have a logical interface since both have common goals. The audit committee acts on behalf of the board of directors, and the internal auditors serve the operating management. From both perspectives, they are each engaged in an independent assessment of the systems and controls. The audit committee, either directly or through the chief financial officer and other senior management, has a responsibility for oversight of the internal audit function. In turn, the internal auditors are, by extension, the eyes and ears of the committee. An audit committee which had no internal audit staff to rely on would of necessity have to depend on the independent public accountants; the more use made of their services, the higher the fee cost (in many instances a cost that would be prohibitive).

The internal auditor owes to the committee the responsibility for keeping them continually apprised. All significant reports should be prepared for their review, and they should be kept promptly informed of developments involving system breakdowns and other failings that can have a material effect on the corporation.

Interface with Independent Accountants

Historically, the relationship between the independent accountant and the internal auditor has been one of mutual wariness. Since the internal auditor is not considered innately independent, the outside accountant has approached the internal work product with some hesitation. But the growing realization of the substantive independence of internal audit has led to expanding reliance upon their work.

In 1975 the auditing standards division of the American Institute of Certified Public Accountants solicited comments on a proposed statement "Using the Work of Internal Auditors." The statement on auditing standards (then existant) indicated that the work of the internal auditor should be considered as a supplement to but not a substitute for test by outside auditors. But the rapid escalation of outside audit fees on one hand and the increasing sophistication of the internal audit effort on the other clearly mean that middle ground has to be created, and in many cases this has been accomplished. The scope of work of the independent auditor with respect to audit tests can and should be meaningfully restricted when the qualified internal auditor, for example, observes and tests inventory, confirms receivables, or makes financial audits of branches or subsidiaries.

There is undoubtedly a natural bias on the part of the independent auditor that his staff is more technically proficient. Although the Institute of Internal Auditors confers the designation of Certified Internal Auditor (CIA) upon those passing a rigorous examination and meeting educational and other requirements, there is no requirement for certification in order to be an internal auditor. And, in addition, there are no mandatory standards for practice. But to adopt the attitude that internal auditors have little use in the outside audit is limiting. The independent auditor should be obliged to test the work of the internal audit staff to the extent necessary to make an evaluation as to their competence and quality of their work. So satisfied, the outside auditor then would utilize the internal audit program, working papers and related reports.

A positive cost/benefit is generally available any time an internal auditor can substitute for an outside auditor, since average billing rates for medium to large CPA firms average two to three times the cost of internal personnel.

Most CPA firms are increasingly agreeable to using internal auditors, up through the senior auditor level, assuming qualifications comparable to those of their own staff, as members of the same team. Although such substitutions can result in outside audit time savings on an hour for hour basis, dollar savings do not tend to be optimized, simply because lower level staff have the lowest billing rates. Substitutions of higher staff, that is, supervisor and manager, present more of a problem to the CPA firm not because of the loss of hours at higher billing rates but because, at the supervisor level and above, independence, as well as judgment, is required for key accounting and auditing decisions. Quite naturally, the outside firms want their own people making those decisions, notwithstanding the qualifications of the internal auditors.

Therefore, while using an internal auditor as a member of the outside audit team has the apparent benefit of hour-for-hour time swapping, it probably should be avoided. The internal auditor may well be given the more menial assignments, and this results in underutilization of talent even though there is apparent cost/benefit. The cost/benefit, however, may be illusory if too much emphasis is placed on reducing outside audit fees rather than providing service to management.

The better arrangement is when the outside auditor sets his scope, determines which functions or locations are required to be visited, and then gives some of those assignments to the internal auditor. Although this method may not result in hour-for-hour swapping, it does have the benefit of higher cost savings because internal audit supervisory personnel can be utilized in an appropriate management capacity. And clearly, this approach provides more meaningful assignments to internal auditors.

Joint and cooperative effort on the part of both audit staffs reinforces the concept of working independence on the part of the internal auditors and enhances their professionalism. At the same time the independent auditor gains an ally within the company, permitting a better sense as to the credibility of management representations. He also gains assurance that the system of internal accounting controls, on which he is relying in the performance of his examination, has been monitored and tested by a group more intimately acquainted with the operations and affairs of the company than he will ever be.

Meaningful cooperation between independent and internal auditors must be strived for continually if duplication of effort and audit inefficiency is to be minimized. In their engagement proposal the independent auditing firm should be required to outline how it intends to utilize the efforts of internal auditors in their examination, and they must then follow through as the audit unfolds.

OPERATIONAL AUDITING

As a somewhat logical outshoot to traditional financial auditing, operational auditing has been adopted by many companies as a natural area of work for the internal auditor. Operational auditing may be simply defined as the application of the techniques of financial auditing to nonfinancial aspects of business operations. It is an operational management tool and has a unique work content. Since the auditor has a natural aptitude for observation and a background as an analyst, it is practical to apply the basic approach and techniques of auditing to a range of business functions beyond the purely financial. The auditor is not an expert in any "thing," but his qualifications lie in developing and reviewing controls and verifying history. Every operating area of a business has (or needs) controls, and the auditor is in a position to make authoritative recommendations. There are differing opinions as to the extent of operational auditing that should be done by financial auditors, but there are clearly those areas where the traditional auditor can help measure results of nonfinancial activities. Such areas tend to be those that are readily susceptible to either a common sense evaluation or where results are objectively determinable. But all areas beyond the traditional financial audit required a high degree of coordination between the internal auditor and the operations people involved to make certain that desired areas of investigation and expected results are clearly understood.

At this point, it should be noted that internal auditors are not all trained accountants. One large company assigns engineers, marketing specialists, and other operating personnel to its internal audit department as a means of increasing their financial awareness. There certainly should be qualified specialists on the internal audit staff if there are desires to delve into nonfinancial areas.

One obvious reason for using internal auditors in areas other than financial auditing is that they probably visit operating locations more often than others on the corporate staff. Since they are already on site, it may make sense to broaden their charge.

There are differing views about what should be the result of the internal auditor's work in the area of operational auditing. Some hold that he should be concerned primarily with pointing out deviations from generally accepted standards and management policies. Under this view, the auditor leaves to those more closely connected with the activity involved the task of bringing perceived weaknesses up to standard.

On the other hand, there are those who feel that internal auditors in the area of operational investigations should be akin to management consultants in that they not only point out weaknesses but also devise solutions and implement recommendations. Clearly, in this latter mode, they will find themselves far afield both in time and responsibility from their traditional roles.

The operational audit must begin with the auditor's clear understanding of management's objectives. In nonfinancial areas, management has a great deal of latitude in determining those parameters of control that it deems necessary or desirable in the overriding interest of promoting the efficiency of the business. And this, of course, differs from the financial audit interest in ensuring the safeguarding of assets and the compliance with applicable laws and regulations, as well as with company policy.

And so, with the above caveats, there are a number of examples where the skills of the financial internal auditor can be well utilized.

Monitoring central cash collection routines.

Reviewing purchasing department practices relating to the securing of bids.

Checking physical security of installations to reduce outside theft and reviewing internal practices to eliminate pilferage.

Testing of personnel files to determine if new employee screening practices have been complied with.

Determining compliance with corporate credit policies.

There are myriad activities that are subject to audit because the use of common sense and an inquisitive mind can result in identifying operational deficiencies and effecting efficiencies.

SPECIAL PROJECTS

While the type of special projects which internal auditors may be qualified to perform is broad, caution needs be exercised toward their involvement in jobs or projects that operating personnel instead should be doing. Without constraints, it will be found that the audit staff is being used as participants (fire fighters) in operating functions as opposed to their correct role as auditors of operating functions.

Special purpose projects can be divided into those that are essential or obviously cost-effective, areas where management desires comfort, and projects which, while perhaps necessary or desirable, should really be made the responsibility of some other group.

The most difficult of all special projects is the fraud or theft investigation. It is natural to assume that internal auditors are the most logical ones to investigate corporate irregularities. To a large extent this may be true but auditors are generally not trained criminal investigators. Delicate matters, such as interrogations of personnel, are best dealt with by company or outside security personnel.

What auditors are good at is detecting improper transactions that are recorded in the books of account, or not recorded but detected through such evidence as interruptions in document sequence. It is, however, generally not possible for them to quantify theft or unrecorded transactions, not involving sequentially numbered documents, simply because there is no documentary trail of evidence to follow.

The preinstallation review of data processing hardware or software is a most worthwhile project. It makes good sense to have computer audit specialists involved in reviewing design and implementation of new systems to be sure that appropriate controls have been provided. The alternative of postinstallation review runs the risk of patch controls being belatedly attached.

One area of specialized project work is the businessman's review or acquisition audit. The internal auditor is professional, well trained in audit techniques and, in this case, not independent. Internal audit is a logical group to assist in the evaluation of a potential acquisition. And certainly they are more knowledgeable about their own company and how the acquiree would fit in than would be the outside accounting firm.

In acquisition reviews the auditors work for, and intimately with, those responsible for the acquisition activity. The due diligence process has some unique features in that work is directed more toward fact finding than review of systems and controls, and it is generally done under severe time constraints. It requires that the audit staff so assigned be knowledgeable and mature. Qualified auditors have been known to blow deals; inexperienced ones have done the same!

COMPUTER AUDITING

There is no area of auditing which is more challenging and difficult for the financial auditor to ensure compliance with good, sound internal control policies than that of computer-based management information systems. Paradoxically, the discipline and structure required to build a viable computer system seems to provide ways to electronically circumvent transactional control. The ability of programmers to introduce deviant data or manipulate correct data could be endless if there were not established controls built into the system architecture to shut out improper transactions.

The auditing of computer activities should not be considered as a separate function because its most effective utilization is as an integral part of the overall audit effort. If computer auditing and the computer audit staff were to be treated as separate entities, coordination and cooperation with the financial audit staff may decrease.

Computers, per se, have no impact on internal audit objectives or thought processes. Whether a system is a manual one or utilizes highly sophisticated data processing hardware and programs, the auditor still must deal with the same basic questions—what can go wrong, and does it matter.

But intelligently addressing these two questions in an environment of electronic data processing (EDP) requires auditors with a different set of skills.

The EDP auditor must not only be able to evaluate the controls surrounding the computer (general controls) but, more importantly, must be able to determine and evaluate what goes on inside the computer. The latter process deals with internal applications controls. A meaningful risk assessment can only be made by understanding what goes on inside the box.

Traditionally, functional responsibilities were defined largely along departmental lines with the operating manager being held accountable for adherence to particular controls. In an electronic data processing environment, however, functional departments may tend to give up their accountability for adherence to processing controls and delegate the task to EDP. The EDP auditor must make sure that this does not happen. Computer programs now make decisions that were previously made by departmental managers. Whereas controls could previously be seen and physically monitored, EDP requires management to rethink its approach to control. It is clear that mechanisms must be introduced to ensure that internal controls—now organizationwide as compared to department limited—are not impaired when just the opposite effect was thought to be the beneficial result of electronic systemization.

An internal auditor, versed only in financial compliance testing of manual systems is, per se, ill-prepared to plunge into a world of ever-changing technology without specialized training. A decision which has to be made very early in the establishment of a computer audit function is whether or not a separate staff should be organized. Experience has proved that financial auditing and computer auditing are each sufficiently comprehensive disciplines to warrant specialization. Although some contend that future internal auditors will all be computer auditors, most companies are not yet at that stage. But there is no doubt that financial auditors without some computer literacy will be unable to perform their duties.

If the recommended decision to have full-time computer audit specialists is made, the next question is whether to take computer specialists and make them auditors or to take auditors and make them specialists. There is no clear cut answer to the question, but more and more accounting graduates have had extensive data processing course exposure, so the latter approach may be easier in the future.

No matter which course of staff selection is taken, the key to success requires a well-coordinated, overall audit effort.

PEER REVIEW

All of the discussions thus far have assumed an appropriately high level of professional competence and independence. However, like any other corporate activity, the auditors must be audited, to be sure they are doing what they should be doing, with appropriately high standards.

The nature of a review of the audit department depends upon the expectations for the activity. The Institute of Internal Auditors and several well-known CPA firms have advocated peer review of the corporate audit department, and the former organization has published guidelines for such reviews.

The person or group conducting the review should have audit experience that is relevant to the function being reviewed. If the internal auditors are engaged primarily in financial compliance auditing and if it is expected that they will function somewhat like a public accounting firm, then a practicing CPA would be a good choice to perform the review. If operational auditing comprises a significant portion of the internal audit effort, then a practicing internal auditor from another company may be the more appropriate reviewer.

To add credibility to the findings, the reviewer must be independent of the function in appearance as well as fact.

The approach to the review, as with any audit, should be structured to produce the desired results. The reviewer should meet with senior corporate management and the audit director, prior to beginning work, and obtain an understanding of management's expectations of the internal auditors and the desired results of the review.

After the initial meeting(s), the reviewer should prepare a formal written work plan (or audit program) for review and acceptance by management. Agreement as to the scope of the review in advance will avoid subsequent misunderstandings as to the meaning of the results. Once the scope is set, the reviewer should have unrestricted access to all information relating to the internal audit function. The review should include the detail working papers, staff selection, continuing education, promotion, and any other areas or policies that have an effect on the quality of the internal audit group.

Arrangements should be made to have the internal audit staff available to assist or respond to questions from the reviewer as his work progresses.

At the conclusion of the review, there should be a closing conference with internal audit department management to clarify and convey findings. Subsequent to the closing conference, the reviewer should prepare a written report for distribution to senior management and the audit committee of the board.

Upon receipt of the report, the function manager should respond to each finding and recommendation and prepare an appropriate action plan, if necessary.

In summary, the audit of the auditors should be handled the same way as any other audit.

SUMMATION

Internal auditing as a full-fledged function of the modern corporation has fully come of age. But it is not yet so constrained by dogma or taboos that it cannot be shaped to fit precisely the imprint that an individual corporation wishes to place on it. It represents a separate function and distinct force within the company to ensure that policies and procedures are being carried out as management intends. The internal auditor can represent a corporate strikeforce working at the direction of the audit committee of the board of directors, the chief executive or chief financial officer, and other senior personnel. It can act as eyes and ears for the monitoring of corporate actions, a task which is particularly difficult in decentralized organizations. Through their travels, they may be the one unit able to compare differing practices throughout the company and compare them to a predetermined norm. It is a group which can be used in any way that senior management would direct.

The effective internal audit group must be well trained and well directed. They must have a clear understanding as to their mission and as to the methods to be used to attain their goal. Although they are responsive to many constituencies, they should be responsible to very few. They should have the authority to wield a big stick, and yet their purpose will be defeated if they are perceived as an antagonist. Their goal must be to assist those whom they audit in understanding the necessity for internal systems controls and the constructive methods required to institute and maintain them. It is no small task to develop and maintain a professional organization, and it is even more difficult to foster independence of outlook and evenhandedness of execution. Yet these are the necessary ingredients for success.

Index